D0232895

Outback
Australia

Denis O'Byrne
Ron & Viv Moon
Hugh Finlay
Jeff Williams

Outback Australia

2nd edition

Published by
Lonely Planet Publications
Head Office: PO Box 617, Hawthorn, Vic 3122, Australia
Branches: 155 Filbert St, Suite 251, Oakland, CA 94607, USA
             10 Barley Mow Passage, Chiswick, London W4 4PH, UK
             71 bis rue du Cardinal Lemoine, 75005 Paris, France

Printed by
SNP Printing Pte Ltd, Singapore

Photographs by

Simon Bracken	Gareth McCormack	Denis O'Byrne	Tony Wheeler
Tim Burke	Ron & Viv Moon	Peter Robinson	Jeff Williams
David Curl	Jon Murray	David Sherman	Great Barrier Reef Marine
Roger Fenwick	Bernard Napthine	Shoot	Park Authority
Hugh Finlay	Richard Nebesky	Richard Timbury	NT Tourist Commission
Richard I'Anson	Mark Norman	Rob van Driesum	Qld Tourist & Travel Corporation

All DESART slides in the Aboriginal Art section taken by Barry Skipsey

Front cover: West of Jupiter Well, heading for Sandy Blight Junction (Ron & Viv Moon)

First Published
November 1994

This Edition
February 1998

**Although the authors and publisher have tried to make the information as
accurate as possible, they accept no responsibility for any loss, injury or
inconvenience sustained by any person using this book.**

National Library of Australia Cataloguing in Publication Data

2nd ed.
Includes index
ISBN 0 86442 504 X.

1. Australia – Guidebooks.
I. O'Byrne, Denis 1947-.

919.40463

Denis O'Byrne

Denis was the coordinating author of this edition, and wrote much of the material on central Australia, including the Oodnadatta and Birdsville tracks, MacDonnell Ranges, Finke Gorge, Simpson Desert and Plenty and Sandover highways, as well as the Gulf Track. Born and raised in country South Australia, Denis first ventured into the outback as an army surveyor. After a couple of years in Africa and Europe, he worked in Western Australia's Pilbara before arriving in Alice Springs on a round-Australia trip in 1978. He's lived in the

Alice ever since, and currently struggles to keep up the mortgage payments by working as a freelance writer. Denis is a columnist and regular contributor of outback travel features to the national 4WD magazine *Overlander*. (Denis would like to thank Phil Brennan of Adelaide, and Bob Kessing, Marie Kilgariff and Louise Tiller of Alice Springs for their kind assistance with this book's research).

Ron & Viv Moon

Ron and Viv wrote the sections dealing with Cape York, the Kimberley and Flinders Ranges, as well as the Canning Stock Route, Gunbarrel, 'Bomb Roads', Strzelecki, Silver City and Matilda highways, Torres Strait, the Kidman Way and Kennedy Highway. They have spent much of their lives exploring and writing about Australia's wild and remote areas. They founded the magazine *Action Outdoor Australia*, where they were editor and assistant editor for a number of years. Ron is now well entrenched as editor of the national 4WD magazine *4X4 Australia*, and Viv is a freelance travel writer

specialising in the more isolated and untamed places of Australia and overseas. Together they also write and publish their successful adventure guidebooks to Cape York, the Kimberley and Flinders Ranges.

Hugh Finlay

Hugh wrote the sections on the Stuart Highway and Top End, the Tanami, Finke and Old Andado Tracks, and the separate feature on Aboriginal art. Parts of the introductory chapters were based on *Australia*, of which Hugh is the co-ordinating author. While working his way around Australia, he spent two years driving through outback South Australia and the Northern Territory prospecting for diamonds (without success), and a further year in Western Australia's remote Mt Augustus region working on a 1¼ million-acre cattle station. He currently lives in central Vic-

toria with Linda and their two daughters, Ella and Vera, trying to juggle the demands – and pleasures! – of family life, travelling and writing, rearing sheep, gardening and lengthy phone calls from Lonely Planet editors!

Jeff Williams

Jeff wrote the sections on the Eyre Highway and the Pilbara, as well as the Gold Fields & Ghost Towns chapter. He was born in Greymouth, New Zealand, and currently lives with his wife Alison and son Callum in Brisbane, Queensland. He is variously author, coauthor or contributor to Lonely Planet's *Western Australia*, *South Africa, Lesotho & Swaziland*, *New Zealand*, *Tramping in New Zealand*, *Australia*, Virginia for the US *Capital Region* guide and bits of West Africa for *Africa on a shoestring*. Jeff has had a love affair with the Outback since his first trip to Alice

Springs and Ayers Rock over 20 years ago. To update this book and *Western Australia*, he drove 12,500km and saw a sprightly and septegenarian Cliff Young running 75km a day in his pursuit to circumnavigate Australia on foot.

This Book

The 1st edition of Outback Australia was coordinated by Rob van Driesum, who compiled the introductory chapters from material supplied by the authors. Jim Hart wrote the sections on Flying Yourself and the Birdsville Races, and Julian Barry wrote most of the material on Aborigines and Aboriginal languages in the introductory chapters.

John Weldon, Lonely Planet's favourite Elvis impersonator, updated the information on Cairns for this 2nd edition (John would like to thank Andy Taylor and Raffi Shlomi for their help).

From the Publisher

This book was edited by Rowan McKinnon, Paul Harding, Rebecca Turner and Chris Wyness. The maps were drawn by Lyndell Taylor. Lyndell also designed the book and the colour sections. Michelle Lewis designed the Australian Ecosystems section, and the cover was designed by Margaret Jung and David Kemp. Matt King compiled the material for the Aboriginal Art & Crafts section. Thanks to Mary Neighbour and to Rob van Driesum for some last-minute information.

Thanks

Many thanks to the following travellers who used the last edition and wrote to us with helpful hints, useful advice and interesting anecdotes:

Suzanne Crowe, Annette James, Mike Kupfer, Bob Madigan, Kerry McGinnis, Tooshey Netz, Sonya Nightingale, Kathryn Purnell, Ruth Ridgway, David Vile, NA Walker, Dimity Williams, Ronald Wolff and Nick Zafer.

Warning & Request

The outback is not to be treated lightly. The isolation, harsh climate and lack of water make it one of the few places in the world where survival can still depend completely on you – where you literally take your life into your own hands. If you are well prepared, outback travel can be highly enjoyable and can provide a great sense of achievement; if you prepare poorly, you may pay the ultimate price.

The outback infrastructure is highly volatile: waterholes dry up or become polluted; tracks that are fine one day could be washed away the next and may be abandoned as a result; new tracks are pushed through by the authorities and private individuals; and areas that have unrestricted access may suddenly become restricted to all but a select group of people. The outback is still a land of pioneers, which means that services, too, change all the time – farmers open up resorts or roadhouses, schedules change, prices go up, good places go bad, and bad places go bankrupt. So if you find things better or worse, recently opened or long since closed, please write and tell us and help make the next edition better.

Your correspondence will be used to help update future editions and, where possible, important changes will also be included in updates on our Web site. Julie Young coordinates a small team that reads and acknowledges every letter, postcard and email, and ensures that every morsel of information finds its way to the appropriate authors, editors and publishers. Everyone who writes to us will receive a free subscription to our quarterly newsletter, *Planet Talk*, and the very best contributions will be rewarded with a free Lonely Planet guidebook. Excerpts from your correspondence may appear in new editions of this guidebook; in our newsletter, *Planet Talk*; or in updates on our Web site – so please let us know if you don't want your correspondence published or your name acknowledged.

Contents

Map Legend

BOUNDARIES

.... International Boundary
.... State Boundary
.... Disputed Boundary

ROUTES

.... Major Road
.... Minor Road
.... Minor Road - Unsealed
(Well-maintained dirt road suitable for a normal car driven with care)

(4WD Only) .... 4WD Track
.... City Road
.... City Street
.... City Lane
.... Train Route, with Station
.... Metro Route, with Station
.... Ferry Route
.... Walking Track

AREA FEATURES

.... Building
.... Cemetery
.... Beach
.... Market
.... Park, Gardens
.... Aboriginal Reserves
.... Pedestrian Mall
.... Urban Area

HYDROGRAPHIC FEATURES

.... Canal
.... Coastline
.... Creek, River
.... Lake, Intermittent Lake
.... Rapids, Waterfalls
.... Salt Lake
.... Swamp

SYMBOLS

☼ **CAPITAL** .... National Capital
◉ **CAPITAL** .... State Capital
● **CITY** .... City
● **Town** .... Large Town
● Town .... Small Town

■ .... Place to Stay
Å .... Camping Ground
⌐♊ .... Caravan Park
⌂ .... Hut or Chalet

▼ .... Place to Eat
🍺 .... Pub or Bar
☕ .... Cafe

✈ .... Airport
.... Ancient or City Wall
❸ .... Bank
⬈ .... Beach
⌒ .... Cave
⛪ 🏛 .... Church
.... Cliff or Escarpment
◿ .... Dive Site
○ .... Embassy
⛳ .... Golf Course
✛ .... Hospital
※ .... Lookout
⚑ .... Monument
◐ .... Mosque
▲ .... Mountain or Hill
🏛 .... Museum
♣ .... National Park

← .... One Way Street
🅿 .... Parking
)(...................... Pass
🅿 .... Petrol Station
★ .... Police Station
✉ .... Post Office
∴ .... Ruins
❖ .... Shopping Centre
◎ .... Spring
🏄 .... Surf Beach
🏊 .... Swimming Pool
☎ .... Telephone
🏛 .... Temple
▣ .... Tomb
❶ ..... Tourist Information
⬤ .... Transport
🦘 .... Zoo

Note: not all symbols displayed above appear in this book

Introduction

Out 'back o' Bourke', way 'beyond the black stump', is Australia's outback. It may be hard to define but you'll certainly know it when you see it. It's the mythical Australia – the Australia of red dust, empty tracks, strange wildlife, endless vistas, tall tales and big thirsts. And, myth or not, it's ready and waiting for anyone with a spirit of adventure and some suitable transport.

Some of the routes that take you through the outback are modern sealed roads, like the east-west Eyre Highway or north-south Stuart Highway, but most of them are not. Some of them are not even maintained and it's only the passing of an occasional vehicle which keeps them open. Some of them are long and dreary, others provide a kaleidoscope of changes, but all of them traverse some of the most remote country on earth.

Improved equipment, from more reliable and readily available vehicles to better long-range radios, plus better track maintenance have made all the outback routes more accessible in recent years. Thirty years ago the Birdsville Track required a sturdy 4WD, and a breakdown in summer could easily be a prelude to disaster. Today, with a little care, you could drive the Birdsville in the same car you use for suburban supermarket runs, although breaking down in the heat of summer is still not recommended. Thirty years ago it was only Aborigines and a handful of hardy explorers with camels that ever made it across the Simpson Desert. Today there is a steady trickle of 4WD parties crossing this awe-inspiring stretch of land. Even the Canning Stock Route, the three week-long ultimate outback trip, is

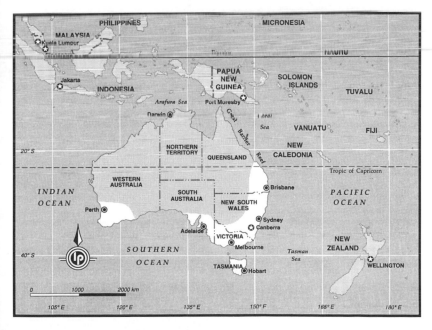

11

feasible for any well-equipped group to tackle.

This book covers all the outback; it explores the easily accessible places like Alice Springs and Kakadu but it also comes to grips with the 'real' outback, the rough and tough tracks where you'd better be equipped with plenty of fuel, plenty of water and plenty of spare tyres. There are full details on when to go (many of the tracks are strictly for the cooler months), what vehicle to use (hardy travellers have even conquered some of the tracks on bicycles or on foot), equipment requirements (tools, radios, spare parts), supplies (on the Canning Stock Route it's even necessary to arrange a fuel drop) and safety (foolhardy travellers sometimes still pay with their lives).

Facts about the Outback

HISTORY

Australia was the last great landmass to be discovered by the Europeans. Long before the British claimed it as their own, European explorers and traders had been dreaming of the riches to be found in the unknown – some said mythical – southern land (*terra australis*) that was supposed to form a counterbalance to the landmasses north of the equator. The continent they eventually found had already been inhabited for tens of thousands of years.

Aboriginal Settlement

Australian Aboriginal (which literally means 'indigenous') society has the longest continuous cultural history in the world, with origins dating back to the last Ice age. Although mystery shrouds many aspects of Australian prehistory, it seems almost certain that the first humans came here across the sea from South-East Asia. Heavy-boned people whom archaeologists call 'Robust' arrived 70,000 years ago, and more slender 'Gracile' people around 50,000 years ago.

These early colonisers arrived during a period when the sea level was more than 50m lower than it is today. This created more land between Asia and Australia than there is now, but watercraft were still needed to cross some stretches of open sea. Although much of Australia is today arid, the first migrants found a much wetter continent, with large forests and numerous inland lakes teeming with fish. The fauna included giant marsupials, such as kangaroos that were 3m tall and huge flightless birds. The environment was relatively non-threatening – only a few carnivorous predators existed.

Because of these favourable conditions, archaeologists suggest that within a few thousand years Aborigines had populated much of Australia, although the most central parts of the continent were not occupied until about 24,000 years ago.

The last Ice age came to an end 15,000 to 10,000 years ago. The sea level rose dramatically with the rise in temperature, and an area of Greater Australia the size of Western Australia was flooded during a process that would have seen strips of land 100km wide inundated in just a few decades. Many of the inland lakes dried up, and vast deserts formed. Thus, although the Aboriginal population was spread fairly evenly throughout the continent 20,000 years ago, the coastal areas became more densely occupied after the end of the last Ice age and the stabilisation of the sea level 5000 years ago.

The Development of Culture Areas

The stabilisation of the sea level led to more stable patterns of settlement and the emergence of broad culture areas – Aboriginal groups which exhibited similarities in terms of language, social organisation, tools, art and the environment in which they lived. There is some disagreement among anthropologists about the definition of these areas, and their exact number. The Australian Institute for Aboriginal Studies recognises 11 regional subdivisions in Aboriginal Australia today, while individual anthropologists have identified up to 21.

Traditionally, most Aboriginal people either lived in the desert, in the inland non-desert areas, on the coast, or in Tasmania. Throughout the desert, Aborigines exhibited a similar foraging pattern, spreading out over large tracts of land after rain, and retreating to permanent waterholes during dry periods. In the desert and inland non-desert areas, they foraged on insects, birds, reptiles and mammals. They also ate many different fruits, and collected various seeds which were ground and mixed with water before being either baked in the coals to make damper, or eaten as a paste.

Coastal Aborigines ate roots, fruits, small game, reptiles, fish and shellfish. In the Torres Strait Islands, between Cape York and New Guinea, people ate fish, shellfish, dugong (a relative of the manatee and walrus), and various fruits and yams. Many Aborigines and Torres Strait Islanders still eat large amounts of traditional foods.

Aboriginal Society

The Aborigines were tribal people living in extended family groups. Many still live in clans, with clan members descending from a common ancestor. Tradition, rituals and laws link the people of each clan to the land they occupy. Each clan has various sites of spiritual significance on their land, places to which their spirits return when they die. Clan members come together to perform rituals to honour their ancestral spirits and the Dreamtime creators. These traditional religious beliefs are the basis of the Aborigines' ties to the land they live on.

It is the responsibility of the clan, or particular members of it, to correctly maintain and protect the sites so that the ancestral beings are not offended and so will continue to protect and provide for the clan. Traditional punishments for those who neglect these responsibilities can still be severe, as their actions can easily affect the wellbeing of the whole clan – food and water shortages, natural disasters or mysterious illnesses can all be attributed to disgruntled or offended ancestral beings.

Many Aboriginal communities were semi-nomadic, others sedentary, one of the deciding factors being the availability of food. Where food and water were readily available, the people tended to remain in a limited area. When they did wander, it was to visit sacred places to carry out rituals, or to take advantage of seasonal foods available elsewhere. They did not, as is still often believed, roam aimlessly and desperately in search of food and water.

The traditional role of the men was that of hunter, tool-maker and custodian of male law; the women reared the children, and gathered and prepared food. There was also female law and ritual for which the women were responsible. Ultimately, the shared effort of men and women ensured the continuation of their social system. This is still

the view of many Aborigines, particularly in northern and central Australia.

Wisdom and skills obtained over millennia enabled Aborigines to use their environment to the maximum. An intimate knowledge of animal behaviour and the correct time to harvest the many plants they utilised ensured that food shortages were rare. Like other hunter-gatherer peoples of the world, Aborigines were true ecologists.

Although Aborigines in northern Australia were in regular contact with the farming and fishing peoples of Indonesia who came to Australian shores to collect trepang (bêche-de-mer, or sea cucumber), the farming of crops and domestication of livestock held no appeal. The only major modification of the landscape practised by the Aborigines was the selective burning of undergrowth in forests and dead grass on the plains. This encouraged new growth, which in turn attracted game animals. It also prevented the build-up of combustible material in the forests, making hunting easier and reducing the possibility of major bush fires. Dingoes assisted in the hunt and guarded the camp from intruders. (It's still unclear whether dingoes came with their prehistoric human masters from South-East Asia or were introduced later by Indonesians.)

Similar technology – for example the boomerang and spear – was used throughout the continent, but techniques were adapted to the environment and the species being hunted. In the wetlands of northern Australia, fish traps hundreds of metres long made of bamboo and cord were built to catch fish at the end of the wet season. In the area now known as Victoria, permanent stone dams many kilometres long were used to trap migrating eels, while in the tablelands of Queensland finely woven nets were used to snare herds of wallabies and kangaroos.

Aborigines were also traders. Trade routes crisscrossed the country, dispersing goods and a variety of produced items. Many of the items traded, such as certain types of stone or shell, were rare and had great ritual significance. Boomerangs and ochre were other important trade items. Along these trading

First Contact in the Western Desert

The Anangu people of the Western Desert were the last Aborigines to have contact with non-Aboriginal people. The last Anangu to abandon their autonomous hunter-gatherer lifestyle were a small group of Pintupi, who in 1984 walked into Kintore, a community 350km north-west of Uluru (Ayers Rock).

First contact in other parts of the Western Desert is also relatively recent, even in the Uluru region where today over 250,000 tourists visit annually. Although Giles passed through the Western Desert region in the 1870s, during the following 50 years non-Aboriginal visitation was so infrequent that many Anangu didn't see a white person until the 1930s or '40s or even later.

By the early 1950s most Anangu were living permanently or semi-permanently on missions, or on pastoral properties where they often worked for no payment other than food and clothing. Up until the late 1960s they continued to spend considerable periods travelling around on foot or on camels, in many cases still hunting with *kulata* (spear) and *miru* (spear thrower).

Up until the 1960s, government patrol officers searched out groups of Anangu, many of whom had experienced little or no contact with non-Aborigines, and trucked them from remote parts of the Western Desert to various settlements. This was part of a government policy which stated that Aborigines should be encouraged to abandon their traditions and become assimilated into mainstream white society. Also, in the Uluru area and on the roads leading to it, authorities claimed that Anangu were having a negative impact on the growing tourist industry.

In other parts of the Western Desert, Anangu were forcibly removed to make way for the testing of military hardware. In 1946 a guided-missile range was established at Woomera, within what was then the Central Desert Aboriginal Reserve. Until at least 1966, groups of Anangu were brought in from areas where testing had taken place. In some cases these people had been traumatised by rockets but had not experienced face-to-face contact with whites.

As well as testing conventional weapons, in the 1950s the Australian government permitted the British to detonate atomic devices at Emu Junction 500km south-west of Uluru, and at Maralinga a little further south. The authorities claimed that prior to detonation two patrol officers combed thousands of sq km, ensuring that no Anangu people were harmed by the tests. Anangu have another story: they say that as a result of these tests many people became sick and died.

Yami Lester is a Yankunytjatjara man who was a child at the time one of the British nuclear devices was detonated 180km from his home. As a result of radioactive fallout, Yami saw many of his relatives sicken and die; some years later, he went blind. *Yami – The Autobiography of Yami Lester* (IAD Publications, Alice Springs) provides an excellent insight into many aspects of early Western Desert contact history, and the struggle for land rights which took place some decades later. ■

networks, large numbers of people would often meet for 'exchange ceremonies', where not only goods but also songs and dances were passed on.

Aboriginal Ceremonies

The perceived simplicity of the Aborigines' technology contrasts with the sophistication of their cultural life. Religion, history, law and art are integrated in complex ceremonies which depict the activities of their ancestral beings, and prescribe codes of behaviour and responsibilities for looking after the land and all living things.

The links between the Aborigines and the ancestral beings are totems, each person having their own totem, or Dreaming. These take many forms, such as caterpillars, snakes, fish and magpies. Songs explain how the landscape contains these powerful creator ancestors, who can exert either a benign or a malevolent influence. They tell of the best places and the best times to hunt, where to find water in drought years, and can also specify kinship relations and correct marriage partners.

Many Aborigines living an urban life in towns remain distinctively Aboriginal – they still speak their indigenous language (or a creolised mix) on a daily basis, and mingle largely with other Aborigines. Much of their knowledge of the environment, bush medicine and food ('bush tucker') has been retained, and many traditional rites and ceremonies are being revived.

See the later Religion section for more on Aboriginal ceremonies and sacred sites.

'Discovery' & Colonisation

Portuguese navigators had probably come within sight of the coast in the first half of the 16th century, and the Chinese may well have visited long before that – a Chinese book, *Classic of Shan Mai*, written before 338 BC, notes kangaroos and dark-skinned people using boomerangs in a land to the south. In 1606 the Spaniard Torres sailed through the strait between Cape York and New Guinea that still bears his name, though there's no record of his actually sighting the southern continent.

In the early 1600s, Dutch explorers began to map parts of the coastline, and the southern continent became known to the world as New Holland – a name that stuck until the second half of the 19th century when British settlers began using the label 'Australia'. Traders first and foremost, the Dutch found little of value in this barren continent with its 'backward' inhabitants, and saw it mainly as an obstacle to be avoided on their hazardous sea voyages to and from the rich East Indies.

Heading east from the Cape of Good Hope, Dutch captains intent on making time rode the Roaring Forties, the icy but powerful winds of the sub-Antarctic, for as long as they dared before changing course to the north. 'Dared' because longitude calculations were very much guesswork before the invention of the chronometer, and many of the more reckless captains smashed their ships into the Western Australian coast.

During the colonisation drive of the 18th century, French and British explorers began to take a stronger interest in New Holland. Captain James Cook 'discovered' the relatively fertile eastern coast that earlier explorers had overlooked, and the British government, to head off French claims, established a penal colony there in 1788 under the name of New South Wales.

Devastation of the Aborigines

When Sydney Cove was first settled by the British, it is believed there were about 300,000 Aborigines in Australia and around 250 different languages were spoken, many as distinct from each other as English is from Chinese. Tasmania alone had eight languages, and tribes living on opposite sides of present-day Sydney Harbour spoke mutually unintelligible languages.

In such a society, based on family groups with an egalitarian political structure, a coordinated response to the European colonisers was not possible. Despite the presence of the Aborigines, the newly arrived Europeans considered the new continent to be *terra nullius* – empty land, or a land belonging to no-one. Conveniently, they saw no recognisable system of government, no commerce or permanent settlements and no evidence of landownership. (If the opposite had been the case, and if the Aborigines had offered coordinated resistance, the English might have been forced to legitimise their colonisation by entering into a treaty with the Aboriginal landowners, as happened in New Zealand with the Treaty of Waitangi.)

Many Aborigines were driven from their land by force, and many more succumbed to exotic diseases such as smallpox, measles, venereal disease, influenza, whooping cough, pneumonia and tuberculosis. Others voluntarily travelled to the fringes of settled areas to obtain new commodities such as steel and cloth, and experience hitherto unknown drugs such as tea, tobacco and alcohol.

The delicate balance between Aboriginal people and the environment was broken, as the European invaders cut down forests and introduced numerous animals – by 1860 there were 20 million sheep in Australia. Sheep and cattle destroyed waterholes and ruined the habitats which had for tens of thousands of years sustained the Aborigines' food resources.

Competition for water and land led to warfare between Aborigines and white settlers. Starving Aborigines speared sheep and cattle, and often settlers, and then suffered bloody reprisal raids. For the first 150 years of 'settlement' very few Europeans were prosecuted for killing Aborigines, although the practice was widespread.

In many parts of Australia, Aborigines defended their lands with desperate guerrilla

TIM BURKE

HUGH FINLAY

Top: Wind-rippled sand, near Uluru, NT
Bottom: Old homestead near Arltunga, NT

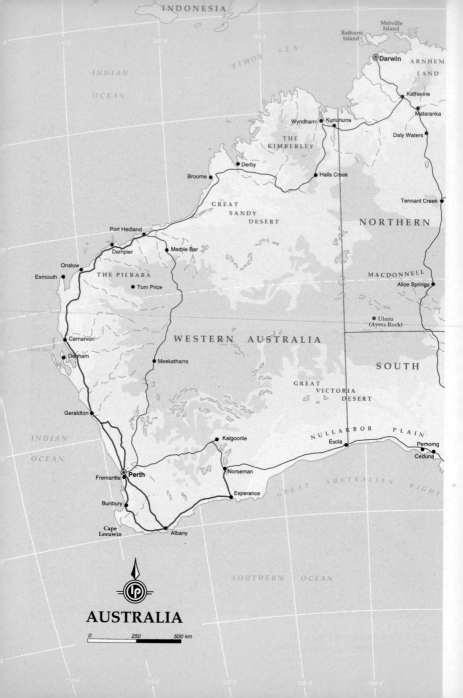

AUSTRALIA

0   250   500 km

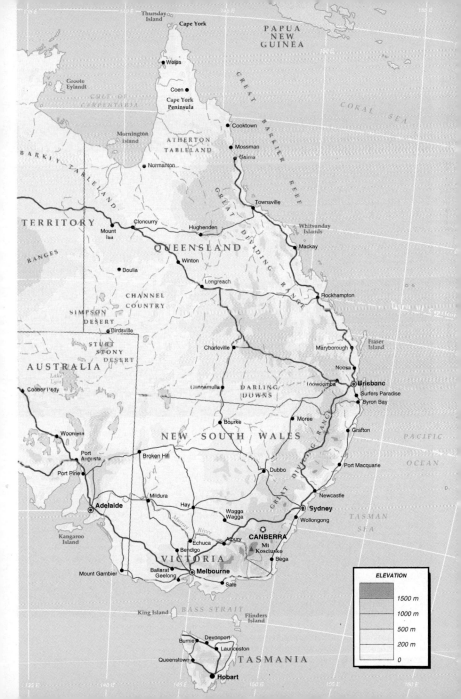

R & V MOON

TIM BURKE

R & V MOON

Top: Open plains south of Normanton in the evening light, Qld
Middle: Sunrise over Dalhousie thermal pond, Simpson Desert, SA
Bottom: A camel trek is a great way to experience the sun setting over Cable Beach, Broome, WA

tactics. Warriors including Pemulwy, Yagan, Dundalli, Jandamarra (known to the whites as 'Pigeon') and Nemarluk were feared by the colonists for a time, and some settlements had to be abandoned. Until the 1850s, when Europeans had to rely on inaccurate and unreliable flintlock rifles, Aborigines sometimes had the benefit of superior numbers, weapons and tactics. However, with the introduction of breech-loading repeater rifles in the 1870s, armed resistance was quickly crushed (although on isolated occasions into the 1920s, whites were still speared in central and northern Australia). By 1900 traditional Aboriginal society survived only among relatively small groups in central and northern Australia.

'Protection' & 'Assimilation' By the early 1900s, legislation designed to segregate and 'protect' Aboriginal people was passed in all states. The legislation imposed restrictions on the Aborigines' rights to own property and seek employment, and the Aboriginals Ordinance of 1918 even allowed the state to remove children from Aboriginal mothers if it was suspected that the father was non-Aboriginal. In these cases the parents were considered to have no rights over the children, who were placed in foster homes or childcare institutions. Many Aborigines are still bitter about having been separated from their families and forced to grow up apart from their people. However, the ordinance had an up-side in that it gave a degree of protection for 'full-blood' Aborigines living on reserves, as non-Aborigines could enter only with a permit, and mineral exploration was forbidden.

The processes of social change were accelerated by WWII, and after the war 'assimilation' became the stated aim of the government. To this end, the rights of Aborigines were subjugated even further – the government had control over everything, from where Aborigines could live to whom they could marry. Many people were forcibly moved to townships, the idea being that they would adapt to European culture which

would in turn aid their economic development. This policy was a dismal failure.

In the 1960s the assimilation policy came under a great deal of scrutiny, and white Australians became increasingly aware of the inequity of their treatment of Aborigines. In 1967 non-Aboriginal Australians voted to give Aborigines and Torres Strait Islanders the status of citizens, and gave the national government power to legislate for them in all states. The states had to provide them with the same services as were available to other citizens, and the national government set up the Department of Aboriginal Affairs to identify the special needs of Aborigines and legislate for them.

In 1972 the assimilation policy was finally dumped to be replaced by the government's policy of self-determination, which for the first time enabled Aborigines to participate in decision-making processes by granting them rights to their land. See the Government section, later in this chapter, for more on Aboriginal land rights.

Although the latest developments give rise to cautious optimism, many Aborigines still live in appalling conditions, and alcohol and drug abuse remains a huge problem. Aboriginal communities have taken up the challenge to try and eradicate these problems – many communities are now 'dry', and there are rehabilitation programmes for alcoholics, petrol-sniffers and others with drug problems. Thanks for much of this work goes to Aboriginal women, many of whom have found themselves on the receiving end of domestic violence.

All in all it's been a bloody awful 200 years for Australia's Aborigines. One can only admire their resilience, which enabled them to withstand the pressures placed on their culture, traditions and dignity, and that after so many years of domination they've been able to keep much of that culture intact.

White Exploration
Twenty-five years after the establishment of New South Wales, Blaxland, Lawson and Wentworth crossed the mountains west of Sydney Cove, and the white exploration of

inland Australia began. Already the coast was fairy well known, with Matthew Flinders making his great circumnavigation of the continent in 1803 and Phillip Parker King's voyages between 1817 and 1822 filling in most of the blanks.

By the 1840s Oxley, Hume, Hovell, Sturt and Mitchell had blazed their trails of exploration across the south-east of Australia, opening up the land between Sydney and the new settlements of Melbourne and Adelaide. Over in the west, explorers had set out from Perth to survey the land southwards close to present-day Albany and northwards to the Gascoyne River. In 1838 a group of men under Charles (later Sir) Grey landed on a rugged stretch of coast in the Kimberley at Hanover Bay and got nowhere, barely escaping with their lives in the forbidding terrain.

It is ironic that some explorers of inland Australia died of thirst and starvation in a land where Aborigines have survived for thousands of years. Rather than living with the land, they chose to conquer it the only way they knew: with weapons and supplies.

The 'Inland Sea' While trying to find a way into the centre of the continent, Edward John Eyre explored the Flinders Ranges in South Australia in 1840. A vast salt lake that he called Lake Torrens blocked his way, but in reality it was a number of lakes now called Torrens, Eyre and Frome, to name a few. It was this so-called impassable barrier that forced Sturt, a few years later, to head east and then north.

Giving up on his quest for the centre of Australia, Eyre, in an epic feat, crossed from Port Lincoln in South Australia to Albany in the west. Although he was a little more successful than Grey and travelled a darn sight further, he too nearly died along the way. One of the only things he proved was that it was not possible to drive cattle from Adelaide to Perth via the coast.

In 1844, Charles Sturt, already a well-known and respected explorer, set out from Adelaide on his greatest expedition, to find what many thought would be an 'inland sea'. Following the Murray and Darling rivers that

he knew so well to a point near Menindee, his team struck north-west. Trapped by unbelievable heat and lack of water, the men spent months at Depot Glen, near present-day Milparinka, before pushing further inland, finally reaching a spot on Eyre Creek north of today's Birdsville. Forced back by the unrelenting conditions, it was thanks to Sturt's skills that only one man died on this 18-month journey into and out of hell. Sturt's health never fully recovered, and although he was welcomed back to civilisation a hero and promoted to government positions, he soon had to retire because of deteriorating eyesight.

The Tropics In south-east Queensland, the opening up of the Moreton Bay area to white settlement in 1842 soon led to pioneer pastoralists pushing further north and west. In 1845 the enigmatic Ludwig Leichhardt led his men from Brisbane to Port Essington (near present-day Darwin) in one of the great sagas of exploration, while Mitchell crossed the Darling River and pushed north into central Queensland. Mitchell went on to be knighted, but Leichhardt vanished without trace somewhere in central Australia soon after.

In 1848 Edmund Kennedy set off from Rockingham Bay, just south of Cairns, and headed north towards the tip of Cape York through the mountains and jungles of northern Queensland. Forced to split his men and leave them at camps along the way, Kennedy met his death when he and his Aboriginal friend Jackey-Jackey were attacked by Aborigines near the headwaters of the Escape and Jardine rivers, just a few kilometres south of where a boat was waiting for them. There were only two other survivors from the 14 people who had set out, and they owed their lives to Jacky-Jacky who led the ship and the crew back to where they had been left.

In the mid to late 1850s AC Gregory blazed a trail from the Victoria River, near the border of Western Australia and the Northern Territory, across the top of the continent and down the coast to Brisbane. A member of the team was Thomas Baines, an artist who had done extensive work in southern Africa, and his paintings of their adventures with crocodiles and hostile Aborigines in northern Australia still exist. Meanwhile, AC Gregory's brother Francis discovered good pastoral land in Western Australia between Geraldton and the De Grey River, 1000km further north.

Burke & Wills In 1860 the stage was set for the greatest act in the white exploration of Australia. Some would say today that it was the greatest folly, but the Burke and Wills expedition was the largest, most lavish and best equipped expedition ever to attempt to solve the riddle of inland Australia.

The lure of being the first to cross the continent was only part of the story. In 1859 the wonder of the telegraph line had reached India and was soon to head for Darwin. Depending on the route forged across the continent by an explorer, an overland telegraph line would finish either in Adelaide or Melbourne. Melbourne was the brashly rich capital of the colony of Victoria, where a gold rush fuelled the fires of progress. In South Australia, however, the government was offering £2000 to the first explorer who crossed the continent.

From Adelaide, John McDouall Stuart, who had been with Sturt on his central Australian expedition, was pushing his way further and further north in a series of small expeditions. The race was on!

With much fanfare Robert O'Hara Burke led the Victorian Exploring Expedition north out of Melbourne on 20 August 1860. Chosen by a committee of the Royal Society, Burke was neither an explorer nor surveyor, had no scientific training, had never led an expedition of any kind, had never set foot out of Victoria since arriving there just a few years previously, and was considered to be, if anything, a very poor bushman. He also ignored the advice of earlier explorers to enlist the help of Aboriginal guides. So much for committees.

Leaving most of his group at Menindee (then at the outer limits of civilisation), Burke and his new second-in-command, William John Wills, pushed north to Cooper Creek where they set up a depot. From there Burke chose Wills, Charles Grey and John King to accompany him to the Gulf of Carpentaria, leaving the depot and the remainder of the expedition on 16 December 1860. At the height of summer, these men set out to walk 1100km through central Australia to the sea! It says something of their fortitude and sheer guts that they made it, reaching the mangroves that barred their view of the Gulf of Carpentaria on 11 February 1861. Camp No 119 was their northernmost camp and can be visited today.

Robert O'Hara Burke

William John Wills

Turning their backs on the sea, the rush south became a life-and-death stagger with Grey dying at a place later called Lake Massacre, just west of the Cooper Creek depot. When Burke, Wills and King arrived at the depot they were astonished to find that the men there had retreated to Menindee that very morning! The famous 'Dig Tree', one of the most significant historic sites in inland Australia, still stands on the banks of Cooper Creek. The name relates to the message carved into its trunk by the departing men: 'DIG 3FT N.W. APR. 21 1861.'

Trapped at Cooper Creek the explorers wasted away, dying on the banks of this desert oasis. Only King, who had been befriended by some Aborigines, was alive when the first of the rescue parties arrived in September 1861.

These rescue expeditions really opened up the interior, with groups from Queensland, South Australia and Victoria crisscrossing the continent in search of Burke and Wills. Howitt, McKinlay, Landsborough and Walker were not only better explorers than Burke, but experienced bushmen who proved that Europeans, cattle and sheep could survive in these regions.

Meanwhile, the determined Stuart finally crossed the continent, reaching Chambers Bay, east of present-day Darwin, in July 1862. So well planned and executed were his expeditions that the Overland Telegraph Line followed his route, as did the original railway line and road.

The Jardines Over in Queensland, the Jardine brothers battled their way north through the wilds of Cape York to the new settlement of Somerset in 1864. They took nine months to drive their mob of 300-odd cattle and 20 or so horses through plains wracked by the dry season in the south-western Cape, across rivers flooded by the wet season in the central and northern Cape, while fighting with hostile Aborigines all the way. Frank Jardine, the leader of the small group, was to stay on at Somerset, where he died in 1919 after building an empire of cattle and pearls.

The 'Empty' West Between 1869 and 1875 John Forrest crossed from Perth to Fowlers Bay in South Australia and from Geraldton to the Overland Telegraph Line. Meanwhile, William Gosse, leaving from the telegraph station at Alice Springs, had happened upon Ayers Rock while trying to find a route westwards.

Major John Warburton was also in the Alice around the same time trying to find a route to the west. Pushed north by the harsh deserts and finally existing on a spoonful of flour and water for breakfast, a tough strip of dried camel meat for lunch and whatever they could collect from bushes for dinner, his team finally made it to the Oakover River. At one stage they were forced to eat the hide of the camels as well. As Warburton wrote in his book, *Journey Across the Western Interior of Australia*, camel hide needed 'about forty hours continuous boiling and is then very good'!

At the same time Ernest Giles was also trying to be the first to cross the western half of Australia. He was the first white man to see Kata Tjuta, naming it the Olgas after the queen of Spain. The lake that blocked his path he named Lake Amadeus, after the king. Forced back after the loss of his companion, Alf Gibson, Giles finally crossed the deserts further south. A few months later he crossed the continent again, this time from the Gascoyne River in the west to the Olgas and the telegraph line in the east. The year was 1876 and Giles died 20 years later, unknown, in the gold-rush town of Coolgardie. His two-volume book, *Australia Twice Traversed*, is regularly reprinted as a facsimile.

By this stage the big picture of Australia was filled in. Some of the detail still needed completing, and during the 1890s the first of the 'scientific expeditions' sallied forth looking for minerals and studying the flora, fauna and the Aboriginal people who still lived their tribal ways in the vast interior.

The 1891 Elder Scientific Exploring Expedition, under David Lindsay, explored the area to the north-east of Coolgardie, and the 1894 Horn expedition explored south and west of Alice Springs. The Calvert Expedition, led by Lawrence Wells, met tragedy in the Great Sandy Desert of Western Australia in 1896, about the same time as a young gold prospector, David Carnegie, was blazing a trail north from Coolgardie to Halls Creek and back again. Carnegie died a few years later, not in the waterless wastes of Australia, but after being wounded by a poisoned arrow in Nigeria.

In 1906 Alfred Canning, using the knowledge of these explorers, mapped and then constructed his famous stock route from Wiluna to Halls Creek. Today this line of wells is one of the greatest 4WD adventures left on the planet.

The 20th Century Around the turn of the century, Baldwin Spencer, a biologist, and Francis Gillen, an anthropologist, teamed up to study the Aborigines of central Australia and Arnhem Land. The result was one of the most detailed records ever of a now-vanished way of life. Other expeditions to northern Australia and Arnhem Land were led by the British polar explorer GH Wilkins (in 1923) and Donald Mackay (in 1928). Donald Thomson led his first expedition to Arnhem Land in 1935 and his work in northern Australia still receives accolades from anthropologists and naturalists.

In the 1930s, aerial mapping of the Centre began in earnest, financed by Donald Mackay. Surveys were carried out over the Simpson Desert, the only large stretch of the country still to be explored on foot. In 1939, CT Madigan led an expedition that crossed this forbidding landscape from Old Andado to Birdsville; today his unmarked route attracts experienced adventurers.

In 1948 the largest scientific expedition ever undertaken in Australia was led by Charles Mountford into Arnhem Land. Financed by the National Geographic Society and the Australian government, it collected over 13,000 fish, 13,500 plant specimens, 850 birds and over 450 skins, along with thousands of Aboriginal implements and weapons.

During the 1950s the Woomera Rocket Range and the atomic-bomb test sites of Emu

Junction and Maralinga were developed. This vast region, which had been seen by few whites since Gosse, Giles and Canning, was opened up by the surveyor Len Beadell, widely regarded as the last Australian explorer. It was, as one of his books is called, the 'End of an Era'.

GEOGRAPHY
Australia is the world's sixth-largest country. Lying between the Indian and Pacific oceans, it measures about 4000km from east to west and 3200km from north to south, with a coastline 36,735km long. Its area is 7,682,300 sq km, about 5% of the world's land surface and similar in size to the 48 mainland states of the USA, and half as large again as Europe excluding the former USSR (Perth to Melbourne is the same distance as London to Moscow). Over 75% of the continent is generally referred to as 'the outback' (ie very sparsely settled and remote from the coastal plains of the east, south-east and south west, which are where over 90% of Australians live.)

Worn down by time, the often monotonous landscape of this island continent is the result of gradual changes wrought over many millions of years. Parts of the outback are among the world's oldest land surfaces. Its last great mountain-building events took place over 300 million years ago, and as a result its once-mighty highlands have long since been eroded down to their stumps.

Most of the outback is taken up by the Western Australian Shield, which lies west of a line drawn south from the east coast of Arnhem Land, around the western margin of the Simpson Desert and on to Eyre Peninsula in South Australia. The shield is a vast plateau with an average elevation between 300 and 460m. It has been fractured into blocks, or cratons, some of which have subsided to form lowlands while others have been raised to form rugged uplands.

The latter include the Hamersley Ranges in the west, the ranges of the Kimberley region in the north-west, and the MacDonnell and Musgrave ranges of central Australia. At 1531m above sea level, Mt Zeil in the West MacDonnells is the country's highest point west of the Great Dividing Range. Scattered over large areas are striking flat-topped hills (mesas), such as Mt Conner in central Australia, whose tops represent the ancient land surface, now largely removed by erosion.

The shield's lowlands include the Nullar-bor Plain in the south – its name is derived from the Latin for 'no trees'. This flat, dry limestone area is largely devoid of scenic interest but has extensive cave systems, several of world class. Other arid lowlands are the Great Sandy and Gibson deserts in the north-west and the Great Victoria Desert in the central shield area. Shaped by the

Archaeological Treasures

The early Aborigines left no stone build-ings or statues to tickle our fancy, but archaeologists have unearthed many other treasures. The best known site by far is **Lake Mungo**, in the dry Willandra Lakes system in the south-west of New South Wales.

Mungo (the name is Scottish) is a living, evolving excavation. The archae-ologists here are time and weather. This area was once a vast system of inland lakes, dry now for some 20,000 years. The embankment of sand and mud on the eastern fringe of the ancient lake system, named the 'Walls of China' by homesick Chinese workers, has been eroded by the wind in recent years, revealing human and animal skeletal remains, ancient campfires and evidence of trading.

SIMON BRACKEN

Walls of China in Lake Mungo

The remains prove that ritual burial was practised here 15,000 years before the construction of the Egyptian pyramids. The fireplaces reveal that sophisticated, tertiary-chipped stone implements were fashioned by the dwellers at the edge of this now dry lake. The food they ate can be discovered in the fireplaces, and the long-extinct animals they preyed on are found in skeletal form on the dunes. This area is so important that the Willandra Lakes are now a World Heritage area.

Another fascinating area of study has been **Kow Swamp** in northern Victoria. This site has a rich collection of human remains which date from the late Pleistocene epoch. One body, buried 12,000 years ago, had a headband of kangaroo incisor teeth. In the lunette of **Lake Nitchie**, in western New South Wales, a man was buried 7000 to 6500 years ago with a necklace of 178 pierced Tasmanian-devil teeth.

The west and north of Australia have many significant sites. Groove-edged axes dating back 23,000 years have been found in the **Malangangerr** rock-shelter in Arnhem Land. Other rich sources of artefacts are **Miriwun** rock-shelter on the Ord River in the Kimberley; the **Mt Newman** rock-shelter in the Pilbara; and the **Devil's Lair** near Cape Leeuwin in the far south-west of the continent. Fragments and stone tools dating back 38,000 years were found in the nearby **Swan Valley**.

Ice-age rock engravings (petroglyphs) are found throughout the continent. Those in **Koonalda Cave**, on the Nullarbor in South Australia, are perhaps the oldest. Flint miners often visited the cave 24,000 to 14,000 years ago, and unexplained patterns were left on the wall – perhaps they are art, perhaps not. Other places where petroglyphs are easily seen are on the **Burrup Peninsula** near Dampier, Western Australia; **Mootwingee National Park**, between Tibooburra and Broken Hill in far western New South Wales; the **Lightning Brothers** site, Delamere, Northern Territory; and at the **Early Man Shelter** near Laura in Queensland.

Josephine Flood's *Archaeology of the Dreamtime* (Collins, Sydney, 1983) provides a fascinating account of archaeological research into Australia's first inhabitants.

Warning: In Australia it is illegal to remove archaeological objects or to disturb human remains – look but don't touch. ■

prevailing winds, whose direction they parallel, the long, linear dunes of these inhospitable areas, and the Simpson Desert further east, were formed about 10,000 years ago during a period of peak aridity.

East of the shield and butting onto the Great Dividing Range is a world of vast plains with few significant uplands – the spectacular Flinders Ranges in South Australia is a notable exception. Known as the Central Lowlands, this region overlies the world's largest reservoir of artesian water: the Great Artesian Basin. Its central west includes the Simpson and Tirari sand-ridge deserts and the gibber-plated desolation of Sturt Stony Desert, all in Australia's driest area. Even here artesian water makes low-density sheep and cattle grazing possible where the native vegetation is palatable.

While the Western Australian Shield is generally lacking in surface drainage, except in the ranges of the north, central west and south-west, the Central Lowlands has the Cooper Creek and Diamantina River systems. These mainly dry, inland rivers rise in central and north-west Queensland respectively and wend their way for around 1500km to Lake Eyre, in north-eastern South Australia. Covering 9700 sq km, Lake Eyre is the largest of a number of huge, mainly dry salt lakes in this part of the state – at 15m below sea level, its bed is the continent's lowest point. These lakes are the remains of a shallow inland sea that once stretched south from the Gulf of Carpentaria.

More than one-third of the continent lies north of the Tropic of Capricorn and is thus technically within the tropics. However, only the extreme north – the Kimberley, Cape York and the northern part of the Northern Territory (the so-called Top End) – lies within the monsoon belt. While the long dry season and infertile soils – not to mention remoteness from markets – have acted against the far north becoming a major agricultural producer, suitable areas for farming do exist and are being developed. The most important is the Ord River irrigation scheme in the Kimberley, and there are others near Katherine and Darwin.

GEOLOGY

Along with Africa, South America, Antarctica and India, Australia once formed part of the supercontinent Gondwana. It only became a continent in its own right about 100 million years ago when it broke away from Antarctica. Since then it has been drifting north – its current rate of drift is about 55mm per year – and in another 100 million years will collide with Indonesia. So in a very short time (geologically speaking) the continent will cease to exist as a separate entity.

Australia can be divided into two broad geological zones: the Tasman Fold Belt and the Australian Craton. These lie east and west respectively of a line drawn roughly between Kangaroo Island in South Australia and Princess Charlotte Bay, near Cooktown in far north Queensland.

Virtually the entire area generally referred to today as 'the outback' lies on a huge crustal block called the Australian Craton. The craton is geologically ancient, its basement metamorphic and igneous rocks ranging in age from 570 million to 3.7 billion years. Its oldest rock formations – in Western Australia's Pilbara region – contain crystals that formed 4.3 billion years ago, making them part of the earth's original crust. At North Pole, also in the Pilbara, are the fossil remains of stromatolites that lived 3.5 billion years ago. Still in existence after all this time, stromatolites are the world's oldest known form of life – see the Palaeontology section later in this chapter.

The Australian Craton is actually made up of several small crustal blocks of igneous material such as granite that became welded together about a billion years ago. Today these blocks are mostly buried by sedimentary material, although they emerge at places like Mt Isa, Broken Hill and in the Tanami Desert. All these areas contain rich mineral deposits that today sustain major mining developments. The eroded remnants of the original sandstone blanket form the rugged landscapes we now admire in the north-west Kimberley region and Kakadu, in the Top End. In the Pilbara, marine sediments laid down 2500 million years ago form huge deposits of iron oxide now being mined at Mt Tom Price, Mt Newman and elsewhere.

Other rocks in this ancient mantle include reminders of the vast ice sheets that covered Australia during ferocious Ice ages 750 and 670 million years ago. Although much of this evidence is buried, exposures of glacial debris called tillite can be seen at Ellery Creek in the MacDonnell Ranges and Tillite Gorge, near Arkaroola in the Flinders Ranges. Deposits of tillite reach 5.5km in thickness in the northern Flinders. This was probably where the ice sheet met an inland sea, melting at the bottom and so dropping its load of rubble.

At this time Australia was still drifting around as a separate entity – during the Ice ages it was actually in the tropics. Gondwana was formed about 600 million years ago when its various components bumped into each other and bonded together. The collisions created shock waves that are thought to have caused the Petermann Event in central Australia. These forces buckled the crust into a chain of mighty mountains that stretched 2000km from the north-west to Broken Hill. Over millions of years, snow-fed torrents gouged deep into the mountains, washing huge quantities of debris into a shallow sea on their northern flank.

Today the original Petermann Ranges are mere hills, best seen on the road between Uluru National Park and Laverton, in Western Australia. The outwash material originally deposited in the sea has likewise largely been stripped away by erosion, although several spectacular remnants still rise above the sand plain. Kata Tjuta (the Olgas) are formed of large rocks, so this area must have been quite close to the original mountains. Eastwards, and further out in the ancient sea, Uluru (Ayers Rock) is composed of coarse sand and gravel while Mt Conner is capped by fine sand and silt.

During the Petermann Event the Tasman Fold Belt was a deep sea basin with volcanic islands. Then, about 500 million years ago, the first of a series of mountain-building episodes threw up an Andes-like mountain range along the Australian Craton's eastern side. (Its remnants are the Transantarctica Mountains of Antarctica and the Flinders Ranges.) Over a period of 110 million years these events gradually pushed the coastline 1000km eastwards.

Meanwhile, the Australian Craton has been relatively stable, which helps explain why it is generally so flat. Over the past 500 million years the major interruptions to this stability have been periods of inundation by shallow seas, and the earth movements that formed the ancestral MacDonnell Ranges about 320 million years ago.

On the heels of this event, another period of global cooling brought glaciers and extensive ice sheets to Australia's southern half. Later bursts of warm moist climate encouraged the growth of dense forests. Buried under thick layers of sediment, their remains turned into huge coal seams, producing huge reservoirs of oil and gas. These are now being tapped around Moomba in northeastern South Australia and in south-west Queensland.

Most of the Australian Craton was dry land between 250 and 140 million years ago, following which a major rise in sea level created an inland sea covering a third of the continent. Marine siltstones from this period contain precious opal, now mined at a number of places including Coober Pedy in South Australia and White Cliffs in New South Wales. Another inundation occurred 10 to 15 million years ago, creating the limestone deposits that today make up the Nullarbor Plain.

For further reading, *The Voyage of the Great Southern Ark* by Reg & Maggie Morrison (Lansdowne Press) tells the fascinating story of the four-billion-year journey of the Australian continent, and explains the evolution of its landscapes, plants and animals. The book is easy to understand and lavishly illustrated.

CLIMATE

Australian seasons are the antithesis of those in Europe and North America. It's hot in December, and midwinter in July and August. Summer starts in December, autumn

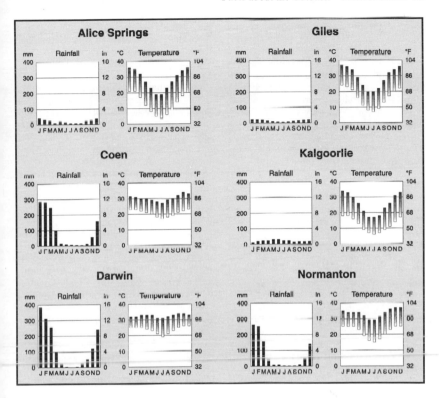

in March, winter in June and spring in September.

The climatic extremes aren't too severe in most parts of Australia. Even in Melbourne, the southernmost capital city on the mainland, it's rare when the mercury hits freezing point, although it's different in the mountains in Canberra, the national capital.

As you head north the seasonal variations become less pronounced until, in the far north around Darwin and up in Cape York, you're in the monsoon belt where there are just two seasons: hot and wet, and hot and dry. The centre of the continent has a typical desert climate – hot and dry during the day but often bitterly cold at night in the 'winter' months, when temperatures below freezing are not uncommon.

See the Planning section in the Facts for the Visitor chapter for information on the best times to visit the outback. See also the Bicycle section in the Getting Around chapter if you want to take advantage of the prevailing winds, which can make a big difference in fuel costs.

FLORA

Australia's tropical north is largely covered with forest despite the fact that at least seven months of the year are hot and dry. The climate is much harsher in the arid inland, of course, but even the Simpson Desert is well vegetated – tourists coming to Australia expecting to marvel at endless expanses of naked sand and rock will be disappointed. The MacDonnell Ranges near Alice Springs, close to the Simpson's north-west corner, contain nearly 600 native plant species, including a number of rainforest relicts.

Plants have to be tough to cope with the harsh conditions, which might seem ideal for succulent plants such as the cactus. However, Australian deserts, unlike most of those overseas, have very few true water-holding plants and none are related to the cactus. This type of plant requires a reliable supply of water – even if it is scanty – and Australian deserts don't provide this.

Origins

Australia's distinctive vegetation began to take shape about 100 million years ago when Australia broke from the southern supercontinent of Gondwana, drifting away from Antarctica to warmer climes. At this time, Australia was completely covered by cool-climate rainforest, but due to its geographic isolation and the gradual drying of the continent, rainforests retreated, plants like eucalypts (gum trees) and wattles (acacias) took over and grasslands expanded. Eucalypts and wattles were able to adapt to warmer temperatures, the increased natural occurrence of fire and the later use of fire for hunting and other purposes by Aborigines. Now many species benefit from fire and even rely on it to crack open their tough seed casings.

The arrival of Europeans two centuries ago saw the introduction of new flora, fauna and land-management practices. Even in the outback, native vegetation has been displaced by pasture grasses or degraded by grazing pressure, Aboriginal burning practices have largely ceased, and soils have been severely damaged by hoofed imports such as cows, sheep and goats. As a result, there have been major, usually detrimental changes to the native vegetation and its dynamics over vast areas.

Interesting books on Australian flora are *Field Guide to Native Plants of Australia* (Bay Books) and *The Greening of Gondwana* (Reed Australia) by Mary E White. Good places to see outback plants are Brisbane's Mt Coot-tha Botanic Gardens,

the Adelaide Botanic Garden, Port Augusta's Australian Arid Lands Botanic Garden and the Alice Springs Desert Park.

Eucalypts

Large eucalypts, or gum trees, are one of the most distinctive features of the Australian landscape, and the smell of burning eucalyptus leaves and twigs is guaranteed to make any expatriate Aussie homesick. The gum tree features in Australian folklore, art and literature, its flowers support the bee industry, its wood has many uses and its oil is used for pharmaceuticals and perfumed products.

There are around 560 species of the eucalyptus genus in Australia but only 60 or so are found in the arid zone, where, not surprisingly, most are rather stunted. However, some species can grow into huge trees that make a spectacular sight in their dry setting. **Mallee**, a multi-stemmed form of gum, is very common, and the roots of fallen mallees will burn seemingly forever in a campfire.

River red gums, usually called river gums or red gums, are generally confined to watercourses where their roots have access to a reliable supply of moisture. Given good conditions they can grow to 40m high and may live for 1000 years. This species is fairly easily identified from its habitat and its smooth, often beautifully mottled grey, tan and cream bark. River gums are found throughout Australia. They have a habit of dropping large limbs, so while they may be good shade trees it's certainly not wise to camp under them.

The **ghost gum** is a great favourite thanks to its bright green leaves and glossy white bark. Although these often majestic, spreading trees are common in tropical northern Australia, it's around Alice Springs where they've achieved most of their fame through the work of artists such as Albert Namatjira. In central Australia they're found on alluvial flats and rocky hills where they make a vivid contrast to their red surroundings.

Coolabahs are a common feature of watercourses, swamps and flood plains right through the outback's drier areas. They are typically gnarled, spreading trees with a rough, dark-brown bark and dull, leathery leaves. Coolabahs can grow to 20m high and often provide excellent shade. All eucalypts are hardwoods and this species is said to have the hardest timber of all. It is also very strong and termite-resistant, which made it extremely useful for building fences and stockyards in the days before steel became readily available.

One of the dominant Top End gums is **Darwin woollybutt**, which occurs on sandstone and lowland country from Broome right across to the east coast. This tall, spreading tree has rough, fibrous, dark-coloured bark on its lower trunk and a smooth white upper trunk and branches. Woollybutt is noted for its large clusters of bright orange flowers which occur from May to August.

Acacias

The Australian species of the acacia genus are commonly known as wattle – and they are common indeed. There are 660 species in Australia, but only about 120 are found in the arid zone. They tend to be fast-growing, short-lived and come in many forms, from tall, weeping trees to prickly shrubs. Despite their many differences, all wattles have furry yellow flowers shaped either like a spike or a ball. If you see a plant with a flower like this you'll know it's a wattle.

Most species flower during late winter and spring. Then the country is ablaze with wattle and the reason for the choice of green and gold as Australia's national colours is obvious. Wattle is Australia's floral emblem.

Mulga, probably the most widespread of the arid-zone wattles, occurs in all mainland states except Victoria. Although young mulga can look a little like small pines, the adults, which are 10m tall at their best, are more of an umbrella shape with a sparse crown of narrow grey leaves. Mulga sometimes forms dense thickets (the explorer John McDouall Stuart complained how the scrub near Alice Springs tore his clothes and pack saddles to bits) but usually is found as open woodland. Mulga leaves are very resistant to water loss, and the tree's shape directs any rain down to the base of the trunk where

roots are most dense. With these attributes mulga is a great drought survivor, but being good fodder for stock puts it at risk from overgrazing.

Spinifex

Spinifex – the dense, dome shaped masses of long, needle-like leaves that you find on sandy soils and rocky areas – is among the hardiest of desert plants. There are many species but most share an important characteristic: in dry times their leaves roll into tight cylinders to reduce the number of pores exposed to the sun and wind. This keeps water loss through evaporation to a minimum, but even so, most plants will succumb during a really bad drought. Spinifex grasslands are very difficult to walk through – the explorer Ernest Giles called it 'that abominable vegetable production'. They cover vast areas of central Australia and support some of the world's richest populations of reptiles.

Saltbush

Millions of sheep and cattle living in the arid zone owe their survival to dry shrubby plants called saltbush, which get their name from their tolerance to saline conditions. Saltbush – there are 30 species – is extremely widespread and can be dominant over vast areas. For example, on the Oodnadatta and Birdsville tracks you'll often see nothing else for considerable distances.

Desert Oak

Its height, broad shady crown, dark weeping foliage and the sighing music of the wind in its leaves make the desert oak an inspiring feature of its sand-plain habitat. These magnificent trees are confined to the western arid zone and are common around Uluru and Kings Canyon, near Alice Springs. You'll also see many along the Gunbarrel Highway. Young desert oaks resemble tall, hairy broomsticks; they don't look anything like the adult trees and many people think that they're a different species altogether.

Wildflowers

After good autumn rains the normally arid inland explodes in a multicoloured carpet of vibrant wildflowers that will literally take your breath away. The most common of these ephemerals, or short-lived plants, are the numerous species of daisy.

In a miracle of nature, the seeds of desert ephemerals can lie dormant in the sand for years until exactly the right combination of temperature and moisture comes along to trigger germination. When this happens, life in the desert moves into top gear as the ephemerals hurry to complete their brief life cycles and woody plants likewise burst into bloom. The sandhills, plains and rocky ridges come alive with nectar-eating birds and insects, which adds up to a bumper harvest for predators as well. Everywhere the various forms of wildlife are breeding and rearing their young while food supplies are abundant. For nature lovers this is definitely the best time to tour the inland.

Water Lilies

Although the Top End can't match the visual spectacle of the desert in full bloom, it nevertheless has many spectacular wildflowers. One such is the water lily, which forms floating mats of large, roundish leaves on freshwater lagoons and swamps right across the tropical north. Its root stock is prized as a food by Aboriginal people.

Boabs

The grotesque boab is only found from the south-western Kimberley to the Northern Territory's Victoria River, where it grows on flood plains and rocky areas. Its huge, grey, swollen trunk topped by a mass of contorted branches make it a fascinating sight, particularly during the dry season when it loses its leaves and becomes 'the tree that God planted upside-down'. Although boab trees rarely grow higher than 20m, the circumference of their moisture-storing trunks can be over 25m. The large, gourd-shaped fruits are edible and have a pleasant, fizzy taste similar to cream-of-tartar. Boabs are closely related to the baobab of Africa.

Weeds

By the 1920s the introduced prickly pear had choked millions of hectares of central Queensland before an effective biological control was found in the form of the cactoblastic moth. Today, in tropical Australia, weeds such as mimosa bush and rubber vine are threatening huge areas, while salvinia has begun to choke waterways. In central Australia, the Finke River has been invaded by athel trees which threaten to swamp its entire ecosystem. Introduced weeds can destroy wildlife habitats as well as make pastoral and cropping land unusable. Right across Australia, their cost in environmental and economic terms is incalculable.

Preventing the Spread of Weeds Studies have shown that motor vehicles are a major culprit in the spread of weeds. In 1990, a check of 222 tourist vehicles entering Kakadu National Park revealed that 70% were carrying a total of 1511 seeds from 84 different species.

The implications of this are obvious when you consider the millions of vehicles that travel Australia's roads and tracks each year. The question is: How can you avoid being responsible for an outbreak?

First, you need to be able to identify the various weeds as well as their seeds and seed capsules. This is easy: get hold of a weeds pamphlet from a state department of primary production or shire office. Second, if possible avoid driving through weed infestations – pay particular attention to quarantine signs, which should be observed to the letter. Third, immediately after leaving an infested area give your vehicle a thorough check for seeds and pieces of plant which may propagate. It's a good idea to carry out such checks on a regular basis regardless of whether you think you've been near weeds. As well, always carefully check the dog, your clothing, tent and bedding for burrs and seeds whenever you go walking or camping in the bush.

Seeds can become lodged in various places in the vehicle such as its undercarriage, engine compartment, radiator, wiper blades, gutters and around lights and doors. Don't forget the interior. For safety's sake, vehicles should only be washed on a proper wash-down area complete with sump and hard stand, not in places where weeds can grow.

If you find any seeds of noxious plants, seal them in a plastic bag and hand them in to the appropriate authorities for disposal; simply throwing them on the campfire is inadvisable as fire promotes the germination of some species. It's always a good idea to inform the authorities of isolated outbreaks in remote areas as they may not be aware of them. Take along a cutting – which ideally will include fruit, seeds or flowers – if you're uncertain about identification.

FAUNA

What can you say about the wildlife of an area with such a tremendous range of habitats and climates as the Australian outback? Obviously some areas are more rewarding than others when it comes to observing the local fauna. For example, the Top End rivers are like giant aviaries, particularly in early morning, and national parks inside the Dog Fence (see the following section on dingoes) seem inundated with kangaroos. Even the barren gibber plains of northern South Australia have much to offer those prepared to put some time and effort into their wildlife-watching.

In most areas away from water the casual observer will wonder if anything lives there at all apart from bushflies and ants. This is because the birds tend to be small and secretive, and native outback mammals are mostly nocturnal as a means of avoiding heat stress and water loss. It's unusual to see reptiles in winter south of the Tropic of Capricorn as cold weather sends them into hibernation.

Almost all Australian native mammals apart from seals, bats, rodents and dingoes belonged to the order of **marsupials**. Marsupials are also found in Central and South America (opossums), but have had evolution to themselves in Australia where they were isolated from the rest of the world for 55 million years or so. Marsupials are a primi-

tive order of mammals who lack a placenta; the young are born in an immature state, barely more than an embryo, climb through their mother's fur to her pouch (*marsupium*) and attach themselves to a teat to continue their development.

Australia is also home to the even more primitive order of **monotremes** (egg-laying mammals), which consists of only the platypus and echidna. The semi-aquatic platypus lives in eastern Australia and Tasmania, but within that area it can be found from near-freezing southern mountain streams to the sub-tropical rivers of Queensland; it has a duck-like bill and lays eggs in grass-lined nests. When the first reports of the platypus were sent back to England, the eminent scientists of the day thought they were a hoax.

The echidna, or spiny anteater, is a small, four-legged creature, covered on the back with long, sharp spines but on the underside by fur. It feeds on ants and termites, and is found in a great range of habitats, from hot, dry deserts to altitudes of 1800m in the Australian Alps, and also in New Guinea. The female carries her eggs in a pouch, and on hatching, the young remain there and suckle, only being evicted when their spines become too sharp for mum!

Since European settlement of Australia, many mammal species once widely distributed through the outback's drier parts are now either extinct or endangered. Some, such as the greater stick-nest rat, are now found only on offshore islands. The reasons for this unhappy record seem to be competition from and predation by introduced animals, and the cessation of Aboriginal fire-stick farming throughout the spinifex grassland areas.

Kangaroos & Wallabies

Australia's national symbol and its smaller relative, the wallaby, generally spend the daylight hours in hidden places sheltering from the sun. For this reason they are seldom seen by most outback travellers except as road kills or as large shapes that suddenly appear in the headlights at night. Kangaroos tend to inhabit open woodlands and plains, while wallabies are more at home in dense scrub and forests – some kangaroos and wallabies actually prefer rocky habitats.

There are six species of kangaroo, of which the red kangaroo is the largest with adult males weighing an average of 66kg. Kangaroo numbers have exploded in many outback pastoral areas owing to the extermination of dingoes and the increase of watering points and grasslands for sheep and cattle. To the horror of many animal-lovers, about three million are shot each year as a means of population control.

Kangaroo meat is a favourite traditional food of Aboriginal people but is only just beginning to be accepted by other Australians. Until recently, it could only be sold as pet food in some states due to the lack of quality inspections.

Although kangaroos generally are not aggressive, males of the larger species, such as reds, can be dangerous when cornered. In the wild, boomers, as they are called, will grasp other males with their forearms, rear up on their muscular tails and pound their opponents with their hind feet, sometimes slashing them with their claws. Such behaviour can also be directed against dogs and, very rarely, people. If there's a dam or waterhole available, a boomer being pursued by dogs may hop into deep water and hold its tormentors under water until they drown.

Kangaroos are a serious hazard to motorists driving at night on outback roads – be careful.

Bandicoots

The small, rat-like bandicoots have been one of the principal victims of the introduced fox and pussy cat. A number of species have either been totally wiped out or are in danger of heading that way.

Bandicoots are mainly nocturnal, but can occasionally be seen scampering through the bush. They are largely insect eaters but do also eat some plant material. Their large claws are put to good use scratching for insects, including centipedes and scorpions.

One of the most common varieties is the short-nosed bandicoot, which is found in

eastern and western Australia. Others, such as the eastern-barred bandicoot, are these days found in very limited areas. The rare bilby, or rabbit-eared bandicoot, survives mainly in northern Western Australia and the Northern Territory. Efforts are being made to ensure its survival.

Dingoes

Whether they tagged along with early Aborigines migrating from South-East Asia or were introduced fairly recently by Indonesian fishermen, the dingo, or wild dog, has been here long enough to be considered a native animal. (Perhaps one day they'll say the same about cats and rabbits.)

Dingoes differ from domestic dogs in various subtle ways – for example, dingoes breed only once a year while domestic dogs breed twice – but they can interbreed and this is the main threat to their survival as a pure strain. They are considered a threat to the sheep industry and in some areas have a price on their heads.

Dingoes are most numerous north and west of the Dog Fence, the world's longest artificial barrier. Between 1.4 and 2.4m high, the fence runs for about 5400km from near the Gold Coast in Queensland to near Ceduna in South Australia. Largely patrolled by government inspectors, the fence's sole purpose is to protect the sheep flocks of south-eastern Australia. A pair of dingoes acting together can kill dozens of sheep in a night, so any that make their way through the fence are vigorously pursued with bullets, traps and poison baits. Although dingoes do prey on calves, their depredations aren't considered a serious threat to the beef-cattle industry, which becomes dominant outside the fence.

Crocodiles

There are two species: the large **saltwater**, or estuarine crocodile and the smaller **freshwater** variety. 'Salties' are found in northern coastal areas from Broome around to Mackay, though there have been sightings further south. Contrary to their name, salties aren't confined to salt water; they can be found in freshwater habitats more than 200km inland. Salties, which can grow to 7m, will attack and kill humans.

'Freshies' are smaller than salties – anything over 3m should be regarded as a saltie. They are also more finely constructed and have much narrower snouts and smaller teeth to suit their fish diet. Though generally harmless to humans, they have been known to bite in defence of their nests; keep children and pet dogs away from them.

Both species of crocodiles were once hunted almost to extinction, but since they were proclaimed a protected species they have become abundant. By some miracle, very few people are killed by salties and attacks still make headlines.

There are simple rules to avoid being attacked and the most important one is to stay out of the water whenever you're in saltie territory. This can be rather difficult after a hot, muggy day's travel along a dusty track, but you'll just have to put up with it. Observe the guidelines contained in national park brochures and you'll be quite safe.

Snakes

Although only about 10% of Australia's 140 snake species are genuinely dangerous to humans, many of the world's most venomous snakes are Australian. The most toxic land snake is the so-called fierce snake or inland taipan of south-western Queensland and north-eastern South Australia – one dose of its venom is enough to kill a quarter of a million mice. It's a relative of the more famous and almost equally deadly taipan. The tiger snake is highly venomous too, and death adders, copperheads, brown snakes and red-bellied black snakes should also be avoided at all costs.

Many people spend months travelling in the outback without seeing a snake other than the occasional dead one on the road. Snakes tend to keep a low profile, but to minimise your chances of being bitten, always wear boots, socks and long, heavyweight trousers when walking through undergrowth where snakes may be present. Walking in dry grass without shoes or long

trousers in warm weather is inadvisable. Tramp heavily and they'll usually slither away before you come near. Don't put your hands into holes and crevices, and be careful when collecting firewood.

Always leave snakes alone – most people are bitten while doing something silly like trying to kill them, or stepping over them when they're asleep. In the unlikely event that you see a snake, the best approach is either to walk around it at a safe distance or to stand quietly until it's made its escape. In most cases it'll be as frightened as you, although if it feels cornered it may well strike in self-defence.

There are 30 species of sea snakes in Australian coastal waters. Although their venom can be 10 times as toxic as that of a cobra, they are shy creatures and usually won't attack if left alone.

First Aid Contrary to popular belief, snake bites do not cause instantaneous death. A snake bite is often shallow and injects little venom – the fangs may not penetrate the skin properly for many reasons (thick clothing, or the victim pulled away at the last moment), and a snake rarely injects a full dose of the stuff anyway. Don't panic. Antivenenes are usually available but may not be close to hand. Tourniquets and sucking out the poison are now completely discredited.

Instead, keep the patient calm and still. This is very important, as excitement and movement accelerate the spread of the venom. Wrap the bitten limb tightly, as you would for a sprained ankle. Start at the bite, work your way down to the fingers or toes, and then back up to the armpit or groin. Finally, attach a splint to immobilise the limb. This has the effect of localising the venom and slowing its spread. Then seek medical help, if possible with the dead snake for identification. Don't attempt to catch the snake if there is even a remote possibility of being bitten again.

Ideally, the patient should not be moved, but if you're in the middle of nowhere you may have no choice. Never leave the patient alone. If the bite is serious, the patient may experience breathing problems requiring artificial respiration, and you should be prepared for this.

Lizards

The outback hosts an amazing variety of lizards, from giant perentie goannas (Australian *iguanas* or monitor lizards) to tiny skinks and geckoes. The ones you're most likely to see are the various large goannas and dragons, which like to sun themselves in exposed situations such as bitumen roads. Unable to generate their own heat, most lizards need to lie in the sun on cool days until their blood reaches the desired temperature for hunting etc.

Goannas are sleek, heavily built lizards with longish, narrow heads. The perentie – the world's second-largest lizard – is found in the kinder habitats of central Australia and is easy to identify by the regular pattern of large yellow spots on its back. Perenties can grow to 3m long but you'd be most unlikely to see one over 2m, which is still a big lizard. The large grey goannas found along the banks of northern rivers are water monitors.

Two of the more common **dragons** are the bearded dragon of arid Australia and the Top End's famous frilled lizard. Some people like to tease the latter to make its neck frill stand out (an attempt to make itself look large and fierce) but such behaviour is pretty thoughtless. You'll notice how the bearded dragon flattens its body when sunbaking so as to warm up in the shortest possible time.

Another unusual lizard is the **thorny devil**, or mountain devil. Found on the sandy plains of the western arid zone, this fat, brightly coloured little creature has an almost indescribably ferocious appearance thanks to its armour-plated coat of horns and spikes. However, it's quite harmless to humans as it lives entirely on tiny black ants.

Finches

Australia has 18 species of native finch, of which most are found in the tropics – only two (the zebra finch and painted firetail) have adapted to arid conditions. **Zebra finches** are most commonly seen near permanent water as, being seed-eaters, they need to drink most days when it's cool and every day when it's hot. If you run out of water in hot weather and there are zebra finches around, you can be fairly sure there's a supply within a short distance.

The **Gouldian finch's** gorgeous colours make it one of Australia's most stunning birds. It was once common across the far north from the Kimberley to Cape York but is now scarce, largely because of its vulnerability to an introduced parasite that affects its respiratory tract. Trapping may also have contributed to its decline.

Honeyeaters

Arguably the most common and widespread variety of bird in scrubland and timbered areas, Australia's 67 species of honeyeaters come in many shapes, sizes and colours, from large, drab, bald-headed friarbirds to the small, brilliantly coloured scarlet honeyeaters. They are generally active, noisy birds with longish curved bills designed for extracting insects and nectar from flowers. Their morning wake-up calls are a feature along inland watercourses, where they are often dominant.

Parrots & Cockatoos

There is an incredible assortment of these birds in the outback. With the exception of the galah, cockatoos tend to be large, loud and not very colourful. The raucous screeching of cockatoos grates on the nerves, and makes you wonder why they're so popular as cage birds.

Parrots, on the other hand, are inoffensive and often very beautiful: the mulga parrot of the southern arid zone and the north's hooded parrot are typical examples. The latter, which nests in termite mounds, is now rare so it's a treat to see one. Budgerigars are extremely widespread and often occur in vast flocks as they follow the favourable seasons across the arid inland.

Birds of Prey

Being on top of the feathered food chain, the various eagles, goshawks, kites, harriers, falcons and kestrels are usually the most commonly seen of all outback birds. Largest of all is the **wedge-tailed eagle**, which you'll often notice feeding on road kills. With a wingspan approaching 3m they soar high on the thermals while scanning the ground for prey such as rabbits and young kangaroos. Their eyesight is so keen that they're thought to be able to see a rabbit quite clearly from a distance of 1.5km. On remote coasts, watch for ospreys and white-bellied sea eagles.

Emus

The world's second-largest bird, the flightless emu is found in large numbers in less inhabited areas inside the Dog Fence. These birds tend to be mobile and will often create problems for cereal growers when drought forces huge numbers in from their outlying haunts. They are extremely curious and you can sometimes attract them right up to the vehicle by waving a handkerchief or flashing a mirror. Attempts are being made to farm them for their meat, hides and feathers. The emu features with the kangaroo on Australia's coat of arms.

Insects

It will come as no surprise to outback campers that Australia has by far the world's largest number and richest diversity of **ant** species. In fact, scientists come from all over the world to study them.

These do not include white ants, which are more correctly called **termites** and aren't related. Termite mounds (each mound is the upper part of a nest) are often a spectacular feature of the tropical north. One species builds a large tombstone-shaped mound that points north-south, as a means of regulating the temperature within the mound. Another builds an immense pillar-like mound over 6m high.

Bushflies can be an unbelievable nuisance and at such times your arm will feel like dropping off from giving the great Aussie salute. Why do they persist in crawling on you? The main answer is that they want to drink your sweat and tears to obtain protein, but they're also waiting for you to go to the toilet behind a bush. Flies lay their eggs in fresh animal droppings, which gives the maggots food to grow until they pupate. A single cow on good pasture can drop enough in one day for 2000 flies to develop. Bushflies become even more numerous after rain, and are at their worst during the warmest months.

Some shops sell the Genuine Aussie Fly Net (probably made in Korea), which is rather like a string onion bag but is very effective. Repellents such as Aerogard and Rid go some way to deterring the little bastards. Fortunately they disappear when it gets dark, which makes those outback nights around the campfire all the more enjoyable.

Mosquitoes can be a problem too, especially in the warmer tropical and subtropical areas. The risk of malaria is negligible but there is a small risk of Ross River Fever, a debilitating virus with symptoms similar to glandular fever. Avoid bites by covering bare skin and using an insect repellent. Insect screens on windows and mosquito nets on beds offer protection. Mosquito coils give mixed results.

Most Australian **spiders** bite but very few are actually dangerous. One outback species to watch out for is the red-back spider, a relative of the American black widow. It's widespread, extremely poisonous and has a legendary liking for toilet seats. First-aid treatment is as for snake bite.

There are three species of **scorpion** in Australia, but they are not very venomous compared with overseas varieties; so far only one human is recorded to have died as a result of an Australian scorpion sting. Scorpions often shelter in shoes or clothing – always give your shoes a good shake-out before donning them in the morning, especially when camping.

Fish

Best known of all the outback's fish is the mighty **barramundi** of northern Australia. See Barramundi Fishing under Activities in

TONY WHEELER
Parakelias

DENIS O'BYRNE
Desert oak

DENIS O'BYRNE
Sturt's desert pea

JON MURRAY
Wattle in bloom

R & V MOON
Mulla mullas

DENIS O'BYRNE
Boab trees

PETER ROBINSON
Water lily

DENIS O'BYRNE
Ghost gums

DAVID CURL
Saltwater crocodile

DENIS O'BYRNE
Red kangaroo

PETER ROBINSON
Frill-necked lizard

JOHN CHAPMAN
Dingo

DAVID CURL
Blue-winged kookaburra

CHRIS KLEP
Echidna

DAVID CURL
Jabiru

PETER ROBINSON
Yellow-footed rock wallaby

the Facts for the Visitor chapter for more about this prized catch.

Surprisingly, the arid zone also has its share of fish, although most are very small. The major exception is the **yellowbelly**, or golden perch, which can grow to over 20kg. Yellowbellies are found in the Cooper Creek and Diamantina River systems, both of which drain into Lake Eyre.

The outback's most widespread fish is the **spangled perch**, which grows to about 0.5kg and occurs in coastal and inland streams of all mainland states – it's one of the largest of the 10 species found in central Australia's Finke River. Among the least widespread are three species known only from the hot pools of Dalhousie Springs, on the edge of the Simpson Desert.

Box Jellyfish

One sea creature you should be aware of is the box jellyfish, also known as the stinger or sea wasp. It inhabits coastal waters and estuaries north of the Tropic of Capricorn, and is particularly prevalent between October and mid-May. Its bell-shaped, translucent body is often difficult to spot, and its long, sticky tentacles discharge a highly potent venom that kills an average of one person a year and causes excruciating pain in many others.

If someone is stung, they are likely to run out of the sea, screaming, and collapse on the beach, with weals on their body as though they've been whipped. They may stop breathing, in which case artificial respiration is called for.

Douse the stings with household vinegar (available on many beaches or from nearby houses); this will deactivate the tentacles, which can then be carefully removed with tweezers. Apply a compression bandage over the affected area to localise the venom as for a snake bite, and then seek medical help as soon as possible. Above all, stay out of the sea when the sea wasps are around – the local people are ignoring that lovely water in the muggy season for an excellent reason.

Introduced Animals

Soon after foxes and rabbits were introduced to Australia for sport in the mid-1800s it became apparent that a dreadful mistake had been made. Both spread far and wide with remarkable speed and it wasn't long before they became pests. **Rabbits** have had a devastating effect on native plants and animals, particularly in the arid zone, while **foxes** – along with **domestic cats** gone wild – have chewed great holes in the populations of Australia's smaller marsupials. Feral cats are now found throughout the mainland but rabbits and foxes have yet to establish themselves in the tropical north. There are hopes that the recently introduced calicivirus, which is specific to European grey rabbits, will provide a permanent control on the feral rabbit population. Researchers are working on a biological control for foxes and cats.

At least 18 introduced mammal species are now feral in Australia and many have become pests. Oddly enough, the **dromedary**, or one-humped camel, seems to have had the smallest impact even though it's the largest feral animal. Australia's estimated 100,000 wild camels are descended from those released by their owners when the camel trains that supplied the outback for 50 years were replaced by motor vehicles in the 1920s and '30s. Now forming the world's only wild populations of this species (the other 13 million or so in North Africa and the Middle East are domesticated), Australian camels are being exported to the Middle East to improve the local gene pool.

Other introduced feral pests include the pig, goat, donkey, water buffalo, horse, starling, sparrow, blackbird and cane toad, all of which have multiplied rapidly in the wild through lack of natural enemies. Sparrows and starlings have yet to reach Western Australia – starling-shooters are employed on the border near the south coast to prevent them entering the state and posing a threat to agriculture. The vast herds of water buffalo that devastated large areas of the Northern Territory's Top End have now been shot out – these days the only buffalo you're likely to see are tame ones in a paddock.

Australian Ecosystems

The expanse of the island continent embraces a variety of ecosystems: dynamic interactions of the physical environment and living organisms. The following representations are composed 'snapshots'. Tropical rainforests and wetlands are found in the north of Australia, as are offshore coral reefs; eucalypt forests dominate in the south-east and south-west; and deserts and arid lands feature in the vast centre.

The typical image of Australia, of a mostly dry and harsh landscape, is largely true; but it wasn't always this way. The familiar arid-land flora and fauna had rainforest-dwelling ancestors – their fossil remains are imprinted in the rocks of the outback. Living and recognisable descendants of this wetter past flourish in the wet tropics of the north and the temperate rainforests of the south-east; a few reside in the deep gorges of central Australia. Contemporary ecosystems reflect this Gondwanan ancestry, the effects of continental drift and a gradually drying climate, the influence of Ice-age events, and, more recently, migrations of other animals (including humans) and plants from the Eurasian continent.

Nourlangie Rock and Anbangbang Billabong,
Kakadu National Park

Tropical Wetland

The tropical wetlands of northern Australia witness remarkable seasonal change. Growing,
flowering, feeding and breeding are all governed by the annual cycle of Wet and Dry.
Towards the end of the Dry, the receding swamps and lagoons attract thousands of water
birds; noisy flocks of whistling ducks and magpie geese are joined by fish-hunting jabiru
and pied herons. A series of spectacular storms precedes the Wet. By the end of December
heavy rains have arrived, signalling the estuarine crocodiles to nest and forcing the
antilopine wallaroos to higher ground. In the warm, wet environment, plant growth is rapid.
Many water birds now nest among the rushes and wild rice. Further storms flatten the tall
grasses, and by about May, the Wet is over. As the land dries, natural fires and Aboriginal
hunting fires continue to shape this environment.

Left: Brolgas and magpie geese
Right: Darter drying its wings in the sunshine

Left: Red lily
Right: Magpie geese and egrets gather on the edge of a drying floodplain

Left: Estuarine crocodile eating a file snake
Right: Kakadu's floodplains during the Wet

A diverse rainforest understorey of palms, ferns and
saplings at Cape Tribulation National Park

Tropical Rainforest

There is scarcely a niche in the warm, damp environment that is not occupied by lush, green
vegetation. The tree canopy filters sunlight and resounds to the calls of birds and fruit bats.
The trunks of trees support lichens, ferns and orchids, and the understorey and forest floor
are a profusion of palms, more ferns and the essential fungi and micro-organisms that
decompose the rich forest litter. Pythons, bandicoots, cassowaries and native mice are the
largest inhabitants of the forest floor, while among the tree branches clamber possums,
clumsy tree kangaroos and monkey-like cuscuses. Interrupting the almost uniform green
are brightly coloured birds and butterflies, often seen near water or displaying themselves
in patches of sunlight.

Most of Australia's tropical rainforest is restricted to a few mountain ranges and along
river courses on the north-east coast. The wet tropic region supports many endemic species
of plants and animals, some of which closely resemble the inhabitants of the cool rainforest
that once covered much of Australia.

Left: King parrot
Right: The brightly coloured cassowary

Left: Bracket fungi
Right: Epiphytic ferns and vines in the rainforest midstorey

Left: Green tree frog
Right: Ulysses butterfly

The coral environment offers a dazzling array of colours

Coral Reef

Unlike other ecosystems of great diversity, coral reefs do not have a conspicuous flora. There are, however, symbiotic algae living within coral, encrusting coralline algae which help to hold the reefs together, and a thin algal turf covering most of the reef. Close to the mainland, in shallows protected from ocean swells by the reef, are seagrass meadows, home to dugongs and a nursery for many fish. Six of the world's seven species of sea turtle feed and breed in these waters. Swimming and crawling among the coral are many unrecorded varieties of fish, crustaceans, echinoderms and molluscs. Above and along the reef edge prowl barracuda, sharks and sailfish. Overhead, gannets, terns, shearwaters, gulls and frigatebirds search for a feed of fish; the isolated coral cays provide a relatively safe nesting ground for thousands of seabirds.

MARK NORMAN

GBRMPA

Left: Gorgonian coral
Right: False clown anemonefish

MARK NORMAN

GREAT BARRIER REEF MARINE PARK AUTHORITY

Left: Regal angelfish
Right: Dugong and calf

ROGER FENWICK

TONY WHEELER

Left: Green turtle
Right: Black noddy

RICHARD I'ANSON

Mountain ash with a fern understorey

Eucalypt Forest

The eucalypt tree is typically Australian but there is no typical eucalypt forest. Depending on climate and soil, you may find mountain ash (the world's tallest flowering plant), stunted alpine gum, hardy arid land ironbark or desert gum. Understorey ranges from moist ferns to dry acacias, sedges and grasses. Eucalypt-associated faunas reveal similar variety. Although there are over 600 species of eucalypt, only a handful of species in the south-east of the continent are eaten by the koala. Less particular are the common possums, the brushtail and the ringtail, who both supplement their diets of eucalypt leaves with fruits and insects. Announcing its presence with a familiar laugh, the kookaburra is a daytime hunter of lizards, snakes, frogs and small mammals. Grey kangaroos and wallabies may be seen moving into open forest in the evenings to browse shrubs and graze native grasses. Also out for a nightly forage, the common wombat, a relative of the koala, grazes its home range before returning to one of its large and conspicuous burrows.

RICHARD I'ANSON

Alpine gums are hardy enough to survive the climatic extremes
of Australia's alpine regions

RICHARD TIMBURY

Eucalypt forest covers vast expanses of Australia's landscape.
There are over 600 varieties of eucalypt, or gum tree.

Right: Despite there
being hundreds of
species of eucalypt in
Australia, the koala
only eats the leaves of
a select few

Far Right: Eucalypt in
flower

RICHARD I'ANSON

RICHARD I'ANSON

Typical flora of the Red Centre: mulga, spinifex and desert oaks

Central Desert

In the arid centre of Australia life is most conspicuous in shaded gorges and along dry river courses where river red gums, home to colourful and noisy parrots, are able to tap deep reserves of water. On this ancient, eroded landscape, sparse vegetation and red sandy soils are infrequently and temporarily transformed by rain into a carpet of wildflowers. Tell-tale tracks in the sand lead to clumps of spinifex grass and burrows. Small marsupials and mice are mostly nocturnal; the rare and endangered bilby was once common to much of Australia but is now only found in the deserts of central Australia. A few of the lizards, such as the thorny devil, will venture out into the heat of the day for a feed of ants. Among the scattered mulga and desert oak, mobs of kangaroos, the males brick-red and over two metres tall, seek shelter from the sun; but seemingly impervious to the heat, emus, with an insulating double layer of feathers, continue the search for seeds and fruit. In the evenings rock-wallabies emerge from rocky outcrops to browse on nearby vegetation. Most animals breed in the cooler winter – their eggs and young attracting the attention of dingoes, eagles and perenties.

Flora and fauna of the central deserts – emus, Sturt's desert pea
and kangaroos

Left: River red gums line a dry creek bed
Right: Major Mitchell cockatoos

Thousands of years ago, as the climate changed and lakes dried up,
animals like the thorny devil adapted to life in the arid desert

PALAEONTOLOGY

Australia has abundant evidence of earlier life forms, but the search is not easy as much of it is conducted in outback regions where conditions are harsh. (See the Palaeontological and Archaeological Sites map.)

Palaeontologists distinguish four main eras – Precambrian (2300-570 million years old), Palaeozoic (570-225 million years), Mesozoic (225-65 million years) and Cainozoic (65 million years to the present) – and many more periods which are sub-divisions of the four eras.

The theory of continental drift says that the earth's landmass started as a supercontinent called Pangaea. About 200 million years ago, Pangaea broke into the northern and southern continents of Laurasia and Gondwanaland respectively; the latter consisted of what we now call Africa, South America, Australia, Antarctica and the Indian subcontinent. It eventually broke apart too, and Australia began its lonely journey northwards – see the preceding Geology section.

In the Beginning...

The layered, mainly limestone deposits known as stromatolites, in the saline Hamelin Pool near Shark Bay in Western Australia, are still formed by the blue-green algae that are believed to have developed over three billion years ago. This makes them the oldest form of life on earth.

Australia also has some of the oldest rocks on earth and embedded in them are some of the oldest fossils. Australia's most primitive vertebrate (back-boned) fish, *Arandaspis* from the Ordovician period (500-435 million years ago), were found in the Stairway sandstone deposits of the Amadeus Basin in the Northern Territory.

Australia is also known for its cornucopia of Devonian fish (395-345 million years ago). The Devonian Reef national parks of the Kimberley are a good source of fossils. Gogo Station, near Fitzroy Crossing, is the site of bony-plated placoderms such as the vertebrate *Rolfosteus canningenis*, which fed on fish and invertebrates in the ancient reef environment of the Devonian period.

In 240-million-year-old (Permian) coal deposits near Blackwater, central Queensland, curious fish with an upturned snout (*Ebenaqua ritchiei*) were uncovered in a large open-cut mine.

Amphibian life forms thrived during the Triassic period (230-195 million years ago). The Blina Shale of the Erskine Range, between Fitzroy Crossing and Derby, has revealed two interesting examples: *Deltasaurus kimberleyensis*, a fish predator similar to a crocodile in appearance; and *Erythrobatrachus noonkanbahensis*, another fish-eater with an elongated skull.

The first *dicynodont* ('two canine teeth') fossil was found in an area known as the Crater, near Carnarvon Gorge, Queensland. It was the first mammal-like reptile (theraspid) known to Australia, and became known as the 'Creature from the Crater'.

Dinosaurs & Friends

The Jurassic period (195-140 million years ago) was the heyday of the dinosaurs. There are possibly three groups: saurischians, ornithischians and a mixture of those two. In 1924 a fair amount of bone material of a four-footed, long-necked, long-tailed reptile (or sauropod) known as *Rhoetosaurus brownei* was found near Roma in Queensland, the first Jurassic example in Australia.

Other creatures of the Jurassic period were the pliosaurs and plesiosaurs – marine reptiles. Remains of a freshwater pliosaur were found near Mount Morgan in Queensland and the remains of two plesiosaurs were recovered from the Evergreen formation, 70km north of Wandoan in south-east Queensland.

One interesting tale of the naming of bones relates to the opalised skeleton of Eric, a pliosaur from the Cretaceous period (140-60 million years ago) who tours the country feted like a celebrity. Eric was unearthed near Coober Pedy, South Australia, and after a national campaign, purchased for all Australians. Why 'Eric'? Well, the person who

Legend:
- ● Archaeological Site
- ■ Palaeontological Site

Kakadu
Darwin

Orri River • ■
Delamere ■

Early Human Shelter, Laura ●

Chillagoe ■

Blina Shale ■
Gogo Station ■
Dinosaur Footprints ■

NORTHERN
TERRITORY

Riversleigh Station ■

Burrup Peninsula ■

Richmond ■
Hughenden ■

Mt Newman ■

Alcoota ■
Lake Amadeus ■
Uluru ● (Ayers Rock)

Lark Quarry ■
Boulia ■
Muttaburra ■

QUEENSLAND

Blackwater ■

Simpson Desert

Carnarvon Gorge ■ (The Crater)

Mt Morgan ■
Wandoon ■

WESTERN
AUSTRALIA

SOUTH
AUSTRALIA

Minmi ■
Roma ■

Chinchilla ■

Brisbane ●

Stromatolites, Shark Bay

Keanalda Cave ●
Andamooka ■
Human Footprints ●

Lake Callabonna ■
Lake Frome

Meatwingee ■
Lake Mungo

Lightning Ridge ■

Swan River ■
Perth ●
Devil's Lake

Adelaide ●

N E W
SOUTH
WALES

Lake Talbragar ■
Sydney ●

Ossuaries, Naracoorte

Kow Swamp

Canberra ◎

V I C T O R I A

Melbourne ●

**Palaeontological &
Archaeological Sites**

Kutakina Cave, Franklin River

Hobart ●

TASMANIA

0   500   1000 km

lovingly pieced together the jigsaw of bones was a John Cleese fanatic: the fish bones found in the plesiosaur's stomach contents were named Wanda, and the devourer of the fish, Eric.

The skeleton of a bulky dinosaur, *Muttaburrasaurus langdoni*, was found in a cattle-mustering area on the banks of the Thomson River near Muttaburra, 100km north of Longreach, Queensland. The bones surfaced in early Cretaceous marine deposits and before they were gathered up, cattle had trodden into the dust what local souvenir hunters had failed to gather.

After a public appeal the jigsaw began to take shape and the bone-detectives realised that they had chanced upon an ornithischian (bird-hipped) dinosaur of the Ornithopoda, or 'Bird-foot', suborder. What was more, it was closely related to the group of iguanodontids of the northern hemisphere. See for yourself when passing through Brisbane, as 'Mutta' is now displayed in the Queensland Museum (an artist's rendition in steel and plaster lives outside the general store-cum-petrol station in Muttaburra).

A spectacular Cretaceous reptile is *Kronosaurus queenslandicus*. Its first frag-

Muttaburrasaurus (Queensland Museum)

ments were found near Hughenden, Queensland. It is thought to be the largest known marine reptile, and the name is derived from the Greek god Kronos who ate his children so they could not take over his throne. 'Krono' is a bulky pliosaur with its head making up for a quarter of its length.

Bones of Cretaceous ichthyosaurs have been found in a number of places; the broad-finned *Platypterygius australis* was found near Richmond, Queensland, and other sites throughout the Great Artesian Basin.

Only two specimens of Cretaceous sauropods have been found and one named: *Austrosaurus*. Their bone fragments were found in central Queensland. Two of the impressive carnivorous theropods, similar to the overseas *Allosaurus*, lived in the Cretaceous: *Rapator ornitholestoides*, found near Lightning Ridge; and *Kakuru kujani*, found near Andamooka.

There is also evidence of where these huge creatures passed. Preserved footprints of a 3m-high specimen are found at Gantheaume Point near Broome. More spectacular is the dinosaur stampede discovered at Lark Quarry south of Winton, Queensland. The prints were made when about 130 small dinosaurs were scared at a waterhole by a 5m-long carnosaur dinosaur.

In the air, Australia boasted some mean-looking pterosaurs, or winged reptiles. In 1979, fossils were excavated near Boulia in west Queensland which occurred in early Cretaceous marine limestones, and more recently, jaws were discovered near Boulia and Richmond. The pterosaurs had a wingspan of 2m and were small sea-going fish-eaters.

During the Eocene period (38-26 million years ago), the giant lungfish *Neoceradotus gregoryi*, known from central Australia and south-east Queensland, would have been crunching on water plants and freshwater snails. In the middle Miocene (16-14 million years ago), *rhabdosteids*, a type of river dolphin, inhabited the inland waterways. The bones of about six of them have been found in sediments in the Lake Frome district of South Australia.

There were huge flightless birds as well, such as 'giant emus' – the Mihirungs of Aboriginal mythology, which fossil evidence now seems to substantiate. *Dromornis stirtoni* was probably the world's largest bird. At 3m in height and over 300kg in weight it was much larger than Madagascar's extinct elephant bird; fossils from the Miocene were found at Alcoota Station near Alice Springs.

Alcoota has been a rich source of fossil material of the late Miocene (14 to 7 million years ago). It has provided information on the oldest known meat-eating thylacinids: a marsupial lion called *Wakaleo alcootaensis*, and a cow-sized diprotodontid, *Plaisiodon centralis*.

Mammals

In Europe, mammals have been known for 200 million years (from the Triassic onwards), but in Australia they are relative newcomers. Australia's oldest fossil mammal is a relatively recent discovery; it is a monotreme, *Steropodon galmani*, found in Cretaceous opal near Lightning Ridge and believed to be 110 million years old. Until then, the oldest known monotreme was *Obdurodon insignis*, similar to a modern-day platypus, revealed from 15-million-year-old deposits from the Simpson Desert.

Marsupials that have long since become extinct include the Diprotodonta and related families – for example, *Ngapakaldia*, whose 14-million-year-old remains were retrieved from Riversleigh in north-west Queensland; or *Neohelos*, a browsing herbivore found in the Lake Eyre Basin, Bullock Creek in the Northern Territory and Riversleigh.

The biggest of the marsupials was *Diprotodon optatum*, about 3m long and 2m high at the shoulder. This bulky creature ranged all over the continent and is thought to have disappeared between 25,000 and 15,000 years ago. Evidence of the largest of the wombats, *Phascolonus gigas*, from the Pleistocene, has been found at Cooper Creek, Lake Callabonna and Lake Eyre.

Riversleigh Station is a treasure trove of fossils. The remains of *Wabularoo naughtoni* joins a number of other species of kangaroo found here. It is a type of rat-kangaroo which became extinct when browsing kangaroos evolved 10 to five million years ago.

Also found in recent times at Gag Site, Riversleigh, is an entirely new order of mammals, loosely named *Thingodonta* for a while but now known as *Yalkaparidon coheni*. The fossil remains of a 7m long snake were given the name *Montypythonoides*.

The Queensland Museum in Brisbane has the country's best collection of outback-related fossil and dinosaur material. Read more about this fascinating subject in *Prehistoric Australia* by Brian Mackness (Golden Press, Sydney, 1987); *The Antipodean Ark*, edited by Suzanne Hand & Michael Archer (Angus & Robertson, Sydney, 1987); and *Prehistoric Animals of Australia*, edited by Susan Quirk & Michael Archer (Australian Museum, Sydney, 1983). The latter two contain excellent illustrations by Peter Schouten.

NATIONAL PARKS

Australia has more than 500 national parks – non-urban protected wilderness areas of environmental or natural importance. Each state defines and runs its own national parks,

Stromatolites

The dolphins at Monkey Mia didn't contribute to the listing of Shark Bay as a World Heritage area; one of the main reasons was the existence of stromatolites (rocky formations) at Hamelin Pool. These structures are several thousands of years old but are built by the oldest living things on this planet, the blue-green algae (one-celled plants) that evolved over 3.5 *billion* years ago.

Hamelin Pool is suited to the growth of stromatolites because of the clarity and hypersalinity of the water; the latter prevents other organisms from attacking the algae. In essence, each stromatolite is covered in a form of cyanobacterial microbe shaped like algae which waves around during daily photosynthesis. At night the microbes fold over, trapping calcium and carbonate ions dissolved in the water. The sticky chemicals they exude add to the concretion of another layer on the surface of the stromatolite.

These are the most accessible stromatolites in the world, spectacularly set amidst the turquoise waters of Hamelin Pool. Don't disturb them. ■

but the principle is the same throughout Australia.

While public access is encouraged, safety and conservation regulations must be observed. The codes of behaviour may vary slightly from state to state and park to park, but essentially all plants and animals are protected, and you're asked to do nothing to damage or alter the natural environment. Among other things, this means driving only on established tracks, camping only in designated areas, disposing of rubbish properly and taking care with fire.

Some outback parks and reserves, such as South Australia's Gammon Ranges National Park, are so isolated, rugged or harsh that they aren't recommended unless you're an experienced bushwalker or 4WD motorist. Others, however, are among Australia's major attractions; some of the most beautiful have been included on the World Heritage List – a United Nations list of natural or cultural places of world significance that would present an irreplaceable loss to the planet if they were altered.

The World Heritage List includes the Taj Mahal, the pyramids, the Grand Canyon and several areas in the Australian outback: the Great Barrier Reef; Kakadu and Uluru national parks in the Northern Territory; the Willandra Lakes region of far western New South Wales; and Shark Bay on the Western Australian coast. The Australian Conservation Foundation is one of a number of bodies lobbying to have further places listed. In the outback these are the Lake Eyre Basin and Cape York Peninsula.

The outback's national park landscapes include rainforests, wetlands, sandy deserts, coastal cliffs and dunes, and rugged ranges. Most are accessible to vehicles, although many are restricted to 4WD only. While camping is generally allowed, facilities at the more remote, less-visited parks are either minimal or non-existent; details on camping are found in the descriptions of tracks and destinations later in this book. For details on outback parks, contact the appropriate state management body – see under Useful Organisations in the chapter on Facts for the Visitor.

South Australia has several enormous conservation areas. They include Witjira National Park (7770 sq km), which protects a unique concentration of artesian mound springs on the edge of the Simpson Desert. In the state's north-east, the Innamincka Regional Reserve (14,000 sq km) has plenty of variety – you'll see gibber plains of the Sturt Stony Desert, sandhills of the Strzelecki Desert, and semi-permanent wetlands and large permanent waterholes along the Cooper Creek system. Other South Australian parks include the beds of huge, mainly dry salt lakes (eg Lake Eyre National Park and Lake Torrens National Park) and vast tracts of sand ridge desert country (eg Unnamed Conservation Park in the west, and the Simpson Desert Regional Reserve).

Parks in Western Australia's Hamersley Ranges, South Australia's Flinders Ranges and the Northern Territory's MacDonnell Ranges near Alice Springs offer some of the Australian arid zone's most dramatic landscapes, including a surprising variety of plant species. Also near Alice Springs, Finke Gorge National Park contains lush remnants of a vanished rainforest along one of the world's oldest river systems. Mootwingee National Park near Broken Hill is a good place to learn about Aboriginal traditions in an arid environment.

As can be expected, the main features of the parks and reserves in tropical northern Australia typically reflect the monsoonal climate of the region. Right up the east coast from Cairns to the tip of Cape York, a series of parks offers rainforests, wetlands or the wonders of the Great Barrier Reef. These include Lakefield (Queensland's second-largest national park) and Lizard Island (one of its most beautiful).

Kakadu National Park near Darwin is famous for its Aboriginal heritage, not to mention the teeming birdlife that congregates around its wetlands come the late dry season. Gregory National Park in the Territory's north-west has a network of remote 4WD tracks; further west, the Kimberley region's Purnululu (Bungle Bungle) National Park is best known for its sandstone 'beehive' formations and deep narrow gorges.

Finally, for a place with no trees, hills or rivers at all, try the Nullarbor National Park and adjoining regional reserve on the Nullarbor Plain in south-western South Australia. Nullarbor is from the Latin for 'no trees', and that's no exaggeration here. The plain seems endlessly flat and bare, and there's a mind-blowing sense of space and isolation.

GOVERNMENT & POLITICS

Australia is a federation of six states and two territories. Under the written constitution, which came into force on 1 January 1901, the colonies joined to form the independent Commonwealth of Australia. The federal (central) government is mainly responsible for the national economy and Reserve Bank, customs and excise, immigration, defence, foreign policy and the post office. The state governments are chiefly responsible for health, education, housing, transport and infrastructure, and justice. There are both federal and state police forces.

Australia has a parliamentary system of government based on that of the UK, and the state and federal structures are broadly similar. In Federal Parliament, the lower house is the House of Representatives (with 147 members, divided among the states on a population basis), and the upper house is the Senate. Elections for the House of Reps are held at least every three years; voting is by secret ballot and is compulsory for citizens aged 18 and over. Senators serve six-year terms, with elections for half of them every three years. Queensland does not have an upper house: it was abolished in 1922. The Commonwealth government is run by a prime minister; the state governments are led by a premier, and the Northern Territory by a chief minister. The party holding the greatest number of lower house seats forms the government.

Australia is a monarchy, but although Britain's king or queen is Australia's head of state, Australia is fully autonomous. The British sovereign is represented by the governor general and state governors, whose nominations for their posts by the respective governments are ratified by the monarch of the day. Increasing numbers of people feel that the continued constitutional ties with Britain are no longer relevant. There's still a deal of soul-searching to be done before the governor-general is replaced by a president of a Republic of Australia, but change seems inevitable.

The Federal Parliament is based in Canberra, the capital of the nation. Like Washington DC in the USA, Canberra is in its own separate area of land, the Australian Capital Territory (ACT), and is not under the rule of one of the states. Geographically, however, the ACT is completely surrounded by New South Wales. The state parliaments are based in each state capital.

In the Federal Parliament, the two main political groups are the Australian Labor Party (ALP) and the coalition between the Liberal Party and the National Party. These parties also dominate state politics but sometimes the Liberal and National parties are not in coalition. The latter was once known as the National Country Party since it mainly represents country seats. The only other political party of any real substance is the Australian Democrats, which has largely carried the flag for the ever-growing 'green' movement.

Aboriginal Land Rights

As we have seen, Britain founded the colony of New South Wales on the legal principle of *terra nullius*, empty land or land belonging to no-one, which meant that Australia was legally unoccupied. The settlers could take land from Aborigines without signing treaties or providing compensation. The European concept of land ownership was completely foreign to Aborigines and their view of the world in which land did not belong to individuals: people belonged to the land, were formed by it and were a part of it like everything else.

After WWII, Australian Aborigines became more organised and better educated, and a political movement for land rights developed. In 1962 a bark petition was presented to the federal government by the Yolngu people of Yirrkala, in north-east Arnhem Land, demanding that the government recognise Aboriginal peoples' occupation and ownership of Australia since time immemorial. The petition was ignored, and the Yolngu people took the matter to court – and lost. In the famous Yirrkala Land Case 1971, Australian courts accepted the government's claim that Aborigines had no meaningful economic, legal or political relationship to land. The case upheld the principle of *terra nullius*, and the common-law position that Australia was unoccupied in 1788.

Because the Yirrkala Land Case was based on an inaccurate (if not outright racist) assessment of Aboriginal society, the federal government came under increasing pressure to legislate for Aboriginal land rights. In 1976 it eventually passed the Aboriginal Land Rights Act (Northern Territory) – often referred to as the Land Rights Act.

Australian Land Rights Acts The Aboriginal Land Rights Act, which operates in the Northern Territory, remains Australia's most powerful and comprehensive land rights legislation. Promises were made to legislate for national land rights, but these were abandoned after opposition from mining companies and state governments. The act established three Aboriginal Land Councils, which are empowered to claim land on behalf of traditional Aboriginal owners.

However, under the act the only land claimable is unalienated Northern Territory land outside town boundaries – land that no-one else owns or leases, usually semi-desert or desert. Thus, when the traditional Anangu owners of Uluru (Ayers Rock) claimed traditional ownership of Uluru and Kata Tjuta (the Olgas), their claim was disallowed because the land was within a national park and thus alienated. It was only by amending two acts of parliament that Uluru-Kata Tjuta National Park was handed back to the Anangu owners on the condition that it was immediately leased back to the federal government as a national park.

At present almost half of the Northern Territory has either been claimed, or is being claimed, by its traditional Aboriginal owners. The claim process is extremely tedious and can take many years to complete, largely because almost all claims have been opposed by the Territory government. A great many elderly claimants die before the matter is resolved. Claimants are required to prove that under Aboriginal law they are responsible for the sacred sites on the land being claimed. Once a claim is successful, Aboriginal people have the right to negotiate with mining companies and ultimately accept or reject exploration and mining proposals.

The Pitjantjatjara Land Rights Act 1981 (South Australia) is Australia's second-most powerful and comprehensive land rights law. This gives Anangu Pitjantjatjara and Yankunytjatjara people freehold title to 10% of South Australia. The land known as the Anangu Pitjantjatjara Lands is in the far north of the state.

Just south of the Anangu Pitjantjatjara Lands lie the Maralinga Lands, and they comprise about 8% of South Australia. The area, largely contaminated by British nuclear tests, was returned to its Anangu traditional owners by virtue of the Maralinga Tjarutja Land Rights Act 1984 (South Australia).

Under these two South Australian acts, Anangu can control access to land and liquor consumption. However, if traditional owners cannot reach agreement with mining companies seeking to explore or mine on their land, they cannot veto mining activity – an arbitrator decides if mining will go ahead. If the arbitrator gives mining the green light, he/she will bind the mining company with terms and conditions and ensure that reasonable monetary payments are made to Anangu.

Outside the Northern Territory and South Australia, Aboriginal land rights are extremely limited. In Queensland, only 1.85% of the state is Aboriginal land, and the only land that can be claimed under the

Aboriginal Land Act 1991 (Queensland) is land which has been gazetted by the government as land available for claim. Under existing Queensland legislation, 95% of the state's Aborigines can't claim their traditional country.

Since the passing of the Nature Conservation Act 1992 (Queensland), Aborigines in the state also have very limited claim to national parks. If Aborigines successfully claim a Queensland park, they must permanently lease it back to the government without a guarantee of a review of the lease arrangement or a majority on the board of management. This is quite different from the arrangements at Uluru-Kata Tjuta National Park, where the traditional owners have a majority on the board, with a 99-year lease-back that is renegotiated every five years.

In Western Australia, Aboriginal reserves comprise about 13% of the state. Of this land about one-third is granted to Aborigines under 99-year leases; the other two-thirds are controlled by the government's Aboriginal Affairs Planning Authority. Control of mining and payments to communities are a matter of ministerial discretion.

In New South Wales, the Aboriginal Land Rights Act 1983 (New South Wales) transferred freehold title of existing Aboriginal reserves to Aborigines and gave them the right to claim a minuscule amount of other land. Aborigines also have limited rights to the state's national parks, but these rights fall short of genuine control and don't permit Aborigines to live inside parks.

Mabo & the Native Title Act In May 1982, five Torres Strait Islanders led by Eddie Mabo began an action for a declaration of native title over the Queensland Murray Islands. They argued that the legal principle of *terra nullius* had wrongfully usurped their title to land, as for thousands of years Murray Islanders had enjoyed a relationship with the land that included a notion of ownership. In

---

Vincent Lingiari & the Wave Hill Stockmen's Strike of 1966

Aboriginal stockmen played an essential role in the early days of the pastoral industry in the Northern Territory. Because they were paid such paltry wages (which often never even materialised), a pastoralist could afford to employ many of them, and run his station at a much lower cost. White stockmen received regular and relatively high wages, were given decent food and accommodation, and were able to return to the station homestead every week. By contrast, Aboriginal stockmen received poor food and accommodation, little or no money, and would often spend months in the bush with the cattle.

In the 1960s Vincent Lingiari was a stockman on the huge Wave Hill station, owned by the British Vesteys company. His concern about the way Aboriginal workers were treated led to an appeal to the North Australian Workers' Union (NAWU), which had already applied to the federal court for equal wages for Aboriginal workers. The federal court approved the granting of equal wages in March 1966, but it was not to take effect until December 1968. The decision led Lingiari to ask the Wave Hill management direct for equal wages – it was refused, and, on 23 August 1966, the Aboriginal stockmen walked off the station and camped in nearby Wattie Creek. They were soon joined by others, and before long only stations which gave their Aboriginal workers not only good conditions but also respect, were provided with workers by Lingiari and the other Gurindji elders.

The Wattie Creek camp gained a lot of local support, from both white and Aboriginal people, and it soon developed into a sizeable community with housing and a degree of organisation. Having gained the right to be paid equally, Lingiari and the Gurindji people felt, perhaps for the first time, that they had some say in the way they were able to live. This victory led to the hope that perhaps they could achieve something even more important – title to their own land. To this end Lingiari travelled widely in the eastern states campaigning for land rights, and finally made some progress with the Whitlam government in Canberra. On 16 August 1975, Whitlam attended a ceremony at Wattie Creek which saw the handing over of 3200 sq km of land, now known as Daguragu.

Lingiari was awarded the Order of Australia Medal for service to the Aboriginal people, and died at Daguragu in 1988. ■

June 1992 the High Court of Australia rejected *terra nullius* and the myth that Australia had been unoccupied. In doing this, it recognised that a principle of native title existed before the arrival of the British.

The High Court's judgment became known as the Mabo decision, one of the most controversial decisions ever handed down by an Australian court. It was ambiguous, as it didn't outline the extent to which native title existed in mainland Australia. However, it was hailed by Aborigines and then-Prime Minister Paul Keating as an opportunity to create a basis of reconciliation between Aboriginal and non-Aboriginal Australians.

To define the principle of native title, the federal parliament passed the Native Title Act in December 1993. Its intention was to limit the application of native title to land which no-one else owns or leases, and to land with which Aborigines have continued to have a physical association. The act stated that native title is extinguished by existing freehold title, but did not adequately address the issue of native title and pastoral leases. It also stated that where land is successfully claimed by Aborigines under the act, they will have no veto over developments including mining.

The Wik Decision Several months prior to the Native Title Act becoming law, the Wik and Thayorre peoples had made a claim in the Federal Court for native title to land on Cape York Peninsula. The area claimed included two pastoral leases. Neither had ever been permanently occupied for that purpose, but the Wik and Thayorre peoples had been in continuous occupation of them. They argued that native title coexisted with the pastoral leases.

In January 1996 the Federal Court decided that the claim could not succeed as the granting of pastoral leases under Queensland law extinguished any native title rights. The Wik people appealed that decision in the High Court, which subsequently overturned it.

The High Court determined that, under the law that created pastoral leases in Queensland, native title to the leases in question had

not been extinguished. Further, it said that native title rights could continue at the same time that land was under lease, and that pastoralists did not have exclusive right of possession to their leases. However, it did not decide what the native title rights of the Wik and Thayorre peoples were.

The Wik decision brought a hue and cry from pastoral leasees across Australia, who claimed that the security of their leases was under threat. They demanded that the Federal Government step in to protect them by legislating to limit native title rights, as was intended in the original act. Aboriginal leaders were equally adamant that native title must be preserved. Whatever the Federal Government's response to Wik, it's obvious that an unnegotiated settlement of this issue will put new and extravagant meaning into 'lawyers' picnic'.

ECONOMY

Australia is a relatively affluent, industrialised nation but most of its wealth still comes from agriculture and mining. It has a small domestic market and a comparatively weak manufacturing sector. Nevertheless, a substantial proportion of the population is employed in manufacturing, and for much of Australia's history it has been argued that these industries need tariff protection from imports to ensure their survival.

Today, however, tariff protection is on the way out and efforts are being made to increase Australia's international competitiveness. This has become more important as prices of traditional primary exports have become more volatile.

In the outback, where so much of the economy is dependent on wool, meat and mining, this volatility has resulted in a roller-coaster ride of boom and bust. Alongside the huge cattle and wool enterprises and the billion-dollar mining conglomerates, there are thousands of struggling cow cockies, hard-partying opal diggers and reclusive gold-panning hermits. More often than not, these interesting characters fight a hard battle for survival in a harsh environment, but very

The Cattle Kings

More than any other enterprise, it was pastoral activity in general and the cattle industry in particular that led to white settlement in much of Inland Australia. Given the vast distances, the often marginal country and the harsh climate, it was an arduous and often risky business to develop stations and rear cattle. Yet there was no shortage of triers prepared to give it a go, and some went on to make major contributions.

Sir Sidney Kidman Sid Kidman was the undisputed cattle king of Australia. He was born in Adelaide in 1857 and ran away from home at the age of 13. He headed north for the 'corner country' of north-western New South Wales where he found work on outback stations. Over the years he became an expert bushman and stockman.

It was in the latter part of the last century that the vast expanses of outback Australia were settled. The infrastructure was virtually nil and getting cattle to markets in good condition was a major problem. Kidman came up with a bold yet superbly simple solution: 'chains' of stations along strategic routes which would allow the gradual movement of stock from the inland to the coastal markets – in effect, splitting the entire outback into a number of paddocks.

Starting with £400 which he inherited at the age of 21, Kidman traded in cattle and horses, and later Broken Hill mines, and gradually built up a portfolio of land-holdings which gave him the envisaged 'chains'. Eventually he owned or controlled about 170,000 sq km of land (an area 2½ times the size of Tasmania, or about the size of Washington state) in chains, one which ran from the Gulf of Carpentaria south through western Queensland and New South Wales to Broken Hill and into South Australia, and another from the Kimberley into the Northern Territory and then down through the Red Centre and into South Australia.

Sir Sidney Kidman (1857-1935)

Such was Kidman's stature as a pastoralist that at one time the north-western area of New South Wales was known as 'Kidman's Corner'. His life was portrayed, somewhat romantically, in Ion Idriess's book *The Cattle King*. Kidman was knighted in 1921, and died in 1935.

The Duracks Another name that is firmly linked with cattle and the opening up of inland Australia is the Durack family. Brothers Patrick (Patsy) and Michael Durack took up land on Cooper Creek in western Queensland in the 1860s, and were soon joined by members of their extended family.

With the discovery of good pastoral land in the Kimberley, the Duracks took up land in the Ord River in 1882. A huge cattle muster was organised and in June 1863 four parties of drovers with a total of 7500 head of cattle set off from the Cooper Creek area. On the map the trip was a neat 2500km, but in 'drover's miles', meandering from water to water and grass to grass, it was much further. It took 28 months to make the journey, and men and cattle suffered greatly along the way – at one point they were held up for months at a waterhole waiting for the drought to break. Many cattle were lost to pleuropneumonia and tick fever.

Nevertheless, the party reached the Ord in September 1885 and still had enough cattle to establish three stations: Rosewood, Argyle and Lissadel.

Patsy Durack's granddaughter, Mary, became a popular author, and many of her novels were set in the Kimberley. Her most well-known work is *Kings in Grass Castles*, in which she describes the great trek.

Patrick (Patsy) Durack (1834-1898)

(Continued on next page)

Nat Buchanan Although Nathaniel Buchanan was not a great land-holder in the mould of the Duracks or Sidney Kidman, he was a great cattleman and drover, responsible for the settlement of huge areas of the outback.

Known as Old Bluey because of his shock of red hair, Buchanan led many drives through Queensland and the Northern Territory, and was responsible for what was probably the largest cattle drive ever to be undertaken in Australia: the movement of 20,000 head from Aramac in Queensland to Glenco Station near Adelaide River in the Northern Territory.

In 1896, at the age of 70, Buchanan set off from Sturt Creek, in northern Western Australia, trying to find a direct route across the Tanami Desert to Tennant Creek which was suitable for cattle, rather than having to take them much further north. Although the cattle route didn't eventuate, this was probably the first European crossing of the Tanami Desert.

Buchanan was accompanied on some of his drives by his son, Gordon, who wrote about his experiences in the book *Packhorse & Waterhole*. ∎

few of them would dream of surrendering their freedom.

A typical cattle or sheep station in the outback covers tens if not hundreds of thousands of hectares, and the larger ones are the size of small countries – Anna Creek station in South Australia is the size of Belgium! Large stations may have one or more semi-independent outstations. The headquarters of a station is the homestead, which is where the owner (or manager) and staff live. The livestock is often left to fend for itself, though the owner will ensure that there are sufficient watering points where additional fodder and salt may be left. Once or twice a year the livestock is mustered to check on their general welfare and take stock of births and deaths, but they may be mustered more often for sale or to move them to other paddocks. Sheep are shorn twice a year – firstly the main shearing and then later on the stragglers; cattle are mustered once a year for ear-marking.

One of Australia's greatest economic hopes is tourism, with the numbers of visitors rising each year and projections for even greater numbers in the future. The other bright spot is the booming economies of South-East Asia. Australia is perfectly positioned to enter these markets, providing goods and services.

The government has sought to restrain real wages and is trying to stimulate new manufacturing and service industries. This policy has seen the creation of new jobs while many people employed in traditional sectors joined the dole queues, and unemployment is currently around 9%. However, prospects for the future are cautiously optimistic.

Although most non-Aboriginal Australians enjoy a relatively high standard of living, the same cannot be said for most of their Aboriginal counterparts. Many Aborigines still live in deplorable conditions, with infant mortality and outbreaks of preventable diseases running at an unacceptably high rate – higher even than in many Third World countries. Progress has definitely been made with the recent Native Title legislation (see the previous Government section), but there is still a very long way to go before Aborigines can enjoy the lifestyle of their choice.

POPULATION & PEOPLE

Australia's population is about 17 million. The most populous states are New South Wales and Victoria, each with a capital city (Sydney and Melbourne) with a population of around three million. Nationwide, the population is concentrated along the east-coast strip from Adelaide to Cairns and in the smaller coastal region of south-west Western Australia. The centre of the country is very sparsely populated.

Until WWII, Australians were predominantly of British and Irish descent with a sprinkling of Chinese settlers, but that has changed dramatically since the war. First there was heavy migration from Europe creating major Greek and Italian populations but also adding Germans, Dutch, Maltese, Yugoslavs, Lebanese, Turks and other groups.

More recently, Australia has had large influxes of Asians, particularly Vietnamese after the Vietnam war. In comparison to the country's population, Australia probably took more Vietnamese refugees than any other Western nation. On the whole these 'new Australians' have been remarkably well accepted and 'multi-culturalism' is a reality.

There are around 220,000 Aborigines, most of whom are concentrated in northern and central Australia. Most of the 10,000 Torres Strait Islanders, primarily a Melanesian people, live in north Queensland and on the islands of Torres Strait between Cape York and New Guinea.

If you come to Australia in search of a real Australian you will find one quite easily – they are not known to be a shy breed. He or she may be a Lebanese cafe owner, an English used-car salesperson, an Aboriginal artist, a Malaysian architect or a Greek greengrocer. And you will find them in pubs, on beaches, at barbecues, mustering yards and art galleries. And yes, you may meet a Mick (Crocodile) Dundee or two telling the same tall stories – a popular activity in outback pubs.

ARTS
Outback Literature

For white Australian writers, a somewhat undelineated outback has always been an important source of inspiration, with its 'frontier' image. For Aborigines, however, the outback was not remote or dangerous: it was their life, and the focus of a rich oral tradition; creeds and practicalities were passed on from generation to generation by word of mouth in songs, stories and accompanying rituals.

Aboriginal Song & Narrative These oral traditions are loosely and misleadingly described as 'myths and legends'. Their single uniting factor is the Dreamtime, when the totemic ancestors formed the landscape, fashioned the laws and created the people who would inherit the land. Translated and printed in English, these renderings of the Dreamtime often lose much of their intended impact. Gone are the sounds of sticks, didjeridu and the rhythm of the dancers which accompany each poetic line; the words fail to fuse past and present, and the spirits and forces to which the lines refer lose much of their animation.

At the turn of the century, Catherine Langloh Parker was collecting Aboriginal legends and using her outback experience to interpret them sincerely but synthetically. She compiled the book *Australian Legendary Tales: Folklore of the Noongah-burrahs* (1902).

TGH Strehlow was one of the first methodical translators, and his important works include *Aranda Traditions* (1947) and *Songs of Central Australia* (1971). Equally important are the combined efforts of Catherine & Ronald Berndt. There are 188 songs in the collection *Djanggawul* (1952), 129 sacred and 47 secular songs in the collection *Kunapipi* (1951), and *The Land of the Rainbow Snake* (1979) focuses on children's stories from western Arnhem Land.

More recently, many Dreamtime stories have appeared in translation, illustrated and published by Aboriginal artists. Some representative collections are *Joe Nangan's Dreaming: Aboriginal Legends of the North-West* (Joe Nangan & Hugh Edwards, 1976); *Milbi: Aboriginal Tales from Queensland's Endeavour River* (Tulo Gordon & JB Haviland, 1980); *Visions of Mowanjum: Aboriginal Writings from the Kimberley* (Kormilda Community College, Darwin; 1980); and *Gularabulu* (Paddy Roe & Stephen Muecke, 1983).

As you drive through the outback, realise that many of the features you see in the landscape have an oral history. They live, have a past and a present. You are, in effect, driving through the pages of the world's most ancient, illuminated manuscript!

Modern Aboriginal Literature Modern Aboriginal writers have fused the English language with aspects of their traditional culture. The result is often carefully fashioned to expose the injustices they have been subjected to, especially as urban dwellers. The first Aboriginal writer to be published was David Unaipon in 1929 (*Native Legends*).

Aboriginal literature now includes drama, fiction and poetry. The poet Oodgeroo Noonuccal (Kath Walker), one of the most well known of modern Aboriginal writers, was the first Aboriginal woman to have work published (*We Are Going*, 1964). *Paperbark: A collection of black Australian writings* (1990) presents a great cross-section of modern Aboriginal writers, including dramatist Jack Davis and novelist Mudrooroo Narogin (Colin Johnson). This book has an excellent bibliography of black Australian writing.

There are a number of modern accounts of Aboriginal life in remote parts of Australia. *Raparapa Kularr Martuwarra: Stories from the Fitzroy River Drovers* (1988) is a Magabala Books production. This company, based in Broome, energetically promotes Aboriginal literature. Autobiography and biography have become an important branch of Aboriginal literature – look for *Moon and Rainbow* (Dick Roughsey, 1971) and *My Country of the Pelican Dreaming* (Grant Ngabidj, 1981). *Yorro Yorro*, a joint project by photographer Jutta Malnic and David Mowaljarlai (interpreter of the Wandjina sites photographed in the West Kimberley), is another excellent production of Magabala Books.

The Aborigine in White Literature The Aborigine has often been used as a character in white outback literature. Usually the treatment was patronising and somewhat short-sighted. There were exceptions, especially in the subject of interracial sexuality between white men and Aboriginal women.

Rosa Praed, in her short piece *My Australian Girlhood* (1902), drew heavily on her outback experience and her affectionate childhood relationship with Aborigines. Jeannie Gunn's *Little Black Princess* was published in 1904, but it was *We of the Never Never* (1908) which brought her renown. Her story of the life and trials on Elsey Station includes an unflattering, patronising depiction of the Aborigines on and around the station.

Catherine Martin, in 1923, wrote *The Incredible Journey*. It follows the trail of two black women, Iliapo and Polde, in search of a little boy who had been kidnapped by a white man. The book describes in careful detail the harsh desert environment they traverse.

Katharine Susannah Prichard contributed a great deal to outback literature in the 1920s. A journey to Turee Station in the cattle country of the Ashburton and Fortescue rivers, in 1926, inspired her lyric tribute to the Aborigine, *Coonardoo* (1929), which delved into the then almost taboo love between an Aboriginal woman and a white station boss. Later, Mary Durack's *Keep Him My Country* (1955) explored the theme of a white station manager's love for an Aboriginal girl, Dalgerie.

Undoubtedly, one of the most hauntingly beautiful examinations of Aboriginal mythology is Bruce Chatwin's recent classic, the partly fictional *Songlines*. It is hard to describe – it is simply one of those indispensable books that should be in the non-drivers' seat during a trip to the outback.

Outback Explorers When John Oxley published an account of his discoveries in 1820, he stimulated the myth of the 'inland sea', and others set about to find it. Charles Sturt gave the first written description of places in the interior such as the Simpson Desert.

Other accounts worth mentioning are the journals recalling Edward John Eyre's epic journey in 1841 across the Great Australian Bight; the account by Aboriginal Jackey-Jackey (Galmarra) of the death of Edmund Kennedy during an expedition to Cape York in 1848; and the writings of Ernest Giles from the period 1874 to 1876. Giles' matter-of-fact, unembellished descriptions of remote parts of Australia's arid heart, like the Gibson Desert, are among the most literary and perceptive of explorers' writings.

Much more recent is Robyn Davidson's description in *Tracks* of her solo journey, accompanied only by camels and a dog, into the outback. Her accounts of the characters she encounters along the way reveal that Australia's dead heart is still populated by mythical 'bushies'.

You can find most of these accounts, either in full or in condensed form, in major public libraries.

Bush Ballads & Yarns The 'bush', in particular the outback, was a great source of inspiration for many popular ballads and stories. These were particularly in vogue at the turn of the century but they have an enduring quality.

Adam Lindsay Gordon was the forerunner of this type of literature, having published *Bush Ballads and Galloping Rhymes* in 1870. This collection of ballads included his popular *The Sick Stockrider*.

The two most famous exponents of the ballad style were AB 'Banjo' Paterson and Henry Lawson. Paterson grew up in the bush in the second half of the last century and went on to become one of Australia's most important bush poets. His pseudonym 'The Banjo' was the name of a horse on his family's station. His horse ballads were regarded as some of his best, but he was familiar with all aspects of station life and wrote with great optimism. *Clancy of the Overflow* and *The Man From Snowy River* are both well known, but The Banjo is probably most remembered as the author of Australia's alternative national anthem, *Waltzing Matilda*, in which he celebrates an unnamed swagman, one of the anonymous wanderers of the bush.

Henry Lawson was a contemporary of Paterson, but was much more of a social commentator and political thinker and less of a humorist. Although he wrote a good many poems about the bush – pieces such as *Andy's Gone with Cattle* and *The Roaring Days* are among his best – his greatest legacy

are his short stories of life in the bush, which seem remarkably simple yet manage to capture the atmosphere perfectly. Good examples are *A Day on a Selection* (a selection was a tract of crown land for which annual fees were paid) and *The Drover's Wife*; the latter epitomises one of Lawson's 'battlers' who dreams of better things as an escape from the ennui of her isolated circumstances.

There were many other balladists. George Essex Evans penned a tribute to Queensland's women pioneers, *The Women of the West*; Will Ogilvie wrote of the great cattle drives; and Barcroft Boake's *Where the Dead Men Lie* celebrates the people who opened up never-never country where 'heatwaves dance forever'.

Standing alone among these writers is Barbara Baynton. She is uncompromising in her depiction of the outback as a cruel, brutal environment, and the romantic imagery of the bush is absent in the ferocious depiction of the lot of *Squeaker's Mate* in *Bush Studies* (1902). Squeaker's mate, crippled while clearing her selection and powerless to do anything, has to endure the indignity of her husband flaunting his new mistress. More terrifying is the murder of a mother by a marauding swagman in *The Chosen Vessel*, also in *Bush Studies*.

Outback Raconteurs Many journalists and travel writers proudly proclaimed the outback to be the 'true' Australia. One of the least known is CEW Bean, Australia's official war historian of WWI. Two of his books, *On the Wool Track* (1910) and *The Dreadnought of the Darling* (1911), evocatively describe the outback of far western New South Wales.

Ion Idriess was an immensely popular writer in his time. His string of stories were eagerly awaited and their heroes were unashamedly outback: *Cattle King: Story of Sir Sidney Kidman, Flynn of the Inland* and *Lasseter's Last Ride*. In *Nemarluk: King of the Wilds* (1941) he chronicles the exploits of an Aboriginal resistance fighter in the Top End.

One of the best known travel writers was

Ernestine Hill, whose *The Territory* (1951), it was said by the prolific Western Australian writer JK Ewers, 'ought to be in the swag of every Australian'. Her first publication, *The Great Australian Loneliness* (1937), described five years of travel through the outback.

Another writer in the vein of Idriess was Bill Harney. He married an Aborigine and was exposed to many aspects of Aboriginal culture. Much of his knowledge of the Top End was learned from the 'school of hard knocks', including a session in the Boorooloola lock-up for cattle-duffing. He later became a ranger near Ayers Rock for many years. His books, written in the 1940s and '50s, include *Tales from the Aboriginals, To Ayers Rock and Beyond, Songs of the Songmen: Aboriginal Myth Retold* and *Life among the Aborigines*.

George Farwell's *Ghost Towns of Australia* is a great source of outback yarns and history, and his travel books include *The Outside Track, Cape York to Kimberley* and *Traveller's Tracks*. Bill Wannan's *Hay, Hell and Booligal, A Dictionary of Australian Folklore* and *Bullockies, Beauts & Bandicoots* all have good titbits on the outback.

HM Barker's *Droving Days* (1966) looks into the exploits of the droving pioneers, the Aboriginal stockmen who accompanied them, and colourful characters such as horsebreakers and drifters.

More recently, Patsy Adam-Smith covered the outback in her popular titles *The Shearers* (1982), *The Rails go Westward* (1969), *Across Australia by Indian Pacific* (1971) and her examination of famous and ordinary lives in *Outback Heroes* (1981).

The applecart was finally overturned in 1996 when a Generation-Xer, Sean Condon, described his (and a mate's) foray into the outback in *Sean and David's Long Drive*, one of the first titles in the Lonely Planet 'Journeys' series. To a certain extent it debunks the myth of the 'great beyond' which lies a few hours' drive from the eastern seaboard. Still, the characters are out there, some of them not very pretty, and the journey is fuelled by alcohol, brawling, sex and distance. Has anything really changed?

Outback Novelists The author's name if not the content would have encouraged many overseas visitors to read DH Lawrence's *Kangaroo* (1923) which, in places, presents his frightened images of the bush. Later, Nevil Shute's *A Town Like Alice* (1950) would have been the first outback-based novel that many people read. Other Shute titles with outback themes were *In the Wet* (1953) and *Beyond the Black Stump* (1956).

Perhaps the best local depicter of the outback was the aforementioned Katharine Susannah Prichard. She produced a string of novels with outback themes into which she wove her political thoughts. *Black Opal* (1921) was the study of the fictional opal mining community of Fallen Star Ridge; *Working Bullocks* (1926) examined the political nature of work in the karri forests of Western Australia; and *Moon of Desire* (1941) follows its characters in search of a fabulous pearl from Broome to Singapore. Her controversial trilogy of the Western Australian gold fields was published separately as *The Roaring Nineties* (1946), *Golden Miles* (1948) and *Winged Seeds* (1950).

Xavier Herbert's *Capricornia* (1938) stands as one of the great epics of outback Australia, with its sweeping descriptions of the northern country. His second epic, *Poor Fellow My Country* (1975), is a documentary of the fortunes of a northern station owner. Herbert uses the characters to voice his bitter regret at the failure of reconciliation between the white despoilers of the land and its indigenous people.

One of the great non-fiction pieces is Mary Durack's family chronicle, *Kings in Grass Castles* (1959), which relates the white settlement of the Kimberley ranges. Her sequel was *Sons in the Saddle* (1983).

Australia's Nobel prize-winner, Patrick White, used the outback as the backdrop for a number of his monumental works. The most prominent character in *Voss* (1957) is an explorer, perhaps loosely based on Ludwig Leichhardt; *The Tree of Man* (1955) has all the outback happenings of flood, fire and drought; and the journey of *The Aunt's Story* (1948) begins on an Australian sheep station.

Kenneth Cook's nightmarish novel set in outback New South Wales, *Wake in Fright* (1961), has been made into a film. And the script for the road movie *The Adventures of Priscilla, Queen of the Desert* – it would take a brave chronicler to categorise this gem into any canon of outback literature.

Pictorial Art

Rock Art Petroglyphs, or rock drawings and engravings, are found widely in Australia, and western New South Wales, north-eastern South Australia and central Australia have many places of significance. These include such well-known sites as Ewaninga, south of Alice Springs; Chambers Gorge in the Flinders Ranges; Cooper Creek in the far north-east of South Australia; and Mootwingee in western New South Wales. All these locations can be visited by travellers, while other spots, such as at Sturt Meadows in New South Wales and Panaramitee near Yunta in South Australia are basically out of bounds.

The ancient art was pecked into the rock with simple tools, yet the designs at these remote places cover large areas of exposed rock. Thousands of engravings have been recorded at some sites: the Sturt Meadow engravings number over 14,000 separate designs, while the Yunta one contains over 8000. The designs consist mainly of concentric circles, other circles and animal tracks.

There are many variations on these themes, and each site is always slightly different from another. In some areas the dominant footprints are those of the wombat, while in others it could well be the emu or kangaroo. Some of the designs give glimpses into the recent past through what seem to be engravings of tracks made by recently extinct animals, such as diprotodonts and giant kangaroos. They lived when inland Australia was a wetter, more friendly place, and Aboriginal people lived side by side with these giant mammals.

At the Olary engravings in South Australia early this century, station children discovered what is thought to be an engraving of a crocodile head. It is now on view in the South Australian Museum. The crocodile interpretation has added strength when you consider that one of the legends of the inland tribes was of an animal called Kadimakara that lived in the pools of the lakes and rivers and ate anyone that came too close.

Much effort has been put into dating these engravings. There seems to be little knowledge about this art among today's Aboriginal elders, but the places are still important to them. Recent efforts at the Olary site and a breakthrough in dating the age of the 'desert varnish' (a natural substance that covers rocks in the desert country) have given an age of some of these engravings of around 43,000 years. That makes them by far the oldest art in the world!

Take the time and effort to visit these places, but remember that these engravings are important to Aboriginal people and that all artefacts, including these ancient art sites, are protected by law. (See the Aboriginal Arts section on pages 65-84.)

The South Australian Museum, North Terrace, Adelaide, has probably the best collection of Aboriginal artefacts in Australia.

Recent Painting In the 1880s a group of young artists developed the first distinctively Australian style of watercolour or oil painting. Working from a permanent bush camp in Melbourne's (then) outer suburb of Box Hill, the painters of the so-called Heidelberg School captured the unique qualities of Australian life and the bush. In Sydney, a contemporary movement worked at Sirius Cove on Sydney Harbour. Both schools were influenced by the French plein-air painters, whose practice of working outdoors to capture the effects of natural light was very appropriate in capturing the fierce light and pastel hues of the Australian landscape. The main artists were Tom Roberts, Arthur Streeton, Frederick McCubbin, Louis Abrahams, Charles Conder, Julian Ashton and, later, Walter Withers. Their works can be found in most of the major galleries of the country and are well worth seeking out.

In the 1940s another revolution took place

when a new generation of young artists rede-fined the direction of Australian art. Included in this group are some of Australia's most famous artists, including Sir Sidney Nolan and Arthur Boyd. More recently the work of painters such as Fred Williams, John Olsen, Robert Juniper, Russell Drysdale, Lloyd Rees and Brett Whitely has also made an impression on the international art world.

Broken Hill has been the popular focus of outback art for a number of years. Local painter Pro Hart has achieved an international reputa-tion for his idiosyncratic style and his son, landscape artist Kym Hart, is following the family tradition. In 1995 Kym Hart teamed up with other talented locals Shane Gehlert, Howard Steer and Geoff De Main to form the acclaimed 'Arid Zone Artists'. The group has already held a number of successful exhibitions in New South Wales and interstate.

Based in Alice Springs, Kaye Kessing is achieving national recognition with her unique style of environmental caricature. She aims to increase public awareness of the problems facing nature in the outback, with popular themes being feral cats and the vanishing bilby.

Cinema

Many people overseas (and probably most Australians) have been introduced to the outback through films like *Crocodile Dundee* and the *Mad Max* series which depict the outback in all its glory.

Earlier and lesser known films like *The Chant of Jimmy Blacksmith* and *Walkabout* tell of the political and social problems faced by those who live in the outback. Both films deal with interracial relationships, but the spectre of the outback and how it affects one's survival and culture is ever present.

Some outback films have the 'pioneering' feel of a John Ford Western. Stories of conflict and struggle, of innocence and the loss of innocence abound. Look out for *Mr Electric*, about the effect of the first light bulbs on a very remote farm. *The Last Picture Show Man* tells the tale of a travelling projectionist who is constantly driven further up the road by the advance of technology.

For outback horror, see *Razorback*, the story of a giant killer hog; for a psychological thrill, see *Wake in Fright* and a man mysteri-ously unable to leave the eerie, sweltering town in which he finds himself marooned. *The Adventures of Priscilla, Queen of the Desert* is the often hilarious, sometimes sad story of several outrageous gay men and their travels in a pink bus through the macho outback.

Music

Australia's participation in the flurry of popular music since the 1950s has been a frustrating mix of good, indifferent, lousy, parochial and excellent. However, even the offerings of the most popular acts have done little to remove the cultural cringe: often the highest praise is 'it's good enough to have come from the UK/USA'. Not too much of the popular music created here has been noticeably different from overseas music (there are exceptions). Which is why the recent success of Aboriginal music, and its merging with rock, is so refreshing. Some of this music really is different (and some of it is very deriva-tive). The most obvious name that springs to mind is Yothu Yindi. Their song about the dis-honoured white man's agreement, *Treaty*, perhaps did more than anything else to popular-ise Aboriginal land-rights claims. The band's lead singer, Mandawuy Yunupingu, was pro-claimed Australian of the Year in 1993.

Other Aboriginal names include Coloured Stone, Kev Carmody, Archie Roach, Scrap Metal, the Sunrise Band, Christine Anu (from Torres Strait), and the defunct bands that started it all, No Fixed Address and Warumpi Band.

White outback music owes much to Irish heritage and American country influences, often with a liberal sprinkling of dry outback humour. Names to watch out for include Slim Dusty, Ted Egan, John Williamson, Chad Morgan, Lee Kernaghan, Neil Murray, and Smokey Dawson. Bush folk bands are popular, with fiddles, banjos and tin whistles featuring prominently. Many folk bands use the indigenous 'lagerphone', a percussion instrument made from beer-bottle caps nailed to a stick, which is shaken or thumped on the floor. Another popular instrument is the single-string, tea-chest bass.

Art has always been an integral part of Aboriginal life, a connection between past and present, between the supernatural and the earthly, between people and the land. The initial forms of artistic expression were rock carvings, body painting and ground designs, and the earliest engraved designs known to exist date back at least 30,000 years.

Aboriginal art has undergone a major revival in the last decade or so, with artists throughout the country finding a means to express and preserve ancient Dreaming values, and a way to share this rich cultural heritage with the wider community.

While the so-called dot paintings of the central deserts are among the more readily identifiable and probably most popular form of contemporary Aboriginal art, there's a huge range of material being produced – bark paintings from Arnhem Land, wood carving and silk-screen printing from the Tiwi Islands north of Darwin, batik printing and wood carving from central Australia, dijeridus and more.

*Title Page: **Devil Devil Man** by Djambu Barra Barra; acrylic on canvas; 1997; Ngukurr, NT; represented by Alcaston House Gallery, Melbourne*

Below: Ewaniga rock engravings, south of Alice Springs; courtesy of the NT Tourist Commission

Art & the Dreaming

All early Aboriginal art was based on the various peoples' ancestral Dreaming – the 'Creation', when the earth's physical features were formed by the struggles between powerful supernatural ancestors such as the Rainbow Serpent, the Lightning Men and the Wandjina. Codes of behaviour were also laid down in the Dreaming, and although these laws have been diluted and adapted in the last 200 years, they still provide the basis for today's Aborigines. Ceremonies, rituals and sacred paintings are all based on the Dreaming.

A Dreaming can relate to a person, an animal or a physical feature, while others are more general, relating to a region, a group of people, or natural forces such as floods and wind. Australia is covered by a vast network of Dreamings, and any one person may have connections to several. ■

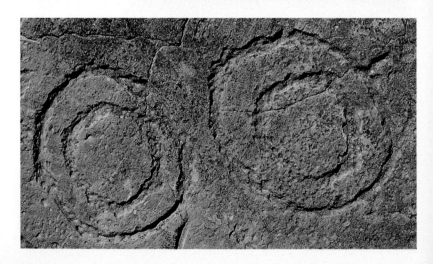

Lightning Brothers rock art site at Katherine River; courtesy of the NT Tourist Commission

Rock Art

Arnhem Land

Arnhem Land, in Australia's tropical Top End, is possibly the area with the richest artistic heritage. Recent finds suggest that rock paintings were being made as early as 60,000 years ago, and some of the rock art galleries in the huge sandstone Arnhem Land plateau are at least 18,000 years old.

The art of Arnhem Land is vastly different from that of the central deserts. Here, Dreaming stories are depicted far more literally, with easily recognisable (though often stylised) images of ancestors, animals, and even Macassans – early Indonesian mariners who regularly visited the north coast long before Europeans arrived.

The paintings contained in the Arnhem Land rock art sites range from hand prints to paintings of animals, people, mythological beings and European ships, constituting one of the world's most important and fascinating rock art collections. They provide a record of changing environments and lifestyles over the millennia.

In some places they are concentrated in large galleries, with paintings from more recent eras sometimes superimposed over older paintings. Some sites are kept secret – not only to protect them from damage, but also because they are private or sacred to the Aboriginal owners. Some

Hollow-Log Coffins

Hollowed-out logs were often used for reburial ceremonies in Arnhem Land, and were also a major form of artistic expression. They were highly decorated, often with many of the Dreaming themes, and were known as *dupun* in eastern Arnhem Land and *lorrkon* in western Arnhem Land.

In 1988 a group of Arnhem Land artists made a memorial as their contribution to the movement highlighting injustices against Aborigines – this was, of course, the year when non-Aboriginal Australians were celebrating 200 years of European settlement. The artists painted 200 log coffins – one for each year of settlement – with traditional clan and Dreaming designs, and these now form a permanent display in the National Gallery in Canberra.

are believed to be inhabited by dangerous beings, who must not be approached by the ignorant. However, two of the finest sites have been opened up to visitors, with access roads, walkways and explanatory signs. These are Ubirr and Nourlangie in Kakadu National Park.

The rock paintings show how the main styles succeeded each other over time. The earliest hand or grass prints were followed by a 'naturalistic' style, with large outlines of people or animals filled in with colour. Some of the animals depicted, such as the thylacine (Tasmanian tiger), have long been extinct on mainland Australia.

After the naturalistic style came the 'dynamic', in which motion was often cleverly depicted (a dotted line, for example, to show a spear's path through the air). In this era the first mythological beings appeared, with human bodies and animal heads.

The next style mainly showed simple human silhouettes, and was followed by the curious 'yam figures', in which people and animals were drawn in the shape of yams (or yams in the shape of people and animals!). Many fish were depicted in the art of this period, and the so-called 'x-ray' style, which showed the creatures' bones and internal organs, made its appearance.

Below: Rock paintings, Nourlangie Rock, Kakadu National Park; courtesy of the NT Tourist Commission

By about 1000 years ago many of the salt marshes had turned into freshwater swamps and billabongs. The birds and plants which provided new food sources in this landscape appeared in the art of this time.

From around 400 years ago, Aboriginal artists also depicted the human newcomers to the region – Macassan fisherpeople and, more recently, the Europeans – and the things they brought, or their modes of transport such as ships or horses.

The Kimberley

The art of the Kimberley is most famous for its images of the Wandjina, a group of ancestor beings who came from the sky and sea and were associated with fertility. They controlled the elements and were responsible for the formation of the country's natural features.

Wandjina images are found painted on rock as well as on more recent portable art media, with some of the rock images being more than 6m long. They generally appear in human form, with large black eyes, a nose but no mouth, a halo around the head (representative of both hair and clouds), and a black oval shape on the chest.

North Queensland

In North Queensland rock art again predominates. The superb Quinkan galleries at Laura on the Cape York Peninsula, north-west of Cairns, are among the best known in the country. Among the many creatures depicted on the walls, the main ones are the Quinkan spirits, which are shown in two forms – the long and stick-like Timara, and the crocodile-like Imjim with their knobbed, club-like tails.

Local Aboriginal people run tours of the Quinkan rock art sites; for further information call ☎ 1800 633933.

Quinkan rock art, Laura, far north Queensland; photograph reproduced with the permission of the Aboriginal community of the Quinkan district, Cape York Peninsula

Painting

Western Desert Painting

The current renaissance in Aboriginal painting began in the early 1970s at Papunya ('honey ant place'), at the time a small, depressed community 240km north-west of Alice Springs, which had grown out of the government's 'assimilation' policy. Here the local children were given the task of painting a traditional-style mural on the school wall. The elders took interest in the project, and although the public display of traditional images gave rise to much debate among the elders, they eventually participated and in fact completed the *Honey Ant Dreaming* mural. This was the first time that images which were originally confined to rock and body art came to be reproduced in a different medium.

Other murals followed this first one, and the desire to paint spread through the community. In the early stages paintings were produced on small boards on the ground or balanced on the artist's knee, but this soon gave way to painted canvasses and acrylic paints. Canvas was an ideal medium as it could be easily rolled and transported, yet large paintings were possible. With the growing importance of art, both as an economic and a cultural activity, an association was formed to help the artists sell their work. The Papunya Tula company in Alice Springs is still one of the relatively few galleries in central Australia to be owned and run by Aboriginal people.

Painting in central Australia has flourished to such a degree that it is now an important educational activity for children, through which they can learn different aspects of religious and ceremonial knowledge. This

Possum Dreaming by Eunice Woods; acrylic on canvas; 100cm x 102cm; 1997; Kaltjiti Crafts, Fregon; courtesy of DESART

Possum, Snake, Potato Dreaming by Paddy Japaljarri Sims and Bessie Nakamarra Sims; acrylic on linen; 91 x 153cm; 1992; Warlukurlangu Artists Association, Yuendumu, NT; courtesy of DESART

is especially true now that women are so much a part of the painting movement.

Dot-painting partly evolved from 'ground paintings', which formed the centrepiece of dances and songs. These were made from pulped plant material, and the designs were made on the ground using dots of this mush. Dots were also used to outline objects in rock paintings, and to highlight geographical features or vegetation.

While dot paintings may look random and abstract, they usually depict a Dreaming journey, and so can be seen almost as aerial landscape maps. Many paintings feature the tracks of birds, animals and humans, often identifying the ancestor. Subjects are often depicted by the imprint they leave in the sand – a simple arc depicts a person (as that is the print left by someone sitting), a *coolamon* (wooden carrying dish) is shown by an oval shape, a digging stick by a single line, a camp fire by a circle. Males or females are identified by the objects associated with them – digging sticks and coolamons for women, spears and boomerangs for

Kadaitja Man by Ronnie Tjampitjinpa; acrylic on linen; 122 x 61cm; 1993; Papunya Tula Artists Pty Ltd, Alice Springs, NT; courtesy of DESART

men. Concentric circles usually depict Dreaming sites, or places where ancestors paused in their journeys.

While these symbols are widely used, their meaning within each individual painting is known only by the artist and the people closely associated with him or her – either by group or by the Dreaming – and different groups apply different interpretations to each painting. So sacred stories can be publicly portrayed, as the deeper meaning is not evident to most viewers.

The colours used in dot paintings from central Australia include reds, blues and purples which may seem overly vivid but which can be seen in the outback landscape.

Bark Paintings

While bark painting is a more recent art form, it is still an important part of the cultural heritage of Arnhem Land Aboriginal people. It's difficult to establish when bark was first used, partly because it is perishable and old pieces simply don't exist. European visitors in the early 19th century noted the practice of painting the inside walls of bark shelters.

The bark used is from the stringybark tree (*Eucalyptus tetradonta*), and it is taken off the tree in the wet season when it is moist and supple. The rough outer layers are removed and the bark is dried by placing it over a fire and then under weights on the ground to keep it flat. In a couple of weeks the bark is dry and ready for use. A typical bark painting made today has sticks across the top and bottom of the sheet to keep it flat.

The pigments used in bark paintings are mainly red and yellow (ochres), white (kaolin) and black (charcoal). The colours were gathered from special sites by the traditional owners, and they were then traded. Even today these natural pigments are used, giving the paintings their superb soft and earthy finish. Binding agents such as birds' egg yolks, wax and plant resins were added to the pigments. Recently these have been replaced by synthetic agents such as wood glue. Similarly, the brushes used in the past were obtained from the bush materials at hand – twigs, leaf fibres, feathers, human hair and the like – but these too have largely been replaced by modern brushes.

One of the main features of Arnhem Land bark paintings is the use of

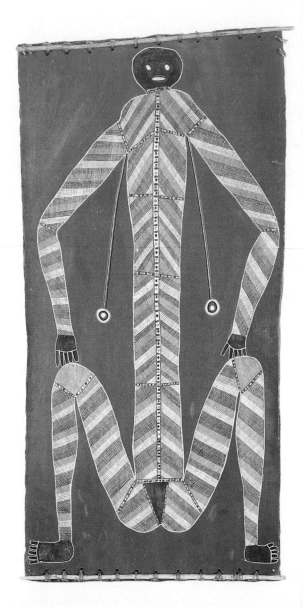

Namarrkon, Lightning Spirit *by Curly Bardagubu, c. 1931-87, Born clan; Kunwinjku language, Namokardabu, western Arnhem Land; earth pigments on bark; 156 x 75cm; 1987; purchased through the Art Foundation of Victoria with assistance from Alcoa of Australia Limited, Governor 1990; National Gallery of Victoria*

Kumoken (Freshwater Crocodile) with Mimi Spirits by Djawida, b.c. 1935, Yulkman clan; Kunwinjku language, Kurrudjmuh, western Arnhem Land; earth pigments on bark; 151 x 71cm; 1990; purchased 1990; National Gallery of Victoria

Tiwi Island Art

Due to their isolation, the Aborigines of the Tiwi Islands (Bathurst and Melville islands, off the coast of Darwin) have developed art forms – mainly sculpture – not found anywhere else, although there are some similarities with the art of Arnhem Land.

The *pukumani* burial rites are one of the main rituals of Tiwi religious life, and it is for these ceremonies that many of the art works are created – *yimwalini* (bark baskets), spears and *tutini* (burial poles). These carved and painted ironwood poles, up to 2.5m long, are placed around the grave, and represent features of the deceased person's life.

In the last 50 or so years the Tiwi islanders have been producing sculptured animals and birds, many of these being Creation ancestors (the Darwin Museum of Arts & Sciences has an excellent display). More recently, bark painting and silk-screen printing have become popular, and there are workshops on both islands where these items are produced. ■

cross-hatching designs. These designs identify the particular clans, and are based on body paintings of the past. The paintings can also be broadly categorised by their regional styles. In the west the tendency is towards naturalistic images and plain backgrounds, while to the east the use of geometric designs is more common.

The art reflects Dreaming themes that vary by region. In eastern Arnhem Land the prominent ancestor beings are the Djangkawu, who travelled the land with elaborate *dilly* bags (carry bags) and digging sticks (for making waterholes), and the Wagilag Sisters, who are associated with snakes and waterholes. In western Arnhem Land the Rainbow Serpent, Yingarna, is the significant being (according to some clans), but one of her offspring, Ngalyod, and Nawura are also important. The *mimi* spirits are another feature of western Arnhem Land art, both on bark and rock. These mischievous spirits are attributed with having taught the Aborigines of the region many things, including hunting, food gathering and painting skills.

Contemporary Painting

Ngukurr Since the late 1980s the artists of Ngukurr ('nook-or'), near Roper Bar in south-eastern Arnhem Land, have been producing works using acrylic paints on canvas. Although ancestral beings still feature prominently, the works are generally much more modern, with free-flowing forms and often little in common with traditional formal structure.

The Kimberley Contemporary art in the eastern Kimberley also features elements of the works of the desert peoples of central Australia, a legacy of the forced relocation of people during the 1970s. The community of Warmun at Turkey Creek on the Great Northern Highway has been particularly active in ensuring that Aboriginal culture through painting and dance remains strong.

Facing page: Pukamani funerary poles and bark baskets installation; Milikapiti, Melville Island, NT; represented by Alcaston House Gallery, Melbourne

Urban Art While traditional works by rural artists have a higher profile, city-based Aboriginal people also produce some important work. Much of this work has strong European influences and it was once regarded as an inauthentic form of Aboriginal art, but this view has changed.

A major impetus in the development of urban art was the Aboriginal land rights movement, which started to gain momentum in the 1970s. Images depicting the dispossession of the Aborigines and the racist

treatment they had received became powerful symbols in their struggle for equality.

Although much of the work being produced still carries strong political and social comment, these days the range has become broader.

Artefacts & Crafts

Objects traditionally made for practical or ceremonial uses, such as weapons and musical instruments, often featured intricate and symbolic decoration. In recent years many communities have also developed non-traditional craft forms that have created employment and income, and the growing tourist trade has seen demand and production increase steadily.

Dijeridus

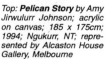

*Top: **Pelican Story** by Amy Jirwulurr Johnson; acrylic on canvas; 185 x 175cm; 1994; Ngukurr, NT; represented by Alcaston House Gallery, Melbourne*

Above & right: Dijeridu by Djambu Barra Barra; private collection; Ngukurr, NT; represented by Alcaston House Gallery, Melbourne

The most widespread craft items seen for sale these days are dijeridus. There has been a phenomenal boom in popularity and they can be found in shops around the country.

Originally they were used as ceremonial musical instruments by Aboriginal people in Arnhem Land (where they are known as *yidaki*). The traditional instrument was made from particular eucalypt branches which had been hollowed out by termites. The tubes were often fitted with a wax mouthpiece made from sugarbag (native honey bee wax) and decorated with traditional designs.

Although they may look pretty, most dijeridus made these days bear little relation to traditional ones: they may be made from the wrong or inferior wood, have been hollowed out using mechanical or other means, have poor sound quality, and most have never had an Aboriginal person anywhere near them! (See Buying Aboriginal Art & Artefacts, below.)

Boomerangs

Boomerangs are curved wooden throwing sticks used for hunting and also as ceremonial clapping sticks. Contrary to popular belief, not all boomerangs are designed to return when thrown – the idea is to hit the animal being hunted! Returning boomerangs were mostly used in south-eastern and western Australia. Although they all follow the same fundamental design, boomerangs come in a huge range of shapes, sizes and decorative styles, and are made from a number of different wood types.

Wooden Sculptures

Traditionally most wooden sculptures were made to be used for particular ceremonies and then discarded. Arnhem Land artists still produce soft-wood carvings of birds, fish, animals and ancestral beings, which were originally used for ceremonial purposes. The lightweight figures are engraved and painted with intricate symbolic designs.

Early in this century, missionaries encouraged some communities and groups to produce wooden sculptures for sale.

Scorched Carvings

Also very popular are the wooden carvings which have designs scorched into them with hot fencing wire. These range from small figures, such as possums, up to quite large snakes and lizards, although none of them have any Dreaming significance. In central Australia one of the main outlets for these is the Maruku Arts & Crafts centre at the Uluru-Kata Tjuta National Park Cultural Centre, where it's possible to see the crafts

Below: Decorative central Australian scorched carvings made from river red gum root; Maraku Arts & Crafts; Uluru (Ayers Rock), NT; courtesy of DESART

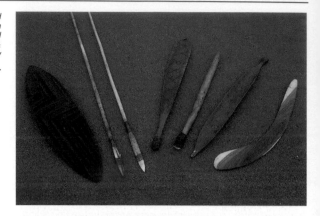

Traditional weapons and tools from the western desert region of central Australia; Maruku Arts & Crafts; Uluru, NT; courtesy of DESART

being made. Although much of the artwork is usually done by women, men are also involved at the Maruku centre. The Mt Ebenezer Roadhouse, on the Lasseter Highway (the main route to Uluru), is another Aboriginal-owned enterprise and one of the cheapest places for buying sculpted figures.

Ceremonial Shields

Around the country many types of weapons were traditionally produced, including spears, spear-throwers (*woomeras*), clubs (*nulla nullas*) and shields. The shields were made from timber or bark in different shapes and sizes, and were often richly decorated with carved and painted surfaces showing the owner's ancestry or Dreaming. They were mainly used for ceremonial purposes, but they were also put to practical use when fighting between clans occurred.

Fibre Craft

Articles made from fibres are a major art form among women. String or twine was traditionally made from bark, grass, leaves, roots and other materials, hand-spun and dyed with natural pigments, then woven to make dilly bags, baskets, garments, fishing nets and other items. Strands or fibres from the leaves of the pandanus palm (and other palms or grasses) were also woven to make dilly bags and mats. While all these objects have utilitarian purposes, many also have ritual uses.

Textiles

The women of Utopia, 260km north-east of Alice Springs, have become known in recent years for their production of batik material. In the mid-1970s the Anmatyerre and Alyawarre people started to reoccupy their traditional lands around Utopia cattle station, and this was given a formal basis in 1979 when they were granted title to the station. A number of scattered outstations, rather than a central settlement, were set up, and around this time the women were introduced to batik as part of a self-help program. The art form flourished and Utopia Women's Batik Group was formed in 1978 (the group was later incorporated and is now called Utopia Awely Batik Utopia Women's Centre Aboriginal Corporation, trading as Utopia Silks). The brightly coloured silk batiks were based on traditional women's body-painting designs called *awely*, and on images of flora and fauna.

In the late 1980s techniques using acrylic paints on canvas were introduced at Utopia, and Utopian art is now receiving international acclaim.

Other Crafts

The Ernabella Presbyterian Mission in northern South Australia was another place where craftwork was encouraged. A 1950 mission report stated that: 'A mission station must have an industry to provide work for and help finance the cost of caring for the natives'. As the mission had been founded on a sheep station, **wool craft** techniques of spinning, dyeing and weaving were introduced. The Pitjantjatjara ('pigeon-jara') women made woollen articles such as rugs, belts, traditional dilly bags and scarves, using designs incorporating aspects of women's law (*yawilyu*). With the introduction of batik fabric dyeing in the 1970s, weaving at Ernabella virtually ceased.

The Arrernte people from Hermannsburg have recently begun to work with **pottery**, a craft which is not traditionally Aboriginal. They have incorporated moulded figures and surface treatments adapted from Dreaming stories.

Bush Tucker and Flowers, silk scarf by Rosemary Petyarre; courtesy of Utopia Awely Batik, Utopia Women's Centre Aboriginal Corporation, NT

Another art form from the western Kimberley is the engraved **pearl-shell pendants** which come from the Broome area. It is believed that the Aboriginal people of the area were using pearl shell for decoration before the arrival of Europeans, but with the establishment of the pearling industry in Broome late last century the use of pearl shell increased markedly. The highly prized shells were engraved and used for ceremonial purposes, as well as for personal decoration and trade – examples of this art have been found as far away as Queensland and South Australia.

The designs engraved into the shells were usually fairly simple geometric patterns which had little symbolic importance. The practice of pearl-shell engraving has largely died out, although the decorated shells are still highly valued.

Buying Aboriginal Art & Artefacts

One of the best and most evocative reminders of your trip is an Aboriginal work of art or artefact. By buying *authentic* items you are supporting Aboriginal culture and helping to ensure that traditional skills and designs endure. Unfortunately much of the so-called Aboriginal art sold as souvenirs is either ripped off from Aboriginal people or is just plain fake. Admittedly it is often difficult to tell whether an item is genuine, or whether a design is being used legitimately, but it is worth trying to find out.

The best place to buy artefacts is either directly from the communities which have craft outlets or from galleries and shops which are owned and operated by Aboriginal communities (see the list below for some suggestions). This way you can be sure that the items are genuine and that the money you spend goes to the right people. There are many Aboriginal artists who get paid very small sums for their work, only to find it being sold for thousands in big city galleries.

Below: Detail of hand-painted silk fabric, Kathleen Wallace; 1997; Keringke Arts; Santa Teresa, NT; courtesy of DESART

Dijeridus are the hot item these days, and you need to decide whether you want a decorative piece or an authentic and functional musical instrument. Many of the dijeridus sold are not made by Aboriginal people, and there are even stories of backpackers in Darwin earning good money by making or decorating dijeridus. From a community outlet such as Injalak or Manyallaluk in the Northern Territory you could expect to pay $100 to $200 for a functional dijeridu which has been painted with ochre paints, and you may even get to meet the maker. On the other hand, from a souvenir shop in Darwin or

Cairns you could pay anything from $200 to $400 or more for something which looks pretty but is really little more than a painted bit of wood.

Dot paintings are also very popular, although they tend to be expensive. As with any art, works by lesser known artists are cheaper than big-name works. A dot painting measuring 1 sq m could be as little as $200, but you can be sure it's no masterpiece. Bargains are hard to find and basically it comes down to whether you think you are getting value for money.

Above: A collection of handpainted gumnut necklaces; 1993; Keringke Arts; Santa Teresa, NT; courtesy of DESART

*Left: **My Country** by Elaine Namatjira; terracotta with underglazes; Hermannsburg, NT; represented by Alcaston House Gallery, Melbourne*

Major Aboriginal Craft Outlets

The following are some Aboriginal owned and operated places where you can buy artefacts and crafts:

Alice Springs

Aboriginal Art & Culture Centre

86 Todd St (☎ (08) 8952 3408, email: aborart@ozemail.com.au) – gallery and craft outlet with a good variety of dot paintings and other desert crafts

Papunya Tula Artists

78 Todd St (☎ (08) 8952 4731; fax 8953 2509) – specialising in western desert dot paintings; high prices but good quality

DESART

Suite 1, Heenan Building, Gregory Tce (☎ (08) 8953 4736) – a resource and advocacy organisation representing 22 owner-operated Aboriginal art centres in central Australia

Cairns

Tjapukai Aboriginal Cultural Park

Kamerunga Rd, Smithfield (☎ (07) 4042 9999; fax 4042 9900) – located at the Skyrail terminus in Cairns with a good range of art, craft and fabrics from a variety of sources

Darwin

Raintree Aboriginal Art Gallery

18 Knuckey St (☎ (08) 8981 2732; fax 8981 8333) – one of the major commercial outlets in Darwin, with medium to high prices but top quality paintings and artefacts

Kakadu National Park

Injalak Arts & Crafts

Oenpelli (☎ (08) 8979 0190; fax 8979 0119) – just over the East Alligator River from Ubirr in Kakadu National Park, Injalak has probably the best selection of Top End arts and crafts anywhere; prices are very reasonable and the staff can pack and ship orders (permits required to visit, but easily available on the spot)

Warradjan Aboriginal Cultural Centre

Kakadu National Park (☎ (08) 8979 0051) – high exposure and consequently high prices, but good fabrics, T-shirts and dijeridus

Katherine Region

Manyallaluk Community

PMB 134, Katherine (☎ (08) 8975 4727; fax 8975 4724) – this small community of Top End Aboriginal people, 100km from Katherine, has a small but impressive array of artefacts including dijeridus and bark paintings, and some of the best prices you'll come across anywhere

Uluru National Park

Maruku Arts & Crafts

Uluru-Kata Tjuta Cultural Centre (☎ (08) 8956 2153; fax 8956 2410) – good for artefacts, especially scorched wood carvings, and craftspeople usually work on the site.

OUTBACK LIVING

While life in remote communities has been much improved by modern developments such as the Royal Flying Doctor Service, the School of the Air and the expanding national telephone network, all outback places are still affected to a greater or lesser degree by the tyranny of distance. Not many city people can imagine living 200km or more from the nearest doctor and supermarket, or their children sitting down in front of a high-frequency (HF) radio transceiver to go to school.

School of the Air

Until recent times, outback children living away from towns either attended boarding school or were educated through written correspondence lessons. In 1944, Adelaide Meithke recognised that HF radio transceivers could be used to improve the children's education as well as their social life by giving them direct contact both with trained teachers and their fellow students. Her idea for a classroom of the airwaves, using the Royal Flying Doctor Service (RFDS) radio facilities, became a reality when Australia's first

School of the Air opened in Alice Springs in 1951.

Today there are 14 Schools of the Air scattered about the outback and most use the RFDS network as their classroom. The major education method is still correspondence lessons – materials and equipment are sent to students, who return set written and audio work by mail – which are supplemented by radio classes lasting 20 to 30 minutes. Students speak to their teachers daily and each has a 10-minute personal session with their teacher once a week. Although face-to-face contact is limited, students and teachers do meet at least once a year on special get-togethers, and teachers visit each of their students on patrols by 4WD vehicles and light aircraft.

With 14 teachers and eight support staff, the Alice Springs School of the Air teaches about 140 children in nine grades, from pre-school to year seven, over a broadcast area of 1.3 million sq km. The student living furthest away is 1000km from Alice Springs. In 1992 the school broke new ground once again when it beamed 'live' lessons by satellite to its students.

Blue Heelers

As you travel around the outback you'll probably see a 4WD traytop or utility with a medium-sized, blue-speckled dog with a red or black face and white-striped forehead sitting alertly in the back. This is the Australian cattle-dog, or blue heeler, the world's only pure breed of cattle-dog.

The blue-heeler breed was established in 1890 to suit large-scale cattle raising under Australian conditions. It had originated some 50 years earlier, when a NSW squatter named Hall crossed smooth-coated Scottish collies with dingoes and produced a type that proved very suitable for cattle. The dogs were silent and tireless, with the instinct to creep up behind an obstinate beast and nip it on the heel.

However, these early 'Hall's heelers' were deficient when it came to working the head of a mob, and to standing guard over their master's horses and gear. So dog breeders crossed them with Dalmations to give them the instinct for guarding, and kelpies (an Australian breed of sheep-dog) so that they'd work a mob from the head as well as the back and sides.

The standard for blue heelers was drawn up in 1897 and has been only slightly varied since then. ∎

Flying Doctor

Established by the Reverend John Flynn with a single aircraft in 1928, the original Flying Doctor has grown into a national organisation, the Royal Flying Doctor Service, which provides a comprehensive medical service to all outback residents. Where people once feared sickness and injury, even the most isolated communities are now assured of receiving expert medical assistance within two or three hours instead of weeks.

Almost as important is the social function of the RFDS's HF radio network, which allows anyone without a telephone to send and receive telegrams and to take part in special broadcasts known as galah sessions. Like party lines, these open periods of radio time allow distant neighbours to keep in touch with each other and events around them in a way the telephone can never rival.

Shopping

Many small communities are far from even the most basic facilities such as post offices, libraries and shops, and often neighbours can be 50km or more apart. They may only receive mail and newspapers either weekly or fortnightly when the mail plane or mail truck does its rounds. Perishable groceries and minor freight can be sent out with the mail, but for really isolated people a major shopping expedition can mean a round trip of 1000km or more to the nearest decent shops.

It's not all Bad

The outback presents its share of difficulties.

The Flying Doctor

Before the late 1920s the outback's far-flung residents had little or no access to medical facilities. The nearest doctor was often weeks away over rough tracks, so if you fell seriously ill or met with a bad accident, your chances of recovery were slim. Difficult pregnancies and illnesses, such as rheumatic fever and acute appendicitis, were almost a death sentence. If you were lucky you fell ill near a telegraph line, where your mates could treat you (or operate) under instructions received in morse code. This pointed to another harsh truth of life in the outback: reliable and speedy communications over long distances were available to very few.

In 1912 the **Reverend John Flynn** of the Presbyterian Church helped establish the outback's first hospital at Oodnadatta. Flynn was appalled by the tragedies that resulted from the lack of medical facilities and was quick to realise that the answer lay in radios and aircraft. However, these technologies – particularly radio – were still very much in their infancy and needed further development.

Flynn knew nothing of either radios or aviation but his sense of mission inspired others who did, such as radio engineer **Alf Traeger**. In 1928, after years of trial and error, Traeger developed a small, pedal-powered radio transceiver that was simple to use, inexpensive and could send and receive messages over 500km. The outback's great silence was broken at last.

Aircraft suitable for medical evacuations had become available in 1920 but it was the lack of a radio communication network that delayed their general use for this purpose. Traeger's invention was the key to the establishment of Australia's first Flying Doctor base in Cloncurry, Queensland, in 1928. Cloncurry was then the base for the **Queensland and Northern Territory Aerial Services** (Qantas), which provided the pilot and an aircraft under lease.

The new service proved an outstanding success and areas beyond the reach of Cloncurry soon

Reverend John Flynn

Most of these can be attributed to isolation, but as the famous Australian poet AB 'Banjo' Paterson wrote in *Clancy of the Overflow*, bush people do 'have pleasures that the townsfolk never know'. One of these is the ready access to wide-open spaces untainted by air pollution, traffic noise and crowds. Another is the sense of self-reliance and independence that's still strong in the outback.

Being forced to make their own entertainment encourages people living hundreds of kilometres apart to get together (usually on the RFDS radio network, although increasingly by telephone) to organise social functions such as horse-race meetings, camp drafts (rodeos) and gymkhanas. This strong sense of community spirit, even when the 'community' may be spread over a vast area, means that even neighbours who don't get on will more than likely assist each other in a crisis. It's these aspects of outback life that help to make the hardships worthwhile.

SOCIAL CONDUCT
Cross-Cultural Etiquette

Many of the outback's original inhabitants lead lives that are still powerfully influenced by ancient traditions. These will be almost incomprehensible to the average tourist, who is almost entirely ignorant of Aboriginal social customs – let's face it, even most Australians have never even met a traditional Aboriginal person. Aborigines will make allowances for the ignorance of white people, but it does no harm to observe a few simple rules. One of the most important of these is to act naturally.

You won't go far wrong if you treat

---

began to clamour for their own Flying Doctor. However, the Presbyterian Church had insufficient resources to allow a rapid expansion. In 1933 it handed the aerial medical service over to 'an organisation of national character' and so the **Royal Flying Doctor Service** (RFDS) was born. Flynn's vision of a 'mantle of safety' over the outback had become a reality.

Today, 12 RFDS base stations provide a sophisticated network of radio communications and medical services to an area as large as western Europe and about two-thirds the size of the USA. Emergency evacuations of sick or injured people are still an important function, but these days the RFDS provides a comprehensive range of medical services, including routine clinics at communities that are unable to attract full-time medical staff. It also supervises numerous small hospitals that normally operate without a doctor; such hospitals are staffed by registered nurses who communicate by telephone or radio with their RFDS doctor.

The administration of RFDS bases is divided between seven largely independent sections, each of which is a nonprofit organisation funded by government grants and private donations.

Facts & Figures To get an idea of the RFDS's scope of operations, let's take a look at its Central Section, which covers virtually the entire outback of South Australia and the Northern Territory's bottom half. With its headquarters in Adelaide and base stations at Port Augusta, Alice Springs and Yulara, the Central Section operates 10 sophisticated twin-engined aircraft and employs around 80 staff. They include 20 pilots, 7 aircraft engineers, 6 doctors, 22 flight nurses and 7 radio operators.

In the 1995-96 financial year the section's aircraft flew 2.9 million km on medical-related matters. These included 2763 medical evacuations and 3300 hospital-to-hospital transfers. It had 32,333 patient contacts, including 26,270 patients attended to at regular clinics and remote locations; there were 67 HF radio consultations and 7962 consultations by telephone. The two main bases (Port Augusta and Alice Springs) made a total of 6461 radphone connections, in which HF outpost radio stations were 'patched in' to the national telephone network. Their emergency alarms were activated 185 times, mostly by callers seeking medical or other assistance.

So the service established by the Reverend John Flynn nearly 70 years ago is still a powerful force in the outback, enabling its residents to live secure in the knowledge that medical help is just a telephone or radio call away. However, there is talk of transferring the RFDS's HF radio network to a single OTC Maritime base on the eastern seaboard as a cost-cutting measure. This proposal is viewed with scepticism if not horror by many outback people, who appreciate the efficiency, local knowledge and experience of RFDS radio operators. They feel that such a radical change will degrade the service on which their lives and wellbeing often depend. ■

outback Aborigines as potential friends. Also, remember that Aborigines generally have great senses of humour and love a good laugh.

Paying a Visit You've arrived at a small Aboriginal community on a back road in the middle of nowhere. The front area outside each dwelling is the occupants' private space, a sort of outdoor living room. Park at a reasonable distance (say, 30m) so as not to intrude on this space, then get out of the vehicle and wait for someone to come over. That person will most likely speak at least reasonable English and will be able to point you in the right direction. If this approach yields no results, try walking over to the nearest house or shelter and calling out to attract attention.

Sometimes you'll find the residents sitting around in a circle, which usually indicates some sort of business in progress. Instead of barging in, stand a little way off – you may be beckoned over, or someone may come up. Don't hang around if it's obvious that your presence isn't wanted.

Most larger communities have a store staffed by white people, and this is the place to go first for information. The store may not be easy to find, in which case ask someone rather than head off on an unauthorised sightseeing tour. One sure way to wear out a welcome is to drive around taking photographs without permission. Aborigines are people, not celebrities.

Many tourists feel extremely uncomfortable when visiting their first Aboriginal community, and this can find expression in rudeness. For example, there's a tendency for tourists to race down the road with their faces expressionless and eyes fixed straight ahead. Aborigines won't think you're immoral if you smile and wave; the fact is they'll generally appreciate it and you'll get a positive response.

People Skills Having got to first base, you need to watch your body language. For example, wrinkling your nose at someone else's odour is unlikely to win any friends.

Desert dwellers naturally place washing well down on the list of priorities; people who eat a lot of kangaroo meat can also develop a distinctive and fairly strong body odour. To put a different perspective on this, the well-soaped white person can smell unpleasantly like a wet sheep to desert Aborigines. However, being invariably polite, they'll give no indication that they find your personal aroma to be anything other than what you imagine it to be.

Western society regards a firm handshake and eye contact as important in creating a favourable first impression – just ask any salesperson. However, both are signs of aggression in Aboriginal society. Their usual greeting is a soft clasp of the hands with little or no arm movement, and there may be no eye contact at all until a friendly relationship is established. The best approach to eye contact is to take it as it comes. If the other person isn't looking directly at you, it's polite not to look at them.

It's also unwise to rush or be pushy, as the usual Aboriginal way is to engage in sociable small talk before getting down to the matter at hand, even if this takes time. While they won't expect you to waffle on at length about the drought or scarcity of kangaroos, a pleasantry or two gets the conversation flowing and establishes your unselfish interest in that person. This works well in white outback society too.

It's also important to remember that English is very much the second language on most remote communities and may not be spoken at all well. This doesn't mean you should lapse into broken pidgin to make yourself understood. Not only is such behaviour demeaning to the audience, but they might think you're some sort of idiot. The correct approach is to speak distinctly and reasonably slowly, using straightforward English and a normal tone of voice. Be careful not to make the mistake of addressing your audience as you would a slow learner with a hearing problem. See the Language section later in this chapter for more advice on communicating with Aborigines.

Purchasing A visit to an Aboriginal community presents an ideal opportunity to purchase traditional paintings or other works of art directly from the artist. However, bargaining such as takes place in an Indian bazaar is foreign to this society, and in any case the prices asked are usually very reasonable.

If you're tempted to drive the price down, remember that there's no sport in this as the seller's inherent politeness may force him or her to accept your unreasonably low offer rather than offend you. On the other hand, Aboriginal artists are waking up fast to the value of their work and the devious ways of many tourists.

Alcohol Many Australians believe that most Aborigines drink to excess, but this is not so. In actual fact, a smaller percentage of Aborigines drink than do non-Aborigines.

However, Aborigines who consume alcohol are more likely than their non-Aboriginal counterparts to drink in public. One reason for this is the fact that Aboriginal councils have banned the possession and consumption of alcohol on many Aboriginal communities. As a result, many outback Aborigines have irregular access to alcohol, and only drink when they go to town. Unfortunately, this is the only time many non-Aboriginal people (and tourists) see Aborigines.

Throughout Australia, Aboriginal people are actively involved in the fight against alcohol. They have persuaded some outback hotels and takeaway outlets not to sell alcohol to local Aboriginal people, and signs at such outlets explain that Aboriginal elders ask tourists to not buy alcohol for Aborigines. Also, some outlets may refuse to sell you alcohol if you're heading towards an Aboriginal community. Please respect such efforts to combat alcoholism.

Pastoral Properties

It's a hot, sweaty day out on the wide brown land and you're bouncing along a dusty road in your 4WD. You've never felt more in need of a bath, particularly after changing that last tyre back in the bulldust.

Then you spy a lonely windmill in the scrub beside the track. There's a large steel tank beside it and the thought of a bath brings instant good cheer. Off come your clothes, you climb onto the edge and with a glad cry leap into the water. To your horror the concussion bursts the wall, but you manage to escape fearful mutilation by clinging to the edge as the tank's precious contents gush out through the jagged hole.

This sort of thing doesn't happen very often (thank goodness) but it's an example of how people from an urban environment can come undone in the unfamiliar world of the outback. Most visitors want to do the right thing and here are some simple rules on how to avoid upsetting the people who live there.

Water Most pastoralists are happy for travellers to make use of their water supplies, but they do ask that they be treated with respect. This means washing clothes, dishes and sweaty bodies in a bucket or basin, not in the water supply itself. Always remember that animals and people may have to drink it when you've finished.

Camping right beside watering points is also to be avoided. In the outback the stock is often half wild and will hang back if you're parked or have your tent pitched right where they normally drink. They'll eventually overcome their fear through necessity, which means you'll be covered in dust and develop grey hair as the thirst-crazed mob mills around your camp at midnight. If you must camp in the vicinity, keep at least 200m away and stay well off the pads that animals have worn as they come in to drink.

Much the same applies if you drive up to a bore or dam and find the stock having a drink. Stay well back until they've finished, then you can move in for your share. The thing to remember at all times is that this isolated pool or trough might be the only water in a radius of 30km or more.

For more about water, see Health in the Facts for the Visitor chapter.

Gates The golden rule with any gate is to *leave it as you find it*. You must do this even if a sign by an open gate says to keep it closed – it may have been left open for any number of reasons, such as to let stock through to water. It's fairly common for animals to perish because tourists have closed gates that a pastoralist left open.

Unfortunately, some home-made wire gates can seem like the work of the devil and on occasion will turn nasty, entangling you in barbed wire as you struggle to close them. When you arrive at one of these things, take careful note of how it works while opening it; closure should then be a relatively simple matter. Never throw up your hands in defeat and drive off leaving it either insecurely fastened or, worse, lying on the ground. Having opened it, you must persevere until you've worked out how to close it.

If you're driving in a convoy it's accepted procedure that, on coming to a gate, one of the lead vehicles remains on the spot until all others are through. That way, there won't be any mistakes with gates not being left as they were found.

Floods Sometimes the outback receives a large part of its annual rainfall in a matter of days. When this happens, unsealed roads and tracks become extremely slippery and boggy. The correct thing to do in this event is either to get out before the rain soaks in or to stay put on high ground until the surface dries out. To do otherwise may see your vehicle gouging great ruts in the road surface, which of course won't endear you to the locals who must live with the mess you've made. Quite apart from that, you'll probably get well and truly stuck in some dreadful place far from anywhere. This is one of the reasons to carry plenty of extra stores on an outback trip. If a road is officially closed because of heavy rain, you can be fined for travelling on it – the norm is $1000 per wheel!

Fire The outback usually experiences drought, during which time many grasses dry off to form standing hay. This, along with the foliage of trees and bushes, carries the stock through to the next rains. Under extreme weather conditions a careless camper can start a bushfire that might destroy the vegetation over many hundreds of sq km of grazing land. To avoid being responsible for such a disaster, always take care with your campfire by siting it at least 5m from flammable material, keeping it small and making certain it's out before you leave camp. The best way to guarantee the latter is to completely cover the ashes with soil.

For more about fire, see Dangers & Annoyances as well as Camping and Food in the Facts for the Visitor chapter.

Dogs The tourist's best friend is a contentious issue in the outback at the best of times. There's no doubt that the best way to avoid dog-related hassles is to keep your pet on a leash at all times when in sheep and cattle country. If nothing else, this will save it from an untimely and unpleasant end.

First, dogs like to chase things. After a day cooped up in the back of a vehicle you'd probably want to chase something yourself, but the difference is that Rover might put a flock of sheep through the fence while he's trying to round it up. The distress caused through being chased and worried by domestic dogs is a major contributing factor in stock deaths each year. For this reason, pastoralists who find a strange dog on their properties tend to shoot first and ask questions later.

Second, dogs are great scavengers and no matter how well fed or bred they are they'll gobble up any old piece of meat or carcass they find lying around. Fox and dingo poisoning is widely practiced throughout the outback, with bite-sized chunks of meat being a common bait. Rover won't be able to resist that one last meal.

Rubbish The best way to dispose of all non-burnable rubbish is to store it in a heavy-duty plastic bag and carry it with you to deposit at an authorised dumping place. Many tourists believe they're doing the right thing by burying their garbage, but few dig a deep enough hole. Anything buried under less than 1m of soil will be dug up by goannas and dingoes, which are attracted by the food scraps. Crows will then scatter it everywhere and the end result is an unsightly mess. If you must bury your rubbish, any cans or other food containers should always be burned first to get rid of the tantalising smells.

See also Camping in the Facts for the Visitor chapter.

Common Courtesy These days most outback pastoralists are on the telephone and it's a common courtesy to contact them before you invade their property. Straight-through travel on established roads is not a problem, but if you're thinking of going camping or fishing in some remote spot, the landholder will expect you to ask permission. You'll usually rise in the estimation of the more isolated people if you drop off some very recent newspapers, or ask if there's anything they'd like brought out from town. Always remember to take-your-own-everything, as station folk seldom organise their shopping around the needs of ill-prepared visitors.

RELIGION

A shrinking majority of people in Australia are at least nominally Christian. Most Prot-estant churches have merged to become the Uniting Church, although the Church of England has remained separate. The Catho-lic Church is popular (about a third of Australian Christians are Catholics), with the original Irish adherents boosted by the large numbers of Mediterranean immigrants.

Non-Christian minorities abound, the main ones in order of magnitude being Muslim, Buddhist and Jewish.

Aboriginal Religion

Traditional Aboriginal cultures either have very little religious component or are nothing but religion, depending on how you look at it. Is a belief system which views every event, no matter how trifling, in a

non-material context a religion? The early Christian missionaries certainly didn't think so. For them a belief in a deity was an essen-tial part of a religion, and anything else was mere superstition.

Sacred Sites Aboriginal sacred sites are a perennial topic of discussion. Their presence can lead to headline grabbing controversy when they stand in the way of developments such as roads, mines and dams. This is because most other Australians still have great difficulty understanding the deep spir-itual bond that Aborigines have with the land.

Aboriginal religious beliefs centre on the continuing existence of spirit beings that lived on Earth during the Dreamtime, which occurred before the arrival of humans. These beings created all the features of the natural world and were the ancestors of all living things. They took different forms but behaved as people do, and as they travelled about they left signs to show where they passed. Most Australians have heard of rainbow serpents carving out rivers as they slithered from A to B. On a smaller scale you can have a pile of rocks marking the spot where an ancestor defecated, or a tree that sprang from a thrown spear.

Despite being supernatural, the ancestors were subject to ageing and eventually they returned to the sleep from which they'd awoken at the dawn of time. Some sank back into the ground while others changed into physical features including the moon and stars. Here their spirits remain as eternal forces that breathe life into the newborn and influence natural events. Each ancestor's spiritual energy flows along the path it trav-elled during the Dreamtime and is strongest at the points where it left physical evidence of its activities, such as a tree, hill or claypan. These features are sacred sites.

The ancestors left strict laws that deter-mine the behaviour of people and animals, the growth of plants, and natural events such as rain and the change of seasons. Although all living things are considered to be con-scious beings with their own language and way of life, they are still required to live in accordance with their ancestors' laws.

Every person, animal and plant is believed to have two souls – one mortal and one immortal. The latter is part of a particular ancestral spirit and returns to the sacred sites of that ancestor after death, while the mortal soul simply fades into oblivion. Each person is spiritually bound to the sacred sites that mark the land associated with his or her ancestor. It is the individual's obligation to help care for these sites by performing the necessary rituals and singing the songs that tell of the ancestor's deeds. By doing this, the order created by that ancestor is maintained.

However, the ancestors are extremely powerful and restless spirits and require the most careful treatment. Dreadful calamities can befall those who fail to care for their sites in the proper manner. As there is nowhere beyond the influence of an angry ancestor, the unpleasant consequences of either disrespect or neglect at a single site may stretch far and wide.

Some sacred sites are believed to be dangerous and entry is prohibited under traditional Aboriginal law. These restrictions often have a pragmatic origin. One site in northern Australia was believed to cause sores to break out all over the body of anyone visiting the area. Subsequently, the area was found to have a dangerously high level of radiation from naturally occurring radon gas. In another instance, fishing from a certain reef was traditionally prohibited. This restriction was scoffed at by local Europeans until it was discovered that fish from this area had a high incidence of *ciguatera*, which renders fish poisonous if eaten by humans.

Unfortunately, Aboriginal sacred sites are not like Christian churches, which can be desanctified before the bulldozers move in. Neither can they be bought, sold or transferred. Other Australians find this difficult to accept because they regard land as belonging to the individual, whereas in Aboriginal society the reverse applies. In a nutshell, Aborigines believe that to destroy or damage a sacred site threatens not only the living but also the spirit inhabitants of the land. It is a

distressing and dangerous act, and one that no responsible person would condone.

Throughout much of Australia, when pastoralists were breaking the Aborigines' subsistence link to the land, many Aborigines sought refuge on missions and became Christians. However, becoming Christians has not, for most Aborigines, meant renouncing their traditional religion. Many senior Aboriginal law men are also devout Christians, and in many cases ministers.

LANGUAGE

Any visitor from abroad who thinks Australian (that's 'strine') is simply a weird variant of British or American will soon have a few surprises. For a start, many Australians don't even speak Australian – they speak Italian, Lebanese, Vietnamese, Turkish or Greek (Melbourne is said to be the third-largest Greek city in the world).

Those who do speak the native tongue are liable to lose you in a strange collection of Australian words. Some have completely different meanings in Australia than they have in English-speaking countries north of the equator; some commonly used words have been shortened almost beyond recognition. Others derive from Aboriginal languages, or from the slang used by early convict settlers.

There is a slight regional variation in the Australian accent but it's minute compared with variations in, say, the USA. The main difference between city speech and that in the country or outback is speed.

Some of the most famed Aussie words are hardly heard at all – 'mates' and 'pals' are more common than 'cobbers'. Rhyming slang is used occasionally ('hit the frog and toad' for 'hit the road', 'Oxford scholars' for 'dollars'), so if you hear an odd expression that doesn't seem to make sense, see if it rhymes with something else that does.

If you want to pass for a native, try speaking slightly nasally, and shorten any word of more than two syllables and then add a vowel to the end of it (garbage contractors become 'garbos', worker's compensation becomes 'compo'). Make anything you can into a diminutive (the Hell's Angels become 'bikies'), and pepper your speech with as many expletives as possible. The Glossary in the back of this book will help.

Aboriginal Languages

Before the Europeans arrived, there were about 250 Aboriginal languages comprising about 700 dialects. It is believed that all the languages evolved from a single language family as the Aborigines gradually moved out over the entire continent and split into new groups. There are a number of words that occur right across the continent, such as *jina* (foot) and *mala* (hand), and similarities also exist in the often complex grammatical structures. Today there remain at least 100 distinct Aboriginal languages, many of which have a number of dialects. Some languages are actually growing as populations expand and dominant languages replace others.

Most Aboriginal languages have about 10,000 words – about the same number of words used by the average English speaker. Many words reflect the close relationship that Aboriginal people have with their environment. For example, the Western Desert Pintupi dialect has 18 words for 'hole': an ant burrow, a rabbit burrow, a goanna burrow, a small animal burrow etc. Traditionally, all Aboriginal adults could identify and name hundreds of plants and animals. This is still the case in many parts of outback and northern Australia, and one reason why Aboriginal people are central to much contemporary scientific research.

Dozens of Aboriginal words have been incorporated into Australian English: barramundi, boomerang, budgerigar, brolga, coolabah, corroboree, dingo, galah, jarrah, kangaroo, kookaburra, mallee, mulga, perentie, quandong, wallaby and yakka, to name a few. Similarly, Aboriginal languages have absorbed many English words, which are invariably adapted to suit Aboriginal grammars and sound systems. For example, English words used by many Central Australian Aboriginal people include 'taraka' (truck), 'tiipii' (TV), 'rrupula' (rifle) and 'ruuta' (road).

Aboriginal Kriol is a new language that has developed since European arrival in Australia. It is spoken across northern Australia and has become the 'native' language of many young Aborigines. It contains many English words but, once again, grammatical usage is along Aboriginal lines. For example, the English sentence 'He was amazed' becomes 'I bin luk kwesjinmak' in Kriol.

Lonely Planet's *Australian Phrasebook* gives a detailed account of Aboriginal languages.

Pitjantjatjara As it's pointless to try and explain the many different languages, we'll focus on Pitjantjatjara (sometimes known as Pitjantjara). This is the best known dialect of Aboriginal Australia's largest language group, the Western Desert language. Western Desert dialects are spoken widely throughout central Australia, from 1000km or so north-west of Alice Springs down almost to the Great Australian Bight, east almost to Queensland, and 1000km or so west of the Northern Territory/Western Australia border. Speakers of Western Desert dialects call themselves Anangu.

Pitjantjatjara is not the traditional language of Alice Springs, but it is often heard in Alice Springs and on some communities west of Alice. It is spoken extensively on Aboriginal communities from the Northern Territory/Western Australia border, through Uluru National Park to the eastern edge of the Simpson Desert, and throughout the Anangu Pitjantjatjara freehold Aboriginal lands of northern South Australia.

Pitjantjatjara means the dialect that has the word *pitjantja*, a form of the verb 'to come', and *tjara*, which means 'to have'. Other dialects use different words instead of *pitjantja* – for example Yankunytjatjara speakers use the word *yankunytja*. Despite these differences, Pitjantjatjara and Yankunytjatjara sound systems are identical, and most of their words are identical or very similar.

Aboriginal cultures are traditionally oral, and the languages were not written down

Aboriginal Languages

0   500   1000 km
(The only languages shown are
those spoken by 500 people or more)

until well after European contact; many languages were lost forever when their speakers were exterminated or died out. Pitjantjatjara was one of the first Aboriginal languages to be comprehensively transcribed, at Ernabella in South Australia in the 1930s in the context of Bible translation and bilingual education. Written Pitjantjatjara now has a standardised phonetic spelling system, which is an integral part of the signage at Uluru National Park.

Aspiring Pitjantjatjara-learners and those with an interest in the language can buy the Pitjantjatjara/Yankunytjatjara-to-English dictionary. This is a nicely illustrated publication available from the Institute for Aboriginal Development, PO Box 2531, Alice Springs, NT 0871. A number of dictionaries of Central Australian languages are also available from the institute, as are a range of language-learning tapes and manuals.

Pronunciation Like most Aboriginal languages, Pitjantjatjara has three vowels:

a   as 'u' in 'sun'
i   as 'i' in 'bin'
u   as 'oo' in 'look'

These vowels also have a long form – eg, kaanka (crow), nyii-nyii (zebra finch), and uulinanyi (to tease).

There are 17 Pitjantjatjara consonants: p, m, w, tj, ny, ly, y, t, n, l, r, t̲, n̲, l̲, r̲, k and ng. Consonants with lines under them (which can happen to t̲, n̲, l̲ and r̲) are retroflexed, which means that when they are articulated the tongue is curled back. Thus when you pronounce the word 'mina' (arm) you must curl your tongue back when you pronounce the 'n'. If you fail to do so you will say 'mina', which means water.

Words & Phrases The following list will help you communicate with Anangu people in the south of the Northern Territory, the north of South Australia, and the south east of Western Australia:

Yes.	*uwa.*
No.	*wiya.*
Sorry.	*munta.*
Sorry, I don't. (ie if someone asks if you smoke or for cigarettes)	*munta, ngayulu ngurpa.*
OK/No worries.	*palya.*
Are you OK?	*nyuntu palya?*
Where can we find water?	*kaapi yaaltjl?*
Do you have any water?	*nyuntu kaapi kanyini?*
Do you have a lot of water/petrol?	*nyuntu kaapi/petrol pulka-tjara?*
sick	*pikatjara*
When?	*yaalara?*
Where?	*yaaltjingka?*

Communicating with Outback Aborigines In many parts of outback Australia, including the Western Desert region and Arnhem Land, many Aborigines do not speak English regularly or fluently. There are many reasons for this. There are virtually no high schools in outback Aboriginal communities and many people emerge from school without basic English literacy or oracy. Many Aborigines seldom have to use English on their communities, and use their own languages when speaking to non-Aborigines with the expectation (or hope) that, with time and like other Aboriginal people, non-Aborigines will learn to understand and possibly speak their language. When they go to towns or shops, they can usually get by without speaking English. Many visitors to outback Australia see Aborigines in shops, selecting what they want and going through the checkout with eyes lowered, passing their money silently over the counter.

Because of all this, and the great differences between Aboriginal and English sound systems, many Aborigines have difficulty pronouncing English words. For example, many Aboriginal languages do not include the sounds 's', 'z', 'v', 'sh' or 'th' and do not distinguish between a 'b' and a 'p', or a 'd' and a 't'. Keep this in mind when you talk to Aboriginal people who have difficulty speaking English. Conversely, it is difficult for some English-speaking people to roll their r's, or to distinguish between the retroflexed and non-retroflexed sounds typical of most Aboriginal languages.

Most Aboriginal languages have no words for hello, please or thank you – these niceties are simply not part of traditional Aboriginal culture. However, these words have been adopted to some extent and people will appreciate you using them, as they show your friendly intentions.

People who come into contact with Aborigines should also be aware that Aboriginal people of mixed descent usually identify as Aborigines and don't like being referred to as half-castes. Refer to Aboriginal people as Aborigines, or Aboriginal people – words such as 'Abos' or 'coons' are grossly insulting.

However, many Aborigines have terms which they use to refer to themselves. For example, many Queensland Aborigines refer to themselves as Murris, many New South Wales and Victorian Aborigines call themselves Kooris, Western Desert speakers are Anangu, Warlpiri speakers Yappa, and north-east Arnhem Landers Yolngu. Nunga is used to refer to the people of coastal South Australia, and Nyoongah is used in the country's south-west. Aborigines appreciate non-Aboriginal people using these terms – provided that the correct term is used to refer to the appropriate group. If you call an Anangu from Uluru a Koori you will probably receive a blank stare.

See the Social Conduct section in this chapter for advice on meeting Aborigines.

Facts for the Visitor

PLANNING

The success of any trip to a vast, remote and sparsely populated area like the Australian outback will depend largely on the research and planning you do before you go. Among other things, you need to find out about the best time to go, the availability of drinking water, services and facilities, the likely condition of roads and tracks, and whether or not your vehicle will be suitable. As is so often the case, you'll probably regret it if you leave your planning until you get there.

When to Go

Roughly speaking, January is the middle of summer in the lower three-quarters of Australia and July is the middle of winter (see Climate in the Facts about the Outback chapter). Up in the monsoon belt, where the temperature remains relatively constant all year, 'summer' is the wet season and 'winter' is the dry season. The best time to visit the Centre and northern Australia is May to September; mid-winter is ideal, but everyone knows that and the popular spots fill up fast.

The Centre isn't recommended in summer unless you love extreme heat, carry plenty of water, and stick to the busy routes – every year inexperienced travellers die or become extremely ill because of heat and dehydration. Daytime shade temperatures usually hover around 40°C at the height of summer and can reach 50°C in the hotter parts. On hot days, physical activities such as cycling and walking are pretty much out of the question unless you do them early.

The northern wet season occurs somewhere between November and May – the rains can be late or early and their unpredictability is a popular topic of discussion. Once the wet sets in, tracks can become bottomless mud, dry creeks become raging torrents and low-lying areas are flooded. Vast areas can be cut off from the rest of the world for weeks at a time.

However, the wet season can be a good time to visit the far north: the vegetation is at its best, the waterfalls and rivers are at their most spectacular, and you'll never forget those fierce electrical storms. If you can handle hot and humid conditions and don't plan on driving (or can stay on sealed roads), you'll find quiet tourist facilities and bargain package deals. The biggest drawback is that you can't cool off in the sea because of the dreaded 'stingers', or box jellyfish (see the Fauna section in the Facts about the Outback chapter).

Another major consideration is school holidays. Australian families take to the road (and air) en masse at these times and many places are booked out, prices rise and things generally get a bit crazy. Holidays vary somewhat from state to state – see the Holidays section later in this chapter.

What Kind of Trip

As public road transport in the outback is limited to main through routes such as the Stuart and Eyre highways, the only real option if you want a good look around is to have your own vehicle. This being the case, you will probably want to do a fair amount of camping, particularly in the more remote areas where there is little or no commercial accommodation. In any case, bush camping is cheap, and it's a wonderful way to experience the real outback.

If you have a 4WD but don't want to drive the tougher tracks by yourself, consider a tag-along tour led by an expert guide. If time is a problem, consider one of the more adventurous coach options, or do a combination of localised tours/car rental with bus/plane travel between major centres.

The Getting Around chapter gives details on transport options including buying your own vehicle, car rental and organised tours.

Maps

Maps are absolutely essential on any outback trip. The maps in this book will give you a good overview of the various tracks – the individual track descriptions list some of the most appropriate maps on a case-by-case basis, and you'd be well advised to try and get hold of them.

There's no shortage of touring maps available, although many are of pretty average quality. The various oil companies – Shell, BP, Mobil etc – publish road maps and these are available from service stations. They're quite good for major roads but begin to let you down off the beaten track.

The state motoring organisations (see Useful Organisations, later in this chapter, for addresses) produce maps that are often free (if you're a member) or cheaper than the oil company maps. Their maps and track-note sheets of outback regions in their own states can be very good indeed. Don't forget the state tourist offices listed later in this chapter either: they sometimes have lovingly produced outback maps that are virtual works of art, though they won't be free.

Westprint maps are excellent and provide copious detail on points of interest, tracks and historical and tourist information. The Westprint catalogue of over 20 mainly outback maps covers many of the tracks mentioned in this book. They're available from specialist map shops, local information centres and various other outback outlets, such as service stations, or through Westprint Heritage Maps (☎ (03) 5391 5233; fax 5391 5221) at RMB 33, Nhill, Vic 3418.

Hema's regional touring maps are attractive, informative and give a wide coverage of the outback, including the gulf country, Cape York, the Kimberley, the Flinders Ranges and central Australia. They're usually available at local outlets, or contact Hema Maps (☎ (07) 3290 0322; fax 3290 0478) at PO 2660, Logan City DC, Qld 4114.

If you want the best, get the topographic sheets put out by the national mapping agency, the Australian Surveying & Land Information Group (AUSLIG). They may be many years out of date, with indicated tracks long since abandoned and new ones formed, but their detail is staggering. The more popular sheets are often available over the counter at shops that sell bushwalking gear and outdoor equipment. AUSLIG also has special interest maps showing various types of land use such as population densities or Aboriginal land. For more information, or a catalogue, contact AUSLIG (☎ (02) 6201 4201), Department of Administrative Services, PO Box 2, Belconnen, ACT 2616, or its interstate sales outlets.

In every state capital there is at least one good shop that specialises in maps and guidebooks. In Adelaide there's the Map Shop (☎ (08) 8231 2033), Brisbane has World-Wide Maps & Guides (☎ (07) 3221 4330), while Melbourne has the Melbourne Map Centre (☎ (03) 9569 5472) and Mapland (☎ (03) 9670 4383). In Perth there's the Perth Map Centre (☎ (08) 9322 5733), while in Sydney, Map World (☎ (02) 9261 3601) has four outlets in the city and suburbs. All have mail-order services.

What to Bring

What you should bring with you will largely depend on what sort of trip you're doing and where you're doing it. At one extreme is independent travel into the middle of nowhere, where you'll need to BYO everything. At the other end is an organised bus trip (see the Coach Options section in the Getting Around chapter) – all you may need to bring here is appropriate clothing.

The check lists at the back of this book will give you some ideas.

HIGHLIGHTS

In an area as broad and geographically diverse as Australia's outback the list of highlights is virtually endless, although one person's highlight can easily be another's disappointment. There are, however, a number of features in each state which shouldn't be missed.

In northern Queensland there's **Cape York Peninsula**, with tracts of rainforest that run right down to the beach, and the **Great Barrier Reef** just offshore. In central Queensland, the **Stockman's Hall of Fame** in Longreach is a moving testimony to the people who opened up the outback.

The Northern Territory has the obvious attraction of **Uluru** (Ayers Rock), probably Australia's most readily identifiable symbol after Sydney's Opera House. There's also the World Heritage-listed **Kakadu National Park** with its wealth of flora and fauna and superb wetlands. The Territory is also where Australia's Aboriginal cultural heritage is at its most accessible – the **rock-art sites** of Kakadu, and Aboriginal-owned and run tours of **Arnhem Land**, **Manyallaluk** (near Katherine) and Uluru are just a few of the possibilities.

Then there's Western Australia with its vast distances and wide open spaces. The remote **Kimberley region** in the far north is as ruggedly picturesque as any you'll find – the **Bungle Bungles (Purnululu) National Park** here is unforgettable. The 1700km **Canning Stock Route** across the Gibson and Great Sandy deserts is the nation's longest 4WD track – a true adventure.

South Australia's major outback drawcard is the **Flinders Ranges**, which offer superb bushwalking and stunning scenery. Further afield you can get a real taste of the outback along the **Strzelecki Track**, **Oodnadatta Track** and **Birdsville Track**. There's also the unique opal-mining town of **Coober Pedy**, where many people both work and live underground.

New South Wales has the outback mining town of **Broken Hill**, once the world's largest silver-lead zinc mine and now a convenient base for outback excursions. Nearby is a treasure trove of early Aboriginal history at **Mungo National Park**.

TOURIST OFFICES

There are various sources of information available to visitors to Australia and, as with a number of other tourist-conscious western countries, you can easily drown yourself in brochures and booklets, maps and leaflets.

Local Tourist Offices

Within Australia, tourist information is handled by the various state and local offices. Most states and the Northern Terri-

tory have a main office in the capital cities, as well as regional offices in main tourist centres and also in other states.

As well as supplying brochures, price lists, maps and other information, the state offices will often book transport, tours and accommodation for you. Unfortunately, only a few of the state tourist offices maintain information desks at the airports and, furthermore, the opening hours of the offices in the city are very much of the 9-to-5 weekdays and Saturday-morning-only variety. Addresses of the main state tourist offices relevant to the outback are:

New South Wales
    NSW Government Travel Centre, 11 York St, Sydney, NSW 2000 (☎ 13 2077)
Northern Territory
    Northern Territory Tourist Commission, 43 Mitchell St, Darwin NT 0800 (☎ (08) 8999 3900)
Queensland
    Queen St Mall Information Centre, corner Adelaide and Albert Sts, Brisbane, Qld 4000 (☎ (07) 3229 5918)
South Australia
    South Australia Travel Centre, 1 King William St, Adelaide, SA 5000 (☎ toll-free 1800 882 092)
Western Australia
    Western Australian Tourist Centre, Forrest Place, Perth, WA 6000 (☎ (08) 9483 1111)

A step down from the state tourist offices are the local or regional tourist offices. All major outback towns and many minor ones maintain a tourist office or visitor information centre of some type or other. These often have a great deal of information not readily available from the larger, state offices. Otherwise check hotels, police stations, park ranger offices and roadhouses.

Tourist offices will be happy to provide bookings and put you on to tour operators, but usually know little about independent outback travel. The automobile associations (see the Useful Organisations section below) are a better bet; their head and regional offices are usually well stocked with maps and brochures of the outback in their own state.

Tourist Offices Overseas

Overseas, tourist promotion is handled by the Australian Tourist Commission (ATC). It has a useful free magazine-style booklet called *Travellers' Guide to Australia* which is a good introduction to the country, its geography, flora, fauna, states, transport, accommodation, food and so on. It also has a handy free map. This literature is intended for distribution overseas only; if you want copies, get them before you come to Australia. Addresses of ATC offices for literature requests are:

Australia
    80 William St, Woolloomooloo, Sydney, NSW 2011 (☎ (02) 9360 1111)
Germany
    Neue Mainzerstrasse 22, D0311 Frankfurt/Main 1 (☎ (069) 274 00 60)
Hong Kong
    Suite 1501, Central Plaza, 18 Harbour Rd, Wanchai (☎ 2802 7700)
Japan
    Australian Business Centre, New Otani Garden Court Building 28F, 4-1 Kioi-cho, Chiyoda-ku, Tokyo 102 (☎ (03) 5214 0720)
    Twin 21, MID Tower 30F, 2-1-61 Shiromi, Chuo-Ku, Osaka 540 (☎ (06) 946 2503)
New Zealand
    Level 13, 44-48 Emily Place, Auckland 1 (☎ (09) 379 9594)
Singapore
    Suite 1703, United Square, 101 Thomson Rd, Singapore 1130 (☎ 255 4555)
UK
    Gemini House, 10-18 Putney Hill, London SW15 6AAA (☎ (0181) 780 2229)
USA
    Suite 1920, 204 Century Park East, Los Angeles, CA 90067 (☎ (310) 229 4870)

Canadians should contact the Los Angeles office, and visitors from Ireland, France or the Netherlands, should contact the London office.

VISAS & DOCUMENTS

Except New Zealand nationals, who receive a 'special category' visa on arrival, all visitors to Australia need a visa.

Visa application forms are available from travel agents or Australian diplomatic missions overseas, and you can apply by mail or in person. There are different types of visas, depending on the reason for your visit.

Tourist Visas

Tourist visas are issued by Australian consular offices; they are generally valid for a stay of either three or six months within 12 months of the date of issue. The three-month visa is free and the six-month visa has a $35 processing fee.

When you apply for a visa, you need to present your passport and a passport photo, as well as sign an undertaking that you have an onward or return ticket and 'sufficient funds' – the latter is obviously open to interpretation.

Working Visas

Young, single visitors from Canada, Japan, the Netherlands and the UK may be eligible for a 'working holiday' visa. 'Young' is fairly loosely interpreted as around 18 to 25, although exceptions may be made – people up to 30, and young married couples without children, may be eligible.

A working holiday visa allows a stay of up to 12 months, but the emphasis is supposed to be on casual employment rather than a full-time job, so you are only supposed to work for three months. This visa can only be applied for outside Australia (preferably in your country of citizenship), and you can't change from a tourist visa to a working holiday visa.

Conditions attached to a working holiday visa include having sufficient funds for a ticket out, and taking out private medical insurance; a fee of around $140 is payable when you apply for the visa.

See the section on Work, later in this chapter, for details of what sort of work is available and where.

Visa Extensions

The maximum stay allowed to visitors in Australia, including extensions, is one year.

Visa extensions are made through Department of Immigration & Ethnic Affairs offices in Australia and, as the process takes some time, it's best to apply about a month before your visa expires. There is an application fee of $135 and if they turn down your application they keep your money! To qualify for an extension you are required to have medical insurance to cover the period of the extension, and a ticket out of the country.

If you're trying to stay for longer in Australia, the books *Temporary to Permanent Resident in Australia* and *Practical Guide to Obtaining Permanent Residence in Australia*, both published by Legal Books, may be useful.

Driving Licences

While overseas licences are acceptable for genuine overseas visitors, an International Driving Permit in conjunction with your overseas licence might be more hassle-free.

Travel Permits

If you intend to travel through the outback on your own, see the Getting Around chapter for the permits you may need to enter Aboriginal land or camp in national parks.

EMBASSIES
Australian Embassies Overseas

Australian embassies and consular offices overseas include:

Canada
Suite 710, 50 O'Connor St, Ottawa K1P 6L2 (☎ (613) 236 0841; fax 236 376)
– also in Toronto and Vancouver
China
21 Dongzhimenwai Dajie, San Li Tun, Beijing 100600 (☎ (10) 532 2331; fax 532 6959)
– also in Guangzhou and Shanghai
Denmark
Kristianagade 21, DK 2100 Copenhagen (☎ 3526 2244; fax 3543 2218)
France
4 Rue Jean Rey, 75724 Paris Cedex 15 Paris (☎ 01 40 59 33 00; fax 01 40 59 33 10)
Germany
Godesberger Allee 107, 53175 Bonn 1 (☎ (0228) 81 030; fax 810 3130)
– also in Frankfurt and Berlin
Greece
37 Dimitriou Soutsou St, Ambelokpi, Athens 11512 (☎ (01) 644 7303; fax 646 6595)
Hong Kong
23/F Harbour Centre, 25 Harbour Rd, Wanchai, Hong Kong Island (☎ 2827 8881; fax 2827 6583)

India
Australian Compound, No 1/50-G Shantipath, Chanakyapuri, New Delhi 110021 (☎ (11) 688 8223; fax 688 5199)
– also in Bombay
Indonesia
Jalan HR Rasuna Said Kav C 15-16, Jakarta Selatan 12940 (☎ (021) 522 7111; fax 522 7101)
– also in Denpasar
Ireland
Fitzwilton House, Wilton Terrace, Dublin 2 (☎ (01) 676 1517; fax 678 5185)
Italy
Via Alessandria 215, Rome 00198 (☎ (06) 85 27 21; fax 8527 2300)
– also in Milan
Japan
2-1-14 Mita, Minato-ku, Tokyo 108 (☎ (03) 5232 4111; fax 5232 4149)
– also in Kyushu, Nagoya, Osaka Sapporo and Sendai.
Malaysia
6 Jalan Yap Kwan Seng, Kuala Lumpur 50450 (☎ (03) 242 3122; fax 241 5773)
Netherlands
Carnegielaan 4, 2517 KH The Hague (☎ (070) 310 8200; fax 310 7863)
New Zealand
72-78 Hobson St, Thorndon, Wellington (☎ (04) 473 6411, 498 7118)
– also in Auckland
Papua New Guinea
Independence Drive, Waigani NCD, Port Moresby (☎ 325 9333; fax 325 6647)
Philippines
Dona Salustiana Ty Tower, 104 Paseo de Roxas, Makati, Metro Manila (☎ (02) 817 7911; fax 817 3603)
Singapore
25 Napier Rd, Singapore 1025 (☎ 737 9311; 733 7134)
South Africa
292 Orient St, Arcadia, Pretoria 0083 (☎ (012) 342 3740; fax 342 4222)
– also in Cape Town
Sweden
Sergels Torg 12, Stockholm (☎ (08) 613 2900; fax 24 7414)
Switzerland
29 Alpenstrasse, CH-3006 Berne (☎ (031) 351 0143; fax 352 1234)
– also in Geneva
Thailand
37 South Sathorn Rd, Bangkok 10120 (☎ (02) 287 2680; fax 287 2029)
UK
Australia House, The Strand, London WC2B 4LA (☎ (0171) 379 4334; fax 465 8210)
– also in Edinburgh and Manchester

USA
>1601 Massachusetts Ave NW, Washington DC, 20036 (☎ (202) 797 3000; 797 3168)
>– also in Atlanta, Boston, Chicago, Denver, Honolulu, Houston, Los Angeles, New York and San Francisco

Foriegn Embassies in Australia

The principal diplomatic representations to Australia are in Canberra. There are also representatives in various other major cities, particularly from countries with major connections with Australia like the USA, UK or New Zealand; or in cities with important connections, like Darwin which has an Indonesian consulate. Big cities like Sydney and Melbourne have nearly as many consular offices as Canberra has embassies, although visa applications are generally handled in Canberra. Look up addresses in the Yellow Pages phone book under 'Consulates & Legations'.

Embassies and high commissions in Canberra (telephone code 02) include:

Canada
>Commonwealth Ave, Yarralumla (☎ 6273 3844)

Germany
>119 Empire Court, Yarralumla (☎ 6270 1911)

India
>3 Moonah Place, Yarralumla (☎ 6273 3999)

Indonesia
>8 Darwin Ave, Yarralumla (☎ 6250 8600)

Japan
>112 Empire Circuit, Yarralumla (☎ 6273 3244)

Malaysia
>7 Perth Ave, Yarralumla (☎ 6273 1543)

Netherlands
>120 Empire Circuit, Yarralumla (☎ 6273 3111)

New Zealand
>Commonwealth Ave, Yarralumla (☎ 6270 4211)

Norway
>17 Hunter St, Yarralumla (☎ 6273 3444)

Papua New Guinea
>39 Forster Crescent, Yarralumla (☎ 6273 3322)

South Africa
>Cnr State Circle and Rhodes Place, Yarralumla (☎ 6273 2424)

Thailand
>111 Empire Circuit, Yarralumla (☎ 6273 1149)

UK
>Commonwealth Ave, Yarralumla (☎ 6270 6666)

USA
>21 Moonah Place, Yarralumla (☎ 6270 5000)

CUSTOMS

When entering Australia you can bring most articles in free of duty provided that Customs is satisfied they are for personal use and that you'll be taking them with you when you leave. There is also a duty-free allowance for each person of one litre of alcohol, 250 cigarettes and dutiable goods up to the value of A$400.

With regard to prohibited goods, there are two areas that need particular attention. Number one is, of course, dope – Australian Customs have a positive mania about the stuff and can be extremely efficient when it comes to finding it. Unless you want to make first-hand investigations of conditions in Australian gaols (not very good), don't bring any with you.

Problem two is animal and plant quarantine. You will be asked to declare all goods of animal or vegetable origin – wooden spoons, straw hats, the lot – and show them to an official. The authorities are naturally keen to prevent weeds, pests or diseases getting into the country – Australia has so far managed to escape many of the agricultural pests and diseases prevalent in other parts of the world. Fresh food is also unpopular, particularly meat, sausages, fruit, vegetables, flowers and flower bulbs (there are even restrictions on taking fruit and vegetables between states within Australia).

Weapons and firearms are either prohibited or require a permit and safety testing. Other restricted goods include products made from protected wildlife species (such as ivory), non-approved telecommunications devices and live animals.

There are duty-free stores at the international airports and their associated cities. Treat them with healthy suspicion. 'Duty-free' is one of the world's most overworked catch phrases, and it is often just an excuse to sell things at prices you can easily beat by a little shopping around.

MONEY
Currency

Australia's currency is the Australian dollar, which consists of 100 cents. There are coins for 5c, 10c, 20c, 50c, $1 and $2, and plastic notes for $5, $10, $20, $50 and $100.

There are no notable restrictions on importing or exporting currency or travellers cheques except that you may not take out more than A$5000 in cash without prior approval.

Exchange Rates

In recent years the Australian dollar has fluctuated quite markedly against the US dollar, but it now seems to hover between 70c and 80c – a disaster for Australians travelling overseas but a real bonus for inbound visitors.

Canada	C$1	=	A$0.99
France	FF1	=	A$0.23
Germany	DM1	=	A$0.77
Hong Kong	HK$10	=	A$1.18
Japan	¥100	=	A$1.16
New Zealand	NZ$1	=	A$0.88
UK	UK£1	=	A$2.20
USA	US$1	=	A$1.39

Changing Money

Changing foreign currency or travellers cheques is no problem at most city banks and licensed money changers.

However, banks in small outback towns aren't always geared up for complicated transactions and it can be a long way between banks. Before heading bush make sure you have sufficient Australian funds, preferably a mixture of travellers cheques, credit cards and cash. Add a Commonwealth Bank passbook (see below) and you'll have money at your disposal almost anywhere.

Travellers Cheques

As long as you remember that there aren't many banks in the outback, travellers cheques are the most straightforward option if your stay is limited, and they generally enjoy a better exchange rate than foreign cash. American Express, Thomas Cook and other well-known international brands are all widely used.

A passport will usually be adequate for identification, although it would be sensible for identification, although it would be sensible to carry a driver's licence, credit cards or other acceptable form of identification in case of problems.

Commissions and fees for changing foreign currency travellers cheques vary from bank to bank and year to year. It's worth making a few phone calls to see which bank currently has the lowest charges, as they can add up.

Buying travellers cheques in Australian dollars is a good option; they can be exchanged immediately at the bank cashier's window without being converted from a foreign currency or without incurring fees, commissions and exchange-rate fluctuations. As well, unlike travellers cheques made out in foreign currencies, they are generally accepted without question by outback businesses.

Credit Cards

While credit cards are widely accepted in the outback, they're by no means accepted everywhere – this particularly applies to remote small businesses, which may insist on travellers cheques and/or cash. The most common credit card is the Australian Bankcard system, but American Express, Diners Club, MasterCard and Visa are also common.

Cash advances from credit cards are available over the bank counter and from many automatic teller machines (ATMs), depending on the card. If you're planning to rent cars while travelling around Australia, a credit card is looked upon with much greater favour by rent-a-car agencies than nasty old cash; many agencies simply won't rent you a vehicle if you don't have a card.

Local Bank Accounts

If you're spending a few months in Australia, it's worth considering other ways of handling money that give you more flexibility and are more economical. This applies equally to Australians setting off to travel around the country.

Most travellers these days opt for an account which includes a cash card. This can be used to access your cash day or night from

ATMs found all over Australia (though not so widely in the outback yet). Westpac, ANZ, National and Commonwealth bank branches are found nationwide, and it is possible to use the machines of some other banks: Westpac ATMs accept Commonwealth Bank cards and vice versa; National Bank ATMs accept ANZ cards and vice versa. A card takes about a week to issue and you'll need an Australian address.

Even in the outback many businesses are linked into the EFTPOS system (Electronic Funds Transfer at Point Of Sale). At places with this facility you can use your bank cash card to pay for services or purchases direct, and sometimes withdraw a limited amount of cash as well. Bank cash cards and credit cards can also be used to make local, STD and international phone calls in special public telephones found in many towns.

Opening an Account Opening an account at an Australian bank is not all that easy these days. A points system operates and you need to score a minimum of 100 points before you can have the privilege of letting the bank take your money. Passports and birth certificates (with a certified translation if they're not in English) earn 70 points and driver's licences 40 points; minor IDs such as Medicare cards and credit cards earn 20 points. Just like a game show really! Foreigners need only present their passport to open a bank account within six weeks of arriving in Australia. After that, the same rules apply.

If you don't have an Australian Tax File Number, 48% of interest earned from your funds will be collected by our old mate, the Deputy Commissioner of Taxation.

Passbook Account The easiest way of obtaining cash in the outback is with a Commonwealth Bank passbook. This is one of those old-fashioned booklets that you may have had when you were a kid, where your transactions are typed in. All post offices or post-office agencies are agencies for the Commonwealth Bank. While not all post-office agencies have the electronic facilities

to handle cash cards, every one of them will handle a passbook, which makes this option particularly useful.

A passbook account can be opened on the spot at any Commonwealth Bank branch. Make sure you get a passbook with a black-light signature or you may not be able to use it everywhere. You usually have to return to the same branch to close the account when the time comes to leave Australia, but many people don't worry about reclaiming that last dollar.

Costs
Compared with the USA, Canada and European countries, Australia is cheaper in some ways and more expensive in others. Manufactured goods tend to be more expensive if they're imported, and if they're locally manufactured they suffer from the extra costs entailed in making things in comparatively small quantities. Thus you pay more for clothes, cars and other manufactured items. On the other hand, food is generally cheaper, and accommodation is also very reasonably priced.

The biggest cost in any trip to Australia is transport, simply because it's such a vast country. If there's a group of you, buying a second-hand car is probably the most economical way to go. Fuel is cheap, though more expensive than in the USA and you'll need lots of it.

Freight charges increase the cost of everything in the outback, adding 20% to 30% to city prices even in a major centre like Alice Springs. Fuel is also more expensive, not just because of freight but because most roadhouses and the like have to produce their own electricity using diesel generators.

Another problem is the difficulty of attracting reliable labour; relatively few people who aren't intent on escaping something (whether it be the law, their spouse or personal problems) are interested in leaving the comforts of town life to work in the bush. Tourists who complain at the high prices charged by remote roadhouses seldom have any appreciation of what it costs to provide the service.

Tipping & Bargaining

Tipping isn't entrenched in Australia the way it is in the USA or Europe. It's only customary to tip in more expensive restaurants and only then if you want to. If the service has been especially good and you decide to leave a tip, 10% of the bill is the usual amount. Taxi drivers don't expect tips (of course, they don't hurl it back at you if you decide to leave the change).

Bargaining is not common, and most times you'll have to pay the indicated price. On the other hand, although not in the big chain stores, it's common practice to ask for a discount on expensive items – not that you're guaranteed to get one. You can try bargaining in markets and second-hand shops.

POST & COMMUNICATIONS

Post

Australia's postal services are reasonably efficient. It costs 45c to send a standard letter or postcard anywhere within Australia, while aerogrammes cost 70c. Airmail letters/postcards cost 75/70c to New Zealand, 85/80c to Singapore and Malaysia, 95/90c to Hong Kong and India, $1.05/95c to the USA and Canada, and $1.20/1 to Europe and the UK.

Post offices are open from 9 am to 5 pm Monday to Friday, but you can often get stamps on Saturday mornings from post-office agencies that operate from local newsagencies or general stores, or from the Australia Post shops found in large cities.

Receiving Mail All post offices will hold mail for visitors. You can also have mail sent to you at American Express offices if you have an Amex card or carry Amex travellers cheques. Although Australia Post's delivery speed compares favourably with that in many other countries, you may have to add one or two weeks for mail to/from isolated outback towns – always specify air mail.

Mail Runs One of the great outback traditions is the weekly mail run. For many isolated people, their visit from the mailman (or woman) may be the only regular contact

with other people for weeks or even months on end. Even with the rapid advances in communication technology, the mailman is still an important link in the spread of information – not to mention gossip – in the outback.

During the northern wet season, when roads are often cut for weeks and long-distance travel by vehicle is not possible, the weekly mail plane becomes the only traffic in and out of many communities.

Other mail runs are done by truck, usually along hundreds of kilometres of often dusty and bumpy roads. The arrival of the mail truck is a keenly awaited event, for not only does it bring the mail, but also much needed station supplies – everything from groceries to vehicle spare parts to a new refrigerator come with the mail.

Joining a mail run is a great way to experience the outback. See the Getting Around chapter for details.

Telephone

Australia's telephone system is efficient and easy to use. Thanks to advances in satellite communication technology, even the outback is well serviced by telephones.

Local Calls Local phone calls cost 40c for an unlimited amount of time. You can make local calls from gold or blue phones (often found in shops, hotels, bars etc) and from payphone booths. Calls from private phones cost 30c.

STD Calls Long-distance (STD – Subscriber Trunk Dialling) calls can be made from virtually any public phone. Many public phones accept Telstra phonecards, which are very convenient. The cards come in $5, $10, $20 and $50 denominations, and are available from retail outlets such as newsagents and pharmacies which display the Phonecard logo. You keep using the card until the value has been used in calls. Otherwise, make sure you have plenty of 20c, 50c and $1 coins, and be prepared to feed them through at a fair old rate. STD calls are cheaper in off-peak hours – see the front of a local telephone book for details.

Some public phones are set up to take only bank cash cards or credit cards – you need to keep an eye on how much the call is costing as it can quickly mount up. The minimum charge for a call on one of these phones is $1.20.

International Calls From most STD phones you can also make ISD (International Subscriber Dialling) calls. All you do is dial 0011 to get out of Australia, then the country code (44 for Britain, 1 for the USA or Canada, 64 for New Zealand etc), the city code (171 or 181 for London, 212 for New York etc), and finally the subscriber number. Have a phonecard, credit card or plenty of coins to hand.

Overseas calls from Australia are cheap by international standards. Off-peak times, if available, vary depending on the destination – see the back of any White Pages telephone book for countries where off-peak times are available and dial ☎ 0102 for details. Sunday is usually the cheapest time to ring.

Country Direct is a service that gives travellers in Australia direct access to operators in around 50 other countries. You can talk to an operator in your home country in your own language and make collect (reverse-charge) calls, have calls charged to your phone-company credit card or perform other credit feats. Call Telstra (☎ toll-free 1800 801 800) for a full list of the countries hooked into this system.

Countries listed include: Canada (☎ 1800 881 150), Germany (☎ 1800 881 490), Japan (☎ 1800 881 810), New Zealand (☎ 1800 881 640) and the UK (☎ 1800 881 440 for BT and 1800 881 417 for Mercury). To the USA, you can go through AT&T (☎ 1800 881 011), BellAT (☎ 1800 881 152), IDB WorldCom (☎ 1800 881 212), MCI (☎ 1800 881 100) or Sprint (☎ 1800 881 877).

Toll-Free Calls Many businesses and some government departments operate a toll-free service, which means it's a free call no matter where you are ringing from around the country. These numbers have the prefix 1800. Many companies, such as the airlines,

have six-digit numbers beginning with 13, and these are charged at the rate of a local call. Often they'll be Australia-wide numbers but sometimes are applicable only to a specific STD district; unfortunately there's no way of telling without actually ringing the number.

Mobile Phones Numbers with the prefix 014, 015, 016, 018, 041 and 0418 are mobile or car phones. Calls to and from mobile numbers are charged at special STD rates and can be expensive.

Information Calls You may come across numbers starting with 0055 and 190. The 0055 numbers, usually recorded information services and the like, are provided by private companies, and your call is charged in multiples of 25c (40c from public phones) at a rate selected by the provider (Premium 70c per minute, Value 55c per minute, Budget 35c per minute).

Numbers beginning with 190 are also information services, but these are charged on a fixed fee basis varying between 35c and $30.

Radio Communications

Radio communications play an important role in the outback. Most travellers manage perfectly well without a radio, but in the more remote areas it is an important safety feature. When travelling in convoy, the ability to communicate with each other on the move can make the trip more enjoyable too.

CB Radio CB radio comes in two forms, working in two frequency bands. The cheaper of the two is AM in the 27MHz frequency range, while the dearer is UHF in the 477MHz band. Both bands have 40 channels to choose from; channel 9 is reserved for emergency contact on the 27MHz band, and channel 5 on the UHF sets.

The cheapest sets on the market are the pure AM sets (from under $100), but these are limited in what they can do. The better 27MHz set is an AM/SSB (single sideband) unit ($250 to $300), and while both units can talk to one another and are good for inter-vehicle communication, the SSB facility gives a longer range. This function may be unreliable and completely unpredictable, but is of some use as a safety feature.

The UHF sets can be expensive ($500 to $800), and while they give good and clear inter vehicle communication, they are only a line-of-sight device. In the more settled areas of Australia their range has been improved by the use of repeater towers, but you need to know the required channels in the respective areas.

For anybody travelling with another vehicle, a CB radio is a great boon. You can yarn to one another, warn the second vehicle of the need to close a gate, of a large dip in the road, or whatever. CBs don't need to be licensed, and there are no restrictions on normal day-to-day operations.

Call signs use the radio alphabet, ie call sign 7VAB would be spoken as 'Seven Victor Alpha Bravo'.

HF Outpost Radio For those travelling the remote areas of Australia, a HF (high-frequency) radio is the way to go. 'Outpost' refers to any building or vehicle that doesn't have direct contact with the normal telephone service. People without radio qualifications can get units that are set up for the Royal Flying Doctor Service (RFDS) or the government controlled Telstra (OTC) frequencies, or several other professional safety organisations. For emergency situations the RFDS HF set is your best option.

These radios are expensive: a reliable second-hand unit can cost at least $1000, while a new unit is up to $3500. However, they can be hired from the RFDS or from radio outlets in the capital cities and major outback centres for about $50 a week. Whether you buy one or hire one, you'll need a Mobile Outpost Station Licence issued by the Spectrum Management Agency – it has offices in each state capital as well as some major regional centres.

HF sets are mainly meant for long-distance communication up to 3000km. You can

talk from one mobile unit to another or to an RFDS or Telstra base.

The RFDS system provides emergency medical aid right throughout the outback and is on call, for an emergency, 24 hours a day, 365 days a year. Its bases also provide a radio-telephone (radphone) service where, for a small charge, you can call the base and have a call put through to the telephone service. This service operates during business hours, five days a week.

Telstra operates from its six bases around the Australian coastline. It provides a number of communication services including a radphone service. This is available 24 hours a day, 365 days a year.

Each Telstra and RFDS base operates a number of channels and these are detailed in the individual track descriptions later in this book. With the RFDS, each individual base you intend to communicate with must be contacted beforehand, an account raised, and then you can use that station for radphone calls. With Telstra you only need to register with one base, once, and you are away. For more information, call ☎ 1800 81 0023.

If you are planning to travel along a particular track, it's a good idea to contact the relevant RFDS or Telstra base beforehand to ask whether there's anything you need to know (channel changes, road closures etc). The RFDS in particular is usually very up to date with its road information.

Calling a Station Before using the radio, spend a while listening to traffic so you become familiar with what's normal for each channel. Though you need to use call signs and the like, the base operators aren't going to get upset if you make mistakes. Select the RFDS or Telstra station closest to you, choose the 'primary' or 'on call' channel, tune the antenna to that channel and listen before making your call. If the channel is busy, wait until the channel is clear or select another.

When it is free, make a call such as, if to the Telstra base in Sydney, 'Sydney Radio this is Seven Victor Alpha Bravo calling. How do you read? Over.' If calling an RFDS base, such as Broken Hill, include its call sign by saying something like 'VJC Broken Hill this is Seven Victor Alpha Bravo calling. How do you read? Over.' Once you have established contact, ask for whatever you require.

Tonecall facilities (basically a distress signal) should be available on any HF set worth its salt. Selcall (a more complex version of Tonecall, which allows the base to call *you*) is available on the better sets and this does make it easier to call the required station.

If you don't succeed first time, try again. If you have no luck on one channel, try another. The time of day and other cyclic factors (seasons, sunspot cycles etc) affect radio communication. Remember the rule of thumb: the higher the sun, the higher the channel number (or frequency). Longer distances also mean higher frequencies so you may have to try a few. You'll soon get the hang of it.

The Future HF radio will be a part of the communication scene for a long time to come, and will get better as new options and service providers come on stream. Contact Spectrum Management Agency for an update on service providers in your area of interest.

Cellular (mobile) phone services cover 85% of Australia's population but only 4% of its landmass, which makes them pretty useless in the outback. However, you can use mobile phones in many of the more important centres such as Alice Springs, Mt Isa and Port Hedland – Telstra can provide details.

In 1997 Telstra launched a personal mobile satellite telephone (MiniSat), which offers voice, facsimile and data functions and can be used anywhere beyond the reach of cellular and fixed communications. About the size of a lap-top computer, it retails for around $5450 and calls cost from $2 per minute.

BOOKS

In almost every specialist bookshop in the country you'll find a section devoted to Aus-

traliana. The outback features prominently, especially among the coffee-table books: Penny van Oosterzee's *The Centre – The Natural History of Australia's Desert Regions* is one of the more affordable and informative; the two-volume *Australia's Wilderness Heritage*, published by Angus & Robertson, is quite affordable in its paperback version and is filled with stunning photographs. At the Wilderness Society shops in each capital city and the Government Printing Offices in Sydney and Melbourne you'll find a good range of wildlife posters, calendars and books.

Aborigines

The Australian Aborigines, by Kenneth Maddock, is a good cultural summary. The award-winning *Triumph of the Nomads*, by Geoffrey Blainey, chronicles the life of Australia's original inhabitants, and convincingly demolishes the myth that the Aborigines were 'primitive' people trapped on a hostile continent – the book is an excellent read.

For a sympathetic historical account of what happened to the original Australians since whites arrived, read *Aboriginal Australians* by Richard Broome. *A Change of Ownership*, by Mildred Kirk, covers similar ground to Broome's book, but does so more concisely, focusing on the land rights movement and its historical background.

The Other Side of the Frontier, by Henry Reynolds, uses historical records to give a vivid account of an Aboriginal view of the arrival and takeover of Australia by Europeans. His *With the White People* identifies the essential Aboriginal contributions to the survival of the early white settlers. *My Place*, Sally Morgan's prize-winning autobiography, traces her discovery of her Aboriginal heritage. *The Fringe Dwellers*, by Nene Gare, describes just what it's like to be an Aborigine growing up in a white-dominated society.

Don't Take Your Love to Town, by Ruby Langford, and *My People*, by Oodgeroo Noonuccal (Kath Walker), are also recommended reading.

History

For a good introduction to Australian history, read *A Short History of Australia*, a most accessible and informative general history by the late Manning Clark, the much-loved Aussie historian, or *The Fatal Shore*, Robert Hughes' best-seller account of the convict era.

Geoffrey Blainey's *The Tyranny of Distance* is an engrossing study of the problems of transport in this harsh continent and how they shaped the pattern of white settlement: transporting produce 160km by bullock cart from an inland farm to a port cost more than shipping it from there around the globe to Europe – a handicap that only wool and later gold were profitable enough to overcome.

Finding Australia, by Russel Ward, traces the story of the early days from the first Aboriginal arrivals up to 1821. It's strong on Aborigines, women and the full story of foreign exploration, not just Captain Cook's role. There's lots of fascinating detail, including information about the appalling crooks who ran the early colony for long periods, and it's intended to be the first of a series.

The Exploration of Australia, by Michael Cannon, is coffee-table book in size, presentation and price, but it's a fascinating reference book about the gradual European uncovering of the continent.

Cooper's Creek, by Alan Moorehead, is a classic account of the ill fated Burke and Wills expedition which dramatises the horrors and hardships faced by the early explorers.

The Fatal Impact, also by Moorehead, begins with the voyages of Captain James Cook, regarded as one of the greatest and most humane explorers, and tells the tragic story of the European impact on Australia, Tahiti and Antarctica in the years that followed Cook's great voyages. It details how good intentions and the economic imperatives of the time led to disaster, corruption and annihilation.

To get an idea of life on a Kimberley cattle station last century, *Kings in Grass Castles* and *Sons in the Saddle*, both by Dame Mary Durack, are well worth getting hold of. Other books which give an insight into the pioneering days in the outback include *Packhorse & Waterhole* by Gordon Buchanan, son of legendary drover Nat Buchanan who was responsible for opening up large areas of the Northern Territory; *The Big Run*, a history of the huge Victoria River Downs cattle station in the Northern Territory; and *The Cattle King* by Ion Idriess, which details the life of the remarkable Sir Sidney Kidman, the man who set up a chain of stations in the outback early this century.

There are a number of books on the outback's natural history, one of the best being *The Centre – the Natural History of Australia's Desert Regions* (Reed), by Penny van Oosterzee and Reg Morrison. This excellent reference has a wealth of information on the arid zone, including its geological history, landscapes and ecosystems.

Fiction

There's no shortage of excellent Australian fiction with an outback theme. See the Literature section under Arts in the Facts about the Outback chapter.

Travel Accounts

Accounts of travels in Australia include *Tracks* by Robyn Davidson. It's the amazing story of a young woman who set out alone to walk from Alice Springs to the Western Australia coast with only her camels for company – proof that you can do anything if you try hard enough.

Quite another sort of travel is Tony Horwitz's *One for the Road*, an often hilarious account of a high-speed hitchhiking trip around Australia (Oz through a windscreen). Another humorous, off-beat road book is *Sean & David's Long Drive*, by young Australian author Sean Condon and published by Lonely Planet as part of its new 'Journeys' travel literature series.

Travel is also possible while standing still, as described in *Our Year in the Outback* by Michael & Susan Cusack, published by Australian Geographic. It chronicles their experiment of living in complete isolation on the Kimberley coast, and contains some fascinating insights into human relationships in adversity, illustrated with stunning photographs. Unfortunately it's out of print, but most libraries will have it.

The late Bruce Chatwin's *The Songlines* tells of his experiences among central Australian Aborigines. It's an interesting book, with its pithy anecdotes about modern Australia probably its best feature.

The journals of the early European explorers can be fairly hard going but make fascinating reading. The hardships that many of these men (and they were virtually all men) endured is nothing short of amazing. These accounts are usually available in the main libraries. Men such as Sturt, Eyre, Leichhardt, Davidson, King (on the Burke and Wills expedition), Stuart and Jardine kept detailed journals.

Travel Guides

Burnum Burnum's Aboriginal Australia is subtitled 'a traveller's guide'. If you want to explore Australia from the Aboriginal point of view, this large and lavish hardback is the book for you.

The track descriptions in this book mention literature relevant to the particular tracks. For more general reading, the late Brian Sheedy's *Outback Australia on a Budget* includes lots of practical advice and anecdotes. By the same author, *Outback on your Doorstep* describes the more accessible outback tracks within one or two days' drive from Sydney, Melbourne and Adelaide. Malcolm Gordon's *Outback Australia at Cost* focuses on the Centre, Top End and Kimberley; it's full of practical information but is a bit unwieldy.

Peter & Kim Wherrett's large-format hardback, *Explore Australia by Four-Wheel Drive*, is beautifully laid-out with a wealth of illustrations and maps (including a detailed road atlas of Australia), and offers solid advice on planning and vehicle preparation. However, this book does omit quite a few of the tracks, and the information on the tracks it does cover is sketchy and at times inaccurate. There are several other books on

this topic including Ron & Viv Moon's *Discover Australia by 4WD* and Viking's *Explore Australia by Four-Wheel Drive*, and both of them include a number of outback tracks.

Safe Outback Travel, by Jack Absalom, is a practical little book with basic advice on vehicle preparation and troubleshooting, general rules of outback travel, and the most important survival skills.

There are a number of other books about vehicle preparation and driving in the outback, as well as survival skills and general bushcraft. In the latter category, *Stay Alive*, by Maurice Dunlevy, gives practical advice on survival techniques and first aid. *The Outdoor Companion* by Q & J Chester, Paddy Pallin's *Bushwalking & Camping* and Lex Lannoy's *The Australian Bushcraft Handbook* (endorsed by the Scout Association) are all good but mainly aimed at bushwalkers and cross-country skiers. The Western Australian police force produces an excellent book titled *Aids to Survival*, which covers map reading, first aid and survival techniques.

Lonely Planet's *Bushwalking in Australia* describes 23 walks of different lengths and difficulty in various parts of the country, though only a few of them are in outback areas. LP also has guidebooks to the various states and territories, and the *Australian phrasebook* with detail on Aboriginal languages.

Jeff & Mare Carter's *The Complete Guide to Central Australia* has some beautiful photographs and provides lots of knowledgeable background on flora & fauna. There are also state-by-state Reader's Digest guides to coasts and national parks, and Gregory's guides to national parks.

Australian Geographic has several excellent publications dealing with life and travel in the outback. They include *The Red Centre*, *Cape York* and *The Canning Stock Route*.

NEWSPAPERS & MAGAZINES

Once upon a time, virtually every Australian town of any significance had its own newspaper; many outback centres still do, and these are a must if you want to know what's happening locally.

Respected big-city newspapers such as the *Sydney Morning Herald* and the Melbourne *Age* become harder to get the further you move into the outback. However, any reasonable newsagent will have that day's (or at least yesterday's) edition of the *Australian* (the country's only national daily) and the major big-city newspaper for that particular state. Rural newspapers such as *The Land*, *Stock Journal* and *The Weekly Times* are widely available. They often have information relevant to the outback, such as employment and vehicle sales.

Weekly newspapers and magazines include an Australian edition of *Time* and a combined edition of the Australian news magazine the *Bulletin* with *Newsweek*. The *Economist* and *Guardian Weekly* are sometimes available and are excellent for international news. Most of the outback newsagencies stock a wide variety of special-interest magazines.

RADIO & TV

The national advertising-free TV and radio network is the ABC. In most state capitals there are a couple of ABC radio stations and a host of commercial stations, both AM and FM, featuring the whole gamut of radio possibilities, from rock and talkback to 'beautiful music'. There's also a wide variety of community radio stations that rely on volunteers and listener subscriptions.

In Sydney and Melbourne there are the ABC, three commercial TV stations and SBS, a government-sponsored multicultural TV station that beams to the state capitals and a small number of regional centres. Around the country the number of TV stations varies from place to place; there are regional TV stations but in some remote areas the ABC may be all you can receive.

Imparja is an Aboriginal-run TV station that operates out of Alice Springs and has a 'footprint' that covers one-third of the country. It broadcasts a variety of programmes, ranging from soaps to pieces made by and for Aborigines.

PHOTOGRAPHY & VIDEO

Australian film prices are not too far out of line with those of the rest of the western world. Including developing, 36-exposure Kodachrome 64 or Fujichrome 100 slide film costs from around $25, but with a little shopping around you can find it for around $20 – even less if you buy in quantity. Remember that slide film probably won't be available in small outback towns, so make sure to carry plenty of film with you.

Most major outback towns have at least one specialty camera shop, and maybe even a camera repairer. They'll also generally have places offering one-hour developing of print film.

When taking photographs in the outback, allow for the exceptional intensity of the light. Best results are obtained early in the morning and late in the afternoon, when colours are 'warmer' and shadows softer. As the sun gets higher, colours appear more washed out, which you can compensate for to some extent with a polarising filter. You must also allow for the intensity of reflected light.

Do your best to keep film cool, particularly after exposure – don't store it in the car's glove compartment. Other film and camera hazards are dust and, in the tropical regions of the far north, humidity.

As in any country, politeness goes a long way when taking photographs – ask before taking pictures of people. Some traditional Aborigines may not like to have their photographs taken at all, even from a distance.

TIME

Australia is divided into three time zones: Western Standard Time (Western Australia) is plus eight hours from GMT/UTC, Central Standard Time (Northern Territory, South Australia and the Broken Hill area in New South Wales) is plus 9½ hours, and Eastern Standard Time (Tasmania, Victoria, New South Wales, Queensland) is plus 10. When it's noon in Western Australia it's 1.30 pm in the Northern Territory and South Australia, and 2 pm in the rest of the country. During the summer, things get slightly screwed up as daylight-saving time (when clocks are put forward an hour) does not operate in Western Australia, the Northern Territory or Queensland, and in Tasmania it lasts a month longer than in the other states.

ELECTRICITY

Australia runs on 240V, 50Hz AC. The plugs are three-pin, but not the same as British three-pin plugs. Sockets often come with their own power switch, so if your appliance doesn't work, try turning on the power at the socket. Buy your adapter before coming to Australia; the ones available locally are intended for Australians going overseas and won't be of any use to you. You can bend US plugs to a slight angle to make them fit, but beware of the difference in voltage.

WEIGHTS & MEASURES

Australia uses the metric system. Petrol and milk are sold by the litre, apples and potatoes by the kilogram, distance is measured by the metre or kilometre, and speed limits are in kilometres per hour (km/h). Many outback people still think in miles and (imperial) gallons and pints. Australia-wide, fuel consumption is still often referred to in miles per gallon (29mpg is roughly 10km per litre), and almost everybody still quotes tyre pressures in pounds per square inch (28psi is roughly 2kg per sq cm).

For those who need help with metric, there's a conversion table at the back of this book.

LAUNDRY

Most major outback centres have at least one dry cleaning business and 7-day laundromat, and you'll usually find coin-operated washing machines and driers at the better caravan parks. Otherwise there'll generally be at least a wash trough and cold-water tap, although remote parks and reserves may have no facilities whatsoever. If you're camping away from it all, carry a 10L bucket to wash your clothes in.

An alternative washing machine when you're travelling is a heavy-duty, sealable 20L plastic container, filled with water,

soiled clothing and detergent, and either carried in the boot of the car or on the roof rack. The agitation as you drive along gets your clothes remarkably clean, particularly on corrugated roads.

HEALTH

Australia is a remarkably healthy country considering that such a large portion of it lies in the tropics. Tropical diseases such as malaria and yellow fever are unknown, diseases of insanitation such as cholera and typhoid are unheard of, and even some animal diseases such as rabies and foot-and-mouth disease have yet to be recorded. However, there are some venomous creatures that you need to beware of – see the Fauna section in the Facts about the Outback chapter.

So long as you haven't visited an infected country in the past 14 days (aircraft refuelling stops do not count) no vaccinations are required for entry. There are, however, a few routine vaccinations that are recommended worldwide whether you're travelling or not, and for the outback you might want to check whether your tetanus booster is still up to date.

Medical care is first-class and only moderately expensive; a typical visit to the doctor costs from around $30 without a Medicare card. If you have an immediate health problem, contact the casualty section at the nearest public hospital or outback medical clinic. For those equipped with a HF radio able to reach the nearest Flying Doctor base, expert medical advice is available 24 hours a day via the radio's emergency call button.

Travel Insurance

Ambulance services in Australia are self-funding (ie they're not free) and can be frightfully expensive in the outback, so you'd be wise to take out travel insurance. Make sure the policy specifically includes ambulance, helicopter rescue and a flight home for you and anyone you're travelling with, should your condition warrant it. Also check the fine print: some policies exclude 'dangerous activities' such as scuba diving,

motorcycling and even trekking. If such
activities are on your agenda, you don't want
that policy.

Medical Kit

Doctors and hospitals are few and far
between in the outback, so you'd be wise to
carry a first-aid handbook and a basic
medical kit – ideally, at least one person in
your party will be a competent first-aider.
Some items to be included in the kit are:

- Aspirin or paracetamol for pain or fever
- Antihistamine (such as Benadryl) – useful as a
  decongestant for colds, allergies, to ease the itch
  from insect bites or stings or to help prevent motion
  sickness. There are several antihistamines on the
  market, all with different pros and cons (eg a
  tendency to cause drowsiness), so it's worth dis-
  cussing your requirements with a pharmacist or
  doctor. Antihistamines may cause sedation and
  interact with alcohol so care should be taken when
  using them
- Kaolin preparation (Pepto-Bismol), Imodium or
  Lomotil – for stomach upsets
- Antiseptic such as Betadine, which comes as
  impregnated swabs or ointment, and an antibiotic
  powder or similar 'dry' spray – for cuts and grazes
- Multivitamins are a worthwhile consideration,
  especially for long trips when dietary vitamin
  intake may be inadequate. Men, women and children each have different vitamin requirements, so
  obtain multivitamin tablets which are specific to
  age and gender.
- Calamine lotion or old-fashioned Tiger Balm – to
  ease irritation from bites or stings
- Eye drops
- Sterile gauze bandages (50 and 75mm)
- Triangular bandages – to support limbs and hold
  dressings in place
- Assortment of other bandages and Band-aids – for
  minor injuries
- Adhesive tape, cotton wool, tissues
- Elastic or crepe bandages – for sprains and snake
  bite
- Scissors, tweezers, safety pins and a thermometer
  (note that mercury thermometers are prohibited by
  airlines)
- Insect repellent, sunscreen, chapstick, perhaps
  water purification tablets
- Pencil and note pad

Optional items include:

- Cold and flu tablets
- Mylanta tablets, or similar, for indigestion

- Ear drops (Aquaear if you're heading for the
  tropics)
- Rubber-pointed eye probe, eye wash
- Vinegar for jellyfish stings (in tropical waters)
- Temporary tooth-filling mix to replace fillings,
  loose caps
- Toothache drops
- Burn cream
- Cream/ointment for bruises and swelling due to
  injury
- Strepsils or similar
- Methylated spirits
- Airsplint – for broken limbs, or immobilising
  limbs after snake bite

St John Ambulance Australia has a selection
of first-aid kits for car drivers, motorcyclists
and bushwalkers, ranging in price from $45
to $85. They include a first-aid handbook
and are well worth considering as a base kit
to which you can add some of the above
items. They're available at St John offices
and at the motoring organisations.

Don't forget any medication you're
already taking, and include prescriptions
with the generic rather than the brand name
(which may not be available locally).

Health Precautions

Travellers from the northern hemisphere
need to be aware of the intensity of the
outback sun. Those ultraviolet rays can have
you burnt to a crisp even on an overcast day,
so if in doubt wear protective cream, a wide-
brimmed hat and loose-fitting cotton
clothing that gives maximum skin coverage.
Loose clothes allow the air to circulate
around your skin and you'll find cotton to be
much more comfortable and cooler than syn-
thetics. Smother all exposed areas of skin
with a sunscreen (protection factor 15 or
higher). Australia has the world's highest
incidence of skin cancer, a fact directly connected to exposure to the sun, so be very
careful.

Remember also that too much sunlight,
regardless of whether it's direct or reflected,
can damage your eyes. The outback is noted
for its strong sunlight, so some good-quality
sunglasses are pretty well essential – 'good-
quality' ones are treated to filter out harmful
ultraviolet radiation. Poor-quality glasses

have limited filtering, and actually allow more ultraviolet light to be absorbed than if no sunglasses were worn at all. Excessive ultraviolet light will damage the surface structures and lens of the eye.

If you wear glasses or contact lenses, take a spare pair and your prescription. A Medic Alert tag is worth having if your medical condition is not always easily recognisable (heart trouble, diabetes, asthma, allergic reactions to antibiotics etc).

The contraceptive pill is available on prescription only, so a visit to a doctor is necessary. Doctors are listed in the Yellow Pages phone book or you can visit the outpatients section of a public hospital. Condoms are available from chemists, many convenience stores and often from vending machines in the toilets of pubs.

Basic Rules

Heat With the exception of southern areas, you can expect the weather to be hot throughout the outback from October to April inclusive, and travellers from cool climates may feel uncomfortable even in winter – 'hot' is a relative term depending on what you're used to. The sensible thing to do on a 'hot' day is to avoid the sun between mid-morning and mid-afternoon. Infants and elderly people are most at risk from heat exhaustion and heat stroke (see below).

Water People who first arrive in a hot climate may not feel thirsty when they should; the body and 'thirst mechanism' often need a few days to adjust. The rule of thumb is that an active adult should drink at least 4L of water per day in warm weather, more when walking or cycling. Use the colour of your urine as a guide: if it's clear you're probably drinking enough but if it's dark you need to drink more. Remember that body moisture will evaporate in the dry desert air with no indication that you're sweating.

Tap water is generally safe to drink in the settled parts of Australia, but in the outback it may be unfit for human consumption – check with the locals before gulping it down.

Bore water is often OK even if it tastes unpleasant, but children's stomachs in particular may have trouble coping with the high mineral content. (Note how soap often won't lather in outback showers.) There's nothing you can do short of actually distilling it – or carrying your own supply of drinking water. Outback residents normally save rainwater for drinking and use bore water for other purposes.

Be careful of drinking from streams and waterholes as they may be polluted by humans or animals. The surest way to disinfect water is to boil it – vigorous boiling for ten minutes should be satisfactory (it takes that long to kill giardia).

Simple filtering won't remove all dangerous organisms, so if you cannot boil water, treat it chemically. Chlorine tablets (Puritabs, Steritabs or other brand names) will kill many pathogens, but not those causing giardia and amoebic cysts. Iodine is very effective and is available in tablet form, such as Potable Aqua, but follow the directions carefully and remember that too much iodine can be harmful. If you can't find tablets, tincture of iodine (2%) can be used. Two drops per litre or quart of clear water is the recommended dosage, and the treated water should be left to stand for 30 minutes before drinking. Cordial or flavoured powder will disguise the taste of treated water and is a good idea if you're travelling with children.

Salt Sweating will also lead to loss of salt. Excessive salt loss manifests itself in headaches, dizziness and muscle cramps. Salt tablets are not a good idea as a preventative, but will quickly restore the balance if you show symptoms of salt loss. Add salt to your food to prevent this happening – a teaspoon a day should normally be enough in hot climates. If you're on a low-salt diet, check with your physician before you leave.

Food If you don't vary your diet, are travelling hard and fast and therefore missing meals, or simply lose your appetite, you can soon start to lose weight and place your health at risk, just as you would at home.

If you rely on fast foods dished out by roadhouses and takeaways, you'll get plenty of fats and carbohydrates but little else. Remember that overcooked food loses much of its nutritional value. If your diet isn't well balanced, it's a good idea to take vitamin and iron pills. Fresh fruit and vegetables are a good source of vitamins, provided they're available of course.

Health Problems

Prickly Heat Prickly heat is an itchy rash caused by excessive perspiration trapped under the skin. It usually strikes people who have just arrived in a hot climate and whose pores have not yet opened sufficiently to cope with greater sweating. Keeping cool, bathing often, using a mild talcum powder or even resorting to air-conditioning may help until you acclimatise.

Heat Exhaustion Dehydration or salt deficiency can cause heat exhaustion. Take time to acclimatise to high temperatures and make sure you to drink lots of (non-alcoholic) liquids – good old water is best. Think of your salt level too.

Anhydrotic heat exhaustion, caused by an inability to sweat, is quite rare. Unlike the other forms of heat exhaustion it is likely to strike people who have been in a hot climate for some time, rather than newcomers.

Heatstroke This serious, and sometimes fatal, condition can occur if the body's heat-regulating mechanism breaks down and the body temperature rises to dangerous levels. Long, continuous periods of exposure to high temperatures can leave you vulnerable to heatstroke. You should avoid excessive alcohol or strenuous activity when you first arrive in a hot climate.

The symptoms are feeling unwell, not sweating very much or at all and a high body temperature (39°C to 41°C or 102°F to 106°F). When sweating has ceased, the skin becomes flushed and red. Severe, throbbing headaches and lack of coordination will also occur, and the sufferer may become confused or aggressive. Eventually the victim will become delirious or convulse. Hospitalisation is essential, but meanwhile get patients out of the sun, remove their clothing, cover them with a wet sheet or towel and fan them continually.

Fungal Infections Hot-weather fungal infections are most likely to occur on the scalp, between the toes or fingers (athlete's foot), in the groin (jock itch or crotch rot) and on the body (ringworm). You get ringworm (a fungal infection, not a worm) from infected animals or by walking on damp areas, like shower floors.

To prevent fungal infections, wear loose, comfortable clothes, avoid artificial fibres, wash frequently and dry carefully. Always wear plastic sandals or thongs in showers you can't completely trust. If you do get an infection, wash the infected area daily with a disinfectant or medicated soap and water, and rinse and dry well. Apply an antifungal powder like the widely available Tinaderm. Try to expose the infected area to air or sunlight as much as possible, wash all towels and underwear in hot water and change them often.

Motion Sickness Eating lightly before and during a trip will reduce the chances of motion sickness. If you are prone to motion sickness, try to find a place that minimises disturbance – near the wing in aircraft, near the centre in cars and buses. Fresh air and looking at a steady reference point like the horizon usually help, whereas reading or cigarette smoke don't. Commercial antimotion-sickness preparations, which can cause drowsiness, have to be taken before the trip commences; when you're feeling sick it's too late. Ginger (available in capsule form) and peppermint (including mint-flavoured sweets) are natural preventatives.

Diarrhoea Major causes of diarrhoea (sometimes referred to as 'gastro' or 'the trots') are drinking mineralised bore water, eating contaminated food and handling contaminated objects (eg money, door handles). Some 'gastro' disorders, such as shigella and giardia, are endemic in parts of the outback including Alice Springs and many Aboriginal communities. Hepatitis A – another locally endemic virus – can also be transferred from person to person on money, door handles and food as well as in water.

Small children are most at risk from diarrhoea and Hepatitis A – with the former they can quickly become dehydrated if fluids are not kept up. The best prevention is to be strict about personal hygiene: always wash your hands (or use 'wet ones') after going to the toilet, and before preparing meals or eating. Wash all fruit and veg as well, and try to keep the flies off your food – you never know where they've been!

Ross River Fever This debilitating virus is spread by mosquitoes, mainly across northern Australia but also in the south. While not life-threatening, its effects are comparable to chronic fatigue syndrome and can (rarely) last several years. The best prevention is to avoid being bitten by mosquitoes – wear loose-fitting, light-coloured long pants and long-sleeved shirts, and apply repellent to exposed skin and clothing edges.

Worms These parasites are common in outback animals. The steak that you buy at the butcher's or get served in the roadhouse will be perfectly safe, but kangaroo or wild goat that hasn't been checked by the proper authorities can be risky, especially if undercooked. Worms may also be present on unwashed vegetables, and you can pick them up through your skin by walking in bare feet, particularly in the north.

Infestations may not show up for some time, and though they are generally not serious, if left untreated they can cause severe health problems. A stool test is necessary to pinpoint the problem, and medication is often available over the counter.

Sexually Transmitted Diseases The outback is generally a bastion of sexual conservatism, but there's a lot of alcohol about and a lot of short-term residents who don't mind partying on. Take care. Abstinence is the only 100% preventative, but using condoms is also effective (though not against pubic lice known as crabs).

Gonorrhoea and syphilis are the most common of these diseases; sores, blisters or rashes around the genitals, discharges or pain when urinating are common symptoms. Symptoms may be less marked or not observed at all in women. Syphilis symptoms eventually disappear completely but the disease continues and can cause severe problems in later years. The treatment of gonorrhoea and syphilis is by antibiotics.

Unfortunately there is no cure for herpes and there is also currently no cure for HIV/AIDS. Remember that it is impossible to detect the HIV-positive status of any person without a blood test.

There are numerous other sexually transmitted diseases, for most of which effective treatment is available. If you suspect anything is wrong, go to the nearest public hospital or medical clinic.

Cuts & Scratches Skin punctures can easily become infected in hot climates and may be difficult to heal. Treat cuts with an antiseptic solution like povidone-iodine. Where possible, avoid bandages and Band-aids, which can keep wounds wet. Coral cuts are notoriously slow to heal, as the coral injects a weak venom into the wound. Avoid coral cuts by wearing shoes when walking on reefs.

Snakebite For first-aid information, see Snakes in the Flora & Fauna section of the Facts about the Outback chapter.

Women's Health
Poor diet and even contraceptive pills can lead to vaginal infections when travelling in hot climates. Maintaining good personal hygiene, and wearing skirts or loose-fitting trousers and cotton underwear will help to prevent infections.

Yeast infections (thrush), characterised by a rash, itch and discharge, can be treated with a vinegar or even lemon-juice douche or with yoghurt. Nystatin, miconazole or clotrimazole suppositories are the standard medical prescription. Trichomoniasis and gardnerella are more serious infections; symptoms are a discharge and a burning sensation when urinating. If a vinegar-water douche is not effective, medical attention should be sought. Flagyl is the prescribed drug. In both cases, male sexual partners must also be treated.

Some women experience irregular periods when travelling because of the upset in routine. Don't forget to take time zones into account if you're on the pill. If you run into intestinal problems, the pill may not be absorbed. Ask your physician about these matters before you go.

WOMEN TRAVELLERS
Australia is generally a safe place for women travellers, although it's probably best to avoid walking alone late at night in any of the major towns – particularly near hotels. Sexual harassment is unfortunately still second nature to some Aussie males, and it's generally true to say that the further you get from 'civilisation' (ie, the big cities), the less enlightened your average Aussie male is going to be about women's issues. Outback women tend to give as well as they get, and the unenlightened outback male will show great respect for creative swearing.

Female hitchhikers should exercise care at all times. See the section on Hitching in the Getting Around chapter.

DISABLED TRAVELLERS
Generally speaking, disabled travellers are poorly catered for in the outback, although most towns, modern roadhouses and major parks have facilities designed for wheelchair access. These days there is a more enlightened appreciation of the needs of disabled travellers, however, and the situation is improving all the time.

There are a few organisations that can supply advice to disabled travellers, but almost all of them only operate within a single state. The major exception is NICAN (PO Box 407, Curtin, ACT 2605; ☎ toll-free 1800 806 769), which can help with advice on most matters of interest to disabled travellers. For example, they can answer specific queries and provide information on state-level organisations, specialist travel agents, wheelchair and equipment hire, and access guides. NICAN would be grateful if you send at least the cost of return postage.

USEFUL ORGANISATIONS
Automobile Associations
Australia has a national automobile association, the Australian Automobile Association, but this exists mainly as an umbrella for the various state associations and to maintain international links. The day-to-day operations are all handled by the state organisations which provide breakdown service, literature, excellent maps and detailed guides to accommodation and campsites. The material they produce is usually of a very high standard, and is relatively cheap or often free.

The state organisations have reciprocal arrangements with each other and with similar organisations overseas. So, if you're a member of the National Roads & Motorists Association (NRMA) in New South Wales, you can use the facilities of the Royal Automobile Association of South Australia (RAA). Similarly, if you are a member of the AAA in the USA or the RAC or AA in the UK, you can use any of the state organisations' facilities. But you'll need to bring proof of membership with you and, if you come from overseas, a letter of introduction.

The most useful state offices are:

New South Wales
    NRMA, 151 Clarence St, Sydney, NSW 2000 (☎ 13 2132)
Northern Territory
    Automobile Association of the Northern Territory (AANT), 79-81 Smith St, Darwin, NT 0800 (☎ (08) 8981 3837)
Queensland
    Royal Automobile Club of Queensland (RACQ), 300 St Pauls Terrace, Fortitude Valley, Qld 4006 (☎ toll-free 1800 811 911)
South Australia
    RAA, 41 Hindmarsh Square, Adelaide, SA 5000 (☎ (08) 8202 4500)

Western Australia
  Royal Automobile Club of Western Australia (RACWA), 228 Adelaide Terrace, Perth, WA 6000 (☎ (08) 9421 4444)

4WD Organisations

Each state has an umbrella organisation for its various 4WD clubs. They can provide information on many 4WD tracks, including conditions and permit requirements and will usually be happy to answer specific queries on outback touring. Not only that, they can put you in touch with any 4WD clubs in the area of interest to you.

The most useful addresses for the outback are:

New South Wales
  Recreational 4WD Clubs Association of NSW & ACT, PO Box 1371, Parramatta, NSW 2124 (☎ (02) 4448 7359)
Northern Territory
  NT Association of 4WD Clubs, PO Box 37476, Winnellie, NT 0820 (☎ (08) 8985 3573)
Queensland
  Queensland Association of 4WD Clubs, PO Box 174, Brisbane Markets, Qld 4106 (☎ (07) 3801 1410)
South Australia
  South Australian Association of 4WD Clubs, PO Box 178, Blair Athol, SA 5084 (☎ (08) 8263 1979)
Western Australia
  Western Australian Association of 4WD Clubs, PO Box 6029, East Perth, WA 6892 (☎ (08) 9399 7275)

National Parks Organisations

The Environment Australia Biodiversity Group (EABG), formerly the Australian Nature Conservation Agency, is a commonwealth body which is responsible for Kakadu and Uluru national parks in the Northern Territory, national parks in the ACT, some offshore areas such as the Cocos (Keeling) Islands and Norfolk Island, and also international conservation issues such as whaling and migratory bird conventions. It's based at 153 Emu Bank, Belconnen, ACT 2617 (GPO Box 636, Canberra 2601; ☎ (02) 6250 0200).

The individual national park organisations in each state are state-operated, not nation-

ally run. They can be hidden away in their capital-city locations, but if you search them out they have excellent literature and maps on the parks. In the bush, national park offices are much more up-front – they are usually the best places for local information. The state offices for outback parks are:

New South Wales
  National Parks & Wildlife Service, 41 Bridge St, Hurstville, NSW 2220 (☎ (02) 9585 6333)
Northern Territory
  Parks & Wildlife Commission of the Northern Territory, Gaymark Building, Mansfield Lane, Palmerston NT 0830 (PO Box 496, Palmerston 0831; ☎ (08) 8999 4401),
  Parks Australia North (an arm of EABG), 81 Smith St, Darwin, NT 0800 (GPO Box 1260, Darwin 0801; ☎ (08) 8946 4300)
Queensland
  National Parks & Wildlife Service, 160 Ann St, Brisbane, Qld 4000 (PO Box 155, Brisbane Albert St 4002; ☎ (07) 3227 8186)
South Australia
  Department of Environment & Natural Resources, 77 Grenfell St, Adelaide, SA 5000 (GPO Box 1047, Adelaide 5001; ☎ (08) 8204 1910)
Western Australia
  Department of Conservation & Land Management, 50 Hayman Rd, Como, Perth, WA 6152 (Locked Bag 104, Bentley DC, WA 6983; ☎ (08) 9334 0333)

Australian Conservation Foundation

The Australian Conservation Foundation (ACF) is the largest non-government organisation involved in conservation. Only about 10% of its income is from the government; the rest comes from memberships and subscriptions, and from donations (72%), which are mainly from individuals.

The ACF covers a wide range of issues, including the greenhouse effect and depletion of the ozone layer, the negative effects of logging, preservation of rainforests, the problems of land degradation, and protection of the Antarctic. It frequently works in conjunction with the Wilderness Society and other conservation groups.

The ACF (☎ (03) 9416 1166) is based at 340 Gore St, Fitzroy, Vic 3065.

Wilderness Society

The Tasmanian Wilderness Society was formed by conservationists who were determined to prevent the damming of the Franklin River, one of Australia's first major conservation confrontations. In 1983, after the High Court decided against the proposal, the group changed its name to the Wilderness Society because of its Australia-wide focus on wilderness issues. There are Wilderness Society shops in all states (not in the Northern Territory) where you can buy books, T-shirts, posters, badges etc.

The society's head office (☎ (03) 6234 9799) is at 130 Davey St, Hobart, Tas 7000.

Australian Trust for Conservation Volunteers

This non-political, non-profit group organises practical conservation projects for volunteers (including travellers) to take part in, such as tree planting, track construction and flora and fauna surveys. It's an excellent way to get involved with the conservation movement and, at the same time, visit some interesting areas. Past volunteers have found themselves working in outback places such as Finke Gorge, the MacDonnell Ranges, Kakadu and Broken Hill.

Most projects are for a week and all food, transport and accommodation is supplied in return for a contribution to help cover costs. Volunteers who are already in Australia can join the Banksia Package, which lasts four weeks. The cost is $560, and further weeks can be added for $140. For volunteers applying from outside Australia there's the six-week Echidna Package ($840). Both packages include a variety of projects at different locations

For details contact the head office (☎ (03) 5333 1483) at PO Box 423, Ballarat, Vic 3353, or the following state offices:

New South Wales
    2 Holt St, Stanmore, NSW 2048
    (☎ (02) 9564 1244)
Northern Territory
    4 Burnett Place, Myilly Point, Darwin, NT 0800
    (☎ (08) 8981 3206)

Queensland
    Old Government House, QUT Grounds, George St, Brisbane, Qld 4000 (☎ (07) 3210 0330)
South Australia
    TAFE College, Brookway Dve, Campbelltown, Adelaide, SA 5000 (☎ (08) 8207 8747)
Western Australia
    1 Baron-Hey Court, South Perth, WA 6151 (☎ (08) 9474 3445)

WWOOF

There are about 350 WWOOF (Willing Workers On Organic Farms) associates in Australia, although only a handful qualify as 'outback'. The idea is that you do a few hours' work each day on a farm in return for bed and board.

As the name says, the farms are supposed to be organic but that isn't always so – some places aren't even farms. However, whether they have a farm, a vegetable patch or a pottery, most participants in the scheme are concerned to some extent with alternative lifestyles.

To join WWOOF (☎ (03) 5155 0218), send $25/30 for singles/couples (A$30/35 from overseas) and a photocopy of your passport data page to WWOOF, Buchan, Vic 3885. They'll send you a membership number and a booklet listing WWOOF places all over Australia.

ANZSES

The Australian & New Zealand Scientific Exploration Society is a non-profit organisation which undertakes extended scientific expeditions into wilderness areas of Australia. Each year it runs a youth expedition for 17 to 25 year olds, an all-women expedition and an open-age, mixed gender expedition. All general expeditioners are volunteers, who pay a fee to cover transport, food and equipment.

The expeditions are a great opportunity for nature lovers from all walks of life (you don't have to be a scientist) to participate in the collection of scientific data and to experience living and working in remote areas. As a bonus, the places visited are generally not accessible to the average traveller. The far north of Queensland and South Australia's arid zone are popular target areas.

ANZSES (☎ (03) 9381 2775; fax 9381 2776) can be contacted at PO Box 174, Albert Park, Vic 3206.

DANGERS & ANNOYANCES

Fortunately, Australia is free of carnivorous wild mammals that tear you to shreds at night, but it does have its fair share of other potentially dangerous creatures such as crocodiles and snakes, and more annoying flies than you ever thought possible. See the Fauna section in the Facts about the Outback chapter.

Other dangers include the climate and the extreme isolation if something goes wrong in a remote area. Plan your outback trips carefully. Beware of abandoned shafts in old mining areas – the holes are often very deep and can be difficult to see.

On the Road

Collisions with cattle, sheep and kangaroos are all too common (as the many carcasses by the side of the road will attest) but there's a simple solution: don't drive at night. Unfortunately, other drivers are even more dangerous, particularly those who drink – which happens a lot in the outback. See the Getting Around chapter for more on driving hazards.

Bushfires

Bushfires happen every year in Australia. Don't be the idiot who starts one. In hot, dry, windy weather, be extremely careful with any naked flame – no cigarette butts out of car windows, please. On a Total Fire Ban Day (listen to the radio or watch the billboards along the roads), it is forbidden even to use a camping stove in the open. The locals will not be amused if they catch you breaking this particular law; they'll happily dob you in, and the penalties are severe.

If you're unfortunate enough to find yourself driving through a bushfire, stay inside your car and try to park off the road in an open space, away from trees, until the danger has passed. Lie on the floor under the dashboard, covering yourself with a wool blanket if possible. The fire front should pass quickly.

Bushwalkers should take local advice before setting out. On a Total Fire Ban Day, don't go – delay your trip until the weather has changed. Chances are that it will be so unpleasantly hot and windy, you'll be better off anyway in an air-conditioned pub sipping a cool beer.

If you're walking in the bush and you see smoke, even at a distance, take it seriously. Bushfires move very quickly and change direction with the wind. Go to the nearest open space, downhill if possible. A forested ridge is the most dangerous place to be. Eucalypts burn easily because of their high content of volatile oil and may literally explode into flames. Heat radiation is a big killer, so cover yourself up, preferably in a less flammable material such as wool.

Fire is a part of nature, and many Australian plants have come to rely on it for reproduction. In outback areas in particular, the authorities often leave bushfires to burn themselves out if there's no danger to humans.

EMERGENCY

In the case of a life-threatening situation, dial ☎ 000. This call is free from any phone and the operator will connect you with either the police, ambulance or fire brigade. To dial any of these services direct, check the inside front cover of any local telephone book.

For other telephone crisis and personal counselling services (such as sexual assault, poisons information or alcohol and drug problems), check the front pages of the local telephone book.

If you have a CB or HF radio, see Radio Communications in the Post & Telecommunications section earlier in this chapter.

SURVIVAL

The key to safe travel anywhere is preparation, and the only way you can be prepared is to research your destination – see the earlier Planning section. If you're unsure, particularly if you're heading off the beaten track, seek expert advice from local police, park rangers and so on; you may not like what they say but you would be foolish to ignore it.

There are plenty of books on bushcraft and survival, and it's worth buying one in advance and reading it – you never know when one of those neat little tricks may save your life. See the earlier Books & Maps section.

There are a number of general survival tips to remember regardless of whether you're driving or bushwalking – and despite the outback's fierce reputation, there is plenty of excellent walking on offer.

Water

See the earlier Health section about your water needs and sources. The main thing is to carry sufficient water to get you through to the next resupply point and still have plenty in reserve for emergencies – don't forget additional supplies for washing purposes and for refilling the vehicle's radiator. If you're planning a trip, allow 4 to 5L drinking water per day per person. On most tracks, around 20L per person is a sensible amount to carry, provided you top it up when you can, and store it in more than one container. Food is less important – the space might be better allocated to an extra spare tyre.

If your vehicle breaks down and you run out of water, use the water in your radiator only if it's free of chemical additives. When walking, it's wise to carry at least one full canteen per person even on a short walk – you never know when you might need it. Tough army-style canteens are ideal, while flimsy plastic bottles such as fruit-juice containers are not.

Register Your Intentions

In the remote outback you should always let a responsible person know details of your proposed activities so that the police will know where to look for you. Generally the best person to use as your insurance policy is someone who cares about you rather than a casual acquaintance – obviously you'd register your intentions with a ranger if walking

in a national park. Leave a map showing where you're going, how you're getting there and how long you expect to take. Always check in as arranged, otherwise you may spark an unnecessary search and rescue operation – in which case you'll be expected to pay the costs.

Safety in Numbers

It's better to travel in company, firstly for the social advantages of sharing experiences and secondly for safety. The minimum recommended number when bushwalking is three people: if someone is hurt, one person can stay to assist while the other goes for help. The silliest thing to do is to go bushwalking by yourself and not tell anyone your plans.

Getting Lost or Breaking Down

The best way to avoid getting lost is to have current large-scale maps of the area and to keep track of where you are at all times. When walking in unfamiliar terrain, always take note of the landmarks around you (including those behind in case you want to return by the same route) and the direction of the sun; use a compass if you can't tell north any other way.

It's a good idea to keep a detailed running log when driving on remote tracks. Simply note each point of interest (for example a track intersection, windmill, gate or any obvious feature) and its distance from your starting point. Running logs enable you to backtrack with confidence and can also be used to advise fellow travellers.

If you do get hopelessly lost or your vehicle breaks down beyond repair it's essential not to panic, as this will more than likely make things worse. You will have told someone where you're going so the best idea is to sit quietly in the shade and conserve water supplies until the search party arrives. If you call for help on the radio, remember that the most protracted searches are often for people who confidently claim to be where they are not; only report an approximate position of which you can be absolutely sure.

To assist aerial searchers, you can lay out

a large 'V' (the recognised ground-to-air visual signal for requiring help) in an open area using any material of contrasting colour to the ground. As a general rule, *never* leave your vehicle and wander off to seek help: the car is much larger than you and will more easily be seen by searchers.

BUSINESS HOURS

Most shops close at 5 or 5.30 pm weekdays, and either noon or 5 pm on Saturday. In most larger centres Sunday trading is catching on, particularly where tourism is an important industry. In many cities there are one or two late-shopping nights – usually Thursday and/or Friday – when the doors stay open until 9 or 9.30 pm.

Banks are open from 9.30 am to 4 pm Monday to Thursday, and until 5 pm or later on Friday. Of course there are exceptions to Australia's unremarkable opening hours. Some places stay open late and all weekend – particularly delicatessens, service stations and supermarkets.

HOLIDAYS

The Christmas holiday period is part of the long summer school vacation, but as this is the outback's slow season for tourism you're unlikely to be bothered by booked-out accommodation and long queues. There are three other, shorter school-holiday periods during the year but they vary by a week or two from state to state, falling from early to mid-April, late June to mid-July, and late September to early October. Generally, by far the outback's busiest tourist season is the mid-year break.

Like school holidays, public holidays vary quite a bit from state to state. The following is a list of the main national and state public holidays:

New Year's Day
1 January
Australia Day
26 January
Labour Day (Vic)
first or second Monday in March
Labour Day (WA)
second Monday in March

Easter
Good Friday and Easter Saturday, Sunday and Monday (and Tuesday in Victoria)
Anzac Day
25 April
Labour Day (Qld)
first Monday in May
May Day (NT)
1 May
Adelaide Cup (SA)
third Monday in May
Foundation Day (WA)
first Monday in June
Queen's Birthday (Qld, NT, Vic)
second Monday in June
Bank Holiday (NSW)
first Monday in August
Picnic Day (NT)
first Monday in August
Queen's Birthday (WA)
first Monday in October
Labour Day (NSW, ACT & SA)
first Monday in October
Melbourne Cup (Vic)
first Tuesday in November
Christmas Day
25 December
Boxing Day
26 December

SPECIAL EVENTS

Some of the most enjoyable Australian festivals are, naturally, the ones that are most typically Australian – like the outback rodeos, race meetings and bachelor-and-spinster balls, which draw together bush folk from hundreds of kilometres around including more than a few eccentric characters.

The following is just a brief overview of some of the more famous 'cultural' events in the Centre and Top End. Check the track descriptions later in this book for more events, and contact the relevant state tourist authorities for exact dates, which tend to vary a bit from year to year:

July
NT Royal Shows – Agricultural shows in Darwin, Katherine, Tennant Creek and Alice Springs
August
Darwin Rodeo (NT) – This includes international team events between Australia, the USA, Canada and New Zealand
Darwin Beer Can Regatta (NT) – Boat races for boats made out of beer cans, of which there are plenty in the world's beer-drinking capital

Shinju Matsuri (Festival of the Pearl, WA) – Held in the old pearling port of Broome, this week-long festival is a great event and includes Asiatic celebrations

September

Birdsville Cup (QLD) – The tiny town of Birdsville hosts the country's premier outback horse-racing event on the first weekend in September

October

Henley-on-Todd Regatta (NT) – A series of races for leg-powered bottomless boats on Alice Springs' (usually) dry Todd River

ACTIVITIES

There are many great walks in the various national parks, where you can do bird-watching and other nature-based activities. Water isn't a feature of the arid zone, although there are plenty of swimming holes in its various river systems. You can go snorkelling and scuba diving at a number of places around the coast such as on the Great Barrier Reef and Western Australia's Ningaloo Reef. Canoeing is a possibility on many tropical rivers.

In northern Queensland you can hire a horse and ride it through rainforests and sand dunes, and swim with it in the sea. Camel riding is available in several places, such as Alice Springs and Coward Springs (on the Oodnadatta Track). If you've done it in India or Egypt or you just fancy yourself as the explorer/outdoors type, then here's your chance.

You can cycle anywhere in the outback, although much of it is pretty boring when seen from a bike; for the well-prepared enthusiast there are long, challenging routes and for the not so athletic there are plenty of great day trips. You can generally hire bikes in major tourist centres, such as Broome and Alice Springs. Most states have helpful bicycle societies with maps and useful tips and advice on outback cycling.

Windsurfing, paragliding, rafting, hot-air ballooning and hang-gliding are among the many other outdoor activities. For more information, see the Activities sections in the track descriptions in this book or contact any of the state tourist bureaus.

Two activities that draw many people to the outback are fossicking (hunting for gem stones and gold) and barramundi fishing (in the north). In fact, they're so popular that we'll deal with them separately below.

Fossicking

Generally, the best places to fossick for gem-stones are in areas where mountain-building has taken place. The rocks of such areas are often formed under conditions that are ideal for the development of large crystals.

Most important of these are pegmatites, which are the major hosts for a whole range of gemstones such as aquamarine, tourmaline, garnet, quartz and topaz. Pegmatites originate as molten, mineral-rich material which is injected into cracks in the earth's crust. Being more resistant to erosion they often form wall-like structures across the landscape.

Also important are rocks, particularly limestone, which have been chemically changed through coming into contact with an invading body of super-heated material – a process known as contact metamorphism. Rocks altered in this way are major hosts for many types of gems including sapphire, ruby, aquamarine, garnet, epidote, sphene and zircon.

About 30% of Australia's land area consists of basins which have been filled with sediments; with the notable exception of precious opal, these are poor in gemstones. Only about 15% has potential for fossickers and this lies in three interrupted zones that run roughly north-south across the continent. The western zone includes the Kalgoorlie gold fields, the Pilbara and the Kimberley. The central zone runs from Kangaroo Island to Darwin and includes the northern Flinders Ranges, the Harts Range in central Australia and the Top End gold fields; an offshoot covers the Broken Hill area. The eastern zone runs up the eastern highlands from Tasmania to Cape York.

Research A successful fossicking trip is usually dependent on good research. Without local information, an area's potential is best discovered in your armchair with large-scale geological maps, mines-department reports and any other literature you can find. The most popular areas are likely to be written about in the various fossicking guides available from mines departments and bookshops.

State-produced geological maps – the larger their scale the better – are essential as they show the types of surface rock and thus give a hint of the kinds of gems and minerals you may find there. They also show roads, homesteads, watercourses and the locations of old mines, prospecting areas and any interesting mineral occurrences. Make sure you get hold of the explanatory booklet that accompanies each map as this will contain additional information.

Fossicking Tools Successful fossicking doesn't require a trailerful of equipment, but you must have some basic tools. A minimum would include: a small spalling hammer or sledgehammer; a pick and shovel; nest of aluminium sieves; prospecting dish; large basin or cut-down drum to wash gravel in; and a small crowbar. Most of these will earn their keep in other ways. If you can fit in a pry bar, a selection of rock chisels, a magnifying glass and a gardening trowel, so much the better. A book on mineral identification is essential, of course.

Prospecting dishes come in a range of sizes and can be either metal or plastic; the best ones have a groove around the edge which is designed to catch heavy particles such as gold as material is washed out of the pan. A shiny metal pan should be blackened first so that the gold stands out – the easiest way to do this is turn it upside down on a smoky fire. You need water to use a pan effectively, but few outback gold deposits have a supply right next to them. This is where the cut-down drum or large basin comes in handy.

Sieves are essential when fossicking for gems in dirt or gravel. The most convenient ones are the small round aluminium sieves that can be fitted together to form a combination – three sieves of 12mm, 6mm and 3mm mesh fitted together are ideal for most

purposes. Fossickers who are really serious and want to move a lot of material usually prefer a large wooden-framed sieve mounted on a tripod. The sieved material needs to be washed so that any gems will be easily seen.

Where to Look River deposits are good places as running water and gravity have already done the hard work of concentrating nature's treasures in one spot. Any situation that causes a drop in flow rate, hence deposition of heavier materials, should be checked. Rock bars often yield exciting finds as gold and gems, being heavy, move along the bottom during a flood and may become trapped in potholes or crevices in the bar. If necessary use your crowbar to gain access to crevices, which should be cleaned out using your trowel and a brush. All material obtained should be either panned or sieved depending on whether it's gold or gems you're after.

The use of a prospecting dish is straightforward but requires some practice with ball bearings or steel shot to perfect the art. First, the dish must be submerged in water as it is water that helps concentrate the heavy particles on the bottom. Second, grasp the rim of the dish with both hands (one on either side) and tilt it slightly, the groove being downwards. Third, agitate the contents by gently shaking the dish sideways and back and forth so that the backwash carries the lighter material over the edge – don't be too vigorous or you'll lose the gold. As you progress you can sweep the larger stones out with your hand.

Eventually all that remains will be heavy particles, which you concentrate further by slowly rotating the dish so that the gold forms a tail. To remove the gold, simply moisten the end of a finger and press it on the specks, which you then transfer to a jar of water – just dip your finger in the water and the gold will drop off.

Digging and sieving around the base of suitable rock outcrops, particularly pegmatites, is worth trying. There are some outstanding areas of gem-yielding pegmatite in the outback, including the Pilbara region near Marble Bar, the Harts Range near Alice Springs and the northern Flinders Ranges.

Mine dumps that date from last century – or at least no later than the 1930s – are fruitful sources of all kinds of secondary minerals, including gemstones. High costs and the inefficient methods used during the early days often meant that only high-grade ore was worth mining. Anything of poorer grade, including fine specimens, was usually thrown out with the waste, as were secondary minerals. A good example is the Harts Range mica field, where magnificent gems were tossed away because they had no monetary value. On the opal fields, precious opal with orange fire was out of favour late last century so the gougers threw most of it away.

The best way to fossick on old dumps is to either sieve material from untouched areas or drag down the sides with a rake. You can also find gemstones by closely examining the surface without necessarily disturbing it. This is best done soon after rain when the dust has been washed away leaving the gems readily visible.

Abandoned mines are dangerous. *Never* enter workings where the roofs are held up by old timbers or where there are signs of rock falls, and always stand well back from old shafts as your weight may trigger a collapse.

Mining Law Mining law differs between the states and territories but all have one thing in common: a fossicker must be in possession of a miner's right or fossicking permit to search for gems and minerals on crown land. Permission to fossick on freehold land and mineral leases must usually be obtained from the owner or leaseholder. A miner's right may allow access to pastoral leases, but this should be checked with the relevant authority. Sadly, the actions of the thoughtless minority has brought the hobby into disrepute in many areas, and fossickers are no longer always welcome.

Information Contact the following state departments for information on mining law

and the availability of geological maps, reports and fossicking guides:

New South Wales
  Department of Mineral Resources, 29-57 Christie St, St Leonards NSW 2065 (PO Box 536, St Leonards 2065; ☎ (02) 9901 8888)
Northern Territory
  Department of Mines & Energy, Paspaley Centre Point, Smith St Mall, Darwin NT 0800 (PO Box 2901, Darwin 0801 (☎ (08) 8999 5511)
Queensland
  Department of Minerals & Energy, QMEC Building, 61 Mary St, Brisbane Qld 4000 (GPO Box 194, Brisbane 4001; ☎ (07) 3237 1435)
South Australia
  Department of Mines & Energy, 191 Greenhill Rd, Eastwood, SA 5063 (PO Box 151, Eastwood 5063; ☎ (08) 8274 7500)
Western Australia
  Department of Minerals & Energy, Minerals House, 100 Plain St, East Perth WA 6004 (☎ (08) 9222 3333)

Barramundi Fishing

For many visitors to northern Australia, one of the primary motivations for getting off the beaten track is to find a waterhole where they can catch Australia's premier native sport fish, the barramundi. It seems that every other 4WD you come across has a 'tinny' (aluminium dinghy) on the roof.

The 'barra' is highly prized mainly because of its great fighting qualities: once it takes a lure or fly, it fights like hell to be free. As you try to reel one in, chances are it will make some powerful runs, usually leaping clear of the water and shaking its head in an attempt to throw the hook. Even smaller fish (3 to 4kg) can put up a decent fight, but when they are about 6kg or more you have a battle on your hands which can last several minutes.

Catching a barra is a challenge, but that's only half the fun; the other half is eating it! The barramundi is a prized table fish, although the taste of the flesh does depend to some extent on where the fish is caught. Those caught in saltwater or tidal rivers generally have the sweetest flavour; those in landlocked waterways can have a muddy flavour and soft flesh if the water is murky. Naturally, everyone has their own theory as to where, when and how barramundi are most likely to be caught. The fish is found throughout coastal and riverine waters of the Kimberley, Top End, Gulf Country and Cape York. The best time to catch them is the post-Wet, ie around late March to the end of May. At this time the rivers are receding and the fish tend to gather in freshwater creeks, where there is plenty of food. The best method is to cast a lure around snags (eg fallen trees) or places where food might be concentrated, such as creek junctions or channels below waterfalls.

The period from June to September is the Dry. While it's not the best season for barra, many roads and tracks which are impassable at other times of the year are open, and so the opportunities of finding a good spot are much enhanced. Trolling close to banks, snags or rock bars with lures is best at this time as the barra tend to stay deep and are relatively inactive as the water is cool.

The build-up to the Wet, from October to late December, is another good fishing time. The water temperature is on the rise, and there are occasional storms, so the fish are more active. Coastal inlets and tidal rivers offer the best fishing at this time. Trolling lures is the best method, although live bait also gets good results.

During the Wet, from January to March, fishing is generally done from boats as many tracks and roads are flooded, making access by vehicle difficult. Casting lures into floodwater run-off or channels is the best method, but even fishing from a river bank or into large channels which feed the rivers is often successful.

In tidal rivers the barra seem to strike most during the last hour or so of the ebb tide, particularly if this is late in the day. The same applies to saltwater areas, although the first couple of hours of the rising tide are also good.

Life Cycle of the Barramundi Early in the Wet, the female barras spawn around the river mouths. The high tides wash the eggs into the coastal swamps. At the end of the Wet, juvenile fish migrate up the rivers to the freshwater areas. By the end of the first year, a barra weighs around 0.5kg and measures around 30cm. Here they stay until they are three to four years old (around 3.5kg and 65cm).

Maturing males start to head downstream at the beginning of the Wet, and once in the open water, mature males undergo an amazing transformation as they turn into females and start spawning! By the time the fish are about seven years old they weigh upwards of 7kg (around 90cm), and fish of up to 20kg are not uncommon.

Bag & Size Limits It's in everyone's interest to follow the legal restrictions when fishing for barra. In the Northern Territory and Western Australia, the minimum size limit is 55cm, and the bag limit is five fish per person. Barramundi may not be retained on a tether line at any time. Certain areas of the Northern Territory are closed to fishing between 1 October and 31 January. In Queensland, the closed season lasts from 1 November to 31 January, the minimum size is 50cm and there's a bag limit of five fish per person. Western Australia has no closed season.

Good Fishing Practices Apart from following the legal restrictions, there are a number of ways to enhance the quality of barra fishing for yourself and others who follow.

When releasing fish, try to remove the hook while the fish is still in the water; use a net to land the fish for dehooking and weighing. Where it's necessary to handle the fish, grip it firmly by the lower jaw ensuring your fingers don't get under the gill cover.

To store fish in top condition, they should be killed and bled as soon as possible. Bleeding by cutting the gills or throat is the best method, and if the fish is then placed in ice water this reduces clotting and aids bleeding. Rapid cleaning also preserves the quality, and it's helpful if you can avoid cutting into the flesh surrounding the gut region or rupturing the intestines. Chill the cleaned fish as soon as possible, as this slows the rigor mortis process; when rigor mortis takes place rapidly, violent muscle contractions result in loss of natural juices and the flesh has a tendency to fall apart when filleted.

Clean and rinse fish in a container if possible; doing so in the river may attract crocodiles.

Information The following addresses can provide all the local rules and regulations relating to barramundi fishing:

Amateur Fishermen's Association of the Northern Territory, PO Box 4705, Casuarina, Darwin NT 0801 (☎ (08) 8981 5991, mobile 014 471 600)

Northern Fisheries Centre, 38-40 Tingira St, Portsmith, Cairns, QLD 4870 (☎ (07) 4052 9888)

Fisheries Department, Broome District Office, Broome, WA 6725 (☎ (08) 9192 1121)

Organised Fishing Trips Various commercial operators across northern Australia offer barra fishing trips, either day or safari style, and in fresh or salt water – there's over a dozen in Darwin alone. Contact state and local tourist bureaus for details, and check the Yellow Pages for those that aren't registered with the tourist offices.

WORK

If you come to Australia on a 'working holiday' visa you can officially only work for three out of those 12 months. Working on a regular tourist visa is strictly *verboten*. Many travellers on tourist visas do find casual work, but with a national unemployment rate of around 8.5%, and youth unemployment as high as 40% in some areas, it's becoming more difficult to find a job – legal or otherwise. In outback areas, however, the difficulty of attracting labour means that there's still a fair bit of casual work available and potential employers won't ask too many questions about your background.

To receive wages in Australia, you must have a Tax File Number (TFN) issued by the Taxation Department. Forms are available from post offices and you'll need to show your passport and visa – processing takes about four weeks. If you don't have a TFN,

tax will be deducted from your wages at the maximum rate (currently 48.5%).

The best prospects for casual work in the outback include bar work, waiting on tables or washing dishes, other domestic chores at roadhouses, and nanny work. Health professionals, chefs (or just plain cooks), and tradespersons are also in demand.

Still, short-term work is not as easy to find as it once was, even in the outback, and many travellers who have budgeted on finding work are forced to return home early. If you are coming to Australia with the intention of working, make sure you have enough funds to cover you for your stay, or have a contingency plan if work is not forthcoming.

To find out what's available and where, check the classified section of local papers under Situations Vacant. The various backpackers' publications and hostels are other good information sources – some local employers even advertise on hostel notice boards. Also keep an eye out for notices posted in shop windows, and ask around at pubs and roadhouses.

ACCOMMODATION

A typical outback town of any importance will have a basic motel at around $40/45 for singles/doubles, an old hotel with rooms (shared bathrooms) at $25/35, and a caravan park with tent sites for $8 to $15 and on-site vans or cabins for $25 to $30 for two people. If the town is a major centre, it'll probably have several of each as well as backpacker accommodation. Even many small towns have backpackers' 'bunkhouses' these days, particularly if there's a fair degree of tourist traffic. If there's a group of you, the rates for four or more people in a hotel or motel room are worth checking; often there are larger 'family' rooms or units with two bedrooms.

It's worth remembering that accommodation prices often vary depending on the time of year. 'High season' or peak holiday rates can be 75% or more above 'low season' rates, so it might be worthwhile timing your visit to coincide with quieter times. Unless stated otherwise, the prices given in this book are low season.

For comprehensive accommodation listings, the state automobile clubs produce directories of hotels, motels, holiday flats, caravan parks and even some backpackers' hostels in almost every city and town in the country. They're updated every year so the prices are generally fairly current. They're available from the clubs for a nominal charge if you're a member. Alternatively, some state tourist offices put out guides to local accommodation.

Camping

The camping story in Australia is partly excellent and partly rather annoying. The excellent side is that you can camp almost anywhere out in the bush for free, or at national park campsites for next to nothing. Roadhouses often have showers for a nominal fee. If you prefer hot showers and laundry facilities when camping, there's a great number of caravan parks where – peak periods aside – you'll almost always find space available.

One of the drawbacks is that professional campsites are often intended more for caravans (house trailers for any North Americans out there) than for campers, and the tent campers get little thought in these places. The fact that in Australia most of the sites are called 'caravan parks' indicates who gets most attention.

Equally bad is that campsites in most large towns are well away from the centre. This is not inconvenient in small towns, but in general if you're planning to camp around the outback you really need your own transport – apart from anything else, you have to get between towns. Still, it's not all gloom. Australian caravan parks tend to be well kept and excellent value. Many also have on-site vans and cabins which you can rent for the night.

Bush Camping Camping in the bush, either freelance or at designated spots in national parks and reserves, is for many people one of the highlights of a visit to Oz. Nights spent around a campfire under the stars are unforgettable.

Except in the far north, where the mossies can be ferocious even in winter, you won't need a tent most of the time – in the north, tents with plenty of insect-screened windows (fine mesh is best) are recommended. Elsewhere, another option is a stretcher (camp bed), as follows: park your vehicle about 3m from a tree or bush; between the two, erect the stretcher and roll out your sleeping bag, string up a mosquito net and tuck it in under the bag. This way you'll sleep off the ground, safe from creeping insects, mosquitoes and early-morning flies, and you can still look at the blazing stars as you doze off.

There are some basic rules to camping in the wild (also see the Social Conduct section in the Facts about the Outback chapter):

- Most of the land in Australia belongs to someone, even if you haven't seen a house for 100km or so. They own it – it is their back yard. You need permission before you are allowed to camp on it. In national parks and on Aboriginal land, you will need permits. On public land, observe all the rules and regulations.
- Select your camping spot carefully. Start looking well before nightfall and choose a spot that makes you invisible from the road. You'll notice any number of vehicle tracks leading off the main road into the bush: explore a few and see what you find.
- Keep to constructed vehicle tracks – never 'bush bash'. Avoid areas that are easily damaged, such as sand dunes.
- Some trees (for instance, river red gums and desert oaks) are notorious for dropping limbs. Don't camp under large branches.
- Ants live everywhere, and it's embarrassingly easy to set up camp on underground nests. Also beware of the wide variety of spiny seeds on the ground which can ruin your expensive tent groundsheet with pinprick holes – sweep the ground first, and erect your tent on a layer of thick agricultural plastic sheeting.
- Carry out all the rubbish you take in, don't bury it. Wild animals dig it up and spread it everywhere.
- Observe fire restrictions and make sure your fire is safe – dig a trench and keep the area around the fire clean of flammable material.
- Don't chop down trees or pull branches off living trees to light your fire. If the area is short of dead timber, go back down the track a little and collect some there. If that is not possible, use a gas stove for cooking.
- Respect the wildlife. This also means observing crocodile warnings and keeping away from suspect river banks.

R & V MOON

R & V MOON

ROB VAN DRIESUM

JEFF WILLIAMS

JEFF WILLIAMS

A	B
C	D
	E

Proving there's more than one way to travel around the outback...
A: Taking the traditional 4WD approach
B: The *Gulflander*
C: Looking down the 'barrel', Gunbarrel Highway
D: Cliff Young jogging around Australia at the age of 74!
E: Walking around Australia

PETER ROBINSON

HUGH FINLAY

HUGH FINLAY

JON MURRAY

BERNARD NAPTHINE

A	B
C	D
E	

Art in the outback
A: Emus painted on an unusual canvas, Silverton, NSW
B: Painted letterbox, NT

C: Albert Namatjira's headstone, NT
D: Sculpture, Broken Hill, NSW
E: Wall mural in Broken Hill, NSW

- Don't camp right beside a water point as you'll scare off the stock and wildlife that normally drink there – stop at least 200m away.
- Don't camp close enough to a river or stream to pollute it. In most parks the minimum distance is 20m.
- Don't use soap or detergent in any stream, river, dam or any other water point.
- Use toilets where they are provided. If there isn't one, find a handy bush, dig a hole, do the job and then fill in the hole. If you're staying a few days, dig a trench (long, narrow and deep) and use that as a toilet pit for everyone, with each individual covering their waste with a little dirt. Burning used toilet paper is a good idea, but don't start a wildfire in the process. Bury all human waste well away from any watercourse.
- If you have small children, disposable nappies are anything but disposable and are becoming a major item of pollution in the bush. Carry used disposables away with you in a heavy-duty plastic bag on the roof rack (they won't smell much if rolled up tight).

If you're doing your own cooking, see Campfire Cooking in the following Food section.

Hostels

Australia has very active state Youth Hostel Associations (YHAs) and you'll find hostels all over the country, including the major centres in the outback. YHA hostels provide basic accommodation, usually in small dormitories or bunk rooms although more and more of them are providing twin rooms for couples. The nightly charges are rock bottom (usually between $8 and $15 a night) and there are no age limits – in fact, the YHAs are campaigning actively to attract an older clientele.

Many take non-members, although there may be a small 'temporary membership' charge. To become a full YHA member in Australia costs $44 for the first year, with renewals $27 (international visitors can join by purchasing a 12-month non-renewable international guest card for $27). You can join at a state office or at any youth hostel.

YHA hostels are affiliated with Hostelling International (HI), formerly known as the International Youth Hostel Federation (IYHF), so if you're already a member of the YHA in your

own country, your membership entitles you to use the Australian hostels. Hostels are great places for meeting people and often function as travel centres where you can sign up for good-value tours. The annual *YHA Accommodation Guide* booklet, available from any YHA office in Australia and from some YHA offices overseas, lists all the YHA hostels around Australia, with useful little maps showing how to find them.

You must have a regulation sleeping bag sheet or bed linen – for hygiene reasons a regular sleeping bag won't do. If you don't have sheets they can be rented at many hostels (usually for $3), but it's cheaper, after a few nights' stay, to have your own. YHA offices and some larger hostels sell the official YHA sheet bag.

All hostels have cooking facilities and 24-hour access, and there's usually a communal area where you can sit and talk. There are usually laundry facilities and often excellent notice boards. Accommodation can usually be booked directly with the manager or through a Membership & Travel Centre. The YHA handbook tells all.

The Australian head office (☎ (02) 9565 1699) is in Sydney, at the Australian Youth Hostels Association, 10 Mallett St, Camperdown, NSW 2050. If you can't get a YHA hostel booklet in your own country, write to them, but otherwise deal with the following Membership & Travel Centres:

New South Wales
    422 Kent St, Sydney, NSW 2001
    (☎ (02) 9261 1111)
Northern Territory
    Darwin Hostel Complex, 69A Mitchell St, Darwin, NT 0821 (☎ (08) 8981 6344)
Queensland
    Northpoint Building, 231 North Quay, Brisbane, Qld 4000 (☎ (07) 3236 1680)
South Australia
    38 Sturt St, Adelaide, SA 5000 (☎ (08) 8231 5583)
Western Australia
    236 William St, Northbridge, Perth, WA 6003 (☎ (08) 9328 4793)

Not all of the 130-odd hostels listed in the handbook are actually owned by the state

YHAs. Some are 'associate hostels', which generally abide by hostel regulations but are owned by other organisations or individuals. You don't need to be a YHA member to stay at an associated hostel. Others are 'alternative accommodation' and do not totally fit the hostel blueprint. They might be motels which keep some hostel-style accommodation available for YHA members, caravan parks with an on-site van or two kept aside, or even places just like hostels but where the operators don't want to abide by all the hostel regulations.

Backpackers' Hostels

In recent years the number of backpackers' hostels in the outback has increased dramatically. Some are run-down hotels where the owners have tried to fill empty rooms. Others are purpose-built as backpackers' hostels; these are usually the best places in terms of facilities, although sometimes they are simply too big and lack any personalised service. The best places are often the smaller, more intimate hostels where the owner is also the manager. These are usually the older hostels that were around long before the backpacker boom.

Prices at backpackers' hostels are generally in line with YHA hostels, typically $12 to $15, although the $9 bed is still alive and well in some places. You can usually get a small discount if you hold a YHA or VIP card.

As with YHA hostels, the success of a hostel largely depends on the friendliness and willingness of the managers. One practice that many people find objectionable – in independent hostels only, since it never happens in YHAs – is the 'vetting' of Australians and sometimes New Zealanders, who may be asked to provide a passport or double ID which they may not carry. Some places will actually only admit overseas backpackers. This is because the hostel in question has had problems with locals treating the place more as a dosshouse than a hostel – drinking too much, making too much noise, getting into fights and the like. If you're an Aussie and encounter this kind

of reception, the best you can do is persuade the desk people that you're genuinely travelling the country and aren't just looking for a cheap place to crash for a while.

Hotels & Pubs

For the budget traveller, hotels in Australia are generally older places – new accommodation usually means motels or Hilton-style hotels. However, not every place called a hotel will necessarily have rooms to rent. If there's nothing that looks like a reception desk or counter, or if it doesn't appear to be staffed, just ask at the bar. A 'private hotel', as opposed to a 'licensed hotel', really is a hotel and doesn't serve alcohol. A 'guesthouse' is much the same as a 'private hotel'.

You'll generally find hotels in the middle of town – in historic centres like the goldmining towns, they can be magnificent. The rooms themselves may be pretty old-fashioned and unexciting, and will rarely come with private facilities, but the hotel facade and entrance area will often be quite extravagant. In country towns the hotel is often a place of real character – the real 'town centre' where you'll meet all the local eccentrics.

A bright word about hotels (guesthouses and private hotels, too) is that their breakfasts are usually excellent – big and 100% filling. If your hotel is still into serving a real breakfast you'll probably feel it will last you until breakfast comes around next morning. Generally, hotels will have rooms from around $20 or $30. When comparing prices, remember to check if breakfast is included.

Motels

If you want a more modern place with your own bathroom and other facilities, then you're moving into the motel bracket. Unlike hotels, motels are usually located away from the town centres. Roadhouse accommodation along outback roads generally falls in this category; many roadhouses also have camping facilities.

Prices vary, and with the motels, unlike most hotels, singles are the same price as doubles. The reason is quite simple: in the old hotels many of the rooms really are singles, relics of the days when single men travelled the country looking for work. In motels, the rooms are almost always doubles.

You'll sometimes find motel rooms for less than $35, and in most places will have no trouble finding something for around $45. They generally have tea/coffee-making facilities and a small fridge, and often a TV. Many motels will deliver breakfast to your room for a fee, but very few do main meals as well.

Stations

The outback is a land of large sheep or cattle farms ('stations') and one of the best ways to come to grips with Australian life is to spend a few days on one. With commodity prices falling daily, mountainous wool stockpiles and a general rural crisis, tourism offers the hope of at least some income for farmers, at a time when many are being forced off the land. Some stations have switched almost entirely to tourism. Many offer accommodation where you can just sit back and watch how it's done, while others like to get you more actively involved in the day-to-day activities.

Accommodation can range from campsites and dormitories to four star bungalows, and prices are pretty reasonable. Many stations that take guests are listed in the track descriptions later in this book, and the state tourist offices can also advise you on what's available.

Other Possibilities

One organisation that sometimes offers accommodation is the Country Women's Association (CWA), but this is usually for women only. The CWA is a powerful institution in country and outback Australia, with strong input into local legislation and community projects.

If you want to stay somewhere for more than a few days, it might be worth sharing a holiday unit or serviced apartment with a few travelling companions, though in the outback this sort of accommodation is generally only available in the major tourist centres like Alice Springs, Darwin and Broome. For longer term accommodation, the first place to look for houses to share or rooms to rent is the classified ad section of the local newspaper; notice boards in hostels, supermarkets and certain popular bookshops and cafes are also good places to look.

FOOD

Australia's food (mighty steaks apart) used to have a reputation for being like England's, only worse. Miracles happen and Australia's miracle was immigration. The Greeks, Yugoslavs, Italians, Lebanese and many others who flooded into Australia in the 1950s and '60s brought, thank God, their food with them. More recent arrivals include the Vietnamese, whose communities are thriving in several cities.

In the larger outback towns you can have Greek moussaka, Italian saltimbocca and pastas, German dumplings, or maybe even Middle Eastern treats. The Chinese have been sweet & souring since the gold-rush days, while more recently Indian, Thai, Vietnamese and Malaysian restaurants have been making their way into the Australian interior.

Australian Food

Although there is little real Australian cuisine, there is some typically Australian food. For a start there's the meat pie – every bit as sacred an institution as the hot dog is to a New Yorker. Some places make this classic dish on their premises and do a great job of it, but the standard factory pie is an awful concoction of anonymous meat and dark gravy in a soggy pastry case. A 'vegetarian' alternative is the pasty – pastry folded over a vegetable filling that sometimes contains meat as well (ask if you want to be sure).

Even more central to Australian eating habits is Vegemite. This dark-coloured yeast-extract substance looks like tar and is spread on bread. It's similar to Marmite or Promite but tastes less salty. Empty Vegemite jars make handy wine glasses – as you may discover in many an outback household.

Everybody knows about good Australian

steaks. They may be a bit tough in the outback (like the cattle) but they taste terrific and you'll seldom complain about the size. Fish like John Dory and the esteemed barramundi are often available far inland, as are superb lobsters and other crustaceans like the engagingly named Moreton Bay bugs! Yabbies are delicious crayfish that often thrive in outback dams and waterholes.

While vegetarians will find their options limited in the outback, most good roadhouses, cafes and pubs will have a vegetarian dish on the menu. Even in the outback a salad will usually be fresh – provided, of course, it hasn't spent too long on the truck getting there.

Where to Eat

Eating options are obviously more limited in the outback than in the big cities. Some towns will have an Asian restaurant, and in the larger towns there may be other styles, too. Many restaurants allow you to bring your own wine or beer, for which you may be charged a small 'corkage' fee.

For a quick meal, roadhouses and local takeaway shops offer straightforward fish and chips, and many different sandwiches that might be a more wholesome alternative. A 'hamburger with the lot' comes with egg, cheese and salad and provides a filling meal for around $5 – ask them to hold the beetroot if you don't share the Australian fetish for this red vegetable.

Be warned that roadhouse fare is often ordinary at best. On the main trucking routes, check which roadhouse has the most trucks parked outside at mealtime. The truckies tend to congregate where the tucker is best.

For a 'proper' meal, roadhouses will oblige but better value is usually to be found in the pubs. Look for 'counter meals', so called because they're eaten at the bar counter. Some places are fancier, almost restaurant-like, with serve-yourself salad tables where you can add as much salad, French bread and so on as you wish. Most pubs have a 'lounge' area where you can sit at a table. Good counter meals are hard to beat for value for money, and although the food is usually of the simple steak-salad-chips variety, the quality can be excellent.

Counter meals are usually served as counter lunches or counter teas, the latter a hangover from the old northern English terminology where 'tea' meant the evening meal. One catch with pub meals is that they usually operate fairly strict hours. The evening meal time may be just 6 to 7.30 or 8 pm. Pubs doing counter meals often have a blackboard menu outside but sometimes not – just ask at the bar. Counter meals vary enormously in price but in general the better class places with good serve-yourself salad tables will be in the $6 to $16 range for all the traditional dishes: steak, veal, chicken, fish and so on.

Preparing Your Own

Roadhouse and pub meals can get a bit boring (and expensive) after a while, so you may prefer to prepare your own food. Most outback supermarkets have at least a reasonable range of supplies, although the freshness and availability of fruit and veg may not be all you could wish for. This particularly applies to small, remote centres such as Birdsville and Oodnadatta.

For this reason, it's usually best to stock up on perishables such as tomatoes, cheese, meat and milk at every opportunity. You have to be super cautious with fresh fish and poultry, but most other perishables can be kept for a few days in an ice container known as an 'esky' after a leading Australian brand; ice is often available at service stations, general stores and pubs.

Fruit-fly roadblocks can be a problem when you're travelling interstate, as the movement of fruits, vegetables, plants and even honey is often restricted. There are a number of fruit-fly inspection stations to police quarantine regulations; otherwise there are 'honesty pits' where you're expected to dump all fruit and vegetable matter. The Department of Primary Industries & Energy, Australian Quarantine & Inspection Service has produced an informative booklet called *Traveller's Guide to Plant Quarantine*. To obtain a copy, write to or phone the appropriate state department. Stiff penalties apply for not obeying the rules.

Cooking in the Bush While it's nice to be able to cook your meal on the coals like a real bushie, this is a vanishing option in many parts of the outback – particularly in conservation areas and the more popular bush camping sites. In some areas open fires are prohibited during summer fire danger periods. As well, fallen timber is a habitat for many wildlife species (eg reptiles, insects). For these reasons it's best to plan on cooking most of your meals on a portable gas stove – you'll be able to fill your bottle at most roadhouses and service stations.

If you must cook on an open fire there are a few basic rules to follow. Firstly it's much better to have good-quality cast-iron or steel pots rather than aluminium, which isn't recommended for campfire cooking – it tends to heat unevenly. A steel grate is useful to put your pots on. Next you should use dry solid hardwoods (dead timber, of course) and allow plenty of time for them to burn down to a bed of coals. Avoid cooking over flames unless you're in a hurry, or simply boiling the billy.

Dig a trench in which to lay your fire. The width and length will depend on your own cooking needs and size of your fire grate, but it should be about 30cm deep.

Bush Cooking in Style, by Gayle Hughes, explains all you need to know about bush cooking, including planning and packing. For a good range of basic recipes, get hold of *Rabbit on a Shovel* by Herb ('Lummo') Lummis. Jack & Reg Absalom's *Outback Cooking in the Camp Oven* has exotic recipes like kangaroo, and gives all the details on how to use a camp oven.

See the Checklists in the back of this book for general cooking equipment and campfire cooking items.

DRINKS

In the non-alcoholic department, Australians knock back soft drinks and flavoured milk like there's no tomorrow. Tea and coffee in the outback usually means teabags and instant, though many places are now sophisticated enough to offer espresso and cappuccino. There are a number of brands of mineral water if you prefer that to tap water.

Beer

Beer plays an integral role in the social fabric of the outback. Australian beer will be fairly familiar to North Americans and is similar to what's known as lager in the UK. Some brands may taste like lemonade to the Continental beer addict, but don't say this out loud in an outback pub. It's always chilled before drinking.

Fosters is, of course, the best known international brand with a worldwide reputation, but its share of the home market is in decline. Each Australian state has its own beer brands: XXXX (pronounced 'fourex') and Powers (Queensland), Swan and Emu (Western Australia), Tooheys (New South Wales), and VB (Victoria Bitter, Victoria). Although most big-name beers are associated in particular with one state, they are available across the country. The smaller breweries tend to produce better beer – Cascade (Tasmania), Coopers (South Australia) and Matilda Bay (Western Australia) being three examples; Coopers Sparkling Ale is similar to some Belgian Trappist beers, including the sediment.

A word of warning to visitors: Australian beer has a higher alcohol content than British or American beers. Standard beer is generally around 4.9% alcohol, although most breweries also produce 'lite' beers with an alcohol content of between 2% and 3.5%. And another warning: people who drive under the influence of alcohol and get caught lose their licences (unfortunately, drink-driving is a real problem in Australia). The maximum permissible blood-alcohol concentration for drivers in Australia is 0.05%.

All around Australia, beer, the containers it comes in, and the receptacles you drink it from are called by different names. Beer comes in stubbies, echos, long necks, bottles, tinnies and twisties, depending on where you are. Tinnies are cans, bottles contain 750ml, and stubbies, echos, long necks and twisties are small bottles (375ml), usually with a handy twist-off cap.

Ordering at the bar can be an intimidating business for the newly arrived traveller. A 200ml beer is a seven in Queensland (seven ounces); a 285ml beer is a pot or a tenner in Queensland, but a middy in New South Wales and Western Australia; in New South Wales they also have the 425ml schooner, but in South and Western Australia a 425ml glass is called a pint. In New South Wales they're likely to ask if you want new or old, 'new' being ordinary beer and 'old' being stout. A low-alcohol beer is called a light, while regular strength beer can be called a heavy, or super.

Australians are generally considered to be heavy beer drinkers, however per capita beer consumption even in the notoriously hard-drinking Northern Territory has been falling faster than in any other developed country.

Wine

If you don't fancy beer, then turn to wines like many Australians are doing. Australia has a great climate for wine-producing and makes many superb wines that are reasonably cheap and readily available. Wine is generally sold in 750ml bottles or 2 and 4L 'casks'.

It takes a little while to become familiar with Australian wines and their styles, especially since the manufacturers are being forced to delete generic names from their labels as exports increase; the biggest victim is 'champagne', which is now mere 'sparkling wine'. White wines are almost always drunk chilled, and in the outback many people chill their reds too – room temperature is just too hot!

Australia produces excellent ports (perfect at a campfire) but only mediocre sherries.

THINGS TO BUY

There are lots of things definitely *not* to buy: plastic boomerangs, fake Aboriginal ashtrays and T-shirts, and all the other terrible souvenirs that fill the tacky souvenir shops. Most of them come from Taiwan or Korea anyway. Before buying an Australian souvenir, turn it over to check that it is actually made here!

Often the best souvenirs are the ones that have special meaning: the fly-net hat bought at Urandangi when the flies were driving you insane, the beautiful shell from the beach on the Gulf of Carpentaria, the gold nugget found near Kalgoorlie, or the 'antique' glass insulator picked up along the old Overland Telegraph Line north of Alice.

Aboriginal Art

Top of the list for any real Australian purchase would have to be Aboriginal art. Theirs is an amazingly direct and down-to-earth art that has finally gained international appreciation. If you're willing to put in a little effort, you can see superb examples carved or painted on rocks and caves in many parts of the outback. Now (and really just in time) skilled Aboriginal artists are also working on their art in a more portable form. Have a look at the spectacular Aboriginal artworks hanging in the respected art galleries before you make your choice.

Prices of the best works are way out of reach for the average traveller, but among the cheaper artworks on sale are prints, baskets, small carvings and some very beautiful screen-printed T-shirts produced by Aboriginal craft co-operatives. There are also a large number of commercial rip-offs – be prepared to shop around and pay a few dollars more for the real thing. See the Cross-Cultural Etiquette section in the Facts about the Outback chapter if you want to purchase works of art on Aboriginal communities.

Australiana

The term 'Australiana' is a euphemism for souvenirs that are supposedly representative of Australia and its culture, although many are extremely dubious. Some of the more worthwhile items are wool products such as hand-knitted jumpers, sheepskin products, and jewellery made from opal. The seeds of many of Australia's native plants are on sale all over the place; try growing kangaroo paws back home. Australian wines are well known overseas, but why not try honey (leatherwood honey is one of a number of powerful local varieties), macadamia nuts (native to Queensland), or Bundaberg rum with its unusual sweet flavour – a 'Bundy & Coke' is a popular drink in the outback.

Aussie Clothing

While you're here, fit yourself out in some local clobber – made in Australia for Australian conditions. Start off with some Bonds undies and a singlet, a pair of Holeproof Explorer socks and Blundstone elastic-sided work boots. Slip on a pair of Stubbie shorts or Thomas Cook moleskin trousers and an RM Williams stockman's shirt, then slap on an Akubra hat and you've got the complete Aussie outback working uniform. If this is totally impractical for the cold, wet climate back home, invest in a Driza-bone waxed-cotton overcoat.

Opals

The opal is Australia's national gemstone, and opals and jewellery made with it are popular souvenirs. It's a beautiful stone, but buy wisely and shop around – quality and prices can vary widely from place to place.

Gold and silver follow world prices and aren't as cheap as you would expect in a country that mines so much of the stuff.

Getting There & Away

Getting to or from Australia generally means flying, although it is possible to book a berth on a freighter or hitch a ride on a yacht.

AIR

The basic problem with travel to Australia is that it's a long way from anywhere. Coming from Asia, Europe or North America, there are lots of competing airlines and a wide variety of air fares, but there's no way you can avoid those great distances. Australia's current international popularity adds another problem: flights are often heavily booked. If you want to fly to Australia at a particularly popular time of year (the middle of summer, ie Christmas time, is notoriously difficult) or on a particularly popular route (like Hong Kong-Sydney or Singapore-Sydney), then plan well ahead.

Australia has a number of international gateways. Sydney and Melbourne are the two busiest international airports with flights arriving from everywhere. Perth also gets many flights from Asia and Europe and has direct flights to New Zealand and Africa. Other international airports include Hobart in Tasmania (New Zealand only), Adelaide, Port Hedland (Bali only), Darwin, Cairns, Townsville and Brisbane. One place you can't reach directly from overseas is Canberra, the national capital.

Although Sydney is the busiest gateway, it makes a lot of sense to avoid arriving or departing there. Sydney's airport is stretched way beyond its capacity and flights are frequently delayed on arrival and departure. Even if you can organise your flights to avoid Sydney, unfortunately many intercity flights (Melbourne in particular) still go via Sydney. If you're planning to explore the outback, then starting at a quieter entry port like Cairns or Darwin can make a lot of sense.

Discount Tickets

Buying airline tickets is like shopping for cars, stereos or cameras: five different travel agents will quote you five different prices. Rule number one if you're looking for a cheap ticket is to go to an agent, not directly to the airline. The airline can usually only offer the official regular fare. An agent, on the other hand, can offer all sorts of special deals, particularly on competitive routes.

Fortunately, airlines would rather have a half-price passenger than an empty seat. If they can't fill seats, they will either let agents sell them at cut prices or occasionally make one-off special offers on particular routes – watch the travel ads in the press.

Of course, what's available and what it costs depends on what time of year it is, what route you're flying and who you're flying with. If you're flying on a popular route (like from Hong Kong) or one where the choice of flights is very limited (like from South America or Africa), then the fare is likely to be higher or there may be nothing available but the official fare.

Similarly, the dirt-cheap fares are likely to be less conveniently scheduled, to go by a less convenient route or be with a less popular airline. Flying London-Sydney, for example, is most convenient with airlines like Qantas, British Airways, Thai International or Singapore Airlines. They have flights every day, operate the same flight straight through to Australia and are good, reliable, comfortable, safe airlines.

At the other extreme, you could fly from London to an Eastern European or Middle Eastern city on one flight, switch to another flight from there to Asia and change to another airline from there to Australia. It takes longer, there are delays and changes of aircraft along the way, the airlines may not be so good and furthermore, the connection only works once a week and means leaving London at 1.30 on a Wednesday morning. The flip side is it's cheaper.

Round-the-World Tickets

Round-the-World (RTW) tickets are very

popular and many of them will take you through Australia. The airline RTW tickets are often real bargains and, since Australia is pretty much at the other side of the world from Europe or North America, it can work out at the same price, or even cheaper, to keep going in the same direction around the world than to do a U-turn to return.

The official airline RTW tickets are usually put together by two airlines and permit you to fly anywhere on their route systems so long as you do not backtrack. Other restrictions are that you (usually) must book the first sector in advance and cancellation penalties then apply. There may be restrictions on how many stops you are permitted and usually the tickets are valid from 90 days up to a year. A typical price for a South Pacific RTW ticket is around £695 or US$1160.

An alternative type of RTW ticket is one put together by a travel agent using a combination of discounted tickets from a number of airlines. A UK agent like Trailfinders can put together interesting London-to-London RTW combinations including Australia for between £895 and £1099.

Circle Pacific Tickets

Circle Pacific tickets use different airlines to circle the Pacific – combining Australia, New Zealand, North America and Asia. Examples include Qantas/Northwest and Canadian Airlines International/Cathay Pacific. As with RTW tickets, there are advance purchase restrictions and limits to how many stopovers you can make. Typically, fares range between US$1780 and US$2330. Possible Circle Pacific routes are Los Angeles-Bangkok-Sydney-Auckland-Honolulu-Los Angeles or Los Angeles-Tokyo-Kuala Lumpur-Sydney-Auckland-Honolulu-Los Angeles.

To/From the UK

The cheapest tickets in London are from the numerous 'bucket shops' (discount ticket agencies) that advertise in magazines and papers like *Time Out*, *Southern Cross* and *TNT*. Pick up one or two of these publications and ring round a few bucket shops to find the best deal. The magazine *Business Traveller* also has good advice on air-fare bargains. Most bucket shops are trustworthy and reliable, but there's the occasional sharp operator – *Time Out* and *Business Traveller* give useful advice on precautions.

Trailfinders (☎ (0171) 938 3366) at 194 Kensington High St, London W8 and STA Travel (☎ (0171) 937 9962) at 86 Old Brompton Rd, London SW7, and 117 Euston Rd, London NW1 (☎ (0171) 465 0484), are good, reliable agents for cheap tickets.

The cheapest London to Sydney or Melbourne bucket-shop (not direct) tickets are about £375 one-way or £530 return. Cheap fares to Perth are around £340 one-way and £675 return. Such prices are usually only available if you leave London in the low season – March to June – which ties in well with the outback season. In September and mid-December, fares go up about 30% while the rest of the year they're somewhere in between. Average direct high-season fares to Sydney or Melbourne are £459 one-way, £879 return; to Perth, £439 one-way and £839 return.

Many cheap tickets allow stopovers on the way to/from Australia. Rules – such as how many stopovers you can take, how long you can stay away and how far in advance you have to decide your return date – vary from time to time and ticket to ticket. But recently, most return tickets have allowed you to stay away for any period between 14 days and one year, with stopovers permitted anywhere along your route.

From Australia, using a budget carrier such as Garuda, you can expect to pay from A$900 one-way and A$1400 return to London and other European capitals, with stops in Asia on the way. Prices increase by up to 30% in the European summer and at Christmas.

To/From North America

There is a variety of connections across the Pacific from Los Angeles, San Francisco and Vancouver, including direct flights, flights via New Zealand, island-hopping routes and more circuitous Pacific rim routes via Asia. Qantas, Air New Zealand and United all fly USA-Australia; Qantas, Air New Zealand and Canadian Airlines International fly Canada-Australia.

To find good fares to Australia, check the travel ads in the Sunday travel sections of papers like the *Los Angeles Times*, *San Francisco Chronicle-Examiner*, *New York Times* or *Toronto Globe & Mail*. You can usually get a one-way ticket from the west coast for US$876, or US$1190 from the east coast. At peak seasons – particularly the Australian summer/Christmas period – seats will be harder to get and the price probably higher.

In the USA, good agents for discounted tickets are the two student travel operators, Council Travel and STA Travel, both of which have many offices around the country. Canadian west-coast fares out of Vancouver start at C$1615. From Toronto, fares go from around C$1909 return.

If Pacific island-hopping is your aim, check out the airlines of Pacific Island nations. For example, Qantas can give you Fiji or Tahiti along the way, while Air New Zealand can offer both and the Cook Islands. See the Circle Pacific section for more details.

Low season one-way/return fares available from Australia include: San Francisco and Vancouver A$1150/1550; and New York A$1300/1800.

To/From New Zealand

Air New Zealand and Qantas operate a network of trans-Tasman flights linking Auckland, Wellington and Christchurch in New Zealand with most major Australian gateway cities. You can fly directly between many places in both New Zealand and Australia.

Fares vary, depending on the cities and the season, but from New Zealand to Sydney, you're looking at around NZ$390 one-way and NZ$510 return and to Melbourne, NZ$529 one-way and NZ$720 return. There is a lot of competition on this route, with United, British Airways, Qantas and Air

New Zealand flying it, so there is bound to be some good discounting.

Cheap fares to New Zealand from Europe will usually apply to flights via the USA. A straightforward London-Auckland return bucket-shop ticket costs around £615. Coming via Australia you can continue right around on a RTW ticket which, with a comprehensive choice of stopovers, will cost from around £695 to £895.

To/From Asia

Ticket discounting is widespread in Asia, particularly in Singapore, Hong Kong, Bangkok and Penang. There are a lot of fly-by-nights in the Asian ticketing scene so a little care is required. Also, the Asian routes have been particularly caught up in the capacity shortages on flights to Australia. Flights between Hong Kong and Australia are notoriously heavily booked, while flights to/from Bangkok and Singapore are often part of the longer Europe-Australia route and are also sometimes very full. Plan ahead.

Typical one-way fares to Australia from Singapore are S$894 to Darwin, S$375 to Perth and S$610 to Sydney or Melbourne.

You can also pick up some interesting tickets in Asia which include Australia on the way across the Pacific. Qantas and Air New Zealand offer discounted trans-Pacific tickets.

From Australia, low-season return fares from the east coast to Singapore, Kuala Lumpur and Bangkok range from A$600 to A$1000 and to Hong Kong from A$1100 to A$1300.

The cheapest way out of Australia is to take one of the flights operating between Darwin and Kupang (Timor, Indonesia). Currently one-way fares start at A$244 and return fares at A$396.

To/From Africa

There are a number of direct flights between Africa and Australia, but only between Perth and Harare (Zimbabwe) or Johannesburg (South Africa). Qantas, South African Airways and Air Zimbabwe fly this route.

Other airlines which connect southern

Africa and Australia include Malaysia Airlines (via Kuala Lumpur) and Air Mauritius (via Mauritius). Both have special deals from time to time.

From East Africa, you can fly via Mauritius or the Indian subcontinent and connect from there to Australia.

To/From South America

Three routes operate between South America and Australia. The Chile connection involves LanChile's Santiago-Easter Island-Tahiti twice-weekly flight, from where you fly Qantas or another airline to Australia. Another route skirts the Antarctic Circle, flying Buenos Aires-Auckland-Sydney, operated twice weekly by Aerolineas Argentinas in conjunction with Qantas. Then there's Malaysia Airlines, which has some good deals from Australia to Buenos Aires via Kuala Lumpur and Johannesburg.

ARRIVING & DEPARTING
Arriving in Australia

Australia's dramatic increase in visitor arrivals has caused some severe bottlenecks at the entry points, particularly at Sydney where the airport is often operating at more than full capacity and delays on arrival or departure are frequent. One answer to this problem is to make Brisbane, Cairns, Darwin or another gateway city your arrival point.

First-time travellers to Australia may be alarmed to find themselves being sprayed with insecticide by the airline stewards. It happens to everyone. Beware of the strict rules relating to the importation of plant and animal matter, including food.

Leaving Australia

The $27 departure tax is incorporated into the price of your air ticket and not paid as a separate tax.

WARNING

This chapter is particularly vulnerable to change – prices for international travel are volatile, routes are introduced and cancelled, schedules change, rules are amended, and special deals come and go. Airlines and governments seem to take a perverse pleasure in making price structures and regulations as complicated as possible and you should check directly with the airline or travel agent to make sure you understand how a fare (and ticket you may buy) works

In addition, the travel industry is highly competitive and there are many lurks and perks. The upshot of this is that you should get opinions, quotes and advice from as many airlines and travel agents as possible before you part with your hard-earned cash. The details given in this chapter should be regarded only as pointers and cannot be any substitute for your own careful, up-to-date research.

Getting Around

AIR

There are two major domestic carriers within Australia – Qantas (Australia's international carrier) and Ansett. Domestic airline travel is expensive and the choices of flights limited, particularly on the low-volume routes to places like Alice Springs and Darwin. However, deregulation in the 1980s has brought more discounting than in the past.

Note that all domestic flights in Australia are non-smoking. Because Qantas flies both international and domestic routes, its flights can leave from either the international or domestic terminals at Australian airports. Flights with flight numbers from QF001 to QF399 operate from international terminals and flight numbers QF400 and above from domestic terminals.

Cheap Fares

Random Discounting The airlines sometimes offer substantial discounts on selected routes. Although this seems to apply mainly to the heavy-volume routes, it's not always the case.

To make the most of the discounted fares, you need to keep in touch with what's currently on offer, mainly because there are usually conditions attached to cheap fares – such as booking 21 days in advance, only flying on weekends or between certain dates. Also, the number of seats available is usually fairly limited. The further you can plan ahead the better. Because the situation is so fluid, with special deals coming and going all the time, booking through a travel agent who knows what's on offer will usually get you a better fare than doing it yourself direct with the airline.

Some Possibilities If you're planning a return trip and have 21 days up your sleeve, you can save 50 to 55% by travelling Apex. You have to book and pay for your tickets 21 days in advance and you must stay away at least one Saturday night. Flight details can be changed with 21 days notice, but the tickets are non-refundable. If you book 14 days in advance, the saving is 40 to 45% off the full fare.

For one-way travel, if you can book five days in advance, the saving is 15 to 20%.

University or other higher education students under the age of 26 can get a 25% discount off the regular economy fare. An airline tertiary concession card (available from the airlines) is required for Australian students. Overseas students can use their International Student Identity Card.

All non-resident international travellers can get a 40% discount on internal Qantas flights simply by presenting their international ticket and passport (or good photocopies) when booking. It seems there is no limit to the number of domestic flights you can take, it doesn't matter which airline you fly into Australia with, and it doesn't have to be on a return ticket. However, the discount applies only to the full economy fare; in many cases it will be cheaper to take advantage of other discounts offered. The best advice is to ring around and explore the options before you buy.

There are also some cheaper deals with local and regional airlines (see Other Airline Options below). On some lesser routes these operators undercut the big two.

Another thing to keep your eyes open for is special deals at certain times of the year. January and early February, May and early June, and November and the first half of December are slack periods during which the airlines will try to lure passengers. Extra flights are put on for special events such as the Melbourne Cup horse race in early November and the Aussie Rules football Grand Final (also in Melbourne) at the end of September. These flights would normally be nearly empty when departing Melbourne, so special fares are offered to people wanting to leave Melbourne when everybody else wants to go there.

Air Passes

With discounting, air passes do not represent the value they did in pre-deregulation days, so much so that Qantas doesn't even offer them.

Ansett still has its Kangaroo Airpass, which gives you two options: 6000km with two or three stopovers for $949 ($729 for children) and 10,000km with three to seven stopovers for $1499 ($1149 for children). A number of restrictions apply, but the pass can be a good arrangement if you want to see a lot of country in a short period of time. You don't need to start and finish at the same place: you could start in Sydney and end in Darwin, for example. You must make at least one stopover of a minimum four nights in a non-capital city.

Other Airline Options

Kendell Airlines services country areas of Victoria, South Australia and Tasmania, as well as Broken Hill and Ayers Rock, and there are numerous other, smaller operators. See the track descriptions in this book for details.

Outback Air Tours

Scenic flights are available in small aircraft at the more popular outback destinations. Prices are very reasonable, sometimes including pick-up and drop-off from where you're staying, and the experience is unforgettable – nothing beats the sight of Ayers Rock or the Bungle Bungles from the air. See the track descriptions in this book for more information or contact the state or local tourist offices.

If you have money to burn, there are tour operators who will take you to the highlights of the outback in six-seater Piper Aztecs and larger aircraft, such as 10-seater Piper Chieftains. Itineraries range from four-day trips to the Flinders Ranges from around $1500 per person to two-week, six-state outback tours for $5000 to $6500. Accommodation is included and you may even have some input into the itinerary. The state tourist offices can provide details. Two operators who have been around for a while are: Aviatour (tel/ fax (03) 9589 4097), 524 Balcombe Rd, Beaumaris, Vic 3193; and Air Adventure Australia (☎ toll-free 1800 033 160; fax (03) 5572 5979), PO Box 339, Hamilton, Vic 3300.

Other Tour Options See the Mail Runs section later in this chapter for details on mail planes. At most outback airfields there will be someone who will take you flying, enabling them to get their hours on the board while you cover the costs. Just ask around.

Flying Yourself

If you are a pilot, flying yourself can be an interesting option and a fairly efficient way to cover large distances.

Many flying schools and clubs hire out planes for private use and are the best places to meet other pilots and find out about local flying conditions. They are listed in the Yellow Pages phone book or you can just go out to the local airport and ask around. Most capital cities have a separate suburban airport for general aviation, such as Bankstown airport in Sydney or Moorabbin in Melbourne.

Typical single-engine hire charges start at around $100 an hour for a Cessna 152, or $135 for a Cessna 172 or Piper Warrior. From there, they increase roughly in proportion to cruising speed. If you want a twin, a Seminole is about $240 an hour. Rates are usually 'wet VDO', ie engine hours inclusive of fuel and oil. You get a credit for any fuel you buy along the way, but only at the operator's local price, not what you paid for it. If you want to take the aircraft away overnight, the operator will probably expect a minimum average usage.

Flying Conditions Anyone planning to fly in Australia will need more information than can be covered in these general comments. Any flying school or hire company will have instructors who are qualified to explain local conditions and regulations. They will also brief you on current airspace rules, which are being reviewed to bring them into line with international standards.

Australia has a fairly low level of air traffic, especially compared with North America and Europe, mainly concentrated around a few cities and a couple of tourist areas. Elsewhere, the sky is pretty empty but unfortunately navigation facilities are equally sparse. Radar coverage is limited to regions around the major cities, with much of the country outside the range of VOR transmitters, so you have to rely on dead reckoning and the ADF for cross-country flying, especially in the outback, unless you are GPS-equipped.

Much of central Australia is classified as a 'Designated Remote Area' because of its inaccessibility or being beyond the range of VHF communications; flights here must carry a higher level of on-board equipment, such as HF radio or an ELB. Australia generally uses metric measurements but some imperial units are used in aviation for consistency with other countries. The result is a mixture, with altitudes in feet, winds and airspeeds in knots, long distances in nautical miles, short distances like runway lengths in metres and fuel in litres. Don't worry, it's not as confusing as it sounds.

Flight Planning Charts and other planning documents can be obtained from the Airservices Australia (ASA) Publications Centre in Melbourne (☎ (03) 9342 2000, toll-free 1800 331 676; fax 9347 4407) or from aviation supply shops at the larger general aviation airports.

Most large country towns have a local airport with sufficient facilities for regional commuter airlines. Many smaller towns offer a licensed aerodrome, even if it's only a gravel strip, a windsock and (with luck) a public phone. ASA's *En Route Supplement – Australia* (commonly known as *ERSA*) has details of all licensed aerodromes, including runway diagrams, navaids and fuel availability.

There are also a number of private and unlicensed aerodromes (some of them mentioned in *ERSA*) and, further down the scale, there are numerous private strips and landing areas. Prior permission to land at these is usually required from the owner of the plane and also from the landowner if it is private property.

Avgas is widely available but prior notice may be required in some places. The price varies from around 80c a litre in the cities, increasing with distance to almost double in remote outback towns. Expect to pay a call-out fee (typically $20) to refuel outside normal hours. As well, small suppliers (such as roadhouses) may expect you to purchase full 200L drums – you will be expected to pay for whatever you don't need from the last drum.

Licences Licensing and all other regulations are controlled by the Civil Aviation Safety Authority (CASA), which has regional offices at airports in most capital cities and larger regional centres. The head office (☎ (02) 6268 4114; fax 6268 4426) can be contacted at GPO Box 2005, Canberra, ACT 2601.

If you have a current foreign licence, CASA will issue a Certificate of Validation which allows you to fly for up to three months. It costs $55 and is available over the counter from any regional office. While no medical or flying tests are required for visual flying, you must undertake a flight review with a qualified instructor and be able to speak English.

For longer periods, a Special Pilot Licence is available for private operations for a fee of $50. Again there is no theory exam or flight test for VFR operations, but you do need a current overseas medical certificate and to have had a flight check within the previous two years. You can apply at any CASA regional office and the licence is mailed to you from Canberra.

With either method, if you have an instrument rating you will generally need to pass a written exam and flight test before flying IFR in Australia.

In addition to CASA's legal requirements, any company hiring you an aircraft will require a check flight with an instructor to get you familiar with local conditions.

Instructor rates are usually around $60 an hour on top of the normal hire cost.

Airport Transport

There are private or public bus services at major towns, but at smaller airports you may have to rely on taxis or friendly locals. If you've booked a motel or other accommodation, they might pick you up. Quite often, a taxi shared between three or more people can be cheaper than the bus.

BUS

Bus travel is generally the cheapest way from A to B, other than hitching of course. The bus networks are far more comprehensive than the rail system, though they tend to stick to the main, sealed highways. The buses all look pretty similar and are similarly equipped with air-conditioning, toilets and videos. See the track descriptions later in this book for specific bus services.

There is only one truly *national* bus network: Greyhound Pioneer Australia.

McCafferty's, operating out of Brisbane, is probably the next biggest, with services all along the east coast as well as the loop through the Centre to Adelaide, Alice Springs and Darwin to Townsville.

There are many smaller bus companies operating locally or specialising in one or two main intercity routes. They often have the best deals. In South Australia, Stateliner operates around the state, including trips to the Flinders Ranges. Westrail in Western Australia operates bus services to places the trains no longer go.

Bus Passes

Greyhound Pioneer Australia has a variety of passes, so it's a matter of deciding which suits your needs.

Set-Distance Version The Greyhound Getaway Pass is probably the most flexible as it gives you 12 months to cover the distance you select along any of the Greyhound Pioneer routes. The main advantage of these passes is that they give you the flexibility to put your own itinerary together. Getaway

Passes are valid for 12 months and can be used on any Greyhound Pioneer service. The passes are issued in multiples of 1000km (minimum 2000km, no maximum) and the cost is $176 for 2000km, $311 for 4000km, $784 for 10,000km, $1344 for 20,000km.

Many travellers find that to make proper use of the passes, they have to travel faster than they would wish. This particularly seems to apply to people who buy their passes before they arrive in Australia.

Set-Route Version Another option is the set-route Aussie Explorer Pass, which gives you six or 12 months to cover a set route. You don't have the go-anywhere flexibility of the set-km bus pass, but if you can find a set route which suits you – and there are 20 to choose from – then it generally works out cheaper than the set-km pass.

The main limitation with this kind of pass is that you can't backtrack, except on 'dead-end' short sectors such as Darwin to Kakadu, Townsville to Cairns and Ayers Rock to the Stuart Highway.

Aussie Highlights allows you to loop around the eastern half of Australia from Sydney, taking in Melbourne, Adelaide, Coober Pedy, Ayers Rock, Kings Canyon, Alice Springs, Darwin (and Kakadu), Cairns, Townsville, the Whitsundays, Brisbane and Surfers Paradise for $840.

There's also an All Australia pass which takes you right around the country, including up or down through the Centre, for $1420.

Set-Duration Version The set-duration pass is known as the Aussie Pass. It allows travel on a set number of days during a specified period. There are no restrictions on where you can travel. The passes range from $475 for seven days of travel in one month to $935 for 21 days of travel in two months. It's hard to see what advantages these passes have over the others already mentioned.

TRAIN

Before Australia became independent, it was governed as six separate colonies, all administered from London. When the colony of

Victoria, for example, wanted to build a railway line it checked not with the adjoining colony of New South Wales but with the colonial office in London. When the colonies were federated in 1901 and Australia became a nation, by a sheer masterpiece of misplanning not one state had railway lines of the same gauge as a neighbouring state! The immense misfortune of this inept planning has dogged the railway system ever since.

In 1970, a standard-gauge rail link was completed between Sydney and Perth and the very popular *Indian-Pacific* run was brought into operation. The old *Ghan* railway line between Adelaide and Alice Springs was only replaced by a new standard-gauge line in 1982. See below for more details about these famous trains.

Apart from different gauges there's also the problem of different operators – although none of this affects passengers travelling between the major cities. The individual states run their own services and in certain cases (for example, Sydney to Brisbane) combine for interstate services. Australian National Railways operates the *Ghan*, the *Indian-Pacific* and the *Overlander* between Adelaide and Melbourne.

Train travel in Australia today is something you do because you really want to – not because it's cheaper (especially now with cheap bus and reduced air fares) and certainly not because it's fast. The train is generally the slowest way to get from anywhere to anywhere. On the other hand, the trains are comfortable and you see Australia at ground level in a way you wouldn't be able to otherwise.

Rail Passes

There are many passes which allow unlimited rail travel either across the country or just in one state. With the Austrail Pass you can travel anywhere on the Australian rail network, in either 1st class or economy seats. The cost is $780/460 in 1st/economy class for 14 days, $985/595 for 21 days and $1270/720 for 30 days.

The Austrail Flexipass differs in that it allows a set number of travelling days within a specified period. While this pass offers greater flexibility, it cannot be used for travel between Adelaide and Perth or Alice Springs. The cost is $650/380 in 1st class/economy for eight days of travel in 60 days, or $915/550 for 15 days' travel in 180 days.

Surcharges are payable on sleeping berths in both classes and on certain trains, such as the *Ghan* and the *Indian-Pacific*, there are compulsory meal charges on 1st class.

For travel within a limited area, the passes that just cover one state may be more suitable. They are available for Victoria, Queensland and Western Australia. They can be purchased at major train stations and from travel agents. For details of passes and conditions, contact Rail Australia on ☎ (08) 8217 4321.

As the railway booking system is computerised, any station (other than on metropolitan lines) can make a booking for any journey throughout the country. For reservations, contact ☎ 13 2232 during office hours; this will connect you to the nearest mainline station.

The Ghan

The *Ghan* saga started in 1877 when authorities decided to build a railway line from Adelaide to Darwin. The railhead reached Marree in 1883, Oodnadatta in 1889 and Alice Springs in 1929. They're still thinking about the final 1500km to Darwin.

By the early 1970s, the South Australian state railway system was taken over by the federal government and a new line to Alice Springs was planned. This opened in 1982, with the old line then torn up. While the old *Ghan* took 140 passengers and, under ideal conditions, made the trip in 50 hours, the new *Ghan* takes twice as many passengers and does it in less than half the time. It's still the *Ghan*, but not the trip it once was.

For more on the history of the old *Ghan* see the Oodnadatta Track section of the Central Deserts chapter.

Fares The *Ghan* costs $144 in coach class (no sleeper or meals); holiday class gives you a sleeper with shared facilities and no meals for $325 ($291 low season); 1st class costs $500 ($450), which includes meals and a self-contained sleeper. Check the availability of promotional or discount fares.

The train departs from Adelaide on Thursday at 2 pm, arriving in Alice Springs the next morning at 9.55 am. It departs from Alice Springs on Friday at 2 pm, arriving in Adelaide the next day at 10.30 am. From April to October, there's a second departure from Adelaide on Monday and Alice Springs on Tuesday, both at 2 pm. You can also join at Port Augusta, the connecting point on the Sydney-Perth route. Fares between Alice Springs and Port Augusta are $116 coach, $293 ($263 low season) holiday and $464 ($416) 1st class.

You can transport cars between Alice Springs and Adelaide for $195. Double-check the times you need to have your car at the terminal for loading: it must be there at least two hours prior to departure. Be prepared for a wait at the Adelaide end, as unloading can take an hour or more.

Bookings can be made from anywhere in Australia by phoning ☎ 13 2232 during business hours.

The Indian-Pacific

Along with the *Ghan*, the *Indian-Pacific* run is one of Australia's great train journeys: a 65-hour trip between the Pacific Ocean on one side of the continent and the Indian Ocean on the other. Travelling this way, you really appreciate the immensity of the country (or, alternatively, are bored stiff).

From Sydney, you cross New South Wales to Broken Hill and then continue on to Adelaide and across the Nullarbor. From Port Augusta to Kalgoorlie, the seemingly endless crossing of the virtually uninhabited centre takes well over 24 hours, including the longest straight stretch of railway line in the world (478km).

History The promise of a transcontinental railway link helped to lure gold-rich Western Australia into the Commonwealth in 1901. Port Augusta in South Australia and Kalgoorlie in Western Australia were the existing state railheads in 1907, when surveyors were sent out to map a line between the two. In 1911, the Commonwealth legislated to fund north-south (*Ghan*) and east-west (*Indian-Pacific*) routes across the continent.

The first sod was turned in Port Augusta in 1912 and, for five years, two self-contained gangs, a total of 3000 workers, inched towards each other. They endured sandstorms, swarms of flies and intense heat as they laid 2.5 million sleepers and 140,000 tonnes of rail. The soil and rock was removed with pick and shovel and the workers were supplied by packhorse and camel. The job was completed with a minimum of mechanical aids, one of the few machines being the Roberts track-layer.

As Australia was embroiled in WWI, there was no great opening celebration when the track gangs met in the sand hills near Ooldea. The first Transcontinental Express pulled out of Port Augusta at 9.32 pm on 22 October 1917, heralding the start of 'the desert railway from Hell to Hallelujah'. It arrived in Kalgoorlie 42 hours 48 minutes later after covering 1682km.

The participants in the struggle to get the railway started are reflected in the names of the stations along the straight stretch: Forrest, Deakin, Hughes, Cook, Fisher, O'Malley and Barton; Bates commemorates Daisy Bates, who devoted herself to the welfare of Aborigines and for a time lived alongside the line near Ooldea; Denman was the governor-general who turned the first sod in 1917.

A good read is Patsy Adam Smith's *The Desert Railway*, which has many photographs of the building of the line. The line's history is covered exhaustively in *Road through the Wilderness* by David Burke.

Fares To Perth, one-way fares from Adelaide are $468 ($420 low season) for an economy sleeper, $722 ($652) for a 1st-class sleeper or $220 in an economy seat with no meals. From Sydney, they're $727 ($653) economy, $1116 ($1010) 1st class or $360 seat only. Ask about promotional and discount fares.

Melbourne passengers from the *Overlander* connect with the *Indian-Pacific* at Adelaide. Cars can be transported between Adelaide and Perth for $290, a good option for those not wishing to drive the Nullarbor in both directions.

The distance from Sydney to Perth is 3961km. You can break your journey at any stop along the way and continue later, as long as you complete the one-way trip within two months; return tickets are valid for up to nine months. Westbound, the *Indian-Pacific* departs Sydney on Thursday and Monday. Heading east, the train departs Perth on Thursday and Sunday. Book at least a month in advance.

The main difference between economy and 1st-class sleepers is that 1st-class compartments are available as singles or twins, economy as twins only. First-class twins have showers and toilets; 1st-class singles have toilets only, with showers at the end of the carriage. In the economy-seating compartments, the showers and toilets are at the end of the carriage. Meals are included in the fare for 1st-class only; economy-berth and economy-seat passengers have the option of purchasing meals from the restaurant car. First-class passengers also have a lounge compartment with piano.

Reservations are made with Australian National in Adelaide and Port Augusta, both on ☎ 13 2232.

TRAVEL PERMITS

If you wish to travel through the outback on your own, you may need special permits to pass through or visit Aboriginal land or to camp in conservation areas.

Aboriginal Lands

A glance at any up-to-date land-tenure map of Australia shows that vast portions of the north, centre and south are Aboriginal land. Generally, the land has either government-administered reserve status or may be held under freehold title vested in an Aboriginal land trust and managed by a council or cor-

poration. With either format, the laws of trespass apply just as with any other form of private land, but the fines attached can be somewhat heftier.

In some cases, permits won't be necessary if you stay on recognised public roads that cross Aboriginal territory. However, as soon as you leave the main road by more than 50m, even if you're 'only' going into an Aboriginal settlement for fuel, you may need a permit. If you're on an organised tour, the operator should take care of any permits – check before you book.

Applications To make an application, write to the appropriate land council or government department, as outlined below, enclosing a stamped, self-addressed envelope and giving all details of your proposed visit or transit. In general, the following information is required: the names of all members of the party; details of all vehicles (colour, make, model and registration number); the dates of travel; route details; purpose of the visit; and contact address and telephone number.

Allow plenty of time: the application process may take one or two months as the administering body generally must obtain approval from the relevant community councils before issuing your permit. Keep in mind that your application may be knocked back for a number of reasons, including the risk of interference with sacred sites or disruption of ceremonial business. As well, some communities simply may not want to be bothered by visitors.

Specific permit requirements are explained in the track descriptions in this book. However, the general requirements are as follows:

Western Australia The Aboriginal Affairs Department is responsible for all Aboriginal land. People wishing to travel on these lands, including transit on the Giles-Laverton road, should write to the Permits Officer (☎ (08) 9235 8000; fax 9235 8033) at PO Box 7770, Cloisters Square, Perth, WA 6850.

South Australia Outside the Woomera Prohibited Area, virtually the entire region bordered by the Transcontinental Railway, the Stuart Highway and the Northern Territory and Western Australia borders is Aboriginal-owned. The northern portion of this region is taken up by the Anangu-Pitjantjatjara Lands, while to the south are the Maralinga-Tjarutja Lands. The two are separated on the map by a line drawn east-west through Mt Willoughby on the Stuart Highway, about 230km south of the Northern Territory border.

For a permit to visit the Anangu-Pitjantjatjara Lands, contact the Permits Officer (☎ (08) 8950 1511; fax 8950 1510) at the AP office in Umuwa. You can also take a look at this area and meet the people on a guided tour with Yulara-based Desert Tracks. For information on Desert Tracks, see the Organised Tours section later in this chapter.

Permits to visit the Maralinga-Tjarutja Lands, which include access to the Unnamed Conservation Park and tracks in the Emu Junction area, can be obtained from the Administration Officer, Maralinga-Tjarutja Inc (☎ (08) 8625 2946; fax 8625 3076) at PO Box 435, Ceduna, SA 5435.

Northern Territory The Central Land Council administers all Aboriginal land in the southern and central regions of the Territory. Write to the Permits Officer (☎ (08) 8951 6320/6321; fax 8953 4345) at PO Box 3321, Alice Springs, NT 0871.

Arnhem Land and other northern mainland areas are administered by the Northern Land Council in Darwin. Write to the Permits Officer (☎ (08) 8920 5178; fax 8945 2633) at PO Box 42921, Casuarina, NT 0811.

Queensland There is no formal permit system for entry onto Aboriginal land in Queensland. Instead, you obtain permission directly from the community, as you would with most other land-holders. Addresses and telephone numbers for the various community councils can be obtained from the Aboriginal Coordinating Council (☎ (07) 4031 2623) at PO Box 6512, Cairns Mail Centre, Qld 4870.

National Parks

You usually need a permit to camp in, or sometimes even to visit, a national park and permits may have to be obtained in advance. Details of required permits are provided in the individual track descriptions in this book. If you're spending a lot of time in a particular state's national park, it pays to check if there's an annual pass system in operation, what it covers and how many parks it is valid for. It could save you money.

Desert Parks Pass To visit the parks and regional reserves in the north of South Australia, you must have what is called a Desert Parks Pass. These areas include the Simpson Desert Conservation Park, the Simpson Desert Regional Reserve, Witjira National Park, Innamincka Regional Reserve and Lake Eyre National Park. The pass allows you to visit and camp in these parks and also provides an information package on natural and social history and travel, including useful maps.

The pass costs $60 ($40 renewal) per vehicle and while that may sound expensive, it's good value if you're touring the region and planning on spending a few nights in its parks and reserves. Special passes ($15) are available for single-night stops at Dalhousie Springs, Lake Eyre and Innamincka.

The pass is available from a number of outlets in northern South Australia, as well as good map shops Australia-wide. The desert parks headquarters is in the Department of Environment & Natural Resources regional office at 9 Mackay St, Port Augusta (PO Box 78, Port Augusta 5710; ☎ (08) 8648 5300).

Alternatively, if you're visiting other regions of South Australia as well as the outback, you can obtain an Annual Statewide Pass. This incorporates the Desert Parks Pass for a cost of $140 per vehicle, $70 per motor cycle and reduced costs for pensioners. Ring the department's Port Augusta office on ☎ toll-free 1800 816 078 for more information on both passes.

CAR

Public transport is almost non-existent in most parts of the outback and for this reason alone, having your own transport is the way to go. Buying or hiring a car need not cost a fortune if there are three or four of you and, provided you don't have a major mechanical problem, the benefits are great.

Inexperienced drivers conquer some of the most difficult tracks in unsuitable vehicles, but they just happen to do so under perfect conditions and have more than their fair share of luck (or help from passers-by). Other keen souls never make it and some even perish. Everyone needs a bit of luck now and then; just be aware that your life is at stake if your luck runs out. There's simply no substitute for careful planning.

Road Rules

Driving in Australia holds few real surprises. Australians drive on the left-hand side of the road just like in the UK, Japan and most countries in south and east Asia and the Pacific. There are, however, a few basic rules to keep in mind.

The main one is 'give way to the right'. This means that if you're driving along a road and somebody appears on your right, you may have to give way to them – unless they are facing a give-way or stop sign, or are coming out of a driveway. At uncontrolled intersections, traffic on major roads generally has right of way over that on minor ones. Road rules vary from state to state, but attempts are being made to standardise them. Get hold of a copy from any police station and study them.

The general speed limit in built-up areas in Australia is 60km/h and out on the open highway it's usually 100 or 110km/h depending on where you are. In the Northern Territory there is no speed limit outside of built-up areas, although you might still be booked for driving at a 'speed inappropriate to the prevailing conditions' (for instance 160km/h at dawn/dusk/night). The police have radar speed traps and speed cameras, tending to use them from concealed locations. Oncoming drivers who flash their lights may be giving you a friendly indication of a speed trap ahead.

The wearing of seat belts is compulsory. All new cars in Australia are required to have seat belts back and front and if your seat has a belt, then you're required to wear it. You're liable to be fined if you don't. Small children must be belted into an approved safety seat.

The average Aussie considers driving a right rather than a privilege and because there's no compulsory driver training as such (merely a 'Learner Period'), driving standards aren't exactly the highest in the world. Drink-driving is a real problem too, especially in country areas. Serious attempts have been made in recent years to reduce the road toll – random breath tests are not uncommon in built-up areas. If you're caught with a blood-alcohol concentration of more than 0.05%, be prepared for a court appearance and the loss of your licence.

On the Road

You can drive all the way round Australia on Highway 1 or through the middle from Adelaide to Darwin on 'the bitumen'. But you don't have to get very far off the beaten track to find yourself on dirt roads.

If you've ever travelled on unsealed roads in Africa or South America, you'll be pleasantly surprised by their counterparts in the outback. The major roads are graded fairly regularly, although heavy road trains can cause the surface to break up rather quickly. You may not even need a four-wheel-drive (4WD) vehicle – a well-prepared, conventional 2WD car with sufficient ground clearance is usually quite suitable on the more established unsealed routes. The individual track descriptions in this book give an indication of the type of vehicle required.

Signposting on the main roads between cities is quite OK and on the more important outback tracks, you'll usually find signposts where they matter. Be careful, though, as what matters to you may not matter to an outback road crew and a missed turn-off can have serious consequences. This is all the more reason to keep a running log when travelling in the outback (see Survival in the

Facts for the Visitor chapter) and to have good maps.

Cattle, sheep and kangaroos are common hazards on outback roads at night; a collision is likely to kill the animal and seriously damage your vehicle. Kangaroos tend to seek shade during the day but are active at night, especially at dawn and dusk when they often come to feed along the road verges – there's usually more feed there because the drains act as traps for even light showers falling on the bitumen. The roos move in groups, so if you see one hopping across the road in front of you, slow right down – its friends are probably close behind. If one hops out right in front of you, hit the brakes and only swerve to avoid the animal if it is safe to do so. Each year, numerous people are killed or injured in accidents caused by swerving to miss an animal. For this reason, it's recommended that you avoid travelling altogether between 5 pm and 8 am on outback roads.

Cattle grids take the place of gates on most major unsealed routes and these should be approached with care. Often there are potholes beside the grids, or they might be raised above the road level. Others may be on top of sharp humps which will cause your vehicle to 'take off' if you hit them at speed.

Another hazard that's not so obvious is driver fatigue. Driving long distances (particularly in hot weather) can be so tiring that you might fall asleep at the wheel. Not only that, people can become so mesmerised by the road stretching endlessly ahead that they forget to turn the next corner! The best approach on a long haul is to stop and rest every two hours – do some exercise, change drivers or have a coffee.

The bitumen (asphalt, tar) on some outback roads is only wide enough for one vehicle, which begs the question: what to do when someone comes towards you. First of all, slow down. It's common to move the left half of the vehicle off the edge and expect the oncoming vehicle to do the same. Wrong, because this gives either party the worst of both worlds. Outback residents usually wait and see what the other vehicle does: if it

moves off the edge, they'll stay on the bitumen and risk a broken windscreen from flying gravel; if it stays on the bitumen, they'll move off the edge and wear out their suspension and tyres. Everyone moves aside for an oncoming truck or road train.

Finally, if an oncoming vehicle throws up so much dust that you can't see the road ahead, slow down (and turn on the lights) or stop. *Don't* pass in dust clouds.

Accidents

Generally speaking, if you have an accident with livestock on an outback road, it'll be you that's considered at fault, not the owner of the animal you've collided with. You'll be expected to pay for the repair/replacement of gates, fencing and other property that you may damage with your vehicle. This makes third-party property insurance a good idea even if you are driving a bucket of bolts.

The best approach after you've had an accident of any sort involving property damage (including to your vehicle) is to inform the police as soon as possible – your vehicle insurance policy will probably require you to do this, anyway.

Fuel

Service stations generally stock diesel, super and unleaded, although the more remote ones may not stock unleaded. Liquid petroleum gas (LPG, Autogas) is frequently unavailable, even at larger service stations along the main sealed roads (check current availability with the state's automobile association). Prices vary from place to place and from price war to price war, but generally they're in the 85c to 95c-per-litre range and $1 a litre is not uncommon (diesel sometimes costs a few cents more and LPG significantly less). In the remote outback, the price can soar and some service stations are not above exploiting their monopoly position (then again, their costs are high too).

Distances between fill-ups can be long, and in some really remote areas deliveries can be haphazard – it's not unknown to finally arrive at that 'nearest station x hundred km' only to find there's no fuel until next week's delivery! Ring ahead if you want to be sure.

The track descriptions in this book will give an indication of the required fuel ranges. There are a few tracks where your vehicle will need a long-range fuel tank, but on many others you'll be able to scrape by on your vehicle's standard tank with, say, one or two 20L jerry cans as backup.

Popular Tracks

There are many tracks to choose from, and this book describes most of them. To help you narrow down your choice, here are a few of the more popular ones:

Birdsville Track Running 517km from Marree in South Australia to Birdsville just across the border in Queensland, this is one of the best-known routes in Australia and these days is quite feasible in a well-prepared conventional vehicle.

Strzelecki Track This track covers much the same territory, starting south of Marree at Lyndhurst and going to Innamincka, 460km north-east and close to the Queensland border. From there you can loop down to Tibooburra in New South Wales. The route has been much improved due to work on the Moomba gas fields. It was at Innamincka that the hapless Burke and Wills died.

Oodnadatta Track This runs parallel to the old *Ghan* railway line to Alice Springs. It's 429km from Marree to Oodnadatta and another 216km from there to the Stuart Highway at Marla. There are many historical sites and it's worth taking your time to see them. So long as there's no rain, any well-prepared vehicle should be able to manage this route.

Simpson Desert Crossing the Simpson Desert from the Stuart Highway to Birdsville is becoming increasingly popular but this route is still a real test. Four-wheel drive is definitely required and you should be in a party of at least three or four vehicles equipped with HF radios. There are several routes: the French Line or a couple of easier but longer alternatives. Silence and space are the main attractions.

Warburton Road/Gunbarrel Highway This route runs west from Ayers Rock via the Aboriginal settlements of Docker River and Warburton to Laverton in Western Australia. From there you can drive down to Kalgoorlie and on to Perth. A well-prepared conventional vehicle can complete this remote route through the typical red desert landscape of central

Australia, although there are a few sandy sections and ground clearance can be a problem. For 300km near the Giles Meteorological Station, the Warburton Road and the Gunbarrel Highway run on the same route. Taking the old Gunbarrel north past Warburton all the way to Wiluna in Western Australia is a much rougher trip requiring 4WD. The Warburton Road is now commonly but incorrectly referred to as the Gunbarrel – just to make life simple.

Tanami Track Turning off the Stuart Highway just north of Alice Springs, the Tanami Track goes north-west across the Tanami Desert to Halls Creek in Western Australia. It's a popular short-cut for people travelling between the Centre and the Kimberley. The road has been extensively improved in recent years to the WA border and conventional vehicles are quite OK, although there are occasional sandy stretches on the WA section. Be warned that the Rabbit Flat roadhouse in the middle of the desert is only open from Friday to Monday.

Canning Stock Route This old stock trail runs south-west from Halls Creek to Wiluna in Western Australia and is one of the country's great 4WD adventures. It crosses the Great Sandy and Gibson deserts and since the track has not been maintained for over 30 years, it's a route to be taken seriously. Like the Simpson Desert crossing, you should only travel in a well-equipped party, and careful navigation is required.

Plenty & Sandover Highways These two remote routes run east from the Stuart Highway north of Alice Springs to Boulia or Mount Isa in Queensland. Though often rough, they provide a significantly shorter alternative to the sealed Barkly Highway heading east above Tennant Creek and are usually suitable for robust conventional vehicles.

Cape York The Peninsula Development Road up to the tip of Cape York, the northernmost point in mainland Australia, is a popular route through a unique part of the country. There are a many rivers to cross and the track can only be attempted in the dry season, when the water levels are low. The original Cape York Track along the old telegraph line definitely requires 4WD. Conventional vehicles can take the new 'Heathlands' road to the east beyond the Wenlock River, which bypasses the most difficult sections, but the Wenlock itself can be a formidable obstacle that often blocks conventional vehicles even at the driest time of year.

Gibb River Road This is the 'short cut' between Derby and Kununurra, running through the heart of the spectacular Kimberley in northern Western Australia. Although very rough and badly corrugated in places, it can sometimes be negotiated by conventional vehicles in the dry season.

Buying a Car

Australian cars are not cheap to buy. Locally manufactured cars are made in small, uneconomical numbers and imported cars are heavily taxed so they won't undercut the local products. If you're buying a second-hand vehicle, reliability is all important. Mechanical breakdowns in the outback can be dangerous and at least very inconvenient – the nearest mechanic can be a hell of a long way down the road.

Shopping around for a used car involves much the same rules as anywhere in the western world. For any given car, you'll probably get it cheaper by buying privately through newspaper private ads or youth-hostel notice boards than through a car dealer. Buying through a dealer does give the advantage of some sort of warranty, but a warranty is not much use if you buy a car in Sydney and set off for Perth via the outback. Used-car warranty requirements vary from state to state – check with the local automobile organisation.

You also need to stop and think about what sort of vehicle will suit your trip. While many of the routes mentioned in this book are suitable for conventional vehicles, others are recommended 4WD only. This doesn't mean that any 4WD will do. The smaller, more car-like 4WDs such as Mitsubishi L300s and Subarus are better for rough dirt roads than the average conventional vehicle, but their low ground clearance and high gearing make them unsuitable for rocky going and heavy sand. Suzuki Sierras will go anywhere, but on a long trip their lack of cargo space can be a telling deficiency.

Another important consideration when choosing a particular make and model is the availability of spares. When your fancy German car goes kaput somewhere back of Bourke, it's likely to be a long wait until the new bit arrives fresh from Stuttgart. In the 4WD category, Toyotas and Nissans are a dime a dozen and there's usually a local mechanic who knows how they work. Old Toyota Landcruisers, in particular, are common outback workhorses and easier to repair than the newer models. Not so

common in the backblocks are Land Rovers, Mitsubishi Pajeros, Holden Jackaroos and the like, although parts are generally available in major towns.

The further you get from civilisation in a 2WD vehicle, however, the better it is to be in a Holden or Ford. New cars can be a whole different ball game of course, but if you're in an older vehicle, something that's likely to have the odd hiccup from time to time, then life is much simpler if it's a car for which you can get spare parts anywhere from Bourke to Bulamakanka. When your rusty old Holden goes bang, there's probably another old Holden sitting in a ditch with a perfectly good widget waiting to be removed. Every scrap yard in Australia is full of good ole Holdens and Ford Falcons.

Expect to pay $1000 to $3500 for an old Holden or Ford and $3000 to $10,000 for an old 4WD. Obviously the closer you get to the lower figures, the more you need to know about cars and how to fix them. For a 4WD, about $18,000 should get you something reasonably new (five years old) and reliable enough to take you to remote areas.

Depending on which state you're in, registration can cost $250 to $400 a year for a conventional car and $350 to $800 for a 4WD, so it's really worth checking how much registration is still left when you buy second-hand. Note that third-party personal injury insurance is included in the registration cost. This ensures that every vehicle (as long as it's currently registered) carries insurance for hospital expenses inflicted on other road users. But you're wise to extend that minimum to at least third-party property insurance as well – minor collisions with Rolls Royces can be amazingly expensive.

When you come to buy or sell a car there are usually some local regulations to be complied with. In Victoria, for example, a car has to have a compulsory safety check (Road Worthiness Certificate – RWC) before it can be registered in the new owner's name – usually the seller will indicate if the car already has an RWC. In New South Wales and the Northern Territory, on the other hand, safety checks are compulsory every year when you come to renew the registration. Stamp duty has to be paid when you buy a car and, as this is based on the purchase price, it's not unknown for buyer and seller to agree privately to understate the price. It's much easier to sell a car in the same state in which it's registered, otherwise it has to be re-registered in the new state and the authorities may want to take a closer look.

Finally, make use of the automobile organisations – see the Facts for the Visitor chapter for details. They can advise on local regulations you should be aware of, give general guidelines about buying a car and, most importantly, for a fee (around $70) will check a used car and report on its condition before you agree to purchase it. They also offer car insurance to their members.

Buy-Back Schemes One way of getting around the hassles of buying and selling privately is to enter into a buy-back arrangement with a dealer. The main advantage of these schemes is that you don't have to worry about selling the vehicle quickly at the end of your trip. The dealer can usually arrange insurance, which short-term visitors may find hard to get. However, the cars on offer may have been driven around Australia a number of times, often with haphazard or minimal servicing, and are generally pretty tired. As well, dealers will often find ways of knocking down the price when you return the vehicle, even if a price has been agreed in writing – they may point out expensive repairs that allegedly will be required to pass the dreaded safety check.

A company that specialises in buy-back arrangements on cars and motorcycles, with fixed rates, is Car Connection Australia. Also known as Bike Tours Australia, it has been organising motorcycle adventure holidays in the outback for over 10 years and has recently branched into this sideline. Its programme is basically a glorified long-term rental arrangement, where you put down a deposit to the value of the vehicle and in the end get your money back, minus the fixed 'usage' fee.

The bottom line is that a second-hand Ford station wagon or Yamaha XT600 trail bike will cost you a fixed sum of $1950 for any period up to six months; a Toyota Troopcarrier, suitable for serious outback exploration, is $3500, also for up to six months. If you want a more upmarket Toyota HJ60 Landcruiser, the fee is $4500 and you'll be expected to pay a bond of $3000 on collection of the vehicle. Prices include a limited 5000km warranty on engine and gearbox. The company will pick you up at Melbourne airport, throw in a night's accommodation in Castlemaine (Victoria) to help you acclimatise and send you on your way with touring maps and advice. You can also rent camping equipment (no sleeping bags). For information and bookings contact Car Connection Australia (☎ (03) 5473 4469; fax 5473 4520) at RSD Lot 8, Vaughan Springs Rd, Glenluce (near Castlemaine), Vic 3451. Its European branch Travel Action GmbH can be contacted on ☎ (49-2764) 7824; fax 7938, Einsiedeleiweg 16, 57399 Kirchhundem, Germany.

Renting a Car

If you have the cash, there are plenty of car-rental companies ready and willing to put you behind the wheel. The track and city descriptions in this book provide further details.

Competition in Australia is pretty fierce so rates tend to be variable and lots of special deals pop up and disappear again. Whatever your mode of travel on the long stretches, it can be very useful to have a car for some local travel. Between a group it can even be reasonably economical. In the outback, there's seldom any public transport and the distances are too great for walking or even cycling.

The three major companies are Budget, Hertz and Avis, with offices in most of the outback's larger towns. The second-string companies that are also well represented are Thrifty and National. Then there is a vast number of local firms or firms with outlets in a limited number of locations. The big operators will generally have higher rates than the local firms but not always, so don't jump to conclusions. In many cases, local companies are markedly cheaper than the big boys but in others, what looks like a cheaper rate can end up quite the opposite if you're not careful.

One advantage with the big operators is that they're more amenable to one-way rentals – pick up a car in Adelaide and leave it in Sydney, for example. There are, however, a variety of restrictions on these. Usually it's a minimum-hire period rather than repositioning charges and only certain cars may be eligible for one-ways. Check the small print before deciding on one company rather than another. One-way rentals are generally not available into or out of the Northern Territory or Western Australia, and special rules may also apply to one-ways into or out of other 'remote areas'.

The major companies offer unlimited km rates in the city but in country and 'remote' areas, it's a flat charge plus so many cents a km. On straightforward city rentals they're all pretty much the same price. It's on special deals, odd rentals or longer periods that you find the differences. Weekend specials – usually three days for the price of two – can be good value. If you just need a car for three days around Alice Springs, make it the weekend rather than midweek. 'Stand-by' rates and other special deals are also worth investigating.

Daily rates are typically about $70 for a small car (Ford Laser, Toyota Corolla, Nissan Pulsar), about $90 for a medium car (Holden Camira, Toyota Camry, Nissan Pintara) or about $100 to $110 for a big car (Holden Commodore, Ford Falcon), all including insurance. See the following section for 4WD rentals.

There's a collection of other factors with this rent-a-car business. For a start, if you're going to want it for a week, a month or longer, then they all have lower rates. If you're in the really remote outback (Darwin and Alice Springs are only vaguely remote), then the choice of cars is likely to be limited to the larger, more expensive ones. You must be at least 21 to hire from most firms.

And don't forget the 'rent-a-wreck' companies. They specialise in renting older cars – at first they really were old and a flat rate like '$10 a day and forget the insurance' was the usual story. Now many of them have a variety of rates, typically around $35 a day. If you don't want to travel too far out, they can be worth considering.

Many car-rental companies, including some of those renting 4WDs, have serious misgivings about their cars being taken onto dirt roads. A well-maintained dirt road leading to a major tourist site is usually not a problem but if you engage in more serious stuff, you may well find that you're breaking the rental terms in the small print. Cairns rental agencies, for instance, often forbid you taking their vehicles up to Cape Tribulation and they have been known to check with paid informers. Tell the rental company about your plans before signing the agreement; if you let sleeping dogs lie, you could well find yourself in serious financial trouble if something goes wrong.

4WD Rentals Renting a 4WD vehicle is within the budget range if a few people get together. Something small like a Suzuki Sierra costs around $100 a day; for a Toyota Landcruiser you're looking at around $160, which should include insurance and some free km (typically 100km). Check the insurance conditions, especially the excess, as they can be onerous.

Hertz has 4WD rentals, with one way rentals possible between the eastern states and the Northern Territory. Budget also rents 4WD vehicles from Darwin and Alice Springs. Brits: Australia (☎ toll-free 1800 331 454) rents 4WD vehicles fitted out as camper vans. These cost from $150 a day with unlimited km, plus collision damage waiver ($20 a day). Brits has offices in all the mainland capitals, as well as Cairns and Alice Springs, so one-way rentals are also possible.

Brits has a 'backpacker relocation deal' which allows you to ferry a vehicle between stipulated branches in a given time – for example, you may be able to drive between Cairns and Alice Springs and be given five days to do it. The cost is $10 for the driver and $5 for each passenger.

In Western Australia, South Perth 4WD Rentals (☎ (08) 9362 5444) has a large range of vehicles and provides information and maps, as well as extra equipment. See the track and city descriptions later in this book for rental companies closer to your chosen destinations.

Four-wheel-drive hire vehicles tend to be pretty basic. You'll probably have to organise extra equipment if you want to do a Simpson trip but then again, you shouldn't be doing such a hard, remote trip if you don't have any experience. If you're travelling with a tour operator (see Organised Tours at the end of this chapter), they may be able to organise a self-drive vehicle for you.

Trailers & Caravans

These come in all shapes and sizes and what you choose will depend on your wallet and personal preferences. There are many places where you cannot take a caravan (house trailer), but a well-constructed luggage trailer designed for off-road work will go virtually anywhere – with a few big provisos.

First, the trailer must be well made. Every year, dozens fall apart on the tracks up to Cape York or through the Kimberley. Axles bend, springs and spring hangers break, tow couplings snap, chassis fall apart and, if that is not enough, they can make you lose control easier. Second, trailers will slow you down and get you stuck. Third, they are banned in some places, such as Finke Gorge and Gurig national parks. At times they are simply not worth the trouble.

Car Preparation

A well-prepared vehicle is of paramount importance, though you can easily go overboard in setting it up. There are a host of accessories for 4WDs, some of them next to useless. But if you intend to keep your vehicle for a long time, or are planning some of the harder trips in this book, then the following advice becomes useful.

Good driving lights are pretty well essential for night driving in the outback. An aftermarket suspension helps the vehicle cope with heavy loads, while a long-range fuel tank takes the worry out of carrying fuel inside the cabin or on the roof (neither of which are recommended). Roof racks are useful for carrying light, bulky items such as tents and sleeping gear, but don't use them as a trailer.

A dual battery (with isolating switch) under the bonnet is a great help to keep the fridge running, for starting your vehicle when the main battery goes flat or for some emergency welding.

Radios are an important accessory – see Radio Communications under Post & Telecommunications in the Facts for the Visitor chapter.

Items such as spare parts, tools and recovery gear are included in the Checklists in the back of this book and depend, to some extent, on your trip. It goes without saying that someone in your group should know how to use them. You don't have to be a qualified mechanic or Camel Trophy veteran, but some knowledge and experience is a great help, particularly on the more remote tracks.

If your tyres are on their last legs, buy new ones before you set out – six-ply or eight-ply, if you can afford them. Stick to common brands, preferably with solid, narrow profiles – wide-profile 'desert' tyres are more fragile and they tend to damage easily. Buying them in the bush is always expensive.

Spare tyres and tubes? As a rule of thumb, if you travel for a day without passing a supply point, you'll need to carry more than one complete spare. For hard trips like the Simpson, you'll also need a tyre/tube repair kit.

Have your vehicle well serviced before you go. Thoroughly check the cooling system, engine, the complete drive train, suspension and brakes. There are 4WD specialist service centres in each state capital and major regional centres, many specialising in trip preparation.

We could write a whole book on setting up and preparing your vehicle for the outback, but there are already a number around. Specialist magazines such as *4X4 Australia* and *Overlander* are useful sources of up-to-date information on where to go, what the conditions are like, what preparation you need and who to see for specialist advice.

4WD Techniques

Driving a 4WD properly, and to the vehicle's capability, is a skill that needs to be practised. It's certainly not something that can be explained here in a few paragraphs. There are more detailed books and instructional videos around. Above all, take your time to learn and remember to tread lightly wherever you go.

Most pre-1984 vehicles don't have power steering or great brakes. Their suspension is very truck-like, giving a harsh ride, a touch or more of understeer and on rough roads, a fair amount of bump steer. Later-model 4WDs are generally more sophisticated, with many being distinctly car-like in comfort and handling.

The Basics You should understand the operation of such things as free-wheeling hubs and the transfer box gear selection. On bitumen or hard dirt surfaces, the vehicle should be in 2WD, high ratio, or if it's a constant 4WD vehicle such as a Range Rover, leave it in normal without the centre diff locked.

Once the road or track gets sandy, muddy or just slippery, you can engage 4WD high ratio or lock the centre diff of a constant 4WD vehicle. When the going slows and it is rough, sandy, or muddy, you can engage 4WD low ratio, or low ratio with the centre diff locked in a constant 4WD machine. This will give you the ultimate in traction and power.

Remember that a 4WD isn't a guarantee that you won't get bogged, but it will help you get bogged less often. The down side of a 4WD is that when you do get bogged, it is normally deeper and further into the quagmire than a normal car.

Corrugations These are one of the things

you will begin to hate on dirt roads. They can be so bad they will seem to be vibrating the vehicle to pieces. Going too fast can be dangerous, as well as detrimental to you and your car, while going too slow might not be as dangerous but will certainly be tiring on you and wearing on your vehicle. In most cases, a speed of around 80km/h is the optimum, as at that speed the vehicle will tend to 'float' across the hollows, giving a smoother ride. Mind you, what sort of ride you get will all depend on how good your suspension is: poor shock absorbers will make you feel every bump.

In the Bush If you are unsure of the ground ahead, especially if there is mud or water, get out and check.

Keep thumbs outside or on the edge of the steering wheel. Irregularities in the track can suddenly make the steering wheel turn with incredible force, bruising or even breaking a thumb in the process.

Don't change gear in the middle of a tricky section and if in doubt, always choose the lower gear.

Tyre pressures play a very important part in four wheel driving. Too hard and the drive will be uncomfortable and you will get bogged more often; too soft and you will destroy tyres. The load you are carrying will determine what pressure you use, but for general touring, pressures between 210 and 280kPa (30 to 40psi) are a sensible average.

Cross small ridges square-on; ditches should be crossed at a slight angle.

Steep Hills Low second or third gear is generally best for going uphill, while low first is best for steep downhills. Use the foot brake sparingly and with caution and keep your feet well away from the clutch. Don't turn a vehicle sideways on a hill and if you stall going uphill, don't touch the clutch or accelerator. See the later Stall Start section for what to do.

Sand Speed and flotation are the keys to success and high ratio is best, if possible.

Tyre pressures are important in the sand.

Generally 140kPa (20psi) is a good starting point but if you are heavily loaded, this may be too low and 175kPa (25psi) could be more appropriate. If you are lightly loaded, 105kPa (15psi) may be the way to go.

Stick to existing wheel tracks, avoid sudden changes in direction and tackle dunes head-on. When descending a dune, avoid braking at all costs, keep the nose pointing downhill and don't travel too fast, but don't go so slow that the wheels stop turning.

If you do get stuck in sand, rock the vehicle backwards and forwards, building up a small stretch of hard-packed sand that you can move off from. Don't spin the wheels or you'll only dig yourself in deeper.

Water Crossings Always check the crossing before you plunge in. Walk through it first if you're unsure. A 4WD should be able to tackle a crossing of around 60 cm deep without any problems or preparation, but a soft sandy bottom or a strong current flow can change all that.

Spray electrical components with WD40, loosen the fanbelt unless the fan has an auto clutch and in deep water, fit a canvas blind to the front of the vehicle.

Enter the water at a slow, steady pace – low second gear is generally best – and keep the engine running even if you stop.

Don't forget to dry your brakes out after the water crossing and if you had become stuck, check all your oils for contamination.

Mud Speed and power are essential and in deep mud, low second or third are probably best. Keep a steady pace and if possible, keep out of ruts.

Stall Start or Key Start When you stop on a steep hill, don't panic; think and stay calm. Engage both the handbrake and the footbrake. Switch the engine off if it hasn't already stalled, ease the clutch in, select low-range reverse gear and ease the clutch out. Check to see if the track is clear and the wheels are pointing straight ahead, take the handbrake off and the footbrake, but keep your foot close to the brake just in case.

Negotiating the deep ruts in the road

Keeping your feet away from the clutch or the accelerator, start the engine and slowly back the vehicle down the hill. Slight feathering of the brake is possible but take care.

MOTORCYCLE

Much of the previous Car section also applies to motorcycles. One of the major differences is that most of the 4WD tracks don't require an off-road motorcycle. True, the going will be much easier on an enduro or motocross machine, especially in sand, but you won't be able to carry the gear you need. On a motorcycle, it's much easier to pick your way through or around an obstacle and if you get stuck, you can always get off and push.

Many bikers travel the outback alone, but for obvious reasons that's not something we can recommend. The ideal setup for serious outback travel is a small group of bikes with one or two follow-up vehicles for fuel, water and luggage; make sure one of the vehicles can also carry a broken-down bike.

You'll need a rider's licence and a helmet. Some motorcyclists in New South Wales have special permission to ride without a helmet, ostensibly for medical reasons.

Unfortunately, there's no motorcycling organisation that can help with touring advice. The Auto Cycle Council of Australia (ACCA, with state-based Auto Cycle

Unions) deals exclusively with sport, while the various state Motorcycle Rider's Associations busy themselves with legislation issues and social get-togethers; there's no all-encompassing national organisation like the American AMA. The state automobile associations are your best source of information, though they usually don't know much about motorcycles.

Which Motorcycle?

The ideal motorcycle is a large-capacity dual-purpose machine, one that will handle the long distances to and from your chosen track with ease and won't be too disturbed by the track itself. Good choices available in Australia include the Yamaha XT500/550/600 or Tnr models (the 'Land Rovers' of motorcycles – rugged, simple and proven) and the Super Tnr; Honda XL600, XLV650 Transalp or NX650 Dominator (one of the best machines for the outback, but let down by a small tank); Suzuki DR600/650/750; Kawasaki KLR600 or Tengai 650; Moto Guzzi NTX650; Cagiva 750/900 Elefant; Triumph Tiger; and last but certainly not least, BMW 800/1000/1100 GS.

You'll probably meet a few motorcyclists, often Japanese, on small capacity dual-purpose bikes, proof that size isn't always important. A 250cc may be a bit tedious over the long approach roads though – especially if you're carrying gear and aren't lightweight yourself. A sturdy, uncomplicated road bike from the 1970s or '80s with a large front wheel (18 inch or preferably 19 inch) will generally be OK too.

Important points to consider are fuel consumption and tank size. Few bikes have a fuel range of more than 300km in favourable conditions, just enough to get you around and straight through the continent on the sealed roads, but not sufficient for many outback tracks.

An electric start will make life a lot easier: a stalled bike is often reluctant to start and the engine usually floods when you drop it. Water-cooling is fine, but if you're faced with the choice, go for a simpler and less sensitive air-cooled engine. The bike ideally should have spoked wheels as they absorb shocks and corrugations better than cast wheels (which have been known to crack under Australian conditions).

Obtaining a Motorcycle

Bringing your own motorcycle into Australia will require a *carnet de passages* and when you try to sell it here, you'll get less than the market price because it doesn't have Australian approval markings (less of a problem in the Northern Territory and Western or South Australia). Shipping from just about anywhere is expensive, but may be worth looking into if you're serious.

With time up your sleeve, you can easily buy a motorcycle thanks to the chronically depressed market. The start of the southern winter is a good time to strike – perfect timing for the outback season. Australian newspapers and the lively local bike press have extensive classified advertisement sections where $2500 will easily take you around the country if you know a bit about bikes. The main drawback is that you'll have to sell the bike again afterwards.

An easier option is a buy-back arrangement with a large motorcycle dealer in a major city – Elizabeth St in Melbourne is a good hunting ground. They're keen to do business and basic negotiating skills allied with a wad of cash (say, $4000) should secure a decent second-hand road bike with a written guarantee that they'll buy it back in good condition minus $1500 to $2000 after your four-month, round-Australia trip. (Don't be surprised if they'll haggle about what constitutes 'good condition' when you return the bike, so it helps if you don't tell them about your Gunbarrel trip.) Popular brands for this sort of thing are BMWs (cheap ones) and large-capacity, shaft-driven Japanese bikes. Dual-purpose bikes go for a bit less, but the problem is that very few dealers are willing to buy them back. See the earlier Buying a Car section for a company that does buy-backs on Yamaha XT600s.

Preparation & Spares

The owner's manual for your bike often

specifies oils of different viscosity for different conditions; use the highest ('thickest') viscosity listed.

Road-going tyres will generally see you through but dual-purpose tyres are a much better proposition. Off-road 'knobbies' are great on chewed-up tracks with deep ruts like the Cape York telegraph track and are less susceptible to punctures than other types of tyre, but you'll probably wear them out before you get to the start and they're hair-raising in wet weather on bitumen. Tubeless tyres are manageable if they're fairly narrow and you carry at least six carbon-dioxide cartridges in the appropriate repair kit (buy cheap soda-water cartridges and tap the threads or have that done). A tubeless tyre will never seat properly with a hand pump and you'll be pumping forever. Replace the gas in the tyre with air at the earliest opportunity.

The different ways of carrying luggage could fill a separate chapter. Carry your heaviest stuff (tools etc) in a tank bag, which puts the weight between the wheels. Lighter, more bulky gear can be carried over the rear wheel, preferably not high over the rear end but in panniers, or bags, that lower the centre of gravity. Luggage racks should be quite solid and, if necessary, braced to withstand corrugations. Aluminium racks tend to crack and aren't easy to weld. Take plenty of elastic straps (octopus or 'ocky' straps) to tie down your gear, and bring a few spare.

Outback dust, especially the powdery bull dust, has a habit of getting everywhere you don't want it. Most motorcyclists stop oiling their chains in the outback and if you have an O-ring chain, this is probably a good idea. Make sure the air intake is completely sealed: apply silicone sealant to the outside of any connections and grease the contact areas of the air filter and cover.

If you're travelling in sandy or muddy regions, a small steel plate welded to the bottom of the sidestand prevents it sinking, though a flattened can or small wooden plank kept to hand in the tank bag also works.

Ensure that the brake and clutch levers can twist around the handlebars in case of a fall – if you do the clamps up tight, they'll break

off. A headlight protector (plastic cover or steel grid) is a good idea to protect the expensive lens against stones thrown up by oncoming traffic.

It's worth carrying some spares and tools even if you don't know how to use them, because someone else often does. If you do know, you'll probably have a fair idea of what to take. The basics include:

- a spare tyre tube (front wheel size, which will fit in the rear but usually not vice versa); you must know how to fix a tyre
- puncture repair kit with levers and a pump, or tubeless tyre repair kit with a pump and enough carbon dioxide cartridges to fix two or three flats (at least two cartridges per flat)
- a spare tyre valve and a valve cap that can unscrew same
- the bike's standard tool kit for what it's worth (aftermarket items are better); some extra tools – ask at a friendly bike shop if you don't know
- spare throttle, clutch and brake cables
- tie wire, cloth tape ('gaffer' tape) and nylon 'zip-ties'
- a handful of bolts and nuts in the usual emergency sizes (M6 and M8), along with a few self-tapping screws
- one or two fuses in your bike's ratings and a few metres of electrical wire
- a bar of soap for patching-up tank leaks (knead to a putty with water and squeeze into the leak)
- most important of all, a workshop manual for your bike – even if you can't make sense of it, the local motorcycle mechanic can

Minimum clothing requirements are sturdy boots, gloves, trousers and jacket and a helmet, ideally with a peak to cut out the sun early and late in the day. Knee and elbow protectors are seriously worth considering and should be worn under your clothes for best results. Pick up a cheap sheepskin and throw it over the seat to ease the sore-bum syndrome – very effective.

Always carry water – at least 2L on sealed roads where someone is bound to come along soon, much more off the beaten track. Beware of dehydration in the dry, hot air: force yourself to drink plenty of water even if you don't feel thirsty, and keep checking that urine.

Finally, learn something about first aid and carry a first-aid kit. Graze wounds are common in bike get-offs and your kit should contain some special gauze for this.

Riding Techniques

If you've never ridden on unsealed roads, the outback could be a bad place to start because of the serious consequences if something goes wrong. If you're in a group with a few experienced riders, however, it could be great fun.

The first mistake that beginners make is to 'freeze' and lock solid onto the handlebars as soon as they see dirt. Wrong. The bike will want to 'wander' a bit and find its own way – let it. Move your weight slightly back on the seat, keep the power on and guide the bike loosely. If things seem to get out of control, stand on the footpegs a bit; this will lower the centre of gravity and calm things down, and if you grip the tank with your knees at the same time, you'll be surprised how well you can 'steer' the bike. Look reasonably far ahead on the track, not immediately ahead of the front wheel or you'll get nervous.

If a sandy patch comes up, the above techniques are mandatory. It's important to keep the power on; move back on the seat, maybe shift down a gear and open the throttle a bit further. You don't have to accelerate as such; the important thing is to keep enough power onto the rear wheel and maintain momentum. This will help move the centre of gravity to the rear and prevent the front wheel sliding sideways or digging into the sand, twisting sideways and spitting you over the bars – the latter result is guaranteed if you close the throttle and thereby transfer weight to the front. Don't try to 'jump ruts' unless they're shallow; choose a particular rut and try to ride it out. Great fun once you get the hang of it!

The same techniques apply to deep gravel, often encountered on freshly levelled ('graded') roads. Car drivers love these, but to motorcyclists the loose surface can be bad news – a bit like riding on marbles. Keep the power onto the rear wheel, but be careful not to overdo it because the rear will break sideways more easily than in sand; better to shift back on the seat a bit. The less 'off-road' your tyre tread, the more of a problem you'll have with gravel.

You can fight against sand and gravel, but mud is a much more formidable adversary. In theory, the same riding principles apply but, unless you're on an enduro machine with knobby tyres, mud requires a delicate balancing act with the throttle: if the front wheel doesn't slide out from under you the rear wheel will, especially in the slippery red or black soil usually encountered in the outback. 'Soften' the power delivery by selecting a higher gear than you normally would for that speed. Take it slowly with your feet out if things are really wet or look for harder surface off the side of the road. Also beware of mud build-up under the rear mudguard (and the front if it sits low on the wheel): the rear wheel could well lock up and if you try to keep going, you'll burn the clutch. All you can do is stop and clear out the mud, which may be necessary every few hundred metres in blacksoil.

On corrugated roads, car drivers tend to sit on relatively high speeds so they skim over the top and make life more comfortable for themselves and their suspension. The drawback is that the tyres lose grip, which is fine so long as the road is flat and there aren't any corners. But a motorcycle has less inherent stability and you could well find yourself drifting sideways out of control if you don't slow down. See how you go, but if the corrugation is really bad you may have to slow right down and ride on the side of the road or off the road altogether.

Beware: road sides and ditches often contain nails, bits of glass and other meanies that lie in wait for unsuspecting tyres.

BICYCLE

Whether you're hiring a bike to ride around town or wearing out your chain-wheels on a Melbourne-Darwin marathon, you'll find that the outback has some great places for cycling. There are bike tracks in most large towns and thousands of kilometres of open roads which carry little traffic. Especially appealing is that in many areas you'll ride all day without encountering a hill. On the downside, you can ride even further and not see any decent scenery.

Bicycle helmets are compulsory wear in all states and territories.

If you're coming specifically to cycle, it makes sense to bring your own bike. Check your airline for costs and the degree of dismantling/packing required. Within Australia, you can load your bike onto a bus or train to skip the boring bits. Note that bus companies require you to dismantle your bike and some don't guarantee that it will travel on the same bus as you. Trains are easier, but supervise the loading and if possible tie your bike upright, otherwise you may find that the guard has stacked crates of Holden spares on your fragile alloy wheels.

You can buy a reasonable steel-framed touring bike in Australia for about $400 (plus panniers), but if you want quality fittings or a good mountain bike, costs rise sharply. It may be possible to rent touring bikes and equipment from a commercial touring outfit. A touring bike is better than a mountain bike if you're staying on the tar.

Outback cyclists are a rare breed

If you don't want to buy a bike or organise your own tour, there are other options such as Perth-based ROC Tours Australia (☎ (08) 9244 4614). They do outback cycling trips with 4WD support in four stages from Perth to Broome via Uluru, Alice Springs and Darwin – you can do the whole lot or just the stage(s) that take your fancy.

Planning

There are two approaches to seeing the outback by bike. The first is to stay on the few sealed roads. Although these are usually highways, they carry little traffic and generally offer good riding. However, distances between sources of food and water can be great, so plan carefully – for example, heading south on the Stuart Highway, it's 250km between Coober Pedy and the next roadhouse.

The other approach involves planning a trip on one of the unsealed routes. You'll probably need a mountain bike, not only because of the rough surface but also because the wider tyres will help in soft conditions. Some roads might be impossibly deep in sand or dust and the only sure way to find out is to talk to another cyclist, if you can find one. Allow plenty of time and be prepared to change your plans. Riding on dirt roads can be very slow and tiring, so don't underestimate the time it will take to reach the next water supply.

The track descriptions in this book tell you who to contact about road conditions. Police are a good source of information, but they will have to deal with the results if something goes wrong and may try to dissuade you. Don't dismiss their advice lightly: they often know the local conditions better than anyone else.

Always check with the locals if you're heading into remote areas and notify the police if you're about to do something particularly adventurous. That said, don't rely too much on local knowledge of road conditions: most people have no idea of what a heavily loaded bike needs. What they think of as a great road may be pedal-deep in sand

Top: Alice Springs with the MacDonnell Ranges in the background
Bottom: The famous Henley-on-Todd Regatta, Alice Springs

HUGH FINLAY

HUGH FINLAY

HUGH FINLAY

Stuart Highway
Top: Typical outback architecture, this Tennant Creek homestead has a wide verandah providing shade
Middle: The Devil's Marbles near Wauchope in the Davenport Ranges
Bottom: Road trains carry all types of freight across the country

or bull dust, while flooded roads which are closed to cars might not be a problem for bikes. Then again, they might be!

You can get by with standard road maps, but one of the government series (such as AUSLIG) showing topography and handy features such as farm buildings helps you plan routes and gives a better appreciation of the surrounding country. The 1:250,000 series is the most suitable, although you'll need a lot of maps if you're covering much territory. The next scale up, 1:1,000,000, is usually adequate.

Spares

It's rare to find a reasonably sized town that doesn't have a shop stocking at least basic bike parts, although whether they will be compatible with exotic machines is another matter. It might be worth talking with a specialist bike shop in a major city before you set out. They may be able to courier spare parts to you in case of emergency.

Compulsory spares include; puncture repair kit, tubes and tyres (hot roads wear tyres quickly and Michelin World Tours start to get pretty thin after about 2000km), brake and gear cables, spokes (about 10, in the correct gauge), bearings and lubricants plus all the tools required to strip down and clean bearings, and perhaps a spare chain (if you're going a long way) and crank. You obviously should know how to perform routine repairs.

On the Road

Until you get fit, be careful to eat enough to keep you going – remember that exercise is an appetite-suppressant. It's surprisingly easy to be so depleted of energy that you end up camping in the spinifex just 10km short of a shower and a steak.

No matter how fit you are, water is vital. Death by dehydration is a real possibility on a remote track. Summer in inland Australia can be impossibly hot, as can early autumn and late spring. Take it easy, wear a hat and plenty of sunscreen and drink *lots* of water. Six litres a day isn't an unreasonable amount if you're working hard and you may well need more – check the colour of your urine. Heat exhaustion can also kill and you need to be aware of how you body is coping. Obtain good medical advice (perhaps from a sports medical clinic) and learn how to recognise the onset of dehydration and heat exhaustion.

The first time you're passed by a road train will be an interesting experience but if you stick to sealed roads, the most dangerous vehicles are buses, which use a lot of road and are surprisingly quiet. When you haven't seen another vehicle for a few hours, it's easy to be on the wrong side of the road when the Alice Springs express blasts through.

In the eastern states, be aware of the blistering 'hot northerlies', the prevailing winds that make a northbound cyclist's life very uncomfortable in summer. In April, the Southerly Trades begin to prevail and you can have (theoretically at least) tailwinds all the way to Darwin. If you're travelling across the Nullarbor, don't try cycling from east to west against the westerlies: they're pretty strong all year and can soon wear you out. It's not uncommon for trans-Nullarbor trucks to use 30% more fuel heading west rather than east.

Information

In each state there are touring organisations that can help with information and put you in touch with touring clubs and private tour operators. The most useful ones for the outback are:

New South Wales
   Bicycle Institute of New South Wales, 209 Castlereagh St, Sydney, NSW 2000 (☎ (02) 9283 5200)
Queensland
   Bicycle Institute of Queensland, 24 Whynot St, West End, Qld 4101 (☎ (07) 3844 1144)
South Australia
   Bicycle SA, 1 Sturt St, Adelaide, SA 5000 (☎ (08) 8410 1406)
Western Australia
   Cycle Touring Association, PO Box 174, Wembley, WA 6014 (☎ (08) 9349 2310)

HITCHING

Quite a few travellers hitch rides in the outback. The locals are generally pretty easy-going and friendly and often pick up hitchers for company. The drawback is that they may deposit them at the track leading to their property, usually a long way from anywhere – find out before it's too late! On the other hand, most car drivers in the outback are engaged in long-distance travel themselves and aren't able to pick up hitchers. For these reasons, hitching is really only feasible along the main sealed roads, where rides take you from town to town or roadhouse to roadhouse.

Hitching is never entirely safe in any country and it's not a form of travel we can recommend. People who decide to hitch should understand that they are taking a small but potentially serious risk. They will be safer if they travel in pairs and let someone know where they are going. University and hostel notice boards are good places to look for hitching partners.

Just as hitchers should be wary when accepting lifts, drivers who pick up hitchers or cost-sharing travellers should also be aware of the possible risks involved.

Two people is the ideal number for hitching, any more makes things very difficult. Ideally the pair should comprise one male and one female – two guys hitching together can expect long waits. It is not advisable for women to hitch alone, or even in pairs.

The ideal appearance for hitching is a sort of genteel poverty – threadbare but clean. Don't carry too much gear – if it looks like it's going to take half an hour to pack your bags aboard, you'll be left on the roadside. A sign announcing your destination can be useful and if you're visiting from abroad, a nice prominent flag on your pack will help.

Trucks often provide the best lifts but they'll only stop if they are going slowly and can get started easily again. Truckies often say they are going to the next town and if they don't like you, will drop you anywhere. As they often pick up hitchers for company, the quickest way to create a bad impression is to jump in and fall asleep.

BOAT

Not really. Once upon a time there was quite a busy coastal shipping service but now it only applies to freight, and even that is declining rapidly. In south-eastern inland Australia, long-distance freight used to go by river – as evidenced by the admiralty office in the outback New South Wales town of Bourke – but modern rail and road transport have taken over completely. There are still a few ferries in outback regions, such as along the Birdsville and Cape York tracks and up at Thursday Island, and details are provided in the relevant track descriptions.

It is, however, quite possible to make your way round the coast by hitching rides or crewing on yachts. Ask around at harbours, marinas or yacht or sailing clubs – anywhere where boats call. It obviously helps if you're an experienced sailor, but some people are taken on as cooks (not very pleasant on a rolling yacht). Usually you have to chip in something for food and the skipper may demand a financial bond as security. A lot of boats move north to escape the winter, so April is a good time to look for a berth in the southern harbours.

If you know your way around a commercial fishing boat, there's often temporary work available on the many small trawlers operating the remote north-eastern and northern coastline. The pay can be excellent or lousy depending on the catch, but it's quite an experience and you visit parts of the coast that can't be reached by anybody else. Ask around at fishing ports. Trawler crews are often amenable to hiring female cooks and women who pursue this option report good and bad experiences.

MAIL RUNS

It's possible to get a first-hand idea of what a mail run means to the people of the outback by going along for the ride (see Post & Telecommunications in the Facts for the Visitor chapter for an explanation of mail runs). In Coober Pedy, the mail truck leaves on Monday and Thursday, covering 600km of dirt roads as it does the round trip to Oodnadatta and William Creek. There's a no-frills price of $60 or the standard fare, including lunch, of $89. For details, ring toll-free on ☎ 1800 069 911.

Another possibility is the mail planes that service the outback's scattered communities – there are a few that take paying passengers, but they're not cheap. In Port Augusta, Augusta Airways (☎ (08) 8642 3100) does a run on Saturday to Boulia in western Queensland, via Innamincka and Birdsville; the cost (air fares only) is $650. In Cairns, Cape York Air Services (☎ (07) 4035 9399), the local mail contractor, does mail runs on weekdays. Space permitting, you can go along for $195 to $390, depending on the length of the trip. Air Mount Isa (☎ (07) 4743 2844) takes tourists on its mail runs for negotiable fees.

ORGANISED TOURS

There are many operators who offer outback tours in a variety of vehicles and even on foot. Some 4WD safaris go to places you simply couldn't get to on your own without a vehicle and large amounts of expensive equipment. See the individual track descriptions for details.

YHA tours are good value – find out about them at YHA Travel offices in capital cities. In major centres like Darwin and Cairns there are many tours aimed specifically at backpackers – good prices, good destinations, good fun.

Coach Options

A handful of small companies offer flexible transport options aimed at budget travellers. These trips combine straightforward bus travel from A to B with a leisurely organised tour. The coaches are generally smaller and so may not be as comfortable as those of the major operators, but it's a much more interesting way to travel.

You can see the outback with Oz Experience (☎ toll-free 1300 300 028), who go from Adelaide to Darwin via Marree, Coober Pedy and Alice Springs (eight days, $590 including meals and a two-day package to Uluru). Wayward Bus (☎ toll-free 1800 882 823) goes from Adelaide to Alice Springs via

the north Flinders, Oodnadatta Track and Uluru (eight days, $600 all-inclusive). West Coast Explorer (☎ toll-free 1800 651 210) offers a zig-zag trip up the coast from Perth to Darwin (15 days, $1390 including meals, tent and entry fees).

Tag-Along 4WD Tours

If you already have a 4WD and want to experience the remote country safely, easily and in the company of others, there are many guiding services or 'tag-along' operators well worth considering. They may be able to set you up with a 4WD hire vehicle, if necessary, and a few may even take a passenger or two.

Some provide a catering service and can really produce wonderful meals in the scrub, including wine with the evening meal. Most of these operations expect a little help preparing the food, washing dishes and carrying some of the tucker, usually on an informal roster basis.

Other operations only provide a guiding service. These are much cheaper but you need to provide your own food and the enthusiasm and expertise to cook it in the bush.

The tag-along services provide experienced guides who are experts with driving and recovery and will give you all the hints necessary to get you through. Full radio gear and recovery equipment are also carried. As well, many of the operators have areas opened to them that are not open to the private traveller. They know where all the worthwhile attractions are as well as the best camping spots and can take care of your permit requirements.

Once you've decided where you'd like to go, contact the operators servicing that area. Details are usually available from state tourist information centres.

Motorcycle Tours

There are several operators offering outback motorcycling tours, either tag-along or (more often) on bikes supplied by them. Some are mentioned in the track descriptions in this book.

Bike-tour operators tend to come and go. One that has been in business for over 10 years is Bike Tours Australia, offering long-distance tours on Yamaha XT600 trail bikes. These include a variety of outback tours ranging from sightseeing trips on bitumen (their three-week Melbourne to Darwin classic costs around $3000) to expeditions for experienced riders (a five-week adventure diagonally across Australia from Perth to Cape York costs $5400). Most of Bike Tours' clients are Continental Europeans (often German); other nationalities are welcome, but Aussies may have trouble fitting in. The company also operates a car and motorcycle buy-back scheme under the name Car Connection Australia; see the earlier Buying a Car section for details.

Aboriginal Culture Tours

Aboriginal involvement in the tourist industry has increased greatly in the last few years. Considering that outback Aborigines are faced with few employment opportunities and that Aboriginal culture is of major interest for most people who visit outback Australia, this trend is likely to continue.

Such tours often give an introduction to traditional Aboriginal law, religion and lifestyle, all of which remain strong in many parts of outback Australia. These tours often describe how, during the creation period (the 'Dreaming'), Aboriginal creation ancestors travelled the face of the earth, creating the landforms that we see today. Aborigines have also built up an encyclopaedic knowledge of useful plants and animals over the past 50,000 years; 'bush tucker' still forms an important part of the diet of many communities and you can find out about that too.

If you do go on any of these tours, please respect any requests that Aboriginal guides make about appropriate behaviour.

Northern South Australia Desert Tracks (☎ toll-free 1800 621 003) is an Aboriginal-owned organisation that offers one-to eight-day tours from $260 per day of the Anangu-Pitjantjatjara Lands. Few, if any, other tours offer such a deep insight into

traditional Aboriginal culture. Costs include payment to Aboriginal elders as guides and teachers. Contact Desert Tracks well in advance of your preferred date of departure. It departs from Ayers Rock Resort, 20km from Uluru.

Northern Territory – south & centre Uluru-Kata Tjuta (Ayers Rock-the Olgas) National Park's 1½-hour Mala Walk looks at Uluru through Aboriginal eyes. The two-hour Liru Walk, operated by the Aboriginal-owned Anangu Tours (☎ (08) 8956 2123), leaves from the park's cultural centre near Uluru. It focuses on the skills and knowledge passed down by the Liru warriors of the creation time.

Oak Valley Day Tours (☎ (08) 8956 0959) is also Aboriginal-owned and operated – it offers day tours south of Alice Springs.

West of Alice Springs, Wallace Rockhole Aboriginal Community (☎ (08) 8956 7415) offers a 1½-hour walk and talk about Aboriginal culture, including rock engravings; Sahara Outback Tours (☎ (08) 8953 0881) includes Wallace Rockhole for this purpose as part of a five-day tour.

In Alice Springs, Rod Steinert Tours (☎ toll-free 1800 679 418) offers a corroboree (ceremonial dance) and a culture and bush-tucker tour. Pitchi Richi (☎ (08) 8952 1931) is an eclectic establishment that offers Aboriginal guided tours.

Northern Territory – top end Outback NT Air Safaris and Kakadu Parklink (☎ (08) 8979 2411) in conjunction with the Manilakarr people offer excursions to Mikiny Valley in Arnhem Land, where various aspects of Aboriginal culture are covered. Umorrduk Aboriginal Safaris (☎ (08) 8948 1306) flies and drives tourists to Kakadu and north-west Arnhem Land for culture tours that include stunning old rock art. Davidson's Arnhemland Safaris (☎ (08) 8927 5240) offer trips to Mt Borodaile in Arnhem Land, including some of the Top End's most spectacular art sites. Aussie Adventure Holidays (☎ toll-free 1800 811 633) will take you west for a day in the life of Peppimenarti Aboriginal Community. Tiwi Tours (also ☎ toll-free 1800 811 633) will introduce you to the modern culture of Melville and Bathurst islands north of Darwin.

From Katherine, Travel North (☎ (08) 8972 1044) will arrange for you to see traditional dancing at Springvale Homestead or visit the famous Lightning Brothers art site with Aboriginal raconteur and local character Bill Harney. At the Manyallaluk Aboriginal community (☎ toll-free 1800 644 727) out of Katherine the owners offer several award-winning tours centred on ancient and modern culture.

Western Australia At Fitzroy Crossing, in the Kimberley, Darngku Heritage Tours (☎ (08) 9191 5121) offers various tours including a culture cruise of Geikie Gorge and a campfire dinner. From Broome, Flack Track Tours (☎ (08) 9192 1487) visits an Aboriginal community.

Queensland In Rockhampton, you can go on daily guided tours of the Dreamtime Aboriginal Cultural Centre (☎ (07) 4936 1655).

In Far North Queensland, at Kuranda, the Rainforestation (☎ (07) 4093 7251) organises Aboriginal guided walks and traditional performances by the Pamagirri dancers. From Cairns, you can fly or drive to Quinkan country near Laura on Cape York Peninsula for a Quinkan Rock Art Safari and Bush Camp; for details, ring Tresize Bush Guides (☎ (07) 4055 1865), also for 4WD tours out of Cairns. The Ang-Gnarra Aboriginal Corporation (☎ (07) 4060 3214) at Laura offers guided tours of rock galleries in the area by prior arrangement. Ku Ku Yelangi woman Nalba (Hazel) Douglas (☎ (07) 4098 2206) will take you on an excellent one-day 4WD culture/adventure tour to Cape Tribulation from Port Douglas.

There's also the Tjapukai Aboriginal Culture Park (☎ (07) 4042 9900) at Smithfield near Cairns. It has a number of attractions including a museum, traditional dancing and a culture theatre.

The Far North Queensland Promotion Bureau (☎ (07) 4051 3588) can help to arrange most tours in the Cape York region.

The Central Deserts

With its awesome sense of space and few people, central Australia is a land of golden opportunity for getting off the beaten track. The region has all of Australia's deserts, the most inhospitable of which is the Simpson Desert, one of the world's outstanding sand-ridge deserts. These aren't true deserts like the Sahara, but they're extremely dry and only very sparsely populated. Where it occurs, primary production is limited to low-intensity sheep and cattle grazing. The few significant towns are all largely dependent on either tourism (eg Alice Springs) or mining (eg Mt Isa). Because of their isolation, even the smallest towns generally have an excellent range of facilities and services.

The region has some of the nation's remotest touring routes, each with its own unique attractions. For major adventure there are several challenging 4WD tracks, such as the

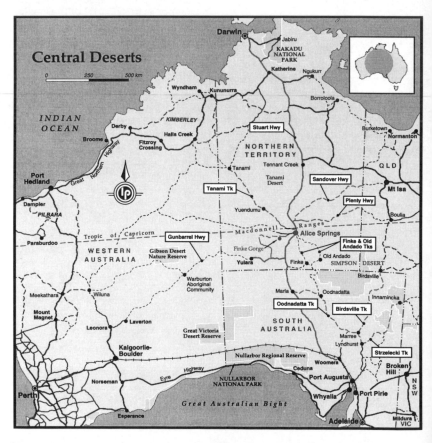

Central Deserts

0   250   500 km

INDIAN OCEAN

Darwin
Jabiru
KAKADU NATIONAL PARK
Katherine   Ngukurr
Wyndham   Kununurra
Borroloola
KIMBERLEY
Derby   Stuart Hwy
Halls Creek   Burketown
Broome   Fitzroy Crossing   Normanton
NORTHERN TERRITORY
Port Hedland   Tanami   Tennant Creek   QLD
Dampier   Tanami Desert   Sandover Hwy
PILBARA   Tanami Tk   Mt Isa
Plenty Hwy
Yuendumu   Boulia
Paraburdoo   Tropic of Capricorn   Macdonnell   Ranges   Alice Springs
Gunbarrel Hwy   Finke Gorge   Finke & Old Andado Tks
WESTERN AUSTRALIA   Gibson Desert Nature Reserve   Yulara   Finke   Old Andado   SIMPSON DESERT
Warburton Aboriginal Community   Birdsville
Meekatharra   Wiluna   Marla   Oodnadatta   Innamincka
Mount Magnet   Oodnadatta Tk   Birdsville Tk
Leonora   Laverton   SOUTH AUSTRALIA
Great Victoria Desert Reserve   Marree   Strzelecki Tk
Kalgoorlie-Boulder   Lyndhurst
Nullarbor Regional Reserve   Broken Hill
Norseman   Eyre   Highway   Woomera   NSW
NULLARBOR NATIONAL PARK   Ceduna   Port Augusta
Perth   Whyalla   Port Pirie
Great Australian Bight
Esperance   Adelaide   Mildura VIC

French Line across the Simpson Desert and the **Anne Beadell Highway** from Coober Pedy to Laverton. Routes such as these have no facilities whatsoever and are only recommended for experienced 4WD travellers. Alternatively, if you haven't got a 4WD, you can discover history in the footsteps of the cattle drovers along the remote **Oodnadatta Track** and **Birdsville Track**.

You can also explore some spectacular places in the central desert region without leaving the bitumen at all. The sealed **Stuart Highway** crosses the continent from Port Augusta in the south to Darwin in the north, with sealed detours leading to **Uluru (Ayers Rock)** and the **MacDonnell Ranges**, near Alice Springs.

Alice Springs

HIGHLIGHTS

- Learning about local Aboriginal culture and the arid zone's plants and animals at the Alice Springs Desert Park

- Visiting the Telegraph Station and stepping back to the earliest days of white settlement in central Australia

Alice Springs (also known as 'the Alice'; population 25,100), a pleasant, modern town with good shops and restaurants, is set among the rugged red hills and ridges of the MacDonnell Ranges. It's the major access point for the many tourist attractions of central Australia.

The growth of Alice Springs has been both recent and rapid. When the name was officially changed in 1933 (it was previously called Stuart), the population had only just reached 200! Even in the 1950s, Alice Springs was still a tiny town with a population in the hundreds. The road to Darwin was sealed during WWII, but it was only in 1987 that the rough dirt road south to Port Augusta

and Adelaide was finally replaced by a sealed highway.

Information

The well-stocked visitor information centre (☎ (08) 8952 5800), operated by the Central Australian Tourism Industry Association (CATIA), is at the river end of Gregory Terrace in the centre of town. It opens at 9 am daily and closes at 6 pm weekdays and 4 pm weekends and public holidays.

The Parks & Wildlife Commission has brochures on all the parks and reserves in the Centre. You'll find them at CATIA as well as at the commission's main office (☎ (08) 8951 8211), just off the Stuart Highway about 7km south of the town centre.

The main post office is at 33 Hartley St (☎ (08) 8952 1020), and there's a row of public phones outside. The telephone area code for Alice Springs is ☎ 08.

There are three good bookshops: the Arunta Gallery on Todd St, just south of Todd St Mall, Dymocks in the Alice Plaza on the mall, and a branch of Angus & Robertson in the Yeperenye Centre off Hartley and Bath Sts.

The Department of Lands, Environment & Planning on Gregory Terrace is a good source for all kinds of maps – it is a sales outlet for AUSLIG products. Also on Gregory Terrace, the Automobile Association of the Northern Territory has touring information including maps.

For camping equipment, try Alice Springs Disposals in Reg Harris Lane, off Todd St Mall. If you want to buy a swag, Red Centre Swags at 38 Elder St produces some really good ones.

Other useful addresses include:

Medical Facilities
> Alice Springs Hospital, Gap Rd (☎ (08) 8951 7777)

Permits
> Central Land Council, 33 Stuart Highway, PO Box 3321, NT 0871 (☎ (08) 8951 6320)

Police
> Parsons St (☎ (08) 8951 8888)

Royal Flying Doctor Service
> Stuart Terrace, PO Box 2210, NT 0871 (☎ (08) 8952 1033)

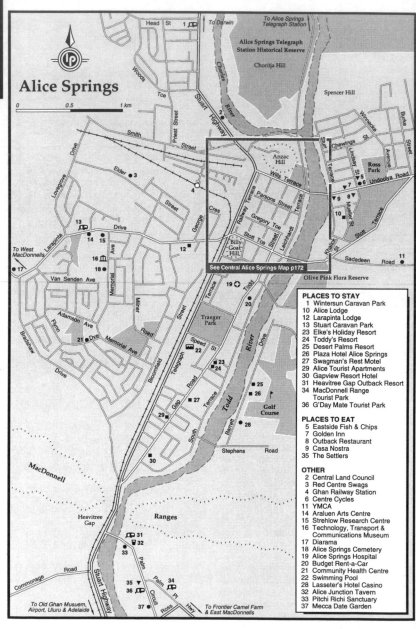

Alice Springs

0   0.5   1 km

To Darwin

Alice Springs Telegraph
Station Historical Reserve

Choritja Hill

Spencer Hill

Anzac
Hill

Wills Terrace

Ross
Park

Parsons Street

Gregory Tce

Billy-
Goat
Hill

See Central Alice Springs Map p172

Olive Pink Flora Reserve

Traeger
Park

Golf
Course

MacDonnell

Heavitree
Gap

Ranges

Stephens   Road

To Old Ghan Musuem,
Airport, Uluru & Adelaide

To Frontier Camel Farm
& East MacDonnells

PLACES TO STAY
1   Wintersun Caravan Park
10 Alice Lodge
12 Larapinta Lodge
13 Stuart Caravan Park
23 Elke's Holiday Resort
24 Toddy's Resort
25 Desert Palms Resort
26 Plaza Hotel Alice Springs
27 Swagman's Rest Motel
29 Alice Tourist Apartments
30 Gapview Resort Hotel
31 Heavitree Gap Outback Resort
34 MacDonnell Range
    Tourist Park
36 G'Day Mate Tourist Park

PLACES TO EAT
5   Eastside Fish & Chips
7   Golden Inn
8   Outback Restaurant
9   Casa Nostra
35 The Settlers

OTHER
2   Central Land Council
3   Red Centre Swags
4   Ghan Railway Station
6   Centre Cycles
11 YMCA
14 Araluen Arts Centre
15 Strehlow Research Centre
16 Technology, Transport &
    Communications Museum
17 Diarama
18 Alice Springs Cemetery
19 Alice Springs Hospital
20 Budget Rent-a-Car
21 Community Health Centre
22 Swimming Pool
28 Lasseter's Hotel Casino
32 Alice Junction Tavern
37 Pitchi Richi Sanctuary
37 Mecca Date Garden

Things to See

Alice Springs has plenty of attractions, and it's worth putting aside a couple of days to see some of the more interesting ones.

The 1870s **Telegraph Station**, one of a string through central Australia, is 2km north of the town; it has a small museum which is open daily. In the nearby Todd River are the **Alice Springs**, from which the town takes its name. The lawns along the river here are a great spot for a picnic or evening barbecue.

Anzac Hill is at the northern end of Hartley St; it offers fine views over Alice Springs, the Todd River and down to the MacDonnell Ranges.

There are a several historic buildings in the central town area including: the Stuart Town Gaol (1907), the Residency (1926) and the Old Courthouse (1928), which now houses the **National Pioneer Women's Hall of Fame**. Adelaide House (1926), the town's first hospital, is preserved as the **John Flynn Memorial Museum** ($3).

Upstairs in Alice Plaza, the **Museum of Central Australia** ($2) has some superb natural history displays. The **Royal Flying Doctor Base** ($3) is close to the town centre in Stuart Terrace; there are tours daily. Also open daily, the **School of the Air** ($3), which broadcasts school lessons to children in remote communities, is on Head St, about 3km north of the town centre.

The **Strehlow Research Centre** ($4), on Larapinta Drive, has an excellent display on the anthropological work of Professor Strehlow among the Arrernte people. Next door, the **Araluen Arts Centre** has a small gallery of paintings by the famous Aboriginal artist Albert Namatjira. **Panorama Guth**, on Hartley St, has a stunning 360-degree panorama painting depicting various local landscapes. The **Diarama**, on Larapinta Drive, has displays featuring Aboriginal mythological heroes.

At the MacDonnell Siding, off the Stuart Highway 10km south of town, the **old Ghan train** ($3 entry only) puffs up and down on a section of the original narrow-gauge railway track. There's plenty of interesting railway memorabilia here. Next door, the

Road Transport Hall of Fame ($3) features early motor vehicles including one of the Northern Territory's first road trains.

The impressive **Alice Springs Desert Park** ($12) backs onto the red walls of Mt Gillen, off Larapinta Drive on the western outskirts of town. Here you can learn first hand about Aboriginal traditions from local Arrernte guides, and get acquainted with arid Australia's unique flora and fauna. There are habitat walks, raptor displays, huge walk-in aviaries and a large nocturnal house. The nocturnal house displays 20 mammal species, about half of which are now either extinct or endangered over the arid zone. They include the western quoll and numbat (both now restricted to the south-west corner of Western Australia), and the rufous hare-wallaby (now found only on islands off the west coast).

If you're interested in natural history you could easily spend four or five hours here – the park has a cafe where you can buy lunch and coffee. Note that the residents of the nocturnal house are most active in the morning.

Organised Tours

There are literally dozens of tours available from Alice Springs. Listed here are some of the more interesting. See also the Organised Tours sections in the individual track descriptions and the Getting Around chapter.

Rod Steinert (☎ toll-free 1800 679 418) operates a variety of tours including his popular $67 Dreamtime & Bushtucker Tour. It's a half-day trip in which you meet some Aborigines and learn a little about their traditional life.

The Frontier Camel Farm (☎ (08) 8953 0444) has plenty of rides on offer. You can do a short one for $10, a day ride for $200, or three/six day safaris for $500/900. Longer rides are only available from April to October.

Sunrise balloon trips are also popular; these cost from $120, which includes breakfast and a 30-minute flight. Outback Ballooning (☎ toll-free 1800 809 790), Ballooning Downunder (☎ (08) 8952 8816) and

Spinifex Ballooning (☎ (08) 8953 4800) are the local operators.

Trec Gondawana (☎ (08) 8952 8248) takes fully equipped bushwalks into the western MacDonnells – day walks cost $95 and extended walks are $155 per person per day and night. They also have a very interesting desert night safari including a campfire dinner for $85.

Special Events

The Camel Cup, a series of camel races, takes place in July. In August there's the Alice Springs Rodeo.

In late September there's the event which probably draws the biggest crowds of all: the Henley-on-Todd Regatta. The boats are all bottomless, so the crews simply run down the (usually) dry riverbed!

Places to Stay

Camping Most of the caravan parks close to town are in the South Alice tourist area, centred on Palm Circuit just south of Heavitree Gap. Those within 5km of the town centre are:

Alice Springs Heritage Caravan & Tourist Park (☎ (08) 8953 1418), Ragonesi Rd off Palm Circuit, 5km from town – camping ($14, $15 with power) and on-site vans ($35)

G'Day Mate Tourist Park (☎ (08) 8952 9589), Palm Circuit, 4km south of the town centre – camping ($14, $16 with power) and cabins ($45)

Heavitree Gap Outback Resort (☎ (08) 8952 2370), Palm Circuit – camping ($12, $15 with power) and motel-style rooms ($39)

MacDonnell Range Tourist Park (☎ (08) 8952 6111), Palm Place, 5km from town – camping ($15, $18 with power) and cabins ($48 to $60)

Stuart Caravan Park (☎ (08) 8952 2547), 2km west of the town centre on Larapinta Drive – camping ($13, $16 with power), on-site vans ($35) and cabins (from $42)

Wintersun Caravan Park (☎ (08) 8952 4080), 2km north of the town centre on the Stuart Highway – camping ($13, $16 with power), on-site vans ($36) and cabins ($41 to $52)

Hostels & Guesthouses There are plenty of hostels and guesthouses in Alice Springs, including the *Pioneer YHA* (☎ (08) 8952 9589) on the corner of Parsons St and Leichhardt Terrace. Dorm beds cost $13 ($15 non-members) and twin/double rooms are $30 ($34 non-members). There's a travel agency on the premises, and a swimming pool.

Other hostels include: the *Melanka Backpackers Resort* (☎ toll-free 1800 815 066) at 94 Todd St, with a variety of rooms ranging from eight-bed dorms at $12 to singles /doubles for $30/32; the relaxed *Alice Lodge* (☎ (08) 8953 1975) at 4 Mueller St, with nightly rates of $12 in the dorm, $25 for a single or $16 per person in a double; *Toddy's Resort* (☎ (08) 8952 1322) at 41 Gap Rd, where it costs $10 for dorms with shared facilities, $12 with bathroom, $34 for doubles and $45 for doubles with bathroom; and the *Queen of the Desert Resort* (☎ (08) 8952 6611), about 2km south of the town centre, which charges $16 for a bed in a six-share, or there are motel rooms for $63/74 singles/doubles.

At 39 Gap Rd, *Elke's Holiday Resort* (☎ (08) 8952 8422) has dorm beds for $13, twin and double rooms for $33 and self-contained rooms from $55. A continental breakfast is included.

Hotels, Motels & Holiday Flats Right by the river at 1 Todd St Mall is the *Todd Tavern* (☎ (08) 8952 1255). This pub gets noisy when there are bands playing, but otherwise it is quite a reasonable place to stay. Room rates are $28 with share facilities and $38 with bathroom.

At 67 Gap Rd, there's the popular *Swagman's Rest Motel* (☎ (08) 8953 1333) with singles/doubles for $60/70. The units are self-contained and there's a swimming pool.

The *Alice Tourist Apartments* (☎ (08) 8952 2788) are also on Gap Rd and have apartments from $72. There's a communal laundry and swimming pool.

On Barrett Drive, next to the Plaza Hotel, the *Desert Palms Resort* (☎ (08) 8952 5977) has spacious rooms, each with a small kitchen, at $78. There's a swimming pool here too.

Motels include: the *Desert Rose Inn*

(☎ (08) 8952 1411), 15 Railway Terrace, with standard rooms at $80 ($75 off season), or deluxe rooms at $105 ($85 off season); and the *Larapinta Lodge* (☎ (08) 8952 7255), 3 Larapinta Drive near the railway station, with singles/doubles for $67/77 ($57/67 off season). There's a communal kitchen and a laundry for guests' use.

Places to Eat

Snacks & Fast Food The town centre has numerous places for a snack or light meal, particularly along Todd St Mall. Several put tables and chairs outside – ideal for a breakfast in the cool morning air. Takeaway addicts will be thrilled to know that fast-food chains such as *McDonalds* and *KFC* are well represented.

The *Jolly Swagman* in Todd Plaza off the mall is a pleasant place with good food. At the southern end of the mall, the *Red Dog Cafe* opens for breakfast (from $5) at 6.30 am and also has burgers, sandwiches etc.

The big *Alice Plaza* has four lunch-time eating places offering Asian, Australian and Italian fare. They share a central seating area – a popular meeting spot for tourists and locals. Across the mall, the Springs Plaza has *Golly It's Good*, with more sandwiches and snacks.

In the Yeperenye shopping centre on Hartley St there's a bakery and several cafes and takeaways. *Charlie's*, beside the main entrance on Hartley St, is popular for lunch.

Across the river on Lindsay Ave, near the corner of Undoolya Rd, *Eastside Fish & Chips* is considered the best fish takeaway in town. There's a French bakery next door.

Pub Meals The most popular place for pub food is the *Todd Tavern*, which has meals daily either in the bar or the slightly more formal *Pub Caf*. The food and serves are good, and there are usually specials from around $6.

Other places worth trying are the *Stuart Arms Bistro*, upstairs in the Alice Plaza on Todd St Mall, and *Uncle's Tavern* on Gregory Terrace.

Restaurants On the corner of Stott Terrace and Todd St, *Dingo's* has an interesting menu and a pleasant atmosphere, including alfresco eating. You can eat in from around $8, or take away. It's convenient to the Greyhound-Pioneer terminal.

The *Eranova Cafeteria*, at 70 Todd St, is a quiet, comfortable place with a good range of meals. It's open for breakfast, lunch and dinner from Monday to Saturday. Main meals range from $10 to $13.

Across the river from the town centre, on the corner of Undoolya Rd and Sturt Terrace, the *Casa Nostra* is a very popular pizza and pasta specialist. You can also get good pasta at *Al Fresco* and next door at *Oscar's*, both at the northern end of the mall. *La Casalinga*, at 105 Gregory Terrace, has a bar and does pizza and pasta from 5 pm to 1 am daily. *Ristorante Puccini*, on the mall is one of town's best restaurants and charges accordingly.

The *Mediterranean Cafe*, in the Fan Arcade off the southern end of the mall, is a very casual, alternative BYO place with an interesting menu and very reasonable prices. Next door, the *Camel Crossing Mexican Restaurant* is also worth trying.

The Alice has several Chinese restaurants. The *Oriental Gourmet* is on Hartley St, near the corner of Stott Terrace. *Chopsticks*, on Hartley St at the Yeperenye shopping centre, is reliable, as is the bright yellow *Golden Inn* on Undoolya Rd, just over the river from the town centre. Aside from the usual items, you can sample some Malaysian and Sichuan dishes.

For steaks you should try the *Overlander Steakhouse* at 72 Hartley St. It features 'Territory food' such as beef, buffalo, kangaroo and camel – a carnivore's delight! It's quite popular, but not that cheap with main courses from $17 to $25. The *Outback Restaurant* on Undoolya Rd is another good place for meat.

For something a little different, there's *Keller's Swiss & Indian Restaurant* on Gregory Terrace, which gives you the chance to try two vastly different cuisines, including vegetarian, in the one place. It's open for dinner nightly, and main courses start from around $11.

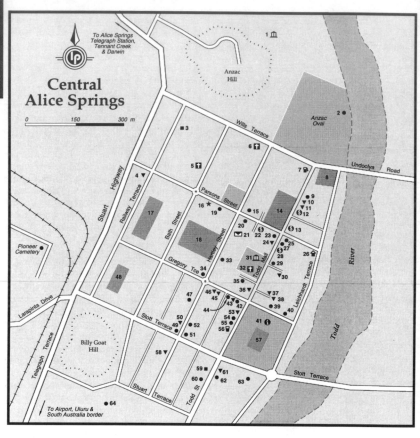

Central Alice Springs

To Alice Springs Telegraph Station, Tennant Creek & Darwin

Anzac Hill

0   150   300 m

Stuart Highway

Railway Terrace

Telegraph Terrace

Larapinta Drive

Pioneer Cemetery

Billy Goat Hill

Bath Street

Hartley Street

Gregory Tce

Stott Terrace

Stuart Terrace

Todd St

Wills Terrace

Parsons Street

Todd St Mall

Leichhardt Terrace

Anzac Oval

Undoolya Road

Todd River

Stott Terrace

To Airport, Uluru & South Australia border

Another interesting possibility is a campfire dinner combined with a ride on the old *Ghan* train at MacDonnell Siding (☎ (08) 8955 5047) for $49. There are different options – style of meal, and with or without a train ride – but their availability depends on numbers.

Entertainment
The local newspaper *The Centralian Advocate* (published Tuesday and Friday) carries details of what's on in and around Alice Springs – check the gig guide in the paper's entertainment section.

At the *Todd Tavern*, the Jam Session has live rock bands on Monday night. Nearby, on Todd St Mall, *Alice Springs Cinemas* has three cinemas with multiple showings daily.

Bojangles is a restaurant and nightclub on Todd St; *Legends* nightclub on the corner of Todd St Mall and Parsons has a disco or live bands four nights a week till 3 am. For country-style music, the *Alice Junction Tavern* on Palm Circuit has live entertainment on Friday and Saturday nights.

Knight Moves is a cabaret/nightclub at the Queen of the Desert Resort with music and dancing to 2 am every night.

PLACES TO STAY
3 Desert Rose Inn
8 Todd Tavern
26 Pioneer YHA Hostel
59 Melanka
   Backpackers Resort

PLACES TO EAT
4 McDonalds
10 Al Fresco
11 Oscar's
24 Ristorante Puccini
30 Jolly Swagman
36 Red Dog Cafe
37 Cafe Mediterranean
38 Camel Café Mexican
   Restaurant
43 La Casalinga
45 Keller's Swiss &
   Indian
   Restaurant
46 Uncle's Tavern
50 Overlander
   Steakhouse
53 Eranova Cafeteria
58 Oriental Gourmet
61 Dingo's

OTHER
1 RSL War Museum
2 Totem Theatre
5 Anglican Church
6 Catholic Church
7 Shell Service Station
   & Centre Car Rentals
9 Cinema
12 Westpac Bank
13 ANZ Bank
14 Alice Plaza
15 Old Courthouse
16 Police Station
17 Coles 24-hr
   Supermarket
18 Yeperenye Centre
19 Stuart Town Gaol
20 The Residency
21 Main Post Office
22 Commonwealth Bank
23 Ansett Airlines
25 Qantas
27 Gallery Gondwana
28 National Bank
29 Original Dreamtime
   Art Gallery
31 Adelaide House
32 Flynn Church
33 Hartley St School
34 Avis

35 Alice Springs
   Disposals
39 McCafferty's Coach
   Terminal
40 Department of
   Lands,
   Environment &
   Planning Offices
41 CATIA Tourist Office
42 AANT
44 Warumpi Arts
47 Department of Mines
   & Energy
48 K-Mart
49 Hertz
51 Territory Rent-a-Car
52 Panorama Guth
54 Outback Auto
   Rentals
55 Papunya Tula Artists
56 Bojangles
57 Library & Council
   Offices
60 Greyhound-Pioneer
   Coach Terminal &
   Thrifty Rent-a-Car
62 CAAMA Shop
63 Jukurrpa Artists
64 Royal Flying Doctor
   Service Base

Chateau Hornsby, a winery 15km out of town, has country or jazz music on Sunday afternoon.

For gambling there's *Lasseter's Hotel Casino*, but dress up as rules are strict. The famous outback character Ted Egan puts on a performance of tall tales and outback songs four nights a week at *The Settlers* on Palm Circuit.

There are all sorts of events at the *Araluen Arts Centre* on Larapinta Drive, including temporary art exhibits, theatre and music performances and films.

Things to Buy

Alice Springs has a number of outlets for Aboriginal art, and there are places where you can buy direct from the artists.

Papunya Tula Artists is on Todd St just south of the mall, you'll find Jukurrpa Artists on Stott Terrace near Leichhardt Terrace, and Warumpi Arts is located on Gregory Terrace near Todd St. These places are owned and

run by the art centres which produce the work.

The Central Australian Aboriginal Media Association (CAAMA) shop at 101 Todd St, just south of Stott Terrace, is another very good place for Aboriginal art.

There are plenty of other outlets, generally more commercial. Two of the better ones are the Gallery Gondwana, next to the Qantas office, and the Original Dreamtime Art Gallery, both on the mall.

Getting Around

The Airport The Alice Springs airport is 14km south of town, about $20 by taxi.

There is an airport shuttle bus (☎ (08) 8953 0310) which meets flights and takes passengers to all city accommodation places and to the train station. It costs $9 ($15 return).

Car Rental A number of car-rental companies, including Hertz, Avis and Brits, have offices in Alice Springs. Most have 4WD vehicles, with available models ranging from Suzuki Sierras to Toyota Troopcarriers. Competition is fierce and different packages are available, but the cheapest rates are usually offered by Territory Rent-a-Car and Centre Car Rentals, the two home-grown firms.

Alice Springs is classified as a remote area so car hire can be expensive, particularly if you want to drive down to Uluru (Ayers Rock) or further afield. Territory, for instance, charges $28 per day plus $0.25 per km for its cheapest 2WD vehicle without air-con. Generally, none of the companies allow their 2WDs to go off sealed roads – if you do, and have a crash, you're liable for all the damage.

A 4WD is much more expensive, but it's the only option if you want to leave the bitumen and visit places like Palm Valley and Chambers Pillar. You'll be looking at around $125 per day for a small Toyota RAV4, including insurance and 100km per day. For a Toyota Landcruiser or similar, the price jumps to around $155 per day. Discounts apply for longer rentals (more than four to seven days, depending on the company).

The 4WD outback specials offered by Hertz are worth investigating if you're flying into Alice Springs and want to do a camping trip. Its Troopcarriers cost $140 per day including 100km per day for seven days or more, and you can hire a full set of camping equipment for four people for an additional $40 per day.

Brits has fully equipped 4WD bush campers accommodating three adults, starting at $160 per day for a trip of four to 20 days. You need the company's written permission before tackling many of the tracks described in this book.

Remember that conditions vary from company to company, and from rate plan to rate plan within the same company. Always read them carefully, particularly insurance matters.

Avis, Budget, Hertz, Territory and Thrifty all have counters at Alice Springs airport. In town, Avis (☎ (08) 8953 5533) is at Shop 5,

52 Hartley St, Hertz (☎ (08) 8952 2644) is at 76 Hartley St, Budget (☎ (08) 8952 8899) is at 10 Gap Rd, Thrifty (☎ (08) 8952 2400) is at 94 Todd St, Brits (☎ (08) 8952 8814) is at the corner of the Stuart Highway and Power St about 4km north of town, Territory Rent-a-Car (☎ (08) 8952 9999) is at the corner of Stott Terrace and Hartley St, and Centre Car Rentals (☎ (08) 8952 1405) is in the service station at the corner of Wills Terrace and Todd St Mall.

Bicycle Alice Springs has a number of bicycle tracks, including a 17km sealed path from Flynn's Grave to Simpsons Gap (see the later MacDonnell Ranges section). There are several places to rent a bike, including most of the backpacker hostels where typical rates are $12 per day. The main cycle shop is Centre Cycles on Undoolya Rd – it also hires bikes.

Stuart Highway

HIGHLIGHTS

- Fossicking for precious opal and visiting a dugout in the unique opal-mining township of Coober Pedy

- At Mataranka, taking a detour to Elsey National Park for a taste of what's to come in the Top End

The 2708km-long Stuart Highway traverses the heart of Australia from the south coast at Port Augusta to Darwin on the north coast. It is one of the most important arteries in the country's highway system, providing the Top End with a direct link to the south.

While it is no longer a true outback track now that it's all sealed and there's a well-developed network of roadhouses, it does go straight through the heart of outback Australia. It also gives access to many of the

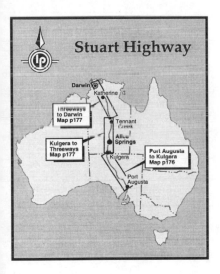

tracks described elsewhere in this book and has a number of worthwhile sights of its own. If you are spending any amount of time travelling in Australia's harsh interior, it's almost guaranteed that some of that time will be spent on 'The Track', as the Stuart Highway is affectionately called.

HISTORY

The highway takes its name from John McDouall Stuart who, in 1862, was the first European to cross Australia from south to north. The road itself is obviously a modern creation. In the early days travellers heading off into the interior were very much dependent on the availability of water, and so the route which initially developed was what is known today as the Oodnadatta Track, some distance to the east of the current highway, where water supplies were more reliable.

With the decline of vehicle traffic along the Oodnadatta Track due to the completion of the railway line to Alice Springs, the discovery of opals in Coober Pedy in 1915 and later the development of the Woomera Rocket Range, the main road developed further west along today's route. Surfacing work on the section from Port Augusta to the

Northern Territory border was only completed in 1987.

From Alice Springs to Darwin the highway basically follows the route of the Overland Telegraph Line, which was built in 1872 largely along the route which Stuart had taken a decade before.

INFORMATION

As you would expect on such a major road, there are no special requirements for travelling on the Stuart Highway. It's two-lane bitumen all the way, there's fuel and accommodation at regular intervals and you're never more than half a day's drive from the nearest pub – civilised indeed! The main thing you need to be aware of is that from Woomera (169km north of Port Augusta) to Glendambo (a distance of 115 km) the highway skirts the southern edge of the Woomera Prohibited Area, and from Glendambo to Coober Pedy (251km) it cuts right through it. Travelling off the main road and into this area is prohibited without a permit from the Area Administrator in Woomera.

Should you strike mechanical trouble, it's unlikely that you'd have to wait more than an hour for another vehicle to pass by. For those with HF radios, the Royal Flying Doctor base at Port Augusta (call sign VNZ) monitors the following frequencies from 6 am to 9 pm daily: 2020, 4010, 6890 and 8165kHz. From Alice Springs (call sign VJD) there's 24-hour emergency coverage on 5410MHz, or the following frequencies are monitored from 7.30 am to 5 pm weekdays: 2020, 5410 and 6950kHz. Darwin is covered by the Aerial Medical Services (call sign VJY) on 2360, 4010, 6840 and 7975kHz daily.

If you have a cassette player, it might be worth getting hold of the taped 'guidebook' produced by Take a Tour Guide. The Stuart Highway is covered in four cassettes: Port Augusta to Alice and Alice to Darwin, and the same sections in reverse direction (because you can't listen to a tape backwards). The tapes cost just $5 including postage and are available by mail order from

TATG (☎ (03) 9555 8419), 38 Beaumaris Parade, Highett, Vic 3190.

THE ROUTE
Port Augusta

The Stuart Highway starts the long haul north from the crossroads town of Port Augusta (population 14,300) at the head of Spencer Gulf. Some useful addresses in Port Augusta include:

Medical Facilities
    Port Augusta Hospital (☎ (08) 8648 5500)
Police
    Commercial Rd (☎ (08) 8648 5020)
Post Office
    50 Commercial Rd (☎ (08) 8642 2779)
Royal Flying Doctor Service
    4 Vincent St (☎ (08) 8642 2044, radphone calls ☎ 8642-5555)
Tourist Office
    Wadlata Outback Centre, 41 Flinders Terrace (☎ (08) 8642 4511)

Port Augusta to Coober Pedy

The first stretch is 169km to the scruffy little settlement of **Pimba**, which sits on a virtually treeless plateau and, despite its accessibility, is one of the most desolate places imaginable. The township of **Woomera** (population 1600) lies 5km north of the highway and in itself is hardly worth the detour, although you can pass through if you intend visiting the opal mining settlement of Andamooka or the huge Olympic Dam mining project (see Detours later in this section). Woomera had its heyday in the 1950s and 1960s when it was the base for military and civil personnel involved in rocket-launching experiments. These days it has something of a ghost-town feel about it, not unlike Canberra on a Sunday afternoon! There's a small museum in the centre of town.

From Pimba the highway swings west for the 115km run to **Glendambo**, along the way passing the usually dry salt lakes of Island Lagoon and Lake Hart. The road once again swings north for 251km until it reaches the opal-mining town of Coober Pedy.

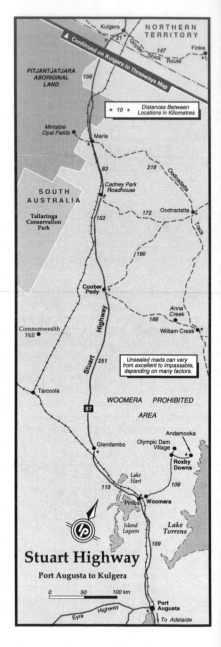

Stuart Highway
Port Augusta to Kulgera

0   50   100 km

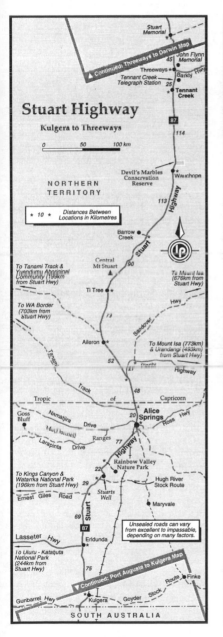

Stuart Highway
Kulgera to Threeways

0 — 50 — 100 km

Stuart Memorial

John Flynn Memorial

Threeways
Barkly Hwy
45

Tennant Creek Telegraph Station
25

Tennant Creek

87

114

NORTHERN TERRITORY

Devil's Marbles Conservation Reserve

Wauchope

113

★ 10 ★ Distances Between Locations in Kilometres

Barrow Creek

Central Mt Stuart
90

To Mount Isa (676km from Stuart Hwy)

To Tanami Track & Yuendumu Aboriginal Community (196km from Stuart Hwy)

Ti Tree

To WA Border (703km from Stuart Hwy)

73

Sandover

Aileron

52

To Mount Isa (773km) & Urandangi (453km) from Stuart Hwy

Plenty

Highway

48

Tropic   of   Capricorn

Tanami Track

Goss Bluff

Namatjira Drive

MacDonnell Ranges

Larapinta Drive

Alice Springs
20

Ross Hwy

77

Rainbow Valley Nature Park
22

Hugh River Stock Route

29

Ernest Giles Road

To Kings Canyon & Watarrka National Park (196km from Stuart Hwy)

Stuarts Well

Maryvale

69

Unsealed roads can vary from excellent to impassable, depending on many factors.

Lasseter Hwy

87

Erldunda

To Uluru - Katatjuta National Park (244km from Stuart Hwy)

75

Gunbarrel Hwy

Kulgera   Goyder   Stock   Route   Finke

SOUTH AUSTRALIA

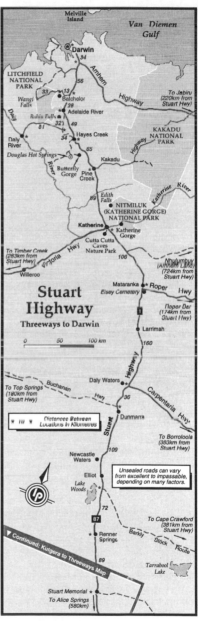

Melville Island

Van Diemen Gulf

Darwin
34

LITCHFIELD NATIONAL PARK

Wangi Falls

56

Batchelor
33   13
28

Adelaide River

Arnhem Highway

To Jabiru (220km from Stuart Hwy)

KAKADU NATIONAL PARK

Robin Falls

81
321
49

Daly River

34

Hayes Creek

85

Kakadu

Douglas Hot Springs

Butterfly Gorge

Pine Creek

89

Edith Falls

NITMILUK (KATHERINE GORGE) NATIONAL PARK

Katherine

Katherine Gorge

Katherine River

To Timber Creek (283km from Stuart Hwy)

Cutta Cutta Caves Nature Park

106

Nhulunbuy (Arnhem Land) (724km from Stuart Hwy)

Willeroo

Stuart Highway
Threeways to Darwin

0 — 50 — 100 km

Mataranka
Eisey Cemetery

Roper
Hwy

1

Roper Bar (174km from Stuart Hwy)

Larrimah

160

Buchanan

Daly Waters

36

Carpentaria Hwy

To Top Springs (180km from Stuart Hwy)

★ 10 ★ Distances Between Locations in Kilometres

Dunmarra

To Borroloola (383km from Stuart Hwy)

Newcastle Waters

109

Unsealed roads can vary from excellent to impassable, depending on many factors.

Elliot

Lake Woods

72

To Cape Crawford (381km from Stuart Hwy)

87

Renner Springs

Barkly Stock Route

89

Tarrabool Lake

Stuart Memorial

To Alice Springs (580km)

Continued: Threeways to Darwin Map

Continued: Port Augusta to Kulgera Map

Continued: Kulgera to Threeways Map

Coober Pedy

Coober Pedy (population 2700) is as close as Australia gets to a having a frontier town. The name is Aboriginal and is said to mean 'white fellow's hole in the ground', which aptly describes the place, as a large proportion of the population lives in dugouts to shelter from extreme temperatures.

The most dominant landmark is the **Big Winch**, which is a lookout over the town and has an extensive display of cut and uncut opals. The **Old Timers Mine** and the **Umoona Mine & Museum** are also worth a look. Several dugout homes are open to visitors – all you have to do is create an eccentric enough abode and you can charge admission!

A must-see is **Crocodile Harry's**, an interesting dugout home about 4km from town which has featured in a number of documentaries and movies, including *Mad Max III*. Not far either side of the Stuart Highway at Coober Pedy you have the world's largest sheep station (Commonwealth Hill at 10,567 sq km) and its largest cattle station (Anna Creek at 30,113 sq km).

Some useful services in Coober Pedy include:

Medical Facilities
    Coober Pedy Hospital (☎ (08) 8672 5009)
Police
    (☎ (08) 8672 5056)
Post Office
    (☎ (08) 8672 5062)

From Coober Pedy, rough and dusty roads lead east to **William Creek** (166km) and north to **Oodnadatta** (190km), both on the Oodnadatta Track. A short distance out of Coober Pedy, the road to Oodnadatta crosses the Dog Fence, and then traverses the flat, eerie and seemingly lifeless Moon Plain (also featured in *Mad Max III*).

Coober Pedy to Alice Springs

The highway continues north from Coober Pedy through fairly unchanging country, passing through **Cadney Park Roadhouse** after 152km, from where a good dirt road

strikes out east to Oodnadatta (172km), an attractive route which passes through the colourful mesa hills known as the **Painted Desert**.

The next settlement on the highway is the small town of **Marla** (population 250), 83km north of Cadney Park, and the head of the Oodnadatta Track (see the Oodnadatta Track section). The opal-mining fields of **Mintabie**, 35km to the west, are worth a quick visit, although permits need to be arranged from the Marla police station.

From Marla it's just a hop, skip and a jump (156km to be exact) to the **Northern Territory border**, and a further 2km to where one of the most famous outback tracks, the **Gunbarrel Highway**, heads off into the great vastness of the western deserts (see the Gunbarrel Highway section later in this chapter).

Kulgera is next, and from here you can strike out east along a dirt road (which can be treacherous in the wet season) to **Finke**, from where there are a number of possibilities: east to Old Andado and then south to Mount Dare and Oodnadatta or north to Alice Springs, or head north to Alice Springs along the Finke Track, also known as the Old Ghan Track (see the Finke & Old Andado Tracks section).

From **Erldunda**, 75km north of Kulgera, you can head west along the bitumen road to **Uluru (Ayers Rock)** (250km) and **Kata Tjuta (the Olgas)** (287km), from where the dirt takes over once again for the journey to **Docker River** and the start of the **Gunbarrel Highway** – see the Gunbarrel Highway section later in this chapter.

The old turn-off for Kings Canyon is 69km north of Erldunda, and from here the final stage into Alice Springs is 118km, passing en route the **Outback Camel Safaris** camel farm at Stuart's Well in the James Ranges.

Alice Springs (see the earlier Alice Springs section), set in the heart of the rugged and spectacular MacDonnell Ranges, is an oasis – a place to rest, restock, eat out and make repairs before heading bush again. It's a lively town with plenty of things to see, and most people find that a few days here are well spent. Being the biggest population centre in the outback, the Alice is also the best place for mechanical repairs and spare parts.

Alice Springs to Tennant Creek

Twenty km north of Alice Springs is the **Tanami Track** turn-off, and the signboard here indicates it's a long and lonely 703km to the Western Australia border. This road gives direct access to the Kimberley and is becoming increasingly popular. Conventional vehicles can pass with care (see the Tanami Track section later in this chapter for details).

The **Plenty Highway** turn-off is a further 48km north, and this road heads east to the Queensland border and on to Mount Isa (773km). The **Sandover Highway**, which leaves the Plenty Highway 27km east of the Stuart Highway, is an alternative to the Plenty, and it heads north-east into outback Queensland, with connections to Camooweal and Mount Isa (see the Plenty Highway and Sandover Highway sections later in this chapter).

Continuing north you pass through the tiny settlements of **Aileron** (65km north of the Plenty Highway turn-off), **Ti Tree** (a further 60km), **Barrow Creek** (90km) and **Wauchope** (113km). It's about here that you pass the last sand dune of the Centre, and start the transition from the red country of the centre of Australia to the more densely vegetated and generally greener Top End. This part of the highway crosses the very eastern edge of the Tanami Desert, where spinifex grass dominates.

The **Devil's Marbles Conservation Reserve**, just a few kilometres north of Wauchope in the Davenport Ranges, consists of unusual spherical boulders scattered haphazardly over a large area. Aboriginal mythology has it that they were laid by the Rainbow Serpent.

Tennant Creek

The town of Tennant Creek (population 3700), 114km north of Wauchope, is, along with Katherine, the only town of any size between the Alice and Darwin. Known as Jurnkurakurr by the local Aborigines, the town has an interesting history. It was on the Overland Telegraph route; there's an old telegraph station here and it was also the site of a small gold rush in the 1930s. The visitor information centre is on **Battery Hill** on Peko Rd, where there are daily tours of a historic gold-crushing plant and underground tunnel. In town there's a **National Trust museum**. Useful addresses in Tennant Creek include:

Medical Facilities
    Tennant Creek Hospital, Schmidt St (☎ (08) 8962 4399)
National Parks
    Parks & Wildlife Commission (☎ (08) 8962 2140)
Police
    Paterson St (☎ (08) 8962 4444)
Post Office
    (☎ (08) 8962 2196)
Tourist Office
    Visitor Information Centre, Battery Hill (☎ (08) 8962 3388)

Tennant Creek to Katherine

Twenty-five km north of Tennant Creek, **Threeways** marks the junction of the Stuart Highway and the Barkly Highway, which is the only bitumen connection between Queensland and the Northern Territory. At this major road junction an ugly brick **memorial** commemorates the Reverend John Flynn, the founder of the Royal Flying Doctor Service.

About 45km north of Threeways there's a **memorial** to Stuart at Attack Creek, where the explorer turned back on the first of his attempts to cross Australia from south to north – see the Oodnadatta Track section later in this chapter. Just a few kilometres further north, and 4km off the road along the old Stuart Highway, is **Churchill's Head**, a rock said to look like Britain's wartime prime minister.

Back on the Stuart Highway, a flat-topped hill known as **Lubra's Lookout** overlooks **Renner Springs**, 89km north from the Stuart Memorial. This is generally accepted as the dividing line between the seasonally wet Top End and the dry Centre, and the highway also divides the Tanami Desert on the west side from the Barkly Tableland on the east. Seventy two km after Renner Springs there's the turn-off to the east of the **Barkly Stock Route**, a dirt road which joins up with the Carpentaria Highway.

The next intersection is 109km up the Stuart Highway, where the **Buchanan Highway**, named after the great cattleman Nat Buchanan, heads north-west to **Top Springs**, **Victoria River Downs** and **Timber Creek** on the Victoria Highway. **Daly Waters**, 36km north of the Buchanan Highway junction and 3km off the highway, was an important staging post in the early days of aviation – Amy Johnson landed here. The **Daly Waters Pub** is an atmospheric place, dating from 1893; it's said to be the oldest pub in the Territory. There's good food available here.

Just south of Daly Waters, the single-lane, sealed **Carpentaria Highway** heads off east to **Borroloola**, one of the best barramundi fishing spots in the Northern Territory, 383km away near the Gulf of Carpentaria.

About 160km north of Daly Waters, the **Roper Highway** branches east from the Stuart Highway. It leads 174km to **Roper Bar**, near the Roper River on the edge of Aboriginal land – an area mainly visited by fishing enthusiasts. All but about 40km is sealed. About 5km south of the Roper junction is the turn-off to the **Elsey Cemetery**, not far off the highway. Here are the graves of characters like 'the Fizzer' who came to life in *We of the Never Never*, Jeannie Gunn's classic novel of turn-of-the-century outback life.

Mataranka is on the Stuart Highway, another 7km north of the Roper Highway turn-off. At **Mataranka homestead**, 7km east of the highway along the turn-off just south of town, a crystal-clear thermal pool in a pocket of rainforest is a great place to wind down after a day on the road – though it can get crowded. It's the major attraction in the **Elsey National Park**, which extends down the Roper River for several kilometres from the hot pool.

From Mataranka the highway curves to the north-west and reaches Katherine after 106km.

Katherine

Katherine (population 9500) has long been an important transit point, since the river it's built on and named after is the first permanent running water if you're coming north from Alice Springs.

The town includes some historic old buildings, such as the **Sportsman's Arms**, featured in *We of the Never Never*. Interesting features of the town include the old **railway station** (owned by the National Trust), the small **Katherine Museum** in the old airport terminal building, and **Springvale homestead**, 8km south-west of town (turn right off the Victoria Highway after 3.8km), which claims to be the oldest cattle station in the Northern Territory. Today, it's also a tourist accommodation centre; free half-hour tours around the old homestead are given once or twice daily.

Katherine is also where the **Victoria Highway**, part of Highway 1 around Australia, joins from the west, connecting the Northern Territory with Western Australia.

Some useful addresses in Katherine include:

Medical Facilities
    Katherine Hospital, Gorge Rd (☎ (08) 8972 9211)
National Parks
    Parks & Wildlife Commission, Giles St (☎ (08) 8973 8770)
Police
    Stuart Highway (☎ (08) 8972 0111)
Post Office
    Stuart Highway (☎ (08) 8972 1439)
Tourist Office
    Katherine Region Tourist Association, Stuart Highway (☎ (08) 8972 2650)

The main interest here, however, is the spectacular **Katherine Gorge**, 30km to the north-east along a bitumen road – a great place to camp, walk, swim, canoe, take a cruise or simply float along on an air mattress. Strictly speaking, Katherine Gorge is

13 gorges, separated from each other by rapids of varying length. The gorge walls aren't high, but it is a remote, beautiful place. It is 12km long and has been carved out by the Katherine River, which rises in Arnhem Land. Further downstream it becomes the Daly River before flowing into the Timor Sea, 80km south-west of Darwin.

Katherine to Darwin

From Katherine it's 89km to **Pine Creek**, an interesting little gold-mining centre and the turn-off for the southern route into **Kakadu National Park** along the recently sealed Kakadu Highway (see the Kakadu section in the Tropics chapter).

At Hayes Creek, 63km north of Pine Creek, a sealed section of the old Stuart Highway makes a loop to the north-west before rejoining the main road 49km on. It's a scenic trip and leads to a number of pleasant spots, but access to them is often cut in the wet season. To reach **Douglas Hot Springs**, turn south off the old highway just after it branches from the Stuart Highway and go about 35km. The nature park here includes a section of the Douglas River and several hot springs – a bit hot for bathing at 40°C, but there are cooler pools, and a pretty camping area.

Butterfly Gorge National Park is about 15km beyond Douglas Hot Springs along a 4WD track. True to its name, butterflies sometimes swarm in the gorge.

The turning to **Daly River** (81km from the turn-off) is 27km further on. There's a **Catholic mission** (the ruins of an 1886 Jesuit mission) and the **Daly River Nature Park** where you can camp. Bird life is abundant at some times of the year, and quite a few saltwater and freshwater crocodiles inhabit the river.

The beautiful 12m **Robin Falls** are a short, rocky walk off the old highway, 18km along. The falls, set in a monsoon-forested gorge, dwindle to a trickle in the dry season, but are spectacular in the Wet.

The old highway rejoins the Stuart Highway at the small settlement of **Adelaide River**, which has a cemetery for those who died in the 1942-43 Japanese air raids on the Top End. The whole stretch of the highway between here and Darwin is dotted with WWII airstrips.

Twenty-eight km north of Adelaide River is the turn-off to the regional centre of **Batchelor**, which is the main access point for **Litchfield National Park**. (See the Litchfield National Park section in The Tropics chapter.) The highway then continues north through cleared farmland for the final 90km stretch into Darwin. The only feature of note along this section is where the **Arnhem Highway**, the access road to Kakadu National Park and Arnhem Land, branches off the Stuart Highway 34km south of Darwin.

See the Darwin section in the Tropics chapter for information on the capital of the Top End.

DETOURS

While most of the detours off the Stuart Highway are tracks in themselves, there's an interesting trip you can make from Woomera to Andamooka and the huge Olympic Dam mine at Roxby Downs. **Andamooka** (population 470) is a rough-and-ready opal-mining community, similar in many respects to Coober Pedy, but on a much smaller scale. However, due to its isolation, it is much less visited. It is 106km north of Woomera, and the road is sealed throughout.

The **Olympic Dam** uranium, gold, silver and copper mine was established in the early 1980s. It is the world's largest copper-uranium mine, and is currently one of only three uranium mines in the country. There are mine tours daily from the BP station at Roxby Downs township.

FACILITIES

Facilities along the Stuart Highway are excellent all the way; the longest stretch without a fuel stop is 251km between Glendambo and Coober Pedy.

There are roadhouses with fuel (all types), food, accommodation and mechanical repairs at most centres along the way. While some roadhouses in the larger towns have 24-hour fuel, the smaller places are typically open from early morning to late evening. Details of accommodation along the Stuart Highway include:

Port Augusta
No shortage of hotels, motels and campsites.
Woomera
Woomera Eldo Hotel (☎ (08) 8673 7867), Kotara Crescent, has single/double rooms from $33/45. The Woomera Travellers Village (☎ (08) 8673 7800), Wirruna Ave, has campsites for $5 per person ($14 for two with power) and on-site caravans from $25 for two.
Glendambo
Glendambo Tourist Centre (☎ (08) 8672 1030 motel and 8672 1035 caravan park) has rooms for $75/85, accommodation in a bunkhouse for $12, on-site vans from $30 a double and campsites from $9.50 for two people ($14.50 powered).
Coober Pedy
No shortage of hotels, motels and campsites.
Cadney Park
Cadney Homestead Motel & Caravan Park (☎ (08) 8670 7994) has rooms at $70/77 and campsites from $6 per person ($16 for two with power). One-bedroom cabins are also available for $35 a double.
Marla
Marla Travellers Rest (☎ (08) 8670 7001) has rooms from $59/65, cabins from $19/28 and campsites from $5 per person ($15 for two with power).
Kulgera
Kulgera Motel & Caravan Park (☎ (08) 8956 0973) has rooms from $38 and campsites from $5 per person.
Erldunda
Desert Oaks Motel & Caravan Park (☎ (08) 8956 0984) has rooms for $64/75 and campsites from $6 per person ($16 for two with power).
Alice Springs
See the earlier Alice Springs section.
Barrow Creek
Barrow Creek Hotel & Caravan Park (☎ (08) 8956 9753) has cabins for $20/35 and campsites from $7.
Wauchope
Wauchope Well Hotel & Caravan Park (☎ (08) 8964 1963) has rooms from $25/55 and campsites from $6.
Tennant Creek
No shortage of hotels, motels and campsites.
Threeways
Threeways Roadhouse Motel & Caravan Park

(☎ (08) 8962 2744) has rooms from $45 and campsites from $4 per person.
Renner Springs
Renner Springs Motel (☎ (08) 8964 4505) has rooms from $40/45.
Elliott
Elliott Hotel (☎ (08) 8969 2069) and the BP Roadhouse (☎ (08) 8969 2018) have rooms from around $35/45. The Midland Caravan Park (☎ (08) 8969 2037) has cabins for $40, campsites from $10 for two people.
Daly Waters
The Daly Waters Pub Hotel & Caravan Park (☎ (08) 8975 9927) on Stuart St, 3km west of the Stuart Highway, has rooms from $28 and campsites from $6 for two people. The Hi-Way Inn & Caravan Park (☎ (08) 8975 9925) has rooms from $45/55 and campsites at $3 per person.
Larrimah
Larrimah Wayside Inn & Caravan Park (☎ (08) 8975 9931) has rooms from $10/20 and free campsites ($5 powered). The Green Park Tourist Complex (☎ (08) 8975 9937) has campsites from $3, or $9 for two people with power.
Mataranka
The Old Elsey Inn (☎ (08) 8975 4512) has rooms for $45/55. The Mataranka homestead (☎ (08) 8975 4544), 9km south-east of town, costs around $79 for a double room and $63 for a 'budget' motel room. You can also camp at the Mataranka homestead from $7 per person plus $4 per site for two, and at the 12 Mile Yards Camping Area (☎ (08) 8975 4789) on John Hauser Drive for $5 per person.
Katherine
No shortage of hotels, motels and campsites.
Pine Creek
Pine Creek Motel & Caravan Park (☎ (08) 8976 1288 motel and (08) 8976 1217 caravan park), Moule St, has rooms from $63/74 and campsites from $10 for two people.
Adelaide River
Adelaide River Inn & Caravan Park (☎ (08) 8976 7047) has rooms from $55/75 and campsites from $6 per person.

ALTERNATIVE TRANSPORT
As you'd expect on such a major highway, there are daily scheduled bus services all the way from Port Augusta to Darwin with both Greyhound Pioneer Australia (☎ toll-free 13 2030) and McCafferty's (☎ toll-free 13 1499). You can also take the Ghan train from Port Augusta to Alice Springs (see the separate entry on the Ghan in the Getting Around chapter).

MacDonnell Ranges

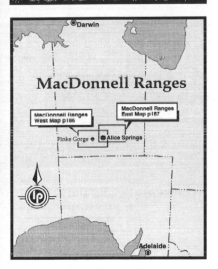

Sweeping east-west for over 400km, the timeless MacDonnell Ranges form a rugged red barrier across the vast central Australian plain. The ranges mainly consist of a parallel series of long, steep-sided ridges that rise 100 to 600m above the valley floors. Scattered throughout are deep gorges carved by ancient rivers that meander south into the Simpson Desert. Here also are the four highest peaks west of the Great Dividing Range. Mt Zeil, the highest, is 1531m above sea level and 900m above the surrounding plain.

Although arid, the ranges are home to a huge variety of native plants, including many tall trees such as the majestic ghost gum. In hidden, moist places are relics of the rainforest flora that covered this region millions of years ago. Wildlife enthusiasts will delight in the chance to observe 167 species of birds, 85 reptiles, 23 native mammals, 10 fish and five frog species; a number of the mammals are rare or endangered elsewhere in the arid zone.

Alice Springs is conveniently situated almost centrally in the ranges. Tourism is big business here, with over 350,000 international and interstate visitors to the town each year. Many of the most spectacular landscapes and most important biological areas are now included in national parks and reserves, which are generally easily reached by conventional vehicle. Largest of these is the 2100-sq-km West MacDonnell National Park, which stretches 160km west from the outskirts of Alice Springs. To the east of town, a string of mainly small parks extends for nearly the same distance.

Most parks have basic picnic facilities, and there are many excellent walks and supurb scenic highlights. However, opportunities for vehicle-based camping are rather limited and most bush camping grounds bulge at the seams during the cooler months. There are commercial facilities to the east at Ross River and Arltunga. Ross River offers a range of services, including meals, motel-style accommodation, camping and fuel. Arltunga is more limited.

INFORMATION
Tourist Offices
The best place for general information on all aspects of the MacDonnell Ranges is CATIA's visitor information centre (☎ (08) 8952 5800) in Alice Springs.

For in-depth information on national parks and reserves, contact the Parks & Wildlife Commission (☎ (08) 8951 8211), PO Box 1046, Alice Springs, NT 0871. Alternatively, contact the rangers direct at:

Simpsons Gap (☎ (08) 8955 0310) for the eastern half of the West MacDonnell National Park

Ormiston Gorge (☎ (08) 8956 7799) for the western half of the West MacDonnell National Park

Alice Springs Telegraph Station (☎ (08) 8952 1013) for Emily & Jessie Gaps Conservation Reserve

Trephina Gorge (☎ (08) 8956 9765) for Corroboree Rock Conservation Reserve, N'Dhala Gorge Nature Park and Trephina Gorge Nature Park

Arltunga (☎ (08) 8956 9770) for the Arltunga Historical Reserve and Ruby Gap Nature Park

Emergency

In the event of an emergency, you can obtain assistance at the park offices listed above. The resort at Ross River has staff trained in first aid and, like the ranger stations, is in telephone contact with the outside world. In more remote areas, hail one of the tourist coaches, which are invariably fitted with HF radios and first-aid kits.

Books

Sadly, there are no good books on the MacDonnell Ranges, although Jeff & Mare Carter's *The Complete Guide to Central Australia* (Hodder & Stoughton, Sydney, 1993) does have a fair-sized section devoted to touring the area. This comprehensive, well-written book is a worthwhile purchase, particularly if you're travelling further afield in the Red Centre.

Penny van Oosterzee's *The Centre – the Natural History of Australia's Desert Regions* (Reed Books Pty Ltd, Sydney, 1991) contains interesting material on the central ranges.

Maps

For topographic information AUSLIG's *Hermannsburg* and *Alice Springs* 1:250,000 sheets are reasonably detailed. For bushwalkers, a 1:50,000 series of orthophoto maps, also by AUSLIG, covers the ranges east of Serpentine Gorge.

The map-guide *MacDonnell Ranges*, by Westprint Heritage Maps, is a useful planning and touring reference. They also produce the map-guide *East MacDonnells*, which covers the ranges from Alice Springs east to Ruby Gap Nature Park. It highlights the 'Explorer Territory' 4WD route from the Ringwood Beef Road through to the Plenty

Highway via Ross River homestead and Arltunga.

For the MacDonnell Ranges west of town, get hold of the *West MacDonnell National Park* map-guide produced by the Department of Lands, Planning and Environment. There's plenty of useful information and a good map at a scale of 1:250,000.

AUSLIG maps are available from the Department of Lands, Planning & Environment in Gregory Terrace, Alice Springs. You can buy the other maps there and from numerous other outlets around Alice Springs, including CATIA, newsagencies and service stations.

Radio Frequencies

As the main roads of the MacDonnell Ranges are fairly busy most of the year, a HF radio isn't generally considered necessary. The major exception would be a visit to remote Ruby Gap in the off-peak season (October to April), when a radio could prove useful.

The MacDonnell Ranges are serviced by the Alice Springs RFDS base (call sign VJD; ☎ (08) 8952 1033), which monitors 5410 and 6950kHz between 7.30 am and 5 pm weekdays. Use 2020 and 5410kHz for after-hours emergency calls.

WEST FROM ALICE SPRINGS

Spearing between high ridgelines, the road from Alice Springs through the West MacDonnells is sealed for the 135km to the Finke River crossing near Glen Helen. From here the 37km past Redbank Gorge to the road between Haasts Bluff and Hermannsburg is rough dirt. Along the way are a number of spectacular red gorges and several deep waterholes, most of which are within the West MacDonnell National Park. In dry conditions, all the main attractions are accessible to conventional vehicles.

Simpsons Gap

Heading out on Larapinta Drive you pass the **Alice Springs Desert Park** on the outskirts of Alice Springs, then you're at the grave of Dr John Flynn, founder of the RFDS and the Australian Inland Mission. On a low rise with ghost gums and a magnificent view of nearby **Mt Gillen**, the great man's last resting place is just outside the eastern boundary of the West MacDonnell National Park.

At **Simpsons Gap**, 22km from town, Roe Creek has gouged a narrow gorge with towering red cliffs through Rungutjirba Ridge. It's popular with picnickers, has some nice walks and a sealed cycle path that winds through the bush from Flynn's Grave (see Activities later in this section). In early morning and late afternoon you may see rock-wallabies among the jumble of huge boulders right in the gap. Simpsons Gap is open 8 am to 8 pm daily.

Standley Chasm

From the Simpsons Gap turn-off, you cross Aboriginal land for the next 30km to Standley Chasm. Owned and managed by the nearby Iwupataka Aboriginal community, this deep narrow cleft has smooth vertical walls and is famous for its midday light display – for a brief period at noon, reflected sunlight causes the rocks to glow red.

The 15-minute walk up the rocky gully from the refreshment kiosk to the chasm is crammed with moisture-loving plants such as river gums, cycad palms and ferns, creating an unexpected lushness in this arid world

of craggy bluffs. It's one of the nicest walks in central Australia but most visitors are in too much of a hurry to notice. For a real walking challenge with many rewards, you can return to Alice Springs along the Larapinta Trail (see Activities). Standley Chasm is open daily 7.30 am to 6 pm, and entry costs $3 per adult.

Ellery Big-Hole & Serpentine Gorge

Leaving the Standley Chasm turn-off, you pass through a scenic gap in the Heavitree Range before swinging right onto Namatjira Drive. Larapinta Drive continues straight on to Hermannsburg, and you can return this way after exploring the West MacDonnells (see Alternative Routes later in this section).

Ten km from the intersection is the **Hugh River** with its large river gums, then you enter a steep-sided valley that takes you all the way to Glen Helen, 75km further on. The Hugh River provided John McDouall Stuart with a route through the MacDonnell Ranges on his expeditions to and from the north between 1860 and 1862. Stuart named the ranges after the then governor of South Australia.

Ellery Creek Big-Hole, 93km from Alice Springs, is a popular swimming hole in summer. However, being shaded by high cliffs it's generally too cold for comfort at other times. There's a small camping ground

---

Central Rock-Rat

There was great excitement among central Australian naturalists late in 1996, when conservation volunteers working on the Larapinta Trail west of Alice Springs trapped an unusual yellow-brown rodent. About the size of a rat, the animal had a swollen hairy tail shaped like a carrot. It turned out to be a central rock-rat (*Zyzomys pedunculatus*), a species so rare that in the past hundred years only five sightings of it had been recorded.

Apparently confined to the rocky ranges around Alice Springs, the central rock-rat was discovered by science in 1894. However, despite intensive searches, no confirmed sightings had been made since 1960, when a single animal was caught raiding a stockman's food supplies about 300km west of town. As a result, it was listed nationally as critically endangered, although many naturalists considered it probably extinct.

Subsequent to its rediscovery, rangers visited the area and managed to trap three adult rats. These are now the nucleus of a captive breeding programme at the Alice Springs Desert Park, where the first litter of three young arrived in April 1997. It's hoped that a secure breeding colony can be established there to enable scientific study of the animal's behaviour and habitat requirements. Provided this captive population continues to grow, the central rock-rat will eventually be put on display in the park's nocturnal house. ■

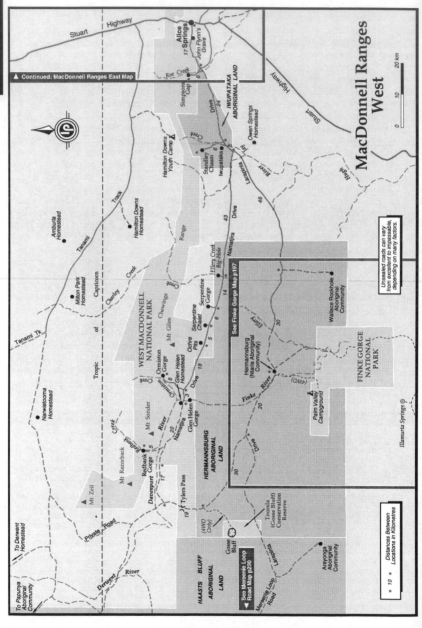

MacDonnell Ranges West

Stuart Highway

Alice Springs
17
John Flynn's Grave

Roe Creek
6

▲ Continued: MacDonnell Ranges East Map

IWUPATAKA ABORIGINAL LAND

Simpsons Gap
Drive
24

Stuart Highway

0   10   20 km

Hamilton Downs Youth Camp

Standley Chasm
Iwupatka
6

Owen Springs Homestead

Creek

Jay
Larapinta

River

Hugh

Hamilton Downs Homestead

Tanami Track

Range

46

Namatjira Drive
43

Amburla Homestead

Milton Park Homestead

Chewings Creek

Ellery Creek Big-Hole

14

Serpentine Gorge
Serpentine Chalet
6

See Finke Gorge Map p197

Unsealed roads can vary from excellent to impassable, depending on many factors.

Tanami Tk

Tropic   of   Capricorn

WEST MACDONNELL NATIONAL PARK

Chewings Range

Mt Giles
Ochre Pits
5

Namatjira Drive
18

Ormiston Gorge
8
Glen Helen Homestead
3

Ormiston Creek

Wallace Rockhole Aboriginal Community

30

Narwietooma Homestead

Mt Sonder

Glen Helen Gorge

Redbank Creek

Namatjira River
20

HERMANNSBURG ABORIGINAL LAND

Hermannsburg (Ntaria Aboriginal Community)

Finke River

(4WD)
20

FINKE GORGE NATIONAL PARK

Illamurta Springs

Redbank Gorge
5

Mt Razorback

Davenport Creek
17

Tylers Pass
19

Private Road

To Derwent Homestead

Mt Zeil

Palm Valley Campground

30

Drive

30

Tnorala (Gosse Bluff) Conservation Reserve
(4WD Only)

Gosse Bluff

Larapinta

Areyonga Aboriginal Community

HAASTS BLUFF ABORIGINAL LAND

To Papunya Aboriginal Community

Derwent River

▼ See Mereenie Loop Road Map p200

Mereenie Loop Road

Distances Between Locations in Kilometres

* 10 *

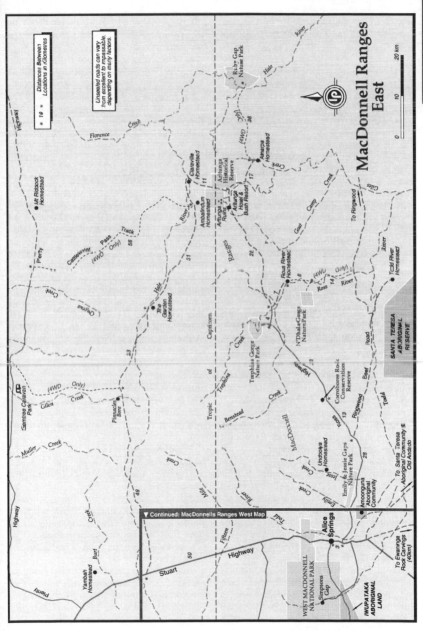

MacDonnell Ranges East

0   10   20 km

Distances Between
Locations in Kilometres

⭑ 10 ⭑

Unsealed roads can vary,
from excellent to impassable,
depending on many factors.

here (see Camping), and the rangers recommend that you do the 20-minute **Dolomite Walk**. An information shelter at the carpark explains the area's fascinating geological history, which is exposed in the creekbanks downstream from the waterhole.

Continuing on you soon arrive at the Serpentine Gorge carpark. From here it's a 1km walk to the main attraction, and this makes a nice introduction to the general area. Most times a waterhole blocks the gorge entrance, but if you swim through (brrr), you can walk up the rocky creek past large cycads to a second water-filled cleft. There is some stunning scenery here, which can also be enjoyed from a lookout above the main entrance. Section eight of the Larapinta Trail (see Activities) starts at the carpark and takes you via **Counts Point Lookout** to the Serpentine Chalet dams and **Inarlanga Pass**, then on to the Ochre Pits.

Ochre Pits

Six km past Serpentine Gorge is the turn-off to the old Serpentine Chalet, where concrete slabs are all that remain of a 1950s tourist venture. The rough 4WD access track takes you past a number of bush campsites suitable for winter use (see Camping). For details of walks in the area, see the brochures for sections eight and nine of the Larapinta Trail.

The nearby Ochre Pits, with extensive parking and picnicking areas, has some interesting information signs relating to ochre and its importance to Aborigines. Except for a small deposit of yellow ochre, which is still used by local Aborigines, the material at this minor quarry site is of poor quality. Nevertheless, the swirls of red and yellow ochre in the walls of this little ravine make an attractive picture in the afternoon sun. From here a walking track takes you to the Larapinta Trail at Inarlanga Pass (see Activities).

Ormiston Gorge

From the Ochre Pits it's 26km to Ormiston Gorge, where soaring cliffs, tall gums, rich colours and a deep waterhole combine to form some of the grandest scenery in the central ranges. Most visitors congregate at the gorge entrance, but for those who want to explore further afield there are several recommended walks (see Activities) that start and finish at the information centre. Ormiston Gorge is a good spot for wildlife enthusiasts thanks to its variety of habitats – they include mulga woodland, spinifex slopes, rock faces, large river gums and permanent water. Its small camping ground (see Camping) makes an ideal base for exploring the western half of the West MacDonnells.

Glen Helen Gorge & Homestead

Glen Helen homestead, 135km from Alice Springs (see Facilities), was closed at the time of this update. Nearby Glen Helen Gorge, where there's another large waterhole, has been carved out by the Finke River; a major flood in 1988 backed up so high that it flooded the tourist accommodation. A 10-minute stroll takes you from the resort down to the gorge entrance, but if you want to go further you'll have to either swim through the waterhole or climb around it. Bush camping is permitted in the Finke River upstream from the crossing on Namatjira Drive (see Camping).

Redbank Gorge

The bitumen ends at Glen Helen, and for the next 20km to the Redbank Gorge turn-off you're on rough dirt with numerous sharp dips.

From Namatjira Drive it's 5km to the Redbank carpark, from where the gorge is a 20-minute walk up a rocky creekbed. Redbank Gorge is extremely narrow, with polished, multihued walls that close over your head to block out the sky. You normally need an air mattress to get through, as its deep pools are freezing even in summer, but it's worth doing – the colours and cathedral atmosphere inside are terrific.

Redbank Gorge is the starting point for section 12 of the Larapinta Trail, which takes you to the summit of nearby Mt Sonder (see Activities). There are two small camping areas in the park (see Camping).

EAST FROM ALICE SPRINGS

The road from Alice Springs to Arltunga is extremely scenic for the most part, taking you through a jumble of high ridges and hills drained by gum-lined creeks. Along the way are several parks and reserves where you can explore a variety of attractions such as rugged gorges, Aboriginal culture and abandoned mining areas.

The Ross Highway from Alice Springs is sealed for the 71km to the Arltunga turn-off, where it becomes a good dirt road for the final 7km to Ross River homestead. Arltunga is 32km from the Ross Highway, and this unsealed road can be quite rough, as can the alternative return route via Claraville, Ambalindum and The Garden homesteads to the Stuart Highway (see Alternative Routes).

Access to John Hayes Rockhole (in Trephina Gorge Nature Park), N'Dhala Gorge and Ruby Gap is suitable for 4WDs only. The region's other main attractions are normally accessible to conventional vehicles.

Emily & Jessie Gaps

Leaving Alice Springs you head south through Heavitree Gap, then turn east onto the Ross Highway. Paralleling a high quartzite ridge to the north, the road heads out through the South Alice tourist and farm area before, finally, you're in the bush.

Emily Gap, 10km from the Stuart Highway, is a beautiful spot with **Aboriginal rock paintings** and a deep waterhole in the narrow gorge. Local drunks have caused numerous problems here over the years, particularly on weekends, so check the situation before leaving your car to go walking or sightseeing. Jessie Gap, 8km further on, is equally scenic, and normally a much quieter and safer place to enjoy nature. The walk along the ridgetop between the two gaps is worth doing (see Activities).

Corroboree Rock

Past Jessie Gap you cross eroded flats with the Heavitree Range looming large on your left, then enter a valley between red ridges. Forty one km from the highway is Corroboree Rock, one of a number of unusual tan-coloured dolomite hills scattered over the valley floor. A small cave in this large dog-toothed outcrop was once used by Aborigines as a storehouse for sacred objects.

Trephina Gorge

At 61km is the **Benstead Creek** crossing, with its lovely big gums. The thousands of young river gums that line the road past here germinated in the mid-1970s, when the region received unusually high rainfall. This delightful scenery, which is totally at odds with the common perception of central Australia, continues for the next 6km to the Trephina Gorge turn-off.

Trephina Gorge Nature Park offers some magnificent scenery, nice walks (see Activities), deep swimming holes, abundant wildlife and low-key camping areas (see Camping). Its main attractions are Trephina Gorge, Trephina Bluff and **John Hayes Rockhole**. The rockhole, a permanent waterhole, is reached by a rough track that wanders for several kilometres up the so-called **Valley of the Eagles**.

With its restful atmosphere and grand views, Trephina Gorge is a great spot for a quiet picnic. There's a colony of black-footed rock wallabies on the cliff above the waterhole – wander down first thing in the morning and you'll usually spot them leaping nimbly about on the rock face.

N'Dhala Gorge & Ross River Homestead

The sealed road ends at the Arltunga turn-off, 71km from Alice Springs and 7km before Ross River homestead. About 1km before the resort is the turn-off to **N'Dhala Gorge Nature Park**; the track winds down the picturesque **Ross River valley**, where a number of sandy river crossings make the going tough for conventional vehicles. As the sign says, towing is costly.

N'Dhala Gorge features hundreds of ancient **rock carvings**, which decorate a deep, narrow gorge 20 minutes' walk from the carpark. You can continue on past the gorge to the dusty Ringwood Beef Road, then head west to rejoin the Ross Highway about 30km from Alice Springs.

Originally the headquarters for Loves Creek station, the Ross River homestead resort boasts a pretty setting and offers a range of services and outdoor activities. For more details, see Facilities later in this section.

Arltunga

Leaving the Ross Highway, the first 12km of the Arltunga road passes through scenic **Bitter Springs Gorge**, where rumpled quartzite ridges tower above dolomite hills. This was the route taken by the early diggers as they walked from Alice Springs to the gold fields at the turn of the century. The road can be quite rough at times and is impassable after heavy rain.

The **Arltunga Historical Reserve** features significant evidence of the gold-mining activity that took place in its arid hills between 1887 and 1913. Its major attraction is a partially restored ghost town containing the remains of a treatment plant and several stone buildings, including a police station and gaol. Walking tracks take you past **old mines**, now complete with bat colonies – two underground mines are open to visitors, so make sure to bring a torch and some old clothes (see Activities).

The richest area was **White Range**, a high quartzite ridge in the eastern part of the reserve. In a remarkable feat of short-sightedness, almost all the historic ruins and small mines that once dotted the ridge were destroyed during a recent opencut mining operation. Joseph Hele, who is credited with the discovery of gold at White Range in 1897, is buried in the nearby cemetery.

Arltunga is a fascinating place for anyone interested in history. To get some idea of what life was like for the early diggers, call in to the information centre. It has displays of old mining machinery and historic photographs, and there are slide shows during the winter months. For details on the various points of interest, see the reserve's informative brochure.

While gold prospecting isn't permitted at Arltunga, there is a **fossicking reserve** in a gully just to the east where you may (with enormous luck) find some gold. A fossicking licence is required; you can obtain one from the Department of Mines & Energy at 58 Hartley St, Alice Springs.

Limited commercial facilities are available at the rustic Arltunga Hotel & Bush Resort near the reserve's main entrance (see Facilities).

Ruby Gap

From Arltunga you head east towards Atnarpa homestead, and turn left at the gate 12km further on. The road now deteriorates and is restricted to 4WD vehicles thanks to its sandy creek crossings and sharp jump-ups. The **Hale River** is 25km beyond the gate; follow the wheel ruts upstream (left) along the sandy bed for about 6km to the turn-around point, which is through Ruby Gap and just short of rugged **Glen Annie Gorge**. These are the main scenic attractions in the **Ruby Gap Nature Park**. If you're first on the scene after a flood, always check that the riverbed is firm before driving onto it, otherwise you may sink into deep quicksand.

In 1886, Ruby Gap was the scene of a frantic ruby rush that crashed overnight when it was found that the rubies were actually worthless garnets. The park's gorge and river scenery is some of the wildest and most attractive in central Australia, and being remote and hard to get to, it doesn't have the crowds that often destroy the atmosphere at more accessible places. Camping is allowed anywhere along the river. The park is managed by the rangers at Arltunga, so check road conditions with them before continuing on.

ALTERNATIVE ROUTES
Gosse Bluff

An alternative return route to Alice Springs once you reach Redbank Gorge is to continue west on Namatjira Drive, then turn south over **Tylers Pass** and link up with the unsealed **Mereenie Loop Road** between Hermannsburg and Watarrka (Kings Canyon).

From the Tyler Pass **lookout** you get a nice view south to Gosse Bluff, the prominent circular remnant of a huge impact crater that resulted when a comet plunged to Earth 130 million years ago. The Aboriginal name for this striking feature is Tnorala; in local mythology it's a wooden dish belonging to some star ancestors that fell from the sky during the Dreamtime. Gosse Bluff is covered by a conservation reserve managed by the rangers at Ormiston Gorge; check with them about access – usually 4WD only.

From Gosse Bluff you can continue east to Hermannsburg, where diesel, super and unleaded petrol are available. For details on Hermannsburg and the Mereenie Loop Road, see the section on Finke Gorge later in this chapter.

Arltunga Tourist Drive

The rough, 123km road from Arltunga via **Ambalindum** homestead meets the Stuart Highway 50km north of Alice Springs and makes an interesting alternative to the Ross Highway. You'll need a range of at least 400km to drive from Ross River homestead to Alice Springs with side trips to Arltunga and Ruby Gap. Check with the rangers at Arltunga for an update on road conditions before continuing on.

En route you can detour to the **Harts Range gem fields** via a 4WD track that turns off opposite Ambalindum. Fuel and camping facilities are available at the Gemtree Caravan Park on the Plenty Highway (see the section on the Plenty Highway for details).

ACTIVITIES – WEST OF ALICE SPRINGS

Walks

The Larapinta Trail By the turn of the century it's expected that 220km of walking tracks, often through remote country, will link Alice Springs to Mt Razorback, at the western end of the West MacDonnell National Park. The following stages (total 169km) were open in 1997:

- Section 1: Alice Springs Telegraph Station to Simpsons Gap (25km)
- Section 2: Simpsons Gap to Jay Creek (24km)
- Section 3: Jay Creek to Standley Chasm (15km)
- Section 8: Serpentine Gorge to the Ochre Pits (19km)
- Section 9: Ochre Pits to Ormiston Gorge (31km)
- Section 10: Ormiston Gorge to Glen Helen (13km)
- Section 11: Glen Helen to Redbank Gorge (33km)
- Section 12: Redbank Gorge to Mt Sonder summit (9km)

Each section has its own distinctive highlights: wildlife, rare plants, high lookouts, gorge scenery, deep waterholes or shady creeks. Experienced enthusiasts will enjoy them all, but if you're a beginner, you'll probably find the Alice Springs to Simpsons Gap and Ormiston Gorge to Glen Helen sections more suitable.

Each of the stages is covered by a detailed brochure ($1) available from the CATIA visitor information centre in Alice Springs, the Alice Springs Telegraph Station and the rangers at Simpsons Gap and Ormiston Gorge.

Simpsons Gap There are many walking opportunities here, with the short track up to the **Cassia Hill lookout** recommended for starters. You can do day walks on the Larapinta Trail – peaceful **Bond Gap** (to the west) and **Wallaby Gap** (to the east) are both worthwhile – or take the Woodland Trail to **Rocky Gap**. This track continues on to Bond Gap via the Larapinta Trail, but it's hard walking through rough hills and won't appeal to many. The flatter wooded country south-east of Simpsons Gap between Rungutjirba Ridge and Larapinta Drive has plenty of potential for off-track walks.

Ochre Pits A three-hour return walk takes you to scenic Inarlanga Pass at the foot of the Heavitree Range. Although the track passes through uninspiring country, the pass itself is interesting, as is the old Serpentine Chalet dam, an hour's walk to the east along the Larapinta Trail. For details, see the brochure on section eight of the Larapinta Trail.

Ormiston Gorge One of the best short walks in the MacDonnell Ranges is the three-hour loop from the information centre into remote

Ormiston Pound and back through Ormiston Gorge. Do it first thing in the morning in an anticlockwise direction so you can enjoy a sunlit view of the big cliffs in front.

Two other excellent but much longer cross-country excursions are mentioned in the *Walks of Ormiston Gorge and Pound* brochure – the return walk up Ormiston Creek to **Bowmans Gap** takes at least one day while the **Mt Giles** route is a two-day affair. If you're an experienced bushwalker, do yourself a favour and spend a night on Mt Giles – the dawn view across Ormiston Pound to Mt Sonder is sensational.

Section 10 of the Larapinta Trail winds over rocky hills and along gum-lined creeks from Ormiston Gorge to Glen Helen, with fine views to Mt Sonder en route.

Mt Sonder The full-day return walk along the ridgetop from Redbank Gorge to the summit of Mt Sonder will appeal to the well-equipped enthusiast. The route is mostly unmarked and the trek itself is nothing to rave about – it's rather monotonous and seems never-ending. However, the view and sense of achievement once you get there are ample reward. The rangers at Ormiston Gorge suggest that you register with them before doing this walk; you'll find route details in the brochure on section 12 of the Larapinta Trail.

Cycling

Simpsons Gap The 17km sealed cycling path between Flynn's Grave and Simpsons Gap wanders along timbered creekflats and over low rocky hills, with occasional kangaroos to keep you company. There are many bush picnic spots en route, and beaut views of Mt Gillen, Rungutjirba Ridge and the rugged Alice Valley. The path is suitable for novice cyclists, but don't go too fast – there are some sharp corners.

Flynn's Grave is 7km from the town centre, and you do this part along Larapinta Drive with an optional detour through the Alice Springs Desert Park. For the best views (not to mention comfort), cycle out in the early morning and return in the afternoon.

Carry plenty of drinking water in warm weather as there is none along the way.

ACTIVITIES – EAST OF ALICE SPRINGS
Walks

Emily & Jessie Gaps For a minor challenge, the 8km walk along the high, narrow ridgetop between these two gaps has much to recommend it. You get sweeping panoramas all the way, and there's usually wildlife including euros (wallaroos), black-footed rock wallabies and wedge-tailed eagles. The idea is to get someone to drop you off at Emily Gap, then have them continue on to Jessie Gap to get the picnic ready. Allow at least 2½ hours for the walk.

Trephina Gorge There are several good walks here, ranging from 30 minutes to five hours, each offering its own attraction. As examples, you can enjoy a relaxing stroll among the big gums along Trephina Creek, take the short, scenic rim walk around Trephina Gorge or, for a rewarding challenge, try the marked route over the main range from Trephina Gorge to John Hayes Rockhole. For details, see the *Walks of Trephina Gorge* brochure.

Arltunga Four interesting walks of under one hour give access to various old mining areas. One track leads to the MacDonnell Range Reef mine, where you can climb down steel ladders and explore about 50m of tunnels between two shafts. The adjoining walk to the nearby Golden Chance mine is also worth doing for its varied content. You'll find details on these walks in the reserve brochure.

Ruby Gap There are no marked walks here, but for the enthusiast a climb around the craggy rim of Glen Annie Gorge features superb views of this beautiful spot. You can climb up on the southern side and return from the north along the sandy floor, or vice versa. The grave of a ruby miner is hidden away at the gorge's northern end.

HUGH FINLAY

RICHARD I'ANSON

Top: Sheer walls tower over 100m above the rocky valley floor at Kings Canyon, NT
Bottom: Ormiston Gorge, MacDonnell Ranges, NT

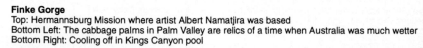

Finke Gorge
Top: Hermannsburg Mission where artist Albert Namatjira was based
Bottom Left: The cabbage palms in Palm Valley are relics of a time when Australia was much wetter
Bottom Right: Cooling off in Kings Canyon pool

ORGANISED TOURS

Day tours of the MacDonnell Ranges are very popular and there are numerous operators and styles to choose from. Costs vary, but expect to pay from $80 for a day tour with lunch included; ask about standby rates during the off season. Extended camping safaris incorporating places such as Palm Valley and Kings Canyon are also available.

See the CATIA visitor information centre in Alice Springs for details of tours in the MacDonnell Ranges and further afield.

FACILITIES – WEST OF ALICE SPRINGS
Glen Helen Homestead

A high red cliff provides a dramatic backdrop to this resort (☎ (08) 8956 7489), which is built on the site of an early homestead of Glen Helen station. It was closed indefinitely for refurbishments at the time of this update, and details of future facilities and prices were unavailable. Previously the resort offered a range of facilities including accommodation, camping, a restaurant, bar and fuel sales.

Camping

In the various parks and reserves, camping areas with basic facilities cost $1/3 per person/family payable into honesty boxes. You have to take your own firewood to most places.

Ellery Gap There's a small, usually crowded camping area with wood-burning barbecues, tables, pit toilet and limited shade within easy reach of the waterhole.

Serpentine Chalet Eleven sites scattered through the mulga and mallee along the track to the old Serpentine Chalet site have wood-burning fireplaces and a sense of isolation. These are ideal for winter camping but are too exposed in hot weather. The first five sites are accessible to conventional vehicles, the last six to 4WD only. No fees are charged.

Ormiston Gorge A small, relatively up-market camping ground offers hot showers, toilets, picnic furniture and gas barbecues, but there is no room for caravans. Fees are $4/10 per person/family. Water restrictions may apply during droughts, when it's recommended that you have your own supplies for drinking.

Finke River Free bush camping is available among big river gums along the Finke River upstream from Namatjira Drive. There are no facilities but the views and atmosphere are first class.

Redbank Gorge A small but pleasant camping ground on a creekflat with shady coolabahs has wood-burning barbecues, picnic tables and pit toilets. An early morning stroll downstream beside the Davenport River, with the sun softly lighting the river gums, is a nice way to start the day. There's another more basic camping ground on an exposed rocky ridge with views across to the main range.

FACILITIES – EAST OF ALICE SPRINGS
Ross River Homestead

Set among rumpled hills beside one of the region's most attractive rivers, Ross River homestead (☎ (08) 8956 9711) has accommodation, meals, a bar, fuel sales (diesel, super and unleaded) and a landing strip. It also offers various activities such as horse rides (from $20), camel rides, sunset wagon rides, overnight safaris, campfire cook-outs, guided walks, boomerang throwing and the obligatory billy tea and damper for morning tea. There's good potential for walks along the river and on the resort's network of tracks.

The homestead complex has spartan but comfortable air-con timber cabins with up to five beds (twin share costs $107 and it's $23 per extra person over 14 years). There are no fridges in the rooms, possibly to ensure that guests buy their drinks at the bar. Meals in the old homestead include buffet, carvery, bistro and barbecue styles, all at reasonable prices. There's also a saltwater swimming pool, for the use of guests only.

Just downstream, at the entrance to a scenic gorge, the resort's camping area has unpowered/powered sites ($8/10 per person) and a bunkhouse with linen supplied ($15). Shade is limited, but there's a small, rustic bar where you can enjoy a cold drink.

Camping

In the various parks and reserves, camping areas with basic facilities cost $1/3 per person/family payable into honesty boxes. You have to take your own firewood to most places.

Trephina Gorge Small camping grounds at Trephina Gorge, The Bluff and John Hayes Rockhole offer a variety of camping experiences. There's normally a heap of firewood just before the first major creek crossing on the Trephina Gorge access road.

The *Trephina Gorge camping area* is in a timbered gully a short stroll from the main attraction, and has running water, pit toilets, wood-burning barbecues and tables. It is suitable for caravans, unlike *The Bluff camp ground* about five minutes' walk away. The Bluff has similar facilities but a more spectacular creekbank setting under tall gums in front of a towering red ridge. *John Hayes Rockhole* has two basically appointed sites just downstream from the waterhole. The most obvious thing about this restricted area is its large population of ants.

N'Dhala Gorge There are three sites at the gorge entrance. Facilities are limited to wood-burning barbecues, tables and a pit toilet; shade is limited.

Arltunga Camping is not permitted within the historical reserve, but the friendly *Arltunga Hotel & Bush Resort* (☎ (08) 8956 9797) has cabins ($35), on-site vans ($30) and unpowered campsites ($5 per person). Counter lunches and teas are served daily.

Ruby Gap Free camping (without facilities) in a beautiful gorge environment is a major attraction of this area. The park is remote and visitors should be self-sufficient in everything. Please take your rubbish with you.

Finke Gorge

HIGHLIGHTS

- Camping under the stars at Boggy Hole and enjoying the atmosphere of central Australia's largest river
- Visiting Palm Valley and stepping back to a time when the now-arid hills were covered in rainforest
- Exploring the traditional German farmhouse architecture at Hermannsburg's historic precinct

The historic Hermannsburg mission is by the Finke River 135km west of Alice Springs. It's the gateway to two 4WD tracks that head south to Palm Valley and Boggy Hole, in the 46,000-hectare Finke Gorge National Park. Both run through Finke Gorge itself, where central Australia's largest river has carved a long, meandering passage through the ranges. For much of the time you're actually driving in the sandy riverbed, so a 4WD vehicle and experience in using it are essential. This particularly applies to the rugged Boggy Hole Track, which continues past Boggy Hole to join up with the Ernest Giles Rd to Watarrka (Kings Canyon) National Park.

Famous for its rare palms, Finke Gorge National Park is one of central Australia's premier wilderness areas. It has plenty to offer those who enjoy bushwalks and remote camping, and the landscape is spectacular and colourful. The main gorge features high red cliffs, stately river gums, cool waterholes, plenty of clean white sand and clumps of tall palms. Combine this tremendous natural beauty with the area's fascinating history and you have an excursion that's packed with interest.

Anyone intending to drive out from Alice Springs to Hermannsburg, visit Palm Valley, and then continue on to Watarrka via Boggy Hole and Illamurta Springs, should have a minimum fuel range of 650km – this allows for heavy going in the Finke River. Otherwise you must refuel at Hermannsburg, as the only other outlet between there and Watarrka is at Kings Creek, 35km before Watarrka.

HISTORY

For thousands of years the Finke River formed part of an Aboriginal trade route that crossed Australia, bringing goods such as sacred red ochre from the south and pearl shell from the north to the central Australian tribes. Far from being desert, the area around Hermannsburg had an abundance of game animals and food plants. It was a major refuge for the Western Arrernte people in times of drought, thanks to its permanent water, which came from soaks dug in the Finke River bed. An upside-down river (like all others in central Australia), the Finke flows beneath its dry bed most of the time. As it becomes saline during drought, the Western Arrernte call it *Lhere pirnte* (hence Larapinta), which means salty river. It was their comprehensive knowledge of its freshwater soaks that enabled them to survive in the harshest droughts.

In 1872, the explorer Ernest Giles travelled up the Finke on his first attempt to cross from the Overland Telegraph Line to the west coast. To his amazement he found tall palms growing in the river, which had been named 12 years earlier by John McDouall Stuart, and went into raptures over the beauty of its scenery. Giles later briefed the Lutheran Church of South Australia on the country he'd visited at the northern end of Finke Gorge. The Lutherans were keen to start missionary work among Aboriginal people in central Australia, and after talking to Giles they applied for a lease over the area.

In 1876, fresh from the Hermannsburg Mission Institute in Germany, pastors AH Kempe and WF Schwarz left Adelaide bound for central Australia with a herd of cattle and several thousand sheep. Eighteen months later they arrived at the new mission site, having been trapped by drought at Dalhousie Springs for nearly a year. It was a nightmarish introduction to the harsh central Australian environment, but the pastors were committed to the task of bringing Christianity and 'civilisation' to the Aborigines.

Despite incredible hardships and difficulties, including strong opposition from white settlers to their attempts to protect the Aborigines from genocide, the missionaries established the first township in central Australia. At one time Hermannsburg had a population of 700 Western Arrernte people, a cattle herd of 5000 and various cottage industries, including a tannery.

The mission continued to operate until 1982, when the Lutheran Church handed its lease back to the Western Arrernte. Since that time most of its residents have left Hermannsburg and established small outstation communities on traditional clan territories. There are now 35 such outstations on the old mission lease. Although about 200 Aborigines still live at Hermannsburg, its main function is to provide support and resources for the outlying population.

INFORMATION
Tourist Offices

The best source of in-depth information on Finke Gorge National Park is the Parks & Wildlife Commission's Alice Springs office (☎ (08) 8951 8211). Alternatively, ring the Palm Valley ranger (☎ (08) 8956 7401).

Brochures on Finke Gorge, Hermannsburg, Wallace Rockhole and local tours are available from CATIA's visitor information centre (☎ (08) 8952 5800) in Alice Springs.

For an update on conditions along the Boggy Hole Track, contact the rangers at Palm Valley.

Emergency

In the event of a medical emergency, you can obtain assistance at the Hermannsburg health clinic, which has registered nursing staff. The rangers at Palm Valley and most coach drivers have training in first aid, and their vehicles are generally equipped with HF radios.

Permits

The Boggy Hole track crosses Aboriginal land for the 16km from Hermannsburg to the national park boundary. Although there is no requirement for a permit to use the road, camping is not allowed in the area and visitors must stay on the main route. Likewise, you can visit the commercial facilities and historic mission at Hermannsburg without a permit, but residential areas are out of bounds.

Maps

The Parks & Wildlife Commission's brochure *Finke River 4WD Route* covers the Boggy Hole Track from Hermannsburg to the Ernest Giles Rd, including the detour to Illamurta Springs. It's available on request from the rangers at Palm Valley and Watarrka.

For topographic detail refer to AUSLIG's *Henbury* 1:250,000 map sheet. It's available from the Department of Lands, Planning & Environment office on Gregory Terrace, Alice Springs, and from AUSLIG sales outlets in all capital cities. The section of track between the Running Waters-Illamurta Springs route and Ernest Giles Rd isn't shown, but you can easily draw it in using the above brochure.

Radio Frequencies

As Palm Valley is a popular tourist attraction, you won't require a HF radio (except possibly in summer, when visitor numbers drop to a few vehicles per day). The Boggy Hole Track is much less used, and there can be a week between vehicles when the weather is hot. It's definitely a good idea to carry a HF radio if you're intending to make this trip in summer.

This region is serviced by the Alice Springs RFDS base (call sign VJD; ☎ (08) 8952 1033), which monitors 5410 and 6950kHz between 7.30 am and 5 pm weekdays. Use 2020 and 5410kHz for after-hours emergency calls.

SPECIAL PREPARATIONS

The Boggy Hole Track is definitely not suitable for low-clearance 4WD vehicles. Even experienced off-road drivers can get bogged on this one, so make sure to pack a high-lift jack and base-plate, long-handled shovel, tyre-pressure gauge and good-quality tyre pump. A winch (or at least a strong tow rope) might also come in handy. Anyone attempting the track in summer should carry plenty of drinking water and travel in company with at least one other vehicle.

THE ROUTE
Hermannsburg

Shaded by tall river gums and date palms, and with a view over the normally dry, shimmering bed of the Finke River, the **old Hermannsburg mission** is a fascinating monument to the skill and dedication of the early Lutheran missionaries. The group of 11 whitewashed stone buildings includes a church, a school and various houses and outbuildings. Dating from 1882, the buildings are probably as good an example of traditional German farmhouse architecture as you'll find anywhere outside that country. They were restored in 1988.

Admission to the historic precinct costs $3.50 per adult and $2.50 per child, and includes a guided tour of the **art gallery**. The gallery provides an insight into the life and times of **Albert Namatjira**, the Western Arrernte artist who opened the world's eyes

Albert Namatjira

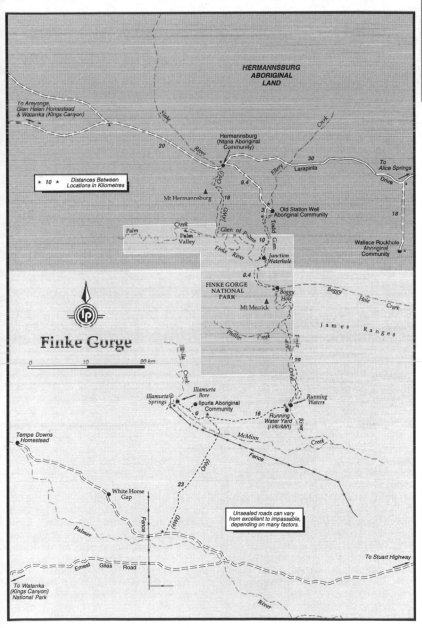

HERMANNSBURG ABORIGINAL LAND

To Areyonga, Glen Helen Homestead & Watarrka (Kings Canyon)

Ellery Creek

Hermannsburg (Ntaria Aboriginal Community)

20

Finke River

Larapinta

30

To Alice Springs Drive

★ 10 ★ Distances Between Locations in Kilometres

9.4

Mt Hermannsburg

18

Old Station Well Aboriginal Community

3

18

Palm Creek

Glen of Palms

Palm Valley

Finke River

10

Junction Waterhole

Wallace Rockhole Aboriginal Community

Finke Gorge

FINKE GORGE NATIONAL PARK

6.4

Boggy Hole

Mt Merrick

Boggy Hole Creek

0   10   20 km

Phillip Creek

James Ranges

Illara Creek

Finke River

28

Illamurta Bore

Illamurta Springs

Ilpuria Aboriginal Community

Running Waters

8

16

Running Water Yard (THRRAM)

Tempe Downs Homestead

McMinn Fence

Finke River

Creek

White Horse Gap

Fence

23

Unsealed roads can vary from excellent to impassable, depending on many factors.

Palmer

Ernest Giles Road

To Watarrka (Kings Canyon) National Park

To Stuart Highway

River

to the striking landscapes around Alice Springs. It contains examples of the work of 39 Hermannsburg water colourists, including three generations of the Namatjira family.

Hermannsburg to Palm Valley (18km)

The Palm Valley track turns off Larapinta Drive on the Finke River's western bank about 1km west of Hermannsburg, and keeps to the riverbed for most of the next 11km. Deep corrugations and soft, sandy sections are normal conditions here, while a flood can close the track for days. However, the major hazards are large 4WD tourist coaches, which have right of way on the narrow track – when you see one heading towards you, either pull right over or reverse back until you can get off the track without bogging yourself. With 65,000 tourists visiting Palm Valley each year, the track can be fairly busy in peak periods.

Finke River Floods After about 1km, the track enters the red-walled confines of Finke Gorge and hits the first patch of soft sand – this is where visitors in conventional vehicles who've ignored the warning signs invariably come to grief. For the next 10km the track dives in and out of the river, passing occasional small waterholes and tall river gums that make a cool contrast to the arid hills on either side.

There were many more big gums in the river prior to 1988, when one of the greatest floods in centuries swept most of them away. The debris piled against surviving trees gives you an idea of the river's force when it's in full flood. Take one look at the scars high up on the trunks and you quickly appreciate that Finke Gorge is no place to be when heavy rain sets in. The river flows on average about once a year, but relatively few floods reach the Stuart Highway bridge south of Alice Springs. Even the largest floods simply vanish into the Simpson Desert which, if you count every twist and turn in the river, is 650km from its headwaters in the MacDonnell Ranges.

Palm Valley

Leaving the Finke at its junction with Palm Creek, you head west past the old ranger station (the houses were flooded in 1988 and are now abandoned), and 1km further on arrive at the Kalarranga carpark. En route there's a small information bay that gives you an introduction to the area and to some of the walks you can do (see Activities). Kalarranga, more usually known as the **Amphitheatre**, is a semi-circle of striking ochre-coloured sandstone formations sculpted by a now-extinct meander of Palm Creek. Be there in early morning or late afternoon for the best views.

Continuing on, the track becomes extremely rough and rocky for the final 3km to Palm Valley. Along the way you pass the camping ground and picnic area before arriving at **Cycad Gorge**, where a chocolate-coloured cliff towers over a clump of tall, slender palms. The gorge is named after the large number of shaggy cycads found growing on and below the cliff face. Lending a tropical atmosphere to their barren setting, the palms and cycads are leftovers from much wetter times in central Australia. They only survive here because a reliable supply of moisture within the surrounding sandstone means they can escape the harsh realities of drought.

Just past Cycad Gorge is the Palm Valley carpark, with the first palms just a stone's throw away. The valley is actually a narrow gorge that in places is literally choked with lush oases of **red cabbage palms** (*Livistona mariae*) up to 25m high. Found nowhere else in the world, the species grows within an area of 60 sq km and is over 1000km from its nearest relatives. There are only 2000 mature individuals in the wild, so the rangers ask that you stay out of the palm groves – the tiny seedlings are hard to see and are easily trampled underfoot. This is probably the reason why there are hardly any of the young palms near the carpark.

The gorge is a botanist's paradise, and home to over 300 plant species, of which about 10% are either rare or have a restricted distribution.

Hermannsburg to Boggy Hole (31km)

Heading out along Larapinta Drive from Alice Springs, you come to the Boggy Hole Track on your left just 50m or so before the signposted turn-off to Hermannsburg. For the first 12km the track is graded but rough, spearing across a red sandy plain past small outstation communities on the old mission lease.

The graded section stops abruptly at an outstation at the entrance to **Todd Glen** on Ellery Creek; go past the houses, ignore the track on the left and continue straight on into the gorge. From this point the track is simply a pair of wheel ruts winding along the mainly stony creekbed. Although the going is often rough, the colourful scenery and sense of discovery make it all worthwhile.

Ten km after entering the gorge you arrive at **Junction Waterhole**, where Ellery Creek meets the Finke River. When full, the hole is a picture to gladden any eye, and as a bonus there are some good campsites under the gums that line its banks. Unfortunately, however, the waterhole is empty as often as not. A few years ago you could drive down the Finke from Palm Valley to Junction Waterhole, but the rangers closed the track which they found they were spending too much time pulling hire cars out of bogs.

Boggy Hole

At Junction Waterhole you continue into Finke Gorge for the slow 8.4km slog to Boggy Hole. A haven for migratory waterbirds such as swans and pelicans, Boggy Hole stretches for 2.5km after a flood but shrinks to only about 300m during extreme droughts. It's one of only a handful of permanent waterholes in the Finke south of the MacDonnell Ranges and so has immense conservation value – believe it or not, 10 species of mainly small fish live here. The bank is rocky and the river gums suffered badly in the 1988 flood, so good campsites with shade are scarce near the water.

In the 1880s, Boggy Hole was a police camp from which Mounted Constable William Willshire and his Aboriginal troopers rode the ranges, quelling black resistance to white settlement. It seems their method of doing this was to shoot as many Aborigines as possible, prompting a Hermannsburg missionary to write in 1885: 'In ten years time there will not be many blacks left in this area and this is just what the white man wants.'

A year later the missionaries were protesting vigorously at the alarming decrease in the Aboriginal male population. It was thanks largely to their efforts that the police were moved to Illamurta Springs in 1893 and Willshire brought to trial for his excesses. He wasn't convicted, but the trial meant the end of his career in the Northern Territory. The stone remains of the police camp (not to be confused with those of a more recent safari camp) are on the waterhole's eastern bank.

Boggy Hole to Ernest Giles Rd (68km)

The river's character changes continuously in the 28km from Boggy Hole to the old Running Water cattle yards. One minute you're driving along a broad valley or through red sandhills, the next you're hemmed in with cliffs on either side. These narrow sections act as dams when the river is in flood, the water banking up to submerge the flats on either side under metres of water. At one point, about 8km past Boggy Hole, scars 8m or more up in the river gums show where flood-borne debris, including huge trees, has bashed against their trunks. Looking around at the normally parched surroundings, it's difficult to imagine that such things can happen here.

Running Waters Twenty km from Boggy Hole you pass through a gate in a grove of desert oaks and enter Henbury station. Five km further on, at the southern end of Finke Gorge, a couple of metal huts on the left mark an Aboriginal outstation at Running Waters. Here the riverbed is littered by tree trunks that were dumped by the 1988 flood. A solitary palm rises from the bulrushes that line the waterhole which, although permanent, is quite shallow in contrast to others in the river. The track continues downstream for a short distance to a set of old timber yards where you turn right (west) along the southern foot of the James Ranges.

Picturesque ghost gums are the major scenic highlights of the 16km to the turn-off to Ernest Giles Rd – continue straight on if you want to visit the Illamurta Springs Conservation Reserve (see Detours). From the turn-off the track heads south-west across red sandhills covered with desert oaks; the going is soft in parts and so badly corrugated in others it'll make your teeth rattle. Around 21km later you arrive at a claypan that heralds the start of the **Palmer River flood plain**. Although devastated by rabbits and cattle over the past century, its desolate claypans, scattered crimson dunes and skeletons of dead trees do have a certain awful beauty.

Another 2km and you swing left (east) onto the Tempe Downs access road. From here it's about 10km to the Ernest Giles Rd, where you turn either east to the Stuart Highway (53km) or west to Watarrka (Kings Canyon) National Park (140km).

DETOURS
Wallace Rockhole
The Arrernte community of Wallace Rockhole, off Larapinta Drive about 30km east of Hermannsburg, offers **rock-art tours** and a chance to sample traditional bush tucker in season. Kangaroo tail cooked in the ground is a speciality. Wallace Rockhole has a pleasant camping area and caravan park, and the general store sells ice and locally produced Aboriginal crafts.

Mereenie Loop Road
Opened to the general public in 1994, the 199km Mereenie Loop Road between Hermannsburg and Watarrka National Park provides an exciting opportunity for a circuit of the western central ranges. Leaving Alice Springs you can drive out through the West MacDonnells National Park, continue on to Watarrka via Gosse Bluff, then return to town via the Boggy Hole Track, Palm Valley and Hermannsburg. The circuit, which covers 800km or more including detours, will appeal to the more adventurous 4WD traveller with time to appreciate the attractions en route. This means allowing seven days for the trip.

The Mereenie Loop Road passes through a variety of semi-desert landscapes. It is, however, generally only suitable either for 4WDs or conventional vehicles with heavy-

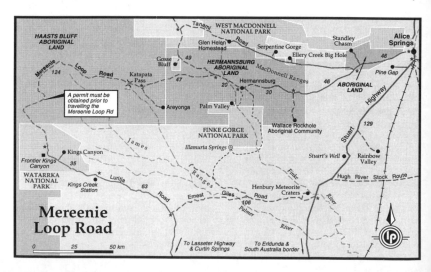

duty suspension and good ground clearance washouts are a hazard after heavy rain, so be careful. The road is not recommended for caravans.

To travel on this route you need a permit called the Mereenie Tour Pass ($2), which doubles as a visitor information guide. It's available at Hermannsburg (the Larapinta Service Station), the Kings Canyon Resort and the CATIA visitor information office in Alice Springs – if the Glen Helen homestead is open, it should be available there too.

You'll need sufficient fuel for at least 300km between Hermannsburg (the last fuel stop) and Watarrka, including a detour to Gosse Bluff. Note that camping is not permitted along the route.

Refer to the MacDonnell Ranges section for details on Gosse Bluff.

Illamurta Springs

At the foot of the James Ranges, 22km west of Running Waters yard, this remote conservation reserve is excellent for bird-watching thanks to its permanent spring and variety of habitats. Hidden away in thick mallee near the spring are the evocative stone remains of what must have been one of the Territory's loneliest police outposts. It makes you wonder what crimes the constables were guilty of to be posted there. The station opened in 1893 and closed in 1912.

There's a small camping area with toilets and powered sites at the nearby Ilpurla Aboriginal community.

Watarrka (Kings Canyon)

Ernest Giles Rd terminates in Watarrka National Park, one of the outback's major scenic drawcards. The park includes a range of environments, from permanent springs with delicate ferns and cycads to red sandhills covered by desert oaks and spinifex. Best of all, however, are the colourful 300m-high cliffs that line Kings Canyon – you get two perspectives of this spectacular landform from walking tracks at the top and bottom. Contact the rangers (☎ (08) 8956 7460) for in-depth information.

Accommodation within the park is confined to the *Kings Canyon Resort* (☎ (08) 8956 7442), which has up-market hotel rooms with private facilities from $240 for a double. Four-bed rooms with shared facilities cost $132 per room, and there are family rooms sleeping five for $115. For meals you have the choice of either the restaurant or cafe – the latter is reasonable value at $11.50 for a two-course meal. The complex includes a well-stocked minimarket, which also sells fuel (diesel, super and unleaded) from 7 am to 7 pm daily.

The *camping ground* won't be everyone's cup of tea, as the idea seems to be to get as many people into a given space as possible. It's also pricey, at $25 per site with power (two persons – extras are $10) and $10 per person without power. For something friendlier and more akin to a bush experience, try *Kings Creek station* (☎ (08) 8956 7474), on Ernest Giles Rd just outside the park's eastern boundary. The very pleasant camping ground is set among large desert oaks, with sites costing $9/8 per person with/ without power. Fuel, ice and limited stores are available seven days a week.

These days there's a fully sealed route from Kings Canyon to the Lasseter Highway to Uluru, which means you can still get there even if heavy rain closes unsealed roads in the area.

ACTIVITIES
Walks

There's good walking in Finke Gorge National Park, although few visitors do more than short walks in the Palm Valley area. A suggested day or overnight walk with plenty of variety is a loop from the Palm Valley camping ground south to Little Palm Creek, then down to the Finke River and back to camp. If you're camped at Boggy Hole, a walk to the top of Mt Merrick is recommended for the view. A stroll along the Finke offers colourful scenery and solitude, particularly in the Glen of Palms between Palm and Little Palm creeks.

Unfortunately, there are no large-scale

topographic maps of Finke Gorge National Park, which is shown in broad detail on AUSLIG's *Henbury* 1:250,000 sheet. Before doing any long walks, you should ask the ranger for advice on routes, conditions and preparation.

Palm Valley Walking Tracks There are several walking tracks in the Palm Valley area, all suitable for families and each with its own particular attractions. The most popular is a 3km loop through Palm Valley and back over the top to the carpark. It offers terrific views down the gorge and gives you a different perspective of local environments.

Another good one is a 5km loop from the Kalarranga carpark that takes in the Finke River, Palm Bend and the rugged Amphitheatre. It leads you in the footsteps of a mythological hero from the Aboriginal Dreamtime, whose adventures are explained by signs along the way.

FACILITIES
Hermannsburg
The best place to start a visit to the historic precinct is the *Kata-Anga Tea Room* (☎ (08) 8956 7402) in the old missionary house. Open seven days a week from 9 am (10 am in summer) to 4 pm, its solid, rough-hewn walls testify to the dedication of those early pioneers. The tea room sells light lunches, or you can relax with a bottomless cup of tea or coffee and a large slice of home-baked cake – the traditional apple strudel is highly recommended.

There's also a range of traditional and watercolour paintings, artefacts and pottery, and all of the items are the work of local Aboriginal people. The quality is often very good, and you'll find the prices more appealing than in most souvenir outlets in Alice Springs.

At the main entrance to town, the well-stocked *Ntaria Supermarket* is open daily from 8 am (10 am on Sunday) to 5.30 pm, as is the service station next door – it sells diesel, super and unleaded petrol and can

help with mechanical repairs. Credit cards are not accepted.

The *Mission Store* near the historic precinct has a better variety of foodstuffs and also sells hardware items and motor accessories such as electric air pumps. It's open during normal business hours weekdays and Saturday morning.

Fuel and mechanical repairs are also available at the Tjuwanpa Outstation Resource Centre, opposite the Palm Valley turn-off. It's open the same hours as the Mission Store, and accepts credit cards.

Palm Valley
A small camping area beside Palm Creek has shady trees, hot showers and gas barbecues, as well as friendly birds which are always on the lookout for a free feed. Otherwise it is a very pleasant place in a scenic setting of red sandstone ridges, and the spectacular Amphitheatre is just a few minutes' walk away.

Overnight charges are $4 per adult or $10 per family, paid into the honesty box; day-trippers have free use of the nearby picnic area and its shade shelters, flush toilets and gas barbecues. Dead timber cannot be collected past the park entry sign in the Finke River. If you want a fire, make sure to collect your firewood in advance.

Bush Camping
You'll find some magnificent campsites with shade, clean sand, firewood and beautiful gorge scenery along the Finke River between Junction Waterhole and Running Waters. The most popular spot (though by no means the best) is Boggy Hole, and this place attracts many Alice Springs residents on weekends.

As waterholes in the Finke are vital to the survival of many wildlife species, the rangers ask that you do your washing in a bucket and camp well back from the water's edge. All rubbish should be carried out, and please don't make new vehicle tracks on the banks – it's unsightly and creates an erosion problem.

Tanami Track

HIGHLIGHTS

- Visiting the Wolfe Creek Meteorite Crater and trying to imagine the explosion that created it

- Experiencing the awesome space and solitude of the Tanami Desert

The Tanami Track cuts right through the heart of the Tanami Desert and some of Australia's least populated country. It connects Alice Springs in the Centre with the Kimberley's Halls Creek in the country's far north-west.

Despite the remoteness, or perhaps because of it, the Tanami Track is becoming an increasingly popular route for those seeking to get off the beaten track, and it can save hundreds of kilometres spent backtracking if you want to visit both the Top End and the Kimberley from Alice Springs. It's also possible to leave the Tanami Track at the Tanami Mine and head north for Lajamanu and Kalkaringi on the Buntine Highway, from where there are a number of possibilities: north-east to Katherine and the Stuart Highway, west to Halls Creek or north along the Buchanan Highway to Victoria River Downs and on to Timber Creek on the Victoria Highway.

The Lajamanu Road is best attempted with a 4WD, although the local Aborigines manage OK with their trusty Ford Falcons. (See Alternative Routes below for more details on the Lajamanu Road.)

The Tanami Track is officially called the Tanami Road in the Territory and McGuires Track in Western Australia but it is universally known as the Tanami Track.

Apart from the sense of achievement which crossing the Tanami Desert gives, the highlights of the track are the Wolfe Creek Meteorite Crater and the sheer vastness of the spinifex plains liberally sprinkled with

millions of red **termite mounds**, many of which are over 3m high. The country is mainly gently undulating plains, with occasional low rock outcrops and areas of sand dunes.

The 1000km track has been greatly improved in recent years; it's possible to cover the track in a well prepared 2WD vehicle. The Northern Territory section is wide and well graded, but between the Western Australia/Northern Territory border and Halls Creek there are some sandy patches which require care – a high-clearance vehicle is advisable. After rain (rare in winter), sections of the track can become impassable.

In the cooler months there is quite a bit of traffic – up to 40 vehicles a day pass through Rabbit Flat – so a breakdown need not be cause for alarm if you are well prepared with food and water. In summer the heat can be extreme – days where the temperature hits 50°C are not uncommon – so think carefully before setting off at this time.

The Tanami Desert is the traditional homeland of the Walpiri Aboriginal people, and for much of its length the Tanami Track passes through Aboriginal land.

HISTORY

The first European exploration of the Tanami Desert was undertaken by the surveyor and explorer AC Gregory (later Sir) in 1855. His party headed south from the Victoria River to what is now Lajamanu, then headed west until they came to a dry watercourse near the present Western Australia/Northern Territory border, which Gregory named Sturt Creek, after the explorer. He followed the creek south-west to a lake south-west of Balgo, which he humbly named after himself, before returning to his Victoria River base.

The first white crossing of the desert was probably in 1896 when the pioneering drover Nat Buchanan crossed from Tennant Creek to Sturt Creek. Buchanan was responsible for some amazing cattle drives from Queensland, and he hoped to find a route suitable for stock so they didn't have to detour so far north. Although he crossed the desert without undue difficulty (largely thanks to his Aboriginal guides), no sources of permanent water were found and the hoped-for stock route never eventuated.

Allan Davidson was the first European to explore the Tanami Desert in any detail. In 1900 he set out looking for gold, and mapped, with amazing accuracy, likely-looking areas. Gold was discovered at a couple of sites in the Tanami and for a few brief years there was a flurry of activity as hopefuls came in search of a fortune. The extremely harsh conditions and small finds deterred all but the most determined, and there were never more than a couple of hundred miners in the Tanami. The biggest discoveries were at Tanami and The Granites, and after many years of inactivity, the latter was reopened in 1986 and is still being mined today; the Tanami Mine closed in 1994.

Pastoral activity in the area has always been a precarious proposition, although some areas are suitable for grazing. Suplejack ('soo-pull-jack') Downs and Tanami Downs, respectively 60km north and south-west of Rabbit Flat, are two which have survived. Suplejack is one of the few pieces of non-Aboriginal land in the Tanami Desert, while Tanami Downs is owned by the Mangkururrta Aboriginal Land Trust.

During the 1920s Michael Terry, a geologist, led a number of expeditions across the northern half of Australia in vehicles as well as on camels, searching for minerals. During his 1928 expedition, when he used a couple of Morris six-wheel trucks on what were the first motorised trips through this part of the continent, he travelled from Broome, via Halls Creek (Old Halls Creek today) down to Tanami and then south-east to Alice Springs. His book, *Hidden Wealth and Hiding People*, recounts the adventures that he and his men had and what life was like for the prospectors and the natives back at that time.

Some of the facts and figures he states regarding his vehicles make interesting reading less than 70 years later. Oil consumption was down to 250 miles to the gallon(!), while fuel consumption was down to less than five miles to the gallon. Mind you, that was across country, as all there was to follow was a camel pad. He also states, regarding tyres, 'the Australian Dunlops stood up very well', even though he recorded 57 punctures and tyre pressures of 80psi! It must have been a hard trip.

INFORMATION

Permits are not required for travel on the Tanami Track, although if you want to venture more than 50m either side of the road, a permit is required. This does not apply if you want to purchase fuel at Yuendumu, which lies 2km off the road.

Although it is not compulsory to register with the police at either end of the Tanami Track, remember that travel in this area is no Sunday-school picnic and you should at least notify someone reliable of your travel plans.

The best map for the track is the Westprint Tanami Track map. It is available from several outlets in Alice Springs, including the visitor information centre on Gregory Terrace.

The Tanami Track is covered by the RFDS in Alice Springs (☎ (08) 8952 1033) and Derby (☎ (09) 9191 1211); Alice Springs (VJD) monitors 2020, 5410 and 6950kHz from 7.30 am to 5 pm weekdays, while the Derby (VJB) frequencies are 2020, 2792, 5300 and 6925kHz, and these are monitored on weekdays from 7 am to 4 pm, and on Saturday from 9 to 9.30 am.

THE ROUTE
Alice Springs to Rabbit Flat

The Tanami Track starts at the Stuart Highway, 20km north of Alice Springs. Here the somewhat daunting sign informs you that it's 703km to the Western Australia border, the first 118km of which are sealed.

The first point of interest is the masts of the Defence Department's **radio receiving station** off to the north of the road (entry prohibited). On the south side of the road is the rugged northern face of the **Western MacDonnell Ranges**.

Shortly after passing the receiver station the road crosses the **Hamilton Downs station** boundary fence, and the turn off to the Apex youth camp at the foot of the ranges. The station was established early this century and named by the explorer John McDouall Stuart. The road then enters Amburla station (and crosses the Tropic of Capricorn) and, 104km from the Stuart Highway, there's the turn-off to the Aboriginal community of **Papunya**, 96km to the west along a good dirt road (permit required).

A further 15km brings you to the crossing of the underground **gas pipeline**, which takes natural gas from near Palm Valley to Katherine and Darwin. It's then another 36km to the first fuel and supply stop along the track, the modern **Tilmouth Well Roadhouse** on the banks of the (usually) dry Napperby Creek.

On from Tilmouth the track passes through the **Stuart Bluff Range**, one of the few outcrops of rock seen along the track, before coming to the turn-off to Mount Wedge homestead after 20km. The boundary of the **Yalpirakinu Aboriginal land** is reached after 15km, and a further 24km brings you to the turn-off to the **Mt Allan (Yuelamu)** community in the Ngalurbindi Hills.

It's then another 45km before you reach the turn-off to the Aboriginal community of **Yuendumu**, which lies 2km north of the track. Visitors are welcome to buy fuel or provisions from the store, but permits are required to visit elsewhere, and alcohol is prohibited. Yuendumu has a thriving art community, and the work put out by the Warlukurlangi artists is highly regarded. It's not possible, however, to visit the artists without a permit. The town also has the highly sophisticated Tanami Network, a satellite TV conference network which can link Yuendumu with Darwin, Alice Springs and even overseas.

From Yuendumu the track crosses into **Mount Doreen station** and soon skirts the southern edge of the **Yarunganyi Hills**. On the northern side of the hills and close to the

Tanami
Track

Unsealed roads can vary
from excellent to impassable,
depending on many factors.

0   50   100 km

road is the site of the abandoned Mount Doreen station. Although originally built in the 1920s, it was later abandoned due to the unreliable water supply. These days the station is run from **Vaughan Springs station**, which lies about 80km west of the track at this point.

The track then enters the vast expanses of the **Central Desert Aboriginal Land Trust**. The spinifex grass and anthills often stretch as far as the eye can see, and there's little to break the monotony – just the occasional acacia tree and the Telecom microwave towers at 50km intervals.

The turn-off to **Mount Theo Outstation** and **Chilla Well** is reached 125km north-west from Yuendumu, and from there it's 58km to **Refrigerator Bore**, off to the right (north) of the track. Up until the early 1970s there was a stock route which went from Refrigerator Bore, passing through Tanami Downs (then Mongrel Downs) and on to Balgo and Halls Creek. This route had been pioneered in the early 1960s and a series of wells dug along its length to supply the cattle. Once trucks took over from droving as the main way to shift cattle, the route was no longer used.

Just before the gold mine of The Granites, you pass a low rocky outcrop on the left of the road where a couple of **old ruins** can be seen. These date back to the 1930s. Nearby are older relics, the most important of which is an ore stamper, or crushing battery. What those early miners went through is vastly different from what the present workers experience, flying in and out from Alice Springs on their weekly shifts.

The Granites Gold Mine is the next major point of interest, 82km along the track from Refrigerator Bore, although there is no public access or facilities. Although small-scale mining had been carried out in the area since the early 1900s, the mine site was first pegged in 1927, and the mine itself operated until 1947. The returns were small, however, with a yield of only about 1000 ounces per year. In 1986 the mine reopened after exploratory drilling by North Flinders Mines proved gold reserves were still there. Production is currently running at around 170,000 ounces of gold per year, from both The Granites site and the area known as Dead Bullock Soak, 45km to the west. The ore from Dead Bullock Soak is carted to The Granites site for treatment along a new bitumen road (definitely the only one for hundreds of kilometres!) on huge four-trailer road trains, each carting well over 100 tonnes of ore. These monsters travel at great speed and require at least 1km to stop.

It's just 48km from The Granites to the most famous place in the Tanami, the **Rabbit Flat Roadhouse**, 1km or so off to the north of the track. The roadhouse was established by Bruce Farrands and his French wife Jacqui in 1969 and has been serving travellers on the Tanami Track ever since. It's certainly not an attractive place – just a couple of breeze-block buildings and a few fuel tanks – but it's the social centre of the Tanami, not least because it's the only place for hundreds of kilometres where people can buy a drink. On Friday and Saturday nights it can get pretty lively with all the workers in from the mines.

Rabbit Flat to Halls Creek

From Rabbit Flat the track continues north-west for 44km to the now-defunct **Tanami Mine**. The story here is much the same as at The Granites – early interest and small yields followed by a period of inactivity from the 1930s to the 1980s, when modern techniques made the prospect viable once again. In 1987 Zapopan NL commenced operations and between then and March 1994, when the mine was once again shut down, around 380,000 ounces of gold were taken from the earth. There are no tourist services or public access to the mine site.

Just 1km or so past the Tanami Mine, the **Lajamanu Road** heads off north (see Alternative Routes below). After the turn-off, the Tanami Track swings due west for the 80-odd km run to the Western Australia border and beyond. In the days of the area's minor gold rush, the track continued north-westerly, passing through Gordon Downs station and on to Halls Creek, but this route was abandoned once the rush was over. The route the current track takes between the Tanami Mine and **Billiluna Aboriginal community** was established in the 1960s by Father McGuire from what was then the Balgo Aboriginal Mission.

It is 78km from the roadhouse to the Western Australia/Northern Territory border, and another 86km will see you at the junction of the road to **Balgo Aboriginal community**, nearly 40km to the south. A fainter track heads north from this point across Aboriginal land to Sturt Creek homestead and finally to the **Buntine Highway**, 70km east of Halls Creek. This 170km trip north to the highway requires a permit.

From near the junction the occasional sand ridge can be seen from the track, which now becomes a little sandier. A car with low clearance could easily become bogged. The track begins to swing north the further west you travel, and 24km from the junction a second road heads south to Balgo.

The track continues to be sandy in places for the next 48km to the crossing of **Sturt Creek**. Here is one of the few reasonable spots to camp along this route, with a couple of pleasant spots on the western bank, just north of the road crossing.

Sturt Creek occasionally flows, its flood-waters ending up in **Lake Gregory**, 100km south of the Tanami Track. When this occurs, the lake becomes one of the great habitats for birds in inland Australia. During one bird-surveying expedition more than 240,000 waterbirds of 57 species were counted, including cormorants, pink-eared ducks, plumed whistle-ducks, coots, darters, egrets and brolgas, to name just a few.

Just 1km past the crossing, a track comes in from the south. This leads a short distance to Billiluna Aboriginal community and is the start (or the end, depending on which way you are travelling) of the **Canning Stock Route**.

From here the road improves and swings almost due north, and the sand ridges slip away to the south-west. The abandoned Carranya Roadhouse comes up on the right 41km north of the Sturt Creek crossing; it marks the turn-off to travel the 20-odd km to

Wolfe Creek Meteorite Crater and the small national park that surrounds it. This station track leads 16km east to the deserted Carranya homestead which you pass close to, before continuing on another 5km to the small parking area at the base of the crater walls.

Wolfe Creek Meteorite Crater This crater is the second-largest of its type in the world. Known to the Aboriginal people as the place where some of their Dreamtime ancestors originated, early explorers and then the first aviators across this vast desert region knew of it long before its significance was recorded by geologists in 1947. It was first gazetted as a reserve in 1969.

The rim of the crater is about 850m across and up to 35m above the surrounding sand plain. While the outer walls of the crater are relatively steep, the inner walls are much more so and descend, in places, via sheer cliffs, over 50m to the crater floor. Once it would have been much deeper, but sand has filled the crater in.

When was it formed? Sometime within the last two million years, and possibly within the last 500,000 years. Scientists tell us that to create such a crater the meteorite would have had to weigh many thousands of tonnes and be travelling at around 900km per minute!

There are no facilities at the crater, not even a tree to cast a patch of shade, but it is worth looking at. The view from the crest of the rim is worth the short walk, and with care you can clamber down into the crater and explore the flat interior. The centre of the crater is a natural water trap and shrubs have grown up in profusion where the water is closer to the surface.

Halls Creek Back on the main road, there is still another 111km of dirt before the major T-intersection with Highway 1 and the bitumen, where you are just 16km west of Halls Creek and all the facilities of this small but major town. There is a choice of fuel outlets, repair places, a supermarket, police station, hospital and more. For information on the facilities, see the section on the Canning Stock Route in The North-West chapter.

ALTERNATIVE ROUTES
Lajamanu Road

The Lajamanu Road heads north off the Tanami Track at the Tanami Mine, although it's not even marked on many maps. It's generally kept in good condition, but it does get sandy towards Lajamanu, and there are numerous creek-bed crossings and the occasional washout. Even so, it is negotiable in the dry by 2WD with care.

The road offers an interesting alternative to the Tanami Track and takes you through country which has very little tourist traffic. It passes through the Central Desert Aboriginal Land and the Lajamanu Aboriginal Land. A permit is not required to traverse the road, or to get fuel and supplies at Lajamanu.

From the Tanami Mine it's 231km to the small Aboriginal community of **Lajamanu**, and the trip takes around six hours. The road goes through some very pretty countryside, especially around Suplejack Downs station, and is generally more interesting than the Tanami Track itself.

The *Lajamanu Service Station* (☎ (08) 8951 1573) sells fuel (super, unleaded, diesel), and there's a supermarket and takeaway food counter. The hours for fuel sales are 10 am to noon and 3 to 5 pm weekdays, and 10 am to noon on Saturday (closed Sunday). The takeaway food shop is open from 10 am to 5 pm Monday to Friday.

Heading north from Lajamanu, the road passes through typical spinifex plains until suddenly, about 10km before the road hits the Buntine Highway, the countryside changes from the red of the Centre to grassed and lightly treed cattle country. The change is quite dramatic – like a line has been drawn delineating the desert and the grazing land.

The Lajamanu Road joins the single-lane bitumen Buntine Highway at an unmarked T-junction 8km east of **Kalkaringi**, which has a pleasant location on the banks of the Victoria River. At Kalkaringi there's a police station (☎ (08) 8975 0790), caravan park,

service station (☎ (08) 8975 0788) with fuel (super, unleaded, diesel), takeaway food and very limited provisions.

From Lajamanu it's 105km to the Buntine Highway and the journey takes about 1½ hours.

ORGANISED TOURS

A couple of tour companies offer the Tanami Desert as part of a wider tour taking in the Kimberley and the Top End from Alice Springs. Neither are cheap. Contact Trek-About Tours (☎ toll-free 1800 818 011) in Alice Springs or Austour (☎ toll-free 1800 335 009) in Victoria.

FACILITIES

Fuel supplies are well spaced out along the eastern end of the Tanami Track, but be warned that Rabbit Flat is only open from Friday to Monday, and that there are no supplies at Carranya Roadhouse. The longest stretch without fuel is nearly 500km from Halls Creek to Rabbit Flat, including a 50km round-trip detour to Wolfe Creek Meteorite Crater.

Although there are a number of bores quite close to the track along the way, the water in some of these is undrinkable, so don't rely on them. Bring your own drinking water.

Tilmouth Well Roadhouse

At the modern *Tilmouth Well Roadhouse* (☎ (08) 8956 8777) there's fuel (super, unleaded, diesel), basic spare parts and accessories. There's also a restaurant with takeaway tucker. Out the back there's a basic campsite for $5 per person (no power), and dongas for $35/50. The roadhouse is open daily from 7 am to 9 pm.

Yuendumu

The *Yuendumu Store* (☎ (08) 8956 4006) has fuel (super, unleaded, diesel) and a fairly well-stocked supermarket. It's open on weekdays from 8.30 am to 5 pm, and on weekends from 9 am to noon. Permits are not required if you just want to get fuel and provisions; however, to visit anywhere else in the town a permit is required.

The other option here is the *Yuendumu Mining Company Store* (☎ (08) 8956 4040). It is well-stocked and has all types of fuel. Opening hours are from 9 am to 5 pm weekdays, as well as Saturday morning and Sunday afternoon.

Rabbit Flat

The quirky *Rabbit Flat Roadhouse* (☎ (08) 8956 8744) stocks fuel (super, unleaded, diesel) and oil. Although your attention will be drawn to it, note that the somewhat antiquated fuel bowsers can only register prices up to \$0.99 per litre. As the fuel currently costs \$1.25 per litre (possibly and not surprisingly the most expensive in the country), the displayed price is only half that and the final price is doubled. The Farrands also sell basic provisions and beer (\$42 for a carton!), and there's a bar. It's also possible to camp here, and there's no charge for this. The roadhouse is only open from Friday to Monday from 7 am to 10 pm, and business is conducted on a cash-only basis.

the entire route and see fewer than a dozen vehicles. Signs of human habitation are rare and facilities are few and far between.

The first 103km are sealed, but after that the road can be extremely rough and corrugated; large bulldust holes are a common hazard on the Queensland side, which is not as well maintained. The unsealed section is suitable for use only in dry weather and is definitely not recommended for caravans.

Diesel, super and unleaded fuel are available at the Gemtree Caravan Park (140km from Alice Springs), Atitjere (215km), Jervois homestead (356km), Tobermorey homestead (570km) and Boulia (812km).

HISTORY

The disappearance of the eccentric German explorer Ludwig Leichhardt and his large, well-equipped party is one of Australia's great unsolved mysteries. Leichhardt vanished somewhere in the interior on his final expedition in 1848, and it's possible that he crossed the area of the Plenty Highway while

Plenty Highway

HIGHLIGHTS

- Taking a detour to an abandoned mica mine and fossicking for gems
- Stopping to photograph the huge termite mound east of Jervois Homestead
- Watching for Australian bustard birds on the Mitchell grass plains in Queensland

Leaving the Stuart Highway 70km north of Alice Springs, the 742km Plenty Highway skirts the northern fringe of the Simpson Desert before terminating at Boulia in western Queensland. Isolation is almost guaranteed as even in winter you can drive

Ludwig Leichhardt

attempting to return to civilisation. The evidence that this actually happened is largely based on the discovery of marked trees in central Australia and far west Queensland.

In 1886 the surveyor David Lindsay, of Simpson Desert fame, found trees in the Harts Range that had been carved with Leichhardt's distinctive mark. Many years later, more such trees were discovered along the Georgina River on Glenormiston station. Also of interest is the fact that the bones of several unknown white men had been found by a waterhole near Birdsville in the early 1870s, before the area was settled.

Leichhardt had intended to cross northern Australia from east to west, but he may have been forced south by the waterless scrub west of the Roper River. Judging by the location of the carved trees, he reached the MacDonnell Ranges, headed east around the top of the Simpson Desert and then, on striking the Georgina, had turned south once more. Reaching the junction of the Georgina and Diamantina rivers, he managed to upset the local Aborigines, who killed him and his remaining companions. No-one knows if the bones found by that lonely waterhole belonged to Leichhardt and his men, but the theory is a fascinating and plausible one.

H Vere Barclay was one of the next Europeans on the scene. In 1878, while carrying out a trigonometric survey from Alice Springs to the Queensland border, he was north-east of the Harts Range when his water supply began to run out. He dug into a sandy riverbed – this being the usual method of finding water in dry outback rivers – and found ample supplies of the precious fluid flowing beneath the surface. That is how the Plenty River got its name, and it's why the present beef road, which was first upgraded from a two-wheel track during the 1960s, is called the Plenty Highway.

INFORMATION
Tourist Offices
The Gemtree Caravan Park (☎ (08) 8956 9855) can advise you on fossicking in the western Harts Range area. The Boulia Shire Office (☎ (07) 4746 3188) is the best source of information on Boulia and the road east of the border.

Road Reports
The Road Report Hotline (☎ (08) 8922 3232) will tell you whether or not the highway is open, but doesn't provide detail and is often dated. The Harts Range police station (☎ (08) 8956 9772), the Boulia police station (☎ (07) 4746 3120 or 4746 3148 if there's no answer) and Jervois homestead (☎ (08) 8956 6307) are better places to ask about current conditions.

Emergency
In the event of a medical emergency, you can obtain assistance from the health clinic at Atitjere Aboriginal community, where there's a registered nurse. The Boulia hospital is under the control of a matron, and an RFDS clinic is held there on a weekly basis. Cattle stations en route have RFDS medical kits and telephones.

Books & Maps
Many of the fascinating reminiscences contained in *A Son of the Red Centre*, by Kurt Johannsen, involve the Plenty Highway area. Johannsen, regarded as one of the fathers of modern road-train transport, mined copper near Jervois and hauled huge loads from his mine to Mount Isa before there was a road. The book will appeal to anyone interested in Australian pioneering history. It's available from bookshops and newsagents in Alice Springs, and also from the author, at 3 Stephen's Place, Morphettville, SA 5043.

If you're intending to look for gems in the Harts Range, you'll need *A Guide to Fossicking in the Northern Territory*, by the Northern Territory Department of Mines & Energy (Darwin, 1986). It describes many of the range's fossicking areas and old mines, including maps; although much of the information about access is out of date, it's still an essential reference. Most areas mentioned are only accessible either on foot or by 4WD vehicle.

At a scale of 1:1,000,000, the map/guide

entitled *Plenty Highway*, by Westprint Heritage Maps, makes a useful planning and touring reference. As a bonus, it includes the short cut from the Plenty Highway to Mount Isa via Urandangi, and the direct route from Boulia to Birdsville. The guides are on sale at numerous outlets around Alice Springs and in good map shops everywhere.

Radio Frequencies
Within the Territory call the Alice Springs RFDS base (call sign VJD; ☎ (08) 8952 1033), which monitors 5410 and 6950kHz between 7.30 am and 5 pm weekdays. Use 2020 and 5410kHz for after-hours emergency calls.

Once into Queensland try the RFDS in Mount Isa (call sign VJI; ☎ (07) 4743 2800) on 5110 and 6965kHz between 8 am and 5 pm weekdays. Use 2020kHz for after-hours emergency calls.

THE ROUTE
Stuart Highway to Harts Range (143km)
From the Stuart Highway to the Harts Range police station, the road parallels the rugged northern flanks of first the Strangways Range and then the Harts Range. The scenery is attractive almost throughout, with several picturesque creeks in the 103km to Ongeva Creek. Most of these are worth stopping at if you feel like boiling the billy under a river red gum and relaxing with nature, although you'll generally need a 4WD vehicle to get away from the road. There's also good potential for quiet walks in the bush, and the chance of finding minerals such as zircon, quartz, garnet and staurolite. The road is single-lane bitumen as far as Ongeva Creek, where it changes to wide formed dirt.

Mud Tank At 70km is the Gemtree Caravan Park on the gum-lined banks of Gillen Creek. This is the only tourist facility of note on the Plenty Highway. Among its services, it offers you the chance to hire fossicking equipment and search for gems at the nearby **Mud Tank zircon field**. Alternatively, you can take their accompanied trip to the zircon deposit

(equipment provided) and get some practical experience with an expert – the cost is $40 per set of equipment. They'll also take you to a garnet deposit for the same price.

At Mud Tank the top 80cm of soil conceals zircons of various colours (including yellow, light brown, pink, purple and blue), ranging in size from small chips to large crystals. Provided they put their backs into it, even novices have a good chance of finding gem material with nothing more complicated than a shovel, a couple of small sieves (minimum mesh size 7mm) and some water for washing the stones. If you find anything worth faceting, Gemtree's gem-cutter can turn your find into a beautiful stone ready to be set in gold or silver.

The turn-off to the zircon field is on the right (south) at the big windmill about 7km east of Gemtree, and the fossicking area is 9km along the track. Deposits of gem-quality garnet also occur in the general area – ask about these at the caravan park. The zircon field and one or two of the garnet deposits can be reached by conventional vehicles, provided it hasn't been raining. Independent fossicking is illegal unless you hold a fossicking licence ($5 per month), available from the Department of Mines & Energy office in Hartley Street, Alice Springs.

Mica Mines The Harts Range starts at Ongeva Creek, where a track on the right takes you to the ominously named Blackfellows Bones mica mine. (Apparently, back in the 1870s, a large group of Aborigines from the Sandover River country was slaughtered nearby in reprisal for an attack on settlers.) From 1888 to 1960, mica was mined from pegmatites throughout the Harts Range, with literally dozens of small mines being developed. The field was never rich thanks to its remoteness, the rugged terrain, lack of water and uncertain markets. However, the miners, most of whom were Italians after the 1920s, persevered until cheaper imports eventually put them out of business. Now the old dumps are a popular target for visiting fossickers, who come in search of the gems that were thrown out with the waste rock.

One of Australia's premier fossicking areas, the Harts Range yields a host of interesting gems and minerals, including mica, smoky and rose quartz, aquamarine, black and green tourmaline, sphene, garnet, sunstone, ruby, iolite and kyanite. However, the area is extremely rugged and the best spots for fossicking are hard to get to – high-clearance 4WD vehicles are required for most tracks. It's also essential to carry plenty of water at all times.

Seven km past Ongeva Creek, a signposted 4WD track leads to garnet deposits en route to Ambalindum homestead, 60km to the south. A massive ochre-coloured ridge looms on your right, its steep bald flanks issuing an invitation to keen hill climbers. It's a tough scramble to the top of **Mt Riddock**, the highest point, but the view is well worth the effort. Before setting out on the walk, you can park your vehicle at Kong Bore, the turn-off to which is about 16km past Ongeva Creek. The dumps of abandoned mica mines in the near vicinity yield various minerals, such as black tourmaline, quartz, hornblende and epidote.

Harts Range High ridges and mountains keep you company for the final 40km to the Harts Range police station. The two police officers based here have the awesome task of preserving law and order over a sparsely populated area of 120,000 sq km – apart from constant travel, they do everything from investigating murders to issuing driving licences. It seems they're kept busy controlling revellers during the annual , which take place over the first weekend in August. This is good entertainment, with a barbecue and bush dance on the Saturday night, but you need to get there early to find a campsite reasonably handy to the action.

From the racecourse, just south of the police station, a 4WD track gives access to a number of mica mines on and around the rocky slopes of **Mt Palmer**. At 600m above the northern plain, this is one of the highest points in the Harts Range and has many large cycads

growing on its southern flank. It's well worth climbing – the atmosphere and sweeping panorama from the top are magnificent.

Mt Palmer first becomes visible past Mount Riddock homestead, 117km from the Stuart Highway. Like a retreat for a goblin king from Tolkien's books, its jagged, misty-blue outline makes a spectacular sight as it rises steeply above the plain. The two white patches you see high up on the western slopes as you get closer are the waste dumps of the Billy Hughes and Oolgarinna mica mines. Two of the field's largest mines, they are best reached by walking along the old camel pads that wind up the mountainside from primitive mining camps at the bottom.

Another of Mt Palmer's mines, the Disputed, is famous in mineralogical circles because of the many fine mineral specimens it has yielded over the years. In the 1930s, miners opened a cave-like cavity in the pegmatite and found it lined top and bottom with huge crystals of black tourmaline, mica, feldspar, quartz and beryl. Apparently the tourmaline crystals stuck up from the floor like fence posts. Known as the Jeweller's Cave, this sparkling wonderland was permanently sealed off by a mine collapse not long after its discovery. A 4WD track takes you from the racecourse to the old Disputed camp, after which it's a half-hour walk along the camel pad to the dumps high above on the mountainside. En route on the pad you pass the Spotted Dog mine, where two miners died in a rock fall in the late 1920s. Their simple grave is nearby, although hard to find.

Harts Range to the Queensland Border (357km)

The first 50km is extremely scenic, with attractive, tall woodlands of whitewood and weeping ironwood fronting the crumpled ranges to the south. Later, mulga and gidgee become dominant. Once past the ranges only flat-topped hills, scattered low ridges and occasional gum-lined creeks break the monotony of the endless plain.

This section's highlight is right beside the road, 50km past the turn-off to Jervois homestead. Here a conical red **termite mound**

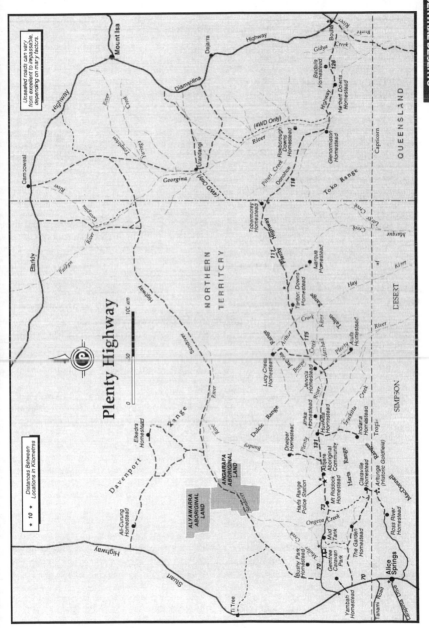

Plenty Highway

Unsealed roads can vary from excellent to impassable, depending on many factors.

Distances Between Locations in Kilometres

* 10 *

nearly 5m high rears like a breaching whale above the surrounding sea of stunted mallees and spinifex. It's the highest point around, and the white splashes on top tell you that it's a favourite perch for hawks. There are lots of similar, if smaller, termite mounds over the next 10km.

Pioneers & Poison Although explored in the 1870s, the area between the Harts Range and Queensland was one of the last parts of Australia to be settled by Europeans. The shortage of permanent surface water kept the pastoralists at bay until bore-drilling equipment became readily available in the late 1940s. Indiana, Jervois, Atula, Lucy Creek, Tarlton Downs and Marqua stations were all first taken up for cattle grazing between 1950 and 1960. Atula, on the Simpson Desert fringe, was recently purchased by the federal government and handed back to its Aboriginal occupants.

Near Mount Riddock homestead you begin to notice clumps of gidgee beside the road. A tough acacia, this generally low, gnarled tree with dark-brown bark and dense grey foliage is the dominant species past Arthur Creek. Although a valuable fodder plant in some areas, gidgee is extremely poisonous to cattle in others. At certain times its pods and young leaves carry a powerful toxin that causes any beast grazing on them to have a heart attack immediately after drinking – the unfortunate animal literally drops dead at the trough. In the early days, stations in this area often suffered devastating stock losses due to gidgee poisoning, but better fencing has brought the problem under control.

Queensland Border
At the Queensland border, the road changes its name and becomes the Donohue Highway. Crossing the border grid, you'll also usually notice a dramatic change in road conditions – the Boulia Shire does its best, but it only takes a few road trains to break the surface and form deep bulldust holes. After the first shattering experiences with these nasties, you soon learn to identify them and take due care.

Queensland Border to Boulia (244km)
Most of this final section is a mix of gidgee scrub and open **Mitchell-grass country**, with variety provided by occasional stony undulations and coolabah creeks. Mitchell-grass habitats, which occur in a great arc from southern Queensland through the Territory's Barkly Tableland to the Kimberley, are the arid zone's most productive in terms of stock grazing. As you'll see along the Plenty and Donohue highways, Queensland has a much greater share of these habitats than does the Territory.

Georgina River At 118km from the border you come to the Georgina River, and other than the vast expanses of empty space, this waterway is the highlight on the Queensland side. Its main channel features shady coolabahs, good campsites and abundant bird life – you'll often see brolgas, emus and bustards as well as large flocks of budgies, cockatiels, galahs and corellas in the immediate area. If there's a down side, it's the **Noogoora burr** that infests the banks. This introduced noxious weed has prickly, cigar-shaped seeds which can easily hitch a ride on your clothing. If you stop here, make sure you're not carrying any unwanted passengers before driving on.

Fed by summer monsoon rains, the Georgina River rises on the Barkly Tableland north-west of Camooweal and heads southwards to join the Diamantina River near Birdsville. A large enough flood will eventually reach Lake Eyre, which is quite a journey by the standards of Australian rivers. A new raised causeway at the crossing means that major floods now close the road for days rather than weeks.

Boulia Eight km from Boulia you meet the bitumen and joyous relief from the bulldust and corrugations. By the time most travellers reach this point, they're ready to kill for a cold beer in the pub.

Straggling down to a large waterhole in the **Burke River**, which the ill-fated Burke and Wills visited on their dash across Aus-

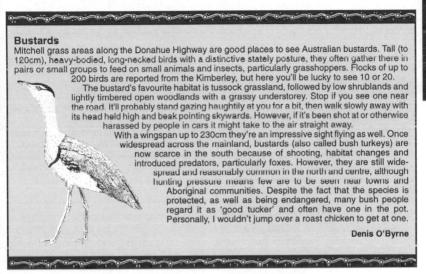

Bustards

Mitchell grass areas along the Donahue Highway are good places to see Australian bustards. Tall (to 120cm), heavy-bodied, long-necked birds with a distinctive stately posture, they often gather there in pairs or small groups to feed on small animals and insects, particularly grasshoppers. Flocks of up to 200 birds are reported from the Kimberley, but here you'll be lucky to see 10 or 20.

The bustard's favourite habitat is tussock grassland, followed by low shrublands and lightly timbered open woodlands with a grassy understorey. Stop if you see one near the road. It'll probably stand gazing haughtily at you for a bit, then walk slowly away with its head held high and beak pointing skywards. However, if it's been shot at or otherwise harassed by people in cars it might take to the air straight away.

With a wingspan up to 230cm they're an impressive sight flying as well. Once widespread across the mainland, bustards (also called bush turkeys) are now scarce in the south because of shooting, habitat changes and introduced predators, particularly foxes. However, they are still widespread and reasonably common in the north and centre, although hunting pressure means few are to be seen near towns and Aboriginal communities. Despite the fact that the species is protected, as well as being endangered, many bush people regard it as 'good tucker' and often have one in the pot. Personally, I wouldn't jump over a roast chicken to get at one.

Denis O'Byrne

tralia in 1861, Boulia is the administrative centre for the vast Boulia Shire. Covering about 60,000 sq km, the shire has a population of 250,000 sheep, 75,000 cattle and about 600 people, 300 of whom live in Boulia. There are a few minor tourist attractions in the town, including a **folk museum** and the last known **corroboree tree** of the Pitta Pitta tribe. About 10km out on the Coorabulka Road is a stand of endangered **waddy trees**, known only in three locations around the margins of the Simpson Desert (the other two are near Birdsville and Old Andado homestead).

If you're camped on a dark night near Boulia, you may be lucky enough to see the famous **Min Min Light**. A ghostly luminous glow resembling a fluorescent football, it's said to float through the air like a lantern being carried in a mist. Many people have seen the light but no-one has ever managed to get close enough to catch it. Apparently it was first noticed many years ago above the graveyard at the old Min Min Hotel on the Winton Road. There is no scientific explanation for the phenomenon, and outsiders tend to scoff that a few ales are necessary before

you'll see it. However, locals have no doubt that the Min Min Light exists.

ALTERNATIVE ROUTE
Mount Isa via Urandangi (280km)

The road to Urandangi, which turns off the Plenty Highway 493km from the Stuart Highway, makes an excellent short cut to Mount Isa, provided the bulldust holes aren't too bad and conditions are dry. Gidgee scrub and open Mitchell-grass plains keep you company for the 96km from the highway to the **Georgina River** crossing, after which tiny Urandangi is only about a minute or two away.

Once an important droving centre, this sleepy little outpost began its slow decline when road trains took over from the drovers in the 1950s and '60s. It has a quaint old pub (☎ (07) 4748 4988) where fuel, meals, basic accommodation and camping facilities are available. Large yellowbelly live in the river, though getting them to bite is usually a challenge. There are plenty of shady campsites near the crossing.

Leaving Urandangi, you endure similar road conditions for a further 110km, then turn onto the bitumen for the final 73km to Mount Isa.

FACILITIES

Gemtree Caravan Park

The *Gemtree Caravan Park* (☎ (08) 8956 9855) offers good shade, a kiosk, public telephone, fuel sales (diesel, super and unleaded) and a range of accommodation options. On-site caravans cost $37 for two people, cabins with air-con are $46 for two, and unpowered/powered sites are $12/16 for two – each additional adult costs $5 and each child $3. Bush camping with access to shower and toilet facilities is $6 per person.

Games of paddymelon bowls, with tea and damper to follow, provide some light-hearted entertainment on Saturday night in the cooler months. Paddymelons, which look like small round watermelons, often occur in large patches beside outback roads.

Atitjere

The *Atitjere Community Store* (☎ (08) 8956 9773) sells basic food requirements and cold drinks, as well as diesel, super and unleaded fuel. Local Aboriginal art is also on offer most of the time. The store opens 9 am to noon and 3 to 5 pm weekdays and 9 am to noon on Saturday.

Jervois Homestead

You can buy diesel, super and unleaded fuel at *Jervois homestead* (☎ (08) 8956 6307) during daylight hours, seven days a week. Shower and toilet facilities are also available. There's no camping at the homestead, but you can stop either at the turn-off, where there's a lay-by, or along the homestead access road between the highway and the first gate (about 1km in). The many magnificent ghost gums growing along the nearby Marshall River make a beautiful setting for a bush camp.

It's worth checking out the huge rocket-proof shelter that was built at the homestead during the 1960s, when Blue Streak rockets were fired in this direction from Woomera. Instead of huddling inside as they were supposed to, the stationfolk preferred to stand on top to watch the fireworks. Similar shelters were provided for all the stations in this area. It seems to have been a waste of taxpayers' money, although a couple of rockets did come down near the highway.

Tobermorey Homestead

Just on the Territory side of the border, *Tobermorey* (☎ (07) 4748 4892 or 4748 4996) is open 24 hours daily for diesel, super and unleaded petrol. There's a small shop, a camping ground with unpowered/powered sites for $10/20 and cabins with air-con sleeping four for $50.

Boulia

This isolated township has a good range of facilities, including a hospital, police station, post office, all-weather aerodrome, hotel, caravan park, two garages, a cafe and a handful of other shops. The *Min Min Store* in the main street sells hardware items and has a minimarket with EFTPOS. Banking facilities are limited to a Commonwealth Bank agency with cash-card facility.

The friendly *Australian Hotel* (☎ (07) 4746 3144) has air-conditioned accommodation in pub and motel-style rooms. Motel rooms with ensuites and TV are $45/55 per single/twin, while single/twin/triple pub rooms are $30/35/45 – other rooms sleep up to four/five people for $55/65. The dining room serves breakfast, lunch and dinner.

It's usually quite peaceful down at the grassy *Boulia Caravan Park* (☎ (07) 4746 3320) beside the Burke River at the eastern end of town. Cabins with two beds and air-con cost $10 per person, powered caravan sites cost $12 for two people plus $2 per extra, and unpowered/powered campsites are $8/10 per person.

Bush Camping

There are numerous good camping sites in the mulga and gidgee scrub en route, although you'll generally need a 4WD vehicle to reach them. The soft, sandy beds of Annamurra Creek (80km from the Stuart Highway), the Plenty River (270km) and Arthur Creek (322km) have excellent campsites among colourful river red gums. The best sites in Queensland are along the Georgina River, where coolabah trees offer good shade and firewood. Roadside stops with small shade shelters, wood-burning barbecues and water tanks are at the turn-offs to Jervois homestead and Urandangi.

Sandover Highway

Leaving the Plenty Highway 96km from Alice Springs, the Sandover Highway heads north-eastwards across flat semi-desert for 552km to terminate at Lake Nash homestead, near the Queensland border. Getting its name from the Sandover River, which it generally follows for about 250km, this wide ribbon of red dirt is an adventurous short cut between central Australia and north-west Queensland.

The Sandover Highway offers a memorable if monotonous experience in remote touring. For almost the entire distance the only signs of human achievement are occasional Telecom communication towers, signposted turn-offs to a handful of isolated homesteads and Aboriginal communities, and the road stretching endlessly ahead. There's often light traffic as far as the Ammaroo turn-off, 218km from the Plenty Highway, but beyond that it's usually a novelty to see another vehicle.

Prolonged heavy rain causes flooding that can keep the highway closed for days. In the late 1980s it was out to all traffic for several months after long sections were washed away in a terrific deluge. Although often rough, the road when dry is normally suitable for conventional vehicles with high ground clearance and heavy-duty suspension. However, it's definitely not recommended for caravans.

While tourist facilities are non-existent along the road, you can buy fuel and supplies at the Arlparra Store (250km from Alice Springs) and the Alpurrurulam Store (643km).

HISTORY

For most of its distance the Sandover Highway crosses the traditional lands of the Alyawarra people, whose lives until recent times focused on the relatively rich environment of the Sandover River. White people arrived in the 1880s, when Lake Nash and Argadargada stations, near the Queensland border, were established for sheep and cattle grazing. The country to the south-west wasn't permanently settled by Europeans until 40 years later. Ooratippra station wasn't taken up until the late 1940s.

As elsewhere in the outback, the loss of food resources and the fouling of precious water supplies by cattle caused bloody conflicts between pastoralists and Aborigines. The so-called Sandover Massacre of the 1920s resulted in the deaths of about 100 Alyawarra, either shot or poisoned for committing the grievous crime of cattle-spearing.

Atartinga station, about 140km north-east of Alice Springs, was taken up by RH (Bob) Purvis, father of the present owner, in 1920. Known as the Sandover Alligator because of his amazing appetite, RH was contracted in the late 1920s to sink wells along the newly gazetted Sandover Stock Route. This was intended to link the stations of far western Queensland with the Alice Springs railhead. However, the water table's increasing depth caused the project to be abandoned near the halfway point. RH's last well, near present-day Ammaroo homestead, struck water at 80m, far too deep for the simple windlasses used in those days.

The stock route was continued from Ammaroo through to Lake Nash after the 1940s, when heavy drilling equipment became readily available in central Australia – this meant that bores could be sunk at regular intervals regardless of depth. Nevertheless, the Sandover Highway was, for the most part, little more than a bush track until the 1970s, when it was upgraded to a standard suitable for road trains.

INFORMATION

The Road Report Hotline (☎ (08) 8922 3232) will tell you whether or not the highway is open, but it doesn't provide details and is often dated. The best places to ask about current road conditions are the Arlparra Store (☎ (08) 8956 9910) and the Alpurrurulam council office (☎ (07) 4748 4800).

Emergency

In the event of a medical emergency, you can obtain assistance at the Urapuntja Health Centre (to the north of the road, 21km past the Arlparra Store), and at health clinics at the Ampilatwatja and Alpurrurulam Aboriginal communities. Homesteads en route have RFDS medical kits and telephones.

Outback Vehicle Recovery (☎ (08) 8952 1087) – the AANT agent in Alice Springs – will come and collect you and your vehicle in the event of a major mechanical breakdown. So will the Mt Isa RACQ agent, Power Automotive (☎ (07) 73 2542).

Maps

There are no useful touring maps of the Sandover Highway and its alternative routes at the Queensland end. The AANT's *Northern Territory* map is the most accurate of those available, but is at a very small scale.

For reasonable detail try the *Alice Springs* 1:1,000,000 topographic sheet produced by AUSLIG – it's way out of date but you can use the AANT map to establish the road's present location. It's available from the Department of Lands, Planning & Environment on Gregory Terrace, Alice Springs, and from AUSLIG sales outlets everywhere.

Radio Frequencies

For most of the way you can call the Alice Springs RFDS base (call sign VJD; ☎ (08) 8952 1033), which monitors 5410 and 6950kHz between 7.30 am and 5 pm weekdays. Use 2020 and 5410kHz for after-hours emergency calls.

Nearer Lake Nash try the RFDS in Mount Isa (call sign VJI; ☎ (07) 4743 2800) on 5110 and 6965kHz between 8 am and 5 pm weekdays. Use 2020kHz for after-hours emergency calls.

THE ROUTE

Plenty Highway to Ammaroo (217km)

Turning off the Plenty Highway 26km from the Stuart Highway, the Sandover crosses a vast plain virtually all the way to the Ammaroo turn-off. Indeed, the landscape is generally so flat that some low granite outcrops about 10km past the Atartinga turn-off become objects of great interest – the highest offers quite a nice view, so it's worth stopping to stretch the legs. You pass occasional attractive patches of shady white-barked gums, but mainly the vegetation is mulga woodland on clay soils and low mallee and spinifex on sandy areas.

This is marginal cattle country – only about 25% of the area of the average station en route is useful grazing land, which explains why they're so huge. For example, Atartinga covers 2240 sq km but its 1200-head herd is concentrated on about 600 sq km. In semi-desert spinifex areas, a typical 10 sq km will support billions of termites but only one cow.

At 127km from the Plenty Highway you cross the western boundary fence of **Utopia station**. Purchased by the federal government in 1976 it's home to about 700 Alyawarra people, who live in 23 small outstations scattered over an area of 2500 sq km. These communities are governed by a council based at **Arlparra**, which you pass 27km further on. The fence 23km past Arlparra marks the boundary between Utopia and Ammaroo stations. Generally, the minor roads that turn off between the two fences lead in to Aboriginal communities and are off limits to the travelling public.

Ammaroo to Lake Nash (335km)

Past Ammaroo, the country soon becomes

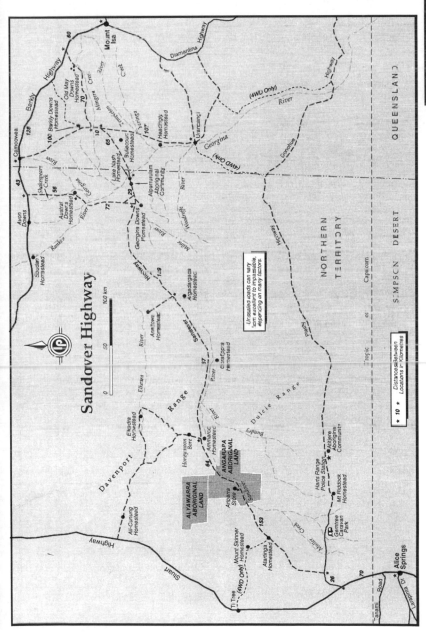

Sandover Highway

Unsealed roads can vary
from excellent to impassable,
depending on many factors.

Distances between
★ 10 ★ Locations in Kilometres

undulating, with stony rises that give sweeping views over an ocean of grey-green scrub. This is the southern end of the **Davenport Range**, which sweeps north-west for 200km to the Devil's Marbles south of Tennant Creek. At this point the **Sandover River** is 5km to the south. It's an extremely scenic watercourse, with attractive gums and a clean sandy bed, but is only rarely visible from the highway.

About 60km past the hills you come to a red sandy plain covered mainly by low mallee and spinifex, a scene that with only minor interruptions takes you almost all the way to Lake Nash. The main variation in plant communities occurs about 200km from Ammaroo, where you cross an outlier of the vast natural grasslands of the Barkly Tableland to the north. As elsewhere, this island of Mitchell grass grows on black clay, more commonly known as blacksoil. Blacksoil roads are typically hard as a rock when dry and incredibly sloppy when wet – it takes only a light shower to turn this short section into a skating rink. Mitchell grasslands occur in a great arc from southern Queensland through the Barkly and on to the Kimberley in Western Australia, and form the arid zone's most productive cattle and sheep country – they cover only about 10% of the Northern Territory yet carry up to 50% of its entire cattle herd.

More blacksoil and Mitchell grass appears 317km past Ammaroo, then the glittering iron roofs of the **Alpurrurulam Aboriginal community** come into view on the left and the end of the highway is just five minutes away, at **Lake Nash homestead**.

Largest of the Sandover's stations, Lake Nash covers 13,000 sq km and carries, on average, 41,000 high-quality beef cattle. Everything about Lake Nash is big: it has the world's largest commercial herd of Santa Gertrudis, the property's bore runs are so long that the vehicles assigned to them travel a total of 96,000km per year, and the average paddock covers several hundred sq kilometres. The station's workforce of 28 is also huge by local standards.

ALTERNATIVE ROUTES

The Sandover Highway ends at Lake Nash homestead, and there you have a choice of three routes: north to Camooweal, east to Mount Isa or south to Urandangi. All are minor dirt roads, and as they include black-soil sections, they become impassable after rain.

Caution must be exercised here, as sign-posting is poor throughout and available maps seldom show the roads' true positions. If in doubt, the best approach is to fill up with fuel at Alpurrurulam and ask for directions and an update on road conditions – if the people at the service station can't help, ask next door at the council office.

Broken Down

I was about 50km past Ammaroo en route to Lake Nash when the engine cut out. I noticed a smell of burning, and a glance at the gauges showed the temperature in the red. With a sinking heart I opened the bonnet. My worst fears were realised: the radiator cap had come off and the radiator had boiled dry. I was carrying a spare cap, but my concern was that the engine might have overheated to the point where it was seriously damaged.

It took the engine over an hour to cool down sufficiently for me to refill the radiator. In the meantime I looked around at the stunted scrub, which offered neither shade nor hope of water. The day was very hot and utterly still, the only sound the incessant buzzing of flies. I hadn't seen another vehicle since the Arlparra Store, over 100km back, and no-one came along while I was stopped. The Sandover Highway is a very lonely road in summer, and although I had plenty of water, the silence and emptiness of the landscape caused my imagination to work overtime.

You can appreciate my immense relief when I finally turned the ignition key and the engine, after coughing a bit, ran as sweetly as before.

Denis O'Byrne

Lake Nash to Camooweal (183km)

The recommended option is to go via Austral Downs homestead, this being a much better road than the alternative route further east via Barkly Downs homestead. The Austral Downs Road turns off the Sandover Highway 13km before Lake Nash. From here the road heads mainly due north over flat terrain, crossing the **Ranken River** and passing Austral Downs at the halfway mark, before meeting the Barkly Highway 43km west of Camooweal.

Most of the way you're on the vast grassy plains of the **Barkly Tableland**, a region notable for its lack of trees. However, there's good shade for a lunch stop or a camp at the Ranken crossing.

Although very small, **Camooweal** offers a wide range of services, including fuel sales, mechanical repairs, hotel accommodation and meals. For details, ring the *Post Office Hotel* (☎ (07) 4748 2124).

Lake Nash to Mount Isa (205km)

From Lake Nash, cross the Georgina River and head north-east for 65km to meet the Camooweal-Urandangi road. Here you veer left towards Barkly Downs and Camooweal. After about 10km you come to a series of three rough creek crossings, where you turn right onto the Old May Downs Road – the turn-off is on a rise just past the third creek and, being unsignposted, is easy to miss. (If you keep going straight on you'll end up at the Barkly Downs homestead.) From here it's a straightforward run of about 70km, past large windmills and the **Old May Downs homestead ruins**, to meet the Barkly Highway about 60km out from Mount Isa. This latter section is relatively scenic, thanks to the stark red ridges that typify the Mount Isa area.

A major regional centre, **Mount Isa** is home to one of Australia's largest mining companies and has a population exceeding 20,000. Contact the Mount Isa Civic Centre (☎ (07) 4744 4200) for information on services, amenities and points of interest in the town and surrounding area.

Lake Nash to Urandangi (172km)

The main route heads north-east from Lake Nash, meeting the road from Camooweal to Urandangi at the 65km mark. Turn right here and drive south for 69km to **Headingly homestead**, where you go around the southern end of the airstrip, keeping the buildings on your right, and head through the gate.

The road is wide and dusty through low gidgee scrub for the final 38km from Headingly to **Urandangi**. For details on this tiny outpost see the Plenty Highway section earlier in this chapter.

FACILITIES
Arlparra Store

The *Arlparra Store* mainly serves the Aboriginal communities of Utopia station. It sells diesel, super and unleaded petrol and has a well-stocked minimarket with all basic food requirements – you can also buy hardware items, tools and vehicle parts. The ladies of Utopia are famous for their batik work, and you may be able to purchase some here. The store opens 9 am to 5 pm weekdays (it closes for an hour at 12.30) and 9 am to noon on Saturday.

Alpurrurulam

The *community store*, which stocks similar lines to the Arlparra Store, is open 8 to 11 am and 3 to 5 pm weekdays and 9 am to 12 noon on Saturday. There's also a service station (open 8 to 11 am and 1 to 4 pm weekdays) selling diesel, super and unleaded petrol, and where minor repairs can be attended to. Although you're welcome to use these facilities, do not proceed further into the community without permission.

Bush Camping

Good campsites near the highway are few and far between, particularly past Ammaroo. One good option near Ammaroo is about 10km up the road to Elkedra and Ali Curung, which turns off north opposite the homestead; a small creek offers pleasant camping with shade and firewood. The spot is just past the big windmill at Honeymoon Bore, where you can refill your water containers.

There are roadside stops with small shade shelters, barbecues and water tanks at the Ammaroo turn-off and about 30km before Lake Nash. As night traffic is virtually non-existent, you're unlikely to be disturbed.

About 5km past Alpurrurulam and within sight of the Lake Nash homestead, you come to a turn-off on the left immediately before a grid. The track heads down to a large waterhole (Lake Nash), where there are some reasonable campsites among scrubby coolabahs near the water's edge. The station manager doesn't mind people camping here, provided they take their rubbish with them. There is no firewood whatsoever, and the blacksoil makes it definitely not the place to be if it starts raining.

Finke & Old Andado Tracks

HIGHLIGHTS

- Getting up early to watch the sun rise on Chambers Pillar

- Spending a night at Molly Clark's atmospheric Old Andado Homestead

This area, south-east of Alice Springs, is full of interest. The countryside is varied, with the red sand-dune country of the western Simpson Desert predominating. However, it's far from boring, and in spring, after rains, the whole area is ablaze with wildflowers.

A number of tracks offer various options: you can do the two main tracks as a loop from Alice Springs, but it's well worth dipping down into South Australia to visit Mount Dare and the Dalhousie Hot Springs in the Witjira National Park.

Old Andado station, on the edge of the Simpson Desert, is a fascinating spot; a visit with the homestead's owner, Molly Clark, is a step back into the 1920s. The Finke Track follows the route of the old *Ghan* railway line between Alice Springs and the small Aboriginal settlement of Finke, the main highlight along the way being a rough detour to the spectacular outcrop known as Chambers Pillar.

The Old Andado Track can successfully be negotiated with care by 2WD, but if you want to head along the old *Ghan* line or down to Dalhousie and on to Oodnadatta, then a well-prepared 4WD is called for.

HISTORY

Archaeological evidence suggests that Aboriginal occupation of this area dates back at least 40,000 years. These days there are communities at Santa Teresa and Finke.

European exploration into the area started in the 1860s with the indefatigable explorer John McDouall Stuart, who passed this way on his travels to and from the north. His route was later followed by the Overland Telegraph Line – see the Oodnadatta Track section later in this chapter for more on Stuart and the Telegraph Line.

The next major developmental stage in this area was the construction of the railway line between Port Augusta and Alice Springs. The line made it as far as Oodnadatta in 1889, and for the next 40 years supplies were carted by camel from the railhead there to outlying districts and Alice Springs. The line eventually reached Alice Springs in 1929, and it remained in use until 1982 when a new line was constructed some distance to the west.

Pastoral activity followed the opening up of the area which the Overland Telegraph Line brought. By the turn of the century most of the workable land was taken up with pastoral leases.

INFORMATION

Permits are not required to travel on any of the tracks listed below. If, however, you are travelling on to the Witjira National Park, permits must be obtained for this. The best place to buy one is at Mount Dare homestead, but they are also available from the

Pink Roadhouse in Oodnadatta if you are coming from the south.

The RFDS base in Alice Springs (☎ (08) 8952 1033) covers this area, and the frequencies monitored are 2020, 5410 and 6950kHz from 7.30 am to 5 pm weekdays.

The best map of the area is once again the excellent Westprint series, this time the *Alice Springs-Oodnadatta* sheet. It is available from several outlets in Alice Springs, including the visitor information centre on Gregory Terrace.

THE ROUTE
Alice Springs to Finke

The first 10km of this route, along the bitumen Stuart Highway, is a breeze. From the airport turn-off a sign points south to Ewaninga and Chambers Pillar. The Old South Rd is well-formed dirt and has quite a bit of traffic as far as Maryvale station, 110km south along the old railway line.

After 30km you come to **Ewaninga Rail Siding** west of the Ooraminna Ranges, and the line from here to Alice Springs is still intact and maintained by the Ghan Preservation Society. The old *Ghan* train makes regular trips out this far from MacDonnell Siding, 5km south of Alice Springs.

Just south of Ewaninga is the **Ewaninga Rock Carvings Conservation Reserve**, a small reserve which protects a number of images carved into the smooth sandstone rocks. The images – of snakes, spirals, animal tracks and other designs – are believed to have been carved between 5000 and 1000 years ago. There's a walking trail with interpretive signs, barbecue facilities and pit toilets. Bring your own firewood.

From Ewaninga the track continues south, past the **Ooraminna Siding**, until after another 37km there's the **Deep Well station** turn-off, and 10km more to the **Hugh River Stock Route**, which heads west for 60km to join the Stuart Highway, and the boundary of the 3200-sq-km Maryvale station. This reasonably well-maintained track is a good alternative access point to the Finke track if you are coming from Kings Canyon or Uluru, or you can use it to make a good day-trip loop from Alice Springs, visiting **Rainbow Valley** and Ewaninga (see Alternative Routes later in this section).

About 20km south of the boundary fence is the ruin of **Rodinga Railway Station**, one of a number you encounter on this route. It is interesting to have a scramble around and get a feel for the loneliness the railway staff must have endured when posted to places such as this.

Maryvale homestead is 13km further south along a side track, which is also the route to take if you want to make the worthwhile 44km detour to **Chambers Pillar**. This trip is highly recommended and well worth the effort (see Detours later in this section).

From Rodinga and the Maryvale turn-off the old railway line and increasingly rough and sandy track continues 40km south-east via sand-dune country known as the Depot Sandhills to **Alice Well**, just off the track on the bank of the Hugh River, although there's no access these days. This was once an important supply depot during the construction of the Overland Telegraph Line, and up until 1928 had its own police station.

After another 13km of pretty sand country the ruins of **Bundooma station**, complete with elevated water tank, are encountered. There are great views from the tank stand, but take care when climbing as the structure is gradually deteriorating.

Another railway station, **Engoordina**, is the next main feature, 23km south of Bundooma, and from here it's a straightforward 61km to the Finke River crossing. The track on this section at times deviates quite a way from the old railway line and it can feel as if you are going in the complete wrong direction, but the two do eventually meet up.

Once over the wide, sandy bed of the Finke River, it's just 4km to the small town of the same name.

When driving along the old *Ghan* track, in many places you have the choice of actually driving on the old rail bed, or on the track alongside. While the old rail bed is obviously level and pretty straight, it is horribly corrugated; often you have to drive at a reckless speed to 'float' over the corrugations. You

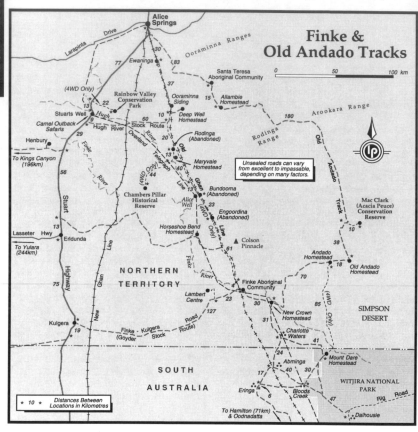

also have to concentrate like crazy and it just doesn't seem worth the effort. The side track, on the other hand, varies from reasonable to sandy, and in some places has the most amazing corrugations which must be at least 50cm deep and 1m long! Imagine a Matchbox car travelling over a sheet of corrugated iron and you'll get the picture! Obviously it's very slow going.

Finke This is another town which owes its existence to the railway line. It started life as a railway siding and gradually grew to have a European population of about 60. With the opening of the new *Ghan* line further west, administration of the town was taken over by the Aputula Aboriginal community. The community store here is also an outlet for the local artists who make crafts such as carved wooden animals, bowls, traditional weapons and seed necklaces. Be aware that this is Aboriginal land – alcohol and photography are prohibited.

Finke is linked to the Stuart Highway, 150km to the west, by the well-maintained dirt road sometimes known as the Goyder Stock Route. It's a fairly dull stretch of road, although the **Lambert Centre**, just off the

HUGH FINLAY

HUGH FINLAY

TIM BURKE

Finke & Old Andado Tracks
Top: The multihued sandstone cliffs of Rainbow Valley
Middle: The cutting for the old *Ghan* line is now a popular 4WD track
Bottom: Chambers Pillar glows red in the evening light

DENIS O'BYRNE

DENIS O'BYRNE

TONY WHEELER

Simpson Desert
Top: Crossing a soft sand dune along the French Line
Middle: Wind-sculpted sand in the Simpson Desert
Bottom: Camping out in the desert

road, is an interesting curiosity (see Alternative Routes).

Finke to Old Andado

The road heads off from Finke to the east, basically following the line of the Finke River. The river was named by Stuart in 1860 after his friend William Finke, who helped fund some of his journeys into the outback.

After 30km you pass right by the **New Crown homestead** (fuel available), and from here there are two choices: south to Charlotte Waters, Abminga and eventually Oodnadatta (with a possible detour to Dalhousie Springs; see Alternative Routes), or north and west to Andado and Old Andado. If you're coming down from the north, this is the first place you'll come across one of Adam and Lynnie Plate's distinctive signs. The Plates run the Pink Roadhouse in Oodnadatta and have worked tirelessly at putting up signs at strategic spots right throughout the western Simpson region, and largely thanks to them, navigation in the area is relatively straightforward.

Shortly after leaving New Crown, the track once again crosses the Finke River and then swings to the north for the 70km run to Andado station. This stretch passes through some beautiful sand-dune country which is ablaze with wildflowers after good rains. For much of the way the track runs along the valleys between the sand dunes, but every now and then it swings up and over a dune to the next valley. The road is in good condition with a firm gravel base; it's no problem at all to roll along at 90km/h, but just keep well to the left when crossing the dune crests.

At **Andado homestead** you are confronted with yet another choice: south along a sandy but very pretty and well-defined 4WD track to Mount Dare (85km; see Alternative Routes below), or east along a *very* corrugated bladed track to Old Andado. Andado station has no tourist facilities and visitors passing through should respect the privacy of the owners. At over 10,000 sq km, Andado is the third-largest station in the Territory.

Old Andado Homestead The 18km track to Old Andado is often in a bad way – it's a private road which is rarely graded. It's quite sandy in places and requires a good deal of concentration if you want to maintain enough speed to get over the corrugations without your fillings coming loose. Mercifully, it's only a short distance.

The homestead, the easternmost on the western side of the Simpson Desert, is situated in a pretty valley between two huge lines of dunes. The homestead is run as a tourist facility by the no-nonsense Molly Clark, one of the great battlers of the Centre.

The Andado pastoral lease was first taken up by Robert McDill in 1909, and he built the bush timber and corrugated-iron homestead in 1922. In 1955 Molly and her husband, Mac, took up the management of Andado station from the 'new homestead', 18km to the west. Pastoral activity on the edge of the desert is an even more marginal activity than elsewhere, and when Mac was killed in a plane crash on the property, and Molly was forced to clear the land entirely of stock for three years as part of the government brucellosis-eradication programme, there was little future in Andado station.

Despite these enormous setbacks, Molly Clark struggled on and eventually sold the property, while keeping the old homestead to run as a small-scale tourist operation. Today, visitors can camp or stay in dongas, and eat meals cooked in the old homestead kitchen on a vintage combustion wood stove. Molly Clark, now in her 80s but still going strong, does all the work around the place herself, and so needs advance warning of guests – don't expect much of a welcome if you just rock up unannounced (see Facilities later in this section).

Old Andado to Alice Springs

At Old Andado the track swings north for the 326km trip to the Alice. It takes around five hours to do in one hit, but it's well worth stopping at the Mac Clark Conservation Reserve along the way. The majority of the track, pioneered by the Clarks and now generally known as the Old Andado Track, runs along a valley between two lines of dunes and is not difficult to negotiate.

Thirty-eight km north of Old Andado is a track that heads eastwards for 10km to the 3042-hectare **Mac Clark (Acacia peuce) Conservation Reserve**. The *Acacia peuce* tree is found in only three places in Australia: near Boulia and Birdsville in Queensland, and, the smallest stand (around 1000 trees), here on the western edge of the Simpson Desert. It's a rare arid-zone tree which can survive in a climate where very little else can – the average annual rainfall is just 150mm and summer daytime temperatures of 40°C are the norm rather than the exception.

From the Mac Clark Conservation Reserve turn-off, the track continues north and slightly west through sand-dune country, looping away to the west around the edges of the Arookara and Rodinga ranges, before arriving at **Allambie station** after 180km. From here the track improves markedly, and it's a further 15km to the **Santa Teresa Aboriginal community**. This community is on the site of the old Catholic mission station which was moved here in the 1950s, having functioned at a site north of Alice Springs for a number of years prior to that. There are no tourist facilities, and a permit is not required to transit straight through. However, visits to the community must be arranged in advance at the council office (☎ (08) 8956 0999).

From Santa Teresa it's just a short hop (83km) to the Stuart Highway 10km south of Alice Springs along an interesting road which skirts the western edge of the Ooraminna Ranges.

DETOURS
Chambers Pillar Historical Reserve

Chambers Pillar is a huge finger of sandstone which towers nearly 60m above the surrounding plain. The sandstone beds which form the pillar were formed over 350 million years ago, and subsequent erosion has left the pillar in its present form.

In the past it was an important landmark, first for European explorers and, later, for travellers heading north to Alice Springs from the head of the railway line before it was pushed all the way through to the Alice. In 1860, on his first attempt to cross the continent, Stuart was the first of these explorers to find the pillar. He named it after James Chambers who, like Finke, was one of Stuart's Adelaide backers. Subsequent visitors included John Ross in 1870, who was on an expedition to determine the future route of the Overland Telegraph Line, and Ernest Giles, who, in 1872, passed the pillar while attempting to cross to the west coast of Australia.

Many of these early visitors carved their names into the rock, leaving a permanent

Acacia Peuce
Acacia peuce trees grow very slowly to a height of up to 17m, and are very long-lived – up to 500 years. The trees, also known as waddies after the Aboriginal fighting clubs carved from their wood, have a very spiky foliage which offers little shade. It's these leaves which are the key to the tree's survival: the moisture loss from such needle-like leaves is very low. The adult trees have a spreading form similar to casuarinas, or she-oaks (but classified as acacias, or wattles, due to the occurrence of seed pods rather than cones), while young trees are far more columnar.

The wood of the *Acacia peuce* is extremely dense and hard (it's impossible to drive a nail into), and so was highly prized. Many trees were felled and used for fence and stockyard posts early this century. Fortunately, the rarity of the tree has been recognised, and the reserve named after pastoralist Mac Clark, who had a great interest in the *Acacia peuce*, is one of a number of measures aimed at ensuring the tree's survival. ∎

reminder of their visit, and this has given the pillar an interesting historical aspect. Unfortunately, many less worthy graffiti artists have added to the gallery in recent times, at the same time defacing much of the historical significance. (Just in case you feel like immortalising yourself in stone, be warned that it will cost you a fine of up to $5000 if you're caught.)

To the Aboriginal people, Chambers Pillar also has great significance. It is said that the powerful gecko ancestor, Itirkawara, killed some of his ancestors and took a girl of a different kin group. They were banished to the desert where both turned to stone – Itirkawara became the pillar and the girl became **Castle Rock**, about 500m away.

The 4WD track to the pillar is signposted from the store at Maryvale station. From the station store to where the track turns left near the boundary fence (12km), there are patches of bulldust, but from here for the next 22km it is less of a problem. After the track does the left turn it climbs a rocky rise and you come to a fork in the track; veer right. The very rocky track continues along the top of the rise, and from here there are excellent views of Chambers Pillar. The track descends and the last 10km are over sand dunes. This track is unsuitable for trailers or caravans.

Note that despite the existence of other station tracks in the area, the route described is the only public access route to the pillar. Do not try to exit the reserve to the new *Ghan* line or Stuart Highway to the west.

Facilities at the reserve consist of a visitor information board, barbecues, picnic tables and long-drop dunnies. Firewood should be brought in from outside the reserve. Camping is permitted but there is little shade and no water.

ALTERNATIVE ROUTES
Alice Springs to Maryvale via Rainbow Valley

The alternative to heading straight for Maryvale station along the Old South Road is to travel south along the Stuart Highway and then cut across to the east along the Hugh

River Stock Route. The main advantage of taking this route is that it allows you to visit the excellent **Rainbow Valley Conservation Park**.

The turn-off to the park is 77km south of Alice Springs, and from here it's 22km along an unsignposted 4WD track which has many sandy patches. Close to the campsite in the park there are a number of claypans, which should be skirted if there is even a hint of moisture in them.

Although colourfully named, the crumbling sandstone cliffs at Rainbow Valley are various shades of cream and red, and late in the day the setting sun can cast some wonderful effects. The red colours are caused by leached iron-oxide staining, while in the lighter parts iron oxide is not present and these areas have been bleached by the sun. If you're lucky enough to visit when there's water in the claypans, you can take some stunning photos.

The park is not as instantly attractive as some of the more spectacular sights in central Australia, but it has a charm which certainly repays any time spent here. Because it doesn't get overrun with visitors, it's a great place to spend a couple of days – wander and scramble in the **James Range**, admire the views and soak up the timeless atmosphere of the Centre.

Facilities at the park are basic. There's a campsite with nothing more than barbecue places, so you'll need to bring all your own supplies, including firewood. Remember to bury all toilet wastes and take other rubbish away when you leave.

Once back on the Stuart Highway, head south for 13km to Noel Fullerton's **Camel Outback Safaris** (☎ (08) 8956 0925) on the highway at Stuart's Well. As well as using the fuel and roadhouse services, you can take a short ride on a camel for a few dollars, or for the more adventurous there are extended trips into the desert; Rainbow Valley is a popular destination.

From the camel farm it's a further 9km south along the highway to the **Hugh River Stock Route** turn-off. This is quite a reasonable track which heads east to the old *Ghan* line (70km), although it is not as well maintained after the new *Ghan* line and the Hugh River crossing about halfway along.

Finke to the Stuart Highway

The other option from Finke is to head due west along the Finke-Kulgera road (sometimes referred to as the Goyder Stock Route) to Kulgera, 150km away on the Stuart Highway. It is a well-maintained (usually) but basically uninteresting road.

The only highlight along the route is the **Lambert Centre**. If you can imagine picking Australia up by the one point where it would balance (ie the centre of gravity), this is it. Yippee! A team from the Queensland University spent two years doing computer calculations to come up with the exact spot. Exactly why they would want to is unclear. For those of you who like precision, the centre is at latitude 25°36'36.4"S and longitude 134°21'17.3"E.

The Lambert Centre is in a shallow gully west of Finke. The signposted turn-off heads north off the Finke-Kulgera road 20km west of Finke. From the road, you head 6.5km north along a well-defined track, passing Mulga Bore on the left, and a further 8km west to the spot, which is marked by a replica of the flagpole atop Parliament House in Canberra!

It was named the Lambert Centre after Bruce Lambert, a surveyor and first head of the National Mapping Council.

Charlotte Waters & Mount Dare Loop

While it is possible to travel direct between Finke and Old Andado, it is much more interesting to head south from New Crown and loop around through Charlotte Waters, Abminga, Bloods Creek and Mount Dare to Andado station. This loop also gives you access to the Dalhousie Mound Springs (94km round trip from Bloods Creek) and the trans-Simpson Rig Road (see the Simpson Desert section for details on Dalhousie and crossing the Simpson).

From New Crown station, a good track heads due south for historic **Charlotte Waters**, 31km away and just shy of the

South Australian border. This once important repeater station and supply depot on the Overland Telegraph Line has all but disappeared – it was demolished to provide building materials for New Crown.

At Charlotte Waters you can either head east the 41km direct to Mount Dare, or continue south and cross into South Australia (border marked by a Pink Roadhouse sign) and head for the ruin of **Abminga**, 24km south from Charlotte Waters. This siding was once the railhead for Mount Dare and Bloods Creek to the east. The track forks here again, the right taking you south to Oodnadatta via Eringa (23km) with its huge and beautifully picturesque billabong, and Hamilton (71km). The left fork, however, is the one you want as it heads direct to the ruins of **Bloods Creek station**, 40km to the southeast. Today, a windmill is all that marks the site of what was an important camping spot for workers on the Overland Telegraph Line. The strategic location meant that the site continued to be used after the line was finished; eventually a pub and store opened up. It was from Bloods Creek that the drover and bushcraft expert Ted Colson set off with six camels and an Aborigine and made the first European return crossing of the Simpson, going to Birdsville and back in 1936.

At the Bloods Creek windmill you can either continue south-east for the 47km run to **Dalhousie Mound Springs**, or head north-east to Mount Dare homestead, 30km away in the **Witjira National Park**. In the late 1960s Mount Dare station became part of the Witjira National Park, but the homestead was leased privately to provide tourist services to the increasing numbers of visitors who were coming through this way.

For details of the facilities at Mount Dare see the Simpson Desert section later in this chapter.

At the homestead there is a track heading north and then west to Charlotte Waters (41km), or you can take the much more interesting route direct to Andado. This route crosses into the Northern Territory after 14km, and for the next 17km follows the course of the Finke River. This section is quite heavily treed, and although the track is good, it winds increasingly through the surprisingly dense scrub, is horrendously dusty, and, at times, is 1m below ground level!

After crossing the Finke River, the track heads on to Andado station, 54km away, passing through a wonderfully varied landscape – high sand dunes and wide-open plains dotted with cattle and crossed by meandering, tree-lined watercourses.

ORGANISED TOURS

There are a couple of outfits in Alice Springs that run organised tours to this area, but these are basically limited to Chambers Pillar and Rainbow Valley.

Oak Valley Day Tours (☎ (08) 8956 0959) is an Aboriginal-owned and run organisation that makes day trips to Oak Valley and Chambers Pillar, both of cultural significance to the Aboriginal people. The cost is $110 ($70 children) and this includes lunch and billy tea.

Another operator is The Outback Experience (☎ (08) 8953 2666), which has day trips from Alice Springs to Chambers Pillar and Rainbow Valley for $95 per person ($65 children).

FACILITIES

Maryvale Station

At *Maryvale station* (☎ (08) 8956 0989) there's a shop selling basic provisions and fuel (diesel and super). It is open daily (except Sunday afternoon) from 10 am to 5 pm. Credit cards are not accepted.

Finke

At the *Aputula Community Store* (☎ (08) 8956 0968) you can buy groceries as well as craft items made by the local artists. Fuel (super, unleaded, diesel) is available and basic mechanical repairs are undertaken. The store is open weekdays from 8 am to noon and from 1 to 4 pm, and on Saturday from 8 to noon. If you want fuel outside these hours there's a $10 surcharge.

There's an unofficial *camping ground* on the outskirts of town, which you can get directed to from the store. Unless you really want power, it's probably better to head out of town a bit further and bush-camp.

New Crown Station

The track from Finke to Andado passes right by the *New Crown homestead* (☎ (08) 8956 0969), so even if you don't need to stop, slow down sufficiently so you don't shower the place in dust.

Fuel supply (diesel, unleaded) is the only service offered to travellers. This is sold during daylight hours; credit cards are not accepted.

Old Andado Station

At *Old Andado station* (☎ (08) 8956 0812) there's reasonably priced twin accommodation available in dongas, and you can get dinner and breakfast. You can also camp nearby, but there's little shade. Booking in advance is essential and rates are available on request; credit cards are not accepted.

There is no fuel or vehicle service here. There's an airstrip but no aviation fuel.

Simpson Desert

HIGHLIGHTS

- Experiencing the solitude of one of the world's great desert regions
- Standing atop 'Big Red', the tallest dune in the desert
- Luxuriating in the warm mineral waters of Dalhousie Springs

Recognised as one of the world's outstanding sand-ridge deserts, the Simpson Desert sprawls across more than 150,000 sq km at the junction of the Northern Territory, Queensland and South Australian borders. The desert's most obvious characteristic is its remarkable system of parallel dunes, which rise to 40m and stretch without a break for up to 200km. Their direction maintained by the prevailing winds, the dunes run from south-south-east to north-north-west and are made up of sand blown in from the flood plains and lakes that border the desert's eastern and southern margins. There are 11 major dune systems and nine minor ones, each with its own physical characteristics – such as dune height, length and width, crest shape, vegetation and the nature of the valleys between the dunes.

Although it receives an extremely unreliable average rainfall of only 130mm per year, the Simpson Desert is by no means biologically boring. Sand ridges aside, it has a number of major habitat types, including spinifex grasslands, gidgee woodlands and coolabah floodouts. Collectively these are home to 800 plant species, over 180 birds, 24 native mammals and probably 90 or more reptiles. In a good season the desert is an exciting place to be for wildlife enthusiasts.

One of Australia's last great wilderness areas, the desert was occupied by Aborigines until 1900 and was not crossed by a white person until 1936. It is only recently that tourists have arrived, using the vehicle tracks that oil explorers carved through the desert during the 1960s. Several of these have since become 4WD routes, popular with increasing numbers of adventurous travellers who come seeking both a challenge and spiritual refreshment in the endless horizons and awesome sense of solitude.

The recreation boom and a new awareness of the desert's fragility and unique values have led to the declaration of several conservation areas over most of South Australia's portion of the desert: Witjira National Park (7770 sq km) centres on Dalhousie Springs in the west, while the combined Simpson Desert Regional Reserve (29,640 sq km) and Simpson Desert Conservation Park (6930 sq km) stretch from Witjira to the Diamantina River on the desert's eastern flank. The Simpson Desert National Park (5550 sq km) occupies the south-west corner of Queensland. All these areas are crossed by one or more of the routes described below.

Before setting out on a Simpson Desert crossing, it's wise to reflect that in recent times several foolhardy travellers have paid the ultimate penalty for failing to prepare for its dangers. The hazards include great heat, lack of water and extreme isolation from human habitation and any facilities. Desert travel is not recommended from October to April, when shade temperatures in excess of 40°C are frequently experienced.

TRACK SUMMARY
The Rig Road
Built during the 1960s to a standard suitable for laden semi-trailers, the Rig Road takes you right across the desert, from Mount Dare homestead to the Birdsville Track. It generally avoids the areas of higher dunes and has been sheeted with clay throughout. However, it is no longer maintained and so is subject to guttering and drift sand – conditions which make a 4WD essential. It is still by far the easiest route across the desert, and the changing colours of its sand dunes (from tomato-red in the west to white in the south-east) and varied topography and vegetation also make it the most interesting. The Rig Road is lined by borrow pits where clay was extracted during its construction. These can hold water for a considerable period after heavy rain and at such times become a focus for desert wildlife.

The French Line & QAA Line
Bulldozed across the desert by the French Petroleum Company in 1963, the so-called French Line runs at right angles to the sand ridges and was never intended to do more than provide temporary access for geological survey work. Kept open by 4WD traffic, its driving conditions are extremely difficult, as it crosses literally hundreds of soft dunes – these are steepest on the eastern side, so travel in a west to east direction is recommended. The QAA Line was constructed in a like manner and also presents difficult conditions, although it is a little easier than the French Line.

ROUTE OPTIONS
There are three major route options between Mount Dare homestead (the last resupply

point on the desert's western side) and Birdsville. All tracks include clay surfaces which are closed when wet.

Via The French Line & QAA Line

This route involves a total distance of 507km, of which 275km includes soft dune crossings. The French Line is not recommended to inexperienced desert motorists.

Via The Rig Road, K1 Line & QAA Line

Covering a total distance of 701km, this route is mainly firm when dry, though 100km of it includes soft dune crossings.

Via The Rig Road & Birdsville Track

Except dune crossings, this route is mainly firm when dry and covers a total distance of 773km.

HISTORY

In 1845 Charles Sturt was attempting to prove the existence of an inland sea near the centre of the continent when he became the first white person to visit the Simpson Desert. Crossing Sturts Stony Desert with a small party on horseback, he followed Eyre Creek (which he named) and struck westwards into the desert. On 14 August, at latitude 24.7-S, near the present border between Queensland and the Northern Territory, he was forced back by the waterless red ocean of sand ridges that stretched before him. Sturt wrote in his journal:

Grass had entirely disappeared and the horses wound about working their way through the pointed spinifex with which the ground was universally covered. Ascending one of the sand ridges I saw a numberless succession of these terrific objects rising above each other to the east and west of me. Northwards they ran away from me for more than fifteen miles, with the most undeviating straightness, as if those masses had been thrown up with the plumb and rule.

Several expeditions nibbled at the desert's fringes in later years, but the first to penetrate it to any extent was led by David Lindsay in 1886. Accompanied by a white station owner and a desert Aborigine, he took camels from Dalhousie Springs via Approdinna Attora

Charles Sturt

Knolls to about latitude 25.5°S on the Queensland and Northern Territory border, where he turned around and returned to Dalhousie. He could easily have continued but didn't bother, as the area to the east was already well known.

Assisted by Aboriginal informants, Lindsay had found water at several of the native wells that were scattered through the desert's southern and eastern parts. The wells, sunk to depths of 7m, were located in depressions between the sandhills and gave access to freshwater soaks. They were the focus of life for the Aboriginal groups who then lived in the desert, providing them with security in drought. After good rains had filled the claypans, Aborigines were able to leave the wells for extended periods and thus exploit the land's resources over a much wider area.

The first white person to cross the Simpson Desert's full width was pastoralist Ted Colson. In 1936, he took camels from Bloods Creek (near Mount Dare homestead) to Birdsville. Colson and his Aboriginal companion travelled close to the Northern Territory border throughout their journey, visiting Approdinna Attora Knolls en route. Having reached Birdsville, the two men turned around and rode back across the desert to Bloods Creek. Colson received no support for this outstanding feat, which was accomplished without fanfare; it seems that he undertook the trek purely in the spirit of adventure.

The first scientific expedition into the Simpson was mounted in 1939 under the leadership of Dr CT Madigan. With eight men and 19 camels, he travelled northwards from Old Andado homestead to the junction of the Hale and Todd rivers, then east to the Queensland border, where he turned southeast to Birdsville. Between the Hale River and Eyre Creek – a distance of 326km – the party crossed 626 sand ridges, many 30m high, and gathered much valuable data. Ten years previously Madigan had made several reconnaissance flights over the desert and recommended that it be named after Allen Simpson, the then president of the South Australian Branch of the Royal Geographical Society of Australasia.

Interest in the desert lapsed until its potential for oil exploration was recognised in the early 1960s, when Dr Reg Sprigg and his company, Geosurveys of Australia, were contracted to carry out gravity surveys in the region. As part of this work, Sprigg and his family completed the first motorised crossing of the desert, travelling from Mount Dare to Birdsville along the Northern Territory border and using fuel and supplies carried in by light aircraft. Two years later, by which time the French Line had been bulldozed, the Spriggs made the first south-north motorised crossing, their route taking them from Cowarie homestead to the Plenty River, on the desert's northern fringe. These feats signalled the beginning of the current recreation boom.

INFORMATION
Tourist Offices

For tourist information of a general nature, contact the Pink Roadhouse in Oodnadatta (☎ (08) 8670 7822), the Mount Dare homestead (☎ (08) 8670 7835) and Birdsville

Auto (☎ (07) 4656 3226). Road reports for the desert's eastern side – in particular conditions at the crossings of Eyre Creek and Warburton Creek – should be obtained from the Birdsville police (☎ (07) 4656 3220). Mount Dare homestead and the Oodnadatta police (☎ (08) 8670 7805) are the best sources of road information for the western half of the desert.

Emergency

Birdsville has a well-equipped hospital staffed by registered nurses. Mount Dare homestead has a comprehensive RFDS medical kit, and in the event of an emergency its staff can administer drugs and perform other procedures by acting on directions they receive over their HF radio.

Registration & Permits

All travellers intending to cross the Simpson Desert should register their intentions with the police at either Birdsville or Oodnadatta, depending on their starting point. The police will be pleased to check your preparedness – if you don't wish to take their advice, they will ask you to sign a waiver. Having registered, don't forget to report in at the other end – otherwise you may trigger an unnecessary search, the cost of which will have to be met by yourself.

Travel in the Simpson Desert within South Australia requires a Desert Parks Pass – for details see the Travel Permits section in the earlier Getting Around chapter. The accompanying booklet contains useful information on Witjira National Park, the Simpson Desert Regional Reserve and the Simpson Desert Conservation Reserve. You can purchase your pass from the Pink Roadhouse in Oodnadatta, Mount Dare homestead, Birdsville Fuel Services and Birdsville Auto in Birdsville, and the Ghan Store in Marree.

A permit from the Department of Environment & Conservation ranger in Birdsville (☎ (07) 4656 3247) is required to travel within the Simpson Desert National Park. This will mainly affect travellers intending to take the QAA Line from near Poeppel Corner east to the old rabbit fence. For information, contact the department's regional office (☎ (07) 4658 1761), PO Box 202, Longreach 4730.

Books

The only worthwhile reference on the desert as a whole is *The Simpson Desert* by Mark Shephard (The Royal Geographical Society of Australasia & Giles Publications, Adelaide, 1992). It covers natural history, Aboriginal life, exploration and conservation issues, as well as giving sound advice on preparing for a crossing.

The *Natural History of Dalhousie Springs*, edited by W Zeidler & WF Ponder (South Australian Museum, Adelaide, 1989), is a fascinating explanation of the ecology and cultural history of these artesian springs on the edge of the Simpson.

Maps

The map-guide entitled *Dalhousie and Simpson Desert*, published by Westprint Heritage Maps, covers the various tracks between Mount Dare and Birdsville and is contained in the Desert Parks Pass package.

For a more detailed coverage, you'll need the *Dalhousie, Poolowanna* and *Pandie Pandie* 1:250,000 topographic maps from AUSLIG. The QAA Line appears on the *Birdsville* sheet, while a small portion of the Rig Road's western end lies on the *Gason* sheet. These maps are available through AUSLIG sales outlets in all capital cities.

Radio Frequencies

An average of about 12 vehicles per day cross the desert in winter, with a dramatic increase to around 50 over the July and September school holiday periods. Having said that, averages are not a reliable indicator, as in the event of a breakdown the next vehicle may be days away. In hot weather you may have to wait weeks for someone to come along. For this reason it's advisable to carry a HF radio fitted with frequencies for the RFDS bases at Alice Springs and Port Augusta or the Telstra Radphone Direct Dial (RDD) antenna at Alice Springs.

To speak to Port Augusta RFDS base (call sign VNZ), use 8165kHz between 7 am and 5 pm, or 4010 and 6890kHz between 7 am and 9 pm seven days. After-hours alarm frequencies are 2020 and 4010kHz. Contact the base (☎ (08) 8642 2044) for more details of its services.

The Alice Springs RFDS base (call sign VJD) can be reached on 5410 and 6950kHz between 7.30 am and 5 pm Monday to Friday, excluding public holidays. For after-hours emergency calls, use 2020 and 5410kHz. For more information on services, contact the base (☎ (08) 8952 1033).

Information on RDD is available from Telstra on ☎ (02) 9901 2000 or freecall 1800 810 023.

SPECIAL PREPARATIONS

For the Simpson Desert driver, lack of traffic, difficult driving conditions and remoteness from all facilities put new emphasis on travel preparation. Carry enough water for at least a week – those in a hurry can cross the desert in two days under ideal conditions, but if you're interested in taking a better look, you'll want to spend longer. Also, don't forget that you might break down and have to wait for rescue. Calculate fuel needs based on the distance of your chosen route, adding at least 30% for unexpected detours and the higher fuel consumption you can expect under 4WD conditions.

The French Line is particularly rough, thanks to the many inexperienced drivers who neglect to deflate their tyres to the recommended 20psi (140kPa) or less on soft surfaces. For this reason, trailers must be robust and all items should be packed to avoid breakages. Always place heavy items (such as full jerry cans and spare wheels) so that they won't raise the vehicle's centre of gravity to a dangerous level – roof racks are not the place!

Owing to the blind crests met with throughout, the lead vehicle in each party should carry a flag (bright orange is ideal) on a long pole fixed to the bullbar. This will warn oncoming vehicles of your approach.

For obvious reasons it's essential to carry ample drinking water at all times in the

Simpson Desert – see the Survival section in the chapter on Facts for the Visitor. You can fill up your jerry cans at Mount Dare homestead and Birdsville as their water supplies are quite acceptable to all but the most sensitive stomachs. The water from Dalhousie Springs and Purni Bore is drinkable at a pinch.

THE ROUTE
Mount Dare Homestead to Dalhousie Springs (70km)

Leaving Mount Dare, the generally rough track to Dalhousie Springs crosses a mix of gibber uplands and sand ridges for the 44km to **Opossum Creek**, where ancient coolabahs and shady gidgees make a pleasant spot to boil the billy. The creek was named after the brush-tailed possums that lived along its banks in earlier times. Sadly, this species has all but vanished from arid Australia over the past 50 years.

Eleven km later and still in gibber country, you cross **Christmas Creek** with its depress-ing graveyard of dead trees. They died after nearby **Crispe Bore**, which flowed into the creek, was capped in 1987. This artesian bore is one of many to be capped in recent years following official awareness that the outback's major source of groundwater – the Great Artesian Basin – was being needlessly depleted. This is the place to collect firewood for a camp at Dalhousie Springs, as there is none further on.

Past Christmas Creek the track climbs up onto a barren gibber tableland from where, 64km past Mount Dare, you look out over an eroded, salt-encrusted basin dotted with dense patches of tall, lush reeds and dark scrub. These are the Dalhousie Springs, the only natural source of permanent surface water in an arid area as large as many European countries. One km further on, you come to a T-intersection, with the lonely stone ruins of Dalhousie homestead 9km to your right and the Dalhousie Springs hot pool and camping area 4km to the left.

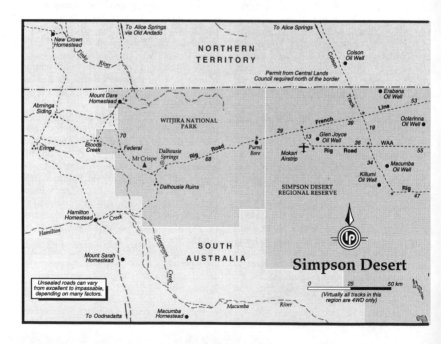

Dalhousie Springs Spread over an area of about 70 sq km, this group of 80 artesian springs is recognised as being of world significance because of its unique geological and biological value. The springs are so isolated from other permanent surface waters that they contain many species of aquatic fauna found nowhere else. This was one of the major reasons the surrounding 776,900-hectare Witjira National Park was declared in 1985.

The main spring is a steaming oasis of deep, dark-blue water measuring about 150m by 50m and fringed by low paperbarks and reeds. A fantastic sight in its desolate setting, the pool attracts a large variety of wildlife, including goannas, water birds and dingoes. The camping area on its banks is bare and uninviting, but a swim in the pool on a cold winter's morning more than makes up for this. From here you can explore other springs in the area, including several – such as the one beside the old Dalhousie ruins –

where the native vegetation has been choked out by tall date palms. The original palms probably grew from seed brought in by the Afghani camel drivers who serviced this area at the turn of the century.

The Rig Road – Dalhousie Springs to the French Line (97km)

Leaving the camping area, you cross the aptly named Gluepot (a terror when wet) and pass extinct mound springs perforated with rabbit burrows, before climbing onto a gibber tableland at the 9km mark. These are the last gibbers you see until Big Red (near Birdsville), so make the most of them. At 20km you enter a large seasonal swamp, where long, deep ruts tell a graphic story of what it's like to drive on when wet.

Ten km after entering the swamp you pass some low mesas and notice the track becoming sandier, with tall saltbush on either side. However, you don't enter the Simpson Desert proper until 52km from the Dalhousie

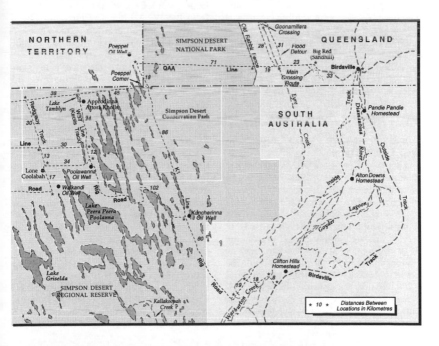

Springs camping ground, when you see low sand ridges topped with cane grass beside the track. The dunes gradually become higher, and spinifex begins to appear on the flanks and in the swales, setting the scene for much of what follows. The distinctive large hoofprints of camels soon become apparent along the track – it's an unlucky traveller who doesn't see at least one of these animals during the crossing.

Purni Bore Cresting a sand ridge 68km from the spring, you arrive without warning at a large pool surrounded by luxuriant beds of reeds and bushy wattles. Clouds of steam and sulphurous smells billow from the near-boiling water that gushes from a pipe beside the track, and native hens scurry into the reeds as you approach. The tracks of camels, dingoes, donkeys, rabbits, hopping mice and many birds cover the nearby sand ridges. This is the little world of Purni Bore, an isolated wetland fed by a flowing artesian bore originally drilled in search of oil and gas. It's a beaut spot for wildlife enthusiasts – over 35 species of birds, including several water birds, have been sighted here, and with time and patience you'll see most of them for yourself. Unfortunately the dingoes haven't learned to fear people, so it's not a good idea to leave food or clothing lying around where they can get it. A toilet and hot shower have been erected here .

The Rig Road – The French Line to the WBY Line (181km)
Twenty-nine km past Purni Bore, the Rig Road turns sharp right (south) at the beginning of the French Line, which spears straight ahead, over a high sand ridge. After 13km of easy travel between the dunes you arrive at **Mokari airstrip**, which was used to service this area during the oil exploration days. The grave of Jaroslav Pecanek, an Oodnadatta identity who fell in love with the desert and asked to be buried here, lies under a low tree near the airstrip's southern end.

From Mokari you head eastwards once more across the sand ridges, with deep washouts running both along and across the road

just to make it interesting. Here the dunes are well vegetated with cane grass, spinifex and bushes, but shade is at a premium. Thirty-six km from Mokari the Rig Road turns southwards at the beginning of the **WAA Line**, which continues due east across the dunes, meeting the **Colson Track** to Alice Springs about 2km from the intersection.

Heading south, the Rig Road passes the faint turn-offs to the Macumba and Killumi oil wells, travelling mainly in open swales, before turning sharply east at 34km from the WAA Line. For the next 47km you cross low, orange dunes whose bare, scalloped crests resemble waves on a choppy sea. There is less vegetation than previously to hold the sand ridges together, and drift sand covers most of the clay sheeting on the dune crossings. These soft patches invariably drop sharply on their eastern side, so a careful approach is warranted. Drift sand worsens the further east you go on the Rig Road.

Lone Gum & Eagles' Nests Eighty-one km from the WAA Line, you turn north up a broad valley with scattered mulga trees, a number of which support the stick nests of wedge-tailed eagles. Some of these nests are an unbelievable size, the result of many generations of use. In winter and spring in a good season, this area used to be alive with eagles, breeding and rearing their young on the bountiful rabbit population. With the near demise of the desert's rabbits due to calicivirus, the eagles' future is unclear.

Continuing on, you pass a **lone coolabah tree** growing on an area of gravel beside the road. Stunted by the harshness of its environment, the tree makes a fantastic sight in its barren setting. Coolabahs are invariably confined to areas that are subject to flooding, so its presence here is a mystery. After 17km heading north, the road swings east again. At the bend, a huge eagle's nest almost covers the crown of a gnarled corkbark, making a fitting climax to this fascinating section.

From the nest, the road heads east across flatter country for 34km to the WBY Line, which makes an ideal detour of about 40km each way to the Approdinna Attora Knolls.

The final 5km on this section winds around small salt lakes, where suspension-busting gutters wait to trap the unwary motorist. At the T-intersection with the WBY Line, you turn left (north) to the knolls or right (south) towards the K1 Line and the Birdsville Track.

The Rig Road – The WBY Line to the Birdsville Track (207km)

About 5km from the WBY Line, you pass the **Poolawanna oil well**, which is conveniently located beside the road. It is one of six (including Purni Bore) to have been drilled in the southern Simpson Desert since the early 1960s.

Past Poolawanna the road wanders among low sand ridges and broad valleys for about 40km before entering a silent, almost coastal world of large, dazzling salt lakes and yellow dunes averaging 25m high. The bigger dunes offer extensive panoramas with Sahara-like foregrounds of bare, wind-sculpted sand, and so are excellent vantage points for scenic photography. The dunes' paler colour indicates that their sand particles are relatively close to their source – as a grain of sand is blown further away, the clay within it weathers, releasing iron oxide (rust) that covers the grain with a red skin.

Here the road skirts the shores of several **lakes**, a feature of which are eroded banks that show how the sand has been deposited in layers over thousands of years. They are a perfect illustration of an environment devastated by rabbits. Large areas of the Simpson have been almost denuded by these pests, but perhaps now that the rabbits have largely gone (hopefully permanently) they may recover.

About 90km from the WBY Line, you leave the lakes and cross high dunes, where the road is covered by deep drift sand. This can be a problem, although tyre deflation will normally get you over without too much effort. Then, at 102km, you arrive at another T-intersection: the K1 Line to Poeppel Corner (see Alternative Routes) and the QAA Line are on your left (north); the Birdsville Track lies to the right.

Warburton Creek Turning south at the intersection, you almost immediately pass the turn-off to Kuncherinna oil well, then commence travelling down broad valleys between low dunes. At about 20km, start watching for patches of bivalves and other shells, indicators of a long-gone wetter age over the desert.

Shortly after leaving these unusual deposits, the road enters a huge area of dead coolabahs and bare white sand. Probably killed by drought, these stark skeletons mark the northern edge of the Warburton Creek flood plain. Some trees have managed to survive, and provide the best shade since Dalhousie Springs. Drift sand now covers much of the road, making it necessary to deflate your tyres for easy progress.

At 60km from Kuncherinna oil well, the road turns abruptly north-east to parallel the main channel of Warburton Creek, which is about 8km to the east. Travelling now over blacksoil flats interspersed with coolabah channels, you reach the main creek crossing 37km further on. From here it is only 8km to the Birdsville Track, where you turn left to Birdsville or right to Marree – see the Birdsville Track section later in this chapter.

ALTERNATIVE ROUTES
The French & QAA Lines: Purni Bore to Birdsville (364km)

Leaving the Rig Road 29km past Purni Bore, the French Line runs eastwards for 175km to meet the K1 Line just past Poeppel Corner. Unlike the Rig Road, the French Line has a natural surface, and cuts at right angles across literally hundreds of soft dunes that average 10 to 15m high. Although the crossings are straightforward when coming from the west (the usual direction of travel), the track's sandy sections have been deeply corrugated, and this makes for slow, rough travelling.

The first 39km from the Rig Road is difficult, thanks to the very soft sand and high, steep ridges. Most travellers bypass this section by taking the Rig Road to the Colson Track, then heading north for 19km to the French Line. This option adds 35km to the total distance. Remember to deflate your tyres to a pressure of at least 20psi (140kPa) before entering this soft sand.

For anyone in a hurry, the French Line is a monotonous experience: as you crest each rise (and on average there are about four of these per kilometre), the view in front is of the track spearing endlessly away across an arid ocean of lesser ridges to reach the horizon at the next highest point. However, the enthusiast with time to spare will find countless opportunities to soak up the desert atmosphere and to discover such small attractions as wildflowers, bird life and innumerable animal tracks in the sand. Many of the valleys contain clumps of shady gidgee trees that provide good shelter for an overnight camp or a meal break.

Approdinna Attora Knolls About 89km past the Colson Track, you cross the northern end of **Lake Tamblyn**, a typical salt lake fringed by gidgees and crowded by red dunes. Reg Sprigg, the first person to cross the desert by motor vehicle, once used the lake as a landing strip, flying tourists in to camp among the gidgees and to experience the desert solitude.

Just past Lake Tamblyn, a turn-off on the right (the WBY Line) takes you about 8km to the Approdinna Attora Knolls. Named by Ted Colson, these two low, flat-topped hills of white gypseous rock are an important landmark in this world of sand ridges and saltpans. They also offer some of the best views in the Simpson Desert. An information sign explains that the knolls were once dunes formed of flour gypsum which later hardened to their present form.

To the south of the knolls lies **Wolporican soak**, one of the rare permanent sources of fresh water that allowed the desert's original inhabitants to survive in this hostile environment. In 1886 David Lindsay found the soak, which was accessed by a well about 4m deep; on being cleaned out, it yielded 40 litres in an hour. Wolporican was a major habitation site for the Wangkangurru people, who inhabited the desert's central and southern sections prior to 1900. Searching around the edge of claypans throughout the Simpson will often reveal evidence of Aboriginal occupation in the form of stone tools and grinding stones, all of which were carried in from far away.

Poeppel Corner For a change in scenery, the track cuts across the northern end of several long, narrow salt lakes in the 45km from the WBY Line to Poeppel Corner. After enduring the corrugations on the dunes, some people can't resist the temptation to go for a drive on the lakes' smooth surfaces, but this is definitely not recommended: the bed may not be as hard as it looks, in which case your vehicle will become deeply bogged in saline mud.

A major objective simply because of its remoteness, the steel marker at Poeppel Corner shows the exact intersection point of the Northern Territory, Queensland and South Australia state borders. Nearby is a replica of the original wooden marker that was installed in 1880 by surveyor Augustus Poeppel – he had just completed the daunting task of marking the border between South Australia and Queensland from Haddons Corner, about 300km to the east. Poeppel's corner post was a 2.1m-long piece of coolabah that he'd cut 90km away in the Mulligan River and dragged by camel to the intersection point.

Poeppel Corner to the Rabbit Fence Shortly after leaving Poeppel Corner, you meet the K1 Line, which runs north-south to link the QAA Line with the Rig Road. Turning north, the track now skirts a salt lake between the dunes, offering much easier going than the chopped-up sandy sections of the French Line. These conditions prevail for the 18km to the QAA Line, where once again you head eastwards over the dunes towards Birdsville.

Surveyed in 1979, the QAA Line crosses several salt lakes before entering the ancient flood plain of **Eyre Creek**. You notice an obvious improvement in the country – soft grasses begin to dominate between the sand ridges, which are higher and further apart than those on the French Line. As a result, driving conditions are somewhat less severe, although the dune crossings are still rough.

The 66km section between the Northern Territory border, which you cross about 5km east of the K1 Line, and the rabbit fence lies within the 550,000-hectare Simpson Desert National Park.

Rabbit Fence Seventy-one km from the K1 Line, you pass through the remains of the great Queensland rabbit fence and enter cattle country. The fence, which once stretched for 800km, was built in the 1890s in an attempt to keep rabbits out of western Queensland; a census taken in 1890 showed 130 men working on its construction near Birdsville. It was maintained by boundary riders stationed roughly 80km apart, until 1932, when they were paid off. Within 20 years much of the fence had either been buried by drifting sand, washed away in floods or corroded by salt, but is still plainly visible where it crosses the QAA Line. Here it forms the present boundary between Adria Downs station and the Simpson Desert National Park.

Eyre Creek Continuing past the rabbit fence, you crest an orange-red sand ridge and suddenly find yourself looking out over a broad valley dotted with large coolabahs. This is part of Eyre Creek's present flood plain. Then, after more high dunes that separate blacksoil flats covered with trees and cane grass, you come to the creek's main channel, 15km from the fence. If the creek is flooded, you must head north on stony ground for 28km to **Goonamillera Crossing** at Dickery Waterhole, then back down along the creek to rejoin the main track. In good seasons the flood plain supports abundant bird life, of which emus, bustards, brolgas, crested pigeons and galahs are the most obvious.

Big Red The country opens out past Eyre Creek, but then 23km later the Simpson Desert's last gasp rises in front of you as a towering wall of pale red sand: the Nap-

panerica Sand Dune, one of Birdsville's major tourist attractions. More commonly known as Big Red, this 40m-high monster is said to be the desert's highest. It's definitely the most difficult to drive over, although a detour of 1km before you get to the ridge heads south and takes you over the same dune at a lower point and straight onto the main road to Birdsville. But the challenge of Big Red is worthwhile. Take the time to climb up to the summit for inspiring views over dry lakes, gibber plains and lesser dunes to distant, shimmering horizons. If you are lucky enough to get over the crest the route turns south near an information shelter about 1km east of Big Red and joins up with the main road to head for Birdsville. That final 33km to town is generally suitable for conventional vehicles.

The WAA Line (85km)
There is no good reason to drive the WAA Line, which parallels the French Line, unless you want a somewhat more difficult run than that offered by the French Line. The track is little used and there are numerous steep ridges along the way, although it is generally less corrugated than the French Line.

The K1 Line (104km)
Forming a scenically attractive link between the Rig Road and Poeppel Corner, this generally firm track runs up broad valleys between orange dunes averaging 13m high. For about 25km at its southern end, you hug the edge of a narrow salt lake; while small compared to others, it makes an impressive sight as you hurtle along at 60km/h. Extensive woodlands of gidgee, where you'll often see dingoes and camels, are another major feature of this route.

FACILITIES
Mount Dare Homestead
Situated in the middle of nowhere in Witjira National Park, *Mount Dare homestead* (☎ (08) 8670 7835; fax (08) 8670 7864) boasts a landing strip, public telephone, ice, liquor licence, minor mechanical and tyre repairs, and fuel sales (diesel, super and

unleaded petrol and Avgas). There is also a small shop selling basic grocery supplies including milk, bread and frozen meat, but no fresh fruit or vegetables. Mount Dare is open every day, from early until late.

Accommodation with share facilities on a dinner, bed and breakfast basis only is offered in the old homestead ($65 a person – rates for children are available on application). The menu is limited (by necessity) but the meals are hearty and the atmosphere is country. Bookings are recommended for casual meals and also for accommodation. Camping in a bush setting, with shower and toilet facilities, is available at $5 per adult and $2.50 per child.

Birdsville

Being a regional centre, if one of only minor importance, Birdsville has a good range of facilities and services, including police, a hospital, hotel, general store, post office, airstrip and mechanical repairs.

The *Birdsville Hotel* (☎ (07) 4656 3244) serves excellent restaurant meals, with a three-course set menu every night. Its air-conditioned, self-contained, motel-style units cost $45/70/75/92 a single/double/triple/quad. The licensee also looks after the airstrip and is the local agent for Avgas – advance orders are not required.

The historic *Brooklands Store* sells limited general goods and all basic food needs, including bread and frozen lines. However, the availability of fresh fruit and vegetables depends on the supply truck, which comes in only once every two or three weeks. The store is one of the few buildings remaining from the town's brief heyday of the 1880s and 1990s.

Birdsville Auto (☎ (07) 4656 3226) sells diesel, super and unleaded petrol, as well as fast food, ice, vehicle parts, tyres and maps. Vehicle repairs are also available and they'll just about go anywhere to recover a stranded vehicle. Opening hours are 8 am to 6 pm seven days a week, and Bankcard, Visa and MasterCard are accepted, and EFTPOS is available. Diesel and petrol are also sold by *Birdsville Fuel Services* (☎ (07) 4656 3263),

which is open from 7.30 am to 7 pm seven days a week.

While lawns are still unknown at the dusty *Birdsville Caravan Park*, it does have a few shady shelters, modern ablution and laundry facilities, electric barbecues, and powered sites with overhead lights and water. Powered sites cost $10 for the first person and $5 for extras (to a maximum of $25), while unpowered sites cost $5 a person, $15 for a family. The park overlooks a lagoon, which is a great spot for bird-watchers.

Banking facilities are limited to a Commonwealth Bank agency in the post office. You can get cash with your Commonwealth Bank keycard during local banking hours and there is also an Express Money Order facility. Business hours are restricted because the manager is often away at the airstrip collecting mail.

Airstrips

Public use of the Dalhousie Springs airstrip (in Witjira National Park) and the Mokari airstrip (in the Simpson Desert Regional Reserve) is permitted only in an emergency. For an update, contact the Department of Environment & Natural Resources in Port Augusta (☎ (08) 8648 5300).

Bush Camping

The only designated camping areas in the desert are found at Dalhousie Springs and Purni Bore, where facilities are limited to a toilet, showers and, at Dalhousie, an information shelter. Dalhousie is by far the more popular and larger *camping area* but it is dusty and exposed. However, it offers ready access to the main hot pool. There is very little shade and no firewood – you can legally collect dead timber from Christmas Creek, 15km away on the road to Mount Dare homestead.

Past Purni Bore you'll find countless good *bush campsites* beside the various tracks described, though firewood and shade are often in short supply, if not absent altogether. For this reason it's a good idea to carry a gas stove, and a tarpaulin or two that you can use to rig up a shelter. A mosquito net over your bed will keep the flies out of your face first thing in the morning; you'll need a net as protection from mosquitoes around wetland areas such as Dalhousie Springs and Purni Bore. The best campsites of all are to be found in the desert's gidgee woodlands, and among the coolabahs on the flood plains of Eyre and Warburton creeks.

Oodnadatta Track

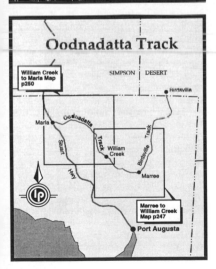

Oodnadatta Track

One of Australia's most interesting outback routes, the 645km Oodnadatta Track links Marree to Marla via Oodnadatta in northern South Australia. Here, as you cross generally flat terrain of desert sand ridges and gibber plains, the sense of space is profound. There is little grand scenery, but in terms of fascinating heritage sites – both natural and cultural – it is well in front of other, more famous routes. Its many attractions include artesian mound springs, Lake Eyre National Park and numerous relics of the Overland Telegraph Line and Great Northern Railway. If you're an enthusiast for such things, allow at least four days for the 429km section between Marree and Oodnadatta. This contains all the notable highlights.

Despite its name, the Oodnadatta Track is actually a fairly good road by outback standards. However, you can still expect plenty of corrugations, potholes and all the other hazards of an unsealed road, while flooded creeks can close the road for days following a big rain. Conditions are usually suitable for robust conventional vehicles with strong suspensions and good ground clearance, but a 4WD is best for some detours. Diesel, super and unleaded petrol are available at Marree, William Creek (220km), Oodnadatta (429km) and Marla (645km). LPG is sold only at Marla.

HISTORY

The track between Marree and Oodnadatta more or less follows the mound springs that occur in an arc from Lake Frome north through Marree and on to Dalhousie Springs, near the Northern Territory border. This region is Australia's driest and the springs are its major natural source of fresh water. For Aborigines, explorers and settlers, they were like stepping stones into the interior. Prior to white settlement the Aboriginal people used them as part of a major trade route that linked the Kimberley and Cape York to the south coast via central Australia. This was the original Oodnadatta Track. For white settlers the springs became the focus of their earliest attempts to develop the arid heart.

In 1858 South Australia's frontier was stalled at Glen's station, about 80km east of the northern tip of Lake Torrens. The country beyond was unknown to white people. Then, in the space of two years, it leapt 300km to reach the Davenport Range, 90km west of Lake Eyre. This was almost entirely due to the explorations of Major Peter Edgerton Warburton (the South Australian Police Commissioner) and Scottish surveyor John McDouall Stuart.

Warburton penetrated as far as Mt Margaret in the Davenports and became the first to report the springs' existence. Stuart added substantially to these discoveries when he led two expeditions into the country west and northwest of Lake Eyre between April 1859 and January 1860. His efforts reduced the unknown by a further 150km – almost to the Macumba River, about 50km north of Oodnadatta.

Stuart was particularly impressed by the height of some of the mound springs and the amount of water flowing from them. He judged that the plentiful good water and grass on the new pastoral leases that he'd surveyed would carry double if not treble the stocking rate of stations further south. What he didn't realise was that he'd seen the country after a succession of good rainfall years. Sadly for those who followed in his footsteps, the grim reality was an average annual rainfall of 130mm and an evaporation rate of 3600mm, and this had reasserted itself by 1865. The grass withered, the sheep and cattle died in their thousands, and the newcomers went bankrupt.

Stuart also saw many well-used native pads, but seldom any of the people who'd made them – those he did see were usually heading at top speed in the opposite direction. To them, the combination of a horse and rider must have seemed like some fearful monster straight from the worst nightmares. Once the explorers came upon an Aborigine hunting in the sandhills. Stuart described the encounter thus:

What he imagined I was I do not know; but when he turned round and saw me, I never beheld a finer picture of astonishment and fear. He was a fine muscular fellow, about six feet in height, and stood as if riveted to the spot, with his mouth wide open and his eyes staring.

Stuart sent his Aboriginal guide forward to speak with the man, but omitted to tell him to dismount. The terrified native remained motionless until the awful apparition was within a few metres, whereupon he threw down his waddies and jumped up into a mulga bush. There, trembling violently on his precarious perch and with one foot only 1m from the ground, he awaited his fate. Imagine his relief when all the creature did was utter a few unintelligible sounds before walking away.

The reports of Stuart's explorations were received with great interest by the South Australian government. This was partly because the colony was keen for Adelaide to be the ultimate destination for a proposed telegraphic link between Australia and Europe via India and Java. For this to happen, however, a practicable route had to be found across the unknown centre of the continent to the north coast; Stuart had fuelled hopes that such a route might exist. Accordingly, the government offered a substantial reward for its discovery.

In March 1860 Stuart departed on what proved to be the first of three epic attempts to win the prize. He passed through the Alice Springs area, but hostile Aborigines and an acute shortage of rations forced his retreat near Tennant Creek. In January 1861 he set out again, only to be turned back by dense, waterless scrub further north, past Newcastle Waters. A final attempt brought success when, on 25 July 1862, he reached the Arafura Sea east of Darwin. Stuart returned in triumph, but the privations he'd suffered caused his premature death just four years later.

The Overland Telegraph Line

Stuart's explorations gave impetus to South Australia's lobbying for the telegraph line to be built entirely within its borders – it had gained control of the Northern Territory from New South Wales in 1863. Eventually, after much heated opposition from Queensland, it won the battle, and signed a contract with the British-Australian Telegraph Company in April 1870.

Under the terms of this agreement, the South Australian government had until 1 January 1872 to construct 3000km of telegraph line to link Port Augusta and Darwin. This would be built and maintained at the government's own cost, and for every day in default it would pay a penalty to the company, which had guaranteed to land the overseas cable in Darwin by that date. The fledgling colony, which then had a white population of only 185,000, had no time to contemplate the enormity of its task. In 1870 the frontier had not progressed past Mount Margaret station. Thus, for about 2000km the wire would be routed through country known only from Stuart's journals.

But with inspired optimism, the government raised a loan to cover the estimated cost and set to work. For the sake of speed, the Overland Telegraph Line was divided into three equal parts, to be built concurrently: the southern, central and northern sections. The former was to go north from Port Augusta to Marree, then follow the mound springs around the western side of Lake Eyre to meet the central section at the Macumba River near Oodnadatta. This was by far the easiest to construct, as the country through which it passed was well known and had been more or less settled. In fact, the only real difficulty proved to be a lack of suitable trees for use as poles. Most of the 10,000 poles required for this section were carted from the Flinders Ranges.

The first pole in the project was erected at Port Augusta on 1 October 1870. By January 1872, the southern and central sections – a total distance of 1890km – were open for traffic, allowing direct contact between Adelaide and Tennant Creek. In the north, however, monsoonal flooding had caused such huge delays that there was still a gap of over 600km. A pony express carried international messages between the operators at either end as 300 men laboured mightily to complete the line. The Telegraph Company made demands for compensation, but these ceased when their cable broke down in June. By the time it was repaired four months later, the two ends had been joined. The governor declared a public holiday to celebrate.

By now the route between Marree and Oodnadatta had become a well-established dray road along the seemingly endless line of white-capped telegraph poles. It was still very lonely country, however. Between the Macumba and Glen's station – a distance of over 500km – there were only four or five rough homesteads, and the new Overland Telegraph Line repeater stations at The Peake and Strangways Springs.

Great Northern Railway

After their remarkable success with the Overland Telegraph Line, it seemed to South Australians that nothing could prevent the development of their north. This belief was strengthened when, in the early 1870s, a run of good seasons created a wheat boom on the semi-arid plains north of Port Augusta. This coincided with a spectacular gold rush near Darwin.

With the bit between their teeth, the optimists now demanded a rail link across the continent. Would-be farmers were convinced that wheat could be grown all the way to the Centre; the plough, they said, would transform the outback into 'a wheat-growers' golden glory'. This kind of emotive nonsense caught the public's imagination, and dissenting voices were drowned out by the ensuing clamour. This reached such a height that the government capitulated, and so the Great Northern Railway was born.

By late 1883, when the narrow-gauge line reached Marree from Port Augusta, normal seasons had returned and the erstwhile wheat farmers were in full retreat to safer ground. It was now recognised that there was little prospect of wheat fields ever stretching to the Territory border. Not only that, the colonies were in the grip of a general depression. In Adelaide alone, there were thousands out of work.

Nevertheless, the South Australian government decided to press on with the railway as a means of relieving unemployment. Trainloads of jobless men were sent north to the railhead, which crept out along the Overland Telegraph Line from newly established Marree in July 1884. The immediate destination was Strangways Springs, although a transcontinental link was still the ultimate goal.

In those days, at least in South Australia, railways were built manually, with picks, shovels and wheelbarrows, assisted by dynamite and horse-drawn scoops. But these new navvies, many of whom were no longer young, were mostly soft-muscled clerks and shop assistants. With the flies swarming about their faces, they must have stared aghast at the shimmering gravel wastes and quailed at the thought of what confronted them. Not surprisingly, the no-hoper element deserted in droves.

Yet many remained and became useful labourers. For some, however, the only reward was a violent death. Gruesome accidents, thirst and murders claimed many lives. In the worst accident, five navvies were killed when a ballast train collided with a mob of cattle. Typhoid epidemics raged, and soon the Oodnadatta Track was dotted with graves.

The Great Northern Railway was built on the cheap, with light rails and minimum ballast. Although hundreds of men were employed on the project, the work progressed at a snail's pace. In 1889 the line eventually reached Oodnadatta, which was then just a place name on the Overland Telegraph Line. It was hardly an epic in the annals of railroad construction.

Oodnadatta remained the railhead until January 1927, when the construction crews moved northwards towards Alice Springs. This time – to the relief of South Australian taxpayers – the federal government was putting up the money. By now the service was known as 'the *Ghan*', after the so-called Afghani camel drivers it had replaced. It had also become legendary for its inefficiency and for the leisurely way in which it operated. After all, which other major train service would stop so that its passengers could pick wildflowers?

In more recent times the *Ghan's* faltering progress, laid-back style and olde-worlde charm made it an anachronism in a modern age of transport. It also offered adventure, because passengers never knew how long their journey was going to take. The line had been built through flood-prone areas, and heavy rains often resulted in washouts that closed the line for weeks. On at least one such occasion, the engineer had to shoot some goats to feed his hungry passengers. The old *Ghan* may have provided an unforgettable experience for the tourists who travelled on it, but the service was a financial nightmare for the treasury bureaucrats in Canberra.

The line closed for good in 1982, when the present rail service to Alice Springs was opened. It has since been dismantled – much of the track went to Queensland to be relaid in the sugar-cane fields – but there are still many fascinating relics left to explore. These, along with remains of the Overland Telegraph Line, had been left to deteriorate until recently, when various restoration projects were launched to save the best examples for posterity.

INFORMATION
Tourist Offices
For up-to-date advice on all touring aspects of the Oodnadatta Track, contact the Oasis Caravan Park (☎ (08) 8675 8352) in Marree, the William Creek Hotel (☎ (08) 8670 7880), the Pink Roadhouse (☎ (08) 8670 7822) in Oodnadatta, and the Marla Travellers Rest (☎ (08) 8670 7001).

Conservation areas along the track are managed by Department of Environment & Natural Resources rangers based at Port Augusta. For the latest information on all public access and other park matters, either call in to the office, write to PO Box 78, Port Augusta, SA 5710, or ring the Desert Parks Information Hotline (☎ (08) 8648 5300).

Emergency
There are well-equipped hospitals, staffed by registered nurses, at Marree, Oodnadatta and Marla. The William Creek Hotel has a very comprehensive RFDS kit, so the staff can administer drugs and perform other medical functions by acting on directions they receive over their HF radio. If an emergency evacuation is required, it only takes the

RFDS 1½ hours to reach William Creek from Port Augusta.

Permits & Registration

There is no requirement to register your intentions with the police. However, it is a sensible precaution to leave a detailed plan of your movements with a responsible person who can give the alarm if you fail to check in.

The entry requirement for conservation areas is possession of a current Desert Parks Pass – for more details see the Travel Permits section in the earlier Getting Around chapter. The pass includes a booklet giving details on the 4WD access routes into Lake Eyre, as well as a few brief facts on the lake and its environs. You can purchase yours from park rangers and selected commercial outlets (including the Ghan Store in Marree, the William Creek Hotel and the Pink Roadhouse in Oodnadatta).

Books

If the dynamics of flooding in the Lake Eyre basin are of interest, you can't go past the lavishly illustrated, large-format *Floods of Lake Eyre* by Victor Kotwicki (Engineering & Water Supply Department, Adelaide, 1986). The text is dry and technical but the photographs are superb. Of particular interest is the series of full-colour satellite shots of Lake Eyre as it dries up after the 1984 flood.

Explorations in Australia – The Journals of John McDouall Stuart, by John McDouall Stuart (Saunders, Otley & Co, London, 1865; facsimile edition by Hesperian Press, Perth, 1984), gives a fascinating day-by-day account of the great explorer's expeditions around Lake Eyre and on to the north coast. It's a must for history enthusiasts.

Basil Fuller's *The Ghan – The Story of the Alice Springs Railway* (Lansdowne, Sydney 1996) makes interesting background reading.

Maps

The map-guide entitled *Oodnadatta Track* published by Westprint Heritage Maps is a very useful basic reference for this trip. It covers the entire route from Lyndhurst (79km south of Marree) to Marla and includes brief details on its various highlights. It's available from various outlets in Alice Springs, Port Augusta, Leigh Creek, Marree, Oodnadatta and Marla.

For a more detailed map coverage of the Marree to Oodnadatta section, you'll need the *Marree, Curdimurka, Billakalina, Warrina* and *Oodnadatta* 1:250,000 topographic maps from AUSLIG. (The *Marree* sheet covers only the first 6km and can be dispensed with.) The *Wintinna* sheet covers the Oodnadatta-Marla section. These maps are available from AUSLIG sales outlets in any capital city.

The RAA's *Northern Areas* map is also quite useful.

Radio Frequencies

The track is well used in the winter months, when you may only have to wait 15 to 20 minutes for another vehicle to come along. However, in summer it's an entirely different story: vehicles can be hours apart, so a HF radio could come in handy. The Port Augusta RFDS base (call sign VNZ; ☎ (08) 862 2044) covers this part of the world. It monitors 8165kHz between 7 am and 5 pm and 4010 and 6890kHz between 7 am and 9 pm daily. Its 24-hour emergency service uses 4010, 6890 and 8165kHz as daytime alarm frequencies, and 2020 and 4010kHz between 9 pm and 7 am.

SPECIAL PREPARATIONS
Water

It's essential to carry ample drinking supplies at all times as most local springs and bores yield unpleasant-tasting water which has a laxative effect. It's pointless attempting to beg or buy rainwater from the locals – not surprisingly, they regard their scant supplies as being more precious than gold. Marree's water supply is undrinkable, as is William Creek's, but the Oodnadatta supply is palatable if served either chilled or in hot drinks. Marla's water is quite acceptable.

Flies & Mosquitoes

Bushfly plagues are the track's downside in warm weather. A fly veil for your face and an insect-screened gazebo for meals are essential at such times; make sure to pack a net to cover any toddlers while they're having their daytime nap. Areas near wetlands (such as around springs and flowing bores) usually swarm with mosquitoes on warm nights.

THE ROUTE

Marree to William Creek (203km)

While there is some nice scenery on this section, the major attractions are old railway sidings, artesian mound springs and the world's sixth-largest lake: Lake Eyre. (See the later Birdsville Track section for details on Marree.)

The Dog Fence Leaving Marree, the track spears westward over rolling gibber downs, passing through a rather ordinary-looking fence 42km from town. This is the world's longest man-made barrier, the Dog Fence – see the Fauna section in the Facts about the Outback chapter.

The Inland Sea Continuing on for a further 26km you pass a high hump-backed range on the right with a cairn on its highest point. This is **Hermit Hill**, climbed in 1858 by Benjamin Babbage, who thus became the first white person to cross the gap between Lake Torrens and Lake Eyre. These two great lakes were previously thought to be joined in a great barrier that would block progress to the north.

Sixteen km past Hermit Hill you come to a rough detour that leads to a nearby **lookout** point above the barren shore of Lake Eyre South. There's another lookout 10km further on, where for a short distance the road runs right beside the lake with the old railway line in between.

Lake Eyre is actually two lakes – Lake Eyre North and Lake Eyre South – joined by the narrow Goyders Channel. Covering a total area of 9700 sq km, the entire lakebed is included within the 13,560-sq-km Lake Eyre National Park. Although the lake has filled to near capacity only three times in the past 150 years (most recently in 1974), it does receive significant flooding once every eight years on average, thanks usually to heavy rains over central and western Queensland.

Lake Eyre is so shallow that even a major flood like that of 1974 takes only two years or so to evaporate. In the meantime the lake becomes a vast breeding ground for swarms of pelicans, seagulls, terns and many other water birds, and such a rare celebration of life in the desert is well worth a special trip. Most times, however, the lake is little more than a flat, blinding expanse of white salt crust. In 1964 Britain's Donald Campbell set a world land-speed record of 648.6km/h on

---

Living with Salt

It's difficult to imagine an environment more harsh than the dry, wind-blown, salt-crust surface of Lake Eyre. In fact, most times it's so inhospitable to life that only a few vertebrate species have adapted to it. One of these is the Lake Eyre dragon (*Ctenophorus maculosus*).

Found only on the salt crusts of South Australia's inland lakes, this small (170mm-long) white lizard feeds mainly on the ants that live around the lake margins, as well as any other insects it can find there. It shelters from temperature extremes by wriggling under the salt crust; two to four eggs are laid in a steep burrow in moist sand at the shoreline. In the rare event of a flood, the dragon moves into adjoining sand dunes – if caught on a low island it can inflate its body and swim to higher ground, even in cold weather.

Unless you're very lucky you won't meet a Lake Eyre dragon in the wild – they're shy and well camouflaged for their life on the open salt crust. However, you can see them at the Alice Springs Desert Park, which is the only place with specimens in captivity. ■

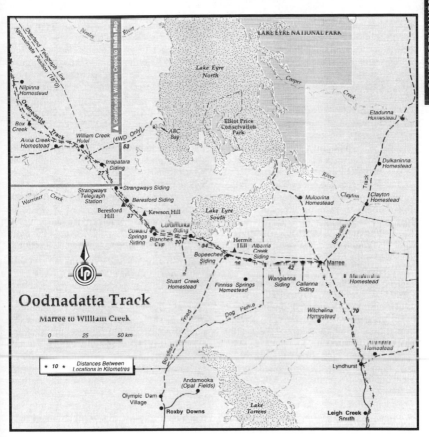

Oodnadatta Track
Marree to William Creek

0   25   50 km

★ 10   Distances Between
         Locations in Kilometres

Lake Eyre North in his jet-powered car *Bluebird II*. It's not a good idea to drive on the lakebed yourself, as your vehicle will soon break through the hard surface and sink deep into black saline slop.

Curdimurka Eight km past Lake Eyre you arrive at Curdimurka Siding, which commemorates the fearsome kadimakara of Aboriginal belief – the kadimakara were thought to live under Lake Eyre and prey on anyone foolish enough to walk on it. This tiny abandoned outpost consists of a nine-roomed stone cottage, an elevated railway

tank and a tower-like **water softener**. (The water tower removed harmful salts from bore water that otherwise caused heavy scaling in locomotive boilers.) It housed a crew of railway fettlers which was responsible for maintaining a 30km stretch of line noted for deep washouts after rain and drifting sand in drought.

In its day, Curdimurka was little different to most other sidings along the railway, but what makes it remarkable now is the fact that it is still in one piece. This is entirely due to the unflagging enthusiasm of the Adelaide-based Ghan Railway Preservation Society which has restored the entire complex, including 4km of railway and an adjacent section of the Overland Telegraph Line. The cottage is of the standard design used for fettlers' quarters along the line. Its bedrooms are quite small, almost like cells, and have whitewashed walls and high ceilings to combat the hellish summers. Looking outside at the empty surroundings, you can easily picture a red dust storm rolling in to bury the place in a gritty, shrieking fury. All in all, Curdimurka is a powerful reminder of a lifestyle better imagined than experienced.

The siding really comes alive in November of even-numbered years, when up to 5000 people in evening dress attend the **Curdimurka Outback Ball**. Tarpaulins are stretched over the desert sands to make a floor, on which revellers dance the night away under the blazing stars.

Mound Springs The road continues westwards for 29km from Curdimurka, at which point you come to a rough, ill-defined detour that heads south for 5km to flat-topped **Hamilton Hill** in Wamba Kadurba Conservation Park. At the foot of this low but prominent feature you find **Blanches Cup**, one of the most remarkable of all the mound springs that line the track between Marree and William Creek.

Mound springs are the natural outlets of the Great Artesian Basin, a vast sandstone aquifer that can be likened to a saucer with one side slightly raised. Rainfall is soaked up where the basin's main water-bearing rocks outcrop, in the eastern ranges of Queensland and New South Wales. From here the water moves towards South Australia, taking an estimated 2.5 million years to reach the Oodnadatta Track.

Mound springs occur wherever the pressure in the aquifer is able to force water to the surface through cracks in the overlying impermeable rocks. The dramatic fall in pressure at the surface causes chemical changes in the water; magnesium, sodium and calcium carbonates are precipitated at the outlet and slowly build up to form hillocks usually several metres high. In this flat, brown land, the white carbonate rock is visible for considerable distances.

Blanches Cup is a classic mound spring, owing to its symmetry and the large circular pool on top. Like other springs in this region, it has suffered greatly from introduced grazing animals and the reduced flow rates resulting from the many bores that have been drilled into the aquifer. Nevertheless, the reed-fringed waterhole remains a beautiful paradox among the sun-baked salt flats and shrubby plants. You can easily appreciate why the early explorers went into raptures when they first laid their eyes on it.

A few hundred metres to the north lies **the Bubbler**, so named because of the frequent eruptions of gas that disturb the tranquil pool over its outlet. In the past, you could wallow about in safety while enjoying a stimulating massage from the upwelling bubbles of sand and gas, but swimming is no longer permitted.

Coward Springs Leaving the Bubbler, you head out along the access track to meet the main road about 8km before the Coward Springs turn-off. This old siding was an exception to the rule, as it once boasted an important little settlement with a hospital, hotel and store as well as several railway houses. The South Australian government established a plantation of date palms, but the bore water proved unsuitable and they failed to thrive.

Today, only the ruins of the station master's and engineer's cottages remain among the saltbush and scrub beside the flowing bore which feeds a pool where you can enjoy a warm bath. The site of the pub is surrounded by tall date palms and shady athel trees. Ask at the camp ground about overnight **camel rides**; if you've got time to spare, you can do a five-day trek to Lake Eyre North (price negotiable). A day visit to Coward Springs costs $2 per vehicle and includes a wallow in the spa.

Extinct Springs Six km from Coward Springs, by which time you're at last heading northwards, the track passes between a tan-coloured mound on the left and a high white hill on the right. The former is an extinct spring; the latter, **Kewson Hill**, is the largest active mound spring along the track. During his 1859 expedition, Stuart bogged his horse on top and had great difficulty getting it out again. An indication of what the flow from these springs must have been like way back in geological time is provided by huge extinct mounds such as flat-topped **Beresford Hill**, which is off on your left 22km past Coward Springs, and Hamilton Hill (behind Blanches Cup).

About 2.5km past Beresford Hill you'll see a rare sight on the Oodnadatta Track: a large clump of shady trees around a **dam**. Built to supply water for steam locomotives, it is now used mainly by cattle and wildlife, most obvious of which are the screeching hordes of corellas that frequently cover the trees.

Strangways Telegraph Station The capped bore 37km from Coward Springs marks the site of the old Strangways Siding. There is no longer any sign of this little settlement (it once had a pub and police station), but if you look to the west you may spot a ruin on the low ridge about 2km away. This was the Strangways Telegraph Station, one of 11 repeater stations constructed between Port Augusta and Darwin in 1871 to boost the morse signals that travelled along the Overland Telegraph Line. Unfortunately, vandals have been busy here: only a large stone tank and some stone-walled sheep pens remain in good condition.

William Creek Two km past Strangways Siding you cross salty Warriner Creek just downstream from a rusty railway bridge – debris heaped against the piles shows what these streams are like in a big flood. The track now leaves the gibber plains behind, and for the next 15km or so passes through large crimson sand ridges separated by clay-pans and gravel flats. Like other sandy areas in the region, this is a great spot for winter wildflowers. The dunes, which cut out 17km before William Creek, are outliers of the Simpson Desert dunefield 100km to the north-east.

The thriving metropolis of William Creek (population 10) is South Australia's smallest town. It consists of the William Creek Hotel and three equally unpretentious houses set on a shimmering saltbush flat between two red dunes. As the rainfall is measured in drops, there isn't much in the way of lawns and gardens. As well, the local bore water is fit only for sheep and cattle. This means that if you've got a thirst (and who wouldn't in a place like this?), you may be forced to make do with a cold ale.

The attraction of bush pubs lies in the fact that what they lack in frills they more than make up for in character and atmosphere, and in this regard the **William Creek Hotel** leaves most modern establishments for dead. Built in 1887 (it was a support station for camel drivers working on the Overland Telegraph Line), the pub's external appearance is undistinguished – its ancient corrugated-iron cladding has been warped by the heat of too many summers and battered by too many dust storms.

Inside, however, is a friendly haven away from the glare and flies. During daylight hours the bar is lit by the golden rays that stream in through holes in the walls. You look up to see a ceiling of sagging planks that threaten to collapse on your head at any moment. Stuck there are strange things, including a pair of sand-filled underpants (a legacy of someone's dip in the Bubbler). Out the front, a parking meter collects donations for the RFDS – a size-58DDD brassiere performs the same function in the bar.

The pub can arrange **scenic flights** costing from $30 each with two passengers; you can fly over Lake Eyre for $80 each with two passengers ($50 with three). Another tourist highlight is the annual **William Creek Cup**, held on the weekend before Easter.

William Creek to Oodnadatta (210km)

On this section the track wanders generally northwards over much the same terrain as before. Although there aren't any mound springs beside the road past William Creek, abandoned railway sidings and other relics provide plenty of interest.

Anna Creek Having torn yourself away from William Creek, you soon pass the turn-off to Anna Creek homestead and Coober Pedy. Anna Creek station covers 30,114 sq km and is the world's largest pastoral lease – most years it runs around 20,000 head of cattle (which, at an average value of $500 per head, is a huge investment in stock). The station also runs nearly 500 working horses, as most of the cattle work is still carried out in the traditional way. The average carrying capacity of this country is less than one beast per sq km and most years you'll wonder how it supports even that many.

Anna Creek is leased by the Kidman Pastoral Company, which was established by the legendary cattle king, Sir Sidney Kidman. The company's holdings have been much reduced since its heyday, but it still operates a string of stations around the southern fringe of the Simpson Desert.

The Peake Telegraph Station You cross a number of mainly small creeks in the 112km between William Creek and the **Ernest**

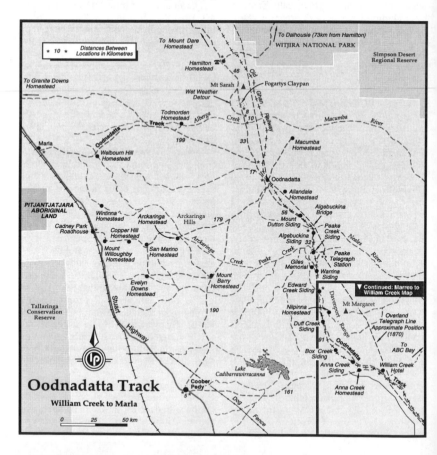

Oodnadatta Track
William Creek to Marla

Giles Memorial. This simple cairn commemorates Giles' arrival here in 1876 after his epic crossing from the west coast. Most streams are lined either by coolabahs, river red gums or gidgees; several offer good shade and camping in welcome contrast to the gibbers on either side. The ruins and water-softening plant at **Edward Creek Siding** (91km from William Creek) are well worth investigating, while the nearby creek is an excellent spot to boil the billy.

Heading east from the Giles Memorial, a rough 4WD track takes you 16km to **The Peake** ruins at Freeling Springs. The Peake homestead was South Australia's northernmost outpost of settlement in 1870, when construction of the Overland Telegraph Line began. A year later a telegraph station was built beside the homestead, and in 1873 a police station was added. This made The Peake a sizeable community for both its time and place, but it was abandoned 18 years later when operations were moved to Oodnadatta.

In recent years, restoration works have been carried out at this fascinating site, which is situated on a rocky terrace overlooking a broad, flat-bottomed valley covered in gidgee. There are a total of nine stone ruins, of which the seven-room telegraph station is the largest and most sophisticated.

In the hills behind are several deep shafts dating from 1898, when mineral lodes assaying 70% copper and several ounces of gold per ton were discovered. Two years later a number of mines were being developed and there was talk of employment for 3000 men, but in the end it came to nothing, and activity ceased in 1904. By that time, the smelter erected at great cost 300m south-west of the telegraph station had treated just 250 tons of ore, averaging 4% copper.

Algebuckina Thirty-two km from the Giles Memorial is the **Neales River**, where channels studded with coolabahs are spread over 1km wide. This is by far the largest watercourse on the Oodnadatta Track, but what really grabs your attention is the 578m-long **Algebuckina railway bridge**, with its soaring steel arches. A common fallacy is that the bridge – the longest in South Australia – was prefabricated for a crossing of the Murray River but was found to be too short. In actual fact it was built specifically for the Neales. The **graves** of three railway workers lie beside the line at the bridge's northern end.

Excitement came to Algebuckina in October 1886 when gold was found on the Neales' northern bank, close to the bridge. A small rush took place and five months later, by which time about 60 ounces had been won, 25 men were on the field. Sadly the rush proved a dud, as did the town site surveyed on the opposite bank at about the same time.

Also of interest here is a large salt **waterhole** on the downstream side (a good spot for bird-watchers). The easy climb up to the cairn above the old **Algebuckina Siding**, which is about 1km south of the bridge, gives a good view over the Neales and surrounding country.

Leaving the river behind, the final 56km stage into Oodnadatta takes you through a mix of gibber plains, ochre-coloured hills and an area of yellow dunes inexplicably called the **Plantation Sandhills**. Some of this country is breathtakingly harsh, and you get a fine view of it from **Cadnaowie Lookout**, 17km from the Neales. With only 20km to go, you pass through **Duttons Gap**, where the sweating navvies toiled with picks and shovels to maintain a suitable gradient. The thought of it gives you a powerful thirst that will last all the way to Oodnadatta.

Oodnadatta

Oodnadatta's heyday lasted from 1889 to 1927, when it was the terminus for the Great Northern Railway. From here, camel trains made round trips of up to 3000km to resupply communities as far away as Newcastle Waters in the Northern Territory. However, the only obvious remaining sign of this relatively prosperous era is an impressive sandstone **railway station**, which houses interesting displays of historic photographs.

To gain entry, ask at either the general store, hotel or roadhouse for a key.

After the railway closed in 1980, most government functions were moved to Marla, on the new line, and the town was expected to die. However, it has managed to hang on and, despite its moribund appearance, remains an oasis of unexpected comforts in a hostile sea of gibbers. Today, half the town, including its hotel and general store, is owned by a council made up of Aboriginal people, who comprise the bulk of the population of about 200.

The council welcomes visitors, and a few drinks in the hotel on pension day is a cross-cultural experience that shouldn't be missed. If you're in town on Adelaide Cup Day (in May), you can attend the **Oodnadatta Cup**.

Oodnadatta to Marla (216km)

Being of much more recent vintage, this final section is lacking in historic appeal. However, there's compensation in the fact that you've a much better chance than previously of seeing interesting wildlife such as emus, bustards, perenties, dingoes and red kangaroos. Most winters you'll see the bright crimson blooms of Sturt's Desert Pea, which form large mats in rare good seasons. The Oodnadatta Track's best displays of wildflowers are seen on this section, particularly in the east, where the soils are generally sandy.

As before, you don't see much variation in the topography, which remains more or less flat throughout with numerous tree-lined creeks in the eastern half and gibber plains thereafter. The first 120km or so makes an interesting drive as the road winds about in the headwaters of **Alberga Creek** and the Neales River. Here you'll find plenty of shady campsites near the road, as well as occasional temporary waterholes after rain. This section is regularly graded but, like the rest of the track, is impassable in wet conditions.

The final 50km past Welbourne Hill homestead takes you along the old Stuart Highway, which was realigned to the west in the early 1980s.

Marla

The little township of Marla (the name is a corruption of the Pitjantjatjara word for red kangaroo) came into existence in 1980 as a regional centre to replace Oodnadatta. Being new and somewhat prefabricated, it has little outback character – it's basically a government town populated by public servants on short-term postings from the city.

DETOURS
ABC Bay (53km one way)

Twenty-seven km past the Strangways Siding bore (7km before William Creek), a 4WD track leads off to the western shore of Lake Eyre North. This straightforward route terminates at ABC Bay, where the desolation literally takes your breath away. Approaching the shore, you cross a wasteland of low breakaways entirely covered by small black stones. It's so ugly and lifeless that at first glance it seems as if some ghastly environmental disaster has befallen the place. On a satellite photograph, the area appears to have been scorched by a bushfire. But on the ground on a hot day, with the stillness and deathly silence working on your imagination, you can tell that in reality it's been seared by the furnaces of hell.

The track forks about 1km before ABC Bay, with the sandy track on the left taking you 10km to the edge of the lake at Halligan Bay. There's a small shade shelter and rainwater tank here, but don't rely on being able to get a drink.

Coober Pedy (166km one way)

The detour from William Creek to Coober Pedy, Australia's opal-mining capital, is worth taking if this is the only chance you'll have to visit the place. Coober Pedy (population about 5000) is a major regional centre and international tourist attraction, with an excellent range of commercial facilities. The turn-off to **Lake Cadibarrawirracanna** (Australia's longest place name) is about 70km from William Creek.

This road is remote, rarely maintained, sees little traffic and has no reliable fresh water. Before setting out, get an update on road conditions from the William Creek Hotel. For more information on Coober Pedy, see the Stuart Highway section earlier in this chapter.

ALTERNATIVE ROUTES

At Oodnadatta you're faced with a number of options which will take you west to the Stuart Highway or north to Mount Dare and ultimately either to Alice Springs or Birdsville. The roads to Mount Dare, Cadney Park and Coober Pedy are normally suitable for conventional vehicles with good ground clearance. Check road conditions at the Pink Roadhouse.

Oodnadatta to Coober Pedy (190km)

The main reason you'd take this road is as an alternative route to Coober Pedy. The country is flat, with gibbers almost all the way, and there are no facilities en route.

Oodnadatta to Cadney Park Roadhouse (179km)

The **Arckaringa Hills**, about 80km from Oodnadatta, make this by far the most interesting alternative route to the Stuart Highway. Numerous colourful mesas provide some of the grandest scenery in outback South Australia, making fantastic subjects for photography in early morning and late afternoon. You're welcome to go for a walk in this area but camping is not permitted.

Also of interest is the *Copper Hill homestead*, 145km from Oodnadatta, where basic tourist accommodation is available – you can drive around on the station tracks and see wildlife and nice scenery. Ring either the Pink Roadhouse or Copper Hill (☎ (08) 8670 7995) for road conditions.

Cadney Park (☎ (08) 8670 7994) offers a range of services, including fuel (diesel, super and unleaded), restaurant and takeaway meals, motel rooms, cabins, camping and mechanical repairs.

Oodnadatta to Mount Dare Homestead via Eringa (250km)

You'd take this slow but interesting road if you wanted to visit Dalhousie Springs (in

Witjira National Park) or head off to either Alice Springs or Birdsville via the Simpson Desert. As an option, you can take the 4WD short cut (73km) from Hamilton homestead to Dalhousie Springs, but this can be extremely rough in places. The turn-off is 1km north of the homestead and about 108km from Oodnadatta. There's a public phone box by the road outside the homestead gates.

ORGANISED TOURS

There aren't many local tour operators on the Oodnadatta Track. You can do overnight and extended camel treks from Coward Springs (☎ (08) 8675 8336) and scenic flights from Marree and William Creek (see The Route earlier in this chapter). Perentie Outback Tours (☎ (08) 8672 5558) of Coober Pedy visits Oodnadatta and the Arckaringa Hills on its camping trips to Dalhousie Springs. Otherwise there's the mail run from Coober Pedy to Oodnadatta and return via William Creek (see Mail Runs in the Getting Around chapter).

Oz Experience and Wayward Bus include the southern part of the track on their trips from Adelaide to Alice Springs (see Organised Tours in the Getting Around chapter). A number of tag-along tours from Sydney, Melbourne and Adelaide incorporate a day or two on the Oodnadatta Track. Details are hard to find, but you can start with the various state tourism offices.

FACILITIES
Marree

See the Birdsville Track section later in this chapter for information on Marree's facilities.

William Creek

The lonely *William Creek Hotel* (☎ (08) 8670 7880) dispenses ice, limited food lines, takeaway liquor, meals, basic motel-style and bunkhouse accommodation, minor mechanical repairs and fuel (diesel, super and unleaded). The choice of meals is surprisingly varied – you can even get quiche and vegetarian fare, as well as crumbed rabbit. Room rates are $30 per person with air-con and $12 without. Alongside is a dusty camping area, with some shade and basic facilities, including limited power, a swimming pool (warmer months only) and barbecues (firewood provided). You pay $5 per person or $10 per family to camp; two on-site caravans are available ($20). Normal trading hours for fuel are 7.30 am to midnight seven days a week.

Oodnadatta

Owing to its location in the middle of nowhere, Oodnadatta's range of facilities is a lot better than you'd expect for a town of its size. It has a hospital, post office agency, general store, garages, roadhouse, hotel, museum, police station and landing ground. There are EFTPOS facilities at the Pink Roadhouse and general store.

The distinctive *Pink Roadhouse* (☎ (08) 8670 7822) is the obvious tourism focus for this region, as all routes leading to Oodnadatta are dotted with the distinctive information signs erected by proprietors Adam and Lynnie Plate. These long-time locals can give sound advice on all aspects of travel in the outback, so drop in for a coffee and a chat. You're welcome to browse through their private library of books, newspaper clippings and maps, all of which will add to your knowledge of the area. The roadhouse is easy to find because it's painted bright pink.

Adam and Lynnie offer fuel (diesel, super and unleaded), takeaway meals, a minimarket, minor mechanical repairs, a post office agency and a Commonwealth Bank agency. There's also a good range of accommodation including backpacker beds in a self-contained seven-bed shack ($9 per person), basic motel-style rooms ($40 per twin room) and powered sites ($9/13/17 and $4 per site for power). All accommodation units are air-conditioned.

The *Transcontinental Hotel* (☎ (08) 8670 7804) offers hearty meals (lunch and dinner only); its air-conditioned but otherwise very basic rooms cost $30/55/70 a single/double/triple. Next door, the *Oodnadatta General Store*, a reasonably priced mini-

market, offers takeaway meals as well as diesel, super and unleaded fuel. Check the fuel prices here and at the Pink Roadhouse, as the store's are usually the more competitive.

Marla

Now the major regional centre in northern South Australia, Marla boasts an excellent range of essential facilities, including a supermarket, hotel-motel, caravan park, garage, police station, medical centre and landing ground.

The commercial hub of this little town is the *Marla Travellers Rest* (☎ (08) 8670 7001), a combination of hotel, motel, roadhouse, supermarket, garage and caravan park, which has everything most people would require. The garage has a qualified mechanic, and fuel (diesel, super, unleaded and LPG) is available 24 hours. After normal hours (6.30 am to 11.30 pm seven days), you can gain entry to the well-stocked supermarket by contacting the night watchman. The Commonwealth Bank agency in the supermarket has an EFTPOS facility.

Tourist accommodation at the Travellers Rest includes air-con motel rooms ($69/75/80/86 with colour TV and telephone, $10 less per person without), backpacker beds in air-con two-berth cabins ($12 per person, no bed linen supplied) and powered caravan and tent sites ($5 per person and $5 per site for power). All guests have access to a swimming pool, and there are shady trees and lawns in the caravan park. The hotel section offers a choice of takeaway, à la carte and restaurant meals.

Bush Camping

The *Coward Springs Camp Ground* (☎ (08) 8675 8336), has toilets and warm-water showers, as well as shady trees and a hot pool. The cost is $10 per vehicle (paid into the honesty box when the manager isn't there, which is most of the time between October and April). In warm weather the place is noted for its mosquitoes. The old workers' cottage at *Curdimurka* has no facilities, but it provides great shelter when it's raining (unlikely) or windy (very likely). A small fee is payable into the honesty box – please clean up before moving out. Sadly, this unique place is beginning to suffer from the actions of the thoughtless minority.

Isolated bush campsites offering good shelter from both sun and wind aren't all that common. Popular spots such as Beresford Siding and the Neales River have generally been degraded by people-pressure, and you should avoid them if for no other reason than to protect your health. The best places to look for private sheltered sites are along creeks and in sandhill areas, but don't leave it too late in the day.

Firewood There's a general lack of trees between Marree and Oodnadatta, but the millions of sleepers along the railway are a great source of firewood. Most are old, easily splintered and make excellent coals for cooking. If you have the space, carry at least one with you, as the country away from creeklines is virtually devoid of dead timber. You'll also find that popular camping areas have long been stripped of firewood.

Birdsville Track

HIGHLIGHTS

- Experiencing the loneliness and armour-plated aridity of Sturt Stony Desert

- Visiting the old mission site at Lake Killalpaninna and wondering at the dedication of the early Lutheran missionaries

- Admiring the determination of the modern-day station folk who live in this world of saltbush, sand dunes and stones

Seared by the relentless sun and scoured by countless raging dust storms, the 517km Birdsville Track between Birdsville and Marree earned notoriety as one of Australia's most hazardous stock routes. Linking a series of unreliable waterholes and artesian bores across one of Australia's harshest regions, it was a droving highway along which up to 50,000 head of cattle a year walked from Queensland to the railway at Marree.

The track's grim reputation was built on death; the lives of many people and entire mobs of cattle have been lost to its great heat and lack of water. Until relatively recent times it was little more than an ill-defined pad, with the bones of dead stock pointing the way to the next drink.

But progress has come to the Birdsville Track and it's now a much tamer version of earlier times. The drovers were replaced by road trains in the 1960s, and as a result the track has been upgraded to the point where it is now mostly a good dirt road. Catering mainly to tourist traffic, the air-con Mungeranie Hotel, near the halfway mark, dispenses fuel and creature comforts such as cold drinks and soft beds. Purists might lament that the spirit of the track is dead, but those who live along it are unlikely to share that sentiment.

For the casual tourist there is little spectacular scenery in this desolate landscape of polished stones, sand ridges and occasional dried-up creeks. Many find the experience crushingly monotonous. For others, the loneliness, silence and vast empty spaces provide the opportunity for a unique and fascinating adventure in outback touring. If you take the time – and an enthusiast could easily spend a week exploring the track – it's an opportunity to appreciate the courage of those who lived and worked here in the days when the drover was king. Those who aren't interested can drive its full length in one day and never know what they've missed.

HISTORY

The Diamantina River system between Lake Eyre and Birdsville was explored by the surveyor John Lewis in 1874. However, the credit for pioneering the Birdsville Track was earned about six years later by EA Burt, the first Birdsville storekeeper. Burt's route gave the stations of south-west Queensland's channel country a link to Adelaide, their closest major market and supply point. In good seasons, mobs of up to 2000 cattle streamed south, taking an average five weeks to travel from Birdsville to Marree.

The drovers' spartan needs were provided for by the isolated stores at Mirra Mitta, Tidnacoordooninna, Cannuwaukaninna and Mulka; these, like the old homesteads at Lake Harry, Mount Gason, Apatoonganie and Oorawillanie, have long since been abandoned. Today, their scant remains and parched surroundings are stark evidence of hard, lonely living and eventual failure in the face of overwhelming odds.

Apart from cattle, its main users until the 1930s were camel trains travelling to and from Marree. In the care of Afghani cameleers, strings of up to 75 animals carried virtually everything that Birdsville and the surrounding stations required in the way of stores, building materials and general cargo. The trek from Marree to Birdsville took about 24 days, with each beast carrying between 250 and 450kg. Camels are superbly adapted to the track's dry conditions, but by the late 1930s they'd been replaced by road transport. Most were set free to wander in the desert.

In a land where water has sacred significance, only the foolhardy tempted fate by walking between the track's far-flung homesteads. Many such travellers were fatally ignorant of local conditions, and their epitaphs, if they were ever recorded, can be found among the terse entries in early police journals. On 22 December 1885 the Birdsville policeman wrote:

Traveller found a dead body. Three or four days old. Ten miles over the border in South Australia. Three men perished 10 miles from Clifton Hills station, ten or twelve days ago. No water.

More recently, the publicity surrounding the Page family's tragic demise only served to enhance the track's fearsome reputation. In late December 1963 the Pages were en route from Marree to Queensland when their vehicle broke down at Dead Man's Sandhill, about 90km from Birdsville. Their water supplies were extremely limited, and in the great heat they waited with increasing desperation for help to arrive. However, in those days travellers were a rarity on the Birdsville Track in summer and the Pages had neglected to advise people of their movements. Tormented by thirst, they finally left their car in a despairing quest for water.

The abandoned vehicle was found several days later by a rabbit-shooter, who raised the alarm. A search party was quickly organised but it was too late for the Pages, whose bodies were located shortly afterwards. The parents and two of their three children had died in a dried-up waterhole, no doubt lured there by the coolabah trees and their false promise of salvation. The eldest son's body was found on a sand ridge about 1km away. Their lonely grave beside the waterhole is marked by a small metal cross bearing the stark inscription: 'The Pages Perished Dec 63'.

INFORMATION
Tourist Offices

For general up-to-date advice, contact the Oasis Caravan Park (☎ (08) 8675 8352) in

Oodnadatta Track
Top: Mail run
Middle: Taking a more unusual form of transport
Bottom: Warrina ruins

SHOOT

Kata Tjuta (the Olgas; NT) is probably the second-most photographed Australian landmark after Uluru (Ayers Rock)

Marree, the Mungeranie Hotel (☎ (08) 8675 8317) and Birdsville Auto (☎ (07) 4656 3226). Road reports are best obtained from the Marree police (☎ (08) 8675 8346) and the Birdsville police (☎ (07) 4656 3220). Just to be on the safe side, you can also check road conditions by ringing the Mungeranie Hotel.

Registration
Despite the popular belief that travellers should register with the police at one end and sign off at the other, the police no longer wish to be involved in these matters except during summer. They suggest that you keep friends or relatives informed of your movements so that they can notify the authorities should you fail to report in on time. However, they're happy to provide advice, and travellers can leave messages with them for others to collect.

Emergency
Marree and Birdsville both have well-equipped hospitals staffed by registered nurses. The Mungeranie Hotel has a comprehensive RFDS medical kit, and in the event of an emergency its staff can administer drugs and perform other procedures by acting on directions they receive over their HF radio.

Books
Mail for the Back of Beyond, by John Maddock (Kangaroo Press, Kenthurst, 1986), tells the fascinating story of the motor mailmen of the Birdsville Track. It gives you an appreciation of how easy the motorists have it today. The Marree-Birdsville mail was carried by camels until 1936, when it was taken over by a truck service which lasted until 1975. Since then the mail has been carried by aeroplane.

Eric Bonython's *Where the Seasons Come and Go* (Illawong Pty Ltd, Yankalilla, 1985) is an absorbing read covering history, lifestyles and adventure in the Cooper Creek country up to the 1950s. The Bethesda Mission on Lake Killalpaninna is featured prominently.

Land of Mirage, by George Farwell (Seal Books, 1972), is a story of cattle-droving and station life along the track in the late 1940s, with plenty of history thrown in. It's definitely worth reading, although now out of print.

Several chapters of *Outback on your Doorstep*, by Brian Sheedy (Roadwrite Publishing, Fitzroy, 1993), are devoted to the Birdsville Track, including history, route descriptions and information on its various highlights. It's recommended as a touring reference.

Maps
The map-guide entitled *Birdsville and Strzelecki Tracks* published by Westprint Heritage Maps is a comprehensive if limited reference covering the major and minor tourist routes of South Australia's northeastern corner. It's available from outlets in Birdsville, Marree, Innamincka and Leigh Creek.

For detailed coverage, you'll need AUSLIG's *Marree, Kopperamanna, Gason* and *Pandie Pandie* 1:250,000 topographic maps – a small section of the track also falls on the *Cordillo* sheet. They're available through AUSLIG sales outlets in all capital cities.

Radio Frequencies
An average of about 30 vehicles use the Birdsville Track each day in winter, so you shouldn't have to wait too long for assistance. In summer, however, the next vehicle can be anywhere up to a week away. It's recommended that anyone travelling the track outside the busy season should carry a HF radio with frequencies for the RFDS bases at Port Augusta and Broken Hill; Port Augusta is the usual base for this region, but it doesn't hurt to have Broken Hill as a backup.

Port Augusta (call sign VNZ; ☎ (08) 862 2044) monitors 8165kHz between 7 am and 5 pm and 4010 and 6890kHz between 7 am and 9 pm daily. Its 24-hour emergency service uses 4010, 6890 and 8165kHz as daytime alarm frequencies, and 2020 and 4010kHz between 9 pm and 7 am.

The Broken Hill RFDS base (call sign VJC; ☎ (08) 8088 0777) monitors 4055 and 6920kHz between 7 am and 6 pm weekdays. Alarm calls are received on 4055 and 6920kHz during business hours and on 2020kHz after hours.

SPECIAL PREPARATIONS
Water
It's essential to carry ample drinking water at all times on the Birdsville Track, as you never know when you may strike trouble. As well, local artesian bores yield river water that smells unpleasant and has a laxative effect when you're not used to it. Marree's water supply is undrinkable, while Mungeranie's is best when chilled or drunk with tea and coffee. The Birdsville supply is quite acceptable and is regarded as the best bore water on the track. Always be careful collecting water from flowing artesian bores, as it usually comes out of the ground at scalding temperatures.

Flies & Mosquitoes
Bushfly plagues are the track's downside in warm weather. A fly veil for your face and an insect-screened gazebo for meals are essential at such times; make sure to pack a net to cover any toddlers while they're having their daytime nap. Unfortunately, areas near wetlands or shallow waterholes usually swarm with mosquitoes, except on cold nights.

THE ROUTE
Birdsville
Queensland's most isolated town sprawls on a barren, stony rise overlooking the Diamantina River, with the great silence of the Simpson Desert just beyond its western edge. So remote that it wasn't visited by a politician for its first 60 years, Birdsville is best known for its tremendous heat waves (temperatures of 50°C are common in summer), its annual race meeting and, of course, its association with the famous Birdsville Track. With a population of about

80, it presents a mere shadow of a more glorious past. This is still evident in several old stone buildings, such as its police station and sole surviving pub.

Within 10 years of its establishment in the late 1870s, Birdsville had a population of 90 whites and 180 Aborigines, as well as three pubs, a cordial factory and a border customs post. Prior to Federation in 1901, a duty was levied on all cattle leaving Queensland and on all goods that came up from Marree; smuggling, particularly of whisky, was apparently a thriving enterprise.

Federation removed the town's status, and the terrible drought that followed saw the population drift away. Finally, a hurricane in 1905 levelled most of the town's less substantial buildings. After that disaster, Birdsville almost expired, but it managed to hang on as a minor regional centre. Today, increasing tourism has restored a glimmer of its old prosperity.

The famous **Birdsville Races**, which take place on the first weekend in September, see the town's population swell to 5000 or more, as visitors from all over Australia fly in for the fun.

Birdsville to Clifton Hills (198km)
Known as the Outside Track, this section is relatively new, having been constructed in the 1960s to allow trucks to detour around **Goyder Lagoon**. Generally the road surface is good, apart from bulldust patches on the Diamantina flood plain and rough sections through Sturts Stony Desert.

Leaving Birdsville, the track drops down onto the Diamantina River's coolabah-studded flood plain and almost immediately crosses its main channel. Rising in western Queensland, where it is fed by monsoonal rains, the river heads south for 800km before flooding out in Goyders Lagoon. This extensive (1300 sq km) seasonal swamp is about 80km downstream from Birdsville. When full, it overflows into **Warburton Creek**, which meanders around the Simpson Desert's southern fringe to Lake Eyre.

Minor floods are fairly common in the Diamantina but cause little inconvenience.

Birdsville Races

Birdsville's big event each year is the two-day race meeting held in early September. Country races are often low key occasions when the locals get together to bet on the horses and have a few beers, but Birdsville attracts thousands of people from all over the country. And they drink more than just a few beers.

The weekend is also notable for the hundreds of light aircraft that fly in. Normally one of the remotest runways in Australia, Birdsville aerodrome gets so busy that the Civil Aviation Safety Authority has to issue special flight rules to help control the traffic. So being a city-based private pilot, I decided that this was an experience we ought to try

Things to Do Getting drunk is the favourite activity, ahead of falling over and wearing tasteless T-shirts. Brawls used to be popular but these days the crowds are fairly good-natured.

Evening entertainment is provided by Fred Brophy's boxing troupe who set up their tent in the centre of town, right across from the pub. This must be one of the last traditional travelling boxing troupes left in Australia, if not the world, and their days may be numbered as such acts are now outlawed in several states but not Queensland. The bass drum booms out across the desert as the spruiker works the crowd ('Here's Mad Dingo. Who reckons he could fight Mad Dingo?'). There's always a few blokes drunk enough to try a few rounds against the professionals, and no shortage of others who will pay to see them try

Oh yes, there are horse races too, on Friday and Saturday. The bookmakers work with speed and efficiency to take your money, though you may find they move a bit slower if your horse wins.

Places to Stay & Eat Put your tent up right beside the plane, or just hang a plastic sheet over the wing. It can get cold at night and the ground is hard and stony so bring a good sleeping bag and mat.

The Diamantina Shire Council provides temporary toilets and showers, complete with hot running water straight from the bore. Your nose will remind you that the sewerage treatment pump runs 24 hours a day.

Don't count on eating at the pub, they're too busy selling beer. Hot dogs and steak sandwiches from the roadside stalls are as good as it gets, so bring your own.

Getting There & Away From Melbourne's Moorabbin Airport to Birdsville is about 1900km as the crow flies, and even further on the route we took in a single-engine Piper Arrow. We had planned a loop through central Queensland, but rain arrived over most of eastern Australia so we headed for Arkaroola in the Flinders Ranges instead. Amended flight plans are a fact of life for small aircraft.

The manager at Arkaroola who refuelled the Arrow was surprised that we were going to the Birdsville Races. He said we seemed too intelligent.

Undeterred, we continued on the last leg, a two-hour flight that took us into a 'designated remote area'. The flat brown uniformity of the desert offers very few recognisable landmarks so we had to trust the instruments and were quite glad when a town finally appeared ahead of us.

This had to be Birdsville if only because no other town would have so many planes at the aerodrome.

Even if you're not a pilot or the friend of one, consider getting a few people together to charter a plane; check the Yellow Pages under 'Aircraft Charter' or 'Flying Clubs'. If you prefer a commercial carrier, Flight West (an Ansett-related airline) flies from Brisbane on Monday and Thursday, while Augusta Airways flies up from Port Augusta on Saturday. You will need to book months ahead.

You can of course go by road, and several outback tour operators offer camping trips to the races. Buses will also take your camping gear if it's too heavy or bulky for the plane.

On Sunday morning the first engines start before dawn, waking everyone except the terminally inebriated, and from first light there is a steady stream of planes taking off. For some, an early start is essential if they are to get home in daylight, even though the passengers might prefer to be sleeping off their hangovers. By midday Birdsville is just about empty again except for the council workers who are already cleaning up.

Getting Around The pub is right beside the aerodrome and you can walk to anywhere in the town in a few minutes. Shuttle buses will take you to the racecourse about 5km south of town for a $2 donation to the local hospital.

Jim Hart

However, major events (above 8m) inundate large areas and can close the track for weeks at a time. The biggest flood in living memory occurred in 1974, when the river level reached 9.5m at Birdsville and completely swept away the Alton Downs homestead. While there have been 14 floods above 6m at Birdsville since 1970, there were none of that magnitude in the 15 years prior to 1970.

Past the Diamantina, the track spears southwards for nearly 100km across broad blacksoil flats hemmed by long, yellow sand ridges. Clumps of coolabahs indicate that you're still on the flood plain, while lines of stunted coolabahs growing on some of the sandhills show how high the water can reach. Generally, however, there is no shade for anything much larger than a rabbit. You may spot a flock of brolgas stalking purposefully among the lignum bushes, but more likely the only moving thing (apart from flies) will be a whirling column of grey dust dancing across the plain.

Dead Man's Sandhill At 85km you're opposite the grave of the Page family, which is about 3km to the east and on the opposite side of Dead Man's Sandhill. There is no track into the site, but you can walk across the plain and climb the sandhill for a view over the normally dry waterhole where they met their appalling deaths. The dune, which parallels the road at this point, earned its macabre name when five stockmen from Innamincka perished on their way to the Birdsville Races in the summer of 1912.

Sturts Stony Desert Approaching the 100km mark the track leaves the flood plain and enters the armour-plated desolation of Sturts Stony Desert. Squeezed between the sand ridges of the Simpson and Strzelecki deserts, this enormous wasteland of polished stones was crossed by the explorer Charles Sturt on his search for the inland sea in 1845. He decided that it had 'no parallel on the earth's surface', and most people would agree with him. Sturt's description is as valid today as it was then:

… the whole expanse appeared to be as level as the ocean, nor had it as far as we could see a single shrub or a blade of vegetation upon it. The stones indeed lay so thick on the ground, that it was impossible for any herb to have forced its way between them.

Sturt's north-easterly route into the Simpson Desert, where lack of water and a wilderness of high sand ridges forced him to turn back, would have taken him across the Birdsville Track about 40km past the Koonchera Sandhill.

Koonchera Soon after entering Sturts Stony Desert, you cross the southern end of the mighty Koonchera Sandhill. Although no monster at this end, it grows to become one of the largest dunes on the Diamantina flood plain. A waterhole near its northern end was the scene of a massacre of Aborigines in the early years of settlement, when a state of open warfare existed in the region. Later, a mob of over 1000 cattle heading towards Marree perished near the sandhill in a ferocious dust storm.

Looking south-eastwards from the crossing point, you can see what appears to be a mighty range of fiery hills shimmering in the distance. The mirage magnifies and deceives, but that red, Sahara-like sand ridge is still a spectacular sight close up. You drive close to it on the 4WD **Walkers Crossing Track** to Innamincka, which turns off 5km past the Koonchera Sandhill – see Detours later in this section. The track may only be used with the permission of Clifton Hills station (☎ (08) 8675 8302).

Clifton Hills Leaving Koonchera, you cross more sandhills and two or three coolabah creeks in the 33km to **Melon Creek**, where there are good sheltered campsites among shady trees. Soon after, the track heads out onto a vast stony plain dotted with distant trees. This is the inhospitable setting for **Clifton Hills homestead**, 43km past Melon Creek, which was built here in the 1940s after an earlier site was buried by shifting sand. Perhaps this is the main reason why the station folk chose a moonscape of brown rocks on which to build. Clifton Hills covers about 12,600 sq km and is the largest station on the Birdsville Track.

Clifton Hills to Cooper Creek (183km)

A few kilometres past the homestead the track crosses several low rises that offer views of much kinder country down on Warburton Creek's broad flood plain. Although it's difficult to imagine in drought times, a good rain or a flood transforms the blacksoil flood plains of this region into the outback's finest cattle-fattening pastures. Between these rare events, the cattle survive on the hardy but nutritious saltbush that dominates much of the local vegetation.

This section is the track's most interesting, thanks to its varied scenery and poignant evidence of human endeavour. Its major highlights are the Mt Gason and Mirra Mitta bores, the Mulka ruins, Mungeranie Gap, Cooper Creek and camping at the Mungeranie Hotel. However, this section of road is also the roughest, with numerous bulldust holes and stony sections; heavy rain can render it impassable for days at a time. Past Mt Gason, the track follows almost exactly in the footprints of the early drovers.

Mt Gason Eleven km past Clifton Hills is the turn-off to the 4WD **Rig Road**, which crosses the southern edge of the Simpson Desert to Mount Dare homestead. Some shady trees in a nearby creek make a good spot to boil the billy before starting out on this remote 564km trek.

For the next 15km the track winds over stony, undulating country on the edge of higher ground before arriving at a rare stand of the endangered **Mt Gason wattle** (*Acacia pickardii*). These low, tough-looking trees are known only from the Mt Gason area and another site near Old Andado homestead in the Northern Territory. The stand has been fenced to determine whether or not cattle and rabbits have any effect on regeneration.

Twelve km further on is the turn-off to **Mt Gason Bore**, on a stony rise 2km to the west. This is the first in a string of artesian bores spaced roughly 40km apart that took the

mobs from Warburton Creek across the gibbers to Marree. Drilled in 1900, it reached a depth of 1350m and is the deepest between Clifton Hills and Marree. As at Mirra Mitta and Cannuwaukaninna, which you pass further south, scalding water smelling of sulphur gushes from a pipe into an open drain that takes it away to cool sufficiently for cattle to drink. In winter the steam billows up like bushfire smoke and is visible for considerable distances. You'll find the stone remains of the old Mt Gason homestead on a rise a few hundred metres west of the bore.

Mt Gason itself is about 5km south of the bore. Rising a mere 35m above the plain, this little mesa is one of the most prominent features along the track. However, it only looks mountainous when it's magnified by the mirage. It was named after Samuel Gason, the first police officer on the Birdsville Track.

Mirra Mitta Bore Leaving Mt Gason Bore, you continue south across Sturts Stony Desert until, at 45km, you see a lush patch of tall reeds sprouting among the gibbers. This is watered by a drain fed by Mirra Mitta Bore, 1km further on. Although its setting is almost unbelievably hostile, the bore once boasted a drovers' store and eating house as well as a thriving vegetable garden. The store was little more than an iron shed, which meant that its occupants froze on winter nights and roasted in hell during the dust storms that lashed it in summer. Modern softies will find it amazing that, of their own free will, people actually spent years living in this unpromising spot.

Mungeranie Twenty-eight km past Mirra Mitta is picturesque **Mungeranie Gap**, a scenic highlight of the Birdsville Track. If you're here in the early morning or late afternoon, it's worth going for a walk among these colourful low hills to capture their stark beauty on film. The country changes to patchy bare gibbers and low sand ridges in the next 8km to **Mungeranie Hotel**, where a

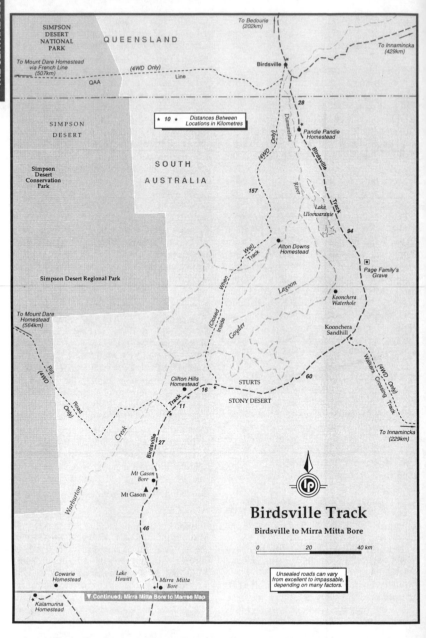

THE CENTRAL DESERTS

SIMPSON DESERT NATIONAL PARK

QUEENSLAND

To Mount Dare Homestead
via French Line
(507km)

QAA Line (4WD Only)

To Bedourie
(202km)

Birdsville

To Innamincka
(429km)

28

SIMPSON DESERT

Diamantina (4WD Only)

Pandie Pandie
Homestead

SOUTH

Simpson
Desert
Conservation
Park

AUSTRALIA

Birdsville Track

River

Lake
Ulloowaranie

157

94

* 10 * Distances Between
Locations in Kilometres

Well Track

Alton Downs
Homestead

Page Family's
Grave

Simpson Desert Regional Park

Lagoon

Koonchera
Waterhole

(Closed Inside

Goyder

Koonchera
Sandhill

To Mount Dare
Homestead
(564km)

Pig (4WD Road Only)

Creek

Clifton Hills
Homestead

16

60

STURTS

STONY DESERT

Walkers Crossing Track (4WD Only)

Track

11

To Innamincka
(229km)

Birdsville Track

27

Warburton

Mt Gason
Bore

Mt Gason

Birdsville Track

Birdsville to Mirra Mitta Bore

0   20   40 km

46

Cowarie
Homestead

Lake
Howitt

Mirra Mitta
Bore

Unsealed roads can vary
from excellent to impassable,
depending on many factors.

Kalamurina
Homestead

▼ Continued: Mirra Mitta Bore to Marree Map

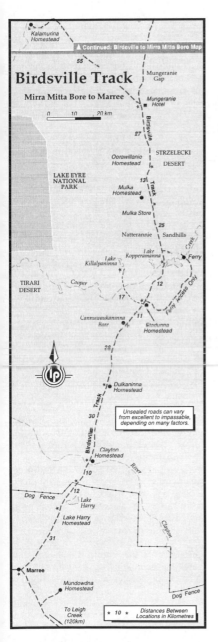

Birdsville Track
Mirra Mitta Bore to Marree

0   10   20 km

cold beer or two does wonders for dust-caked throats.

Among its services (see Facilities later in this section) the hotel offers sheltered camp-sites beside the Derwent River. This perfect oasis of shady trees is watered from a flowing bore and, like other wetland areas on the track, is a beaut spot for bird-watchers. Half-dead coolabahs on the nearby sandhill are roosting places for screeching flocks of corellas. When they land, it seems as if the bleached limbs have miraculously burst into great masses of white flowers, although flowers were never so noisy. Water birds such as ducks, herons and native hens are also common here.

Mulka The gibber plain continues to soften past Mungeranie, with grass and shrubby patches becoming more common. At 27km is the old **Oorawillanie homestead**, now just a pile of rubble and scattered rubbish beside the road. Drought put the station out of business many years ago, and it now forms part of the Mulka lease.

Low sand ridges begin to dominate over the next 13km, then you're at the crumbling stone ruins of the **Mulka homestead** and general store off to your right. Once a sub-stantial building for these parts, it was the home of Mr and Mrs George Aiston who'd previously lived at the Mungeranie police station – George had been a mounted consta-ble there from 1912 to 1924. He'd resigned, bought Mulka station and established the store rather than be posted to Adelaide.

A remarkable man, Aiston co-authored the academic book *Savage Life in Central Australia* and became an honorary consulting anthropologist to the Australian Institute of Anatomy. Mrs Aiston stayed on and ran the store after his death in 1944, but finally abandoned it in the mid-1950s.

Natterannie Sandhills Eight km past Mulka, you say goodbye to the gibbers of Sturts Stony Desert and enter a world of high yellow sand ridges that roll away on either side like jumbled waves on an ocean. Known as the Natterannie Sandhills, this area marks the convergence of the Strzelecki Desert to the east and the Tirari Desert to the west. Parts of the Tirari, which runs onto the eastern shore of Lake Eyre, are the closest thing Australia has to true desert.

These days the sandhills hold no terrors, but in the droving era their numerous boggy patches were a nightmare for anyone travelling in a motor vehicle. Even the famous Birdsville mail officer Tom Kruse – an expert in taking heavy vehicles through difficult country – found them tough going. It usually took him eight hours to get through the worst section of about 12km! Unfortunately, the tyre-deflation method couldn't be used when the truck became bogged, which it frequently did. This was because the effort involved in hand-pumping the big tyres up again put the driver at risk of heat exhaustion or worse.

Kruse was forced to employ various strategies in his attempts to defeat the Natterannie Sandhills. Trucks fitted with dual rear wheels carried 6m lengths of 75mm bore casing which were laid on the sand such that the dual tyres could grip them and so find traction. Otherwise the slopes had to be laid with heavy iron sheets, which were liable to fly up and damage the vehicle's underparts if tackled at speed. He even tried using conveyor belts to create a half-track vehicle, but with limited success. This was a fearful journey in hot weather (which was most of the time), and the mail officers were forced to endure it every fortnight for many years until the road was finally upgraded.

Cooper Creek

After 17km of sand ridges, the timbered Cooper Creek flood plain is a welcome sight, to say the least. Five km wide at the crossing, its outstanding feature is an abundance of spreading coolabahs which invite you to stop and boil the billy. Coolabahs are exceptionally hardy trees, but even they can be killed by drought, as you'll see at the crossing's northern end. On the positive side, this area of standing dead timber is a good source of firewood.

The Cooper rises in the central highlands

of Queensland, and by the time its flood-waters flow into Lake Eyre they've travelled about 1500km. Floods seldom cut off the Birdsville Track, but when they do the only way across is via a ferry 10km upstream from the road crossing. There are two things you must do on the ferry: get out of the vehicle, and wear a life-jacket. These rules are in response to an accident many years ago when a crosswind blowing against the side of a truck caused the ferry to capsize. The driver of the truck, sitting in his cabin, was drowned.

If a crossing on today's modest ferry is an adventure, you can imagine what its predecessor, the MV *Tom Brennan*, must have been like. This tiny steel craft was used to transport supplies across the Cooper after the 1949 flood, which was the first to reach the track in 30 years. After many years of occasional service, the boat is now permanently grounded on the southern bank as a memorial to the motor mail officers.

Cooper Creek to Marree (134km)

This section's major highlights are Cannuwaukaninna Bore, and a lookout and ruins at Lake Harry. Although sandhills and gibbers still dominate, the country is generally kinder south of Etadunna. The road surface is good throughout, if stony in parts.

The Missionaries Leaving the Cooper behind, the track spears across a rolling gibber plain until, at 12.5km from the *Tom Brennan* memorial, it passes a tall metal cross on the roadside at **Etadunna homestead**. This was placed in memory of the dedicated missionaries who came to this area in the 1860s with the intention of converting the local Aboriginal people to Christianity.

In 1866 a Moravian mission station was established at Lake Kopperamanna, 3km north-west of the Cooper Creek crossing. However, faced with a searing drought and an unfriendly reception from the Aborigines, the Moravians departed for good the following year. Just months after the Moravians arrived, Lutheran missionaries from Germany built their Bethesda Mission beside

Historic Sites of the Cooper

Aboriginal Sites Aboriginal rock engravings can be found at the far end of Cullyamurra Waterhole, close to the bottleneck on the Cooper known as the Innamincka Choke. To find this spot, follow the vehicle track out along Cullyamurra Waterhole to its end and then walk along the foot track to the rock area that can be seen on both sides of the creek.

This is a good spot to explore, with a couple of nice swimming holes and some good fishing. If you are camped on the waterhole, there is no better way to get to the site than by canoe.

Explorers Signs of the earliest white explorers can also be seen in this region. While the township has a monument to both Charles Sturt, who discovered and named the creeks in this area during his 1845 expedition, and to Burke and Wills, who perished near here in 1860, it is the latter whose monuments and camps evoke the most poignant memories (see History in the Facts about the Outback chapter for more about Burke and Wills).

Their camp, near a tree now known as the Dig Tree, can easily be visited from Innamincka. Sitting under the shady trees that surrounded the camp and that still exist today, watching a turbid river flow past, you cannot help but be struck by the irony of it all. Here was an area that supported hundreds of Aborigines and yet Burke and his men starved to death.

The blazed Dig Tree that played such an important role in the saga still stands at the site and is probably the most important reminder of early European exploration in Australia. Nearby are a couple of other blazes and carved trees which, although dating back a few years, are not part of the original saga. A memorial to Wills can be found at the western end of Tilcha Waterhole; Durke's memorial is on the edge of Burke Waterhole. The place where Charles Grey died, south-west of Coongie Lakes at a place called Lake Massacre, is not open to travellers.

About 7km west of Innamincka is a marker indicating the place where John King was found alive by Alfred Howitt's party. Howitt's depot camp on the Cooper is marked by a monument on the north side of the river. This spot is best found by crossing the Cooper just below Cullyamurra Waterhole, then walking upstream to the monument. Be prepared for wet feet!

Other Sites In Innamincka itself, the Australian Inland Mission nursing home stood in ruins for many years, but has now been restored. These days it's an office of the National Parks & Wildlife Service, and has interesting displays of old photographs and historic memorabilia. ■

---

nearby **Lake Killalpaninna**. It too was abandoned, but the Lutherans returned and established a permanent presence.

In its heyday in the 1880s, Bethesda had a population of several hundred Aborigines and a dozen whites. It was laid out like a small town, with over 20 mud-brick buildings, including a church with a 12m-high tower complete with steeple. It survived largely on the income derived from its flocks of sheep, but rabbit plagues and drought eventually forced the missionaries to leave forever in 1917. Today only a sad little cemetery and a few timber uprights show that they were ever there. Nevertheless, when full the lake is a magnificent jewel among the sand ridges – you could easily spend several days there bird-watching, bushwalking and dining on yellowbelly and bream.

Lake Killalpaninna is about 17km north-west of Etadunna and is accessible by a 4WD track that turns off opposite the cross. Directions and permission to enter must be obtained from the homestead (☎ (08) 8675 8308). There's an entry fee of $5 per vehicle (this is for a day visit, it's $10 per vehicle per night if you want to camp) and a key deposit of $5.

Cannuwaukaninna Past Etadunna the track crosses a vast saltbush plain for most of the 11km to Cannuwaukaninna Bore, where another small wetland attracts numerous birds. It also attracts swarms of mosquitoes, which makes a good reason not to camp nearby in warm weather. At one time there was a drover's store here, much like the one at Mirra Mitta, but it too has long since been demolished and carted away for use elsewhere. In this isolated country very little recyclable material goes to waste, particularly sheets of corrugated iron.

Leaving Cannuwaukaninna, you pass **Dulkaninna homestead** at 28km; the power line stretching across the gibbers to the house carries electricity generated by a water-driven turbine installed at the flowing bore. Thirty km further on, **Clayton homestead** is on the banks of a sandy creek boasting the largest coolabahs between Marree and Cooper Creek.

Lake Harry Ten km past Clayton is a grid in a rather ordinary-looking fence. This is, in fact, the world's longest artificial barrier: the famous **Dog Fence** – see the Fauna section in Facts about the Outback. The claypan on your left at the grid is Lake Harry.

Soon after, the track passes close to a low mesa with twin wheel ruts climbing to its summit. Although only 40m above Lake Harry, the hill is arguably the most prominent feature seen along the track. From the cairn on top there's a view over a vast patchwork carpet of brown, yellow and dark green, with the road a narrow white ribbon from horizon to horizon.

Eight km further on, the remains of **Lake Harry homestead** are off on the left. Set amid a scatter of low, ochre-coloured hills, with the mirage giving an illusion of water in the nearby lake, this forlorn ruin dates from 1870, when it was an outstation of Mundowdna. Thirty years later it became a camel depot for the bore-sinking gangs then working along the Birdsville Track. Around the same time, the South Australian government established a trial plantation of over 2000 date palms. The experiment looked promising at first, but failed due to poor water quality and a high labour requirement. Today not even a stump remains, but it's said you can still find Lake Harry palms lining the streets of Renmark and Mildura, both on the Murray River.

Twenty-two km past Lake Harry you enter sheep country, as evidenced by the way the vegetation has been eaten out. Then the glittering iron roofs of Marree come into view across the plain and the end of the journey is just minutes away.

Marree

On a barren gibber plain 3km from Hergott Springs, Marree was a thriving railway town of 600 residents just two years after its establishment in 1883. The Great Northern Railway to Port Augusta had made Marree the focus for a vast area of the outback. In 1885 alone, between 40,000 and 50,000 head of cattle from Queensland and the Northern Territory were entrained for Adelaide. Meanwhile, camel trains carried supplies and general cargo to places as far away as the Gulf of Carpentaria. At one time Marree was home to 60 Afghani cameleers and their families, who lived in their own 'Ghantown', complete with mosque. In 1910, around 1500 camels were operating out of Marree.

However, progress sounded the death knell to Marree's role as a major regional centre when first the cameleers and then the droving teams were replaced by motor vehicles. Most people thought the end had come when, in 1980, the narrow-gauge railway to Alice Springs was replaced by the present service, which bypasses the town. Today, with a population of about 100, Marree clings to life as a minor regional centre and survives mainly on welfare cheques and tourism. Several fine old residences, the abandoned railway station and its grand old hotel (1885) are graphic evidence of a more prosperous past.

Other points of interest include the small **heritage museum** in the Arabanna Centre, and a large **sundial** in the form of a squatting camel (it's made of railway sleepers) near the railway station. Book at the Oasis Cafe for one-hour **scenic flights** over Lake Eyre, the northern Flinders and Cooper Creek ($100 per person, $50 child under 15; minimum two passengers). The cafe can also give you a mudmap for the **scenic drive** (4WD only) to Lake Eyre and Goyders Channel via Muloorina homestead.

The **Marree Picnic Races**, held on the Queen's Birthday Weekend in June, attract a good crowd. Also popular is the **Marree Australian Camel Cup**, held on the first Saturday in July on odd-numbered years.

DETOURS
Kalamurina (55km one way)
Camping is permitted at the Kalamurina (pronounced Kalla-murna) homestead (☎ (08) 8675 8310), on the banks of Warburton Creek 52km north-west of the Mungeranie Hotel. There's a choice of a camping ground with toilets and hot showers or bush sites with no facilities among the coolabahs along the creek; both cost $10 per vehicle per night. The creekbank environment offers interesting bushwalking and plenty of bird life, particularly when the big waterhole near the homestead is full – it usually lasts 12 months after a flood and contains many fat yellowbelly and bream. At such times the contrast with the nearby sandhills and gibber flats is nothing short of fantastic.

The Kalamurina road turns off the Birdsville Track 1.5km north of Mungeranie. It's narrow and generally rough, with plenty of bulldust patches, but is usually suitable for conventional vehicles in dry conditions. For information on access and camping, ring the homestead.

Innamincka (229km one way)
The Walkers Crossing Track to Innamincka turns off the Birdsville Track 122km south of Birdsville. Winding across the Cooper Creek flood plain and through the big sandhills of the Strzelecki Desert, it offers a different experience in remote touring. En route are the producing wells of the **Moomba oil and gas field**, which is linked by pipelines to Sydney and Adelaide. While the track is generally good in dry conditions, numerous sandy sections restrict its use to 4WD vehicles only.

It's definitely not recommended in summer, when the heat and lack of water and other traffic create potentially dangerous conditions. Good campsites are reasonably common almost right along the track's length.

Part of the track crosses Clifton Hills station (☎ (08) 8675 8302), and the owner's permission is required to use it. As the track also crosses the **Innamincka Regional Reserve**, you must hold a Desert Parks Pass, which can be purchased in Birdsville, Marree and Innamincka – see the Travel Permits section in the earlier Getting Around chapter.

For track information contact the Innamincka ranger on ☎ (08) 8675 9909. For details of Innamincka see the Strzelecki Track section later in this chapter.

ALTERNATIVE ROUTE
The Inside Track
Until the 1960s the Birdsville Track south to Clifton Hills wound among the channels of Goyder Lagoon. When wet, this blacksoil swamp is a disaster for any sort of vehicle, so the present Outside Track was constructed to avoid it.

Known as the Inside Track, the original part of the old stock route covers about 157km, which makes it 25km shorter than the new road. It is the more scenic of the two, but is also slower, rougher and lonelier – in short, it's an attractive alternative for the more adventurous 4WD traveller. The Inside Track joins the Outside Track 60km west of the Koonchera Sandhill and 16km east of Clifton Hills homestead.

FACILITIES
Birdsville
See the Simpson Desert section earlier in this chapter for information on the facilities in Birdsville.

Mungeranie
The *Mungeranie Hotel* (☎ (08) 8675 8317) offers a wide range of services and amenities, including a landing strip, public telephone, ice, shop (grocery lines and limited hardware items), takeaway liquor, meals, minor mechanical and tyre repairs, and fuel (diesel, super and unleaded). The normal trading hours for fuel are 8 am to 8 pm daily; Avgas should be ordered at least one month in advance.

Beds in the pub's air-con twin units cost $25 each, while campsites are $5 per adult.

Marree

Despite its decline in fortunes in recent years, Marree still has a good range of facilities and services, including a hotel, caravan parks, a landing strip, small supermarkets, mechanical repairs, a post office agency, police and a hospital.

The grand old *Great Northern Hotel* (☎ (08) 8675 8344) offers counter and dining room meals as well as old-style hotel accommodation. Tariffs range from $35 for a single room to $70 for four people sharing.

Marree has two quite reasonable caravan parks. The well-grassed *Oasis Caravan Park* (☎ (08) 8675 8352) in the middle of town has campsites for $5 per person ($2 extra per site with power), and basic cabins with air-con for $10 per person. Alternatively, the somewhat dustier *Marree Caravan & Campers Park* (☎ (08) 8675 8371) is at the start of the Birdsville Track about 1km south of town. Its grassed campsites cost $5 per person (power $4 extra per site), a six-bed bunkhouse with kitchen costs $72 and twin rooms with air-con go for $12/22. It sells diesel and unleaded fuel, and there's a campers' kitchen.

There are two seven-day minimarkets, both with EFTPOS: the *Oasis Cafe* (attached to the Oasis Caravan Park) and the *Ghan Store*, both of which also sell takeaway meals and diesel, super and unleaded fuel. The Ghan Store has the post office and Commonwealth Bank agencies, while the Oasis Cafe has a State Bank agency.

Bush Camping

Roadside campsites offering good shelter aren't all that common, owing to the fact that over vast areas the tallest vegetation is shrubby saltbush. The best places to look are along coolabah creeks and in sandhill areas, but don't leave it too late in the day. There are many excellent campsites on the Cooper Creek flood plain. However, the clay sticks like glue when moist, so don't hang around if it starts raining – at such times the sandhills offer the best option.

Strzelecki Track

HIGHLIGHTS

- Paddling a canoe on Cooper Creek
- Discovering where Burke and Wills met their end along the banks of Cooper Creek
- Sitting on top of a sand ridge and absorbing the special atmosphere of Coongie Lakes

What does a Polish-born, sometime eccentric explorer who called himself a 'count' have to do with inland Australia? Not very much really, but his name is immortalised in the name of the track and the creek it follows through the arid expanse of north-eastern South Australia.

For most modern-day travellers the Strzelecki Track (pronounced 'stres-LEK-ky'), which was originally a stock route, runs from Lyndhurst, a small hamlet on the northern edge of the Flinders Ranges 560km north of Adelaide, to Innamincka on historic Cooper Creek, a total distance of 460km. In days of old this stock route continued north from Innamincka to Arrabury station and on to the meeting of the Windorah-Birdsville road, 60km west of Beetoota.

There is a choice of routes south of Innamincka, but the route described here is the original and best one, heading up Strzelecki Creek. Popular alternatives are included in the Alternative Routes entry later in this section, but none touch the old one for character or adventure.

The Strzelecki traverses extremely arid country. For the most part the track is well defined, graded and, when dry, passable to a normal passenger car. Some sandy sections do occur in the northern areas, but these are usually fairly short.

HISTORY

Long before the arrival of Europeans, Aboriginal people lived along the permanent waters of Cooper Creek. Little remains of their passing in this harsh desert country, but not far from Innamincka a spectacular array of rock engravings testify to the rich culture that was once here.

It was Charles Sturt, one of Australia's greatest explorers, who discovered and named Strzelecki Creek on 18 August 1845, after Paul Edmund de Strzelecki, a self-taught geologist who, among a few other claims to fame, was the first European to discover, climb and name Australia's highest mountain, Mt Kosciuszko, in 1840. Obviously Sturt was impressed by his reputation!

Sturt was on the last legs of his great central Australian trip, trying to find his elusive 'inland sea', when he stumbled across the life-saving waters of this ephemeral creek. Later he followed it north and discovered the more permanent waters of Cooper Creek, which, when in flood, feed Strzelecki Creek. The creek itself flows into Lake Blanche, but water rarely reaches far enough south to flood the salt-encrusted bed.

The area around the junction of Cooper and Strzelecki creeks was to become etched into the Australian psyche, not by the successful exploits of Sturt and his men but by the death of explorers Burke and Wills in 1860 – see the section on White Exploration in the Facts about the Outback chapter.

The route that was to become, for the most part, the Strzelecki Track, runs between the northern extremity of the Flinders Ranges and Cooper Creek, and was blazed by a top bushman who happened also to be a cattle thief.

Cattle-duffing (rustling) and the branding of cleanskins (unbranded cattle) was for many during the early days of settlement an easy way of stocking a station. But Harry Redford had bigger and better plans. With 1000 head of cattle stolen from Bowen Downs, north-east of Longreach in central Queensland, he set out on an ambitious and highly dangerous drive south over untracked country to Adelaide in South Australia. If it wasn't for a distinctive white bull amongst the cattle he had stolen, he would have got away with it, but he was finally caught and

brought back to face justice at the Roma court in Queensland in 1873. However, his exploits in blazing a new track south was such that the jury declared him not guilty! While public outrage followed, Harry went on to freedom and to carve a name for himself as one of the greatest drovers in Australian history, with escapades in the Northern Territory and Far North Queensland.

Relying on waterholes and the very infrequent floods, the Strzelecki was always a much tougher route than the Birdsville Track, and at times the track was not used for years. Travellers also had to cross the infamous Cobbler Desert at the southern end of the track – a sea of deeply furrowed and convoluted sandhills.

Before the discovery of gas and oil in the Cooper Creek basin in the early 1960s, the track was largely unused. But the discovery and the development of the fields throughout this region has transformed the area. While the main roads have been upgraded, a network of lesser roads crisscross the deserts, some heading to wells and camps, while others just peter out in the sea of sand.

INFORMATION
Tourist Information
Lyndhurst The small township of Lyndhurst doesn't have an information centre, but the Lyndhurst Hotel (☎ (08) 8675 7781) can certainly let you know what the track is like.

The nearest medical facilities and police station are at Leigh Creek South, 38km south of Lyndhurst. The Leigh Creek hospital (☎ (08) 8675 2100) and the Leigh Creek South police station (☎ (08) 8675 2004) are in Black Oak Drive.

Innamincka The Innamincka Hotel (☎ (08) 8675 9901) and the Innamincka Trading Post (☎ (08) 8675 9900) can help travellers with information about the surrounding area.

There are no medical facilities or police stations in this remote region, the nearest being Leigh Creek South. However, Innamincka is covered by the RFDS, and in an emergency, RFDS paramedics based at Moomba can be called in.

Other Information

Much of the horror of travelling along the Strzelecki has been nullified since the Moomba gas fields came into operation in the 1960s. The track has been upgraded and rerouted to service these fields and those surrounding the main camp and processing plant at Moomba itself.

For the most part the track is a good dirt road where it is quite easy to travel at 80km/h or faster. Keep out of the way of the road trains thundering either north or south loaded with all the paraphernalia that a vast oil and gas field requires.

Keep to the main track. While some of the oil rig roads may look to be a better route, they are private roads and are not for use by the public. Some lead long distances into the desert and just stop, and you can easily run out of fuel chasing dead ends.

Contact the Northern Roads Condition Hotline (☎ (08) 11633) to check on current road conditions.

While there is no need to register with police, you should be aware that there are no supplies available between Lyndhurst at the southern end of the track and Innamincka at the northern end. Moomba has no facilities for tourists and does not supply anything to passing travellers; only emergency assistance is given. However, there is a public telephone at the security gate at the entrance to Moomba.

As for most of the routes in this book, you need to be self-sufficient to travel this track. Summer can be very hot, you will meet few other travellers, and a breakdown can be life-threatening.

Books & Maps

The best single map for the track is *Birdsville and Strzelecki Tracks* published by Westprint.

There is no other guidebook covering this area and no dedicated book on the track itself. There are a number that cover the history of the surrounding area, including *Drought or Deluge: Man in the Cooper's Creek Region* by HM Tolcher. A small book called *Innamincka – the Town with Two Lives*

(Innamincka Progress Association), by the same author, is a little beauty containing many historic photographs.

For a comprehensive insight into the natural history of the area, the best book is *Natural History of the North East Deserts*, edited by M Tyler, C Twidale, M Davies & C Wells (Royal Society of South Australia).

Radio Frequencies

If you have a HF radio with you, the important frequencies to have are the RFDS bases at Broken Hill, Port Augusta and Mount Isa, and the Telstra (OTC) base in Sydney. While it is not imperative you have all of them, it's certainly the best position to be in.

For Broken Hill (call sign VJC), the primary frequency is 4055 with a secondary frequency of 6920. Port Augusta (call sign VNZ) has a primary frequency of 4010 and secondary frequencies of 6890 and 8165. Mount Isa (call sign VJI) has a primary frequency of 5110 and secondary frequencies of 4935, 6965 and 7392. Remember that Queensland RFDS bases do not have radphone and are only there for emergency medical services.

Sydney's Telstra base (call sign VIS) has the best land mobile operation set-up of all the Telstra bases. You should have no problem getting them during the day. The Selcall for the beacon is 0899 and the operator is 0108. The main radphone OTC channels are 405, 607, 802, 1203 and 1602.

THE ROUTE
Lyndhurst

Lyndhurst, at the start of the Strzelecki Track, is 560km north of Adelaide and is reached by a good bitumen road. It is considered by many to be the stepping-off point for the real outback. Here the bitumen ends, and the dirt road heading north leads to Marree and the Birdsville and Oodnadatta tracks, while the Strzelecki Track heads off to the east.

Turning east just opposite the general store, the bitumen continues a short distance past the pub and over the disused railway line that once took the famous *Ghan* train all the

Strzelecki
Track

Unsealed roads can vary
from excellent to impassable,
depending on many factors.

(Track Closed at Times
Check with NP&WS)

Tu Birdsville
To Birdsville
Cordillo Downs
Homestead
To Betoota &
Windorah

Coongie
Lakes
Innamincka
Regional
Reserve

Arrabury
Homestead

(Private)

Coongie
To Noccundra &
Thargomindah

Kudriemitchie
Homestead

106
Sturt
Stony
Desert
Dig
Tree
Cooper   Creek

Gidgealpa
Oilfield
(Only)
Nappa Merrie
Homestead

Innamincka
17
28
Burke & Wills Bridge

62
Innamincka
Station

24
47

Moomba
40
69

STRZELECKI
DESERT
50
QUEENSLAND

45
Merty Merty
Homestead

43

87
Bollards
Lagoon
Homestead
Cameron Corner
& Border Store

Strzelecki
Creek
Strzelecki
Crossing
15

Lake
Blanche
Cobbler   Desert
55

Montecollina
Bore

Dog
Fence
Blanchewater
21
Tibooburra

Mumpeowie
Homestead
40
Mount Hopeless
Homestead

Marree
50
N E W

Mt Hopeless
S O U T H   W A L E S

30
To
Arkaroola

Mount Freeling
Talc Mine
S O U T H
A U S T R A L I A

Ochre
Quarries
Strzelecki
76

Lyndhurst
Mount Lyndhurst
Homestead

* 10 *   Distances Between
Locations in Kilometres

way to Alice Springs. The track leads away
in front of you.

This small outback town caters for passing
travellers with fuel, food and accommodation (see Facilities later in this section).

One of the characters of the north is Talc
Alf, a local artist whose abode and gallery is
just north of the pub. He carves sculptures
out of the soft talc stone that is mined at
nearby Mount Freeling. Give him a chance
and he'll let you know his fairly strong views
on politics, conservation, tourism, tourists
and life in general.

Five km north of the town, close to the

Marree road, are the **ochre cliffs and quarries** that were once worked by Aboriginal
people. The ochre from these cliffs was
traded as far north as the Gulf of Carpentaria
and south all the way to the coast. Listed on
the Register of the National Estate, these
quarries, unlike many others, have never
been mined by Europeans.

Lyndhurst to Strzelecki Crossing
(272km)

As you head north along the Strzelecki, the
Flinders Ranges are a blue smudge on the
south-eastern horizon. The track passes

through arid pastoral country made famous by Sir Thomas Elder who, in the 1860s, had taken up the expansive Murnpeowie station, where he bred horses for the Indian Army and ran more than 100,000 sheep.

About 76km from Lyndhurst a track heads east off the Strzelecki Track towards the **Mount Freeling talc mine**. Less than 30km further north, the route passes through the **Dog Fence**. Sheep get more scarce as you head north, and once through the fence, you'll see only cattle.

Creek crossings are numerous across these vast plains, but most are kept in good condition and the creeks only flow after rare, heavy rain in the distant ranges. MacDonnell Creek is 50km north of the fence, just north of the road; the ruins of **Blanchewater station** are on the western bank of this occasional waterway.

In 1860, when the Burke and Wills saga was being played out, Blanchewater, then more commonly known as Mount Hopeless, was the northernmost station in South Australia. It was this property that the explorers were trying to reach when they perished. Blanchewater was also where Harry Redford sold his ill-gotten stock, rather than chance the sale at the Adelaide stockyards.

Forty km further on, a track from the south joins the Strzelecki. This track heads down past the eastern flank of the Flinders Ranges to Arkaroola and the Gammon Ranges National Park.

The **Montecollina Bore**, the only bore drilled on the Strzelecki Track for the use of drovers, is just over 20km further north. This is a popular spot to camp, but there are no facilities and you should even bring your own wood if you want the enjoyment of a fire.

Pushing ever north, the Strzelecki Track passes through the **Cobbler Desert**, its eroded forms being blamed on the rabbit plagues and heavy stocking rates of last century.

The creek that the track takes its name from is now just a few kilometres to the west, but the first time you see it will be some 50km further north, and you know then that you are close to the **Strzelecki Crossing**.

About 3km south of the crossing a track heads west off the main road, leading in a short distance to the creek and **Yaningurie Waterhole**. This is a popular spot to camp, and with its water and trees it is hard to beat. Bring your wood in from some distance away and *don't* cut trees down.

The main road, often called the Strzelecki Track but really the **Moomba Road**, swings across the river. See the later Alternative Routes entry for details on this route.

At the crossing itself, just past the track junction, the wide bed of the creek, dotted with its box trees, is a good place to stop and have a brew or even camp. On the northern bank, beside the Moomba Road, a wayside stop and picnic area has been established, but the creekbed is better.

Just before the main road crossing of Strzelecki Creek, a major track heads off to the right. Take this track, which puts you on the original Strzelecki Track heading up the creek to Merty Merty station. This is by far the more enjoyable of the runs north and a little more of an adventure.

Strzelecki Crossing to Innamincka (159km)

From the crossing, the track begins to follow the normally wide dry creekbed north. It makes a pleasant change from the harsh gibber and sand country you passed through further south. For the most part, the track winds up the wide bed of the creek and the run through the box trees can often flush some sample of wildlife, whether it be a solitary kangaroo, a lazy, well-fed wedge-tailed eagle or a scavenging dingo.

This first section of the track between here and Merty Merty station is probably the most unused part of the Strzelecki, and the track is sandy in places.

As you head north, the sand ridges become more pronounced, but because you are heading in the direction in which the dunes are running, they are really no problem.

About 43km north of the crossing, **Merty Merty station** will be seen close to your left-hand side, while a large reddish sandhill is prominent stretching away to the south on your right. Slowly this big dune is swallowing all in its path – it's an impressive dune and a top spot to watch the sun rise or set.

Another track, looking a bit better than the one you are on, joins the Strzelecki from the right, close to the homestead. This leads to **Cameron Corner**, 134km away, via Bollards Lagoon homestead. The *Corner Store* (☎ (08) 8091 3972) located at the Corner has limited supplies and fuel (diesel, super and unleaded).

Just north of Merty Merty station is a signposted track junction. The track coming in from the west is from the Moomba Road, while the Strzelecki Track veers north.

A few kilometres north you will begin to see the first signs of a gas field: large, robotic arms wave to their computer master's beat, pumping the liquid gold across the sand ridges to Moomba. A couple of these pumps can easily be seen just off to the east. Strictly speaking you shouldn't approach them, but most travellers are interested enough to do the short diversion. Please don't interfere with this equipment – the producers are near-paranoid about vandalism, and access would definitely suffer if any damage was done.

Less than 70km north of Merty Merty is a major T-junction and a better class of road. Turn right at the junction and then turn left after a couple of kilometres at another signposted junction. From here it is another 45km of easy running north to Innamincka and the end of the Strzelecki Track.

Innamincka

On the banks of Cooper Creek is the small town of Innamincka. Here you can buy a cold beer, have a meal and fuel up. There's plenty to do in the surrounding area, so allow a bit of time to soak up the atmosphere and enjoy the waters of the historic, picturesque creek.

Close to the Queensland border, Innamincka owes its beginnings to the government's customs post which taxed all the stock travelling from one colony to another. Such a hold-up of stock and thirsty drovers meant that a pub soon followed to help quench the thirst of the hard-working men who pushed the stock south to markets.

With their revelry came a need for a police station and lock up, and by the turn of the century, Innamincka was a town of four or five buildings.

With the advent of free trade between the states as a result of Federation, the customs post went in 1901. But the years that followed were the years that saw Sidney Kidman, the 'Cattle King', build his empire, and the Cooper fairly hummed with the clash of branding irons and the rattle of stirrup and spur. The pub and the police post were still required.

In 1928 the **Australian Inland Mission** (AIM) built a hostel there, and a few years later it and the Strzelecki Track played a part in John Flynn's establishment of the Royal Flying Doctor Service.

Until the beginning of WWII, a mail truck ploughed its way up the track to Innamincka from Farina, now just a few old stone ruins south of Lyndhurst. The war saw an end to that, and afterwards the mail came up every two weeks from Broken Hill via Tibooburra in New South Wales.

In 1951 the AIM closed down the hostel and within a year the police post and the pub had gone as well. The town was dead, and a couple of the stations around the area claimed the remains – the pub becoming stockmen's quarters for nearby Innamincka station, while the hostel was partly demolished and anything worth salvaging transported to Arrabury station, 160km north. About the only thing of substance left was the monster bottle heap that stretched for over 200m and was over 1m high. It was obvious why Innamincka needed a police post.

With the 1960s came the search for oil and gas, and big strikes of both occurred in the surrounding dune country. In 1974, Mike Steel, a tour operator, traveller and part-time author, saw the potential in the area and started what you see today.

Nowadays there are around 12 permanent residents of Innamincka, which is about as big as it's ever been. Mind you, there is a good chance you'll arrive when the place is seemingly overflowing with stockmen from the nearby stations, oil workers from Moomba, road workers from up and down the track, and a few other travellers.

A picnic **race meeting** is held each year, generally towards the end of August, and that really makes the place bounce. Then there may be a few hundred to over a thousand people in town! Needless to say, accommodation is stretched at these times and even camping close to town can be crowded.

Take the opportunity to visit **Coongie Lakes**, a short distance to the north-west. It is a spectacular wetland alive with birds. The lakes form one of the great freshwater lake systems in central Australia and rely on the occasional flooding of the Cooper for their ephemeral waters. Coongie Lake itself is the southernmost lake of this complex and the only one travellers are allowed to visit. It is also the one with the most water. The whole region is a haven for bird life; in the years of plenty when the lakes are full, the area is bursting at the seams with all forms of animal life. Remember that camping fees are payable (see Facilities later in this section).

ALTERNATIVE ROUTES

North of the Strzelecki Crossing there are a number of alternative routes north.

The **Moomba Road** heads north from the Strzelecki Crossing for 95km to Moomba, the high-tech heart of these spread-out oil and gas fields. Some 44km up this main road from the crossing, and 50km south of Moomba, a track heads east, meeting up with the real Strzelecki Track just north of Merty Merty station.

From Moomba you can also head east for 40km and join up with the Strzelecki proper, or head north for 24km before swinging east for the last 60-odd km to Innamincka. All these routes are good dirt roads and are well maintained.

The road north from Moomba is handy for those who want to travel the **Walkers Crossing Track** that gives access, when open, across the Cooper Creek flood plain to the Birdsville Track, 185km north of Moomba. For more details on this route see the Birdsville Track section earlier in this chapter.

Further along the Moomba-Innamincka road, access to a number of historical sites along the Cooper is easy, but as they are also within an easy drive of Innamincka, don't bother heading for them from the old Strzelecki Track.

ACTIVITIES
Canoeing

Canoeing is excellent along the Cooper and at Coongie Lakes. These are both exceptional wildlife experiences, with a host of waterbirds to regale you with their variety and beauty.

One of the best canoe trips starts at the far end of Cullyamurra Waterhole, where the vehicle access ends. From there you can take an easy paddle upstream as far as the Innamincka Choke and check the Aboriginal engravings nearby, or head off downstream all the way to the causeway at Innamincka itself. It makes for a very pleasant day.

The other waterholes in the area also offer some interesting paddling.

If you want to rent a canoe, contact the pub at Innamincka. A two-person Canadian canoe costs $45 for a 24-hour hire.

Fishing

Anywhere there is a decent stretch of water there is the chance of catching a feed of fish.

These days the amateur with a rod and line has a good chance of catching a feed, as nets have been banned. The yellowbelly is the prize catch of these waters, and it tastes delicious.

ORGANISED TOURS

Local tours can be arranged at the hotel or general store in Innamincka. Given enough warning, they can take you out to Coongie Lakes or along the Cooper to the Dig Tree and the other historic places scattered along the waterway.

A number of tour operators include the Strzelecki Track and the area around Innamincka on their tours. Few include it as the total package, but rather as a route to do and a place to see while on their way to somewhere else. That's a pity really, but their loss is the independent traveller's gain. If that is what you want to do, the best spot to start is the South Australia Tourism Commission (☎ (08) 8212 1505, freecall 1800 882 092), 1 King William St (PO Box 1972), Adelaide, SA 5000.

There are a couple of companies that include the Cooper and Coongie Lakes in guided bushwalking trips. EcoTrek (☎ (08) 8383 7198), PO Box 4, Kangarilla, SA 5157, and Exploranges (☎ (08) 8294 6530), 37 Walker St, Somerton Park, SA 5044, have irregular departures.

FACILITIES
Lyndhurst
The *Lyndhurst Roadhouse* (☎ (08) 8675 7782), in the centre of town, is the last chance to buy fuel (diesel, super and unleaded), a hamburger, cool drinks and an ice cream. It also stocks more traditional bushie supplies such as Akubra hats and tins of baked beans, and general food items.

The *Lyndhurst Hotel* (☎ (08) 8675 7781), just a few hundred metres, away offers travellers cold beer, meals and friendly banter. Accommodation is also available in single or triple rooms, ranging from $28 a day for a single to $60 for a triple. A cooked breakfast is available and meals are also served for lunch and dinner. The bar and dining areas are air-conditioned and they are also good spots to find out what the track is like. EFTPOS is also available.

If you need a spare tyre, a battery or limited repairs, the Strzelecki Tyre Service (☎ (08) 8675 7783), close to the roadhouse, can provide all you need.

Lyndhurst has no bank or post office; the nearest such facilities are at Leigh Creek South, 38km south.

For travellers, there are toilets and showers situated close to the main road junction. People heading east may think nothing of them, but those coming west may revel in the luxury.

As far as camping is concerned, there is nothing at Lyndhurst that comes even close to a camping ground. If you are desperate, the closest and best spot to erect a tent is about 5km north of the town, where the main road crosses a grid. Off to the east, a line of low scrub marks a low depression and a spot to camp. It's not brilliant.

Innamincka
The *Innamincka Hotel* (☎ (08) 8675 9901) offers cold beer, meals and accommodation, and it's a good place to obtain information about the surrounding area. If you are there on Sunday evening during the tourist season, don't miss the banquet of roasts at the pub. For $12 there is a great feed, a roaring log fire and plenty of friendly company, including most of the locals. The accommodation is in motel-style, air-con units costing $40/60/80 for single/double/triple.

Right next door is the *Innamincka Trading Post* (☎ (08) 8675 9900). Here you can buy most of your daily requirements such as milk and bread, plus souvenirs, maps and books and the like. They also supply fuel – diesel, super and unleaded, camping gas and Avgas. The Trading Post also has accommodation available for an overnight stop or longer in the *Burke Lodge Cabins*, with three two-bedroom cabins available for $30 a single or $25 per person when there is more than one. Each cabin has four beds, and there is an outside barbecue area for your use.

Innamincka has no banking or post office facilities, but EFTPOS is available. Major credit cards are also readily accepted at the hotel and trading store.

Just a stone's throw away are some excellent toilets and showers which are a boon to travellers and campers. A donation to help in the upkeep is greatly appreciated. A solar-powered telephone nearby is a link with the outside world.

At Innamincka you can also hire a canoe, get some welding done and even get a few things repaired. Contact the Trading Post for details.

Camping is allowed down near the creek on the town common. If you want to camp elsewhere in the area (and there are plenty of magical spots to camp), you will need a Desert Parks Pass ($60) which is available from the ranger at Innamincka if you haven't picked one up beforehand. For more details on the pass, see the Travel Permits section in the earlier Getting Around chapter.

Camping rates per night within the Innamincka zone are $15 per vehicle, $8 per motorcycle and $4 per person with no vehicle. Note that persons walking or travelling by bicycle are not required to pay an entrance fee to the parks.

Camping along the Cooper

There are numerous campsites spread along the river both up and downstream from Innamincka. One of the most popular sites is *Cullyamurra Waterhole*, about 13km east of Innamincka. It is a spectacular waterhole, stretching upriver for at least 6km to a natural rock bar called the Innamincka Choke. This waterhole is reputedly the deepest waterhole in central Australia and has been measured at 28m. It has never been known to dry up. One of the best ways to enjoy this waterhole and any others in the area is by canoe.

Tall, gnarled gums line the creek and offer shade for campsites, but wood for fires is scarce. Much damage has been done in recent years to the magnificent trees along this section of river by unthinking people chopping down branches and even whole trees to feed their fires. If you must have a wood fire, bring in the firewood from elsewhere. In such a popular spot, gas fires are better.

West of Innamincka, along the 15-Mile Track that is also the route to Moomba, is *Queerbidie Waterhole*, 2.5km away. A further 1.5km on, a turn-off towards the river leads to a number of sites spread along a short section of waterway. Some of these sites are a little back from the water, while at others you will need to carry your gear a short distance to get close to the creek.

Less than 5.5km west from the township on the Innamincka-Moomba road, another track heads off to the river and to *Ski Beach*. Camping is also possible further west along this main road at Kings Marker (7km west of Innamincka), Minkie Waterhole (or Minkie WH; 12km) and Tilcha WH (14km).

While most of the abovementioned sites

have rubbish bins, it's a much better idea to take your rubbish to the rubbish pit at Innamincka.

Camping at Coongie Lakes

The trip out to Coongie Lakes, north-west of Innamincka, is 106km each way, and in dry weather a normal car can get there. You need a Desert Parks Pass to travel this road and to camp, the camping rates per night are $15 per vehicle, $8 per motorcycle and $4 per person with no vehicle. You'll pass through a number of different vegetation types on your drive out to the lake. While the return trip can be done in one day, it is better to spend a little longer.

Along the track there are some pleasant camping spots: Bulyeroo WH (37km from Innamincka), Scrubby Camp WH (45km) and Kudriemitchie WH (85km). Up to Kudriemitchie you are allowed wood fires and even generators and dogs; further north they are all banned.

Don't forget that this area is part of a working cattle station and cattle may be seen along the way. Take care.

Just before the track ends at Coongie, a couple of turn-offs to the east lead to some campsites along the lake shore. Remember that only gas fires are allowed out here. Rubbish can be dumped only at the rubbish disposal pits at Kudriemitchie and Scrubby Camp.

Airstrips

Every homestead along the Strzelecki has an airstrip close by. These are meant for light aircraft and can be dotted with anthills, potholes and animals.

Innamincka has a well-used airstrip that sees many people flying in for a weekend or longer. The airstrip is on the highest ground around and is only a short distance from the pub. At times, when the Cooper is running a banker, this is the only way supplies and people can move in and out of the tiny outpost. Avgas is usually available – contact the Trading Post for more details. If you are flying in and will need fuel, it's best to check beforehand.

ALTERNATIVE TRANSPORT

Bus

The Stateliner bus company (☎ (08) 233 2777), 21 Mackay St, Port Augusta, SA 5700, services Copley, south of Lyndhurst three times a week, with a bus departing from Port Augusta for Copley every Wednesday, Friday and Saturday. The return fare is $86.60. Check with them for a current timetable.

Air

Innamincka is serviced by plane each Saturday by the Augusta Airways mail run. A single one-way fare costs $175. Contact them at Port Augusta airport (☎ (08) 8642 3100) for flight details; the mailing address is Port Augusta airport, Port Augusta, SA 5700.

Gunbarrel Highway

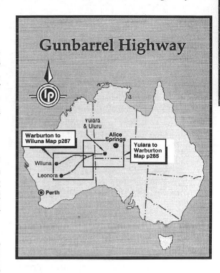

HIGHLIGHTS
• Surviving the corrugations between the Warburton road and Carnegie
• The spectacular Petermann Ranges
• Walking along the gum-lined Hull River to Lasseter's Cave

The Gunbarrel Highway was the first link between central Australia and Western Australia. Built to service the Woomera Rocket Range and the Giles weather station, it was completed in 1958.

Today much of the 'real' Gunbarrel is out of bounds to normal travellers and there is a little confusion as to which of the useable roads is really the Gunbarrel. Some call the Laverton-Warburton road the Gunbarrel, but it is definitely not. The road east from Carnegie station to Docker River is the real Gunbarrel – well, a lot of it is. Some of the original Gunbarrel now passes through an Aboriginal area that to most of us is a 'no go' area. The diversion, via Warburton Aborigi-

nal community, which some call the Gunbarrel, isn't.

Likewise, the stretch of road between Docker River and Uluru (Ayers Rock) is called the Gunbarrel, but in fact it's not. The real Gunbarrel heads south from Giles weather station, crossing into South Australia just south of the Northern Territory border. It then parallels the border before passing back into the Territory and finishing at Victory Downs station. Much of this route is also a 'no go' area for travellers. Confused? Well, aren't we all?

This text looks at the Gunbarrel in today's accepted terms, keeping as much as possible to the original route but obviously staying away from the areas that demand very special permission to enter. In that light, the trip starts at Yulara, the resort servicing visitors to Uluru (Ayers Rock), and heads west to Docker River Aboriginal community before crossing the border to Giles weather station and then striking south-west in a gunbarrel-straight line to Warburton – it's not really all that straight, but that's the general idea. From this point the route swings north, joining with the ridgy-didge Gunbarrel west of Jackie Junction. From there we are on the original highway all the way to Carnegie station.

HISTORY

There was a flurry of activity in this region back in 1873 when three explorers were vying for the honour of discovering what lay between the Overland Telegraph Line, which stretched across central Australia from north to south, and the Western Australian coast. Major Peter Warburton pushed north from Alice Springs, finally making the coast near De Grey, north of present-day Port Hedland, but almost dying in the attempt.

William Gosse left Alice eight days after Warburton had set out, but Gosse and his men, although initially heading in much the same direction as Warburton, swung south. They eventually became the first whites to see Uluru, which Gosse named Ayers Rock. In his journeys south and west from Ayers Rock, Gosse also named the Mann and Tomkinson ranges, before giving up his quest to cross the continent near Mt Squires in the Cavenagh Ranges of Western Australia.

Ernest Giles had already been in the region west of Alice in 1872. Later he tried to cross a vast salt lake he called Lake Amadeus. To the south he could see a cluster of rounded peaks, the highest of which he called Mt Olga. However, it was Gosse who actually got to Kata Tjuta (the Olgas) before him – by a month, a year later.

A year later, from the Kata Tjuta, Giles and his men, who included William Tietkins as his second-in-command, pushed south-west into the desert, establishing a depot at Fort Mueller, west of the Tomkinson Ranges. Retreating back to more permanent waters, at a place he called Circus Water in the Rawlinson Ranges, he tried to push west for the next three months. Time and again he was repulsed.

During March 1874 Giles explored and named the Petermann Ranges and in April, from a depot he called Fort McKellar in the Petermanns, he gave his westward push one last effort. He took with him a young stockman by the name of Alf Gibson, and so one of the great stories of the white exploration of Australia began. About 140km west of Circus Water, Gibson's horse knocked up. Giles gave him his horse and, knowing that it was impossible to continue, sent Gibson back to bring help from their base camp. Gibson never made it. Giles, alone and on foot, with hardly a skerrick of water, did! Arriving at Circus Water, he drank his fill and came upon a dying wallaby. 'I pounced upon it and ate it, living, raw, dying – fur, skin, bones, skull, and all,' he was to write later; his only regret was that he couldn't find its mother!

Two days later, Giles staggered back into the depot at Fort McKellar and, finding Gibson missing, immediately turned back to look for him, taking Tietkins with him. Both nearly died in the effort. Giles named the desert the Gibson Desert. Retreating back to civilisation, Giles arrived back at Charlotte Waters in July 1874, and a couple of months later learnt that both Warburton and Alexander Forrest had crossed the western half of the continent.

Giles was still determined to write his name in the history books. His third expedition, eight months later, was the relatively short trek from Fowlers Bay, on the southern coast, to Finnis Springs south of Lake Eyre. Again he nearly died of thirst, but it proved to him that camels, of which he had two on that trip, were the best animals to use.

His fourth and most successful expedition left a month after his third had finished, in May 1875. Striking north and west from Port Augusta, Giles used the waterholes he had discovered on the previous trip, passing the northern end of Lake Gairdner. Finally, after much hardship, he and his men, Tietkins included, crossed the Great Victoria Desert, discovering a life-saving spring that Giles called Queen Victoria Springs. In November the expeditioners were welcomed into Perth, and the celebrations followed. Giles, though, was still fired with the thought of exploring and finding rich pastoral land.

Leaving the party scene in January 1876, he and his men, with camels, pushed north along the Western Australian coast and then inland to the Ashburton River, about 480km from the coast. From a depot at this point in May, he turned his eyes and thoughts east – almost 800km away was where he and Gibson had parted.

Striking east, he almost lost the camels when they ate a poisonous plant, but once they had recovered, Giles pushed on, finally reaching the Alfred & Marie Range, the furthest point west he had sighted on his 1874 expedition. By late August the group was back on the Overland Telegraph Line at Peake, after passing along the old route through the Rawlinson, Petermann and Musgrave ranges.

While Giles was the first to do a double crossing of the western deserts, he is probably Australia's least known successful explorer. He died penniless and unknown in 1897. His book *Australia Twice Traversed*, originally published in 1889, occasionally appears as a facsimile. It is one of the most readable of all the books written by Australia's explorers.

In 1891 the Elder Scientific Exploring Expedition set forth from northern South Australia, heading west to the Everard Ranges, Fort Mueller and Mt Squires, then south to Queen Victoria Springs and Esperance on the coast before striking north to Lake Wells. Led by David Lindsay, with Lawrence Wells as his lieutenant, it was the first of the 'scientific' expeditions that were to fill in the gaps left by the earlier explorers.

Over the next 40 years, the country along the Overland Telegraph Line and around Alice Springs was taken up as pastoral country. By 1900 gold had been discovered in a couple of isolated regions north-west and east of Alice, and with the discovery of the untold riches at Kalgoorlie and Coolgardie in Western Australia, prospectors looked at the region along the Petermanns. One was Harold Lasseter, who in 1930 led an expedition to find a 'golden reef' he had supposedly discovered 33 years previously.

The legend of the reef and the Lasseter story has been told again and again. While the expedition had struck west from Alice Springs, Lasseter was later to head south, eventually on his own, to Uluru (Ayers Rock) and then west through the Petermann and Rawlinson Ranges to a point somewhere around Lake Christopher.

Lasseter states in his diary that he found and pegged the reef on 23 December. Retracing his steps, his camels bolted when he was about 50km east of present-day Docker River Aboriginal community. Realising he couldn't make it back to Uluru (Ayers Rock) and safety, he stayed in a cave on the edge of a creek for a few weeks, waiting for a rescue party that he was sure would be sent to look for him. Despairing, he finally set out on the impossible task, eventually collapsing and dying beside Irving Creek. His body and diary were later recovered, and while other search parties and gold-prospecting parties went out – and still do – no sign of his fabled reef has ever been found. If it was a hoax, Lasseter paid the supreme price!

Apart from the occasional prospector, the next person on the scene was the late Len Beadell, building the odd road or two for the Woomera Rocket Range.

The Gunbarrel Highway, which he constructed, ran between Victory Downs, west of Kulgera on the Stuart Highway, headed west, and then south along the northern edge of the Musgrave Ranges. From there the Highway followed the Mann and Tomkinson ranges before swinging north to a spot in the Rawlinson Ranges where Len Beadell established Giles as a weather station. Today the station is used to help amass information for weather forecasts and for aircraft flying 13,000m overhead, but its original purpose was to ensure that the day chosen for the big bangs at Emu or Maralinga were perfect and that the wind was blowing in the right direction.

Passing along the southern edge of the Rawlinsons, Beadell's route swung south to Warburton Mission. North of the mission he established a road junction for the last push, which ran west and then slightly north to Mt Everard before swinging south, passing the Mungali Claypan and Mt Nossiter, and finally reaching the easternmost outpost of civilisation in Western Australia, Carnegie station.

Len Beadell – The Last Explorer

Len Beadell was born in 1923 in the Sydney suburb of West Pennant Hills. He was just 12 when he started his career as an unpaid assistant surveyor for the Sydney Water Board. He started working full-time with the board after finishing high school, but was conscripted in 1942. After serving in New Guinea, he rejoined the water board at the end of the war to help map remote Arnhem Land. A little later he was asked to do a job for the Defence Department: lay out a rocket range!

It was the beginning of the town of Woomera and the Woomera Rocket Range, which were later to lead to the A-bomb tests at Emu and Maralinga.

It was also the beginning of the last phase of Australian exploration. Len and his men, whom he later christened 'the Gunbarrel Road Construction Party', carved out a series of roads through 2.5 million sq km of wilderness west of Alice Springs.

He started to survey the Woomera range in 1947; it was not until 1952 that he was called on to find the site for Emu. The next year was taken up with building the road from Mabel Creek (then on the Stuart Highway) to Emu, preparing for the A-bomb tests at Emu, and then picking a new site which was to be called Maralinga. Surveying around Maralinga took up all of 1954 and much of the next year, and the remainder of 1955 was spent making the road between Emu and Maralinga. Late that year the first 160km of the Gunbarrel Highway was completed, from Victory Downs to Mulga Park. This was Len Beadell's first major road, and also his most well known.

In 1956 the site for the Giles weather station was chosen and the Gunbarrel was continued out to this new site. Building an airstrip at Giles was next on the agenda, and the rest of the year was taken up with a new road south from Giles to Emu via Mt Davies, although that road wasn't finished until 1957.

The last section of the Gunbarrel, west to Carnegie Station, a little east of Wiluna in Western Australia, was pushed through during 1958. It was the first road link across central Australia and, as the name suggests, it was as straight as Len could make it – 'to keep the country looking tidy', as he says during his lecture tours.

This road, the first to run east-west across central Australia, took from 1955 to 1958 to survey and build and ushered in the modern world to this ancient landscape. The Gunbarrel Highway, like most of the roads he helped construct, was named by Len Beadell.

INFORMATION
Tourist Information

The best places for tourist information are at Alice Springs or Yulara, or from the Western Australian Tourism Commission.

The Central Australian Tourism Industry Association (CATIA; ☎ (08) 8952 5199) can be contacted by writing to PO Box 2227, Alice Springs, NT 0871.

The Yulara visitor information centre (☎ (08) 8956 2240) can be contacted at PO Box 46, Yulara, NT 0872.

The Western Australian Tourist Centre is in Forrest Place, Perth, WA 6000 (GPO Box W2081; ☎ (08) 9483 1111).

Police

While is not really necessary, you can contact the police in Wiluna and Yulara before you set off and let them know your intended route and time of arrival. They are also a good source of information on the latest conditions of the route. Don't forget to tell the police at the other end that you have made it safely. The Wiluna Police Station (☎ (08) 9981 7024) is in Thompson St. The Yulara Police Station (☎ (08) 8956 2166) is on the Lasseter Highway at Yulara.

Permits

Permits are required to travel the enormous area of Aboriginal land in this region of Australia. For the Gunbarrel route described here, there are few hassles; permits take about three weeks to be issued. Areas that require special permission and permits are much harder to enter, and unless you have good reason to do so, a permit will not be issued.

To travel the full length of the Gunbarrel you require a permit from the Central Land Council in Alice Springs for the Northern Territory section, and another from the Aboriginal Affairs Department in Perth for the Western Australian section. For more details on applications see Travel Permits in the earlier Getting Around chapter. The permits lay down certain conditions for travel which must be adhered to.

Books & Maps
Apart from Len Beadell's books on the area (see the boxed story on this last Australian explorer), there are few others.

Although not really covering the Gunbarrel Highway, *The Great Victoria Desert* by Mark Shephard and published by Reed Books covers the region to the south of Warburton and is an excellent reference to the area.

Westprint publishes a map called *The Gunbarrel Highway*. To do the whole route you'll also need the *Ayers Rock* map. Also good is the Royal Automobile Club of Western Australia's map *Perth to Alice Springs – via Gunbarrel Highway or Warburton Road*. This map is available through the state automobile associations or good map shops Australia-wide.

Radio Frequencies
The need to carry a HF radio may be debated, especially if you are on the well-used Warburton-Laverton road, but for the remote tracks such as the Anne Beadell or the route west of Papunya, the argument for carrying one is greatly reinforced. Certainly it's a good idea for anywhere off the bitumen.

The RFDS base at Alice Springs (call sign VJD) has a primary frequency of 5410 and a secondary frequency of 6950. If you are further south, the Port Augusta base (call sign VNZ) has a primary frequency of 4010; secondary frequencies are 6890 and 8165.

Along the Gunbarrel and Gary highways, the base at Meekatharra is hard to beat. Its call sign is VKJ and its primary frequency is

4010; secondary frequencies include 2280 and 6880. Up towards the Canning Stock Route, the Port Hedland base may be worth a try. Its call sign is VKL and it has a primary frequency of 4030; secondary frequencies are 2280 and 6960.

For those working through the Telstra radphone bases, the best ones to go for depend on where you are. Sydney (call sign VIS) has good reception if you are anywhere in the eastern portion of this trip. Radphone 24-hour channels include 405, 607, 802, 1203, and 1602. Other frequencies for Selcall and Tonecall are also available. The Selcall for the beacon is 0899, while for the operator it is 0108.

In the western portion of these roads, the best station to use is Perth (call sign VIP). Its main 24-hour frequencies include 427, 806, and 1226. Other frequencies are also available. The Selcall for the beacon in Perth is 0799, while for the operator the Selcall is 0107.

Telstra RDD channels are also available, with the bases at Alice Springs and Perth the best to go for. Frequencies are supplied once you have registered with Telstra, (☎ 1800 810 023).

THE ROUTE

This route takes you from the flash resort at Yulara west along the Docker River road to

---

Uluru-Kata Tjuta National Park

The main feature of this 1325-sq-km desert park is world-famous Uluru (Ayers Rock). At 3.6km long, and with steep smooth flanks of red rock that tower 348m above the surrounding sand plain, it's a remarkable sight in its pancake-flat setting. To many Australians 'the Rock' has almost religious significance, and to visit and climb it is like a pilgrimage.

In fact, both the Rock and nearby Kata Tjuta (the Olgas) are of tremendous spiritual significance to the local Aboriginal people. They own the surrounding land, but have leased it to the federal government as a national park. The park is jointly managed by the Aboriginal traditional owners and Parks Australia North (an arm of the Environment Australia Biodiversity Group, the federal government's national parks body).

Kata Tjuta ('many heads') is 30km west of Uluru and, like the name suggests, is a concentration of dome-shaped structures. These are much smaller than Uluru, but are almost as spectacular – the tallest, Mt Olga, is about 200m higher than Uluru. Many visitors find this area to be the more captivating of the two, although the echoing racket of light aircraft doing scenic flights overhead can be a real turn-off.

Uluru-Kata Tjuta offers much more than inspiring scenery, sunset colours and lung-pumping climbs, however. There are some good walks, a superb cultural centre and Aboriginal culture tours, as well as various activities at the nearby resort township of Yulara. It's not at all difficult to spend several days here.

Information The park's cultural centre is 1km before the Rock on the road from Yulara. It has excellent multi-lingual displays which are worth reading before you visit the Rock. There's also a craft outlet where you can watch artists at work (no photos, please) and purchase direct from them. The centre is open 7 am to 5.30 pm (6 pm in summer), and there's a free 1½-hour tour at 3.15 pm on Monday, Tuesday and Wednesday.

The park is open daily from half an hour before sunrise to sunset. Entry permits cost $15 (free for children under 15) and are good for a five-day visit. You can get your permit from the visitor centre at Yulara or at the park entry station between Yulara and Uluru.

For information on the park call the Uluru-Kata Tjuta Cultural Centre on ☎ (08) 8956 3138. The Yulara visitor centre (☎ (08) 8956 2240) can advise on local tours, accommodation and services.

Getting Around All public roads within the national park, including the road to Yulara, are fully sealed.

There is no taxi service at Yulara. However, if you're not an independent traveller you can get to Uluru from Yulara and return for $20 with Sunworth Shuttles (☎ (08) 8956 2152). They'll take you there, drop you off, then come back and get you at a prearranged time.

Giles, then south-west to the Warburton Aboriginal community. Soon after, you veer off the Warburton-Laverton road and head for Carnegie station and Wiluna along the original track of the Gunbarrel Highway. The total distance is 1400km.

Until you are west of Warburton, the track is generally passable to normal cars. Once on the real Gunbarrel, the route deteriorates and a 4WD is advisable.

Travelling times between Yulara and places further west depend on how quickly you like to drive on sandy dirt and corrugated roads. Between Yulara and Warburton, allow eight to nine hours; between Warburton and Carnegie station, allow 10 to 12; from Car-

negie to Wiluna, allow five to six hours. Obviously these figures are for driving times only.

Yulara

The modern Ayers Rock Resort is in the township of Yulara, on the edge of Uluru-Kata Tjuta National Park. While the township caters mainly for the resort, the resort caters mainly for well-heeled tourists who flock to **Uluru (Ayers Rock)** to see it change colour, to photograph it, or video it. Like anything in nature, it doesn't always perform. Even so, the Rock and nearby **Kata Tjuta (the Olgas)** is worth seeing and spending a couple of days enjoying.

Walks Around Uluru There are walking trails around Uluru, and guided walks delving into the plants, wildlife, geology and mythology of the area. It can take five hours to make the 9km walk around the base of the Rock, looking at the caves and rock paintings on the way. Areas of special spiritual significance to local Aborigines are off-limits to visitors – these are marked with fences and signs.

Mala Walk This walk starts at the base of the climb and takes about 1½ hours at a very leisurely pace. The traditional law of the Mala (hare-wallaby) ancestors is a major force in the lives of local people. You can do the walk on your own, or join a free guided walk from the carpark – they leave daily at 10 am (8 am from October to April inclusive).

Liru Walk The two-hour guided Liru Walk starts at the cultural centre and focuses on traditional uses of the area's plant and animal life. Operated by Anangu Tours (☎ (08) 8956 2123), it leaves daily at 8.30 am (earlier from October to March). The cost if you're driving yourself to the start point is $39 ($29 children). Bookings are essential.

Kuniya Walk This short walk takes you from the carpark on the southern side of the Rock to Mutitjulu waterhole. It features the traditional law associated with the clash between Kuniya and Liru, two ancestral rainbow serpents – you'll also learn about the food and medicine plants found along the way. Anangu Tours does guided walks daily (two hours, 4 pm – later in summer). Its self-drive option costs $39 ($29 children)

Climbing Uluru Those climbing Uluru should take care – there have been numerous deaths resulting from falls and heart attacks. In warm weather drink plenty of water and do the climb early in the morning. The climb is actually closed between 10 am and 4 pm on days when the forecast temperature exceeds 38°C, and at times of heavy rain or strong winds.

The climb itself is 1.6km and takes about two hours up and back, with a good rest at the top. The first part is the steepest and most arduous, and many would-be climbers – suddenly becoming aware of how unfit they are and how steep the rock is – wisely choose not to continue. It's often very windy on top, even if conditions are calm on the ground, so make sure your hat is tied on.

It's important to realise that it goes against local Aboriginal beliefs to climb the Rock. In fact, the park's traditional owners would prefer it if you didn't.

Walks at Kata Tjuta The main walking trail is a scenic 6km loop (2½ to four hours) via the aptly-named Valley of the Winds. It's not particularly arduous, but there is some scrambling – be prepared with drinking water and sun protection. Another walk (50 minutes) takes you into Walpa (Olga Gorge). ■

The resort, which includes a camping ground, has hotels that are like any luxury international hotel anywhere. Between them, the camping ground, the Emu Walk Apartments, the Outback Pioneer Hotel, the Desert Gardens Hotel and the Sails in the Desert Hotel can accommodate 5000 people a day, at varying levels of luxury.

Fuel, limited repairs and supplies are available at Yulara, and you can really go overboard on the souvenirs.

Yulara to Warburton (565km)

Pulling out of Yulara, turn left as if heading to the Rock, but 8km down the road, take the turn-off to Kata Tjuta and Docker River.

Heading west, **Kata Tjuta (the Olgas)** dominates the skyline and as you get closer it takes on more and more character. You really should have spent a day exploring there before striking west, but if not, try to make time to stop for an hour before continuing on. With the bulk of Mt Olga off to the right, turn left onto the dirt road at the junction 49km from Yulara.

Irving Creek, where Lasseter died, is crossed 83km further west, and 100m past the crossing, a track on the right leads 750m to a hand-operated water pump. Shaw Creek is crossed 26km further on, while just 9km past Shaw Creek the Churnside Creek is crossed. Neither is any problem.

As you come up to the eastern bank of the **Hull River**, 191km from Yulara, there is a track junction and parking area on your left. You are allowed to camp here. A walking track leads a short distance along the creek to a cave. This is **Lasseter's Cave** where Lasseter waited vainly for rescue. A monument nearby tells the story. You might be lucky enough to see this area when there is water in the Hull. With all the comforts of modern travel and a brew cooking over a small wood fire, it's a pleasant spot. Lasseter probably thought otherwise.

Fourteen km further west, the road begins to pass through an area clothed in desert oaks, and the scenery, with the Petermanns in the background, is spectacular.

The road enters **Docker River Aboriginal community** 26km further on, and a short distance later the service station and store are off to your left. Fuel and limited supplies are available here.

The **Sandy Blight Junction Road** leaves the main road 26km west of Docker River and heads north. Our route veers to the left, keeping to the main road. After a couple of creek crossings a signpost on the left, 13km past the junction, indicates you are at Giles' **Schwerin Mural Crescent**. The panorama of range country around you is magnificent.

At the T-junction 36km past the Schwerin Mural Crescent sign, turn right onto the original Gunbarrel Highway, now heading west towards Giles. Left also takes you along the original Gunbarrel back into South Australia, but you need special permission to travel that route.

Twenty-nine km further on, you come to the **Warakurna Roadhouse** where you can camp, have a meal, refuel and top up with water.

The turn-off to **Giles weather station** is less than 500m west of the roadhouse. This station plays an important part in the forecasting of Australia's weather and is hooked up to the world meteorological network, but was originally established to check on wind conditions before and during the atomic blasts at Emu and Maralinga. With advance permission you can visit the station.

Continuing west along the Gunbarrel for another 16km brings you to where the original Gunbarrel veers off to the right. This is a definite 4WD route and you need a special permit to travel it.

The original Gunbarrel Highway swings along the southern ramparts of the Rawlinson Range and comes to a Len Beadell marked tree, 84km from the junction. Off to the north is Lake Christopher, which is the closest known point to the gold reef that Lasseter talked about.

Another 13km along this route sees you at another marked tree. For the next 163km the road alternates from chopped-up to quite sandy, as it swings further and further south. At Jackie Junction, 276km from the Warakurna Roadhouse, you need to turn

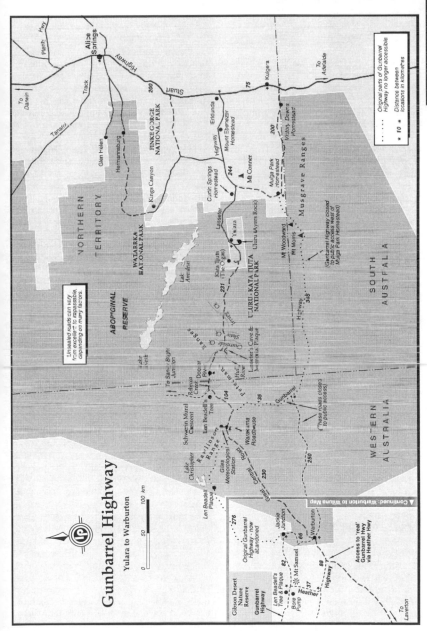

Gunbarrel Highway

Yulara to Warburton

Original parts of Gunbarrel Highway no longer accessible

Distance between locations in kilometres

★ 10 ★

Unsealed roads can vary from excellent to impassable, depending on many factors.

NORTHERN TERRITORY

ABORIGINAL RESERVE

SOUTH AUSTRALIA

WESTERN AUSTRALIA

Musgrave Ranges

FINKE GORGE NATIONAL PARK

WATARRKA NATIONAL PARK

ULURU – KATA TJUTA NATIONAL PARK

Alice Springs

Glen Helen

Hermannsburg

Kings Canyon

Lake Amadeus

Kata Tjuta (The Olgas)

Yulara

Uluru (Ayers Rock)

Curtin Springs Homestead

Mt Conner

Mulga Park Homestead

Victory Downs Homestead

Mt Woodward

Mt Morris

Erldunda

Mount Ebenezer Homestead

Kulgera

To Adelaide

To Darwin

Stuart Highway

Stuart Highway

Plenty Hwy

Tanami Track

Lasseter Highway

Highway

Lasseter's Cave & Australia Plaque

Petermann Ranges

Petermann River

Hull River

Docker River

Shaw Cr

Irving Cr

Olia Cr

Lake Christopher

Lake Hopkins

To Sandy Blight Junction

Len Beadell Plaque

Schwerin Mural Crescent

Ian Beadell's Tree

Rebecca Creek

Docker River

Warakurna Roadhouse

Rawlinson Range

Giles Meteorological Station

Gunbarrel

(These roads closed to public access)

(Gunbarrel Highway closed to public access west of Mulga Park Homestead)

Central Road

Gunbarrel Highway

Gibson Desert Nature Reserve

Len Beadell's Tree & Plaque

Original Gunbarrel Highway – now abandoned

Jackie Junction

Mt Samuel

Bore Pump

Heather

Warburton

Access to 'real' Gunbarrel Hwy via Heather Hwy

Highway

To Laverton

▲ Continued: Warburton to Wiluna Map

200

75

200

244

231

235

104

365

250

230

276

82

66

88

117

0   50   100 km

right (west). Continuing south will take you to the Warburton Aboriginal community, 66km away.

Heading west from Jackie Junction, cross the Todd Range, passing just to the south of Mt Charles. There is a lookout and a cairn on the top of Mt Samuel, which is on the left 76km from Jackie Junction. After another 6km you will meet the Heather Highway coming in from your left. This is the main used route which heads north from the Warburton-Laverton Road to join the 'real' Gunbarrel at this point.

From the junction with the old Gunbarrel, head south-west along the Warburton road; the going is relatively easy, although the corrugations can be wicked. As you approach the **Warburton Aboriginal community** the road swings hard right, leading you past the centre of town and to the Warburton Roadhouse on the right side of the road, 214km from the junction, or 230km from the Warakurna Roadhouse. There is accommodation and a nice camping area.

Warburton to Carnegie Station (486km)

The Heather Highway turns off the Warburton-Laverton road 41km south-west of the community and here you need to turn right. At a T-junction 47km past this major turn-off, turn right, and 37km later the rough old Gunbarrel comes in on the right at a junction where you turn left to head for Carnegie and Wiluna.

A large gum tree, marked by Len Beadell in 1958 and sporting a plaque, is on the right, 11km west of the junction. Less than 300m past the tree, a track off to the left leads 800m to a hand pump and water. It might not be brilliant, but if you were dying of thirst you'd love it.

Camp Beadell, 49km west of Beadell's tree, is a couple of hundred metres off to the left of the road. If you want a large, cleared area for a group camp, this could be it. A hill on the left and a track to it, 6km after the turn-off to Camp Beadell, brings you to **Mt Beadell**, with a monument to Len Beadell and good views of the surrounding country. Twenty-five km later you pass into the

Gibson Desert Nature Reserve. Passing through the Browne Range, another 25km on, the red bluff of **Mt Everard** is on the left. Just 6km further along the road is a major road junction – Everard Junction. At this point you're on a flat plain that is covered in spinifex all round, with scrub in the distance. The Browne Range rises to the east and the Young Range can be seen to the north-east. The Gunbarrel stretches away to the west.

The road north is the **Gary Highway**, which leads to the Canning Stock Route. A Len Beadell plaque can be found on the left. See the section on the 'Bomb Roads' later in this chapter for more details on this route.

You will pass out of the Gibson Desert Nature Reserve 31km from the junction with the Gary Highway. One km later is the Geraldton Historical Society Bore on your left, 150m off the road. The water isn't nice, but it's drinkable.

The sign denoting the boundary of the **Mungali Claypan Nature Reserve** is passed 48km further on, while the claypan itself is crossed just a little over 4km later. Seven km from the eastern boundary of the Mungali Reserve, you cross the western boundary, and just before that you will have passed through a junction with **Eagle Road**.

By now the road has improved as the Wiluna Shire grades it to a point around here. For the next 75km or so the Gunbarrel continues westward and is pretty good, although it can be washed out or rough in places. Sandhill country is met once again 85km from the western boundary sign of the Mungali Reserve; the road is sandy but it is no problem for a 4WD.

Just before you get to the turn-off to **Carnegie station**, you can see the station on your left, with the track junction a short distance later, 67km from first striking the sand ridge country and 486km from Warburton. At Carnegie you can buy fuel and limited supplies, camp, and even stay in the shearers' quarters. This is the end of the 'real' Gunbarrel, where Len and his men finished making their road across central Australia. For most travellers the trip continues westward for another 350km to Wiluna.

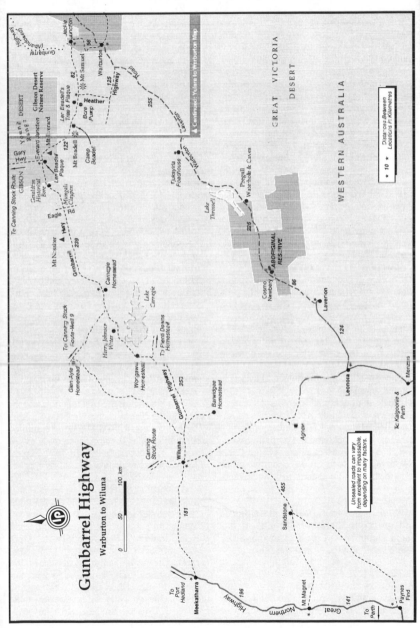

Gunbarrel Highway

Warburton to Wiluna

0   50   100 km

* 10 *   Distances Between
         Locations in Kilometres

Unsealed roads can vary
from excellent to impassable,
depending on many factors.

◄ Continued: Yulara to Warburton Map

GREAT VICTORIA DESERT

WESTERN AUSTRALIA

ABORIGINAL RESERVE

Jackie Junction
56
Mt Samuel
Warburton
82
125 Warburton Highway
Heather
Len Beadell's Tree Plaque
Bore (Pump)
255
Mt Everard
Everard Junction
Gibson Desert Nature Reserve
GIBSON DESERT
Young Range
122
Mt Beadell
Camp Beadell
Len Beadell Plaque
Geraldton Historical Bore
Gary Hwy
To Canning Stock Route
Mungali Claypan
Mangai Rd
Eagle Hwy
Mt Nossiter
239
Gunbarrel
Carnegie Homestead
Lake Carnegie
Tjukayirla Roadhouse
Warburton Road
Peegull Waterhole & Caves
Lake Throssell
226
Cosmo Newbery
86
Laverton
124
To Canning Stock Route-Well 9
Harry Johnson Water
Glen-Ayle Homestead
To Plenti Downs Homestead
Worgawa Homestead
Gunbarrel Highway 350
Banwidgee Homestead
Agnew
Leonora
Menzies
To Kalgoorlie & Perth
Canning Stock Route
Wiluna
181
Sandstone
455
To Port Hedland
Meekatharra
196
Northern Highway
Mt Magnet
Great
141
Paynes Find
To Perth
Gunbarrel Hwy (Abandoned)

Carnegie to Wiluna (350km)

Heading west from Carnegie, the road is formed dirt and generally in better condition than the Gunbarrel. A Y-junction 30km from the station is where those travellers heading for the Canning Stock Route at Well 9 must veer right. The track north goes via Glen-Ayle station for 45km to the stock route. Our route westward to Wiluna is via the left fork.

Continuing towards Wiluna, the road swings more in a southerly direction. At **Harry Johnson Water**, on the right 69km from Carnegie, there's a campsite near the water, and a picnic table, shelter and barbecue.

The road continues to swing south, at one stage skirting the north-western extremity of the salt lake known as **Lake Carnegie**. The turn-off to Wongawol station homestead is on your left, 97km west of the Glen-Ayle turn-off. The station, which has no facilities for travellers, is also on your left.

Heading almost due south, the road passes the turn-off to Prenti Downs on the left, 28km south of Wongawol. The road begins to swing more westerly, and 164km from Wongawol the turn-off to Barwidgee station is on the left. Another 16km further on is a track off to the right which leads north to Glen-Ayle station.

The small community of **Wiluna** is entered another 43km west, 350km west of Carnegie station. For all intents and purposes this town is the end of the road. For travellers, there is the choice of heading north up the Canning Stock Route; continuing westwards 181km to Meekatharra on the Great Northern Highway; or swinging south for 455km through Sandstone to Paynes Find, itself 424km north of Perth on the Great Northern Highway

Wiluna can supply fuel, limited repairs and groceries. For more details on this outback community, see the Canning Stock Route section in the North-West chapter.

ALTERNATIVE ROUTES
Warburton-Laverton Road

Instead of taking the real Gunbarrel west, the shortest distance to Perth and the south-west of Western Australia from central Australia is via the Warburton-Laverton road. The distance between these two communities is 567km and it is all dirt. Allow seven to eight hours as an average driving time.

How long it's been since the graders were last out will determine how bad this run is. It can be badly corrugated and a bit sandy in places, but is still generally passable in a normal car with sufficient ground clearance if driven with care, and if it hasn't rained.

The Route From Warburton, head out on the road west, but at the road junction 41km from the community, keep left towards Laverton, leaving the real Gunbarrel to 4WDs.

The run south is uneventful, through typical desert country. **Tjukayirla Roadhouse** (☎ (08) 9037 1108) is passed about 255km south of Warburton. Here you can get all fuels as well as tyres and tubes, and limited food supplies. Accommodation, camping and powered sites are available.

As you approach a large salt lake called Lake Throssell, visible on your right, the **Peegull Waterhole and caves** are on your left, 336km from Warburton.

The first turn-off to **Cosmo Newbery** is struck 138km further on, and a second road leads the same way a few kilometres later. This Aboriginal community has no facilities for the traveller.

Some 80km past the first junction into the community, you come to the bitumen. Turning left will take you to the mining community of Laverton, just 6km away; turning right will take you to Leonora, 118km further south-west.

ORGANISED TOURS

Nobody really runs tours of the Gunbarrel as a stand-alone destination. The highway is included in a number of operators' itineraries, including AAT King's Tour (☎ (03) 9274 7422 or freecall ☎ 1800 334 009), 29 Palmerston Crescent, South Melbourne, Vic 3205; Amesz Tour (☎ (08) 9250 2577), 4 Elmsfield Rd, Midvale, WA 6056; and Russell Guest's 4WD Safaris (☎ (03) 9481 5877), 38 Station St, Fairfield, Vic 3078. While all carry passengers, Amesz and

RICHARD I'ANSON

SHOOT

R & V MOON

Top: Uluru (Ayers Rock) from a distance, NT
Middle: Not another vehicle in sight, NT
Bottom: Convoy of 4WDs on the Sandy Blight Junction Road, NT

Beautiful wildflowers growing near Mereenie Loop Road, NT

Russell Guest's take people who drive their own vehicle as tag-alongs.

For a complete list of tour operators, contact the Western Australian Tourist Centre (☎ (08) 9483 1111).

FACILITIES

Don't expect fancy all-night supplies of fuel along the Gunbarrel – even at Yulara the service station closes around 7 pm. While most places have unleaded and super, at times some of them run out of unleaded, super, or both. Diesel seems to be more readily available.

Yulara, Warakurna, Carnegie and Wiluna are the most consistent suppliers of fuel and supplies along the route described.

Yulara

If you are camping and you want to stay and see Uluru (Ayers Rock), you have no option but to stay in the well set-up and expensive *camping ground* (☎ (08) 8956 2055) at the Ayers Rock Resort in Yulara. Prices range from $10 a night per person for a campsite ($6 extra for power per site) up to $96.60 per night for four people to stay in a cabin.

Elsewhere at the resort, you have a choice of various levels of luxury – for bookings at any of the following phone the Ayers Rock Resort (☎ 1800 089 622). The *Outback Pioneer Lodge* has beds in 20-bed dorms for $19, while private cabins that have a shared bathroom and sleep four cost $116 a night. In the same complex, the *Outback Pioneer Hotel* has more expensive units with bathroom for $256 plus 5% tax. The *Emu Walk Apartments* offer one and two-bedroom flats which accommodate four and eight people respectively and these cost $260 for the small apartments and $320 for the larger ones. Rooms at the *Desert Gardens Hotel* cost $286 plus 5% tax a double, while at the luxury *Sails in the Desert*, doubles are $350 plus 5% tax.

In the town square of Yulara you will find a small supermarket, takeaway outlets, a newsagency and a tavern.

The service station (☎ (08) 8956 2229) at the resort is next to the camping ground and has unleaded, super, diesel and LPG. Ice is also available, as are spare parts, tyre and mechanical repairs. It's the cheapest fuel you'll see until Wiluna.

Vehicles can be hired from Avis (☎ (08) 8956 2266) and Territory Rent-a-Car (☎ (08) 8956 2030); although you can go anywhere, the vehicle must be returned to a company agent in the Northern Territory. That makes it a little difficult to head west to Wiluna, unless you want to come back as well.

For more information on the facilities, tours and nightlife offered by the resort, contact the Yulara visitor information centre (☎ (08) 8956 2240).

Docker River

This community has a service station that can supply petrol and diesel to passing travellers.

Warakurna Roadhouse

This roadhouse (☎ (08) 8956 7344) is just a short distance from the Giles weather station. Unleaded, diesel and Avgas are available, as are a range of limited supplies and garage repair facilities. A camping ground offers powered/unpowered sites for $12/8 a night while a couple of motel rooms start at $80 a night and sleep three.

Warburton

This large Aboriginal community has the *Warburton Roadhouse* (☎ (08) 8956 7656), with unleaded and diesel fuel as well as Avgas. Camping on the green grass costs $6 per person for a powered site and $5 per person for an unpowered one. A choice of accommodation is available, with self contained motel rooms sleeping two for $90; twin rooms with communal facilities at $70; and budget rooms for $35 a double, $20 a single per night.

Carnegie Station

Carnegie station (☎ (08) 9981 2991) can supply unleaded, super and diesel. It's a good place to camp – green lawns fed by the near unlimited water, hot showers, and hospitality. Camping costs $8 per person per night, while the cabins cost $15, and there are cooking facilities provided. Souvenirs, general food supplies, cool drinks and the like are all you can expect. Emergency repairs are also available.

Wiluna

This is the biggest and best-equipped supply centre you will have seen since leaving Yulara. It has everything you need to keep you going, including food, fuel, general supplies, accommodation and camping.

For details on Wiluna, see the section on the Canning Stock Route in the North-West chapter.

ALTERNATIVE TRANSPORT

Getting to Uluru (Ayers Rock) and the Yulara Resort is relatively easy. It is serviced by air and by bus from Alice Springs with connections to anywhere in Australia from there. Air services include both Ansett and Qantas from all over Australia, with charter flights from Alice Springs as well. The bus service is Greyhound Pioneer Australia.

Beyond the resort, any form of travel, unless it's on an organised tour, is much more difficult. While once there was a bus service that ran between Perth and Uluru (Ayers Rock) using the Laverton-Warburton road, this is not running at present. For the latest information, contact the Western Australian Tourist Centre (☎ (08) 9483 1111).

'Bomb Roads'

HIGHLIGHTS

- Experiencing the extremely remote ever-changing desert country
- Driving along the desert-oak lined Sandy Blight Junction Road

The 'Bomb Roads' cover the desert country of western South Australia and adjoining Western Australia, north of the *Indian-*

Pacific railway line. They were constructed by Len Beadell in the 1950s to provide an infrastructure for the Woomera rocket tests and Emu A-bomb tests. In all, there are over 6000km of desert tracks, the most important being the east-west Gunbarrel Highway. While the Gunbarrel was the first link across central Australia from east to west, others followed, and with an interconnecting grid of north-south roads, this region is a favourite for desert-lovers and 4WD adventurers.

ANNE BEADELL HIGHWAY

This highway runs from Coober Pedy west via the atomic bomb test site of Emu, through Vokes Hill Junction and across the Western Australia/South Australia border into Western Australia, crossing the north-south Connie Sue Highway at Neale Junction. Continuing westward, the Anne Beadell passes through the Yeo Lakes region before reaching Yamarna station and from here it is station tracks to the mining community of Laverton.

For nearly the entire way, the track is sandy and often very narrow. Staking a tyre in the scrub country is a definite possibility. The route is easier than the Canning or the Simpson, as it rarely crosses any sand ridges, however, it is extremely remote – even over the cooler winter months, travellers are few and far between.

It's 1342km from Coober Pedy to Laverton, so you will need to carry a fair amount of fuel.

Permits

To do this trip on your own you will need a number of permits, as the track traverses Aboriginal land, Department of Defence land around Emu and a conservation park.

Permission to cross Mabel Downs station (tel/fax (08) 8672 5204) is also required – contact the manager, PO Box 450, Coober Pedy, SA 5690.

Permission to enter the area around Emu can be obtained from the Area Administration Office, Defence Support Centre (☎ (08) 8674 3370; fax 8674 3308), PO Box 157, Woomera, SA 5720.

To traverse Aboriginal land, you need to contact the Maralinga-Tjarutja Council in Ceduna – see the Travel Permits section of the earlier Getting Around chapter.

The Unnamed Conservation Park in the far west of South Australia is managed by the Dept of Environment and Natural Resources and a permit is required to enter and camp in the park. Contact the department's far west regional office (☎ (08) 8625 3144; fax 8625 3123) at PO Box 569, Ceduna, SA 5690.

The Route

From Coober Pedy, head west towards Mabel Creek on what is a good station track. The 50km run will take just over an hour.

The track to Emu passes a shearing shed 16km from **Mabel Downs homestead** and soon becomes a track, first across gibber country, then in between sand ridges. The Dog Fence is passed at the 102km mark, with the not-to-be-relied-upon Tallaringa Well just off to the left of the road at the 157km point. The 235km drive to Emu from the station will take between five and six hours.

At **Emu** there is little left from the atomic-test days. The sites where the bombs were let off, known as Totem I and Totem II, are 15km east of the actual township and landing ground that was Emu. A crossroads marks the spot. Turning to the left will take you to the low rise where the official 'viewing area' for the blasts was; turning to the right will take you to the actual bomb sites. A few bits of twisted steel and a small depression in the landscape, along with a concrete monument, mark the two spots where the bombs, on tall steel towers, were detonated. Take heed of the radioactivity warning signs around the area.

The airstrip at Emu is occasionally used by mining companies, and there are a few tracks around the old town site, so make sure you are on the right one. When coming from Mabel Downs, the airstrip is off to the right; you do a dogleg to the left then to the right, to get onto the main track west.

The 153km from Emu to Vokes Hill Junction takes between five and six hours on what is a much less used track. About 50km from

Emu a track veers off to the right. This leads into prohibited Aboriginal land – definitely no entry. Keep on the main track west, passing between a long line of dunes covered in spinifex and mulga or low acacia scrub with the occasional stand of mallee. You enter the Unnamed Conservation Park about 124km from the road junction at Emu.

From **Vokes Hill Junction** it is 175km (five hours) to the Western Australia/South Australia border. The road south from the junction leads 250km through Aboriginal land to the small railway siding of Cook, on the *Indian-Pacific* railway line. Heading westward, the track remains much the same as before, and you know you are getting close to the state border when you begin to cross the long, thin expanse of the salt-encrusted **Serpentine Lakes**.

West from the border the track begins to swing north-west and, in the process, begins to cross a few sand ridges before again turning west and running between the east-west dunes. From the border to **Neale Junction**, at the crossroads with the Connie Sue Highway, it is 348km, which should take you between nine and 10 hours. The area from 45km east to 23km west of the Connie Sue Highway junction is proclaimed as the **Neale Junction Nature Reserve**.

From Neale Junction to Yamarna station, it is 235km (about six hours). Around **Lake Yeo** you pass into another nature reserve. There are a few tracks through this region – stick to the main one, which tends to swing north of west, passing through the Pitcher Range and then the rugged mesa country of the Morton Craig Range. The ruins of Yeo station are passed 165km from the junction. As you get closer to **Yamarna station**, 70km further on, the efforts of the gold mining company which owns this property will be evident as there are tracks seemingly in all directions.

From the station, which you pass close to, the road condition improves, and the last 146km to Laverton takes just 1½ hours.

There's fuel and accommodation available at **Laverton** as well as accommodation, a camping ground, and a couple of stores

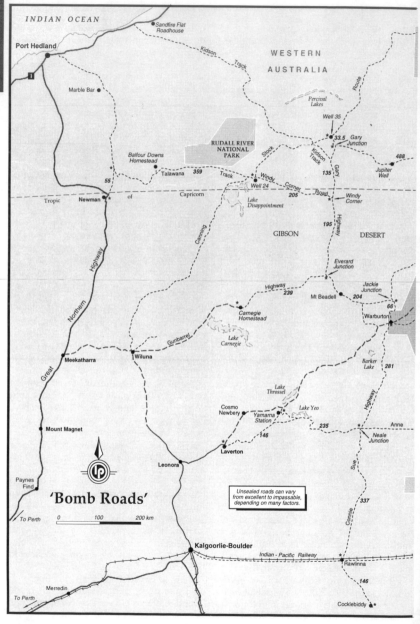

INDIAN OCEAN

Port Hedland

Sandfire Flat
Roadhouse

Kidson   Track

WESTERN

AUSTRALIA

Route

Marble Bar

Percival
Lakes

Well 35

33.5   Gary
Junction

RUDALL RIVER
NATIONAL
PARK

Stock

488

Balfour Downs
Homestead

Talawana   359

Track

Windy
Well 24

Corner

135

Gary

Jupiter
Well

55

Tropic   of   Capricorn

Newman

Canning

Lake
Disappointment

205   Road

Windy
Corner

Highway

195

GIBSON   DESERT

Everard
Junction

Highway
239

Mt Beadell

Jackie
Junction

204   66

Northern

Carnegie
Homestead

Warburton

Meekatharra

Wiluna

Gunbarrel

Lake
Carnegie

Barker
Lake   281

Highway

Great

Lake
Throssel

Mount Magnet

Cosmo
Newbery

Yamarna
Station

Lake Yeo

146

235

Anne

Neale
Junction

Highway

Leonora

Laverton

Sue

Paynes
Find

'Bomb Roads'

0   100   200 km

Unsealed roads can vary
from excellent to impassable,
depending on many factors.

Connie

337

To Perth

Kalgoorlie-Boulder

Indian - Pacific Railway

Rawlinna

146

Merredin

To Perth

Cocklebiddy

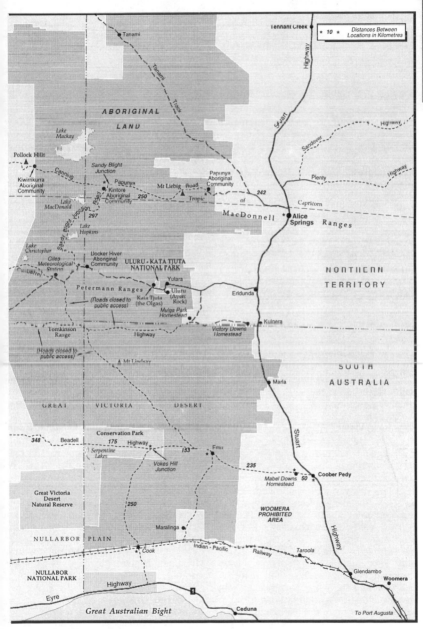

supplying most requirements. From here you can head south on bitumen via Leonora to Kalgoorlie (360km away), or north to Wiluna (a distance of about 400km, depending on which route you take).

CONNIE SUE HIGHWAY

The Connie Sue runs from the railway siding of Rawlinna north to Neale Junction (the intersection with the Anne Beadell Highway), then continues north to meet up with the main Laverton-Warburton Road just a few kilometres west of the Aboriginal community at Warburton. In all it is 618km from Rawlinna to Warburton, and another 66km to the junction with the Gunbarrel Highway.

Permits

To enter Warburton Aboriginal community, you will need a permit from the Aboriginal Affairs Department in Perth (see Travel Permits in the earlier Getting Around chapter).

The Route

Rawlinna, on the *Indian-Pacific* railway line, is 146km north-west of Cocklebiddy, which is 1240km from Perth along the Eyre Highway. While a number of people live at Rawlinna, there is no store to speak of, so don't expect to get fuel or supplies at this small outpost.

Cross the railway line and head for Seemore Downs, 30km north, and then north-east towards Premier Downs Outstation for about 27km. Just before you get to the ruins of the outstation you will come to a major road junction with the Connie Sue stretching away to the north: it's straight as an arrow, like many of Len Beadell's roads.

Once north of the treeless plain that is the Nullarbor, the country turns into arid grasslands dotted with trees, bordering the fringe of the Great Victoria Desert. It's a relatively easy drive for the next 280km to **Neale Junction**, but allow six hours for the trip. A couple of seemingly major sandy roads join and leave the route north but these lead to mining camps or Aboriginal communities, so don't be diverted on your way north. The

bulldust can be thick along these well used sections of track. There is a nice cleared area at the junction for camping, with plenty of room if your group consists of more than a couple of vehicles.

North of the intersection with the Anne Beadell Highway, the track becomes a little sandier and rougher, but is still generally no problem.

About 140km from the Neale Junction you pass into the **Baker Lake Nature Reserve**, named after a salt lake far off to the north-west of the track. The country is a little rockier through this next section, the road skirting such high points as Hanns Tabletop Hill, Skipper Knob and Point Brophy, before entering sandier country again north of Manton Knob, 210km north of the Anne Beadell Highway.

You leave the reserve 30km north of Manton Knob, passing through stands of majestic desert oak, and come to a Y-junction where you need to veer right to continue to Warburton. The left hand track will take you out to the Laverton-Warburton Road, meeting with it south of the Heather Highway junction. Continuing north from the Y-junction you meet the main Laverton-Warburton Road 35km later. Turning right at this point will take you into the **Warburton Aboriginal community**, just 6km along the main road, where you can get fuel and limited supplies.

From Warburton, the Connie Sue Highway continues north 66km to Jackie Junction and ends at the Gunbarrel Highway, but this stretch of the road is through an area of very restricted access and driving it requires special permission. Most travellers head north-east to Giles, Docker River and Uluru (Ayers Rock) on the major dirt road, or from Warburton they turn south-west towards Laverton, where 40km down the road they can head northwards and follow the Gunbarrel Highway through to Carnegie station.

GARY HIGHWAY

The Gary heads north from the Gunbarrel Highway to join up with the Canning Stock

Route at Well 35, before continuing west, as the Callawa Road, to a point north-east of Marble Bar. Since the Kidson Track was graded in 1963, Len's road west of the Canning has fallen into disuse. From the Gunbarrel to the Canning along the Gary Highway, it's 364km.

Permits
No permits are required to use this road.

The Route
The junction of the Gunbarrel and Gary highways, known as **Everard Junction**, is 10km west of the low mountain of the same name, 239km east of Carnegie station and 204km west of Jackie Junction, or 247km from Warburton Aboriginal community via the Heather Highway.

The area surrounding the junction and a vast area to the east is protected in the **Gibson Desert Nature Reserve**. As you head north from the Gunbarrel Highway, the Browne and Young ranges are to the east. Fourteen km north of the junction you pass Charlies Knob. The track is washed away in parts through this range country but, while slow going, is generally no problem.

After you leave the ranges, for the most part the track traverses a flat to slightly undulating plain covered in spinifex and dotted with small trees. It's a very easy run, with nary a sandhill in sight.

Lake Cohen, 84km north of Everard Junction and just to the west of the road, is normally a shallow dry lakebed, but occasionally it does fill with water. Then it is worthy of a camp, and a Mecca for bird life. Ducks, avocets and banded stilts vie with herons, native hens and coots for food in the shallow waters of the lake.

The road junction of **Windy Corner** is 195km north of Everard Junction, a drive of between four and five hours. There's a book to sign at the junction; it's not there for any particular safety reason but everybody seems to fill it in, telling all and sundry how their particular trip is going.

While the Gary Highway continues north, the Windy Corner road strikes west to the Canning Stock Route. For more details, see The Talawana Track-Windy Corner Road later in this section.

The Gary Highway heads across lightly rolling gibber plains for 73km, where a faint track to the east leads to **Veevers Crater**. This crater, 20km off the main track, is another meteorite impact crater. It is only 80m in diameter but is a near perfect circle, 7 to 8m deep.

A short distance later the Gary Highway passes through a 10km-wide swath of sand-ridge country that has the road twisting and turning. Soon, however, it's back into more open country. Twelve km further on, 105km north of Windy Corner, the Kidson Track joins the Gary Highway from the west. This track heads west 65km to join the Canning Stock Route just south of Well 33.

Gary Junction, 30km further north, is 135km (nearly three hours) north of Windy Corner and 330km north of the Gunbarrel Highway. This is where the Gary Highway turns hard left and strikes out for the Canning Stock Route. At Gary Junction you'll find a Beadell plaque on top of a fuel drum: turn right for Alice Springs or left to the Canning.

After passing through another strip of sand-ridge country, and 33.5km beyond Gary Junction, another junction on the right is met. You are now on the main Canning Stock Route. Going straight ahead leads to Well 35, 14km away, while turning right will lead to Well 36 and on to Halls Creek. The drive from Gary Junction to Well 35 will take two to three hours.

SANDY BLIGHT JUNCTION ROAD
This road through the desert country of central Australia strikes north from the Gunbarrel Highway at a point 27km west of Docker River Aboriginal community and finishes at Sandy Blight Junction, nearly 300km north and close to Kintore Aboriginal community. The drive will take you between six and seven hours. From here you are just 500km west of Alice Springs.

Built by Len Beadell, and named after he experienced a particularly bad bout of this desert scourge, the Sandy Blight Road is a relatively easy run north. For most of the way it crosses sandy country, and where it does traverse sand ridges they are generally pretty small and present no problem.

For much of the way the road passes through quite dense stands of desert oak, and these make this drive magnificent.

Permits

You require permits from the Central Lands Council in Alice Springs to traverse this road – see the Travel Permits section in the Getting Around chapter.

The Route

Docker River Aboriginal community, 231km west of Yulara along the Gunbarrel Highway, can supply fuel and limited supplies.

The Gunbarrel Highway around Docker River passes through some of the most spectacular country in central Australia. Travel down this road in the early morning or late afternoon and you will be impressed with the colours and the surrounding ranges.

The junction of the Sandy Blight Road is 26.5km west of Docker River. Veering right off the highway, the road parallels Rebecca Creek and passes the western end of the Anne Range, 13km north of the junction. Fourteen km further on, with the Walter James Range off to the west, there is a track that leads to **Bungabiddy Rockhole**, deep within the range. It's a nice spot and popular with the locals.

The road continues north, and while it can be a little washed out, it is generally fairly easy, but slow, travelling.

Past the track junction to the Aboriginal community at Tjukurla, 66km north of the Gunbarrel, the track swings around the western end of the salty Lake Hopkins, and the first of the sand ridges are crossed 17km further on.

A large desert oak, 143km from Docker River, has an original Len Beadell plaque on it, and a further 53km north another large oak on the right bears one of Len's plaques.

From here the road crosses sand-ridge country and passes through the Sir Frederick Range. The Northern Territory/Western Australia border, with a log blazed by Len on the left, is 203km north of the junction and 230km from Docker River.

From the border the road heads almost due east for 25km, before heading north again and crossing the **Tropic of Capricorn**, 251km north of the Gunbarrel. You'll find yet another Len Beadell plaque and marker at this spot.

Heading on, the horizon is dominated by the bulk of the **Kintore Range**; Mt Leisler (901m) is the highest point around for quite some way. At the far north of the range is Mt Strickland. It's a magnificent scene – one to which your eyes are drawn time and again.

Tietkins Tree, an old, dead tree, blazed by the explorer William Tietkins in 1889, stands below the bluff of Mt Leisler, beside the road 18km north of the Tropic.

With the Kintore Range rearing up to your left, it is a pleasant 28km to the end of the road at Sandy Blight Junction. Turning right at this junction will lead finally to Alice Springs; turning left takes you back into Western Australia and to the Canning Stock Route (see the following section for more details).

CANNING-PAPUNYA ROAD

This road is one of the few that wasn't named by Len, although the section west from Gary Junction to the Canning Stock Route is really part of the Gary Highway. Between Sandy Blight Junction and Gary Junction, Len called the road the Gary Junction Highway, but it is one of the few names that has neither stuck nor been officially recognised. The route east to Mt Liebig was just a minor connecting road.

Built between 1960 and 1962, this road gives access west from Alice Springs to Well 35 on the Canning Stock Route, via Papunya, Sandy Blight Junction, Jupiter Well and Gary Junction.

All up, the distance between the Canning and Alice is 1014km. Like most of Len's roads, this one traverses the easiest country possible. In only a couple of places does it cross sandhills, the rest of the time running down the valleys between the dunes.

Permits

Permits from the Central Land Council in Alice Springs are required for travel west of Papunya to the border – see the Travel Permits section in the Getting Around chapter.

The Route

From Alice Springs the route heads north along the Stuart Highway for 20km, then turns west along the Tanami Track to the Papunya turn-off, 137km from Alice. This is where the bitumen ends; the next 105km to **Papunya** is good dirt. The total travelling time from Alice is two to three hours.

Between Papunya and Kintore Aboriginal communities the road deteriorates slightly, but is still relatively good, well-maintained dirt. Fifty km west of Papunya, off to your left, you will see **Mt Liebig**, the highest peak at the western end of the Amunurungara Range. At this point the road begins to follow Len's route west.

As you begin to approach the Henty Hills and the Ehrenberg Ranges, around the 100km mark, the first of the sandhills begin to appear. The road continues to be sandy, and can deteriorate to the point where it is 4WD only.

Sandy Blight Junction is 250km west of Papunya, and nearby is the Aboriginal community of **Kintore**. The main access to this community, where you can get fuel and limited supplies, is 17km west of the junction. The drive from Papunya to Kintore takes about three hours.

Beyond Kintore the road improves a little and is usually in fair condition. The Western Australia/Northern Territory border is crossed 42km further west, and 170km from Sandy Blight you see the remains of **Len's burnt-out ration truck** on the right side of the road. The story is told in Len's book *Beating About the Bush*.

Just 16km further on you come to the **Kiwirrkurra Aboriginal community**, probably the most remote community in all

Australia. Fuel and limited supplies are available here, but only if you have been in contact with the Kiwirrkurra community first (store ☎ (08) 8956 8615). The trip from Sandy Blight Junction to Kiwirrkurra will take between two and three hours.

To continue to the Canning Stock Route, head west out of town and past the airport. The road quickly becomes a sandy track, showing a definite lack of maintenance. In places it has been washed away and a new track skirts the original. In other spots the sand along the road can be deep, forcing you to crawl along in second gear for kilometre after kilometre. It chews the fuel! Occasionally the track crosses a sandhill, but this shouldn't cause you any problems.

Jupiter Well is found in a magnificent stand of desert oak 327km west of Sandy Blight and about five hours' drive west of Kiwirrkurra. There's an Aboriginal community outstation beside the track just before you get there. No fuel or supplies are available, and don't rely on getting water here either.

Gary Junction and the highway running south are found 161km (about five hours) further west, where you will find a Len Beadell plaque. Continuing westward, you reach Well 35 on the Canning Stock Route. See the earlier section on the Gary Highway for more details.

TALAWANA TRACK-WINDY CORNER ROAD

The last road built by Len and his men, this track heads west from Windy Corner on the Gary Highway to Western Australia's Pilbara region. Travelling via Well 24 and Well 23 on the Canning Stock Route, it is today the main route by which the centre of the Canning is accessed from the west.

Permits

No permits are required to travel this road.

The Route

The Windy Corner Road runs 205km from the Gary Highway to the Canning Stock

Route just a couple of kilometres north of Well 24. The drive takes five to six hours.

For the first 70km the track passes across undulating, gravelly country covered with spinifex. After that, the road begins to pass between low sandhills, but the going is pretty easy. Just over 40km from Windy Corner the road skirts the **Connolly Basin**, an ancient, eroded meteorite-impact crater some 9km in diameter.

The track continues west, and 96km from Windy Corner a drum on the right marks the approximate position of the **Tropic of Capricorn**. Early in the season, when the area has received good rainfall and the spinifex is seeding, the seed stems can be over 1m tall, with seeds so thick in the air that they block up radiators in minutes and make it very difficult to keep engines cool. At one spot the track passes the burnt-out shell of an old Land Rover – obviously one that didn't survive.

The track joins with the Canning Stock Route 205km west of Windy Corner. The route west from here will take you along the Canning to a point 22km south of Well 23. **Well 23** is where most Canning travellers pick up the fuel that has been prearranged and dumped there for their use. Please don't use any that is not yours – a life could easily be lost for such thievery.

The 39km from where the Windy Corner Road meets the Canning Stock Route to the point where you leave the Canning and head west on the Talawana Track is a pretty easy run, taking less than two hours.

West of the Canning, the Talawana Track skirts the southern boundary of the **Rudall River National Park**, a vast area of desert country surrounding the ephemeral Rudall River and the salt lakes of Lake Dora and Lake Blanche. You pass the turn off to Cotton Creek Aboriginal community 60km after leaving the Canning and the country changes between sand dunes and spinifex-covered plains and back again.

Talawana, 205km west of the Canning, is now no more than a water tank on the edge of the track, and from here the main track continues for another 32km to a junction where you need to turn left. Right leads to **Balfour Downs**, a remote cattle station that has no facilities for travellers. Heading south and then west on station tracks for 115km will bring you to the old Northern Highway. The run from the Canning to this junction takes six to seven hours.

You are about 55km (40 minutes) north of the mining community of **Newman**, (where you'll find all the fuel and other supplies you could need) and the bitumen of the Great Northern Highway.

The South

From western New South Wales across South Australia to the eastern fringes of the south-west of Western Australia, 'The South' takes in a vast sweep of semi-arid saltbush and scrub plain that is in the main, flat! Only through the heart of South Australia does a line of spectacular hill country, the Flinders Ranges, provide a different vista to the long straight roads and distant level horizons.

Much of the region is pastoral country with the properties, mainly sheep stations, taking up huge areas. Often the only sign of human habitation are kilometres of straggly wire fences, slowly turning windmills bringing their nectar of water to the surface and the occasional silver galvanised roof of a homestead, glinting in the unrelenting sun. Towns (even small ones) are generally few and far between; the only one of any real significance in the area covered here is the mining centre of Broken Hill.

Distances between towns, although still measured in hundreds of kilometres, aren't as great as other areas of the outback. In the far west of South Australia and across into Western Australia the pastoral land gives way to the spinifex and sand ridges of the Great Victoria Desert. In this region too, the outback meets the sea but the meeting is not a gentle one. Beaches are few; the arc of the Great Australian Bight is mostly an unbroken line of cliffs where the flat Nullarbor Plain plunges into the Southern Ocean.

Eyre Highway

HIGHLIGHTS

- Driving or walking along the beaches of the Great Australian Bight near Eyre Bird Observatory

- Exploring the caves and the lonely expanses of the Nullarbor Plain

- Visiting the old telegraph repeater and weather station in the sandhills near Eucla

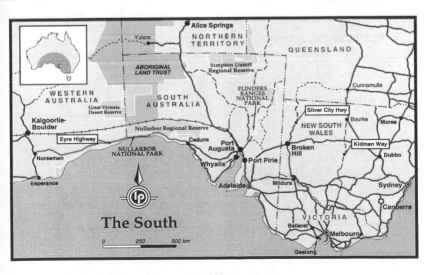

The South

0   250   500 km

Ask most Australians what they think the ultimate road trip is and they will answer 'crossing the Nullarbor'. It's more than 2700km from Perth to Adelaide – not much less than the distance from London to Moscow.

The long and sometimes lonely Eyre Highway crosses the southern edge of the vast Nullarbor Plain. Nullarbor is bad Latin for 'no tree', but though there is a small stretch where you indeed see no trees at all, the road is actually flanked by trees for most of the way, as this coastal fringe receives regular rain, especially in winter.

The surfaced road runs close to the coast on the South Australian side. The Nullarbor region ends dramatically on the coast of the Great Australian Bight, at cliffs that drop steeply into the ocean. It's easy to see why this was a seafarer's nightmare, for a ship driven onto the coast would quickly be pounded to pieces against the cliffs, and climbing them would be a near impossibility.

The *Indian-Pacific* railway runs on the actual Nullarbor Plain, unlike the main road, which only fringes the great plain. One stretch of the railway runs dead straight for 478km – the longest piece of straight (though not flat) railway line in the world.

HISTORY

The highway across the Nullarbor takes its name from John Eyre, the explorer who made the first east-west crossing in 1841. In 1877, a telegraph line was laid across the Nullarbor, roughly delineating the route the first road would take.

Later in the century, miners en route to the gold fields followed the telegraph line across the Nullarbor. In 1896 the first bicycle crossing was made. In 1912 the first car was driven across, but in the next 12 years only three more cars managed to complete the route.

In 1941, the war inspired the building of a transcontinental highway, just as it had the Alice Springs-Darwin route. It was a rough-and-ready track when completed, and in the 1950s only a few vehicles a day made the crossing. In the 1960s, the traffic flow

increased to more than 30 vehicles a day, and in 1969 the Western Australian government surfaced the road as far as the South Australian border. Finally, in 1976, the last stretch from the South Australian border was surfaced, making the Nullarbor crossing a much easier drive, though still a long one.

INFORMATION
Tourist Offices

There's a tourist bureau in Norseman (☎ (08) 9039 0171), at the western end of the highway. It is at 68 Roberts St, and is open daily from 9 am to 5 pm. At the eastern end of the highway, the first tourist office is at Ceduna (☎ (08) 8625 2972), in Poynton St. In Port Augusta the Wadlata Outback Centre (☎ (08) 8642 4511), 41 Flinders Terrace, is also the tourist information centre.

All of the roadhouses have pamphlets relating to tourist sights in the area and to the towns nearby.

Permits

No permits are required to cross the Nullarbor, even though the Yalata Aboriginal Land is crossed at one stage. If you go off road, you will need a permit; contact the Yalata Roadhouse (☎ (086) 25 6990). A permit is also needed to bush camp in the Nullarbor National Park and Nullarbor Regional Reserve; contact the South Australia National Parks & Wildlife Service in Ceduna (☎ (086) 25 3144).

Books & Maps

There are a number of helpful publications which cover the Nullarbor. One of the most comprehensive is the free *Hills Tourist Guide to Western Australia & the Eyre Highway*, available in Perth and Adelaide.

There are details about off-road options on either side of the sealed highway in Peter & Kim Wherrett's *Explore Australia by Four-Wheel Drive*. If you follow the highway, no special maps are required.

Radio Frequencies

If you should strike mechanical trouble, you're unlikely to have to wait long for another vehicle to pass by. For those with HF radios, the RFDS base at Port Augusta (call sign VNZ) monitors the following frequencies from 6 am to 9 pm daily: 2020, 4010, 6890 and 8165kHz. Kalgoorlie RFDS base (call sign VJQ) monitors 5360kHz from 8 am to 5 pm Monday to Friday and from 9 to 10 am on weekends.

SPECIAL PREPARATIONS

Although the Nullarbor is no longer a torture trail where cars get shaken to bits by potholes and corrugations, and where travellers marooned by breakdowns die of thirst waiting for another vehicle, it's still wise to avoid difficulties whenever possible.

The longest distance between fuel stops is about 200km, so if you're foolish enough to run out of fuel midway, you'll have a long trip to get more. The price of unleaded fuel, for example, is about five cents a litre more expensive in Cocklebiddy than in Norseman or Border Village; the variation in the price of other fuels is as marked.

Finding help in the event of a mechanical breakdown can be equally time-consuming and very expensive, so make sure your vehicle is in good shape and that you've got plenty of fuel, decent tyres at the right pressure and at least a basic kit of simple spare parts. Savvy motorcyclists fit a cheap rear tyre for the trip, as the centre of the tread will wear quite markedly.

Carry plenty of drinking water (4L per person), just in case you do have to sit it out by the roadside on a hot summer day. Remember, there are limited supplies of fresh water between Norseman and Ceduna.

There are no banks between Norseman and Ceduna, so take plenty of cash. All roadhouses, except Mundrabilla, have EFTPOS facilities, and most accept major credit cards.

Take it easy on the Nullarbor. Too many people try to set speed records, and plenty have made a real mess of their cars when they've run into big kangaroos, particularly at night. The police also pull out their radar guns every now and then, especially near the Western Australia/South Australia border.

THE ROUTE

From Norseman, where the Eyre Highway begins, it's 727km to the Western Australia/South Australia border, near Eucla, and a further 482km to Ceduna (from an Aboriginal word meaning 'a place to sit down and rest') in South Australia. From Ceduna, it's still another 783km to Adelaide via Port Augusta. It is, in the immortal words of a trans-Australian truck driver, 'a bloody long way'.

Norseman

Most people think of Norseman as just a crossroads where you turn east for the trans-Nullarbor journey, south to Esperance along the Leeuwin Way or north to Coolgardie, Kalgoorlie and Perth. The town, however, also has gold mines, some still in operation. The **Historical & Geological Collection** in the old School of Mines has items from the gold-rush days. It's open weekdays from 10 am to 4 pm; admission is $2.

You can get an excellent view of the town and over the surrounding salt lakes from the **Beacon Hill Mararoa Lookout**, down past the mountainous tailings.

Norseman to Cocklebiddy (440km)

From Norseman, the first settlement you'll reach is **Balladonia**, 191km to the east. After Balladonia, near the old station, you may see the remains of old stone fences built to enclose stock. Clay saltpans are also visible in the area. **Newmann's Rocks**, 50km west of Balladonia, are also well worth seeing. The Crocker family have a fine art gallery (☎ (08) 9039 3456), with paintings of the Eyre Highway. Phone between 9 am and 4.30 pm to arrange a visit.

The road from Balladonia to Cocklebiddy is a lonely section. To Caiguna, it includes one of the longest stretches of straight road in the world – 145km, the so-called 90-Mile Straight.

Caiguna, over 370km from Norseman, is a good place to stop. Some 10km south of Caiguna is the memorial to John Baxter, Eyre's companion, who was killed on 29 April 1841 by hostile Aborigines.

At Cocklebiddy there are the stone ruins of an old Aboriginal mission. **Cocklebiddy Cave** is the largest of the Nullarbor caves. In 1983 a team of French explorers set a new record here for the deepest cave dive in the world.

With a 4WD, you can travel south of Cocklebiddy to **Twilight Cove**, where there are 75m-high limestone cliffs, or to the **Eyre Bird Observatory** (see the later Detours section).

Cocklebiddy to Eucla (274km)

Ninety-three km east of Cocklebiddy is **Madura**, close to the hills of the Hampton Tablelands. At one time, horses were bred here for the Indian Army. You get good views over the plains from the road.

The ruins of the **Old Madura homestead**, several kilometres west of the new homestead by a dirt track, have some old machinery and other equipment. Caves in the area include the large **Mullamullang**

Caves, north-west of Madura, with three lakes and many side passages.

The **Mundrabilla Roadhouse** is on the lower coastal plain, with the Hampton Tablelands as a backdrop. From Mundrabilla it is 66km to Eucla or 79km to the border.

Eucla & the WA/SA Border

Just before the South Australian border is Eucla, which has picturesque ruins (just the chimneys stick out now) of an old **telegraph repeater & weather station**, first opened in 1877. The telegraph line now runs along the railway line, far to the north. The station, 5km from the roadhouse, is gradually being engulfed by the sand dunes. You can also inspect the historic jetty, which is visible from the top of the dunes. The dunes around Eucla are a truly spectacular sight.

The 3340-hectare **Eucla National Park** is only a 10-minute drive from the town. It features the Delisser Sandhills and the high limestone Wilson Bluff. The mallee scrub

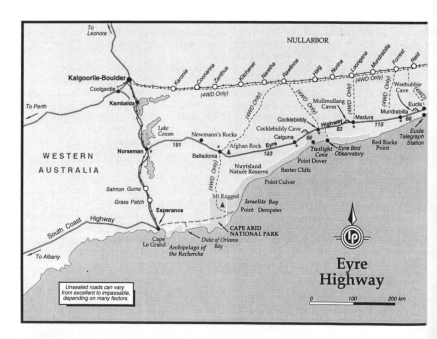

Eyre Highway

and heath of the park is typical of the coastal vegetation in this region.

At Eucla, many people have their photo taken with the international sign pinpointing distances to many parts of the world; it's near a ferro-concrete sperm whale, a species seldom seen in these parts. Another popular photo stop is at the **Travellers' Cross**. This is atop the escarpment which overlooks the ruins of old Eucla.

At **Border Village**, 13km from Eucla, connoisseurs of kitsch will appreciate a 5m-high fibreglass kangaroo. Remember to set your watch forward 1½ hours – or 2½ hours when daylight-saving time operates in South Australia.

Border Village to Nullarbor Roadhouse (185km)

Between the Western Australia/South Australia border and Nullarbor Roadhouse, the Eyre Highway runs close to the coast, and there are six spectacular **lookouts** over the

Great Australian Bight – be sure to stop at one or two.

After about 90km, you reach a turn-off (4WD only) to the well-known **Koonalda Cave**. It has a 45m-high chamber, entered by ladder. Like other Nullarbor caves, it's really for experienced cave explorers only. All caves in this part of South Australia are strictly regulated; to enter them, you usually must be accompanied by a National Parks & Wildlife officer.

Around **Nullarbor Roadhouse** are many caves, which should be explored only with extreme care (again, they are recommended to experienced cave explorers only). Watch out for wombat holes and poisonous snakes in the area. A dirt road leads to a beach, 30km away – ask directions at the roadhouse.

Nullarbor National Park (593,000 hectares) and **Nullarbor Regional Reserve** (2.28 million hectares) contain part of the largest arid limestone landscape in the world. This vast treeless terrain is better appreciated

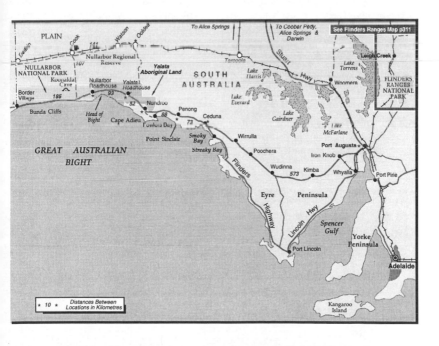

travelling north of the Eyre Highway along the Cook Road.

Nullarbor Roadhouse to Nundroo (145km)

The road passes through the Yalata Aboriginal Reserve (600,000 hectares), and Aborigines often sell boomerangs and other souvenirs by the roadside. You can also buy these in the **Yalata Community Roadhouse**.

Winter and early spring is a good time for whale watching (southern right whales – see Activities in this section). The best viewing point is **Twin Rocks**, at the Head of the Bight, and for 7km west of the rocks. The turn-off to Twin Rocks is about 20km east of the Nullarbor Roadhouse. Get a $2 permit from the Nullarbor or Yalata roadhouses. The edge of the Nullarbor is at **Nundroo**, 52km from Yalata.

Nundroo to Ceduna (161km)

South-east of Nundroo is the ghost town of **Fowlers Bay**. There is good fishing here, and nearby is **Mexican Hat Beach**.

You can make a short detour south of Penong to see the Pink Lake, Point Sinclair and **Cactus Beach**, a famous surf beach with left and right breaks that is a must for any serious surfer making the east-west journey.

Eastbound from Penong to Ceduna, there are several places with fuel and facilities. **Ceduna**, effectively the end of the solitary stretch from Norseman, is equipped with supermarkets, banks and all the comforts of a big town.

DETOURS

Look at any map of the central Nullarbor and you will see that very few roads head south. There are, however, a number leading north to the transcontinental railway line. Two detours from the normal route are described here. One leads south to the Great Australian Bight; the other takes you north to the railway, east along it and back south to the Eyre Highway.

Eyre Bird Observatory

Established in 1977, the Eyre Bird Observatory is housed in the Eyre Telegraph Station. This 1897 stone building in the **Nuytsland Nature Reserve** is surrounded by mallee scrubland and looks up to spectacular roving sand dunes which separate buildings from the sea. A small museum at the rear of the station has exhibits from the days of the telegraph line and of the legendary station-master William Graham.

Full board is the usual arrangement: $55 per person per day (with a $10 discount for YHA and Royal Australian Ornithological Union members).

The observatory (☎ (08) 9039 3450) is about 50km south-east of Cocklebiddy, and if you are travelling independently, you will need a 4WD to get there. The turn-off from the Eyre Highway is 16km from Cocklebiddy, and from there it is 14.5km to the microwave tower. Turn right at the tower and drive to the lookout carpark, about another 5km. Down below you see the sandhills near the station and the road snaking out towards it. From here the road gets rough; keep an

---

The Last Place on Earth

A latter-day visitor to the Eyre Bird Observatory was eccentric US millionaire Harold Anderson. Convinced that some form of nuclear Armageddon was nigh, and that Eyre's isolation made it just the place to sit out the firestorms and nuclear winters that would wrack the rest of the world, he decided to donate to the observatory all the books he thought would form the perfect account of the earth and its history.

Anderson returned to the USA, collated the books and despatched them to Australia. Not long afterwards he was mugged and died, in his early forties, never to see the books on the shelves at the observatory. They are still there, alongside all the written paraphernalia any avid bird-watcher could need. ■

eye out for a small arrow that indicates the track down the escarpment. At the base of the escarpment the drive is through about 12km of sand to the observatory, so tyres may sometimes need to be deflated.

Return transport to the bird observatory from Cocklebiddy or the microwave tower can be arranged for about $30.

From the buildings, there is a 1km walk, via the dunes, to the beach and the lonely Great Australian Bight. You can also drive out here and along the sand.

Into the Nullarbor
Possibly the best detour into the Nullarbor is in South Australia: drive north through the Nullarbor National Park and the regional reserve, east along the transcontinental railway line to Ooldea, and then south through Yalata Aboriginal Land to the Eyre Highway. From Eucla or Border Village, it is a full day of driving, best broken into two days. Take plenty of water. Because of rough sections of road a 4WD vehicle would be preferable.

If you take two days, you will need two permits: a bush-camping permit for Nullarbor Regional Reserve and a permit to cross Yalata Aboriginal Land (see Permits in the Information section earlier). There is a fuel outlet at Cook (☎ (08) 8641 8506), but it is not always open when you need it – phone ahead to find out its hours.

From Border Village, it is 146km to the Cook turn-off. If you go to a few (or all) of the Nullarbor lookouts, this stretch of sealed road will take some time. It is 107km north to Cook.

Turn right and travel along the rough road which parallels the transcontinental railway on its south side to Watson, passing by Fisher and O'Malley stations. Cross to the north side of the line at Watson, follow the improved road to Ooldea and then cross to the south again (the Telstra repeater station should be to your left) – it is about 141km from Cook to Ooldea. Proceed south to the Eyre Highway, crossing Ifould Lake, a large saltpan, on the way. Leave the gates in this section as you found them, and make sure you close the dog-barrier gate.

ALTERNATIVE ROUTES
Esperance to Balladonia
For those travelling in the south-west of WA, there is a good alternative route from Esperance. You can cut north-east to the Eyre Highway from near Cape Arid National Park utilising the 4WD-only Balladonia Road. To get there, head out from Esperance on Fisheries Rd, and when Grewer Rd comes in on the right, turn left. This becomes Balladonia Road and allows you to traverse part of Cape Arid National Park.

On this route you will pass Mt Ragged, the highest point in the Russell Range, where there is a tough walk to the top (3km return, three hours). Good topographic detail is found in the 1:250,000 AUSLIG series *Balladonia* and *Malcolm*. Good information on the national park is in the pamphlet produced by the Department of Conservation & Land Management (CALM) called *Cape Arid & Eucla*.

You have to be self-sufficient with both fuel and water, and after the caravan park at Duke of Orleans Bay (south of the route), there are no facilities until Balladonia.

ACTIVITIES
Bird-Watching
The Eyre Bird Observatory is one of the best places in the country to go bird-watching (see the earlier Detours section).

A wide range of desert flora and fauna is studied. Twitchers can expect to see many pink cockatoos, brush bronzewings and the odd furtive mallee fowl. There are many birds of prey along all sections of the highway, dispensing with road kills. By far the most spectacular is the wedge-tailed eagle.

Cycling
The Eyre Highway is a real challenge to cyclists, who are attracted by the barrenness and distance, certainly not by the interesting scenery. As you drive across, you see many of them, at all times of the year, lifting water bottles to parched mouths or sheltering under the lone large trees that punctuate stretches of the highway.

Obviously, excellent equipment is needed and adequate water supplies must be carried.

The cyclist should also know where all the water tanks are located. And as for the sun, adequate protection should be applied even in cloudy weather. Realise that the prevailing wind for most of the journey will be west to east, the preferable direction to be pedalling.

Spare a thought for the first cyclist to cross the Nullarbor. Arthur Richardson set off from Coolgardie on 24 November 1896 with a small kit and water bag. Thirty-one days later he arrived in Adelaide, having followed the telegraph line. Problems he encountered were the hot winds, '1000 in the shade' and 40km of sandhills west of Madura station.

FACILITIES
Norseman
The *Gateway Caravan Park* (☎ (08) 9039 1500) has tent sites ($13 for two), vans (from $24) and on-site cabins ($33). There is a small guesthouse, *Lodge 101* (☎ (08) 9039 1541), at 101 Princep St; rudimentary backpacker beds are $15. At the *Norseman Hotel* (☎ (08) 9039 1023) singles/doubles are $30/50. The *Railway Motel Hotel* (☎ (08) 9039 1115) costs $20/30, the *Norseman Eyre Motel* (☎ (08) 9039 1130) costs $62/69, and the *Great Western Motel* (☎ (08) 9039 1633) costs $60/69.

Tasty Bits & Pizzas has a wide range of eat-in or takeaway meals and *Pure Health* offers something for the vegetarian cyclist; both of these places are in Robert St. The BP and Ampol *roadhouses*, at the start of the Eyre Highway, have a wide range of food, including tasty fish & chips.

All types of fuel, including LPG, are available. There are banking facilities in town.

Balladonia to Cocklebiddy
The *Balladonia Hotel Motel* (☎ (08) 9039 3453) has single/double rooms from $58/68, and its dusty caravan facility has tent/caravan sites for an exorbitant $10/14. At Caiguna, the *John Eyre Motel* (☎ (08) 9039 3459) has rooms for $50/65 and a caravan facility with tent/powered sites from $5/12 for two.

The *Wedgetail Inn Motel Hotel* (☎ (08) 9039 3462) at Cocklebiddy has a marauding and contrary goat, extremely expensive fuel, overpriced rooms (from $50 to $76 for three), and powered tent/caravan sites in its attached caravan facility (☎ (08) 9039 3462) for $6/12. It also has wedge-tailed eagles overhead!

All types of fuel (including LPG) are available from Balladonia, Caiguna and Cocklebiddy, and there are telephones there too.

Cocklebiddy to Eucla
The *Madura Pass Oasis Inn* (☎ (08) 9039 3464) has double rooms from $49 to $76 and tent/powered sites in the caravan facility from $8/15.

At Mundrabilla, 114km to the east, the *Mundrabilla Motel Hotel* (☎ (08) 9039 3465) has singles/doubles from $45/55, and a caravan facility with tent/powered sites from $4/12 and cabins for $30 for two.

Madura and Mundrabilla have all types of fuel (including LPG).

Eucla & the WA/SA Border
The *Eucla Motor Hotel* (☎ (08) 9039 3468) has single/doubles for $58/68; its Eucla Pass section has rooms for $18/30 and the tent/powered sites in the caravan facility are $4/10 (showers are $1).

The *WA-SA Border Village* (☎ (08) 9039 3474) has tent/caravan sites in its caravan facility from $6/10, cabins from $35 for two and motel units from $60/68.

All types of fuel (including LPG) are available in both Eucla and at WA-SA Border Village.

Eucla to Ceduna
The *Nullarbor Hotel Motel* (☎ (08) 8625 6271) has units from $55/68 (extra persons $10) and a restaurant. Just look for the fibreglass southern right whale. Tent/powered sites in the nearby caravan facility are $5/8, and cabins $15 per person. The *Yalata Aboriginal Community Roadhouse* (☎ (08) 8625 6990) has tent sites and rooms; there's also a restaurant/takeaway.

The *Nundroo Inn* (☎ (08) 8625 6120) has singles/doubles for $55/60 and a caravan park with tent/powered sites for $7/10. There is a restaurant, takeaway food, laundry facilities and a pool.

The *Penong Hotel* (☎ (08) 8625 1050) has some basic singles/doubles from $30/40, and serves counter meals. The service station has a restaurant and takeaway.

All types of fuel (including LPG) can be obtained from Nullarbor, Nundroo and Penong, but not from Yalata.

Eastbound from Penong to Ceduna, there are several places with all types of fuel and other facilities. Ceduna is effectively the end of the solitary stretch from Norseman, and is equipped with supermarkets, banks and all the comforts of an 'end of hell' oasis.

ALTERNATIVE TRANSPORT

As the Eyre is the most important transcontinental route, there are daily scheduled bus services all the way from Perth to Adelaide with Greyhound Australia. There is also a rail option, one of the great railway journeys of the world (see the entry on the *Indian-Pacific* in the Getting Around chapter at the start of this book).

Flinders Ranges

HIGHLIGHTS

- Watching for yellow-footed rock-wallabies in Brachina Gorge
- Experiencing the grandeur of Wilpena Pound
- Discovering the Aboriginal heritage and the old mining relics of the rugged northern Flinders Ranges

For many seasoned travellers the Flinders Ranges in South Australia are the epitome of the outback. Certainly they are, for the vast majority of Australians, the easiest outback destination to get to. Another thing is certain: of all the regions in Australia's outback, the

Flinders have had more glossy coffee-table books produced about them than any other. That does say something about their grandeur and attraction.

While the Flinders officially begin near Crystal Brook, just 195km north of Adelaide, it is further north where they take on their distinguishing outback characteristics. It's also further north where they reach their highest point and are at their grandest.

On these pages we describe the loop route from Hawker north via Wilpena, Blinman and Arkaroola to Lyndhurst. While it could be done as a stand-alone trip, it is also an enjoyable route north to Lyndhurst or Marree and the start of the Strzelecki, Oodnadatta and Birdsville tracks.

Much of the route could be travelled, generally, in a normal car, as the conditions vary from good bitumen to slow but reasonable dirt. Only in the far north, beyond Arkaroola, do the tracks become real 4WD.

All told, this trip covers around 450km of rugged outback range country. You could travel it in a longish day, but you wouldn't see much and you'd enjoy it even less. There are a number of places to stock up with supplies, and you could stay in a motel or hotel every evening you are away.

HISTORY

The Adnyamathanha, meaning 'hill people' have inhabited the Flinders Ranges for many thousands of years. The ranges and the people who lived there were an integral part of the long-distance trade routes that crossed the continent. Ochre and pituri, a mildly narcotic drug, were traded, as were stones for axes and tools, and shell for decoration.

Dotted amongst the hills and valleys are important archaeological sites including ochre quarries (the ochre being used as a paint decoration in ceremonies), rock quarries (sources of tools) and art sites. The Flinders are rich in rock engravings, or petroglyphs, a form of art that probably predates the painted art which, in the Flinders, lacks the richness and variety found at sites in northern Australia.

The last full-blood Adnyamathanha died

in 1973, but all the descendants of the tribal groups that inhabited the ranges and the surrounding country still have strong ties to the land. Most of them live in the towns of the region; Nepabunna, east of Copley, is a small Aboriginal community.

The first white person to see these ranges was Matthew Flinders, from the deck of his ship *Investigator* in March 1802 as it sailed up Spencer Gulf. From his anchorage south of present-day Port Augusta he sent a group to climb the highest peak in the vicinity, naming it Mt Brown after his intrepid botanist.

Edward John Eyre was next on the scene in 1839. Over a two-year period, he explored along the western edge of the range, striking west and north, but ran into a series of salt lakes that he thought were one giant ring of salt blocking his way north. His last expedition saw him push east, from north of Mt Deception, past Mt Aroona and deep into the ranges near Mt Serle, before following the Frome River north out of the labyrinth of gorges and rugged ridges surrounding him. Following the edge of the range north-east, he climbed a low hill that he named, supposedly before he even climbed it, Mt Hopeless, and once again spied a barrier of salt.

Just four years later the pastoral expansion had reached the southern edge of the Flinders Ranges near Gladstone, and slowly but surely pushed north. Wilpena Pound, one of the natural wonders of the Flinders, was discovered soon afterwards by William Chace, who had been sent out by the Browne brothers (both doctors). By 1851 the brothers had taken up the Wilpena, Aroona and Arkaba runs. The runs incorporated some of the best watered and most scenic country in the Flinders Ranges – today Wilpena and Aroona make up the picturesque Flinders Ranges National Park, while Arkaba is still privately owned but operated in part as a tourist lease.

Others followed, and by the early 1860s all of the range country was held under pastoral lease.

Earlier, in 1846, copper had been found near Mt Remarkable and in 1859 it was also discovered at what became known as Blinman. Other discoveries followed, but while some were fantastically rich they were generally only small, and the mines, plagued by long distances from markets, little water, poor or non-existent roads, never made a profit. Today the ruins of those mining ventures are some of the best preserved and poignant reminders of our recent past, scattered throughout the ranges in narrow, forgotten valleys.

From the 1870s the area south of Hawker was opened up to more intensive farming. This was in conflict with the view of the surveyor-general, GW Goyder, whose name is immortalised in Goyder's Line. That line, Goyder said, indicated where the rainfall and the country changed from prospective farming land to pastoral country. A run of good seasons pushed the wheat farmers well north, towards and even into Wilpena Pound, but in the end, normal seasons returned and Goyder was proven right. The scattered stone ruins of old farm houses around Hawker, and the occasional abandoned old wheat harvester, are all that remains of their dreams and aspirations.

In the far north, among the convoluted ridges and gorges of the area we know as the Gammon Ranges, WB Greenwood found a wealth of different minerals, triggering a gem rush that had prospectors combing the hills looking for sapphires and rubies.

His discovery of the uranium-rich ore torbernite in the area around Mt Painter is what he is most remembered for, but it was many years before the new mineral could be identified. Working with Douglas Mawson, later of Antarctica fame, the two pegged many claims in the region. With the ore being used to produce radium, which in 1924 was worth, supposedly, the modern equivalent of $2 million an ounce, other prospectors rushed to secure leases in the rugged range country of the northern Flinders. Bigger, more easily worked discoveries of the ore overseas saw the Flinders mines wane, only to be revived again when the USA was developing the atomic bomb in the 1940s.

Like most of the minerals found in the Flinders, however, these finds were small deposits, far from markets. The most enduring deposits have been the Leigh Creek coal fields, the barytes mine just east of the Flinders Ranges National Park, and the talc mine in the far north at Mt Fitton.

Since the end of the WWII the area has become a major tourist drawcard, and while it is not in the same league as the Great Barrier Reef or Uluru (Ayers Rock), tourism is an important part of the local economy.

INFORMATION
Tourist Offices
The best way to obtain tourist information is to write or phone Flinders Ranges & Outback SA Tourism (☎ freecall 1800 633 060 or (08) 8373 3430; fax 8373 2793), GPO Box 666, Adelaide, SA 5001.

For information on the national parks, contact the Department of Environment & Natural Resources, Far North Region, Hawker office (☎ (08) 8648 4244).

Police & Hospitals
Hawker has a police station (☎ (08) 8648 4028) in Eighth St; the Great Northern War Memorial Hospital (☎ (08) 8648 4007) is in Fifth St.

Leigh Creek South is the only other town in the region with a police station and hospital. The police station (☎ (08) 8675 2004) and hospital (☎ (08) 8675 2100) are both in Black Oak Drive.

Permits
Permits are required if you want to visit or camp in the national parks in the area. They can be obtained at the ranger headquarters at Wilpena (☎ (08) 8648 0048) or the district office in Hawker. Day visitors require a Day Vehicle Entry Pass, which costs $5 per vehicle, $3 per motorcycle – people walking or travelling by bicycle don't need to pay.

If you want to camp you'll need an Annual Regional Pass (which includes camping and entry fees), which covers Mount Remarkable, Flinders Ranges, Gammon Ranges and Dutchman's Stern. Cost is $60 per vehicle and $30 a motorcycle. Alternatively you can obtain an Annual Statewide Pass costing $140/70 for a vehicle/motorcycle, with reduced costs for pensioners and renewal.

Big Moro Gorge is now on Aboriginal land and a permit is required to visit. For an update, see the rangers at Balcanoona (☎ (08) 8648 4829), in the Gammon Ranges National Park.

Books & Maps
There is a good range of books that cover all aspects of the Flinders Ranges. Hawker Motors in Hawker has a good selection for sale.

The Story of the Flinders Ranges, by Hans Mincham (Rigby), is the best book on the history of the area. Most of the towns, including Hawker, Quorn and Port Augusta, have local history books published about them. The murder at Grindell's Hut in the Gammon Ranges is detailed in the book *Cloud over the Gammon Ranges*, by Alan Bailey (Endage Print).

Flinders Ranges – an Australian Aura, by David Berndstoecker (South Australian Government Printer), and *The Flinders Ranges – a Portrait*, with photography by Eduard Domin (Little Hills Press), are just two of the glossy coffee-table books on the region. The latest glossy books, *Flinders Ranges, South Australia: the Art of the Photographer*, and *An Australian Landscape – The Flinders Ranges*, by Stavros Pippos (Endeavour Publishing), are some of the best.

If you are into the natural delights of the area, *The Story of the Flinders Ranges Mammals*, by Dorothy Turnbridge (Kangaroo Press), is worth reading. There's also *Fossils of the Flinders and Mt Lofty Ranges*, by Neville S Pledge (South Australian Museum), and *Corridors Through Time – the Geology of the Flinders Ranges*.

The best guidebooks for those wanting to camp and 4WD is *The Flinders Ranges – an Adventurer's Guide*, by Ron & Viv Moon (Kakirra Adventure Publications), and *Explore the Flinders Ranges*, by Sue Barker and others (Royal Geographical Society of Australasia, SA Branch). Probably the best walking guide is *Grant's Guide to the Flinders Ranges*, by Grant Da Costa (Acacia

Vines). *A Climber's Guide to Moonarie* (South Australian Climbing Club) is available from good outdoor shops in Adelaide.

The *Official Visitor's Guide – Flinders Ranges and Outback* covers all of the Flinders and much of the outback and gives good detail on the facilities, places to stay, commercial tours, etc of the region. It has one big advantage: its free! It is available in many stores in the local area.

The Department of Recreation & Sport publishes maps which cover the length of the Heysen Walking Trail. The best maps of the area for general touring are *Flinders Ranges, South Australia*, produced by the Flinders Ranges & Outback South Australia Tourism Inc, and *The Flinders Ranges* by Hema. These maps are readily available locally or from good map shops, Australia wide.

Radio Frequencies

There is really no need for an HF radio in this region. If you have one fitted to your vehicle, the frequencies to have are the RFDS base at Port Augusta (call sign VNZ; primary frequency 4010; secondary frequencies 6890 and 8165) and the Telstra base in Sydney (call sign VIS). Telstra's radphone 24-hour channels include 405, 607, 802, 1203, and 1602. Other frequencies for Selcall and Tonecall are also available. The Selcall for the beacon is 0899, while for the operator it is 0108.

Other Information

This trip is relatively easy. Distances between facilities are not great, the roads are generally pretty good by outback standards, and well used. Contact the Department of Road Transport's Far Northern Roads Condition Report (☎ (08) 11633) for current details.

THE ROUTE

The route described is one of a number that traverse the ranges from south to north. It offers a good insight into the delights of the ranges, the variety of landforms and the mix of history that lies within these rocky ramparts.

Hawker

The adventure begins at the small township of Hawker, 375km north of Adelaide. You can reach it by travelling the blacktop via Port Augusta and Quorn or via Melrose, Wilmington and Quorn. Or you can take in a short section of excellent dirt road by travelling via Jamestown and Orroroo. The latter route is the shortest from Adelaide, while the route via Melrose is the most picturesque.

Established in 1880, Hawker originally serviced the many wheat farms that were established in the area and now caters for the sheep properties that took their place. Since 1970, when the railway ceased operating, tourism has become an important industry.

Hawker is a good place to use as your major resupply point. It has everything a traveller needs, including a choice of stores, fuel outlets, vehicle repair places and accommodation, but only one pub.

Although there is a choice, **Hawker Motors** in the centre of town is where most tourists go for fuel, minor repairs, souvenirs and information. The business was established by Fred Teague, who was something of a legend in the Flinders. His family, who still run the business, are a good source of information on the area. Inside the store is an informative little museum and a wide range of books for sale.

Many travellers use the town as a base to explore the area, but Quorn is better if you are travelling around the area south of Hawker. Wilpena is more central if you are exploring to the north.

Hawker to Blinman (154km)

Heading north-east on the bitumen to Wilpena Pound, the road initially traverses gently undulating country, with the main range away to the left. Dominating the distant vista to the north are the bluffs of the southern wall of Wilpena Pound. As you progress, the Elder Range off to the west begins to draw the eyes more and more.

Arkaba station The turn-off to the Arkaba station woolshed is 19km north of Hawker. This historic working woolshed is just a few

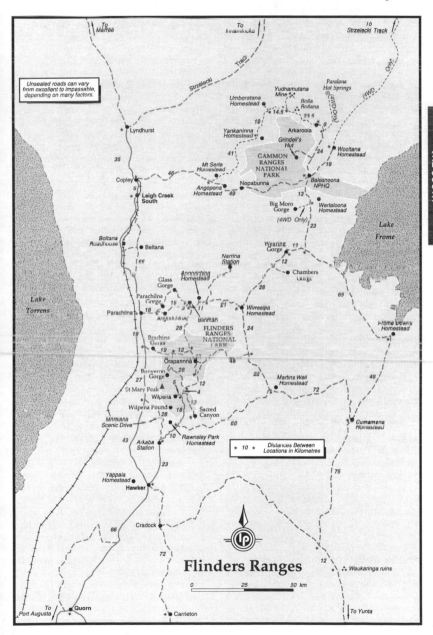

Unsealed roads can vary
from excellent to impassable,
depending on many factors.

To
Marree

To
Innamincka

To
Strzelecki Track

Strzelecki   Track

OTM

(4WD Only)

Paralana
Hot Springs

Umberatana
Homestead

Yudnamutana
Mine

Bolla
Bollana

14.5

33.5

19

Lyndhurst

Yankaninna
Homestead

Arkaroola

Grindell's
Hut

6

41

GAMMON
RANGES
NATIONAL
PARK

24

Wooltana
Homestead

35

Mt Serle
Homestead

46

19

Copley

Angepena
Homestead

Nepabunna

Baloanoona
NPHQ

5

49

13

Leigh Creek
South

Big Moro
Gorge

Wertaloona
Homestead

Boltana
Roadhouse

Beltana

(4WD Only)

23

Lake
Frome

166

Wearing
Gorge

17

Lake
Torrens

Narrina
Station

12

Chambers
Gorge

Glass Gorge

Angorichina
Homestead

Parachilna
Gorge

16

28

65

Parachilna

16

Angorichina

21

Wirrealpa
Homestead

Binman

24

FLINDERS
RANGES
NATIONAL
PARK

19

28

Brachina
Gorge

Frome Downs
Homestead

19

13

Orapannna

28

48

Bunyeroo
Gorge

27

5

12

22

Martins Well
Homestead

48

St Mary Peak

4

72

Wilpena

13

Wilpena Pound

18

Sacred
Canyon

Maraiana
Scenic Drive

28

60

10

Rawnsley Park
Homestead

★ 10 ★   Distances Between
                   Locations in Kilometres

43

Arkaba
Station

23

Oumamana
Homestead

Yappala
Homestead

75

Hawker

Cradock

66

Flinders Ranges

72

12

∴ Waukaringa ruins

0   25   50 km

To
Port Augusta

Quorn

Carrieton

To Yunta

hundred metres off the main road and caters to passing travellers with coffee, scones and cool drinks, as well as a good range of local art, craft and souvenirs. Arkaba runs 4WD tag-along tours, with trips that offer some of the best country in the Flinders along the Elder Range and the southern ramparts of the Wilpena Range. For those without a 4WD, tours can be arranged through the Wilpena Pound Resort.

A cottage is available here for rent and a tent camp is also located on this renowned and strikingly spectacular property.

Arkaba station was one of the first properties taken up in the area, and with its good supplies of spring-fed water it remains one of the best drought-protected properties in the Flinders. Surprisingly, much of the property was completely inaccessible to vehicles up until a few years ago. Then the new owners, members of the well-known Rasheed family who own and manage Wilpena Pound, pushed a couple of tracks into the country bordering the Elder Range and began to control the rabbits and goats that had bred unchecked for generations. The results have been spectacular, and the family were recognised for their work by winning a major state conservation award in 1992.

Those tracks also make much of the range country accessible to keen 4WD travellers, who can join an organised self-drive trip through the property. Trips are usually of just one day, but travellers can camp in idyllic secluded isolation on gum-tree-lined flats beside the ranges. A few goats still exist in the rugged back country, but the native wildlife has flourished. Red kangaroos and the more stockily built hill wallaroo, or euro, are often seen at close quarters, while the natural water points that dot the property are a magnet for animals, including a wide variety of birds.

Arkaba Station to Wilpena Pound Less than 5km further along the bitumen, the **Moralana Scenic Drive** veers off to the left. This road is actually a private road that cuts across Arkaba station; public access is allowed, but straying from the road or camping is not! The 28km (one way) drive gives splendid views of both the Elder Range and the southern wall of Wilpena Pound.

Rawnsley Park station, a sheep property of just over 3000 hectares, on the left of the road 10km further north, offers a large caravan and camping ground, and self-contained cabins and bunkhouse-style accommodation also. It is popular during school holidays but is quiet the rest of the time. Worthy of note is that pets are allowed, provided they are kept under control and there is horse riding, bushwalks, and more.

As you continue north along the bitumen, the southern rampart of the Wilpena Pound Range, Rawnsley Bluff, crowds in from the west. Seven km from the turn-off to Rawnsley Park is a minor signposted track on the left to **Arkaroo Rock**, an Aboriginal art site within the national park. A short walk from the carpark brings you to this small but important site. It's an enjoyable walk through open forest alive with birds. Keen rock climbers can reach the 100m-high sandstone walls of Moonarie via a longer walk from the carpark; there are many routes up the cliffs to challenge even the most dedicated climber.

Back on the bitumen, you enter the **Flinders Ranges National Park** 3km further along the road, with the road now running parallel to the main range of the Pound. The drive is very enjoyable, with a red-gum-lined rocky creek beside the road and a dense forest of smallish native pines crowding the road and the creek.

Wilpena Pound The turn-off to Wilpena Pound Resort, and the only entrance into Wilpena Pound, is 18km north of Rawnsley Park, or 52km north of Hawker. Turning left here will lead you 4km to the main parking area, the ranger's office and the entrance to the resort and the camping ground. Fuel and limited supplies are available. If you can, stop here for at least two days. The walking is superb and there are a number of walking trails you can take, depending on your fitness and keenness; the Heysen Trail passes through the national park.

Wilpena Pound is one of the most sensational visual features of the Flinders, and it's also a spectacular geological structure – a natural amphitheatre 11km long and 5km wide. 'Wilpena' is an Aboriginal word that is taken to mean 'the place of the bent fingers' or 'a cupped hand', both of which are very appropriate.

The range that forms its perimeter slopes gently up from the inside to a line of bluffs and high peaks, which drop steeply on the outside to the surrounding hills and plains. **St Mary Peak** (1190m), the highest peak in South Australia, is on the northern extremity of the Pound. The summit gives fine views of the encircling ranges, as well as occasionally attracting snow.

Only two creeks flow out of the Pound. One is **Wilpena Creek**, which gives the only practical access; where it leaves Wilpena Pound is where you will find the caravan park and all the facilities of the resort. The gums that line the creek here are magnificent and it is no wonder that the area is popular with travellers. The second creek is Edeowie Creek, which leaves Wilpena Pound by a series of waterfalls and a tortuous course through **Edeowie Gorge**, in the far northwest of the Pound's surrounding ramparts.

The flat, well-watered floor of Wilpena Pound was used by the pioneers to graze sheep and cattle; for many years much of it was ploughed and wheat was grown, the tall peaks attracting more than their fair share of rainfall. In 1914 a flood down Wilpena Creek washed away the only track access into the Pound, and wheat growing was abandoned. In 1920, on the expiration of the lease, the area was declared a forest reserve.

In 1945 tourism had reached the stage where Wilpena Pound was proclaimed a National Pleasure Resort. A couple of years later a resort was built at the entrance to the Pound, and this was taken over in the 1950s by Kevin Rasheed, whose family still run this popular operation.

In 1970 the state government purchased Oraparinna station, proclaiming Oraparinna National Park. In 1972 Wilpena Pound was added to the national park to form the Flinders Ranges National Park. Since then, extra additions have taken the park to its present size of 92,746 hectares, but the Pound is still the major drawcard.

Wilpena Pound to Blinman Back on the main road north, the bitumen quickly ends. Just before you cross Wilpena Creek, 1km north of the turn-off to Wilpena Pound, a track heads off to the right to **Sacred Canyon**. This small gorge contains some of the best of the easily accessible Aboriginal rock engravings in the Flinders.

Nearly 5km north of the turn-off to Wilpena Pound, at a major road junction, take the road to the left. This is the start of one of the best drives in the Flinders; early morning, when the sun lights up the walls of the distant Heysen Range, is the time to go. The road is reasonably good dirt with the odd rough patch, so a normal car should have no problems.

For the first 12km to **Yanyanna Hut** the road traverses rolling hills cut by charming, tree-lined creeks. In the early morning, kangaroos and emus are commonly seen, as are flocks of raucous pink and grey galahs and snow-white corellas. Yanyanna Hut and its nearby yards testify to the days when this area was a working property.

From here the road swings in a big arc, the vegetation changes to native pine, and the scenery gets better. The **Bunyeroo Valley Lookout** 2km from the hut is worth a stop to admire the view. The Heysen Range dominates the background to the west, while a lower range of more rounded peaks between the lookout and the main wall of rock is the ABC Range. To the south are the battlements of the eastern wall of Wilpena Pound, dominated by St Mary Peak.

For the next 2km the road traverses a ridge with spectacular views, before descending steeply to run beside **Bunyeroo Creek**. The next 2km is through a winding gorge with the road running, in typical Flinders fashion, along the creekbed. Normally the creek does have water through it, and after heavy rain it is closed to normal traffic. Heed the 'Road Closed' signs if they have been erected.

There are a couple of good campsites along this section, although none have any facilities.

As you leave the gorge, the road swings up out of the creek and heads north. A carpark on the left is a good spot to stop and take a walk down into Bunyeroo Gorge proper. For the next 10km the road heads north, with the rugged Heysen Range off to the left and the ABC Range directly off to the right.

Turn left at the T-junction 10km north of the carpark. (Turning right at this junction will lead you east to a number of good campsites in the Aroona Valley or along Brachina Creek and its tributaries, and from there you can head either north to Blinman or south to Wilpena Pound.) Heading west, the road quickly becomes confined by the surrounding bluffs and cliffs of the Heysen Range into **Brachina Gorge**. The road seems to spend more time in the creekbed than out of it. After heavy rain this road is also closed to normal traffic, so take heed of the warning signs.

There is some excellent camping through here; although it is popular during school holidays, especially in spring and it is one of the best places in the Flinders. The creek is fed by natural springs and it is rare for there to be no water in the gorge. From any of the campsites, there are walks to be enjoyed down along the creek or up the steep hills for a great eagle's-eye view of the surrounds. Brachina Gorge is a good place to see the endangered yellow-footed rock wallaby.

Seven km west of the T-junction, the road crosses the creek for the last time and climbs

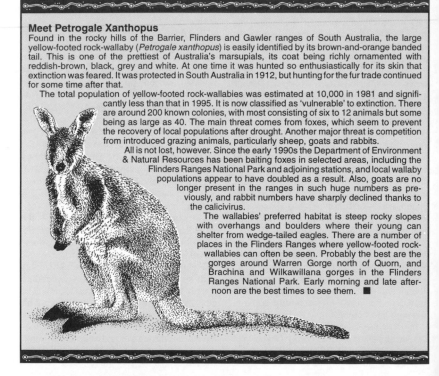

Meet Petrogale Xanthopus

Found in the rocky hills of the Barrier, Flinders and Gawler ranges of South Australia, the large yellow-footed rock-wallaby (*Petrogale xanthopus*) is easily identified by its brown-and-orange banded tail. This is one of the prettiest of Australia's marsupials, its coat being richly ornamented with reddish-brown, black, grey and white. At one time it was hunted so enthusiastically for its skin that extinction was feared. It was protected in South Australia in 1912, but hunting for the fur trade continued for some time after that.

The total population of yellow-footed rock-wallabies was estimated at 10,000 in 1981 and significantly less than that in 1995. It is now classified as 'vulnerable' to extinction. There are around 200 known colonies, with most consisting of six to 12 animals but some being as large as 40. The main threat comes from foxes, which seem to prevent the recovery of local populations after drought. Another major threat is competition from introduced grazing animals, particularly sheep, goats and rabbits.

All is not lost, however. Since the early 1990s the Department of Environment & Natural Resources has been baiting foxes in selected areas, including the Flinders Ranges National Park and adjoining stations, and local wallaby populations appear to have doubled as a result. Also, goats are no longer present in the ranges in such huge numbers as previously, and rabbit numbers have sharply declined thanks to the calicivirus.

The wallabies' preferred habitat is steep rocky slopes with overhangs and boulders where their young can shelter from wedge-tailed eagles. There are a number of places in the Flinders Ranges where yellow-footed rock-wallabies can often be seen. Probably the best are the gorges around Warren Gorge north of Quorn, and Brachina and Wilkawillana gorges in the Flinders Ranges National Park. Early morning and late afternoon are the best times to see them. ∎

a low rise and leaves the park. A lookout on the right gives an enjoyable view of the western battlements of the range, while to the west the flat plains of the desert country begin and sweep away to the shores of Lake Torrens and beyond.

The road improves as it leaves the range country and strikes west for another 12km before reaching the bitumen at a T-junction. Here you turn right (north) towards Parachilna. Hawker is 70km south along the bitumen. In the evening, as you head north, the ranges look superb, rearing up from the plain your are now travelling on.

The small railway siding of **Parachilna** is 19km north of where you joined the bitumen road; you need to turn off to the left to get to the Prairie Hotel or the public showers and toilets that are available. The historic pub can supply accommodation, fuel and a top meal that would do a city restaurant proud.

About 100m past the turn-off to the hotel, take the road that strikes east towards the range and the township of Blinman. Nine km later you enter **Parachilna Gorge**, and 2km further on a road junction is met. Keep right at the junction, although the left-hand route makes a pleasant scenic drive through Glass Gorge to Blinman. Good campsites beside the creek become available just before the road junction off to the left and continue for the next few kilometres.

Parachilna Gorge is not within the national park: it's a recognised camping area maintained by the local shire. A camping permit is not required, and you can take the family pet. Because of that, the spectacular nature of the area, and the almost constant water supply in the spring-fed creek, the gorge is very popular with campers. Even so, you could have a campsite to yourself. The experience of camping here amongst these red-raw ranges, with a trickle of water running past and a lazy wind sighing through the gum trees, is hard to beat.

Camping spots are numerous for the first few kilometres after they appear, but once you arrive at the **Angorichina Tourist Village**, 16km east of the bitumen, you are really out of the best of the camping areas.

Angorichina caters for campers, caravanners and those wanting self-contained cabins, units, on-site vans and bunkhouse-style accommodation. The small general store has fuel, groceries, souvenirs and limited repair facilities.

There is some excellent walking around the gorge, with the **Heysen Trail** heading south from a picnic site close to the road, about 3km before Angorichina. This part of the long-distance walking trail leads along the Heysen Range all the way to Wilpena Pound and, while you don't need to go that far, you can enjoy a day walk. Another walk is along Oratunga Gorge (on the north side of the road, less than 1km before the picnic area), but the best one is along Parachilna and Blinman creeks up to the Blinman Pools and waterfalls.

Blinman

The small township of Blinman is 15km east of Angorichina. At the T-junction on the edge of town, turn left for the hotel, general store, post office and the **old mine**. In reality the main centre of the town is Blinman North. Blinman, a few kilometres south, is deserted and offers no facilities.

Copper was discovered here in 1859 by Robert 'Pegleg' Blinman, and the original town of Blinman was surveyed in 1864. It was too far for the miners to walk from the mine, so in 1867 a new town was established a little closer to the mine, and Blinman North took over as the main centre of the community. In those years the population was around 1000 – about 985 more than at present. The mine closed in 1874 but was worked spasmodically over the next 30 years. About the only person who ever really made any money out of it was Pegleg, when he sold the mine to the Yudnamutana Copper Mining Company for £70,000 – a lot of money in 1862!

An excellent walking trail with information signs has been established around the site of the old mine and smelter, and it is worth more than just a passing glance.

Fuel, a choice of accommodation and meals are available in Blinman and if it's a

The Heysen Trail

The Heysen Trail is one of Australia's premier long-distance walking tracks. It starts far to the south at Cape Jervis, 110km south of Adelaide, and wanders through the Mt Lofty Ranges to Parachilna Gorge in the northern Flinders. The total walking distance is around 1500km and the trail is marked throughout.

In 1967, long before a recognised trail was established, CW Bonython became the first to walk the complete length of the range, a story told eloquently in his book *Walking the Flinders Ranges* (Rigby).

The trail is named after one of Australia's greatest painters, the late Sir Hans Heysen, who painted extensively in the areas around Aroona and Arkaba near Wilpena Pound. He first visited the ranges in 1926, returning again and again to capture the mood of the ranges that he described later as 'the bones of nature laid bare'. Many artists have visited the Flinders, but it was Heysen more than any other who really opened people's eyes to the grandeur and the majestic beauty of the Flinders.

The trail takes you through some of the state's most scenic country, and you don't need to mount an expedition to enjoy it. Good vehicle access via dedicated tracks, or where the trail crosses a public road, means there are plenty of places you can go on a half-day or day walk.

A book and a series of 15 1:50,000 topographic strip maps ($6.50) produced by the South Australian Department of Recreation & Sport give you all the required information. The maps not only provide the normal geographical information, but also give good descriptions of the route, places to see, and some timely reminders about walking in this essentially arid country.

To walk the Heysen Trail you must be fit, have the right equipment, and know how to use it. A good knowledge of map-reading and route-finding is essential. It is surprising how many people get lost following the well-marked trail.

Remember that the trail traverses private land for much of the way. Treat the privilege of crossing it with the consideration it deserves. Be extremely careful with fire, obey all the regulations, leave gates as you find them, don't disturb stock and don't camp right beside water so stock can't come and drink.

The Heysen Trail is closed to walkers from 1 November to 30 March, the only exceptions being a couple of short walks within the Flinders Ranges National Park. Contact the South Australian Department of Environment & Natural Resources (☎ (08) 8226 4000) for details.

Information on the Heysen Trail is available from good map shops throughout Australia and from a number of stores in the Flinders. Alternatively, you can also purchase the strip maps from the Department of Recreation & Sport, PO Box 219, Brooklyn Park SA 5032; ☎ (08) 8416 6677. Another good source in Adelaide is the Natural Resources Information Centre, at 77 Grenfell St. ∎

hot day you can enjoy a swim in the pub's swimming pool. If you have taken the route described, you are 154km north of Hawker, but by the shortest route, directly north from Wilpena, the distance is only 111km.

Blinman to Copley (297km)

To continue on the loop, head south past the road junction you came in on to another road junction 3km south. This is the original township of Blinman. Turn left here, and 6km further east, keep right at the junction. A few kilometres further on, the road begins to wind through a small gorge, and 14km from the Blinman hotel, you pass the turn-off on your left to Narrina station.

The road passes through the Bunkers range before levelling out across lightly undulating country as Wirrealpa homestead is

approached, 35km from Blinman. Just past the homestead, which is on your right, you meet with a major dirt road coming from the south. This is another route, shorter but nowhere near as scenic, to Wilpena Pound and Hawker.

Turn north and follow the road as it traverses a relatively flat plain with the ranges off to the left. Numerous creeks are crossed but these are nearly always dry, except after heavy local rain when they run for a few hours, or maybe a day, before being soaked up by the sands. The turn-off to Chambers Gorge is 28km north of Wirrealpa.

Chambers Gorge Chambers Gorge offers some enjoyable camping in an area vastly different to the gorges further south. Here the country is harsher, the vegetation thinner, and the majestic red gums and the native pine no longer dominate. The gorge itself starts about 9km from the turn-off; within about 400m there is a prominent bluff on the left with a small, normally dry creek coming in from the same direction. Access past this point is 4WD. On the southern rim of the gorge is the cube-capped dome of Mt Chambers, resplendent with scree slopes down its flanks.

While the gorge often has water in it, it should not be counted on, especially as a source of drinking water. Don't camp where there are signs indicating no camping near permanent water, as this is the only water source for wildlife and stock in the vicinity. Most of the camps are close to the creek, before the bluff, while the one at the bluff is the most popular and has the most spectacular setting.

Walking in the gorge is worthy of a few hours, especially in the cool of the morning. Within a few kilometres the gorge opens out and finally, at the edge of the expansive Frome Plains, ends at an impressive rock column known as **Windsor Pillar**.

Back near the first prominent bluff, a short walk up the creek will bring you to one of the best Aboriginal rock engraving sites you will find anywhere. It's worth spending an hour or so here, resting in the shade and pondering on what this country must have been like when these people chipped their designs thousands of years ago. Certainly it was more temperate and water was more abundant than it is now.

Chambers Gorge to Arkaroola On the main route north, 12km beyond the turn-off to Chambers Gorge, the road begins to pass through **Wearing Gorge**. About 2km long, the gorge is a pleasant respite from the sun and heat of the flat plains. Once out of the gorge, the road runs east for 10km, meeting the main access road north from the small township of Yunta. This route south is the shortest to Adelaide from this point, as Yunta is on the main road between Broken Hill and Adelaide.

Turn left at the T-junction and head north

with the immense salt expanse of Lake Frome, occasionally visible, off to the right. Wertaloona homestead, 23km north of the road junction, is off to the right, while almost directly opposite is the track to **Big Moro Gorge**. The track west to the gorge is 4WD and the 15km trip takes around 40 minutes. While the gorge isn't as spectacular as those further south, it's still worth exploring and enjoying – this area is now Aboriginal land, so check with the rangers at Balcanoona (below) as to permit requirements.

Heading ever northwards, you come to a major T-junction, 13km north of the Big Moro Gorge turn-off. This is the main Copley-Balcanoona road. Turning left (west) at this junction will lead you on a good dirt road 95km back to the bitumen at Copley, 5km north of Leigh Creek South and 159km north of Hawker. Turning right will take you across a creek, and on your right is **Balcanoona**, now the main ranger station for the Gammon Ranges National Park. If you want to camp in the park, this is the place to go for information and for a camping permit.

The **Gammon Ranges National Park** covers an area of over 128,000 hectares and takes in a strip of land from the edge of Lake Frome, past and including Balcanoona homestead, mushrooming out to protect all the country from Arkaroola, Bolla Bollana and Umberatana in the north, to Arcoona Bluff, Mt McKinlay and Italowie Gorge in the south.

The park encompasses some of the most rugged country in the Flinders. John McKinlay explored much of the region on his travels looking for pastoral land in 1850, but so rugged and dry was the country that much of it wasn't taken up until later. In 1909 John Grindell secured most of the area in the east and south of what was later to become the national park. The Gammon Ranges themselves were not crossed until Warren Bonython and a friend walked across them in 1947. Today the ranges are a magnet for bushwalkers sufficiently experienced and well equipped to tackle the convoluted gorges and sheer ridges that make up the range country.

There is some excellent camping within the park, and those with a 4WD can enjoy some good camping areas at places such as Grindell's Hut, Lochness Well or Mainwater Well. Walkers have a much wider choice of campsites. Water is often very scarce in the park so travellers need to be self-sufficient.

Back at the creek crossing just before Balcanoona, a main dirt road heading off to the left, just north of the creek, is the main road to Arkaroola and the one to take.

Nine km from the junction the main access road into the Gammon Ranges National Park heads off to the left. From this junction it is about 10km to **Grindell Hut**, about the only spot in the park a normal car has a chance of getting to, driven with care.

Continuing north, the Arkaroola road skirts the main bulk of the range off to the west, running parallel to the national park boundary. Less than 9km further on, you enter the **Arkaroola Sanctuary**, and 24km from the Balcanoona road junction you come to another road junction where you need to keep left. Heading right at this point takes you via a scenic drive to **Paralana Hot Springs**, 26km along the range.

Arkaroola Less than 2km up the Arkaroola road from the junction, you pass the original Arkaroola station, and 6km from the junction, you come to a T-junction in the heart of Arkaroola village. You are 307km north of Hawker by the way you have come, or 248km by the shortest route (via Wilpena Pound, past the barytes mine, and Wirrealpa to Balcanoona and Arkaroola).

Here you can camp, stay in the caravan park or choose from the wide range of other accommodation available. There is a store, service station, licensed restaurant and swimming pool, and a museum, art gallery and an astronomical observatory. You could easily spend a couple of days here.

The **Arkaroola Sanctuary & Resort** was established by Reg Sprigg in 1968 when he took over the 61,000-hectare station lease. He immediately got rid of the sheep, and over the years that followed brought the rampant feral goat and rabbit populations

under control. Now the Arkaroola Sanctuary probably has a better example of the area's flora and fauna than the adjoining national park, all due to the eradication of the vermin on the place.

There are many geological features in this privately owned reserve, many of which, such as **Mt Painter** and the **Armchair**, are registered by the Geological Society as Rock Monuments, while a significant percentage of the area is listed on the Register of the National Estate.

There are many attractions worth visiting, and if you have a 4WD there are some enjoyable drives through the ranges to places of interest. These include Echo Camp Waterhole, Paralana Hot Springs, Bolla Bollana copper mine and smelter in the far northwest of the property, and the Yudnamutana mine and smelter, which is a real highlight. The resort also runs tours to these places for those without a 4WD.

One trip that you can only take in the resort's vehicles is the **Ridgetop Tour**. This tour is highly recommended and takes visitors through some of the most rugged country in the ranges to **Sillers Lookout**, where you can get fabulous views of the surrounding peaks and valleys, out across the plain to Lake Frome.

Even if you are only slightly interested in the stars, you should not miss the **astronomical observatory**. With the clear desert air and no artificial light to impinge on the scene, the views of our galaxy and beyond are unbelievable.

There are many good walks in the reserve. One of the most enjoyable is the 2.5km walk into **Bararranna Waterhole**, and many longer walks are available for those fit and well equipped.

Camping is only allowed in the camping area near the resort, and fires are only allowed in the fireplaces in the camping area.

Arkaroola to Copley The route beyond Arkaroola is really only suitable for 4WDs as it traces a path around the Gammon Ranges National Park. Normal cars will have to retrace their steps to Balcanoona and head to Copley on the main road.

For those wanting to push on, turn left at the T-junction you met as you entered the village and head past the shops, down along Wywhyana Creek, keeping right at the next two track junctions that lead to the caravan and camping areas.

After the second junction, the road continues along Copper Creek and less than 7km from the resort a track heads off to the right to **Bolla Bollana Spring**. A short distance later the road crosses Bolla Bollana Creek and then, on the left, is the turn-off to the parking area for the short walk to the **Bolla Bollana smelter**.

Just a little over 9km from the resort, a turn-off to the right leads to **Nooldoonildoona Waterhole**. This is a pleasant spot, ideal for a lunch break and a bit of exploring.

The road divides 12.4km from the resort, both branches leading to the same place; the right-hand (northern) route is a little rougher, but it's more enjoyable than the left-hand (southern) route. The right-hand route passes along Wild Dog Creek to a track junction 23.5km from Arkaroola. From here, the right branch leads north 6km to the **Yudnamutana mines** and smelter site which are well worth visiting. The left (south) branch is your route to Umberatana homestead.

Keep right at the next couple of track junctions, and 14.5km after you turned south, with **Umberatana homestead** on the right, pass through the gate and keep left. If you look up to the left along the ridgeline once you are past the windmill, you'll see the remains of a stone fence – imagine building it! The fence finishes a couple of kilometres later.

Nearly 19km south of Umberatana homestead you come to **Yankaninna station**. The track passes close to the homestead and outbuildings; keep the house on your left. Less than 1km past the homestead you will pass a track junction on your left, with a sign reading 'Yadnina'. This leads into the Gammon Ranges National Park and eventually back to Balcanoona.

Nine km east of Yankaninna, with the track skirting the ramparts of the **Yankaninna Range**, cross Gammon Creek and then begin to swing more and more south as you pass **Arcoona Bluff**, which at 953m is one of the highest peaks in this part of the range. Just over 5km from the Gammon Creek crossing, a track heads off to the left, entering the national park and leading to a small camping area on Arcoona Creek.

Less than 500m south of this junction the main track you are on crosses the same creek and 2km later passes through an outstation. The numerous small creeks that are crossed as you head south are all spawned in the rugged mountains to your left. Twenty km from the outstation you pass **Mt Serle station** homestead on your right, and 4km later meet the main Copley-Balcanoona road, 46km east of the bitumen at Copley. The total distance from Arkaroola is 98km.

Turn right at this main dirt road and head west an easy 46km to **Copley**. At Copley you can head north 35km to Lyndhurst, or south 5km to Leigh Creek South, or 159km to Hawker. By the way you have come, the total distance is about 450km, but you have seen and experienced much more of these magnificent outback ranges than you would have if you had travelled up the bitumen.

Copley has a hotel and roadhouse and can offer accommodation, fuel, repairs, food and meals. Leigh Creek South offers a more modern extensive shopping facility, and the meals from the licensed canteen are excellent.

ALTERNATIVE ROUTES

There are a number of alternative routes through the ranges, depending whether you want a quick trip or one that's a little different. Some of the shorter alternatives between such places as Wilpena Pound and Blinman, or Wilpena Pound and Balcanoona via the barytes mine road and Wirrealpa, have already been mentioned, but none are as scenic as the route described.

Certainly if you are in a hurry, the 159km run up the bitumen from Hawker is the way to go, but the Flinders Ranges will be just a line of blue mountains off to your right.

If you're coming from Adelaide and you

want the shortest way to the northern Flinders, the quickest route is to head up the Barrier Highway (the Broken Hill road) from Adelaide 313km to Yunta. Here you turn north onto a good dirt road and, travelling via Frome Downs, reach Balcanoona in another 271km.

ACTIVITIES
Walks
Walking is the main activity in the Flinders. There is a host of day walks and marked walking trails, or you can wander the long distance Heysen Walking Trail for a day or more.

Don't forget that this is an arid region and water can be scarce – be prepared!

Some of the walks that can be done in the gorges along the way have been mentioned already. At Arkaroola, in the far north, there are also many walks ranging from an hour to days. It's best to contact the visitor information centre at Arkaroola (☎ (08) 8648 4848) for more details. In the nearby Gammon Ranges National Park there are no marked trails and much of the area is really only for experienced, well-equipped walkers. However, there are a couple of shorter walks, the most popular being a eight-hour 16km walk from Grindell Hut south through the park to the main Copley road at Italowie Gap. Another walk of about 5km heads from Grindell Hut east through Weetootla Gorge and Balcanoona Gorge to a carpark just west of Balcanoona. You should contact the ranger at Balcanoona (☎ (08) 8648 4829) for more information, and to provide details of your walk, route and expected time of return.

Wilpena Pound and the surrounding national park is the best set-up area for walking, and there are a number of marked trails and short walks up to a day for those wanting to better experience the Flinders.

In Wilpena Pound itself, some of the walks include the old homestead and Wangarra Lookout, which take between one and two hours. The popular walk to St Mary Peak is a highlight, but it is a fairly strenuous one, taking eight to nine hours. The walk across Wilpena Pound to Edeowie Gorge takes

about the same amount of time and leads north-west to Edeowie Creek and its waterfalls.

There are other walks in and around Wilpena Pound, while a little further afield, but still in the park, there are a couple of marked trails from the Aroona Ruins. From the ruins, you can follow the Heysen Trail north to Parachilna Gorge, a six-hour, one-way trip. In the east of the park there is Wilkawillana Gorge to enjoy for four to five hours.

At Yanyanna Hut, north of Wilpena and on the route described, there is an enjoyable six to seven-hour walk across the undulating country to Elatina Hut. A little further along the route is a two-hour walk, which includes a little rock-hopping into Bunyeroo Gorge.

ORGANISED TOURS
There is a good choice of organised tours operating along this route. From Hawker, Allan Schultz 4WD Tours (tel/fax (08) 8648 4010) 5 Wonnoka Tce, Hawker, SA 5434, operates 4WD tours through the Flinders and beyond. Other 4WD tour operators include Butler's Outback Safaris (☎ (08) 8642 2188, fax 8642 4498), PO Box 671, Port Augusta, SA 5700, and Intrepid Tours (☎ (08) 8648 6277, fax 8648 6357), 17 Sixth St, Quorn, SA 5433, which have a wide choice of half-day to four-day trips.

Arkaba station (☎ freecall 1800 805 802 or (08) 8648 4195; fax 8648 0028), via Hawker, SA 5434, runs 4WD tag-along tours along the spectacular, picturesque Elder and Wilpena ranges. These are generally day trips and cost $70 a vehicle, cheaper if there is a group. The guide can tell you the history of the place and much about the flora and fauna.

Graham Dunn's Bush Retreat (☎ (08) 8339 1989) is also on Arkaba station. Graham conducts nature walks and tours based at a tented camp in a secluded spot on the property.

Rawnsley Park station (☎ (08) 8648 0030, fax 8648 0013), Hawker-Wilpena Rd, Hawker, SA 5434, operates local 4WD tours to surrounding points of interest, and horse-riding excursions from one hour to full-day

Top: Washing off the dust and unwinding in the thermal pool at Mataranka, NT
Bottom: Well 17 (Killagurra Springs; WA) along the Canning Stock Route is a sacred Aboriginal site

JEFF WILLIAMS

RICHARD I'ANSON

Top: Striking landscape near the Eyre Bird Observatory, SA
Bottom: Aerial view of Wilpena Pound, Flinders Ranges, SA

trips. Scenic flights and bushwalks are also available.

The Wilpena Pound Motel (☎ (08) 8648 0004, reservations freecall 1800 805 802; fax 8648 0028), c/o Wilpena Pound Holiday Resort, CMB Wilpena Pound, SA 5434, operates 4WD tours and coach tours to local points of interest, as well as a half-day and a full-day 4WD trip across parts of Arkaba station.

Scenic flights over Wilpena Pound are readily available for 15 or 30 minutes. Longer flights to Lake Torrens, Arkaroola, Lake Eyre, Andamooka and other outback destinations can also be arranged. Contact the Wilpena Pound Motel for information.

The Bush Safari Outback Camel Co (tel/ fax (08) 8543 2280), operated by well known outback adventurer Rex Ellis, operates one to eight-day camel trips in the Blinman and Wilpena Pound areas between April and October.

The Arkaroola Tourist Village (☎ (08) 8648 4848, freecall 1800 676 042; fax 8648 4846) has its famous Ridge Top Tour, along with 4WD tours to local points of interest. Scenic flights over the rugged ranges and further afield are also available from Arkaroola.

Ecotrek (☎ (08) 8303 7198), PO Box 4, Kangarilla, SA 5157, and Exploranges (☎ (08) 8294 6530), 37 Walker St, Somerton Park, SA 5044, have extensive tours and walking trips. Flinders Rides (☎ (08) 8528 2132), PO Box 19, Stockport, SA 5410, has a good selection of horse-riding trips throughout the region.

FACILITIES
Roadhouses
Hawker Motors (☎ (08) 8648 4014), on the corner of Wilpena and Cradock roads, is not the only place in Hawker for fuel, but it is the biggest and the best known. It is also the service depot for automobile club members and can supply all fuels, including LPG, parts and accessories, batteries and tyres, camping gas refills, souvenirs, books and maps, along with ice and cool drinks.

The *Beltana Roadhouse* (☎ (08) 8675 2744) is just off the main bitumen highway,

north of Parachilna and south of Leigh Creek South. It offers all fuels, ice and groceries along with dining and takeaway foods, and is licensed. Public toilets and showers are also available.

In Leigh Creek South, Leigh Creek South Motors in Black Oak Drive (the main street into the town centre off the highway) is the only place to get fuel. It can also supply tyres as well as LPG and repair facilities, along with a range of food, cool drinks and the like.

The Copley Roadhouse & Caravan Park (☎ (08) 8675 2288) offers very limited supplies and fuel, as well as a basic camping ground.

Fuel Outlets
There are a number of other outlets for fuel in the area that are not associated with roadhouses, as follows:

Hawker
  Range View Motors in Wilpena Rd (☎ (08) 8648 4049) has fuel and repair facilities; it is also the Toyota agent
Rawnsley Park station
  On the way north to Wilpena; has fuel (see below for more details)
Wilpena Pound
  The general store has all fuels and camping gas
Parachilna
  Fuel is available at the hotel – see below
Angorichina Tourist Village
  In Parachilna Gorge; has a store (☎ (08) 8648 4842) which sells all fuels as well as camping gas
Blinman
  The Blinman Hotel (see below for details) and the Blinman General Store sell fuel, but LPG is not available
Arkaroola
  The Arkaroola Resort (☎ (08) 8648 4848) has a wide range of supplies, including all fuels, limited spares and repairs and EFTPOS is available
Copley
  The Packsaddle General Store has the three main types of fuel – see below for details

Camping
Throughout the Flinders there is a choice of bush camping, with few if any facilities, and camping in commercial-type camping grounds. During the school holidays, especially the spring and autumn holidays, and

on long weekends, it pays to book in advance at the commercial camping areas.

At Hawker you can stay at the *Hawker Caravan Park* (☎ (08) 8648 4006), where there are on-site vans ($28 double) and self-contained cabins ($50 double), as well as the normal caravan-park facilities, with powered and unpowered sites costing $13/10. No dogs are allowed. Across from the Railway Station Restaurant on the edge of town is the *Flinders Ranges Caravan Park* (☎ (08) 8648 4266), where there are on-site vans from $28 to $32 and the normal facilities, including ensuites for vans, and free barbecues, with powered/unpowered sites $13/9. Dogs are also allowed.

At *Arkaba station* (☎ (08) 8648 4195) there is some excellent bush camping available for $10 a vehicle. You're guaranteed your own private spot – it's great!

There is a large, pleasant camping ground at *Rawnsley Park* (☎ (08) 8648 0030, fax 8648 0013) with powered sites, on-site vans and cabins. Unpowered sites cost $10 for a family, while powered sites cost $17. On-site vans cost $36 and sleep 4 to 6 people while the self-contained units cost $56 for two people.

At *Wilpena Resort* (☎ (08) 8648 0004) there is a large, idyllic camping area that can be crowded during the school holidays. Powered/unpowered sites are $17/10.50 for two people, with extra adults $3. Backpacker accommodation in a tented camp with shared cooking facilities is also available.

Throughout the national park, there is a wide choice of camping spots. Many people prefer the gorges or the area around Aroona. You need a permit, and camping fees vary. Self-registration, using the 'iron rangers' near the camping areas within the park, costs $3 per vehicle, while permits issued by a ranger from the national parks office cost $2 per adult. Contact the national parks office at Wilpena Pound (☎ (08) 8648 0048) or Hawker (☎ (08) 8648 4244) for further details.

At Parachilna, campers can have a site at the *old rural school* for just $5, while caravanners can stay behind the *Prairie Hotel*

with a powered site costing $12 for two people, $3 for each person there after. It's a good opportunity to sample some excellent Aussie food from the dining room, but space out the back is limited. See below for more details.

In Parachilna Gorge you can camp for nothing. There are no facilities and nobody to pick your rubbish up, so please look after this area – it is popular.

The *Angorichina Tourist Village* in Parachilna Gorge Rd has on-site vans ($30), camping sites ($8) and powered caravan sites ($12). Pets are allowed only at the manager's discretion.

At Blinman, the *Blinman Hotel* (☎ (08) 8648 4867) campers and caravanners can pull up under the peppercorn trees. Price is $5 per person but space is limited.

The *Arkaroola Tourist Resort* (☎ (08) 8648 4848) has a large camping area suitable for tents and vans. Prices are $10 for a site, with another $5 for power.

You can camp in the Gammon Ranges National Park if you have a permit issued by the ranger at Balcanoona (☎ (086) 48 4829). The same camping fees apply as for the Flinders Ranges National Park. The area around Grindell's Hut is the most popular but there are others. Grindell's Hut can also be rented – contact the ranger for details.

The *Copley Caravan Park* (☎ (08) 8675 2288) has basic facilities, and dogs are allowed. An unpowered site is $5 and a powered site is $12 for two people. On-site vans and the solitary cabin both cost $30 and sleep two people.

The *Leigh Creek Caravan Park* (☎ (08) 8675 4214) has powered and unpowered sites, but no pets are allowed.

Hotels, Motels, Cottages & Bunkhouses

In Hawker you can stay at the *Hawker Hotel-Motel* (☎ (08) 8648 4102) or the *Outback Motel* (☎ (08) 8648 4100). Prices range from $25 a single in the hotel to $65 a double in the motels, for a room only.

Two km south of Hawker are the *Windana Cottages* (☎ (08) 8648 4136), which cost $55 a double, but it's cheaper the longer you stay. As is the case with most self-contained flats, you need to bring your own linen, toiletries and food.

Arkaba station (☎ (08) 8648 4195) has a lovely, fully self-contained cottage that sleeps six. Costs range from $100 for two people, extra adults $15, with a minimum stay of two nights.

The *Wilpena Motel* (☎ (08) 8648 0004) has accommodation costing $85/93 single/double, room only. Meals are available in the restaurant. There is a wide choice of activities on offer from the resort and there is a large pool and barbecue area.

The *Prairie Hotel* (☎ (08) 8648 4895) in Parachilna offers cold beer, the best food in the north, and accommodation in single/double rooms for $40/55, or twin $60. Family rooms are also available costing $100 per room, while a double and single room costs $75 (children up to 12 are $10). Breakfast and all meals are available.

The *Old Parachilna School* (☎ (08) 8648 4676, or 8648 4895) in Parachilna offers accommodation in dormitory-style rooms, cost $12 with your own linen, or $16 linen supplied. There are also three separate rooms costing $15 single with own bedding, or $25 with bed made up, twin share per room is $25 with your own linen, or $35 with beds made up. You can also camp at a cost of $5 per person. Facilities include a kitchen, barbecue and shared showers/toilets.

The *Angorichina Tourist Village* (☎ (08) 8648 4842) has bunkhouse accommodation for $12, plus self-contained cabins with five, six or eight beds from $45.

The *Blinman Hotel* (☎ (08) 8648 4867) has rooms with ensuite for $60 a double, those without ensuite for $50 a double. Backpacker dormitory-style accommodation with shared cooking facilities costs $15 each. EFTPOS facilities are also available. Up the road a little and close to the old mine is *The Captain's Cottage* (☎ (08) 8648 4895). This historic circa-1860 cottage offers self-contained accommodation in two separate sections. The study sleeps up to three people and costs $80 a double, while the main part of the cottage, which can sleep two to seven

people, costs $100 for the first two people and $20 extra per person. Breakfast provisions can be provided by arrangement.

Arkaroola Tourist Resort (☎ (08) 8648 4848, fax 8648 4846) has bunkhouse accommodation for $10 per person, while rooms in the motels range from $49 to $99 for two people. There is a licensed restaurant with excellent meals and a bar. There is often a very pleasant barbecue around the pool which goes down well with guests and camping ground visitors.

A few of the sheep stations throughout the Flinders Ranges offer shearers' quarters-style accommodation. Some of these are *Nilpena station* (☎ (08) 8648 4895), 35km north-east of Parachilna, *Oratunga* and *Angorichina* stations (☎ (08) 8648 4863), just out of Blinman, and *Gum Creek station* (☎ (08) 8648 4883), south of Blinman. Prices are in the vicinity of $10 to $15, and there is generally a minimum charge. You will need to bring your own bedding and food.

Shopping

Hawker This is the place to go for supplies as there are a number of stores, including *Gloede's General Store*, the *Hawker Shopping Centre* and the *Sightseer's Cafe & General Store*. All are in the centre of town.

Other Places Apart from the roadhouses and resorts mentioned, there is very little else when it comes to buying supplies. After Hawker, the best place to buy anything is Leigh Creek South. The shopping centre, found just off the main road north, has a couple of well-stocked supermarkets, a newsagency, butcher and post office.

The *Packsaddle General Store* in Copley, just a few kilometres north of Leigh Creek South, supplies fuel and camping gas refills, along with a full range of meat, groceries and smallgoods.

Airstrips

Hawker has a well-maintained private airstrip capable of taking good size aircraft. The strip is run by the Hawker District Council.

No fees are payable and no aviation fuel is available. The strip is unusable after rain. For further information, contact the overseer (☎ (08) 8648 4114) or the district council (☎ (08) 8648 4011).

The Arkapena airstrip at Wilpena Pound is pretty short, so it is recommended that light aircraft land at nearby Oraparinna airstrip. Both strips are under the control of the National Parks Service; contact the Hawker office for further details. The Wilpena Motel can arrange to pick you up from the strip, and you can ring the motel for information on the serviceability of the strip and how to find it.

At Arkaroola there is a good private strip, 700m long and capable of taking most sorts of light aircraft. Avgas is available and there is a collection fee payable to Arkaroola. Contact the Arkaroola Resort for more details.

Leigh Creek South has a public aerodrome which is a major field capable of taking quite large aircraft. Contact Leigh Creek South (☎ (08) 8675 2006) for further information.

ALTERNATIVE TRANSPORT

If you don't have your own vehicle, there are a few ways of getting to and around the Flinders. Some of the tour operators listed in the earlier Organised Tours section have trips running from Adelaide, Port Augusta or elsewhere, but they are organised tours and you go where they want you to go.

Car Rental

There are a couple of places where you can hire vehicles, but neither are very handy to the centre of the Flinders. The closest are Budget (☎ (08) 8642 6040) and Thrifty Car Rental (☎ (08) 8642 2445), both in Port Augusta.

Bus

Stateliner Express (☎ (08) 8642 5055), 21 Mackay St, Port Augusta, SA 5700, has a bus network throughout South Australia and regularly services the main towns in the Flinders, including Hawker, Parachilna, Wilpena Pound and Leigh Creek South. Cost to Leigh Creek South is around $85 return,

to Wilpena Pound is $65 return, both leaving from Port Augusta. Those who want to go through to Arkaroola can be picked up, by arrangement, by a bus from there, the cost being an extra $110 return.

Train

The railway network, whether coming from Adelaide or from the eastern states, can only get you to Port Augusta, and that's it. From there you can hire a vehicle, catch a bus, or hoof it. For more details on timetables, call ☎ 13 22 32.

Air

Augusta Airways (☎ (08) 8642 3100), Port Augusta Airport, Port Augusta, SA 5700, operates scheduled services between Adelaide, Port Augusta and Leigh Creek South. It also has scenic flights and charter flights to anywhere in the outback.

Silver City Highway

For those travelling northwards from Melbourne, the Silver City Highway is one of the best introductions to the vastness and uniqueness of the Australian outback. If you are journeying west from Sydney or east from Adelaide, the Silver City Highway cuts across your course – you would probably meet it at the outback mining town of Broken Hill, from which the highway gains its name. From here, travellers can head south to Wentworth and Mildura, both on the Murray River, or north through Tibooburra into

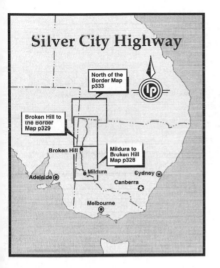

Silver City Highway

North of the
Border Map
p333

Broken Hill to
the Border
Map p329

Broken Hill

Mildura to
Broken Hill
Map p328

Adelaide

Mildura

Sydney

Canberra

Melbourne

HISTORY

For millennia, the region west of the Darling River has been inhabited by Aboriginal people. While the various groups were concentrated on the reliable water resources of the rivers, in the good seasons their wanderings took them across the rocky broken ground of the Barrier Range, where Broken Hill now stands, to the dunes of the sandridge country around Cameron Corner.

Charles Sturt was the first European to penetrate this country, in 1845. He named the Barrier Range but missed the wealth underneath, before pushing north to his Depot Glen near present-day Milparinka. Plagued by hot weather and a lack of water, he and his men continued northwards to a point north of present-day Birdsville, but their effort was in vain. The inland sea that Sturt had set out to find had vanished a few thousand years before, and he and his men retreated the way they came. It was one of the great survival feats of European exploration of Australia, and a stark contrast to the next expedition that passed this way.

In 1860 Burke and Wills led their well-prepared expedition north from Menindee (on the Darling River) to a depot they established on Cooper Creek. From this point, Burke, Wills and two others left the majority of the expedition at the depot and rushed to cross the continent. However, on their return, they discovered that the main party had left the depot just hours before their arrival. The Burke and Wills team were left with just a few stores, and all but one (King) perished on the banks of the Cooper near present-day Innamincka. The search parties that went out looking for them found country that appeared to be ideal for grazing, and their reports soon had pioneer pastoralists moving into the region.

Wentworth, at the junction of the mighty Darling and Murray rivers, 30km from Mildura, became a major port for the steamers plying these rivers from 1850 onwards, and Broken Hill came to prominence when Charles Rasp discovered the silver-lead-zinc deposit there in 1883. It was the richest deposit of its type ever discovered, and by

south-east Queensland, and to Cooper Creek, Birdsville and places beyond.

Broken Hill, the largest town in western New South Wales, is a long way from anywhere: Sydney is nearly 1200km to the east, while Melbourne is 900km to the south. Adelaide, over 500km to the south west, is the closest capital. It's the major source of supplies and the place where most Broken Hill residents go for holidays.

The Silver City Highway starts on the New South Wales side of the Murray, opposite Mildura. From here to 'the Hill', it's 261km, all of it good bitumen. North of the Silver City, the bitumen peters out after 60km. It continues spasmodically, interspersed with sections of well-maintained dirt to Tibooburra, then as pure dirt to Warri Warri Gate on the New South Wales/Queensland border, 393km north of Broken Hill.

This is officially the end of the Silver City Highway, and it shows. The road deteriorates as it heads north-west to Cooper Creek or north-east to Noccundra and Thargomindah, but in normal conditions it is still passable to ordinary vehicles. Although this road is slowly being upgraded, it will be a long time before all of it is sealed.

the 1890s a town of 20,000 had been established. Since then, minerals worth over $2 billion have been extracted from the ground. The mine has been the foundation for Broken Hill Proprietary (BHP), the biggest company in Australia, and for the town of Port Pirie, on the coast of South Australia, where the ore is smelted. Broken Hill is past its peak, the vast ore body stripped of its richest deposits. Within 10 or 20 years the ore will disappear, but the town will remain a tourist destination and an important service centre for this part of the country.

Both Tibooburra and Milparinka, a little further north, owe their existence to the gold rushes that occurred during the 1870s and 1880s. However, the gold was never in huge quantities, and the lack of water was always a problem.

Today Tibooburra is a minor service town offering basic facilities for the surrounding stations and the ever-increasing numbers of tourists who come to experience the 'Corner Country'. Milparinka is, but for the hotel, deserted.

INFORMATION
Tourist Offices
The following tourist centres can supply you with information on the Silver City Highway and the towns and centres through which it passes. The national parks offices listed can help you with details on Mootwingee and Sturt national parks.

Wentworth Tourist Information Centre
    Shop 6, Adams St, Wentworth, NSW 2648 (☎ (03) 5027 3624) – open seven days a week
Broken Hill Tourist & Travellers Information Centre
    cnr Blende and Bromide Sts, Broken Hill, NSW 2880 (☎ (08) 8087 6077, fax 8088 5209) – open from 8.30 am to 5 pm daily (except Christmas Day)
National Parks & Wildlife Service
    Broken Hill District Office, 5 Oxide St (PO Box 459), Broken Hill, NSW 2880 (☎ (08) 8088 5933)
National Parks & Wildlife Service
    Mootwingee Visitors Centre (☎ (08) 8091 2587)
National Parks & Wildlife Service
    Tibooburra District Office, Briscoe St, Tibooburra, NSW 2880 (☎ (08) 8091 3308)

Emergency
You will find police stations and hospitals in the following towns:

Wentworth
    Police (☎ (03) 5027 3102)
    Hospital (☎ (03) 5027 2345)
Broken Hill
    Police (☎ (08) 8087 0299)
    Hospital (☎ (08) 8088 0333)
Tibooburra
    Police (☎ (08) 8091 3303)
    Hospital (☎ (08) 8091 3302)

THE ROUTE
Officially the Silver City Highway starts on the New South Wales side of the border, near Mildura, but it is at Wentworth, 30-odd km further west, that it takes on its distinctive character and leaves behind the Murray River with its citrus groves.

From Mildura you can travel south of the river through Merbein, crossing the Murray 9km east of Wentworth. Alternatively, cross just north of the centre of Mildura, head a short distance north and turn left onto the Silver City Highway at the small hamlet of Buronga. From here it is 24km to Wentworth.

Wentworth to Broken Hill (261km)
The township of **Wentworth** straddles the Darling River just upriver from its confluence with the Murray, but the main part of town is on the western bank of the Darling. Here is a wide choice of accommodation and a good selection of places to handle all your supply requirements.

Just a few hundred metres past the Darling River bridge, turn right and follow the highway north. The manicured orchards and vineyards quickly give way to open grazing country, setting the scene for the drier, more expansive country further north.

The **Anabranch**, a major channel of the Darling River, is crossed 66km north of Wentworth. There is a spot to stop and enjoy the slowly flowing waters close to the road bridge, and at a pinch you could stop here for the night.

Another 50km brings you to a high point

overlooking the low-lake country to the east and **Popiltah Lake**, 121km north of Wentworth. It is a popular spot to stop and enjoy the view. It also makes the best overnight stop on the run north to Broken Hill.

At the *Coombah Roadhouse* (☎ (08) 8091 1502), 16km north of Popiltah Lake, you can get all fuels, takeaway foods and snacks. From the roadhouse it is a steady run north, through country that gets progressively drier, to Broken Hill, 124km further on.

Broken Hill

With a population of over 22,000, Broken Hill has much to offer the first-time visitor. Its rich mining heritage is well recorded in the **Railway & Mineral Museum**, and the mines that are open to the public. These include the **Day Dream Mine** (☎ (08) 8088 5682) 33km north-west of the Hill on the way to Silverton and the **original BHP mine** (☎ (08) 8088 1604), almost in the middle of town.

Broken Hill also offers travellers several of the finest **art collections** in Australia. For some years the town has been the centre for well-known Australian artists such as Pro Hart, Jack Absalom and Eric Minchin. Their galleries, amongst others, are well worth visiting, especially Pro Hart's, which has one of the biggest private collections in Australia.

The **Heritage Trail**, which starts and ends at the tourist centre, can be completed in a couple of hours. This easy and enjoyable drive gives you a good idea of the history and development of the Hill, while the **Heritage Walk** covers about 2km and takes the visitor around many of the original buildings of the central commercial area.

The town is also a major centre for the **Royal Flying Doctor Service** (☎ (08) 8088 0777), and at their base at the airport they have an information shop and museum.

There are far fewer hotels and clubs in the Hill than there used to be, but there's still a very good choice of places to eat and drink. Being a major service town, it has all the supplies you require, and you can get anything repaired here.

It's also an excellent base from which to explore the local area. One place not to miss

is the ghost town of **Silverton**, 21km northwest. Once a rich mining centre, Silverton has been the operational centre for a number of films, and the **Silverton Hotel** and the **Goal Museum** are beauties. Penrose Park, just a stone's throw from the Silverton Hotel, is a pleasant spot for a picnic, and its bushlike camping area is a quiet spot to put the tent up for a night or more. See Facilities for more detail.

South-east of the Hill are the **Menindee Lakes**, Broken Hill's watery playground, and the nearby **Kinchega National Park**. To the north-east of Broken Hill is **Mootwingee National Park**, with its rugged country and Aboriginal heritage, while a little further east is the opal town of White Cliffs.

Broken Hill to Warri Warri Gate (393km)

Wind your way out of town leaving the stark silhouettes of the mining headgear to the south. The Silver City Highway twists and turns through the streets of the Hill before finally heading towards Stephens Creek and places further north, about 2km from the centre of the city.

Stephens Creek, 16km out of the town, was once important to the townsfolk of Broken Hill as a pub and Sunday social centre, but is now just a name on the map, while **Yanco Glen**, another 16km up the road, is nothing more than a hotel. It offers a cool beer and that's about all.

A road junction 23km north (55km from Broken Hill) marks the turn-off for those who want to head east to the Mootwingee National Park, 75km away. This road also leads to the opal-mining community of White Cliffs, 215km from the junction.

Mootwingee National Park This park protects 68,900 hectares of harsh sandstone country of the Byngnano Range, and the surrounding sand and gibber plains that are so characteristic of this part of New South Wales. It is approximately 130km from Broken Hill.

Near-permanent waters tucked into the narrow, rugged gorges that cut through the range made the area a welcome place for

THE SOUTH

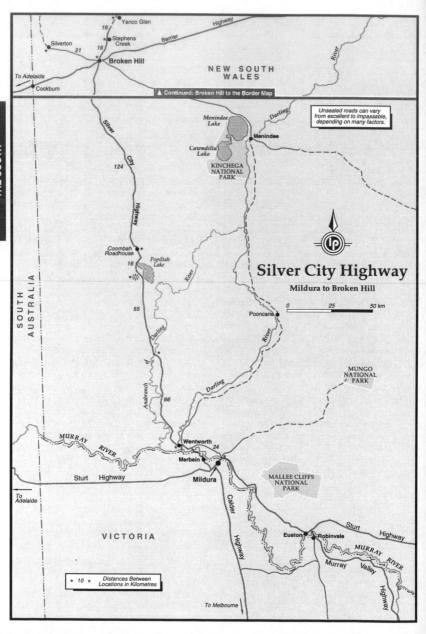

THE SOUTH

Yanco Glen

Silverton

Stephens Creek

Broken Hill

To Adelaide

Cockburn

▲ Continued: Broken Hill to the Border Map

NEW SOUTH WALES

Highway

Barrier

River

Silver

City

Highway

124

Menindee Lake

Cawndilla Lake

KINCHEGA NATIONAL PARK

Menindee

Darling

Unsealed roads can vary from excellent to impassable, depending on many factors.

Coombah Roadhouse

Popiltah Lake

16

55

Darling

River

of

Anabranch

66

Silver City Highway

Mildura to Broken Hill

0   25   50 km

Pooncarie

River

MUNGO NATIONAL PARK

Darling

SOUTH AUSTRALIA

MURRAY RIVER

Sturt Highway

Wentworth

Merbein

Mildura

24

MALLEE CLIFFS NATIONAL PARK

To Adelaide

VICTORIA

Calder

Highway

Euston

Robinvale

Sturt Highway

MURRAY RIVER

Murray Valley

Highway

★ 10 ★ Distances Between Locations in Kilometres

To Melbourne

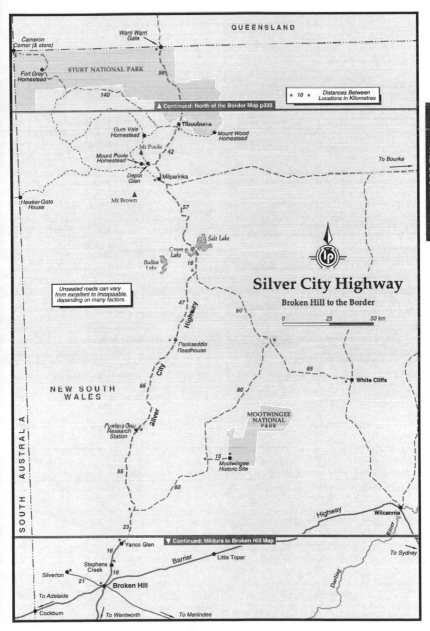

QUEENSLAND

Cameron Corner (& store)

Warri Warri Gate

Fort Grey Homestead

STURT NATIONAL PARK

56

140

★ 10 ★ Distances Between Locations in Kilometres

▲ Continued: North of the Border Map p333

Tibooburra

Gum Vale Homestead

Mount Wood Homestead

Mt Poole

42

Mount Poole Homestead

To Bourke

Depot Glen

Milparinka

Hawker Gate House

Mt Brown

57

Salt Lake

Green Lake

Bullea Lake

16

Unsealed roads can vary from excellent to impassable, depending on many factors.

Silver City Highway

Broken Hill to the Border

0   25   50 km

47

Highway

60

Packsaddle Roadhouse

City

65

NEW SOUTH WALES

65

Silver

90

65

★ White Cliffs

MOOTWINGEE NATIONAL PARK

Fowlers Gap Research Station

15

Mootwingee Historic Site

55

60

Highway

Wilcannia

23

River

★

Darling

To Sydney

▼ Continued: Mildura to Broken Hill Map

Yanco Glen

16

16

Barrier

Little Topar

Stephens Creek

16

Silverton

21

Broken Hill

To Adelaide

Cockburn

To Wentworth

To Menindee

SOUTH AUSTRALIA

Aboriginal people in days gone by, while the 1860 Burke and Wills expedition passed this way as well. There are many Aboriginal sites in the ranges, and the **Mootwingee Historic Site**, surrounded by the park and the most-visited area within it, gives visitors a fine chance to discover this heritage. The Cultural Resource Centre, along with a network of trails and the guided walks led by Aboriginal rangers, help people discover the art and imagine what life must once have been like in this region.

A camping area at *Homestead Creek* offers basic camping facilities and nothing else. A camping fee applies. For further details, contact the ranger at the Mootwingee National Park Visitors Centre (☎ (08) 8091 2587), or the Broken Hill District Office (☎ (08) 8088 5933).

White Cliffs This small outback community is a little different from most: many of the inhabitants live underground. Their homes are extensive, multi-room affairs, some even sporting underground swimming pool areas and the like. Think about it: if you are an opal miner and your house becomes too small, what do you do? Well, you bring home the mining equipment you work with each day and add a room to your underground home – it's as easy as that.

A few houses and buildings aren't underground, and these include the hotel and the general store. The *general store* (☎ (08) 8091 6611) can supply fuel and a good range of foods; it is also the tourist centre. The *White Cliffs Hotel* (☎ (08) 8091 6606) can supply a cold beer or three. There is a *caravan park* in town, as well as the *White Cliffs Dug-Out Motel* (☎ (08) 8091 6677).

Mootwingee Turn-Off to Milparinka Continuing north along the Silver City Highway, the road heads almost due north, dipping through the occasional wide, low creekbed and skirting the infrequent rocky hill or low range. There's the occasional strip of dirt just to bring you back to reality and to give you an idea of what lies ahead.

Fowlers Gap, a research station, lies close to the creek of the same name, 55km north of the Mootwingee road junction, and here you'll find a pleasant wayside stop – if the weather isn't too hot.

Packsaddle, 65km further north, offers a cold beer, very limited supplies and fuel to the passing traveller. Located close to Packsaddle Creek, there is a wayside stop beside the gum-lined creekbed (like most in this part of the world, it rarely has water in it).

A reasonable dirt road joins with the Silver City Highway 47km north of Packsaddle. This road, from the south-east, is the northern access to White Cliffs and Mootwingee National Park.

The road passes through a wide sweep of low sand-ridge country north of Packsaddle, and 63km from this small outpost of civilisation the road winds between a series of lakes. Off to the right is the normally dry Salt Lake, while to the left are the seasonal freshwater swamps of Green Lake, Lake Patterson and Cobham Lake.

Milparinka Milparinka is just a couple of kilometres off the main road, 57km further on. While the main road continues north, you need to turn left at the signposted junction. Cross the gum-lined creek, turn left again at the T-junction, and a few hundred metres on you are at the pub – the life centre and the only inhabited building in Milparinka.

The *Milparinka Albert Hotel* (☎ (08) 8091 3963) is a favourite watering hole. The solid stone building offers a welcome respite from the heat, and the open square, with its water fountain surrounded by the rooms that make up the accommodation, is very pleasant. The pub can also supply meals and fuel.

Milparinka was the centre for a brief, relatively rich gold rush that took miners into the surrounding hills searching for the elusive metal. During those heady days, the pub and the nearby courthouse and police station were built. While the pub survived intact, the other two fine buildings were destined to become a pile of rubble, until the locals got to work a couple of years ago and saved these monuments.

Just a short distance from Milparinka is

Depot Glen, where the explorer Charles Sturt and his party were trapped for months during their 1845 expedition to find the inland sea. So certain were they of finding a vast body of water that they had taken a boat with them – local legend has it that the boat was abandoned near here when the explorers retreated to the Darling River.

Depot Glen today is much the same as when Sturt and his men were there. Gums still line the creek, and corellas and galahs wheel in noisy profusion at the slightest disturbance. Near the creek and where the explorers camped is a blazed tree and a monument to James Poole, Sturt's second in command, who died while the party was trapped here. Just a short distance away, deeper in the hills, the waters of the creek, confined by the rocky range, are deeper and more permanent.

A few kilometres north of the creek, past the homestead, is Mt Poole. A rocky monument crowns its low but lofty prominence; to keep the men in his party occupied during their enforced stay, Sturt had them build a marker on top of this hill, stating in his journal:

I little thought when I engaged in that work, that I was erecting Mr Poole's monument, but so it was, that rude structure looks over his lonely grave and will stand for ages as a record of all we suffered in the dreary region to which we were so long confined.

Although both sites are easy to find, it's best to stop at the pub and get directions.

Tibooburra Back on the main road heading north, it's an easy run to Tibooburra, 42km away. For all intents and purposes, Tibooburra is a single street, which happens to be the main road north, with a few houses, offices and pubs along the way. Even so it's the biggest town since Broken Hill and can supply all the general daily requirements for the traveller, such as food, fuel, basic repairs and a range of accommodation, including a number of hotels, a motel and a caravan park.

The town also acts as the main service centre for the outlying sheep stations and for the nearby Sturt National Park. The Tibooburra District office of the National Parks & Wildlife Service (☎ (08) 8091 3308), Briscoe St, is an excellent place to start if you want to find out a bit about the history and the fauna of the area. Just 1km north of the town, at Dead Horse Gully, a small camping area is run by the National Parks & Wildlife Service, a display of old gold-mining equipment is worth seeing.

Each year over the New South Wales Labour Day long weekend, the town puts on its rodeo and gymkhana.

Sturt National Park This park takes up 344,000 hectares of the very north-west corner of New South Wales, having as its northern and western boundary the Queensland and South Australian borders, marked in this part of Australia by the famous Dog Fence – see the Fauna section in the Facts About the Outback chapter.

The protection the fence offers to sheep also benefits the kangaroos, which abound in the park. With their major predator kept under control and the water points put in for sheep and cattle, the roo numbers have increased since the coming of Europeans, and that makes the park and its inhabitants one of the major attractions of western New South Wales.

Here you will generally see the western grey kangaroo and the red kangaroo. The male of the latter species is easy to identify, but to the uninitiated, the female (or blue-flier) looks similar to the grey roo, a species where the male and female are less easy to tell apart. In the range country that cuts across parts of the park, the heavier-built euro, or hill wallaroo, may be seen.

Wedge-tailed eagles and emus are also common in the park, but many other species of birds, not as big or as majestic, also call this stark country home.

For most travellers who come this way, a visit to Cameron Corner, where the three states of New South Wales, South Australia and Queensland meet, is on the agenda. The Corner lies 140km north-west of Tibooburra and is reached by a good, well-signposted, dirt road. On the way, you will pass through Fort Grey, where Sturt set up a base camp during his 1845 expedition. A camping area near the station of the same name is an ideal spot to enjoy this section of the park.

At Cameron Corner a gate through the Dog Fence leads to a small camping area in South Australia, while just a drive of a few hundred metres will lead you past the Corner post to the Corner Store. Here you can get snacks, a cool drink and fuel. From the Corner, you can head west to the Strzelecki Track and Cooper Creek, covered in the Central Deserts chapter.

There are other places to visit in the park, and other spots to camp, including the old Mount Wood homestead. The **museum** here is well worth a look. To the north of the homestead there is another camping area, at The Gorge.

Continuing north from Tibooburra, the road is good dirt all the way to the border at **Warri Warri Gate**, 56km from Tibooburra. Here you need to open the large gate through the Dog Fence; be sure to close it after you. You're now in Queensland and at the end of the Silver City Highway, but as this is a hell of a place to stop, we'll push a little further north to take you to some form of habitation and a choice of places to go next.

North of Warri Warri Gate

Travelling through Queensland, the country remains much the same as before. A road junction 34km north of the border gives you your first choice of where to go. Turning left here will take you via Santos and Orientos stations north to Nappa Merrie on Cooper Creek, a total distance of 224km. Not so long ago, this was a sandy track, but recent years have seen it steadily upgraded north to Nappa Merrie, with a new bridge across Cooper Creek 5km east of Nappa Merrie.

Nappa Merrie is where the famous Burke and Wills 'Dig Tree' is located, about 50km east of Innamincka – see the Strzelecki Track section in the Central Deserts chapter. From Innamincka you can head north to Birdsville or Betoota, and from there to places further north.

Continuing along the main road north of Warri Warri Gate, **Naryilco** homestead is passed 18km further on, and another track to Santos comes in from the left just north of here. Yet another track to Santos meets the road 45km north from Naryilco. A few kilometres further on, just before the crossing of the normally dry Elizabeth Creek, is the abandoned Bransby homestead on the left.

Noccundra and its famous pub are 88km north of the road junction, 185km north of the border. Here you can get a beer, meals and accommodation. Fuel and emergency repairs are also available, as well as up-to-date information on all the roads in the region.

From Noccundra you can head east on bitumen to Thargomindah, and from there to Cunnamulla and the Matilda Highway (covered in the Tropics chapter). Alternatively, if you want to stay on dirt roads and tracks, you can continue north to Eromanga, Windorah and beyond.

ORGANISED TOURS

Contact the various tourism bodies and regional tourist information centres for details of local tour operators, including Tri State Safaris (☎ (08) 8088 2389) which offers one to 16-day 4WD tag-along tours throughout the region, or Crittenden Air (☎ 08) 8088 5702), based in Broken Hill, which operates mail flights.

FACILITIES
Wentworth

Wentworth is a major town and, as such, offers all facilities, including branches of most banks.

There is plenty of accommodation – travellers can choose from a wide range of hotels, motels, holiday units and caravan parks. The *Cod River Lodge* (☎ (03) 5027 3071) has motel rooms for $35 a double, while the *Willow Bend Caravan Park* (☎ (03) 5027 3213) offers ensuite cabins ($38 a double), self-contained cabins overlooking the river for $32 a double, on-site vans ($25 a double) and powered/unpowered sites ($12/10 a double). For a complete listing and prices, contact the Wentworth

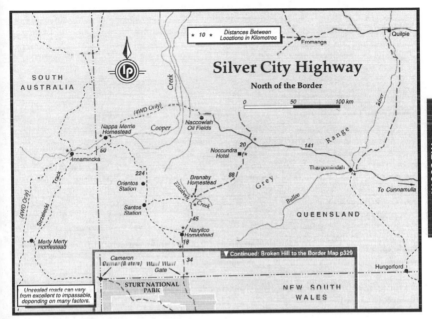

▼ Continued: Broken Hill to the Border Map p329

Tourist Information Centre (☎ (03) 5027 3624).

Broken Hill

This major centre can supply all requirements. All major banks are represented, including New South Wales credit unions.

The Royal Automobile Association of South Australia (☎ (080) 88 4999) handles emergency road services and recovery.

There are over 20 hotels and nearly 20 motels, along with self-contained cottages, hostels and three caravan parks, at varying prices. The budget-conscious can choose from two hostels: the YHA *Tourist Lodge* (☎ (08) 8088 2086), 100 Argent St, and *Astra House* (☎ (08) 8087 7788), 393 Argent St. The Tourist Lodge offers shared kitchen facilities, single rooms for $20; YHA members $18 a night, while in the dorm, a bed will cost $14. At Astra House, backpackers can find accommodation with kitchen facilities from $12.

The two caravan parks, *Broken Hill* (☎ (08) 8087 3841), and *Lake View* (☎ (08) 8088 2250), offer accommodation in cabins (with or without ensuites) and on-site vans. There are powered and unpowered sites that are also available. The prices are around $40 a double for a cabin, $24 for an on-site van and $14/10 for powered/unpowered sites, with small additional charges for extra people. The Lake View allows dogs, under control.

Silverton

The ghost town of Silverton offers limited supplies and fuel. Accommodation and camping are available at *Penrose Park*. Though there are limited amenities and no powered sites, it only costs $2.50 per adult, while kids are free. There are two bunkhouses, both with eight bunks, one with power costing $20, the other without power for $15 – it doesn't matter whether there are one or eight of you; the price is the same.

Tibooburra

The *Tibooburra Supply Store* has EFTPOS facilities, food supplies and all fuels, but not LPG. The post office is also the agency for the Commonwealth Bank, but only passbooks are accepted.

There's a National Parks & Wildlife Service district office (☎ (08) 8091 3308) in Briscoe St.

Accommodation is available at both the hotels. The *Family Hotel* (☎ (08) 8091 3314) in Briscoe St is famous for its walls painted by the late Clifton Pugh. It has dining-room and counter meals, and laundry facilities are available for guests. Singles/doubles cost $20/35 and breakfast can be arranged. The *Tibooburra Hotel* (☎ (08 8091 3310), also in Briscoe St, has rooms available for $30/40. All meals can be arranged.

At the *Granites Motel-Caravan Park* (☎ (08) 8091 3305), on Brown St, there's motel accommodation from $40/50, with use of a communal kitchen. The caravan park has all facilities, including on-site cabins ($44 for a double) on-site vans ($24) an powered/unpowered sites ($12/10 a double). Dogs are also allowed, under control.

ALTERNATIVE TRANSPORT
Air

Southern Australian Airlines (☎ 13 1313), and Kendell Airlines (☎ 13 1300), Broken Hill agent (☎ (08) 8087 1969), both operate flights between Adelaide, or Melbourne, to Broken Hill, via Mildura.

Bus & Train

There are regular bus services, run by private companies as well as by public state transport authorities, from the eastern capital cities to Broken Hill and Mildura.

At the bus terminal in Broken Hill, 23-25 Bromide St, you'll also find the booking office of Greyhound Pioneer Australia (☎ (08) 8087 2735).

Country Link, run by Australian National Rail in New South Wales, operates a rail service to Broken Hill. Contact Country Link (☎ 13 2232) or the Broken Hill Railway Station (☎ (08) 8087 0441), Crystal St, for current timetable details and costs of rail and coach transport.

For details on bus services to Mildura (for connection to Wentworth), contact V-Line (☎ 13 2232), which is run by the Victorian Public Transport Corporation.

Car Rental

If you were hoping to hire a vehicle around Wentworth, you will need to check the hire-car companies based in Mildura.

In Broken Hill, however, all the major car-hire companies are represented; Avis (☎ (08) 8087 7532), Budget (☎ 13 2727) and Hertz (☎ (08) 8087 4838) along with Broken Hill 4WD Hire (☎ (08) 8087 2927).

Kidman Way

HIGHLIGHTS

- Experiencing the outback of some of our earliest poets and writers
- Camping amongst the gum trees along the many rivers on the route

Cutting through the heart of western New South Wales, the Kidman Way offers for northern bound travellers the quickest route from Victoria. As well, many of Australia's best and most loved poets, bush balladeers and writers drew their inspiration from this vast region; Henry Lawson, Will Ogilvie, 'Breaker' Morant and others all lived, worked and wrote about their experiences in this area of New South Wales.

HISTORY

This route is cut by the great rivers of early Australian history, and for generations of Aborigines it was a rich area in which to live before Europeans arrived in the early 1800s.

Across these vast plains and along the great rivers some of Australia's best known early explorers sought to open the country up

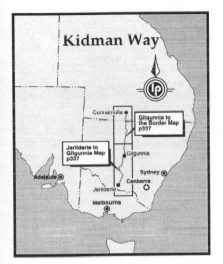

and fought for recognition and knighthood. Thomas Mitchell was one, and he was later knighted for his efforts, while Charles Sturt, who was the first European to discover the Darling River in 1829, never received the acclaim to which he was entitled.

INFORMATION
Tourist Offices
Travellers will find tourist offices or information centres in most towns along the route and these are listed under facilities, later in this chapter.

For more information you can also contact Tourism New South Wales (☎ (02) 9931 1111), 140 George St, Sydney.

Books and Maps
There are numerous books and maps that cover this region of Australia. See the nearest good map shop or local automobile club such as the NRMA in New South Wales, or the RACV in Victoria.

THE ROUTE
Jerilderie
Jerilderie is located on the Newell Highway, 318km north of Melbourne on the main route

to Brisbane. It is famous for wheat, wool, rice and a host of other crops reaped from its verdant irrigation area. For travellers it supplies all one requires and has a good selection of accommodation.

Jerilderie to Griffith (135km)
Head north out of town on the Newell Highway for 16km where you need to turn left for Coleambally. It is only another 51km to the small township of Coleambally. Follow the main road through Coleambally and it is a straight run north, only interrupted by the major cross roads of the Sturt Highway.

Located on the banks of the Murrumbidgee River a couple of kilometres north of the Sturt Highway intersection, and 32km from Coleambally, is **Darlington Point**. This small town was foundered in the early 1860s and can supply a fair range of services.

Follow the signposts out of town to Griffith, 36km north. Once you've entered town, keep a good lookout for roadsigns as the route through Griffith is a little convoluted. Basically head north to the main street, Banna Ave, and turn left (west) keeping a good lookout for signs. At the western end of town you need to get into Griffin Ave and onto Route 87 heading to Warburn, Goolgowi and Hillston.

Griffith
Griffith is by far the biggest town you will go through on this trip north and lies in the heart of the Murrumbidgee Irrigation Area, 680km west of Sydney. Proclaimed when the railway arrived in 1917, it was by 1922 a flourishing town.

There's plenty to see and do in and around the city, with most of the nearby wineries putting on tours and wine tasting, while **Cocoparra National Park** (☎ (02) 6962 7755) 30km from town, is worth a visit. The town has a population of over 20,000 and can supply a wide range of services.

Griffith to Cobar (367km)
Once on the right road out of Griffith it's a 50km run across flat land to **Goolgowi** on

the Mid-Western Highway. This small town can supply the major requirements of all travellers.

It's another 60km to Hillston, and you soon leave the irrigated country behind and enter wheat and grazing country.

Hillston

Situated on the banks of the **Lachlan River**, the town of Hillston offers a wealth of waterborne activities as well as a good range of facilities and supplies. **Willandra National Park** (☎ (02) 6967 8159) is a pleasant day trip from the town where kangaroos and mobs of emus are very common.

North of Hillston From Hillston, you need to turn right at the major intersection in the heart of town, and head for Lake Cargelligo and Mt Hope.

About 20km from town the road turns to a well-maintained sandy road and 15km later you need to veer left, crossing the Lachlan River soon afterwards. You're now getting into more remote country and the road less travelled.

Mt Hope, 96km north of Hillston, can nearly be passed through without being noticed. As the road climbs a small hill you pass the Mt Hope general store and Royal Hotel – that's it!

Heading north the road improves, finally turning to bitumen again about 100km south of Cobar and 60km north of Mt Hope.

You enter Cobar from the south-east, meeting the main east-west Barrier Highway just on the east side of town, where you veer left to the centre of town, past the now closed Great Cobar Copper Mine and the very good regional museum.

Cobar

Located on the Barrier Highway, 705km west of Sydney, 161km north of Mt Hope and 502km north of Jerilderie, Cobar is in the outback. Centre of a large shire, the population of the town is around 4500, and while the town supports a rich grazing industry, it is mining that has been its lifeblood.

The town can supply all a visitor requires

and there is a good range of sporting clubs and activities.

Cobar to Bourke (160km)

Head north onto Bourke Road and you are soon on your way. The first 25km or so is bitumen, but that soon expires and it's good dirt all the way to Bourke through scrub and grazing land. As you get closer to the Darling River town, signs of cotton growing begin to crowd the roadside.

You enter the outskirts of Bourke, cross over the railway line and meet with the main Mitchell Highway. Following the main road north you come to the police station and the heart of town.

Bourke

Located on the banks of the mighty and muddy Darling River, Bourke, with a population of around 3400, is 780km north-west of Sydney, via the Mitchell Highway, and 980km north of Melbourne, via the route you have taken. Brisbane is 950km to the east.

Bourke features deep in the Australian psyche and both Will Ogilvie and Henry Lawson mentioned Bourke and places around this quintessential outback town in their writings, giving it a larger-than-life character for many city people.

The town has a wide range of accommodation and service facilities, and there is plenty to see and do. The Darling River is the lifeblood of the area and being about 2800km long it is the longest river in Australia. Charles Sturt was, in 1829, the first European to see the river and graziers soon followed.

Bourke to Barringun (136km)

Follow the dog-legging Mitchell Highway through town and you soon leave the built-up area behind and cross the Darling River to North Bourke, with its few houses and pub.

You are on bitumen as you head north along the Mitchell Highway and 99km from Bourke you come to the small hamlet of **Enngonia** where the pub can offer accommodation and fuel.

Pushing ever north, it is just 37km to

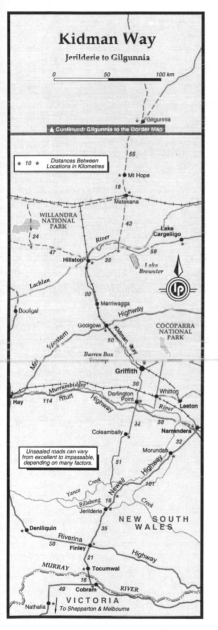

THE SOUTH

Barringun and the end of the Mitchell Highway. Located 136km from Bourke, this small sprawling village straddles the New South Wales/Queensland border, 1116km north of Melbourne and 793km north of Jerilderie. The pub, once a haunt of Henry Lawson, offers a traveller succour, while a roadhouse, just a short distance north, has fuel and food as well.

North across the border is Queensland and the all-bitumen Matilda Highway (for details see The Tropics chapter).

ORGANISED TOURS

Contact the various tourism bodies and regional tourist information centres detailed below for details of local tour operators.

FACILITIES
Jerilderie

The *Jerilderie Budget Motel* (☎ (03) 5886 1301), has rooms from $35/40 a single/double. There is also the *Jerilderie Caravan Lodge & Caro-Tel* (☎ (03) 5886 1366), with caravan sites at $10 a double.

Coleambally

The *Brolga Hotel/Motel* (☎ (02) 6954 4009) has rooms from $30 a single, while the *Kingfisher Caravan Park* (☎ (02) 6954 4100) has caravan sites at $7 a double per night.

Darlington Point

Accommodation and camping is available at the *Riverside Caravan Park* (☎ (02) 6968 4237) with unpowered sites costing $8 a double.

Griffith

There is a wide range of hotels and motels offering accommodation, such as the *Acacia Motel* (☎ (02) 6962 4422), with rooms from $55. The *Griffith Tourist Park* (☎ (02) 6964 2144) offers powered sites costing $14 a double, as well as park cabins from $44 a double.

Tourist information can be obtained from the Griffith Visitor's Centre (☎ (02) 6962 4145), on the corner of Jondaryan and Banna Aves.

Goolgowi

The *Goolgowi Caravan Park* (☎ (02) 6965 1331) has a number of powered and unpowered sites costing $11 and $9 respectively.

Local tourist information can be obtained from the Visitor Information Centre (☎ (02) 6965 1306), on the corner of Cobram and Stipa Sts.

Hillston

There are a number of hotel/motels including the *Kidman Way Motor Inn* (☎ (02) 6967 2151) and the *Club House Hotel* (☎ (02) 6967 2514) with rates from $15/25 a single/double. Caravanners and campers can select a site at the *Hillston Caravan Park* (☎ (02) 6967 2575).

Local tourist information can be obtained from the WG Parker Memorial Library (☎ (02) 6967 2503), on High St.

Mt Hope

The *Royal Hotel* (☎ (02) 6897 7984) has singles for $16 per night.

The *Mt Hope General Store* (☎ (02) 6897 7986) is open seven days a week supplying fuel, groceries and tyre repairs.

Cobar

Cobar has a wide range of accommodation, including the *Copper City Motel* (☎ (02) 6836 2404) which has units from $46 a single, and the *Cobar Caravan Park* (☎ (02) 6836 2425) with cabins from $24, while powered sites are $12 a double.

The Cobar Tourist Information Centre (☎ (02) 6836 1452) is based at The Great Cobar Outback Heritage Centre, on the Barrier Highway.

Bourke

This major town has a range of accommodation to choose from, such as the *Old Royal Hotel* (☎ (02) 6872 2544) with rooms at $27/40 a single/double, and the *Major Mitchell Motel* (☎ (02) 6872 2311) which has rooms starting at $60/69.

Caravanners and campers can stay at either the *Mitchell Caravan Park* (☎ (02) 6872 2791), or the *Paddlewheel Caravan*

Park (☎ (02) 6872 2277) with prices around $12/10 for powered and unpowered sites or cabins at $35 a double.

For more information on Bourke and its surrounding area contact the Bourke Tourist Information Centre (☎ (02) 6872 2280), on Mitchell St.

Enngonia

The *Oasis Hotel* (☎ (02) 6874 7577) has singles for $20, and caters for campers and caravans.

Barringun

The *Bush Tucker Inn* (☎ (02) 6874 7584) in the park has doubles for $20, while camp-sites cost from $4 a double. All fuels are available from the Inn.

ALTERNATIVE TRANSPORT
Air

Air Link (☎ 13 1713 or 13 1300) connects Sydney with Cobar and Bourke, and is also available for charter. Hazleton Airlines (☎ 13 1713), also has flights to Cobar and Bourke from both Sydney and Dubbo.

Bus

There are no bus companies that operate a service along the Kidman Way, although Greyhound Pioneer (☎ 13 2030) does have a service from Dubbo to Cobar, at $52 one way.

Car Rental

Representatives of major car-hire companies such as Avis, can be found in Cobar and Bourke, along with Thrifty Car Rental (☎ (02) 6836 2607) in Cobar.

THE SOUTH

The North-West

With its wide open spaces, stunning scenery and lure of adventure, Australia's north-west is a promised land for outback travellers. It includes the rugged Kimberley and Pilbara regions, spectacular coastlines of red cliffs and lonely beaches and the vast desolate expanses of the Great Sandy Desert. Towns are few and far between – a sprinkle of mining and pastoral centres in the Pilbara and Kimberley and a few ports along the coast. Most famous of these is Broome, once the pearl capital of Australia and still with much of the atmosphere of its colourful past.

Unless you're mainly sticking to the few sealed roads, the north-west isn't really the place for inexperienced outback motorists. The region has numerous remote touring opportunities, including two of Australia's finest long-distance 4WD routes. The most challenging is the Canning Stock Route

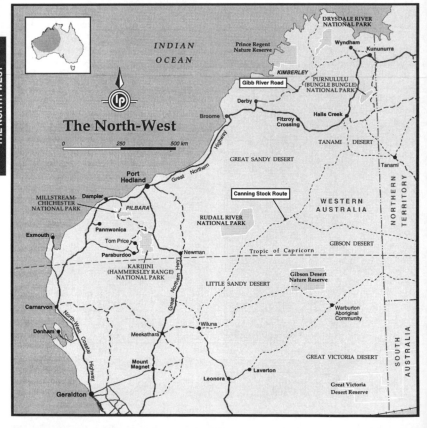

The North-West

(1700km), which cuts through the desert from Halls Creek, in the Kimberley, to Wiluna in the south. There's also the Gibb River Road (710km), running through the heart of the Kimberley between Derby and Kununurra.

If you're in a normal car, you can visit most of the national parks in the north-west, including Geikie Gorge and Tunnel Creek in the Kimberley, and Millstream-Chichester and Karijini in the Hamersley Ranges. The spectacular Bungle Bungles are, unfortunately, only accessible to 4WDs – which is why most visitors confine themselves to a scenic flight. Although the north-west is extremely remote and sparsely populated, there's a good range of visitor facilities and organised tours. The latter includes 4WD tag-alongs on the Gibb River Road, fishing trips at various places, visits to a huge iron-ore mine at Tom Price, canoeing on the Ord River and boat cruises on the vast Lake Argyle.

Gibb River Road

HIGHLIGHTS

- Cooling off in the waterfalls of Bell Gorge
- Discovering the magnificent Aboriginal Wandjina art of the Kimberley
- Walking through Tunnel Creek – don't forget your torch

The Kimberley, that vast chunk of country that takes up the far north-west corner of Australia, is much bigger than the UK or Japan, nearly half the size of Texas and, for those who relate to Australia, bigger than Victoria and Tasmania combined.

It's closer to Asia than most major cities of Australia: Indonesia is less than 500km away and Wyndham, Western Australia's northernmost port, is nearer to Jakarta than

it is to Perth and closer to Singapore than to Melbourne. By road, it is 3400km from Melbourne to Halls Creek, while from Perth to Broome, on the other side of the Kimberley, it is a mere 2300km.

Less than 30,000 people live in the Kimberley, mainly in small towns such as Broome, Derby and Kununurra.

To the north and west, the area is bordered by a torn and twisted coastline and one of the most spectacular stretches of water in the world. Rugged sandstone ranges separate the Kimberley from the sandy desert country that encroaches to the south.

The area represents one of the great outdoor travel destinations in Australia, rich in Aboriginal culture, European history and spectacular natural beauty.

Highway 1 swings north from Broome to Derby and then east to Halls Creek, before heading north to Kununurra, but misses out on the 'real' Kimberley. To see that, you need to travel along the unsealed Gibb River Road, which cuts through the very heart of the region. At 710km, it represents the shortest (but slowest) distance between Derby and Kununurra.

The road has been improved over the years, but one good wet season sees much of the past effort washed away. In 'good' years, after the graders have been out, the road is suitable for a normal car, if you don't mind it losing a few bits along the way. In 'bad' years, after heavy rain and no graders for months, the route is rough even for 4WDs that have been well prepared.

For the most part, the Gibb River Road passes through pastoral country, with some interesting national parks along the way.

HISTORY

The Kimberley was probably the first place on the Australian mainland where Aborigines landed when they arrived from Asia. A number of sites have been found that date back at least 18,000 years, but because the sea level has risen substantially in the past 50,000 years, many early occupation sites would now be under water.

The richness of Aboriginal culture is

vividly portrayed in the art that can still be found in the area – the Kimberley contains some of Australia's greatest collections of prehistoric art. If you are lucky enough to see a rock gallery of the distinctive, vividly painted Wandjina figures, then you, like many before you, will be impressed.

For hundreds of years, Macassan bêche-de-mer (trepang, or sea cucumber) fishermen from islands far to the north were sailing to the Kimberley coast and establishing fishing camps there.

The first European known to have sailed along this coast was the Dutch navigator Abel Tasman, in 1644. He went on to explore Australia's southern coast, where his name is immortalised in the island of Tasmania. The English buccaneer William Dampier was next on the scene, making two visits, in 1688 and 1699. His reports were less than favourable, curtailing English interest in the region until the early 1800s.

Nicolas Baudin's expedition in the ships *Le Geographe* and *Naturaliste* between 1800 and 1804 mapped much of the Australian coastline, resulting in the French names scattered along the Kimberley coast.

Matthew Flinders circumnavigated Australia at the same time without even seeing the Kimberley. Phillip Parker King led four coastal mapping expeditions to the area between 1818 and 1821, naming such places as Careening Bay (after the enforced landing of his ship) and the Buccaneer Archipelago (in commemoration of Dampier's voyage). He also travelled far up the Prince Regent River, sketching King's Cascade, still a favourite spot for remote boat travellers.

In 1837, the famous ship of Charles Darwin, the HMS *Beagle*, under the command of John Wickham and John Stokes, mapped much of the coast, including the area around Derby and Brecknock Harbour.

The first overland trip in the Kimberley was undertaken by George Grey. He landed on 2 December 1837 at Hanover Bay, a spot that is just as remote today as it was then. Although the expedition didn't discover anything of note, Grey waxed so lyrical about the place that later a pastoral company was

formed to establish a settlement near the Glenelg River. Like the expedition, this venture failed. Grey was the first European to see the Wandjina art that dots many of the caves and overhangs of the Kimberley.

By the 1860s, pearlers were plying the coast from Broome and the first tentative steps at a pastoral industry were being taken. In 1879 Alexander Forrest left Beagle Bay and followed the Fitzroy River upstream as far as Geikie Gorge, before heading towards the coast along the ramparts of the King Leopold Ranges. Failing to reach the coast, he returned eastwards and discovered the Ord River. His reports of good grazing land along the Fitzroy and Ord rivers sent settlers scrambling for a slice of the action. These included Nat Buchanan, the Durack family and the MacDonald family, who still own and operate the Fossil Downs station, just outside Fitzroy Crossing.

In the early 1930s, there were less than 10,000 people in the Kimberley, and the cosmopolitan 'capital' of the area was Broome . Hundreds of boats worked out of Broome, searching for pearl shell and pearls. In the late 1930s a plan was developed for the formation of a Jewish home state centred around Argyle station in the eastern Kimberley; it was not until the birth of modern Israel in 1948 that the idea died.

WWII brought raids by Japanese bombers, not only on Broome, Wyndham and Derby but on Aboriginal missions as well. Secret landfalls by Japanese troops occurred during these years, but the rugged terrain that had repulsed Grey and his followers served Australia well.

The population of Broome plummeted after the war and the new use of plastics for buttons saw the demise of the pearling industry. In the 1950s, the main road north of Broome was improved from a horse track to a wide horse track. The road network was so poor that until the late 1950s, all police patrols were by horseback – the sealing of Highway 1 was only completed here in 1987.

In 1963, the Ord Dam wall was completed and Lake Argyle, the largest lake in Australia, began to form. It took over two years to fill, even though the river in full wet-season flood would be capable of filling every dam that supplies Perth with water, from empty to full, in 20 minutes! The dam, and the irrigation area that was set up for it to serve, has only just recently reached its full potential.

Mineral finds resulted in rushes back at the turn of the century, but it was the discoveries of oil at Blina, east of Derby, diamonds near Lake Argyle in the late 1970s, bauxite on the Mitchell Plateau around the same time and oil and gas offshore that really opened up the Kimberley.

While cattle have waned in importance over recent years, much of the land still remains under grazing. Over 30% of the Kimberley is Aboriginal land of one form or

---

Pedalling through the Kimberley in the 1950s

Alex and Jacky Sklenica bicycled through the Kimberley back in 1954. Here's what they had to say about it in 1990, after they had just completed a similar return trip in their trusty 4WD:

Repacking our push bikes, we were considering possible routes from Wyndham to Derby. A shorter but very rough 700km on the Durack and Gibb River track, confusingly crossed by stock routes petering out in the bush and no supply points along the way. Or the 1000km via Turkey Creek, Halls Creek, Fitzroy Crossing. This longer way, still rather a bush track than road in 1954, was used mainly by drovers and station vehicles. A decisive advantage was that food supplies would be available from shops at Halls Creek and Fitzroy Crossing.

The Wyndham Police and locals in the pub offered advice, wished us luck and one grinned: 'You know what I am thinking.'

We had to travel light and live mostly off the land. A limited amount of basic food supplies were bought in Wyndham. Water, still remaining after the previous 'rainy', and some edible plants would have to be found on the way. Not a beginner in the Australian bush, I carried also a few fishing hooks and a line and a single-shot .22 rifle. We hoped to catch fish, but knew that our main food source would consist of pigeon, ibis meat, ducks, galahs and wallabies.

We were unable to ride our bikes over the frequently sandy or rock-strewn stretches, but had to walk, pushing the bikes or sometimes ride on firmer surfaces parallel to the road.

There were no camping grounds, national parks or tourists there. During four months, we met only one car with two Melbourne tourists and one Frenchman riding a motorcycle around Australia. When, on rare occasions, we met with station people, we stopped to boil a billy and to exchange news.

Once a passing stockman from Bohemia Downs stopped his truck near our little campfire for a bit of a talk, sharing with us a billy of tea. Looking our scanty outfit over, he said: 'On bikes ... but how ... what do you eat?'

Pointing to our saddle bags I replied: 'We have some flour, tea, sugar and such here and there is plenty of game around waterholes.'

When leaving our camp, he dropped an apparently empty plywood tea-chest: 'Perhaps you can use this as a table.'

Inside the tea-chest was his present: a loaf of bread and a pound of butter wrapped in sheets of newspaper. Fresh bread and real butter! Immediately, we boiled another billy, spread slices of buttered bread on the tea-chest and read every scrap of newspaper, adverts including. This was indeed a happy camp, still vivid in our memory.

There were no marked tracks through spear grass and spinifex leading to Geikie or Windjana gorges. Near Tunnel Creek, overhanging rock shelters were still periodically inhabited by nomadic natives. We found and left undisturbed spears, stone knives and scrapers.

We met a mounted police patrol and sat till midnight smoking and talking, listening to natives singing around a campfire near the billabong.

A period in our life when we were not tied to conventions and restrictions of crowded civilisation. A time when we were free to walk over the horizon. A slice of damper and roasted wallaby washed down with Bushell's was a repast. A shady tree, the warmth of a small fire on cool nights, bright stars our roof. Unforgettable memories of an unfenced land, of outback people and times past.

Alex Sklenica

Just such a short time ago, and much has changed. Yet so much remains the same. ∎

another, and this percentage is growing. More than 10% of the land is protected in national parks or conservation reserves, but much of this is inaccessible to travellers.

INFORMATION
Tourist Offices
The Derby Tourist Bureau (☎ (08) 9191 1426; fax 9191 1609), 1 Clarendon St, PO Box 48, Derby, is a good source of information. The Kununurra Tourist Bureau (☎ (08) 9168 1177; fax 9168 2598), is found close to the heart of town at 75 Coolibah Drive. Wyndham's Information Centre (☎ (08) 9161 1054; fax 9161 1341) is in the old port area at the Old Port Post Office, O'Donnell St.

The Western Australian Tourist Centre (☎ (08) 9483 1111), 469 Wellington St, Perth, can also provide information on the Kimberley.

The Department of Conservation & Land Management (CALM) has regional headquarters (☎ (08) 9168 0200) at Kununurra, in Konkerberry Drive. You can contact them for any information on the national parks and conservation reserves in the Kimberley.

Permits
There is no requirement for permits if you stick to the main road and the route described.

Emergency
Derby The police station (☎ (08) 9191 1444) is at the corner of Villiers and Loch Sts, while the hospital (☎ (08) 9193 3333) is further west along Loch St.

If you are unfortunate enough to need towing, the Derby RAC of WA agency is the BP Colac Service Station & Roadhouse (☎ (08) 9191 1256), 84 Loch St, while Derby Motorplus (☎ (08) 9191 1844) also has 24-hour recovery.

Wyndham The police station (☎ (08) 9161 1055) is in the old port area, while the hospital (☎ (08) 9161 1104) is in the new part of town.

The RAC of WA agency in Wyndham,

Branko BP Motors (☎ (08) 9161 1305), Great Northern Highway, can arrange towing.

Kununurra The more modern town of Kununurra has its police station (☎ (08) 9169 1122) just west of the main shopping centre, in Coolibah Drive. The hospital (☎ (08) 9168 1522) is in the same street, but a little further west.

Kununurra's RAC of WA agency, Elgee Toyota (☎ (08) 9168 2236), 231 Bloodwood Drive, can help with towing.

Books & Maps
There are a number of good maps of this area. The Hema map *The Kimberley*, Australian Geographic's *The Kimberley* and the Western Australian Department of Land Administration Street Smart Touring maps *East Kimberley* and *West Kimberley* are by far the best for the general tourer.

The best guide books to the area are *The Kimberley – an Adventurer's Guide* by Ron & Viv Moon, published by Kakirra Adventure Publications, and *The Australian Geographic's Book of the Kimberley*.

There are a host of other books that cover different aspects of the Kimberley, its people, history and natural wonders. Many of these are available in bookshops in towns of the region.

Radio Frequencies
For those who have an HF radio, the important frequencies to have are the Royal Flying Doctor Service bases at Derby, Port Hedland and Alice Springs and if possible, the frequencies for the Telstra radphone bases in Darwin and Perth.

For the RFDS base at Derby (call sign VJB), the primary frequency is 5300 with secondary frequencies of 6925 and 6945. Port Hedland's call sign is VKL and its primary frequency is 4030; secondary frequencies are 2280 and 6960. Alice Springs (call sign VJD) is a good base to call from the eastern Kimberley if you can't get through to Derby. Its primary frequency is 5410 and its secondary frequency is 6950.

The Perth Telstra base (call sign VIP) has

radphone channels 427, 806 and 1226. Other frequencies for Tonecall and Selcall include 607, 834, 1229 and 1610. The Selcall for the beacon in Perth is 0799 and for the operator, 0107.

The Darwin Telstra base (call sign VID) has radphone channels 415, 811, 1227 and 1622. These are only available between 8 am and 8 pm as voice call, but 24 hours as Tonecall and Selcall. Other Tonecall and Selcall channels are 607, 834, 1229 and 1610. The Selcall for the beacon at Darwin is 0599 and the operator, 0105.

The Telstra RDD network via Darwin or Perth is very poor, while the Alice Springs base is only fair. Telstra is planning a new RDD base to service the Kimberley. Contact Telstra on ☎ toll-free 1800 810 023 for more information.

There are generally better communications through the RFDS base in Derby, so when it is working (business hours only), it is the one to go for.

SPECIAL PREPARATIONS

Even in the good times, the road is remote and travellers can be thin on the ground. Have a breakdown and you can be waiting for help for a while. Be prepared.

To check on road conditions throughout the Kimberley, contact the Main Roads WA (☎ toll-free 1800 013 314, all hours) or the department's offices at Kununurra (☎ (08) 9168 1755) or Derby (☎ (08) 9191 1133). Alternatively, you could check with the police stations at Derby, Kununurra or Wyndham (see Emergency) or the tourist bureaus (see Tourist Offices).

The country dries out very quickly after the wet-season rains stop and water can be scarce along the way. Those contemplating walking or riding the route, please take note! The road can be very rough and tyre damage is common. Carry at least two spares.

THE ROUTE

For the best views, it's recommended that you drive the Gibb River Road from the Kununurra end and this is the way we've described the trip.

Kununurra

The township of Kununurra is 45km from the Western Australia/Northern Territory border and owes its existence to the construction of the Ord Dam in the 1950s and 1960s. It is the Kimberley's most verdant town, literally awash with green for most of the year, courtesy of the nearby dams.

Today, Kununurra's population owes its living not only to the irrigation area along the river but also to the wealth of minerals in the area, both on land and offshore.

Kununurra is 825km from Darwin, 360km from Halls Creek and 1062km from Broome via Highway 1. There are good facilities here – everything the traveller needs, from camping and caravan parks to hotels and motels.

The town makes a good base for exploring the surrounding area and you could join in the fun at the many local festivals such as the Ord River Festival or the Bushman's Rodeo. Paddle a canoe on the Ord or go fishing for the elusive barra, either on your own or with the help of a guide. A couple of national parks and nature reserves in the area are also worth checking.

Mirima (Hidden Valley) National Park On the edge of town, this small park protects some Bungle Bungle-style rock formations among a maze of cul-de-sacs, amphitheatres and twisting, sheer-sided valleys. There are examples of Aboriginal art in some of the overhangs, but these are not as spectacular as other galleries deeper in the Kimberley.

Animal life includes dingoes, agile wallabies, echidnas and a number of bats. Birds are the most obvious and include numerous birds of prey, finches, pigeons and parrots.

The best way to see the park is by walking and a number of walks, up to 1km long, to points of interest and good lookouts have been established.

Ord River There are two dams on the Ord River. The first, just out of town where Highway 1 crosses this mighty river, is the Diversion Dam, holding back the waters of Lake Kununurra. The main dam is 74km away, via a good bitumen road, and its wall holds back the waters of **Lake Argyle**. It makes an enjoyable day trip, but if you have a boat or a canoe, or like a spot of fishing, you can make something more of it.

Kununurra to the Kalumburu Road (294km)

Heading west along the bitumen on Highway 1 makes an easy start to this trip. A major road junction 45km west of Kununurra has you heading towards Wyndham and leaving Highway 1, the road to Halls Creek, Derby and Broome.

Seven km north-west of this junction, a signposted dirt road turns off to the left (west). This is the start of the Gibb River Road.

If, instead of turning left onto the Gibb River Road, you continue straight ahead, you will reach **Wyndham**, 48km up the road. Despite Kununurra's size and importance, Wyndham is still the official centre for the huge shire of East Kimberley. You may want to visit this historic port while you are in the area (see the later Detours section).

Initially, the Gibb River Road is well maintained and crosses the **King River** 17km from the highway. This river crossing is normally dry, except early in the Dry. The impressive ramparts of Mt Cockburn South can be seen to the north. In fact, for the next 50km, there are wide and expansive views of the **Cockburn Range** and its towering cliffs of red, raw rock. In the evening light it is dramatically impressive.

The turn-off to **Emma Gorge** is another 7km along the road. This is part of El Questro station and at the Emma Gorge Resort you can pamper yourself. You can also drive the 2km off the Gibb River Road to the carpark, walk into the gorge and have a swim, but it will cost you $5. Situated near the gorge is the resort, with a range of bush cabins, a bar and a shop.

The main access track into **El Questro station** is 10km further along the Gibb River Road. This cattle station, 17km off the main road, has opened its doors to tourism in a big way and takes in over 400,000 hectares of typically rough, broken Kimberley cattle country. Camping is available along the Pentecost River or you can stay in some more luxurious accommodation – in fact, fancier accommodation in the Kimberley would be hard to find. Fishing, horse rides and helicopter trips are all on the agenda.

The **Pentecost River** is crossed 58km from the main highway. Once again there is water across the causeway only early in the dry season.

For the next 1km or so, the road parallels the Pentecost River and on a sweeping corner just 9km from the crossing, a track leads off to the right to **Home Valley station**. Visitors are welcome and you can camp or be accommodated here; there's a wide range of activities, from fishing to horse riding, scenic flights to 4WD trips.

Back on the road again, the route climbs the range. Near the top, 2km from the turn-off to Home Valley, a **lookout** gives an expansive view of the entire Cockburn Range. This is a top spot to sit on a cooling Kimberley evening, having a cold beer and enjoying the changing hues of the cliffs. From here you can also see, to the north, the twin Pentecost and Durack rivers, as well as the West Arm of Cambridge Gulf.

Twelve km further is a camping spot. A track on the right leads down to a small camp beside a watercourse that generally has some water in it. There is only a little shade but for an overnight camp, it is fine.

Bindoola Creek is crossed for the first time just over 5km further and a second time 18km after. Both crossings are generally dry and present no problems.

After climbing Gregory's Jump-up at the 122km mark, it is just 3km to the **Durack River homestead** turn-off. This station is owned by the Sinnamon family. The homestead and camping area are less than 1km off the main road. Camping along the river is superb and you can fish, swim or canoe. Overnight accommodation and meals are also available, as are fuel and limited supplies.

Nearly 4km from the turn-off to Durack River homestead is the track to **Karunjie station**, the third of the Sinnamon properties, but it is not open to the public.

From this junction, the road continues to be rough and stony. Spare your tyres by taking it easy. For most of the time, the road winds across flat ground, occasionally climbing a jump-up or escarpment, where the going gets rockier and rougher. After a time on this plateau country, the road descends, via another jump-up, to a flat or creek bed. This country is extremely harsh and unforgiving. Water is scarce between the rivers at any time, except during and straight after the Wet.

The **Durack River** is crossed 152km from the bitumen, just 27km past the Durack River homestead turn-off. This is a wide crossing between quite high banks but is generally no problem. A number of tracks on both banks lead to camping spots up and downstream and there are some nice waterholes in either direction.

The main track to **Ellenbrae homestead** is passed just over 20km further on. Pleasant camping and accommodation are available here.

Dawn Creek is crossed 4km further and here you will find a reasonable campsite and permanent water down to the right. After another 24km of rock and dirt road, a track heads off to the right. Just 100m along this track is a good campsite on the Campbell River that comes with its own shade and water. Walkers and cyclists will appreciate both!

Just before the crossing of Russ Creek, 20km from the Campbell River camp, a track leads off to the right from the Gibb River Road to a fair camp.

At the 242km mark from the highway (294km from Kununurra), 23km from the Russ Creek crossing, you come to a major road junction. To continue on the Gibb River Road, turn left. If you want to take a diversion to the Mitchell Plateau or the Aboriginal community at Kalumburu, turn right (see Detours section). Both places are worthwhile but, while the Gibb River Road is passable for a normal car during good times, the road to the Mitchell Plateau is definitely 4WD and the road to Kalumburu is not much better.

Kalumburu Road to Derby (417km)

Veering left and continuing along the Gibb River Road, there is no appreciable change in the road conditions. They rarely get better and in fact, with the increased traffic that this section carries, heading towards the Mitchell Plateau and Kalumburu, the road may be more chopped up. By this time, if you have been crazy enough to tow a van along this road – and some people do – you'll be wishing you hadn't.

The track into **Gibb River station** is 40km from the Kalumburu junction and it's obvious from the sign on the front fence that they don't have fuel or supplies and want nothing to do with travellers.

Three km further on is the Bryce Creek crossing and another 1.5km brings you to Mistake Creek. Generally both these waterways are as dry as a badger. Nine km past the Mistake Creek crossing is the **Hann River** crossing. This is one of the major rivers in the central Kimberley and you are near its headwaters. The river often has water in it at the crossing. A couple of minor creek crossings follow.

Sixteen km south of the Hann River you come to the turn-off to **Mt Elizabeth station**, run by the Lacey family. Their father pioneered this area of the Kimberley in the 1920s and the family is keenly aware of the heritage, both Aboriginal and European, of this wild place.

The homestead is 30km from the main road, and accommodation and camping are available there. Booking is essential for accommodation and a phone call would be appreciated if you want to camp (see the later Facilities section).

From the homestead, it is possible to travel to the remote western coast around the Walcott Inlet area, but you pay a fee to use the private road. The road is extremely rough and, unless you are experienced or travelling with others who are, we do not recommend it. The Laceys offer trips to Walcott Inlet as part of their Bushtrack Safaris operation and, as they know the art sites and the best fishing spots, it pays to go with them.

Just a little less than 10km down the main

THE NORTH-WEST

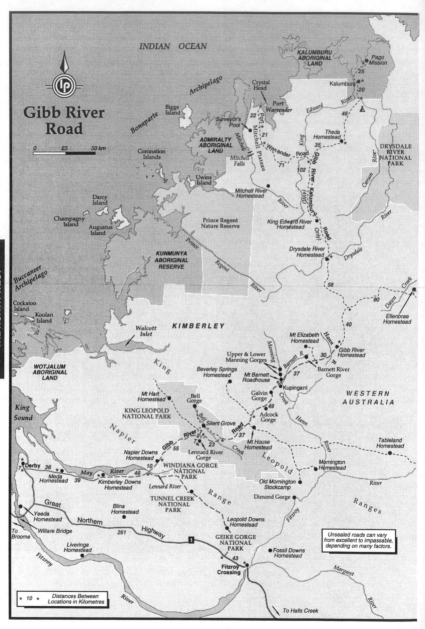

Gibb River Road

0   25   50 km

INDIAN OCEAN

Bonaparte Archipelago

Bigge Island

Coronation Islands

Darcy Island

Champagny Island

Augustus Island

Buccaneer Archipelago

Cockatoo Island

Koolan Island

KIMBERLEY

Walcott Inlet

KUNMUNYA ABORIGINAL RESERVE

Prince Regent Nature Reserve

ADMIRALTY ABORIGINAL LAND

Surveyor's Pool

Uwins Island

Mitchell Falls

Mitchell River Homestead

Mitchell Plateau

Crystal Head

Port Warrender

KALUMBURU ABORIGINAL LAND

Pago Mission

Kalumburu

25

20

46

Theda Homestead

35

DRYSDALE RIVER NATIONAL PARK

Winnender

71

102

King Edward Homestead

Drysdale River Homestead

Drysdale River

Carson River

58

90

Dimm Creek

Ellenbrae Homestead

40

WOTJALUM ABORIGINAL LAND

King Sound

Napier Range

Mt Hart Homestead

KING LEOPOLD NATIONAL PARK

Bell Gorge

Silent Grove

23

Lennard River Gorge

Napier Downs Homestead

10

55

WINDJANA GORGE NATIONAL PARK

Derby

7   36

Meda Homestead

39   46

Kimberley Downs Homestead

May River

Lennard River

TUNNEL CREEK NATIONAL PARK

Blina Homestead

Yeeda Homestead

To Broome

Willare Bridge

Great Northern Highway

261

Liveringa Homestead

Fitzroy River

GEIKE GORGE NATIONAL PARK

1

43

Fitzroy Crossing

Fossil Downs Homestead

To Halls Creek

Margaret River

Leopold Downs Homestead

Dimond Gorge

Old Mornington Stockcamp

Mornington Homestead

Fitzroy River

Leopold Ranges

Tableland Homestead

Mt House Homestead

37

Hann River

Adcock Gorge

49

Galvin Gorge

37

Kupingarri

Barnett River Gorge

30

Gibb River Homestead

Mt Elizabeth Homestead

Barnett River

Upper & Lower Manning Gorges

Beverley Springs Homestead

Mt Barnett Roadhouse

Manning Creek

WESTERN AUSTRALIA

Prince Regent River

Beverley Springs Homestead

Gibb River – Kalumburu Road (4WD)

King Edward River

Edward River

Mitchell River

Unsealed roads can vary from excellent to impassable, depending on many factors.

★ 10 ★ Distances Between Locations in Kilometres

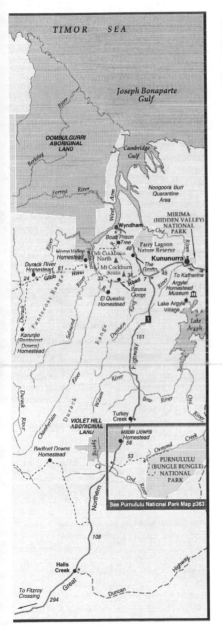

road from the turn-off to Mt Elizabeth is the track to **Barnett River Gorge**. This track heads west, off the road, and winds around a little before you get to the river. The furthest point is about 4km from the road, but it is not the best camping spot, although the walking and the river are excellent. A couple of tracks which veer earlier off this track give access to some exceptional camping. Across the river from the camping area, under an overhang, observant walkers will find some reasonable, but old and faint, Aboriginal art.

The Barnett River is crossed 27km further along the Gibb River Road. It normally has water in it but is generally no problem to a 4WD.

On the right, 1km past the river crossing, is the turn-off to the **Mt Barnett Roadhouse** and camping area. The roadhouse dispenses fuel and all those things that hot, thirsty travellers love. The camping down on the Barnett River must be experienced to be fully appreciated – it's magic, though it can be crowded at times. Pay at the store.

Spend some time lazing around the river – the sandy beaches, scattered rocks, cool water, sheer cliffs 100m upriver, shady trees and lily-covered backwaters make this an idyllic spot. If you have a canoe, the waters of the river also make a pleasurable, gentle paddle. It is even possible to snorkel in the **Lower Manning Gorge**.

There are some Aboriginal art sites around the area. They can be found on the opposite bank of the river, at the end of the walking track.

A longer walk (about an hour each way) takes you to the **Upper Manning Gorge**. This track starts on the bank opposite the camping ground and cuts across country, following a marked trail of old drink cans hanging in trees, and the odd stone cairn.

While the upper gorge has a small, sandy beach, it's the waterfall and huge pool surrounded by cliffs that are the real attractions. Take lunch and spend the whole day up in the gorge – it's great.

Back on the Gibb River Road and heading south, you pass, on your left, the Aboriginal community which owns Mt Barnett. The road improves from here; while it is still stony dirt, the ridges of sharp rock jutting above the road surface that were so common north of Gibb River station have almost disappeared.

The turn-off to **Galvin Gorge** is 14km south of the roadhouse and a reasonable camping area can be found at the end of the track which leads about 1km west from the road. A walk of a few hundred metres takes you to the main pool and waterfall. It is a top swimming spot and will be appreciated by those pedalling a bike or doing the trip on foot. Beside the pool, in the shadiest part of the cliff-face, is a small sample of the local Aboriginal art, in this case a Wandjina head.

As soon as the road passes the turn-off to Galvin Gorge, it begins to climb the Phillips Range. Over the next 10km there are good views of the surrounding country.

The Adcock River is crossed 13km from the Galvin Gorge track and 5km further on, a track leads off to the left to **Adcock Gorge**. The 5km track into the gorge and the small camping area is, apart for the last few hundred metres, pretty good. At the end of the track is a small, idyllic camping area and the refreshing waters of the gorge.

Continuing along the main road, you cross a couple of minor creeks before coming to the turn-off to **Beverley Springs station** on your right, 49km south of the roadhouse. The station, located 43km from the main road, offers accommodation, camping and tours.

Just 4km past here and 160km from the Kalumburu junction, you will find the short access track to **Mt House station** on your left. This large, well-known Kimberley property has limited supplies and fuel for travellers and accommodation is possible if you book beforehand. You can also travel via Mt House to the Old Mornington Stock Camp Resort and the delightful Dimond Gorge and Sir John Gorge (see the later Detours section).

The first permanent water across the road is crossed 25km south of the turn-off into Mount House. This is **Saddlers Spring** and on the left, just 1km past the creek crossing is the **Imintji Roadhouse** and Aboriginal

community. Limited fuel and stores are available here and camping is allowed.

Some 8km south is the turn-off to **Bell Gorge**, probably the most scenic and relatively accessible gorge in the heart of the Kimberley. The 30km run into the gorge is pretty reasonable; it takes about an hour.

The track into Bell Gorge parallels the northern face of the rugged **King Leopold Ranges** coming to the camping ground at **Silent Grove**, 19km from the turn-off. The route swings north soon afterwards, before coming to and running beside Bell Creek. There is some excellent camping along here in designated sites. The shady trees and pandanus palms make a verdant scene, the canoeing and swimming are very enjoyable and you can wet a line for some sooty grunters, or black bream, which make a great meal. Less than 4km on, the track ends beside a large boab tree with a bell carved into its trunk.

From this spot, a walking trail heads north a few hundred metres to the lip of one of the most spectacular waterfalls and gorges in the Kimberley, formed as the river slashes its way through the Isdell Range. Spend a bit of time enjoying the scenery and exploring the falls and the surrounding area.

This area, now managed by the Department of Conservation & Land Management (CALM), was once a part of Mt Hart station and is destined to be a national park.

About 4km from the Bell Gorge junction, the road turns to bitumen for a few kilometres and begins a long climb of the King Leopold Ranges. As the route winds its way up the battlements of the range, you'll have some good views of the surrounding area.

Over the next 10km, the road crosses a number of small creeks before coming to **Dog Chain Creek**, 21km south of the Bell Gorge turn-off. The road continues through the range country and just over 2km from Dog Chain Creek, there is a major road junction with a good dirt road heading off to the left. This is the Millie Windie Road. Two hundred metres along this road, a lesser track heads south into **Lennard River Gorge**.

It is about a 7km drive into the carpark

from where you can access the Lennard River Gorge and the road is often very rough, passable only to 4WDs. The drive and the walk down the hill to the gorge rim are worth it, though.

A trail marked by some small rock cairns leads down to the water at one end of the gorge. Here, in the heat of the Dry, it is cool, the deep, dark water always refreshing.

Seven km south of the Lennard turn-off, a track heads off to the right to **Mount Hart homestead**, some 50km from the Gibb River Road. Accommodation, but no camping, is available at the homestead.

A few hundred metres past this junction, the road crosses Apex Creek, which has a small camping area on its banks, just after the crossing. Less than 1.5km later, you pass through **Inglis Gap**; a small parking area on the left gives extensive views of the surrounding plains and ranges. From here, you descend the final ramparts of the King Leopolds and head across rocky and undulating country towards the Napier Range, the final barrier before reaching the flat plains that border the great rivers of the western Kimberley.

The road gets better all the time and while there are a few minor creek crossings in the next 40km, most of them are bridged. The turn-off to Napier Downs station is 278km from the Kalumburu junction and 53km south of Inglis Gap.

You begin to pass through Yammera Gap just 500m from the turn-off to Napier Downs. This short pass leads through the **Napier Range** – a sheer-sided limestone range that was, millions of years ago, a coral reef.

The Lennard River is crossed 9km south of the pass and a track on the southern side of the river leads a few hundred metres west to a pleasant camp close to the stream.

Just 400m further is the turn-off to **Windjana Gorge**, 21km from the Gibb River Road, and **Tunnel Creek**, 35km further on. This road also leads another 68km east and joins the main highway 43km west of Fitzroy Crossing. Windjana Gorge is perhaps the best place in all of Australia to see freshwater

crocodiles in their natural environment. Windjana Gorge and Tunnel Creek are both national parks, but only the former allows camping. Neither should be missed (see the later Walking section under Activities).

Once south of the Napier Range, the road passes through flat, lightly treed, pastoral country. The turn-off to **Kimberley Downs station** is 46km from the road junction to Windjana Gorge and the bitumen begins just a short distance after the Kimberley Downs turn-off. You'll appreciate it!

The turn-off to Meda station and the **May River** is 39km further on. The access track to the homestead comes close to the May River after 6km. Camping is allowed here; it is a popular spot with the locals and a good fishing area, but be careful where you swim – big saltwater crocodiles have been seen. This is one of the better spots to camp near Derby.

Back on the main road, a major T-junction is reached 36km beyond the May River turn-off; to the right is Derby and you'll hit the outskirts in less than 4km (it's about 7km to the centre of town). You're 416km from the Kalumburu junction and 710km from the green town of Kununurra.

Derby

Derby lies just above the high-tide mark on a low tongue of land in King Sound, just north of the mouth of the Fitzroy River. Mud flats surround the town on three sides. While Derby may lack the all-season green of Kununurra and the razzamatazz of cosmopolitan Broome, it is an honest and friendly place.

Derby was officially proclaimed in 1883, a couple of years after Yeeda station was founded on the banks of the Fitzroy River, 50km south, by George Patterson. By 1890, the town boasted a jetty (used for the shipping of wool), a resident magistrate and a police force.

While European settlement in the eastern Kimberley had been based on cattle brought overland from Queensland, the western Kimberley was opened up by sheep graziers bringing their flocks from the south. By the

The Napier Range

This prehistoric barrier reef that grew in a Devonian sea has a magnetic appeal to travellers. The adjoining Oscar Range and Geikie Range are also part of this ancient reef system and while you can see and experience one aspect of it at Geikie Gorge National Park, just north of Fitzroy Crossing, it is the Napier Range that holds the greater (and less developed) attractions.

Windjana Gorge is 25km east of the Gibb River Road, 127km east of Derby. Geologists consider it of major importance: here, exposed for all to see, are the remains of an ancient reef complex, with all its intricate relationships locked into the rocks.

The Lennard River has cut its way through the range, forming a narrow, picturesque canyon about 3.5km long, up to 200m wide and, in places, nearly 100m deep. The near-vertical walls of the gorge are an impressive backdrop to the line of green along the sandy bed of the dry-season stream. Late in the dry season, when the river does not flow, it forms a chain of pools, home to fish and a few freshwater crocodiles.

In the sediment and ancient river gravels, scientists have found the remains of extinct crocodiles and turtles, as well as ancient mammals, such as the large marsupial wombat diprotodont.

A ranger is based at the gorge during the dry season and there is a pleasant camping area close to the mouth of the gorge. Walking and canoeing are enjoyable ways of seeing the splendour of the gorge, and if you are quiet there is always the chance of seeing a shy croc or agile wallaby. Bird-watching is also rewarding, as a number of species, such as sandstone shrike thrushes and great bower birds, are common.

There are some Aboriginal art sites around the area, but they are a little difficult to find without prior knowledge. Ask the ranger for directions to the red Wandjina figure on the southern wall of the gorge.

Once again, this place has a part in the Pigeon story. Here, he and his men attacked a group of settlers who were about to drive their wagons and cattle through the gorge to open a new endeavour north of the range. Further east along the Napier Range towards Tunnel Creek are the ruins of Lillimilura, where Pigeon started his uprising by killing a policeman and releasing the prisoners he had with him.

Tunnel Creek is 30km east of Windjana Gorge and while camping is not allowed, this is a place not to be missed by anyone travelling through the Kimberley. As its name indicates, Tunnel Creek has carved a tunnel through the Napier Range; it is so big that you can walk through it with no problems during the Dry.

There is always water in the stream, even if there is none (or very little) on the north side, where the carpark is – the amount of water depends on the previous wet season and how much water there is in the tunnel. Sometimes you can walk through the 750m-long tunnel and only get wet up to your knees. At other times, you may need to swim.

Although the roof has collapsed about halfway along the tunnel, you still need a good torch to thoroughly enjoy the walk through the range. Other chasms and offshoots from the main tunnel can also be explored, but the highlight is the far end. Here Tunnel Creek flows out into the open air under a large rent in the cliff face. It's a peaceful place, worthy of an hour or two before you venture back the way you have come, to the far side of the range and the carpark.

Some samples of Aboriginal art can be found near the northern entrance, while the southern end of the tunnel was a site for stone axes and the like.

Tunnel Creek was Pigeon's hideout during his days as an outlaw or freedom fighter, and it was, no doubt, very effective.

For information on these small parks, see the rangers at either Windjana or Geikie Gorge National Park (☎ (08) 9191 5121) or the district ranger at the Department of Conservation & Land Management regional office in Kununurra (☎ (08) 9168 0200). ■

mid-1890s, sheep swarmed over the flat plains, right up to the sheer rock walls of the Napier Range.

The local Aboriginal people resisted the white invasion and took to spearing the Europeans' stock as a way of supplementing their food supply. During this time an Aborigine called Jandamarra, but known to the whites as 'Pigeon', led a revolt that lasted for three years before he was killed near Tunnel Creek. The **Pigeon Heritage Trail** starts in Derby and takes in the cemetery where Pigeon's first victim is buried, plus the gaol and the **Prison Tree**. From there it leads out to Windjana Gorge and the ruins of Lillimilura (once a police post and where Pigeon

SHOOT

R & V MOON

Top: Ruins near the Flinders Ranges, SA
Bottom: Brachina Creek with the Flinders Ranges in the background, SA

R & V MOON

PETER ROBINSON

PETER ROBINSON

Top: The old courthouse at Milparinka, NSW
Middle: Out near the Silver City Highway, NSW
Bottom: A busy day at the Silverton Hotel, NSW

claimed his first victims), then on to Tunnel Creek where the final chapter was played out.

Apart from the heritage trail, there's also **Myall's Bore** (said to be the longest cattle trough in the southern hemisphere) and **Wharfingers House** (which houses the local museum). Derby is a good base for exploring the area – it promotes itself as the 'Gateway to the Gorges'. The **RFDS base** opens its radio section to the public most mornings.

From Derby, you can take a scenic flight over the coast and islands or inland across the range country. Other tours include one around town, another down to Yeeda station or out to a pearl farm as well as fishing trips for a day or longer. Longer tours in 4WD vehicles are also available or you can hire vehicles that come complete with camping gear from the local Avis dealer.

There is some excellent fishing from river, shore, jetty or boat. Boat-fishers will have more luck than the others because they will be able to access more places, including the offshore islands. Barra is prized, but many other species fight just as hard and are equally tasty: threadfin salmon, sawfish, tarpon, catfish and sooty grunters are just some you can catch off the shore, while boaties may get into queenfish or Spanish mackerel.

The jetty is a good spot to cast a line or net for mud crabs; it's also where you will find the best fish & chips in Australia. A small restaurant beside the jetty caters for take-aways and sit-down meals. Note, though, that it is closed on Monday.

Offshore are the 'Iron Islands': Cockatoo and Koolan. **Cockatoo Island** has accommodation as well as fishing and diving. The island is something entirely different from what you have been seeing, but typical of the wild Kimberley coast.

Then there is, of course, the **Fitzroy River**. There are four areas where you can camp on the banks. Access is possible at a number of spots, but elsewhere the river banks are off limits to travellers because most of the river downstream from Fitzroy Crossing is within the Noogoora burr quarantine area.

The most accessible area takes up the southern bank of the Fitzroy River downstream from the **Willare Bridge**, where Highway 1 crosses the Fitzroy River, 58km south of Derby. Camping is popular among the trees within the first few hundred metres of the bridge, but there are spots all the way downstream to the old highway route at Langi Crossing.

Other places to camp by the river are: downstream from Fitzroy Crossing to a point (adjacent to Alligator Hill) about 10km south of the Fitzroy Bridge; east of Liveringa station, along the Camballin-Noonkanbah Road; at the Fitzroy Weir, 155km south-east of Derby; and at Myroodah Crossing just south of Liveringa, 120km from Derby.

Finally, there are the **festivals** that add so much to anyone's trip through the bush. There is the Boab Festival, with country music, a mardi gras, rodeo and more in July, the Derby Race horse race meeting in June and, on 26 December, the annual Boxing Day Sports, which is just a little different to your normal sports day.

The town can provide all a traveller requires. Accommodation ranges from a caravan park to motels. There are supermarkets, butchers, a good range of shops and repair facilities for vehicles, outboard motors and boats. From Derby, it is just 222km to the lights, golden beaches and trendy boutiques of Broome. Or if you want to head further south, you are a mere 2520km from Perth!

DETOURS
Gibb River Road to Wyndham

It's worth making a short detour to visit the historic town of Wyndham, an easy run on bitumen from the turn-off where the Gibb River Road starts. Fifteen km north from this junction, or 22km from Highway 1, you come to **The Grotto**. This secluded spot, just to the left of the road, offers a chance for a swim. Early in the Dry, the falls may still be running, adding more charm to this rocky defile, immersed in the green of trees, ferns and palms.

The **old road** to Wyndham veers off to the

right just metres north of here and heads across the flood plains to Alligator Hole, Marlgu Billabong and Parry Lagoons. Alligator Hole is a fine swimming spot and the latter two areas are ideal for bird-watching. This dirt road joins the bitumen again 12km north of The Grotto. Wyndham is 14km further north.

Wyndham

Wyndham, on the shores of Cambridge Gulf, was founded in 1886 to supply the cattle stations that were being established in the region and to give easier access to the gold fields at Halls Creek.

In 1919, the meatworks opened and this enterprise kept the town going over the next 60 years. The factory closed down in the late 1980s and was gutted by fire soon afterwards.

Wyndham's proximity to South-East Asia meant that many great aviators, setting world air endurance records, passed through the town during the 1920s and 1930s. The Ord River Dam revitalised the area in the 1960s, while in the late 1970s, offshore gas and oil and mineral finds further south maintained the impetus.

Much of the original character of the town has been retained, no doubt due to the fact that the old port area is 5km away from the newer hub of the town.

The selection of accommodation in the town includes a hotel, club and a caravan park. There is also a supermarket, a bakery, a couple of general stores and a few places to buy fuel or get your vehicle repaired. A hospital and police station are also here.

In August, Wyndham stages its **Top of the West festival**, with 10 days of revelry, as well as a music festival, a gymkhana and the Wyndham Cup race meeting, which are a lot of fun for locals and visitors alike.

Check the local **old port area**, which still reeks of the old days when horses and carts rattled down the street and pioneers such as 'Patsy' Durack from Argyle station came into town. The three **old cemeteries** in town are also poignant reminders of days gone by, as is the **Boab Prison Tree** found along the

TONY WHEELER

Boab Prison Tree

Karunjie Road, just after it turns off the Moochalabra Dam Road, 30km from Wyndham.

One place that should not be missed is **Five Rivers Lookout**. From this spot above the old port area, you have a grand spectacle of the old town and of Cambridge Gulf and the rivers that feed it. The view is better in the morning. To the north is the mouth of the mighty Ord River, to the south are the King, Pentecost and Durack rivers, while to the west is the Forrest River.

The **Moochalabra Dam** is Wyndham's main water supply and a pleasant picnic spot. There are also some Aboriginal rock paintings in the overhangs along the tall cliffs that are on your right, just before the picnic area.

The fishing is brilliant around Wyndham, and those with a boat will find it a mecca. Land-based fishers can try the wharf at the old port or any of the rivers in the area. The road out to the dam gives good access to the King River, which is a fine spot for barra. Otherwise, you can charter a boat for some fishing further afield.

If you enjoy bird-watching, the place to go is the **Parry Lagoons Nature Reserve**. To get there, head south along the bitumen for 14km before turning left onto the Old Halls Creek Road, which heads east across the flood plains of the Ord River. Parry Lagoons, along with Marlgu Billabong and Police Hole, holds water long after the dry season bleaches the rest of the plain a dusty gold. The bird life is fantastic.

Gibb River-Kalumburu Road

The road to the Mitchell Plateau and Kalumburu leaves the Gibb River Road 40km north of the turn-off into Gibb River station. There is an immediate decrease in the standard of the road and it certainly doesn't get any better – this is 4WD territory. The route north is nearly always closed for a few months of the wet season and even after the rains have stopped, no vehicles move across the black soil plains for another month or so.

Drysdale River station (☎ (08) 9161 4326), 58km north of the road junction, can supply fuel, limited supplies and accommodation. Riverbank camping is also available close by.

Beyond here, the road continues to be rough and can be really chopped up at times. At the 98km mark north of Drysdale River is the turn-off to the Mitchell Plateau and for most people, this is an interesting and enjoyable side trip.

The Mitchell Plateau The Mitchell Plateau offers excellent scenery, good camping, a chance to get to the coast and a good opportunity to see some fine Aboriginal art.

About 6.5km north-west from the junction is the **King Edward River** and once across the stream, there are some excellent camping spots close to the river. The swimming is very pleasant here and if you walk upstream, the observant will find some exceptional art sites – some of the best in the Kimberley.

As the track continues, it can become even rougher – it really depends on the previous wet season. About 15km from the river crossing, you climb up onto the plateau and begin to see the palms that are so distinctive in this area.

Nearly 71km from the turn-off from the Kalumburu road is the turn-off to **Mitchell Falls**. The Mitchell Falls track terminates, 15km from the turn-off, at Mertens Creek. There is a small camping area with no facilities, except during the tourist season, when a helicopter is normally based there, offering scenic flights over the falls and the surrounding area. From the camping ground, it is a half-hour walk to **Little Mertens Falls**. Ten

minutes later is the spectacular **Big Mertens Falls**, while another 10 minutes will bring you to Mitchell Falls. You'll find some good Aboriginal art and spectacular scenery along the way and the water is delightful – take your bathers.

Back on the main track heading north from the Mitchell Falls turn-off, it's 21km to the turn-off to **Surveyor's Pool**. The side track will take you nearly 7km west and then you need to walk another 4km to the pools. It's a top spot, but lacks the dramatic scenery of the Mitchell Falls walk.

Continuing further north, the track leads to Crystal Creek and the nearby mangrove-lined bay or into Port Warrender, a total of around 43km from the Falls junction. The tracks to either spot can be extremely bad – the track to Port Warrender can have 3 to 6m washaways in it, at which times it is, of course, impassable.

Kalumburu Heading north to Kalumburu from where the Mitchell Plateau road turns off, the road continues as before. **Theda station** is passed 35km north (191km from the Gibb River Road) and another 46km brings you to the **Carson River** crossing, which is another good spot to camp. Twenty km up the road, you enter the friendly Kalumburu Aboriginal community.

You need a permit to enter the Aboriginal reserve as well as a camping permit to take advantage of the excellent camping on the coast. It is worth if for the fishing alone. All enquiries and arrangements for permits should be directed to the Kalumburu Aboriginal Corporation (☎ (08) 9161 4300; fax 9161 4331), PMB 10, via Wyndham, WA 6740.

Visitors to the community are welcome, but you are asked to respect the community's privacy and to follow the rules and guidelines, the most important being no entry to the reserve without a permit (which should be arranged in advance) and no alcohol of any kind to be brought onto the reserve. Entry to the area is only allowed during working hours (Monday to Thursday from 7 to 11 am and 1.30 to 4 pm and Friday from

7 to 11 am). A 14-day permit costs $25 a vehicle.

You can purchase limited food supplies at the general store and fuel (unleaded, super and diesel) is available from the service station (open from 7 to 11 am and 2 to 4.30 pm). Travellers should also note that repair facilities are very limited and virtually no spare parts are available. Cash only is accepted as payment.

There is some great fishing around Kalumburu. If you don't have your own boat, it is possible to hire a fishing guide and equipment – ask at the store.

Kalumburu also has its own airstrip and while there are no landing fees payable, you are required to pay the normal visitor's fees. Those wanting aviation fuel can arrange it through the Kalumburu Mission (☎ (08) 9161 4333). Let them know well in advance so that the fuel can be freighted in by barge if necessary.

Access to Kalumburu is only advisable for 4WDs in the Dry (normally from June to October) and only well-built, off-road trailers should be taken on the trip.

Gibb River to Old Mornington Stock Camp

This route leads east from the Gibb River Road from the Mt House homestead turn-off, 53km south of the roadhouse at Mt Barnett, to Old Mornington station and the small camping resort, 90km from the road junction.

Less than 10km from the Gibb River Road you veer right to Old Mornington. Left leads to the Mt House homestead and store. About 53km from the main road another junction demands you veer right again and just over 10km later you pass the site of the old **Glenroy Meatworks**, a failed scheme that tried to fly processed meat out of the central Kimberley in the 1950s.

The original **Glenroy homestead** is passed another 7km further south and 20km later, you arrive at the tented camp of the **Old Mornington Stock Camp** (☎ (08) 9191 7035; fax 9191 703). You can camp here or be accommodated in the permanent tents

located along the edge of a small delightful creek.

From here it is possible to travel 14km to **Sir John Gorge** on the Fitzroy River, or 26km to Dimond Gorge, further downstream. Both are magnificent places to visit and enjoy. Access to the gorges is only possible by staying at the camp.

Scenic flights and boat and canoe hire are also possible from the camp.

ALTERNATIVE ROUTES

If you've been visiting Wyndham (see the earlier Detours section), you can pick up the Gibb River Road where it crosses the Pentecost River. Head back out of town the way you came for 6km to the airport and the signposted road to Moochalabra Dam. The road turns right, off the bitumen (when coming from town).

The turn-off to **Moochalabra Dam** is 19km further. Turning left here will take you to the dam and some Aboriginal art. Continuing straight ahead, there are some campsites off to your right as you parallel the King River. Five km past the dam turn-off, you will come to the **Boab Prison Tree**, once used by police patrols to hold their prisoners; it's a better example than the famed one at Derby.

Over the next few kilometres the road twists and turns through a few junctions, with few (if any) being signposted. Nine hundred metres from the Prison Tree, turn right, then after 2.1km, turn left. Turn left 1.7km after this junction and pass through a gate. You have covered just 35km from Wyndham.

You are now on the **Old Karunjie Track** and the route is now fairly plain to follow. Stick to the main track, which swings in a large arc around the great red massif of the Cockburn Range. Minor tracks spear off the main one, heading across the salt plains to the West Arm of Cambridge Gulf and some fishing spots. Be careful – get bogged out here and you are in the diabolicals!

You come close to the **Pentecost River** 39km after you pass through the gate. There are a number of campsites on your right but they are for dedicated fishers. There are numerous tracks in this area, but just keep heading south and you'll end up in the right place. Less than 8km after first seeing the river, you pass through another gate. Another 2km will see you at the Gibb River Road, just before the crossing of the Pentecost River.

The distance from Wyndham via this rough route is 83km and you are just 58km from the main highway via the Gibb River Road. From here on, it is the Gibb River Road all the way to Derby.

ACTIVITIES

There is a wide choice of activities in this area. Walking, canoeing (and boating), fishing and bird-watching would have to be at the top of the list of things you can do on your own. See earlier route descriptions for good fishing and bird-watching spots.

Walking

There are some excellent walks beginning just outside of Kununurra. Mirima National Park, on the outskirts of town, has two short marked trails, but you can spend hours wandering through here.

If you camp on El Questro station, there are ample opportunities for walks into some of the magnificent gorges in the area. Once you have a mud map from the store, you can enjoy walks to El Questro Gorge, Moonshine Gorge or Zebidee Springs. Zebidee Springs should not be missed – the springs run with hot water and the small thermal pools and waterfalls they form as they run down the escarpment are divine. Shaded by lush tropical growth, there is no better place to spend a hot Kimberley day.

At Durack River station, hike around Jack's Waterhole and enjoy the bird life.

At the Barnett River Gorge, take the walk up or downstream along the river. The shallow cascades, the deep pools lined with pandanus palms and the bird life are very enjoyable.

If you stop at Mount Barnett Roadhouse and camp down on the river, you will be on Manning Creek. The Lower Manning Gorge, just a stone's throw from the camping area,

is worth exploring. There is some Aboriginal art on the north bank, below the gorge. A longer walk (about an hour each way) is to the Upper Manning Gorge. Once there, you can explore the falls and gorge. This walk is across rocky ground that blasts the heat back into your face at any time, apart from early morning and evening. Spend the day at the top end of the gorge – you won't be disappointed.

In 1992, an expedition led by Peter Treseder, and supported in part by Australian Geographic, walked from Mount Barnett down the Isdell River, through all its gorges to the sea at Walcott Inlet. They used rubber rafts (carried in their backpacks) to get over large sections of water, before heading back up the Charnley River to Mount Elizabeth station. From there, it was down the Barnett River to where they had started.

Galvin, Adcock and Bell gorges, further south along the Gibb River Road, all warrant a little exploration.

At Windjana Gorge, take a walk up the gorge below its towering, shady cliffs. The gorge offers a great opportunity to see freshwater crocs in their natural environment. A wander through the range at Tunnel Creek will probably mean getting wet and you may even have to swim. Carry a torch, preferably one that is going to keep working if it gets wet. The 750m walk through the range can take as little as one hour (return) but is much more enjoyable if you take a bit longer. The far end is worth more than an hour on its own.

Canoeing & Boating

Taking a canoe or a small boat to the Kimberley adds yet another dimension to the adventure.

Chamberlain Gorge on El Questro station is ideal for both a canoe or a small boat but no petrol motors are allowed, so it's a paddle or an electric-motor job only. Be warned that saltwater crocodiles have been known to take up residency in this stretch of water. The waters of the Lower Manning and Windjana gorges are really only suitable for a canoe. On waters such as Jack's Waterhole at

Durack River station, only non-motorised craft are allowed.

The best canoeing and boating, though, is around Kununurra. The waters of Diversion Dam, just outside town, can handle quite large craft, as the ski jumps testify, while Lake Argyle is so big that it is like an inland sea and can be dangerous to canoes.

The shallow waterways that adjoin the open waters of Diversion Dam are locally called 'The Everglades' and the area is ideal for canoeing and bird-watching. There are a couple of places to launch a small boat or canoe adjacent to the highway or the caravan parks that abut the waterway. An evening paddle is great, but take notice of where you paddle: after a couple of hours out here, paddling between reeds and trees, you might have some trouble finding your launching spot.

One of the best trips is down the Ord River, from just below the wall at Lake Argyle to Kununurra, at Diversion Dam. This trip is suitable for a small outboard-powered boat or it's a good two-day paddle in a canoe.

All up, the trip is 55km long. For much of the way, the river is lined with dense stands of paperbarks, coolabahs and pandanus palms. Carlton Gorge is about 15km downriver from the launching spot and there are a couple of reasonable campsites in the gorge on the left. At the 23km mark, a creek joins the Ord and here is another good camp. For the next 10km, there are a couple of good sites to stop overnight, but then the river runs into the top end of Diversion Dam and access to the bank is limited. The water also slows, so it's a paddle without a current to help for the last 20km to the dam wall near the highway.

The Western Australian Department of Sport & Recreation's *Canoeing Guide (No 10)* to this stretch of water is sometimes available in Kununurra.

ORGANISED TOURS

Numerous tour operators around Australia go to the Kimberley. However, there are also quite a few local tour operators based in

Kununurra, Wyndham and Derby who offer more extensive trips exploring the whole of the Kimberley region. For a comprehensive list of all operators, contact the Western Australian Travel Centre.

Local Tour Operators

Kununurra

Desert Inn 4WD Safaris, PO Box 819, Kununurra 6743 (tel/fax (08) 9168 2702)

East Kimberley Tours, PO Box 537, Kununurra 6743 (☎ (08) 9168 2213; fax 9168 2544)

Kimberley Wilderness Adventures, PO Box 564, Kununurra 6743 (☎ (08) 9168 1711; fax 9168 1253) – stand-by prices for backpackers are available on trips into the Bungle Bungles

Belray Diamond Tours, PO Box 10, Kununurra 6743 (☎ (08) 9168 11014; fax 9168 2704)

Duncan's Ord River Tours, PO Box 888, Kununurra 6743 (☎ (08) 9168 1823; fax 9168 1670)

Wyndham

Wundargoodie Aboriginal Safaris, PO Box 302, Wyndham 6740, (☎ (08) 9161 1336; fax 9161 1429)

Cambridge Gulf Fishing & Scenic Tours, (☎ (08) 9161 1305)

Derby

Bushtrack Safaris, (tel/fax (08) 9191 4644)

King Sound Resort Helicopters, (☎ (08) 9191 1044; fax 9191 1649)

Boab Tours, (tel/fax (08) 9191 1237)

General Tour Operators

AAT King's, 108 Ireland St, West Melbourne 3003 (☎ (03) 9274 7422, toll-free 1800 334 009)

Amesz Tours, 4 Elmsfield Rd, Midvale, Perth 6000 (☎ (08) 9250 2577; fax 9250 2634)

Vehicle Guide Services

Bushtrack Safaris, Mt Elizabeth station (☎ (08) 9191 4644)

Peter Murray Kimberley Safaris, PO Box 207, Broome 6725 (☎ (08) 9192 1223; fax 9192 2518)

Russell Guest's 4WD Adventure Safaris, 38 Station St, Fairfield 3078 (☎ (03) 9481 5877; fax 9482 4713)

Boat Tours & Fishing

The Kimberley has the most spectacular and rugged coastline in Australia. The scenery is awe-inspiring and the fishing is fantastic, not only along the coast but also in the inland rivers. A number of boat charters and fishing safaris operate locally. These include:

Alligator Airways, Hangar No 5, Kununurra Airport (☎ (08) 9168 1333; fax 9168 2704) for float-plane fishing safaris
Buccaneer Sea Safaris, PO Box 532, Derby (tel/fax (08) 9191 1991)
Kimberley Coastal Camp, PO Box 146, Glen Forrest (☎ (08) 9161 4410)
Ultimate Adventures, PO Box 442, Kununurra (☎ (08) 9168 2310; fax 9169 1041)

Canoeing Tours
Canoe tours down the Ord River can be organised through Kimberley Canoeing Experience (☎ (08) 9169 1257) based in Kununurra.

Scenic Flights
There are a host of tour and scenic flight operators throughout the Kimberley, such as the Kununurra-based Alligator Airways (☎ (08) 9168 1333) and Kingfisher Aviation (☎ (08) 9168 1626). In Derby, there is Aerial Enterprises (☎ (08) 9191 1132) and Ord Air Charter (☎ (08) 9191 1014). Contact the Kununurra or Derby tourist bureaus for a comprehensive listing.

FACILITIES
Kununurra
Kununurra is a major centre. The town boasts a large supermarket complex, general stores, chemists, a laundry, a bakery, butchers, fishing-tackle shops, service stations and fuel supplies, as well as LPG and major repair facilities. Elgee Toyota (☎ (08) 9168 2236) 231 Bloodwood Drive, is the local agency for the RAC of WA and also does towing.

A number of banks are represented in Kununurra. Both the Commonwealth and BankWest banks have ATM facilities and there is also a National Australia Bank branch.

There's a wide choice of accommodation, from hotels to hostels, as well as numerous caravan parks. The *Country Club Private Hotel* (☎ (08) 9168 1024) has budget rooms for \$50/60 for a single/double and motel rooms with ensuite for \$135 a double, while the *Lakeside Resort* (☎ (08) 9169 1092) comes in at \$103/117. At the *Hotel Kununurra* (☎ (08) 9168 1344), prices range from \$35 a single and \$50 to \$110 a double.

For the budget-conscious, there is the *Kununurra Backpackers* (☎ toll-free 1800 641 998 or (08) 9169 1998; fax 9168 3998), which costs \$14 a single in the dormitory section. Twin rooms are \$18 per person, while triples are \$15 per person but there is a discount if you are a VIP cardholder. Facilities include a swimming pool and spa, fully equipped kitchens and a laundry. Bike hire and 4WD tours can also be organised. The *Desert Inn Backpackers* (☎ (08) 9168 2702) has a pool, a communal kitchen, with a bed in the dorm costing \$15, in a quad room \$16 while a double room is \$40 a night.

There are four caravan parks in Kununurra, as well as another just out of town. The *Kona Lakeside Caravan Park* (☎ (08) 9168 1031), on the edge of Lake Kununurra, has van sites for \$16 a night, camping is \$7 a person, while on-site vans are \$50 a double. Self-contained cabins are also available and range from \$85 a double. The *Town Caravan Park* (☎ (08) 9168 1763), in the centre of town, has powered/unpowered sites for \$18/16 for two people, as well as on-site vans (\$60) and villa units (\$90 a double). *Ivanhoe Village Caravan Park* (☎ (08) 9169 1995) has unpowered campsites at \$7 a person, while a powered van site is \$16. Self-contained villas cost \$85 a double and an on-site van costs \$55 a double. The *Hidden Valley Caravan Park* (☎ (08) 9168 1790) on Weaber Plains Rd has powered/unpowered sites at \$15/13 a double. At the *Kimberleyland Holiday Park* (☎ (08) 9168 1280), also on the shores of Lake Kununurra, powered/unpowered sites cost \$16/14 a double. Cabins that sleep four cost from \$70 a double. Dogs are allowed at Hidden Valley for one week only, but not in the camp area, and also at Kimberleyland, by arrangement.

Wyndham
The northernmost town and harbour in Western Australia, Wyndham has been

developed into two main areas: the old town and the new. While Wyndham lacks the variety and number of services available at Kununurra, the town certainly has a wide range of facilities, including a supermarket, general stores, a hardware store, a bakery, service stations and fuel supplies. The RAC of WA agency is Branko Motors (☎ (08) 9161 1305).

BankWest has an ATM facility here, while the Commonwealth Bank is an agency with passport and keycard facilities.

Accommodation is varied. The *Wyndham Community Club* (☎ (08) 9161 1130) has units costing $45/55 a single/double, while at the *Wyndham Town Hotel* (☎ (08) 9161 1202), prices are from $50 a single, $80 a double in fully self-contained units. You can also stay at the *Gulf Breeze Guest House* (☎ (08) 9161 1401) for $30/45 a single/double, while six in the dorm can bed down for $60.

Campers and caravanners can stop at the *Three Mile Caravan Park* (☎ (08) 9161 1064), which is close to the shops. Powered/unpowered sites cost $15/12 for a double, while those with air-con in their van will be up for $18 a night. Pets are allowed, on a leash.

Emma Gorge Resort

Part of El Questro station, the *Emma Gorge Resort* is only 2km off the Gibb River Road. An airstrip is near the resort. The resort's facilities include tented cabins, a restaurant and bar, a reasonably stocked shop, laundry facilities and a large swimming pool. Emma Gorge itself is just a short walk away.

The tented cabin accommodation costs $62/98 a single/double per night, with family cabins (one double and two single beds) available for $146. For further details, contact El Questro station (see below).

Travellers who want to explore Emma Gorge but are not planning to stay overnight pay a fee of $5 per adult.

El Questro Station

El Questro station is a working cattle station but it also welcomes visitors and offers a range of accommodation, from the most luxurious to secluded riverside camping. It has its own private airstrip for those wishing to fly in.

For the tourist with heaps of money, there is the homestead, with luxury, fully inclusive accommodation at $640 per adult twin share, or $640 per person per night plus an extra $200 single supplement is payable. At a more realistic level, bungalows which sleep up to four people cost $130 adult twin share ($97 for a single person) and $30 per extra person. Meals are available in the Steakhouse, where breakfast, lunch, dinner and morning and afternoon teas are served.

The self-sufficient camper has a choice of two types of sites: some sites are close to shower/toilet facilities and the store, while those who want to get away and have a bit more privacy can choose from a selection of riverside campsites. Nightly cost is $7.50 per person, children under 12 are free.

For groups of four or more, the Brumby Base is available, with a minimum of two nights stay. Cost is $20 per adult. The Base has shower and toilet block facilities, dormitory-style accommodation which sleeps 12 and an outback-style kitchen with dining room.

Travellers wanting to explore El Questro but not intending to stay overnight are charged a fee of $10 per adult.

For more details, contact the station (☎ (08) 9161 4318; fax (08) 9161 4355), PO Box 909, Kununurra, WA 6743. For bookings, ☎ (08) 9169 1777; fax (08) 9169 1383.

Home Valley, Durack River & Karunjie Stations

The Sinnamon family runs three working cattle stations, covering a total of one million hectares (over two million acres), two of which have opened their doors to tourists.

Home Valley station (☎ (08) 9161 4322; fax 9161 4340) is on the Cambridge Gulf, surrounded by some spectacular scenery. Accommodation is available at the homestead, with dinner, breakfast and shared facilities included, for just $75 per person. Pleasant camping is also possible for $5 per adult. The Sinnamons also have a wide range of 4WD tours throughout the Kimberley region available.

Durack River station (☎ (08) 9161 4324) is one of the largest cattle stations in Australia and is also one of the best places to camp along the Gibb River Road. The homestead and camping area are less than 1km from the Gibb River Road, beside a large waterhole. A store provides limited supplies and fuel is also available, as well as minor emergency vehicle repairs. Accommodation costs $50 per person; camping, with toilets and shower facilities, is $6. The camping is very pleasant along the waterhole, which provides the opportunity to swim, canoe or fish. Again, 4WD tours of the area are available.

Mount Elizabeth Station
The Lacey family runs *Mount Elizabeth station* (☎ (08) 9191 4644). Travellers can stay here, enjoy the Laceys' hospitality and join one of the organised 4WD tours. On either, you'll see some of the wildest, most remote country in the Kimberley and some fine examples of Aboriginal art.

The homestead has eight beds available for guests where bed, breakfast and dinner costs $90 a single on a shared basis. Camping is also available, with hot showers and toilets, for $7 a single. A small store provides limited supplies.

Mount Barnett Roadhouse & Manning Gorge
The beautiful Manning Gorge and *Mount Barnett Roadhouse* (☎ (08) 9191 7007; fax 9191 4692) are both on Mount Barnett station on the Gibb River Road.

The roadhouse has a good range of food supplies, snacks and cool drinks and all fuels, but no LPG. The workshop can carry out limited tyre and mechanical repairs. The store is normally open from 7 am to 5 pm.

The roadhouse is also the place to get your permit to camp at Manning Gorge. The pleasant *camping area*, beside Lower Manning Gorge, is a delightful swimming spot.

Toilets and fireplaces are provided. The cost is $5 per person per night.

Mount House Station
At the *Mount House station* (☎ (08) 9191 4649; fax (08) 9191 4703), visitors can stay in the old homestead, with dinner, bed and breakfast, for $67 to $77 per person, or there is a cottage for self-caterers at $25 per person, as well as backpacker-style accommodation at $20 per person. The hire of linen costs extra and prior bookings are essential.

A store offers a range of essential food supplies (including bread, meat and some fresh produce). Diesel and unleaded fuel are available, as well as tyres and batteries. Emergency mechanical repairs can be carried out as well as trailer and tyre repairs, cut and weld etc. There's also a public coin-operated phone at the store.

Derby
Derby is one of the original towns of the Kimberley region and can supply all a traveller's requirements. There are a couple of supermarkets that operate seven days a week, along with a chemist, butchers, a bakery, and hardware and fishing stores, to name just a few of the facilities. There's also a choice of service stations supplying all fuels and LPG; the *BP Colac Roadhouse & Service Station* (☎ (08) 9191 1256) is the RAC of WA agent. There are a number of automotive repair facilities available.

The ANZ Bank has full banking facilities and the post office has both passbook and keycard facilities for the Commonwealth Bank. The Challenge and BankWest banks have agencies here.

Accommodation ranges in price: a unit at the *King Sound Tourist Resort Hotel* (☎ (08) 9193 1044) costs $90/100 a single/double. The *West Kimberley Lodge* (☎ (08) 9191 1031) has a budget room for $35 a double, while other rooms cost from $30 a single, with a family room costing $70. The *Spinifex Hotel* (☎ (08) 9191 1233) offers a range of backpacker accommodation from $11 a single, and self-contained rooms from

$40/$50 a single/double, while motel-type rooms cost $50/65 single/double.

Campers can stay at the *Kimberley Entrance Caravan Park* (☎ (08) 9193 1055); dogs are allowed, on a leash. A powered site costs $9/15 a single/double; a tent site is $6 a single. On-site vans are also available at $40 a double, extra people $6.

Airstrips

There are public aerodromes at Derby and Kununurra, while Wyndham's airstrip (☎ (08) 9161 1002) is owned and maintained by the Wyndham-East Kimberley Shire. Aviation fuel is readily available.

Throughout the Kimberley are small, privately owned and maintained airstrips on station properties. Aviation fuel can often be organised, but you need to give prior notice of your requirements.

The Ibis Aerial Highway is a unique tourist set-up for those who want to fly around the Kimberley and see all the best known places. Contact the tourist centres in each major town or the Department of Conservation & Land Management (CALM) in Kununurra (☎ (08) 9168 0200; fax 9168 2179).

ALTERNATIVE TRANSPORT
Air

A wide choice of aircraft charters operate all over the Kimberley – see the earlier Organised Tours section or contact the Derby or Kununurra tourist bureaus.

Both major towns are also regularly serviced with commercial flights by Ansett Australia from Perth, while local air charter services link Wyndham and Kununurra. Ansett has offices in Derby (☎ (08) 9191 1426) and Kununurra (☎ (08) 9168 1622). For flight details, contact Ansett on ☎ 13 1300.

Bus

Being important centres in the Kimberley region, the towns of Kununurra and Derby are serviced regularly by Greyhound Pioneer Australia (☎ 13 2030). Bookings for the latter can be made in Kununurra at the Visitor Centre (☎ (08) 9168 1177), Coolibah Drive, and in Broome at Broome Travel (☎ (08) 9192 1561), Hammersley St.

Car Rental

There are a number of companies in the Kimberley that hire 4WDs to travellers. Drivers usually need to be over 25 years of age. Some companies also offer camping-equipment packages along with the hire of the vehicle. Avis has offices in Derby (☎ (08) 9191 1357) and Kununurra (☎ (08) 9168 1258). So does Hertz – call (☎ (08) 9191 1348) in Derby and (☎ (08) 9169 1424) in Kununurra.

Purnululu (Bungle Bungle) National Park

HIGHLIGHTS

- Experiencing the awe-inspiring Cathedral Gorge
- Walking into Echidna Chasm

The Bungle Bungle massif and its surrounding national park are now one of the Kimberley's major tourist attractions. Rated by many as one of the scenic wonders of Western Australia, the Bungle Bungles are more often than not viewed from the air, with visitors taking a scenic flight from Kununurra, Turkey Creek or Halls Creek. For the traveller with a 4WD, the diversion off the main highway around Australia is interesting and well worthwhile.

Secluded by distance and the surrounding ranges, the Bungles remained hidden from prying eyes until 1982. Known to a few drovers, helicopter pilots and local Aboriginal people, the area became an instant hit when it was featured in a television documentary on the scenic wonders Western Australia.

In March 1987, the Purnululu (Bungle Bungle) National Park was gazetted (the Kija word 'purnululu' means sandstone). The 210,000-hectare park abuts a 110,000 hectare conservation reserve and while the park takes in much more, the Bungle Bungle massif is really the only place that is readily accessible to the public. The surrounding country along the Ord River is prone to severe erosion – the reason this area and much of the country in the headwaters of the Ord River and surrounding Lake Argyle were proclaimed water catchment reserves as far back as 1967.

Since the park's formation, basic camping facilities have been established at a couple of places close to the range, and a ranger station has been set up.

INFORMATION
Tourist Offices
The Halls Creek Tourist Information Centre (☎ (08) 9168 6262), Great Northern Highway, is open from May to September. The Shire of Halls Creek (☎ (08) 9168 6007) may also have useful information.

In Kununurra, the Visitor Centre (☎ (08) 9168 1177; fax 9168 2598) is at 75 Coolibah Drive, while the regional headquarters of the Department of Conservation & Land Management (CALM) (☎ (08) 9168 0200) is in Konkerberry Drive.

Another source of information is the Western Australian Tourist Centre (☎ (08) 9483 1111), 469 Wellington St, Perth.

Emergency
There are hospitals at Halls Creek (☎ (08) 9168 6002) and Kununurra (☎ (08) 9168 1522). Police stations can also be found at Halls Creek (☎ (08) 9168 6000) and Kununurra (☎ (08) 9169 1122). There are other emergency services in Wyndham (see the earlier Gibb River Road section).

Other Information
The track off the main highway into the national park has been rerouted and upgraded in recent times but still remains a rough, dusty 4WD track.

No permits are required to enter the park, other than an entrance and camping fee, payable at the information bay adjacent to the ranger station. There are a couple of camping areas which have been set up with basic facilities.

THE NORTH-WEST

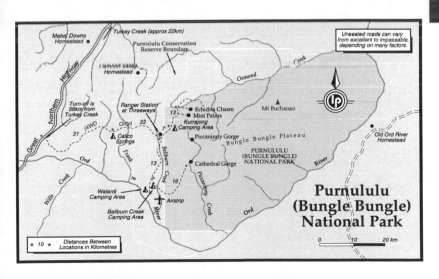

The best maps and books for the area are listed in the earlier Gibb River Road section.

It is not essential to have an HF radio for a trip into the Bungles. If you do have one, the frequencies required are the same as for the Gibb River Road.

THE ROUTE

From Kununurra, head west across the Ord River Diversion Dam wall to the intersection of Highway 1 and the road to Wyndham, 44km from the town centre.

Turn left here and head down the bitumen of Highway 1, admiring the great scenery of rolling hills and rugged mountain ranges. Initially, the Carr Boyd Range is off to the left (east), with the Durack Range far off to the west.

The **Durham River** crossing, about 35km south of the main road junction, offers a reasonable spot to camp, as does the Bow River rest area 95km further south.

Turkey Creek and its roadhouse (☎ (08) 9168 7882) are 152km south of the junction (196km from Kununurra). Fuel and limited supplies are available; and there is also a camping/caravan park (dogs allowed) and accommodation.

Continuing south along the highway, the turn-off to the Purnululu National Park is well signposted, 56km south of the roadhouse. Turn left here onto a dirt road which soon deteriorates into a dirt track. The information sign just past the track junction is worth a read: it will let you know what the latest situation is with the track, camping in the park or whatever.

The first 40km of the east-bound track is across Mabel Downs station property and no diversions off it are allowed. Where there are private station tracks leading off from the main track, it is obvious (or marked) which track to stay on.

Calico Springs, 31km from the bitumen, is a popular camping and rest stop on the run in and out of the Bungles. While permission from the station owner is officially required to camp here, many people don't seem to bother and camp here anyway. It's a top spot, with a couple of tall, rocky bluffs crowding

in on a small area of flat land dotted with trees and palms. A small creek fed by the spring trickles through the gap in the range and with the shade and permanent cool water, this spot is a pleasant interlude from the dust and heat of the surrounding country.

The intersection known as **Three-Ways** is 53km from the bitumen and it is here that the **ranger station** and the self-registration bay are located. The drive in from the highway will have taken you between 2 and 3 hours. Fill in your visitor's form and from here you have a choice of places to go.

The **Kurrajong camping area**, 7km north, gives access to the western side of the Bungle Bungle range. This camping area has toilets, water and separate areas for campers with generators and those without.

This side of the range has a couple of gorges worth exploring, including Echidna Chasm, Froghole and Mini Palms. All three walks are pleasant and less than 3km. Even if you are short of time, don't miss **Echidna Chasm**. As you progress up this gorge, it becomes narrower and narrower and the walls get sheerer. Finally, it is just an arm-span wide and towers upwards well over 100m. It is a spectacular place.

The **Walardi camping area** is 13km south of the ranger station, just a little north of the **Bellburn camping area**, the tour operators' camping area. Walardi is set up similarly to Kurrajong, with toilets and water as well as separate areas for groups and those with generators.

The Walardi and Bellburn camping areas give the easiest access to the southern section of the Bungle Bungle massif and from a track junction just north of the campsites, it is a 16km drive to the end of the vehicle track.

A 2km return walk to **Cathedral Gorge**, arguably one of Australia's most sensational and awe-inspiring natural wonders, takes you past spectacular domes and along an ever-narrowing ravine. Suddenly, around a corner, it opens up into a large amphitheatre. The walls crowd in on all sides, a smallish patch of sky adding to the grandeur of this magical place. This sight makes the trek, and all the dust, worthwhile. A much longer walk

(30km return) leads to **Piccaninny Gorge**, further east along the southern ramparts of the range.

To return to the bitumen and the highway, retrace your steps back the way you have come.

About 5km from the Walardi camping area is the airstrip and helipad. Scenic helicopter flights operate from here in the peak of the tourist season.

ORGANISED TOURS

A number of tour operators, both around Australia and working out of Halls Creek and Kununurra, include the Bungle Bungles as a major destination in their trips around the Kimberley. For more information, see the earlier Gibb River Road section, or contact the appropriate tourist information office or the Western Australian Tourist Centre.

Scenic Flights

There are several scenic-flight operators based in Halls Creek and Kununurra. See the earlier Gibb River Road section, or contact the Halls Creek or Kununurra tourist bureaus.

FACILITIES

For full details on facilities at Halls Creek or Kununurra, see the earlier Gibb River Road section (for Kununurra) or the later Canning Stock Route section (for Halls Creek).

Airstrips

Halls Creek has an airstrip – contact the Halls Creek Shire Council (☎ (08) 9168 6007) for details. Aviation fuel is readily available.

Broome

HIGHLIGHTS

- Celebrating at one of Broome's many annual festivals
- Discovering the town's colourful history
- Enjoying beautiful beaches after a long desert crossing

For many travellers, Broome is Australia's archetypal getaway: palm-fringed beaches, clear, blue waters and a relaxed atmosphere. But it is also noted for its Chinatown and the influences of early Japanese pearlers. For outback travellers, finishing one of the long desert crossings, it is an absolute oasis.

The Roebuck Bay region was known to the local Aborigines of the Djuleun tribes as 'Nileribanjen'. The surrounding mudflats and shallows were rich in shellfish, fish and mudcrabs and the Djuleun traded spears and pearl shell; ironically, the latter eventually contributed to the end of their traditional way of life.

In 1864, a syndicate was formed to investigate the story of a convict that had found gold at Camden Harbour, near Kuri Bay, in 1856. Many eager pastoralists backed this expedition and, when gold was not found, a number of them put together another expedition to introduce sheep to the region.

The Aboriginal inhabitants of Roebuck Bay resented the intrusion of the pastoralists, especially their fencing of traditional waterholes. In November 1864, three members of the pastoralists' expedition were murdered by Aborigines which resulted in open conflict. The pastoralists withdrew in 1867 only to be replaced later on by pearlers, working their way north from Cossack, in the 1870s.

Pearling in the sea off Broome started in earnest in the 1880s and peaked in the early 1900s when the town's 400 pearling luggers, worked by 3000 men, supplied 80% of the world's mother-of-pearl. Today there's only a handful of boats that still operate. The **Japanese cemetery**, near Cable Beach Rd, testifies to the dangers that accompanied pearl diving when equipment was primitive and knowledge of diving techniques limited. In 1914, 33 divers died of the bends, while in 1908 a cyclone killed 150 sailors caught at sea. The Japanese section of the cemetery is one of the largest and most interesting, and was extensively renovated in 1983.

Japan entered WWII in 1941, and the 500 Japanese in Broome were interned for the duration of the war. On 3 March 1942, following the bombing of Darwin in February,

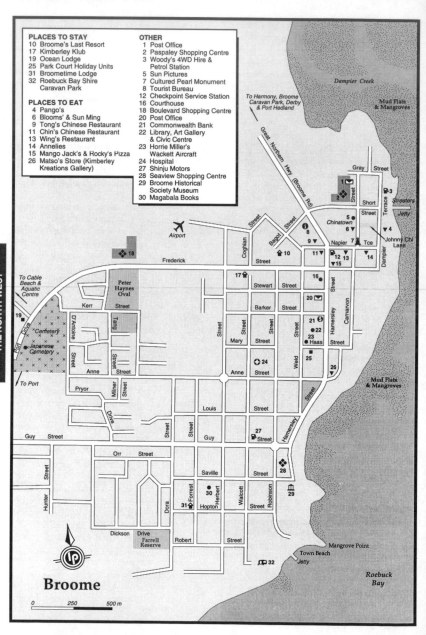

PLACES TO STAY
10 Broome's Last Resort
17 Kimberley Klub
19 Ocean Lodge
25 Park Court Holiday Units
31 Broometime Lodge
32 Roebuck Bay Shire
Caravan Park

PLACES TO EAT
4 Pango's
6 Blooms' & Sun Ming
9 Tong's Chinese Restaurant
11 Chin's Chinese Restaurant
13 Wing's Restaurant
14 Annelies
15 Mango Jack's & Rocky's Pizza
26 Matso's Store (Kimberley
Kreations Gallery)

OTHER
1 Post Office
2 Paspaley Shopping Centre
3 Woody's 4WD Hire &
Petrol Station
5 Sun Pictures
7 Cultured Pearl Monument
8 Tourist Bureau
12 Checkpoint Service Station
16 Courthouse
18 Boulevard Shopping Centre
20 Post Office
21 Commonwealth Bank
22 Library, Art Gallery
& Civic Centre
23 Horrie Miller's
Wackett Aircraft
24 Hospital
27 Shinju Motors
28 Seaview Shopping Centre
29 Broome Historical
Society Museum
30 Magabala Books

THE NORTH-WEST

Broome

0   250   500 m

Dampier Creek

Mud Flats
& Mangroves

To Harmony, Broome
Caravan Park, Derby
& Port Hedland

Great Northern Hwy (Broome Rd)

Gray   Street

Short   Street
Streeters
Jetty
Terrace

Chinatown

Napier   Tce

Johnny Chi
Lane

Dampier

Airport

Coghlan   Street

Bagot   Street

Frederick   Street

To Cable
Beach &
Aquatic
Centre

Peter
Haynes
Oval

Stewart   Street

Barker   Street

Hamersley   Street

Carnarvon   Street

Kerr   Street

D'Antoine   Street

Tang   Street

Mary   Street

Weld   Street

Haas

Cemetery

Japanese
Cemetery

To Port

Anne   Street

Pryor

Milner   Street

Drive

Port   Drive

Anne   Street

Mud Flats
& Mangroves

Louis   Street

Guy   Street

Guy   Street

Orr   Street

Street   Street

Saville   Street

Robinson   Street

Hunter   Street

Dora   Street

Forrest

Herbert   Street

Hopton   Street

Walcott

Magabala Books 30

31

Dickson   Drive

Farrell
Reserve

Robert   Street

Street

32

Mangrove Point

Town Beach
Jetty

Roebuck
Bay

the Japanese bombed Broome. A number of flying boats were destroyed and about 70 Dutch refugees were killed.

Today, tourism and beef processing are the major industries and Broome's attractions and festivals bring hordes of visitors. The Aboriginal community is playing a major part in this renaissance.

The term **Chinatown** is used to refer to the old part of town, although there is really only one block or so that is multicultural and historic. Some of the plain and simple wooden buildings that line Carnarvon St still house Chinese merchants, but most are now occupied with restaurants, pearl dealers and tourist shops. The bars on the windows aren't there to deter outlaws but to minimise cyclone damage.

Information

Broome tourist office (☎ (08) 9192 2222) is just across the sports field from Chinatown. It's open daily from 8 am to 5 pm from April to November, and otherwise from 9 am to 5 pm Monday to Friday and 9 am to 1 pm on weekends. It publishes a useful monthly guide to what's happening in and around Broome, a *Town Map & Information Guide* (50c) and a *Kimberley Holiday Planner*.

Organised Tours

The *Spirit of Broome* (☎ (08) 9193 5025) is a small hovercraft which makes daily one-hour flights around Roebuck Bay ($45), stopping at various points of interest. You can twilight cruise in the original pearl lugger *Cornelius* ($65) and in replica lugger *The Willie* ($45).

There are also some good guided bush-walks. Paul Foulkes (☎ (08) 9192 1371) concentrates on environmental features close to Broome, such as the palaeontologically important dinosaur footprints ($15), the mangroves ($25), remnant rainforest ($25) and a hidden valley ($25).

Places to Stay

Camping Camping in Broome is not particularly cheap. The *Roebuck Bay Shire Caravan Park* (☎ (08) 9192 1366) is conveniently central; tent/powered sites are $14/16.50 for two. *Broome Vacation Village* (☎ (08) 9192 1057), Port Drive, has powered sites/cabins for $15/60 for two; fortunately, it now has new owners. *Broome Caravan Park* (☎ (08) 9192 1776), on the Great Northern Highway, 4km from town, has tent sites for $12, and on-site vans for $35 for two.

Budget On Bagot St, close to the centre and just a short stagger from the airport, is the *Broome's Last Resort* (☎ (08) 9193 5000). It's adequate and has a pool, large kitchen and courtesy bus. The accommodation is not cheap – dorm beds are $12 and twins are $38 for two, all with shared facilities.

Also close to the centre in Frederick St is the new *Kimberley Klub* (☎ (08) 9192 3233), one of the fanciest budget places you could ever hope to stay in. Excellent two/four/eight-bed dorms are $17/15/12 per person and doubles are $40.

Out at the beach, at 33-37 Lullfitz Drive, is the cosy and well-appointed *Cable Beach Backpackers* (☎ toll-free 1800 655 011). A comfortable dorm bed is $14. The staff pick

---

Broome's Special Events

Broome is something of a festival centre, offering visitors and residents many excuses to party.

In March, the town's multicultural population turns out for the *Chinatown Street Party*, an event organised by the Chinatown Progress Committee.

Dragon-boat paddlers from all over Australia meet in Broome each April to take part in the *Dragon Boat Classic* carnival.

Accommodation is hard to find during *Shinju Matsuri* (Festival of the Pearl) in August. This excellent festival commemorates Broome's early pearling years and multicultural heritage, featuring many traditional Japanese ceremonies, including the *Obon Festival*. When it's on, the town's population swells, so book ahead.

That sticky-sweet fruit loved by some, but deplored by mothers with small children is celebrated during the annual *Mango Festival* in November. ∎

up from town, and there is heaps of parking for a 4WD.

The *Broometime Lodge* (☎ (08) 9193 5067), at 59 Forrest St, has small single/twin rooms with fan for $50/70. The *Park Court Holiday Units* (☎ (08) 9193 5887), Haas St, has nine two-bedroom units with all facilities; these are $500 to $600 per week, depending on the season. The *Ocean Lodge* (☎ (08) 9193 7700) is on Cable Beach Rd near the Port Drive turn-off. It has backpackers' beds for $15 and twin rooms for $82.

A really different place, well worth a visit, is *Eco Beach: Yardoogarra* (☎ (08) 9192 4844), about 90 minutes' drive south of Broome at Cape Villaret on Roebuck Bay.

Here the environment is a priority and elaborate steps have been taken to protect the flora and fauna. The private cabins, connected by boardwalks, are elevated to take advantage of the breezes and stunning views; the cost of a twin, which sleeps four, is $100 for two (plus $10 per extra person). Meals can be purchased at *Jack's Bar*. A huge breakfast is $10, lunch is about $10 and a two-course buffet dinner is $20.

Places to Eat

Finding a place to stay in Broome may be a hassle but eating out is no sweat at all. Lots of people go out for coffee after the movies at *Sun Picture Gardens*. *Bloom's*, close by,

---

Dampier Peninsula

It's about 200km from the turn-off, 9km out of Broome, to the Cape Leveque lighthouse at the tip of the Dampier Peninsula. This area features spectacular red pindan cliffs, expansive blue water and is a flora and fauna paradise. The road can sometimes be negotiated by 2WD but in some weather, the road (and especially sidetracks) is only suitable for 4WD.

Originally, the peninsula was inhabited by the Bardi people and during the early pearling days, a number of Aborigines dived for pearl shell. The communities now welcome visitors and offer bush-tucker walks and mud-crabbing tours. An excellent account of the plants and peoples of the Dampier Peninsula is found in the CALM publication *Broome and Beyond* by K Kenneally, Dapne Choules Edinger & T Willing.

North of Broome, on the western coast of Dampier Peninsula, is the **Coulomb Point Nature Reserve**. This conservation area was set up to protect the unique pindan vegetation of the peninsula and may still harbour the endangered rabbit-eared bandicoot (*Macrotus lagotis*) or bilby.

The **Beagle Bay Aboriginal community** (☎ (08) 9192 4913) is a welcome diversion and has a beautiful church in the middle of a green, built by Pallotine monks and completed in 1918. Inside is an altar stunningly decorated with mother-of-pearl. A fee of $5 is charged to enter the community and you must contact the office on arrival. Petrol and diesel are available every day except Sunday. From Beagle Bay, it is 12km to the turn-off to picturesque **Middle Lagoon**, 18km west on a manageable dirt road. The lagoon is a great place for snorkelling and swimming, boating and fishing. Unpowered sites are $8 and there are beach shelters with a pine floor for $30 for two ($10 for an extra person); water is available.

Just before Cape Leveque is **Lombadina Aboriginal community** (☎ (08) 9192 4942), which has a church built from corrugated iron on the outside, lined with paper bark and supported by mangrove timber. There are a number of carved artefacts for sale including trochus shell, ebony carvings and pearl-shell jewellery. One-day and overnight mud-crabbing and traditional fishing tours are available; contact the Broome tourist office for details. Petrol (leaded and unleaded) and diesel are available on weekdays from 8 to 11 am and 1 to 4 pm.

Cape Leveque, about 200km from Broome, has a lighthouse and two wonderful beaches. Beyond it is **One Arm Point**, another Aboriginal community (☎ (08) 9192 4930), where you can get petrol (leaded and unleaded) and diesel. Take note that while you can look around or purchase goods, communities won't want you to stay on their land. Permission to visit other areas must be obtained in advance. Ask at the Broome tourist office about road conditions before setting out.

There is accommodation at Kooljaman (☎ (08) 9192 4970), ranging from backpackers' beds ($12), self-contained units ($50), chalets, bark huts ($30) and camping ($10 per person). Bush-tucker and mud-crabbing tours are available. Unleaded and diesel fuel can be purchased here. The restaurant is open for lunch and dinner from April to November. ■

serves a very generous cappuccino and has excellent croissants.

Mango Jack's, on Hamersley St, has hamburgers and also dispenses the usual sandwiches and fish & chips.

Chin's restaurant, on Hamersley St near Mango Jack's, has a variety of dishes from all over Asia. Prices range from $8 to $13. There's a popular takeaway section. Other Chinese specialists are *Wing's*, on Napier Terrace; *Tong's*, near the corner of Napier Terrace and the Great Northern Highway; *Son Ming* on Carnarvon St; and *Murray's Asian Affair*, on Dampier Terrace.

Annelies is a continental restaurant on Napier Terrace near the Roebuck; reports from locals are all good and the lunches are cheap – eg turkey, camembert and avocado in a huge roll is $4.50. The *Tea House*, in a mud-brick building with an outdoor dining area, is at the end of Saville St. It has a great variety of Thai and seafood dishes and it is BYO.

Cheffy's on the 19th (☎ (08) 9192 2092) is at the golf course overlooking Roebuck Bay; it has meals from $5, a buffet roast dinner for $10 and great garlic prawns. *Pango's* on Dampier Terrace is new and is a little slice of Bali with an Asian menu and Pindan decor; entrees are $9 and a meal from $14.

Getting Around

Car Rental Avis has an office in Broome (☎ (08) 9193 5980) at 14-16 Coghlan St, as does Hertz (☎ (08) 9192 1428) at 29 Frederick St.

Motorcycle Rental Road Runner Motor Cycle Hire (☎ (08) 9192 1971), 7 Farrell St, Broome, has motorcycles and scooters available. Bikes up to 250cc can be hired by any person who has held a motor cycle licence for at least 12 months. Unfortunately, these bikes can only be taken from Broome (and environs) to Derby. For those who just want to explore around Broome itself, you can hire a 50cc scooter, as long as you have held a valid car licence for at least 12 months. Road Runner also offers a free pickup and delivery service.

The Pilbara

The Pilbara region encompasses some of the hottest country on earth. It also contains the iron ore that accounts for much of Western Australia's prosperity. Gigantic machines are used to tear apart the dusty red ranges of this isolated, harsh and fabulously wealthy area. The Pilbara towns are almost all company towns: either mining centres where the ore is wrenched from the earth or ports from which it's shipped abroad.

It is possible to get a feel for the majesty and contrast of this ancient, raw frontier by driving through it. There are no 'classic' outback routes that traverse it, but you can go deep into the arid areas and the fascinating Hamersley Range.

There is no doubt that the ancient Hamersley Range contains some of Australia's most stunning scenery. The landscape is dotted with spectacular red rimmed gorges, occasional waterfalls and palm-fringed waterholes. It is a land synonymous with the Dreamtime and abounds in Aboriginal artefacts. Eroded forms of prehistory are overlaid with the machinery and impedimenta of modern explorers in search of abundant raw materials and minerals.

South of Karratha and the Pilbara coastline are two magnificent interior national parks, one based on the Chichester Range, the other on the Hamersley Range. They contribute to part of an excellent loop journey from the coastal highway.

The description that follows assumes the loop starts in Karratha or Roebourne, passes through the Millstream-Chichester and

THE NORTH-WEST

Karijini national parks, returning to Karratha via the western gorges, Tom Price and the Hamersley Iron (HI) private Dampier-Tom Price railway road. The only backtracking is in and around the national parks. It is, however, a contrived route – there are many other possible points of entry and exit.

INFORMATION
Tourist Offices
In Karratha, the Karratha & Districts Information Centre (☎ (08) 9144 4600), on Karratha Rd just before you reach the T-junction of Dampier and Millstream Rds, has loads of information on what to see and do in the Pilbara. For information on the Pilbara's national parks, contact the Department of Conservation & Land Management (CALM) at its Karratha regional office (☎ (08) 9186 8288) in the SGIO Building, Welcome Rd.

In Roebourne, information is available at the tourist bureau (☎ (08) 9182 1060) in the Old Gaol complex, Queen St.

The 'gem shop' (☎ (08) 9189 7096) on Sixth Ave in the ghost town of Wittenoom acts as a tourist centre – probably until such time as the government succeeds in closing down the town completely (and then bulldozing all evidence of it into the ground).

The Tom Price tourist information centre (☎ (08) 9188 1112) is on Central Rd and the Newman tourist information centre (☎ (08) 9175 2888) is at the corner of Fortescue Ave and Newman Drive. Port Hedland is also a popular starting point for a Pilbara tour. The tourist bureau (☎ (08) 9173 1711) is at 13 Wedge St, across from the post office.

It is good that these services operate, the national park offices of the Department of Conservation & Land Management (CALM) are more often than not unattended; the Millstream visitor centre is much better than the isolated Karijini ranger station on Juna Downs Rd. Fortunately, there is now an interpretive centre (☎ 014 511 1285) near the junction of the Yampire Gorge and Dales Gorge roads. It is run by descendants of the Panyjima, Innawonga and Kurruma Aborig-

inal people, for long the traditional occupiers of Karijini.

Permits
A permit is required to travel on private Hamersley Iron roads. You will need one to travel on the Dampier-Tom Price Rd (used for the homeward part of the described loop). This is obtained easily from the security gate (☎ (08) 9143 5364) at Hamersley Iron's 7-Mile workshop, halfway between Karratha and Dampier. The tourist bureau in Tom Price will tell you how to get permits for the HI railway road at its southern end.

There is a speed limit of 90km/h on this road. A map on the back of the permit shows turn-offs and restricted access roads. Slow down to 25km/h for work crews.

Chances are that you may deviate onto Robe River Iron Associates' private road – it parallels Robe River's railway between the shipping facility at Cape Lambert and mining operations at Pannawonica. Robe River can be contacted at its security gatehouse (☎ (08) 9187 1001) in Wickham.

Books & Maps
There are a number of good publications which cover this route. Productions by the Department of Conservation & Land Management (CALM) are useful and include the pamphlets *Karijini National Park*, *Millstream-Chichester National Park*, *Pilbara National Parks* and *Geology of the Gorges* and booklet *North-West Bound: From Shark Bay to Wyndham*.

The StreetSmart map of the *Pilbara* is also indispensable for this trip.

Radio Frequencies
Should you strike mechanical trouble, it's unlikely that you'd have to wait long for another vehicle to pass by. For those with HF radios, the Royal Flying Doctor Service bases at Derby (call sign VJB, 5300kHz), Meekatharra (call sign VKJ, 4010 and 6880kHz) and Port Hedland (call sign VKL, 4030 and 6960kHz) monitor transmissions from 7 am to 5 pm Monday to Friday and

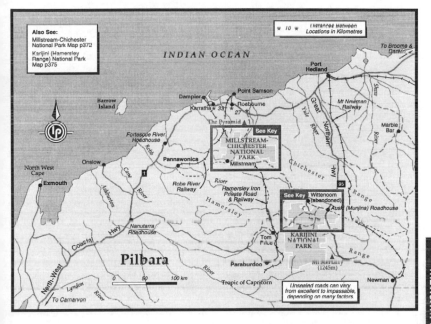

8.30 to 10 am on Saturday, but not on Sunday.

SPECIAL PREPARATIONS

If you are travelling away from the main coastal highway in this area, always carry sufficient water and check you have enough fuel to get to the next refuelling point. When travelling into remote areas, make sure you tell someone your travel plans before you head off and don't leave your vehicle if you become stranded.

Occasionally, the roads are closed after heavy rain. Check road conditions with Main Roads WA (☎ toll-free 1800 013 314).

Fuel is available in a number of locations but is considerably more expensive than in the coastal towns. At the Auski (Munjina) Roadhouse, for instance, it is 5c a litre dearer than in Karratha. Fill up those long-range fuel tanks – the closest fuel to Millstream is in Karratha, Roebourne or at Auski Roadhouse, at the junction of the Great Northern Highway and Wittenoom Rd. Around Karijini, fuel is available at Tom Price, the Auski Roadhouse and a little further away in Newman. (It is likely that Wittenoom will have no refuelling facilities by the time this book is published.)

The only banking facilities in the area are at Tom Price, Newman, Karratha and Port Hedland, so bring plenty of cash to pay for supplies, accommodation and fuel while travelling in the parks.

THE ROUTE
Karratha to Millstream-Chichester

The town of **Karratha** ('good country'), the commercial centre for the area, was developed because of the rapid expansion of the Hamersley Iron operations and the Woodside offshore natural gas project. The rich town is now the hub of the coastal Pilbara. The area around Karratha is replete with evidence of Aboriginal occupation – carvings, grindstones, etchings and middens are all located on the **Jaburara Heritage Trail**, which starts near the information centre.

To get to Roebourne, head for the North West-Coastal Highway from Karratha and turn left; Roebourne is 33km from this turn-off.

Roebourne is the oldest existing town in the Pilbara. It has a history of grazing, gold and copper mining, and was once the capital of the North-West. There are still some fine old buildings to be seen, including an **old gaol**, an 1894 **church** and the **Victoria Hotel**, the last of five original pubs. Roebourne is close to the historic port of Cossack and the fishing village of Point Samson.

From Roebourne, follow the North-West Coastal Highway for 27km to the turn-off for Millstream, then take the signposted gravel road. It passes through grazing land, with the occasional dry creek crossing. The most spectacular natural feature on this route is **The Pyramid**, a symmetrical pile of red rock and yellow spinifex, dominating the landscape to your right.

Millstream-Chichester National Park
The park includes a number of freshwater pools, such as **Python Pool**, which was once an oasis for Afghani camel drivers and still makes a good place to pause for a swim. The turn-off to Python Pool is reached some 61km after you leave the North-West Coastal Highway. The road is now bitumen and climbs up from Python Pool to close to the summit of **Mt Herbert**, from where there are great views of the Chichester Range.

Once down the hill, the road reverts to gravel and you pass through undulating sandstone country. Ten km from the end of the bitumen, the road crosses the Hamersley Iron railway line. At this T-junction, turn left (near Camp Curlewis) and follow the road for about 20km until you reach the Millstream-Yarraloola Rd (to Pannawonica) turn-off. Turn right, and follow the road for 11.5km to the 30km loop road (Snappy Gum Drive) through the park.

The **visitor centre** (☎ (08) 9184 5144) in

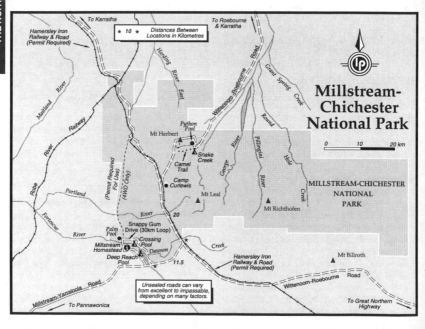

the impressive 200,000-hectare Millstream-Chichester National Park is at Millstream homestead, 150km south of Roebourne, 21km off the road to Wittenoom. The old homestead has been converted into an information centre with a wealth of detail on the Millstream ecosystems and the lifestyle of the Yinjibarndi people, the region's traditional inhabitants.

The **Chinderwarriner Pool**, near the visitor centre, is another pleasant oasis, with pools, palms (including the unique Millstream palm, *Livistonia alfredii*) and lilies; it is well worth a visit. Take time to do the 6km **Cliff Lookout Drive** for great views of the palm-fringed Crossing Pool and the Fortescue River. The lush environment is a haven for birds and other fauna such as flying foxes and kangaroos. Over 20 species of dragonfly and damselfly have been recorded around the pool.

The park also has a number of walking and driving trails, including the half-hour Homestead Walk, the 6.8km Murlunmunyjurna Trail (which links the homestead with Crossing Pool) and the 8km Chichester Range Camel Track.

Millstream Chichester to Karijini

To get to the Auski (Munjina) Roadhouse on the Great Northern Highway, a possible base for exploring the Karijini (Hamersley Range) National Park, return the way you came to the Wittenoom-Roebourne Road. Turn right here and in 28.5km you will cross the Hamersley Iron railway line – keep a lookout for those 1 to 2km-long iron-ore trains.

The next 100km of driving takes you through relatively featureless country, occupied by **stations** such as Tambrey, Mt Florance and Mulga Downs. Mulga Downs was the home of mining tycoon Lang Hancock. The spectacular Hamersley Range looms straight ahead on the other side of the Fortescue basin.

Wittenoom, once a main tourist centre, is at the northern end of the Karijini National Park. Wittenoom had an earlier history as a blue asbestos (crocidolite) mining town, but

mining finally halted in 1966. A number of miners and baggers at the Wittenoom Gorge mine have subsequently 'died of the dust' (or mesothelioma, a lung condition). There are still many potential compensation cases outstanding. It is now virtually a ghost town, although a few inhabitants still cling tenaciously to almost beleaguered homes. It's likely there will be nothing there when you visit as Perth's bureaucrats are trying to close it down for good.

The now-infamous **Wittenoom Gorge** is immediately south of the former town. A surfaced road runs the 13km through this gorge, passing old asbestos mines, smaller gorges and pretty pools.

But, note the following warning and push on to the Auski Roadhouse on the Great Northern Highway, 42km east of Wittenoom. You pass the old northern access road into Karijini – the **Yampire Gorge** (also a site where asbestos was mined) – after 24km. It now looks as though it will either be closed permanently or never repaired (it was extensively damaged by the floods in February 1997).

In Yampire Gorge, blue veins of asbestos can be seen in the rock. **Fig Tree Well**, in the gorge, was used by Afghani camel drivers as a watering point.

Warning Even after 30 years, there is a health risk from airborne asbestos fibres around Wittenoom. Avoid disturbing asbestos tailings in the area and keep your car windows closed on windy days. If you are concerned, seek expert medical advice before going anywhere near Wittenoom or Yampire gorges.

Karijini (Hamersley Range) National Park

Like the gorges in central Australia, those of Karijini are spectacular, both in their sheer rocky faces and varied colours. In early spring, the park is often carpeted with colourful wildflowers.

There is now a sealed road from the Great Northern Highway to the Aboriginal interpretive centre, at the junction of the Yampire

Gorge and Dales Gorge roads. This access road is about 35km south of the Auski Roadhouse and 160km north of Newman. (Eventually, the road will be sealed all the way to Tom Price, on the western edge of the park, and open up the area.) After 26km, turn north, or right, onto the Juna Downs Rd and follow the newly sealed road to the interpretive centre. You pass a self-registration station where you pay entry fees ($5 per car).

Dales Gorge is a good place to start your exploration of the many gorges. The 10km road into Dales Gorge starts just south of the interpretive centre; there is a freshwater tank close to the turn-off to replenish supplies. About 200m along the Dales Gorge track is a turn-off to the right; it takes you to a **giant termite mound**, popular with 'I've been there' snap-shooters.

At the end of this road, you can get to **Circular Pool** and a nearby lookout and, by a footpath, to the bottom of **Fortescue Falls**. The walk from Circular Pool along Dales Gorge to the falls is recommended; you will be surprised by how much water is permanently in the gorge.

Next, head west on the Joffre Falls road. A turn-off, to the right, after 19km leads to **Kalamina Gorge** (6km) and then another (after 30km) leads to **Knox Gorge** (6km). It is only 1km down this road to the often dry, but nonetheless spectacular, **Joffre Falls**. Near Knox Gorge is a 1.5km return walk to Red Gorge lookout.

From the Knox Gorge turn-off, it is 3km west to a T-junction. Head north from this junction for another 14km to the remarkable **Oxers Lookout**, at the point where the **Red**, **Weano**, **Joffre** and **Hancock gorges** meet. This is one of the outback's greatest sights. If you want to go down into the gorge proper, take the steps down to Handrail Pool (turn to the right at the bottom) in Weano Gorge.

The Gorges to Tom Price

At the T-junction on Joffre Falls road, you can head south to Tom Price. Follow Joffre Falls Rd for 26km until it meets Hamersley-Mt Bruce Rd. Turn right, travel for 2km and then head south for 5km until you meet the Marandoo Rd. Turn right on Marandoo Rd and after 35km, it joins the Paraburdoo-Tom Price Rd; it is another 10km north-west to Tom Price. You'll pass **Mt Bruce** (1235m), Western Australia's second-highest peak, on this route. Incidentally, the state's highest mountain is **Mt MeHarry** (1245m), near the south-east border of Karijini National Park.

Tom Price is an iron-ore town, 128km south-west of Wittenoom. Check with Hamersley Iron (☎ (08) 9189 2375) in Tom Price about inspecting the **mine works** – if nothing else, the scale of it all will impress you. **Mt Nameless**, 4km west of Tom Price, offers good views of the area, especially at sunset.

When you have had your fill of a mining town, you can use your permit to travel on the Hamersley Iron railway road back to the North-West Coastal Highway and Karratha (use the map on the back of the permit). There are no real highlights on this 270km road, just the experience of using it.

About 29km north of Tom Price, you can take a sidetrip on the Nanutarra-Munjina road. At 41km on this road you reach the turn-off to the **Hamersley Gorge**, only 4km from the main road. The evidence of the force of nature in the folded ribbons of rock adds to the awe-inspiring landscape. Not far north is the small **Rio Tinto Gorge**, appearing like a dry gulch in those cowboy movies of old.

Return to the Hamersley Gorge turn-off and a little south (perhaps 1km) is a short cut (31km) across to the Hamersley Iron Dampier-Tom Price road; it is quite clearly marked on the StreetSmart *Pilbara* map. From here it is plain sailing to Karratha.

ORGANISED TOURS

There are a number of tour operators in the area. Design-a-Tour (☎ (08) 9144 1460), operating from Tom Price or Auski Roadhouse, offers one/two-day tours of Karijini and the gorges for $70/190. A four-day tour covering Millstream, Tom Price and Karijini starts from Port Hedland; the cost is $550, with all meals.

Snappy Gum Safaris (☎ (08) 9185 1278)

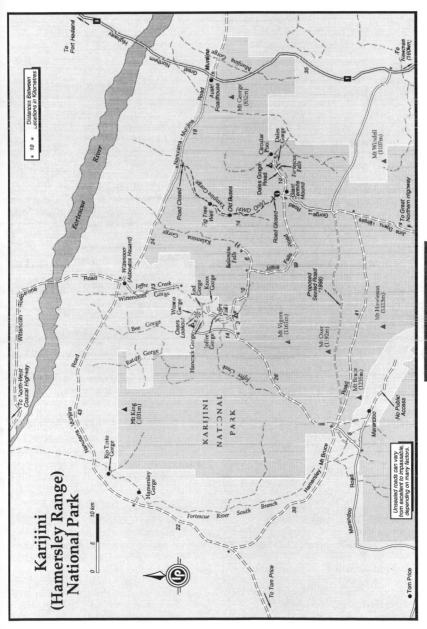

Karijini (Hamersley Range) National Park

THE NORTH-WEST

in Karratha runs various tours to Karijini, Millstream, Marble Bar and Tom Price; a four-day safari is about $695.

FACILITIES
Karratha

There are three caravan parks in town: *Balmoral Rd* (☎ (08) 9185 3628), *Rosemary Rd* (☎ (08) 9185 1855) and *Karratha Caravan Park* (☎ (08) 9185 1012), Mooligunn Rd. The first two have powered/ensuite sites at $16.50/24 for two; the Karratha is a little cheaper. (This author, after a terrible night in an ill-equipped on-site van at Rosemary Rd, vowed never to return).

At the other end of the scale are the *Mercure Inn Karratha* (☎ (08) 9185 1155) and *Karratha International Hotel* (☎ (08) 9185 3111); singles or doubles at both start from $132.

Los Amigos, on Balmoral Rd opposite the BP station, has Mexican specials. For snacks, you can try the cafes and takeaways in the Karratha shopping centre, including *Adrienne's* and *Paradiso Pizza*. A little way out of town, the *Tambrey Centre* has a tavern and serves good counter meals; visitors are welcome to use the swimming pool.

Roebourne

The *Harding River Caravan Park* (☎ (08) 9182 1063), with tent sites at $10 for two, is 1km down a road on the north side of the bridge, just off the North-West Coastal Highway. The *Mt Welcome Motel Hotel* in Roe St is the main place, with singles/doubles for $45/65.

The *Roebourne Diner*, good for eat-in and takeaways, and the fancier *Poinciana Room* are in the Mt Welcome complex.

Millstream-Chichester & Karijini National Parks

In Millstream-Chichester, there are basic *campsites* (☎ (08) 9184 5144) at Snake Creek (near Python Pool), Crossing Pool and Deep Reach; tent sites are $5 for two, plus $3 for an extra person. The latter two places have gas barbecues and fireplaces.

There are also several basic *campsites*

within Karijini, including Fortescue (Dales Gorge), Weano Gorge and the Joffre intersection ($5 for a tent site for two) – contact the rangers (☎ (08) 9189 8157) for more information.

Wittenoom

All of the town's accommodation is basic (and under imminent threat of closure). The *Gorges Caravan Park* (☎ (08) 9189 7075), Second Ave, has tent sites from $12 and cabins from $35 for two.

Wittenoom Bungarra Bivouac Hostel (☎ (08) 9189 7026), 71 Fifth Ave, has beds at $7 per night; it is the base for Dave's Gorge Tour. *Nomad Heights* (☎ (08) 9189 7068), on First Ave, is a small arid/tropical permaculture farm, and beds are available at $6 a night. *Wittenoom Holiday Homes* (☎ (08) 9189 7096) on Fifth Ave has cottages from $55 for two.

You can get basic supplies at the caravan park or local store.

Auski Roadhouse, Munjina

Some 42km from Wittenoom, at Munjina on the Great Northern Highway, is the asbestos-free *Auski Tourist Village* (☎ (08) 9176 6988). Its 'negative' mineral status and the fine hamburgers in the *restaurant* are its only saving graces. The ablution block is a bitterly cold winter's morning walk from the vastly overpriced cabins – $45 for 'the barest of necessities'. Tent sites in the caravan facility are $10 for two and the motel rooms, basking in a lack of competition, are $110 for two.

Tom Price

The *Tom Price Caravan Park* (☎ (08) 9189 1515) has tent/powered sites for $12/14 for two, on-site vans for $35 and chalets for $65. *Hillview Lodge* (☎ (08) 9189 1625) has overpriced rooms for $110.

The *Red Emperor* and the *Karijini Cafe*, both in the shopping mall, provide reasonable food, while the Mercure Inn has a licensed *restaurant*.

Newman

There are several caravan parks in the area, the closest to town being the *Newman Caravan Park* (☎ (08) 9175 1428) on Kalgan Drive; tent/powered sites are $12/15 and cabins are $60 for two. *Dearlove's Caravan Park* (☎ (08) 9175 2802) on Cowra Drive, has tent/powered sites from $12/15, and on-site vans/park cabins from $40/50 for two. If you are over 50, you can get a discount (and will probably need it) on your accommodation from the *Mercure Inn Newman* (☎ (08) 9175 1101) on Newman Drive, which has double rooms for $132.

In addition to the roadhouses, there are a number of takeaway shops including the *Boulevarde Cafe*, *Chicken Treat* and *Chinese Kitchen* in the Boulevarde shopping centre. On Hilditch Avenue, you can choose from the *Kiwi-Inn*, *K's Pizza & Bakery* and *Coxy's Corner*.

Port Hedland

Lately, it has been hard to find accommodation in this bustling, project-laden town. The newly employed hand out their hard-earned bucks for the most basic of doss houses.

The *Cooke Point Caravan Park* (☎ (08) 9173 1271) on Athol St is adjacent to Pretty Pool. This is now one of the best parks in the state, a far cry from its former status. Tidy powered sites are $16 for two, and meticulous cabins (with colour TV) are $65. The dusty but friendly *Port Hedland Backpackers* (☎ (08) 9173 3282) at 20 Richardson St has dorm beds for $14 and twin rooms $32; they organise budget trips to Karijini.

On the corner of Anderson St, there's the *Esplanade Hotel* (☎ (08) 9173 1798), with dank, noisy rooms from $55. The *Pier Hotel* has adequate singles/doubles that cost $65/80. The *South Hedland Motel* (☎ (08) 9172 2222), at 13 Court Place, has rooms at $80/90.

Marg's Kitchen, opposite the tourist bureau, is open till late. *Maureen's Bakehouse* on Richardson St has been heartily recommended for its home-made salad rolls. Nearby is the *Coral Trout*, where you can get fish & chips – the mackerel is superb.

Canning Stock Route

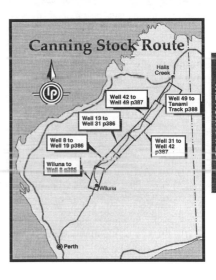

The Canning Stock Route stretches for over 1700km across the arid heart of Western Australia, between Wiluna in the south and Halls Creek in the north. It is the longest stock route in the world, most of it passing through uninhabited country.

Just think: here you can drive the same distance as the complete length of Great Britain and halfway back again, or from Nagasaki in the south of Japan to the island of Hokkaido in the north, or from Los Angeles, across California and Oregon, to

Seattle in Washington state – and hardly see a soul. It's a long haul in anybody's language.

It is the hardest and longest 4WD trip in Australia. The number of sandhills that need to be crossed vary, depending on who you believe and if they counted every hill or just the big ones. There are at least 800, but most people stop counting after day two or three.

The route crosses the Gibson Desert, the Great Sandy Desert and, in its northern part, the western section of the Tanami Desert. Because of that, one may think the country, or the scenery, never changes. Nothing could be further from the truth. The variety of desert landforms and the subtle changes of vegetation weave their magic on all who travel this vast landscape.

Nobody travels the Canning in summer. It usually begins to see the first adventurers in late April or early May and by the middle of October, the season is coming to a close. June to August are probably the best months. If you are the first of the season, you may be plagued by tall spinifex that can block your vehicle's radiator in less than 10 minutes. In places, you may find it difficult to see the track.

Needless to say, you need to be very well set up to travel the Canning. Most would consider the route to be out of the realm of the small 4WDs. The ability to carry the huge amount of fuel, water and supplies for the minimum two-week trip means that anything smaller than a four-cylinder Jackaroo or Pajero is completely out of the question. While the four-cylinder utes, such as the Hilux and Rodeo, do well out here, the real kings of the Canning are the six-cylinder diesel Landcruisers and Patrols.

Mind you, some people have walked the Canning. Alfred Canning, after whom the route is named, and his men did (when they weren't riding camels), but in more recent times, some adventurers looking for a challenge have walked or run the route. The handful who have either pushed a specially designed cart to carry their supplies or had vehicle backup. Either way, it's a hard slog!

Bicycle and motorcycle riders are just as rare. The deep, soft sand and the distances between water tends to turn most off. As the only place you can get fuel dropped is about halfway along the stock route, carrying fuel and water is a problem only overcome by a backup vehicle.

Travelling the stock route in company is much safer than on your own. If you want to travel the Canning but don't know anyone who wants to go, 4WD clubs often have trips and there are a number of tour operators who take tag-alongs. Some of the latter even cook for you and they certainly supply the safety and companionship.

Wiluna and Halls Creek, at either end of the stock route, are only small communities but service vast pastoral regions; you can find or get anything you want, as long as you have the time to wait. Parts may have to be flown in on the weekly mail plane. Forget the cost – you need the parts to keep rolling! The only other option is to sell your truck as it stands, hitch a lift to the more settled parts of the country and give up on exploring the real Australia.

HISTORY

One of the great attractions of travelling the stock route is the strong sense of history that pervades most of the 54 wells dotting its course. You cannot help being touched by the freshness or the closeness of this saga in Australia's history.

Major Peter Warburton crossed from central Australia to the north-western coast in 1873, traversing the stock route's northern section en route. In 1874, John Forrest and his party travelled from the Western Australian coast to the Overland Telegraph Line, naming several points at the southern end.

On 2 June of that year, he found what he described as 'one of the best springs in the colony', naming it Weld Springs. When they were attacked by Aborigines here, Forrest and his men built a small stone fort to protect themselves. That fort still remains at what became Canning's Well 9.

In 1876, Ernest Giles passed just to the north of Forrest's tracks on his return from the west coast. But it was to be another 20 years before another white person travelled this region.

In 1896, two expeditions set on south-to-north crossings. The Calvert Expedition was led by Lawrence Wells, but tragedy struck when two members, including his cousin, became lost and died of thirst. David Carnegie's party had better fortunes: all but one survived a double crossing of the desert (Charlie Stansmore died after a shooting accident). But they failed to find any gold or a cattle route – the main reasons for the trip. Both expeditions advised the government that a cattle route was impossible and the search for one should be stopped. The stage was now set for Alfred Canning.

By the early 1900s, Kimberley cattlemen were clamouring for a stock route to be developed from the north-west station country to the southern gold fields. Earlier, in 1898, the movement of cattle from the East Kimberley to the coast around Derby had been banned to stop the spread of cattle tick. A desert route was seen as a natural barrier to the spread of the ticks.

In April 1906, Canning, already a surveyor with a good reputation, was chosen to lead a group of men to survey a route between Wiluna and Halls Creek.

In April of that year, the party of eight men, 23 camels and two ponies left Perth, heading via Day Dawn to Wiluna. Pushing north across the untracked wilderness, they arrived in Halls Creek at the end of October, spending Christmas there before heading south, back into the desert, at the end of February 1907.

Searching for water all the way, they found and used many rockholes that were sources of water for Aborigines. In April, at a rockhole called Waddawalla (later to be known as Canning's Well 40), party member Michael Tobin was speared to death.

In July, the group returned to Perth and Canning's report that a route could be made through the desert was met with a standing ovation in parliament. Canning was the obvious choice to lead a well-sinking party.

By the end of March 1908, the well-sinking party of 30-odd men congregated at Wiluna, ready to head into the harshness of the desert. By the time they reached Flora Valley station at the northern end of the stock route in July 1909, they had sunk, lined and set up 31 wells. They retraced their route a month later, reaching Wiluna around the end of April 1910, after establishing another 21 watering points.

To line many of the wells, timber had to be cut and carted for long distances. The deepest well on the stock route is Well 5, dug out to a depth of 32m, while the shallowest is Well 42 at just 1.5m.

Canning, on his arrival at Wiluna, sent a three-word telegram back to Perth: 'Work completed – Canning.'

The first stock weren't far behind Canning and his men. In April 1911, two drovers, George Shoesmith and James Thompson, along with one of their three Aboriginal stockmen, were fatally speared near Well 37.

But over the next 30 years, the route was never used to anywhere near its full potential. Cattle were brought down it only occasionally, so in 1929, after much lobbying, the government sent out William Snell to refurbish the route. He only got as far north as Well 35. Canning was called out of retirement at the age of 70 to finish the job!

From then until just after WWII, use of the stock route increased a little, with the last mob of cattle taken down in 1958.

The first vehicle to travel part of the stock route was Michael Terry's on a 1925 expedition. Other sections of the stock route succumbed to the motor vehicle, but it was not until 1968 that a group of surveyors drove the complete length. During the 1970s, a handful of travellers challenged the route and by the end of the 1980s, some 10 to 20 groups a year were travelling its length. Today, maybe a thousand adventurous souls travel the stock route each year.

INFORMATION
Tourist Information, Hospitals & Police
Wiluna The Wiluna Shire Council (☎ (08) 9981 7010) in Scotia St is a good place to seek information on the surrounding area and the stock route.

Flora of the Canning

With luck, your trip up the Canning will coincide with rain somewhere along its course. The chances of that happening are, in fact, pretty good as the stock route traverses such a vast segment of land, from the more temperate south to the subtropical north.

The occasional southern winter storm or tropical thunderstorm brings with it an unexpected bounty as the country bursts into new and colourful life. For those who love wildflowers, the desert can be a wondrous place.

Acacias, or wattles, are one of Australia's most common plants. On the Canning there are a number of species that colour the scenery. Prickly acacia, with its pale-yellow flower, is common along the complete length of the stock route, while gidgee is found along creeks in the southern section. Pindan wattle, found in the north, stands out with its yellow flowers. Another colourful wattle with bright-yellow flowers is locally called elephant-ear wattle; a good stand of these can be seen on the way to Well 38.

Grevilleas are one of the really magnificent Australian flowers. There are about 200 species in Australia and you'll see a few different ones on the Canning. The holly grevillea, or Wickham's grevillea, has yellow flowers, while the similar prickly grevillea, found in the northern section of the stock route, has spectacular red-orange flowers. These plants can be found on rocky hills or sandy plains and dunes, but the desert grevillea and the honey grevillea are found only on dunes and sandy plains. These two plants have bright yellow-orange flowers and are loaded with nectar. If there are not too many ants on them, the flowers are lovely to suck or to drop into a cup of water for a pleasant, refreshing drink.

Hakeas are closely related to the grevilleas and more than 90 of the 110 or so species found in Australia can be seen in Western Australia. The most common hakea on the Canning is the easily identifiable corkwood hakea, named for its distinctive bark. The flowers are a creamy yellow.

About 25 species of **cassia** can be found in the Australian inland, including several along the stock route. These shrubs are usually less than 2m high and all have yellow, buttercup-shaped flowers. The green cassia, desert cassia, blunt-leaf cassia and cockroach bush are just some you might see.

Found throughout the length of the Canning and elsewhere in inland Australia is the fluffy **mulla mulla**, sometimes called pussy tails. These low-growing plants have pink, purplish or white flowers that are commonly seen because they persist for a long time after rain.

Vivid displays of the delicate, star-shaped, pink flower of the **desert-fringe myrtle** can be seen on the dunes and the yellow-green, bird-shaped flower of the **parrot-pea bush** is found north of Well 36.

Daisies of many sorts can also be seen, as well as bright-purple **parakelia**, and if you are lucky, vivid displays of the magnificent **Sturt's desert pea**. ∎

Medical facilities are available from the Wiluna Medical Centre (☎ (08) 9981 7063) in Lennon St. It also has support from the Royal Flying Doctor Service in emergencies.

The police station (☎ (08) 9981 7024) is in Thompson St; travellers are asked to inform the police of their departure/arrival when travelling the Canning.

Halls Creek For information on the surrounding area, visit the Halls Creek Tourist Information Centre (☎ (08) 9168 6262; fax 9168 6467) on the Great Northern Highway; it's open from May to September. The Shire of Halls Creek (☎ (08) 9168 6007) in Thomas St can also supply information, as can the Poinciana Roadhouse (☎ (08) 9168 6164) on the highway.

The hospital (☎ (08) 9168 6003) is in Roberta Ave. The police station (☎ (08) 9168 6000) is on the highway.

Permits

No permits are required if you travel the stock route as detailed.

Both ends of the stock route cross private pastoral land, where the normal restrictions apply.

If you go via Glen-Ayle station (☎ (08) 9981 2990), it costs $10 a vehicle to use the station tracks. It's best to make contact before you leave and visit as you pass through – the house is close to the track.

You need permission from Granite Peaks station (☎ (08) 9981 2983) to use the track between the homestead and the stock route; a fee of $10 per vehicle is payable.

Registration

It is advisable to register with the police at your starting point (either Wiluna or Halls Creek) and complete a form called Notification of Travel in Remote Areas. See the Survival section in the chapter on Facts for the Visitor.

Books & Maps

The best maps of the Canning are those by the Royal Automobile Club of Western Australia, Australian Geographic and Westprint Maps. A full range of 1:250,000 topographic maps is available, but these maps are unlikely to be required unless you are doing something off the beaten track.

Far and away the best books for travellers are the *Canning Stock Route – a Traveller's Guide for a Journey Through History* by Ronele & Eric Gard, published by Western Desert Guides (80 Glenelg Ave, Wembley Downs, WA 6019) and *The Canning Stock Route*, published by Australian Geographic (PO Box 321, Terry Hills, NSW 2084). There is an interesting insight into Canning and his travels on the stock route in a book by E Smith, *The Beckoning West*, published by St George Books. It's hard to get but well worthwhile for history buffs.

Radio Frequencies

The RFDS bases at Meekatharra and Derby are the best radio bases to work through. Don't forget the bases are only open during normal business hours.

The primary frequency for the RFDS base at Meekatharra (call sign VKJ) is 4010, while its secondary frequencies are 2280 and 6880. Derby base (call sign VJB) has a primary frequency of 5300 and secondary frequencies of 6925 and 6945.

If you are working through Telstra, the best bases are Perth (call sign VIP) and Darwin (call sign VID). For Perth the main radphone channels are 607, 806 and 1226, and these are available 24-hours. Selcall for the beacon at Perth is 0799, while the operator's Selcall is 0107. For Darwin, the main voice-call channels are open only between 8 am and 8 pm and include channels 415, 811,

227 and 1622. Darwin can be extremely hard to get, especially in the morning. Selcall for the beacon at Darwin is 0599, while the operator's Selcall is 0105.

For those who have registered with Telstra (☎ toll-free 1800 810 023) and the RDD network, the best bases at present are Perth and Alice Springs.

Warning

This is not an easy trip and you need to be thoroughly prepared and have your vehicle in first-class shape before you start. People still die in this extremely remote region when their vehicle breaks down. In the last 10 years, the number has reached double figures. Others have survived because they either did everything right or luck was on their side. If your vehicle fails out here, you are in real trouble!

SPECIAL PREPARATIONS
Food & Water

Most people take about a fortnight to 'do' the Canning, so you'll need plenty of food and water on board. For more on water, see the Survival section in Facts for the Visitor.

The Canning is rapidly becoming stripped of firewood – many popular camping areas have no dead timber at all – so it's recommended that you take and use a gas stove for cooking.

Fuel

To travel the route and see a few of the sites along the way (some are 50km or more off the main track), a six-cylinder diesel Cruiser will need to carry 280 to 300L of fuel, while a petrol Cruiser will need 350 to 370L. A big V8 Ford may need 500L or more, while a small four-cylinder diesel may get away with 200 to 220L. Basically, that is what you require to travel from Well 23 to Halls Creek or vice versa. From Wiluna to the resupply point at Well 23, a six-cylinder diesel will need about 160 to 180L.

That is a lot of fuel, but you'll only get away with that amount if you organise a fuel drop at Well 23. The **Capricorn Roadhouse** (☎ (08) 9175 1535) just south of Newman is the place to get in touch with, but do it six weeks or so in advance. The fuel comes in 200L drums; work out your consumption before going, so that when you leave Well 23, you are fully fuelled for the run north. What doesn't fit in, leave behind! Considering the remoteness of Well 23, $270 for a 200L drum is pretty good value.

Tyres
Carry at least two complete spares and a couple of extra tubes. A good tyre-repair kit and pump are essential. Tyre pressures will play a very important part in successfully tackling the Canning. Too high and you won't get up the sand hills, too low and you will stake tyres. Because of the loads being carried, it's not necessary to drop pressure as low as you would for a day's run along the beach: 170 to 180kPa (25 to 26psi) should do nicely.

In places, you will be travelling over very rocky and broken ground so extreme care is needed. Take it slowly and you should be OK. Travel too quickly, or with tyre pressures too low, and your tyres will start blowing.

Trailers
The Canning is no place for a trailer. It is possible to take a well-constructed trailer over the stock route but those who have done it once will never do it again.

THE ROUTE
Wiluna
Once considered the wildest town in Australia, Wiluna sits on the edge of the desert country and was gazetted as a town in 1898. During its boom years in the 1930s, the population peaked at around 9000 and the town had four hotels. While its population waned after WWII, recent mining activities have seen the town gain a few more people. Today the population is about 300.

Facilities at this small outback community include fuel, food supplies, limited repairs and accommodation. If you want some fresh fruit, the **Desert Gold Orange Orchard**, just out of town, is worth a visit. You can not only buy oranges, but also grapefruit, tangellos, lemons and some stone fruits.

Wiluna to Well 9 (295km)
This track lies across pastoral land and during times of heavy rain can be officially closed to all traffic. As with travelling across any pastoral land, leave gates as you find them and leave stock alone. Do not camp close to any stock-watering points. From Wiluna, a well-formed dirt road heads north with **Well 1** just 7km from town, while a little further on, and off the main road, is **Well 1A**, called North Pool; it's on the Negara River and is a popular swimming hole with locals.

Just before **Well 2**, you leave the main road and turn right onto a lesser station track reaching the well 3km later, 41km north of Wiluna. The normally dry **Well 2A**, or The Granites, lies another 37km north and was the last one built by Canning and his men.

Water from Well 3, 31km north of Well 2A, is unreliable, while sections of the track between **Well 3** and **Well 4** can become boggy after even quite light falls of rain. The crossing of **Lake Nabberu**, which is really a series of lakes, can be a problem and even Canning and his men built a corduroy road across it from logs. The remains of this crossing can be seen 4.5km west of Well 4; the water from this well, 32km north of Well 3, is salty.

Well 4A lies 2km off the main route, 35km north-east of Well 4 and just a short distance from **Little Windich** and **Windich Springs**. Found and named by Forrest, these springs and waterholes are used today by numerous cattle; it is not the best place to camp, as the water is polluted.

Well 5 is 215km north of Wiluna and 38km from the turn-off to Well 4A. It was the deepest well built by Canning and his men; more than 100 tonnes of rock were blasted and removed by hand during its construction. Because of its depth, the water is hard to get. Here a track heads east to Granite Peaks homestead and can be used as a diversion around a flooded Lake Nabberu. A fee of $10 a vehicle, payable at the homestead passed by the track, is charged for using this route.

Well 6, or Pierre Springs as Forrest called it, is 19km further and was reconditioned by the Geraldton 4WD club in 1991. Its good, reliable water and surrounds make it one of the best spots to camp on the Canning.

Mt Davis, 4km north of Well 6, is worth a climb. Once you have panted your way to the top, you'll have a great view of the surrounding country. Observant travellers may even find some Aboriginal art.

Set in a dense stand of mulga, 100m off the track and 23km from Well 6, **Well 7** is in a dilapidated state but still provides good water. Willy Willy Bore, **Well 8**, with its good water, Scorpion Bore and Canning Bore are all passed on the way to Well 9, a further 39km north.

Well 9 is Forrest's famous Weld Springs and is now contained in a historic reserve. Here, Forrest and his men built a fort to protect them from attack by Aborigines – you can still see the remains. While the spring is now almost dry, the well, fitted with a windmill, still produces a good supply of water. The water looks crystal clear as it overflows out of the tank, but you wouldn't want to drink it once you've looked inside. Pigeons and finches abound.

At this point, the track from Carnegie homestead via Glen-Ayle homestead joins the stock route, this track is often used by those coming from the east along the Gunbarrel Highway. It is also a wet-weather alternative when the track between Wiluna and Well 9 is closed. Permission is required from Glen-Ayle station to use this track; a fee of $10 per vehicle applies. It is about 200km from Carnegie homestead (☎ (08) 9981 2991), where you can get fuel, to Well 9 via Glen-Ayle.

Well 9 to Durba Springs (220km)

Once you leave Well 9, you are approaching the end of pastoral country. Soon the landscape changes and you enter sandhill country, where the real adventure begins.

The Durba Hills, at the very north of this section, are one of the gems of the trip; allow time to enjoy them.

Well 10 was called the Lucky Well by the drovers of old, as they considered themselves lucky to have escaped the sandhill country and reached this far south. It is still in good condition, 20km north of Well 9, and supplies decent water.

Heading for **Well 11**, you cross the first of the sandhills, but they really shouldn't be a problem. At this well on the edge of the salt expanse of **White Lake**, 15km north of Well 10, a sign for travellers has been erected by Australian Geographic. Water from this well is too salty to drink.

Nearly 21km north of Well 11, the first big sandhill will test your skill. If you haven't dropped your tyre pressures, now is the time to do so. Here you'll also see the southernmost patch of desert oaks on the stock route. These trees are a magnificent highlight of the trip. As you head north, the sandhills get bigger. North of Lake Aerodrome, named by Snell, you will find **Well 12**, surrounded by desert oaks. The well has collapsed. The distance between Well 11 and Well 12 is 33km.

There is little remaining of **Well 13**, another 27km north, but it is a good place to camp as mulga and other trees provide shelter. The well has collapsed and is dry.

While **Well 14**, 16km north, has also caved in, there are the remains of the timber fence and stock trough among the tea trees. From here to Well 15, the track is prone to flooding.

Well 15, 25km north of Well 14 and 136km north of Well 9, is also collapsed and dry. About halfway to Well 16, the remains of a trolley can be seen beside the track. It was abandoned by Murray Rankin on his first attempt to walk the Canning in 1974. He succeeded in 1976.

A few hundred metres west off the track, and 38km north of the previous well, **Well 16** is set among picturesque white-gums. This well normally has water, but the water will be unfit for human consumption.

As the track heads north, it begins to skirt

the western edge of the **Durba Hills**. Approaching the hills from the south in the evening is an unforgettable experience, as the rugged escarpment glows fiery red in the rays of the setting sun.

Sunday Well lies 14km north-east from the main track; the turn-off is nearly 9km north of Well 16. Now no more than a hole in the ground and surrounded by tea trees, it can be easily missed. This track also leads out to the Calvert Range, 45km east of Sunday Well, where there are Aboriginal rock engravings.

About 18km north of Well 16, a track leads north-east into the base of the escarpment, below the prominent **Canning's Cairn**. The climb to the top is relatively easy and the view excellent. Aboriginal petroglyphs can be found on the southern wall.

The turn-off, to the north-east, to **Biella Spring** is about 7km north of Canning's Cairn. Once you have travelled the 2km from the junction, it is a pleasant half-hour walk into the gorge to the spring, where you will generally find water. There are a number of Aboriginal rock paintings here.

At the northernmost point of the range is a major track junction, 32km from Well 16. Turning north will keep you on the main stock route, while turning hard right will take you on a track into **Well 17**, also known as Killagurra Springs, named by Canning. Continuing straight ahead, the track leads to Durba Springs, 5km from the main track junction. Killagurra Springs is a registered Aboriginal sacred site – the rock art is the best you will see on the trip. There is permanent water here.

Durba Springs is a place not to miss; you should spend, at the very minimum, two nights here. The camping area now boasts a pit toilet courtesy of the Land Rover Owners Club of Western Australia. From the camping spot, you can explore the head of the gorge and the surrounding country. There are many art sites within the nearby hills and gorges and the area is a haven for birds. If nothing else, just relax and soak in the atmosphere of this tranquil place.

Durba Springs to Well 23 (205km)

Once you head north from the Durba Hills, you enter some of the toughest country on the Canning and further on, you skirt the western margin of the vast salt expanse of Lake Disappointment. North of Well 22, you meet the Talawana Track, a major escape route to the west, and just a little further on is Well 23 – site of the Capricorn Roadhouse fuel dump.

Well 18 lies only 33km north of the Durbas, but it will take you up to four hours to cover that distance. The well, about 1km east off the track, is dry and in disrepair.

Three km further on, a track heads east from the main track to the Terrace Hills and **Onegunyah Rockhole**, found at the base of a small, normally dry waterfall. A few kilometres south of **Well 19**, which is 26km north of Well 18, you will cross the **Tropic of Capricorn**, marked by a survey peg, FX15. Well 19 is on the edge of a claypan and is completely silted up.

Savory Creek, 23km north of Well 19, is often a major obstacle. While it often has water, it is very salty, as you can see from the creek banks. If the main crossing is too risky, there is another 3km west which should be drier and easier.

Once across, the track turns in towards **Lake Disappointment**, but swings north a short distance from the lake shore. A faint track continues to the lake and is worth a detour, but beware of boggy patches. This lake, a vast sea of salt, only has water in it after unseasonable heavy rains. The stock route travels along its western edge for over 70km, but this is about the only place you have a chance to see it at close quarters.

The turn-off to **Well 20** is 15km north of Savory Creek; the well is 10km west from the main track. All that remains is a hole in the ground.

You need to turn right at a track junction, 24km north of the turn-off to Well 20, which leads 8km to **Well 21** and its poor water. This route continues east and joins the other route just south of **Well 22**. Well 22, 40-odd km north-east of Well 21 along this diversion, is

RICHARD I'ANSON

RICHARD I'ANSON

Top: Bungle Bungles, WA
Bottom: Hidden Valley, Gibb River Road, WA

Canning Stock Route
Top: Memorial to Alfred Canning, WA
Bottom Left: Descending a sand dune towards Thring Rock, WA
Bottom Right: Prolific wildflowers just after the rain, near Lake Nabberu, WA

in a picturesque white gum flat between the dunes. The well is dry.

The **Talawana Track**, graded by Len Beadell in 1963, is met some 9km north of Well 22. By heading west here, you can reach the township of Newman within 460km. On the western side of the junction is Georgia Bore with its delightful water from a hand pump – a good spot to camp.

Well 23 – the fuel dump – is another 22km north. Most people stop here for fuel, but the well water is undrinkable.

A 125km diversion route, known as the **Airstrip Track**, leaves the stock route at this point and heads north, then west and finally east, bypassing many of the big dunes the main route crosses north-east of Well 23 and meeting the main track just north of Well 26. While the Airstrip Track is a little easier, the main route is more interesting, so you should stick to that.

Well 23 to Well 33 (271km)
This section of the Canning brings variety and enjoyment as you revel in the waters of Well 26, the beautiful stands of bloodwood and desert oak and the secrets of its water-filled caverns.

Situated just off the track and 14km north, **Well 24** is dry. Three km further north, the **Windy Corner Track**, put in by Len Beadell, joins with the Canning. North of here a vast sea of waving spinifex leads 20km to **Well 25**, once again dry with just a few surface timbers lying around. Just north of this well, a series of three big dunes will test your technique and tyre pressures. There will be plenty more like these between wells 40 and 42. By the time you have covered the 59km to Well 26 from the refuelling point, you'll be looking forward to stopping and enjoying this oasis. You are 760km from Wiluna, barring detours and side trips.

Well 26 was fully restored by a party led by David Hewitt in 1983 to commemorate the route's 75th anniversary. It provides good drinking water and a chance to freshen up. A visitor's book is also at the well and most travellers use it to record their thoughts and adventures.

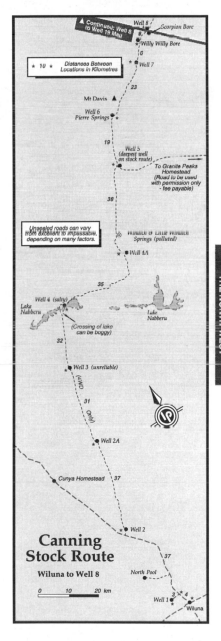

**Canning
Stock Route**

Wiluna to Well 8

0   10   20 km

THE NORTH-WEST

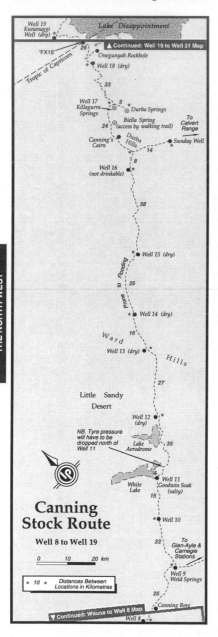

Well 19
Kunanaggi
Well (dry)

Lake Disappointment

'FX15'

26

▲ Continued: Well 19 to Well 31 Map

Tropic of Capricorn

Onegunyah Rockhole

Well 18 (dry)

33

Well 17
Killagurra
Springs

5

Durba Springs

Biella Spring
(access by walking trail)

To
Calvert
Range

24

Canning's
Cairn

Durba
Hills

Sunday Well

14

Well 16
(not drinkable)

8

38

Well 15 (dry)

Prone to Flooding

25

Well 14 (dry)

16

Well 13 (dry)

Ward

Hills

27

Little Sandy
Desert

Well 12
(dry)

NB. Tyre pressure
will have to be
dropped north of
Well 11

35

Lake
Aerodrome

White
Lake

Well 11
Goodwin Soak
(salty)

15

Well 10

22

To
Glen-Ayle &
Carnegie
Stations

Canning
Stock Route

Well 8 to Well 19

0   10   20 km

Well 9
Weld Springs

25

Canning Bore

★ 10 ★ Distances Between
Locations in Kilometres

▼ Continued: Wiluna to Well 8 Map

Well 8

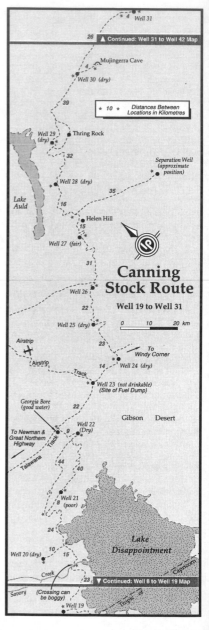

★ 4 Well 31

26

▲ Continued: Well 31 to Well 42 Map

4   Mujingerra Cave

Well 30 (dry)

39

★ 10 ★ Distances Between
Locations in Kilometres

Well 29
(dry)

Thring Rock

32

Separation Well
(approximate
position)

Well 28 (dry)

35

Lake
Auld

16

Helen Hill

15

Well 27 (fair)

31

Canning
Stock Route

Well 19 to Well 31

0   10   20 km

Well 26

22

Well 25 (dry)

23

Airstrip

To
Windy Corner

Airstrip

Track

14

Well 24 (dry)

Well 23 (not drinkable)
(Site of Fuel Dump)

Georgia Bore
(good water)

22

Well 22
(Dry)

To Newman &
Great Northern
Highway

9

Track

Talawana

44

Gibson   Desert

40

Well 21
(poor)

8

24

Lake
Disappointment

Well 20 (dry)

10

15

Creek

Savory

(Crossing can
be boggy)

Capricorn

▼ Continued: Well 8 to Well 19 Map

Tropic of

★ Well 19

23

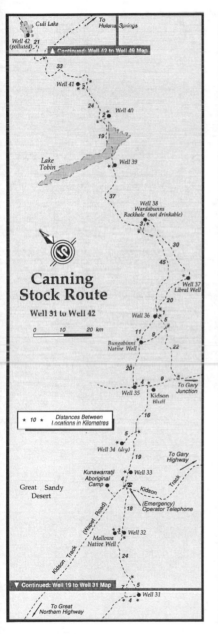

Culi Lake

To Helena Springs

Well 42 (polluted) 21

▲ Continued: Well 42 to Well 49 Map

33

Well 41 2

24

2

Well 40

19

Lake Tobin

Well 39

37

Well 38 Wardabunni Rockhole (not drinkable)

3

30

45

Canning Stock Route

Well 31 to Well 42

0   10   20 km

Well 37 Libral Well

20

Well 36 5

11 9

Bungabinni Native Well

22

20

4

9

Well 35   Kidson Bluff

To Gary Junction

16

★ 10 ★ Distances Between Locations in Kilometres

5

Well 34 (dry)

19

To Gary Highway

Kunawarratji Aboriginal Camp 4 Well 33

Great Sandy Desert

Kidson (Emergency) Operator Telephone

Kidson Track

18

(Wapet Road)

3 Well 32

Mallowa Native Well

24

7 5

▼ Continued: Well 19 to Well 31 Map

7 4 Well 31

To Great Northern Highway

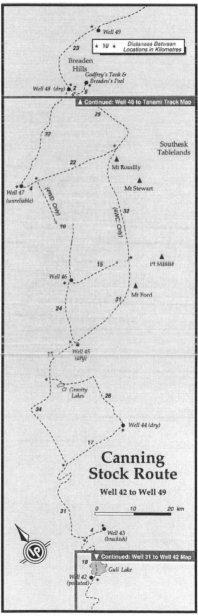

Well 49

23

★ 10 ★ Distances Between Locations in Kilometres

Breaden Hills

Godfrey's Tank & Breaden's Pool

Well 48 (dry) 2 5

▲ Continued: Well 48 to Tanami Track Map

25

32

Southesk Tablelands

22

Mt Romilly

Mt Stewart

Well 47 (unreliable) 4

(4WD Only)

(4WD Only)

32

29

15

Pt Massie

Well 46 5

Mt Ford

24

31

13

Well 45 (dry)

Granity Lakes

26

34

Well 44 (dry)

17

Canning Stock Route

Well 42 to Well 49

0   10   20 km

31

4 Well 43 (brackish)

▼ Continued: Well 31 to Well 42 Map

18 Guli Lake

Well 42 (polluted)

THE NORTH-WEST

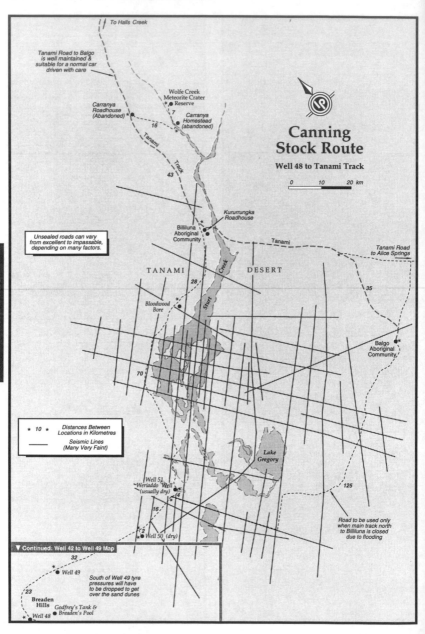

Canning
Stock Route

Well 48 to Tanami Track

0   10   20 km

To Halls Creek

Tanami Road to Balgo
is well maintained &
suitable for a normal car
driven with care

Wolfe Creek
Meteorite Crater
Reserve

Carranya
Roadhouse
(Abandoned)

16

Carranya
Homestead
(abandoned)

Tanami Track

43

Kururrungka
Roadhouse

Billiluna
Aboriginal
Community

Tanami

Tanami Road
to Alice Springs

Unsealed roads can vary
from excellent to impassable,
depending on many factors.

TANAMI   DESERT

28

Stuart Creek

35

Bloodwood
Bore

Balgo
Aboriginal
Community

70

* 10 *   Distances Between
           Locations in Kilometres

           Seismic Lines
           (Many Very Faint)

Lake
Gregory

Well 51
Weriaddo
(usually dry)

Well
14

16

125

Road to be used only
when main track north
to Billiluna is closed
due to flooding

2

Well 50 (dry)

▼ Continued: Well 42 to Well 49 Map

32

Well 49

South of Well 49 tyre
pressures will have
to be dropped to get
over the sand dunes

23

Breaden
Hills

Godfrey's Tank &
Breaden's Pool

Well 48

A steady drive north for 31km leads to **Well 27**, which has fair water in an emergency. A further 15km brings you to a track which heads east for 35km to **Separation Well**. The trip to Separation Well is a slow drive and leads to a shallow depression where members of the 1896 Calvert Expedition split up to head for Warburton's Joanna Spring.

Warburton had plotted the position of Joanna Spring incorrectly and neither Calvert group found the spring. Charles Wells and his companion died, while Lawrence Wells, the leader of the expedition and leading the second group, made it through to the Fitzroy River. Over the following few months, six search expeditions, all with Lawrence Wells as leader or member, pushed into the desert, finally finding both bodies at Discovery Well.

Little remains of **Well 29** and **Well 29**, which are both dry, but there is some good camping just before and just after Well 29, 152km north of Well 23.

What remains of **Well 30** lies 39km north of the previous well and among a glorious stand of bloodwood trees. It is an ideal campsite, although there is no water.

Just 4km east is **Mujingerra Cave**, a limestone cave with crystal-clear water. Reached through a narrow tunnel, it is not for the faint-hearted. Be careful when approaching the entrance and park your vehicle some distance away. Please do not pollute this fragile environment with soap.

Well 31 is 4km east off the main route and dominated by a good specimen of a cabbage-tree gum. The turn-off is 26km north of Well 30 and the route continues, joining up with the main track 5km later. The run 24km north from here to **Well 32** is easy and you may even get a chance to hit top gear for a change. While Well 31 is dry, Well 32, alongside the main track on the east side, normally supplies reasonable water. About 3km west of Well 32, along a distinct track, is **Mallowa Native Well**, set amongst green acacias. Like many of these soaks, you will have to dig for water if there's none that is visible on the surface.

The **Kidson Track** crosses the Canning 17km north of Well 32. Just 3km west along this relatively good road is the Kunawarratji Aboriginal community – keep heading west and, after another 575km, you reach the Great Northern Highway. East will lead to Len Beadell's Gary Highway, Windy Corner and Sandy Blight Junction, all just as remote as the junction you are at. There's a phone booth here that only takes operator-connected calls.

Well 33 is just 4km north of the Kidson-Canning track junction on the east side of the main track. It is a pleasant camp but the dingoes are friendly and will steal anything left lying around – smelly shoes seem to be a real favourite. The water from the well is generally drinkable.

Well 33 to Well 39 (163km)

Some of the most historic and poignant places lie along this section of the stock route. Take your time and make the effort to see it all.

Another good spot to camp is at **Well 34**, 5km west of the main track; the turn-off is 19km north of Well 33. Little remains at this spot and there is no water.

Once you pass Kidson Bluff to the east, a track junction is met, 16km north of the turn-off to Well 34. Here you can turn left and travel 4km to **Well 35**. This well was burnt out (like many on the Canning – a timely reminder to be careful with your own fire), but a bore casing does provide a limited supply of water. You're now just over 1000km north of Wiluna.

From Well 35, you can proceed north on an alternative route through a magnificent stand of desert oaks to **Bungabinni Native Well**, which has a plentiful supply of fresh water and a visitor's book. From there, you pass **Well 36**, with its fair water and nice camping spot among the desert oaks, before rejoining the main stock route just a few kilometres further on, 33km from Well 35.

At the junction before Well 35, you can also turn right, following the **Gary Highway** for 9km before turning north, or left, again back onto the stock route. About 27km north of here, the alternative route described previously joins with the main route.

One km past this junction a track veers off to the east, heading 20km to **Well 37**, or Libral Well. This well produces good water. The surrounding area makes for a pleasant camping spot; the history and the graves close by make for an interesting few hours of exploration.

Well 37 is often called the Haunted Well, which recalls its tragic history. The first stockmen to take cattle down the Canning were attacked and killed by Aborigines at this point. The two drovers, Shoesmith and Thompson, along with their Aboriginal helper, are buried about 50 to 60m almost due north of the well.

The grave of an oil prospector, John McLernon, clubbed to death by Aborigines in 1922, can also be found here. He was killed some distance east of the well and was buried at the base of a desert oak about 250m north-east of the well. The tree is blazed but only the most observant will see the original blaze.

From Libral Well, a diversion track leads for 30km to **Well 38**, also known as **Wardabunni Rockhole**, which is normally dry or, more often than not, green and stagnant. The walls of the rockhole reveal the initials of some of the early explorers.

Just 3km further on from Well 38, you meet up with the old stock route track and swing north. Travelling another 37km north, you reach **Well 39**, which has reasonable water, in an emergency.

Well 39 to the Breaden Hills (300km)

Here, history and a variety of desert landscapes vie with one another for attention and it's easy to spend days soaking up the atmosphere.

A few kilometres north of Well 39, a stand of desert oaks makes a good camp. The crossing of **Lake Tobin** is generally easy and speed across the salt flat is something to enjoy! At the northern extremity of the lake, 19km north of Well 39, is the turn-off to **Well 40**. Two km east from the main track, this well is the site where Michael Tobin, a member of Canning's 1907 survey party, was killed by an Aborigine. This is a good spot to camp; the well supplies reasonable water.

The turn-off to **Well 41** is 24km north of Well 40 and the well itself is another 2km west of the main stock route. Its tannin-stained water is quite good for drinking.

A bumpy scraped track, 33km north of Well 41, leads to David Carnegie's **Helena Springs**. This track leads 88km east to the historic site and there is no water at the end. The track was put in by a group led by Peter Vernon, who has blazed a number of trails out here and, in July 1988, ran the length of the Canning from Wiluna to Halls Creek in 35 days.

On the south-western end of Guli Lake, **Well 42** is 54km north of Well 41 and is the shallowest well constructed on the stock route. The well's timbers and the nearby bush have suffered from unthinking passing travellers looking for firewood. The water is generally polluted.

Well 43 is 4km north-east off the main route. Just a few metres away from the original is a new well which can supply brackish water in an emergency. The old well, which yielded thousands of litres per hour of good water, is now dry.

The distance between the turn-off to Well 43 and the turn-off to **Well 44** is 31km. Well 44 is some 17km east off the main route. It is nothing much more than a hole in the ground and is completely dry.

To continue to Well 45 from Well 44, you can either backtrack to the main vehicle route or continue on a scraped track to join the stock route 26km north of Well 44, near the Gravity Lakes and about 15km south of **Well 45**. On the main route, the distance from the Well 44 turn-off to Well 45, located on the main stock route track, is 49km. Well 45 is caved in and generally dry.

From Well 45, you have the option of following the old vehicle route north-east, a distance of 88km, to a major track junction just south of Well 48. Here, you can turn off to the Breaden Hills. This route from Well 45 bypasses Wells 46 and 47 by up to 22km, but access tracks lead to each well.

A better choice is to head north along a scraped track that follows the original Canning Stock Route directly to **Well 46**, a distance of 24km. This well provides excellent water and is a great spot to camp.

You can head directly east from here, reaching the old vehicle route, 31km north of Well 45, after 15km.

However, by heading north from Well 46 along another bumpy, scraped track for 29km, you will join up with the main access track to **Well 47**. Well 47 lies 4km further west and is a very unreliable water source.

From here, you can head back east, past the scraped track on which you came north, for 26km to join up with the old stock route track, 63km north of Well 45 and 27km south of Well 48. This way, the total distance between Well 45 and Well 48 is 106km, compared to 88km via the main route, but you have seen all the wells along the way.

Alternatively, from Well 47 you can head 32km in a more northerly direction across faint, scraped tracks directly to Well 48, a total distance from Well 45 of about 90km. Whichever way you get to Well 48, it is worth visiting the nearby Breaden Hills.

From the track junction just south of Well 48, a track leads 5km north-east into the heart of the **Breaden Hills**. Breaden's Pool is a 5-minute walk from the parking area, while the walk to **Godfrey's Tank** takes a little longer. Both are named after members of David Carnegie's 1896 expedition and in the rock walls above Godfrey's Tank, there are the initials of members of both the Carnegie and Canning parties. Aboriginal carvings can also be found.

Breaden Hills to Tanami Track (180km)

The end of the stock route looms and once north of the Breaden Hills, you are into pastoral country. Care needs to be taken here because of the large number of seismic survey lines that lead nowhere – several people have died in recent years through taking the wrong track!

The turn-off to **Well 48** is just 2km north of the track junction that takes you into the

Breaden Hills. The well lies a short distance to the west, just off the main route north. It once supplied small amounts of good water but is now dry.

From the carpark at the Breaden Hills to **Well 49** is 30km, 23km east from the turn-off to Well 48. At the well, you'll find the grave of Jack Smith, a stockman, who died here after falling from a horse. This well also has some of the best water on the Canning, but to get a drink you'll need a long rope and plenty of energy.

As you head north, you pass the Australian Geographic's **notice to travellers** and then the last lot of desert oaks on the Canning. You are fast approaching civilisation; this spot is a good one for a last camp on the stock route proper. **Well 50** lies 2km south off the main track, 32km north of the previous well. It is caved in and dry.

The turn-off to **Dalgo Aboriginal community** is 16km further and just 4km past here is **Well 51**, or Weriaddo, the last well on the stock route. The well has caved in and the bore next to it is also usually dry. You are now on Aboriginal-owned **Billiluna station** and there are many tracks and seismic lines throughout the area.

Stick to the main route north. About 70km north of Well 51, you will pass **Bloodwood Bore** and after a further 28km, you'll pass through the outskirts of the Billiluna Aboriginal community, as well as the Kururrungku Store with its fuel and supplies, just before joining up with the **Tanami Track**.

While modern travellers head up or down the Tanami Track, the now-unused original stock route continues northwards along Sturt Creek and its occasional shady waterholes. North of present-day Sturt Creek station the original route leaves the Sturt Creek following Cow Creek, crossing the Elvire River near the Old Flora Valley station before ending at Old Halls Creek, 16km south of present-day Halls Creek.

Turning west at the Tanami Track junction will lead you to **Halls Creek**, 175km away, but just 43km north along the Tanami Track is the turn-off to the **Wolfe Creek Meteorite Crater Reserve**. This is the second largest meteorite crater in the world and is easily accessible being just 23km from the main road. It's worth a visit.

At this stage, you'll feel elated that you have driven and experienced the Canning. If you are like most, you will be a little sad that this great adventure is over.

ALTERNATIVE ROUTES

We've included some minor alternative routes between wells in the main description of the track. As well, there are a number of ways to enter or leave the stock route.

The very southern section of the stock route is liable to be closed to traffic because of flooding around Lake Nabberu (Well 4). The alternative route for travellers during such times, or for travellers approaching from the east along the Gunbarrel Highway via Carnegie station, is to travel to Well 9 via Glen-Ayle station. You will need permission from Glen-Ayle to travel these private roads and be required to pay $10 per vehicle.

Granite Peaks station, almost due west of Glen-Ayle, is reached via the Granite Peaks road from near Wiluna. This route will bring you out at Well 5 or from near Granite Peaks, you may head to Glen-Ayle and join up with the stock route further north. You need permission from Granite Peaks to use the track between the homestead and the stock route; a fee of $10 per vehicle applies.

The Talawana Track joins the stock route 9km north of Well 22 and heads west 460km to the mining town of Newman. It is a relatively good dirt road that traverses remote desert country all the way to civilisation.

North of Well 24, the Windy Corner track, graded by Len Beadell in 1963, joins the stock route. This track leads east 210km to the Gary Highway. See the Bomb Roads section in The Central Deserts chapter for more details.

Just south of Well 33 is a crossroad. West is the Wapet Road that runs over 900km to Broome or Port Hedland on the west coast. East takes you along the Kidson Track, 75km to the Gary Highway.

At the T-junction before Well 35, you can turn west to the well or swing east, then north

to Well 36. Where the Canning swings north, another track continues east 34km to Gary Junction at the northern end of the Gary Highway. From this point you can either head south to the Gunbarrel Highway (300km) or continue east to Alice Springs (900km). Both routes go through remote desert country but the going is easier than the Canning. The latter route passes through Aboriginal land and a permit is required. See the Bomb Roads section in the Central Deserts chapter for more details.

South of Well 51, the last section of the Canning heads north to Billiluna and the Tanami Track. This area can be flooded when Lake Gregory, to the east, overflows. A track heads south-east and then north-east 125km to the Balgo Aboriginal community, which is 35km south of the Tanami Track. Fuel, accommodation and limited supplies are available here. Once again, you should have a permit but if the Canning is flooded, you should receive a sympathetic hearing. Travellers intending to visit the community should contact the Chairman, Balgo Hills Community Aboriginal Corporation, via Halls Creek, WA 6770.

ORGANISED TOURS

Amesz Tours (☎ (08) 9250 2577) was one of the first commercial operators to take travellers along the Canning. Trips are run once or twice a year, carrying passengers as well as leading tag-alongs.

Geoff and Lisa Portman, who operate Portman's Australian Adventures (☎ (03) 5786 1780), generally have at least one trip along the Canning each year. Most begin in Alice Springs. These are tag-alongs only and no passengers are carried.

Russell Guest's 4WD Safaris (☎ (03) 9481 5877) has been operating successful escorted convoys over outback Australia for quite a few years. You can join one of his trips to the Canning, either driving your own vehicle or travelling as a passenger in the escort vehicle.

Western Desert Guides (☎ (08) 9341 2524), 80 Glenelg Ave, Wembley Downs,

WA 6019, is run by Eric and Ronele Gard, who know the Canning better than most. They run tag-along trips and also carry passengers on their regular jaunts along the Canning.

FACILITIES
Wiluna
Located 950km north-east of Perth, the town of Wiluna, you have to say, is remote. Most supplies are available and it is your last chance to stock up before tackling the Canning.

Canning Trading (☎ (08) 9981 7020) in Wotton St is open seven days a week and you'll be able to find just about all of your general requirements in the store. Along with food, it also offers fuel, aircraft refuelling, vehicle hire, ice, camping gas refills as well as mechanical and tyre repairs. It is also the local post office and the agency for the Commonwealth Bank. The store has EFTPOS facilities.

Fuel, general supplies, hardware, clothing and ice are available from the *Ngangganawili Community Store*, also in Wotton St. The store is only open Monday to Friday from 9 am to noon and 1.30 to 4 pm.

The *Club Hotel/Motel* (☎ (08) 9981 7012), on the corner of Wotton and Wall Sts, offers cold beers and a range of meals for breakfast, lunch and dinner, while snacks are available throughout the day. On Sunday, weather permitting, there is a barbecue costing just $8 per head. Accommodation is also available in the hotel, and in air-con motel rooms. The costs for the hotel range from $45 to $55 for a single/twin share room, while twin share in the motel is $80 to $90 per room.

Travellers can also stop over at the *Wiluna Shire Caravan Park* (☎ (08) 9981 7021) in Lennon St. It has powered, grassed caravan and camping sites, laundry and ablution facilities, hot showers and a barbecue area. Dogs are also allowed, on a leash. An unpowered tent site is $5 per person; a powered site for an air-con van for two people is $13.50 a night.

Halls Creek
Halls Creek is a major rural centre, catering reasonably well for the needs of the outback traveller.

The *Kimberley Super Value Store* on the Great Northern Highway has general food supplies, fruits, vegetables and hardware items. It is open seven days a week, with limited trading hours on the weekend and public holidays – on Saturday the store is open from 8 am to noon and on Sunday and public holidays from 9 am to noon.

Halls Creek has a number of other general stores in Halls Creek along with a bakery, butcher and liquor store.

Service stations and roadhouses have fuel supplies and repairs can be carried out in one of the mechanical workshops in town. Aviation fuel is available from the Halls Creek Trading Post (☎ (08) 9168 6107). The cheapest spot for fuel and the service centre that can supply the biggest range of spare parts (especially Toyota parts) is Baz Industries (☎ (08) 9168 6150), located at 137 Duncan Rd.

There is a variety of accommodation available in Halls Creek. You can choose to stay in the *Halls Creek Caravan Park* (☎ (08) 9168 6169), Roberta Ave, which has all facilities. A powered caravan site costs $14 for two people per night, while an unpowered tent site is $6 per person, with power costing an extra $2 per site. Travellers not staying in the park can use the shower facilities for $1.50. Dogs are allowed, on a leash.

Alternatively, there are two motels, both of which offer meals. The *Halls Creek Kimberley Hotel/Motel* (☎ (08) 9168 6101), Roberta Ave, has rooms from $110/130 a single/double, with a family room which sleeps six and costs $160. Prices at the *Halls Creek Motel* (☎ (08) 9168 6001), 194 Great Northern Highway, start from $63/78, room only.

For budget-conscious travellers, accommodation at $15 a single is available at the *Halls Creek Backpackers* (☎ (08) 9168 6101), part of the Kimberley Hotel/Motel. There is a dormitory with shower and toilet facilities, but there is no kitchen.

Airstrips

Wiluna has a private airstrip. Contact the Wiluna Shire (☎ (08) 9981 7010) for details.

Halls Creek also has an airstrip which is run by the Halls Creek Shire Council and well used by charter and scenic-flight operators. Contact the council (☎ (08) 9168 6007) for information. Avgas is available.

The Tropics

The tropical north of Australia contains some of the best scenery in the country, and provides the off-road enthusiast with a number of superb adventures. Darwin is the urban hub of the north and is well serviced – it's a good place to rest and restock before heading bush again. Cairns, on the north Queensland coast, is another major centre with plenty of attractions.

Once off the bitumen roads, the possibilities are many. Top of the list is perhaps the trip to Cape York, an isolated and rugged part of Australia and, along with the Canning Stock Route in WA, one of the great 4WD expeditions. The Gulf Track connects Queensland with the Northern Territory, and offers varied scenery, a bit of history and great fishing.

In the Northern Territory itself you can venture off to one of the most remote corners

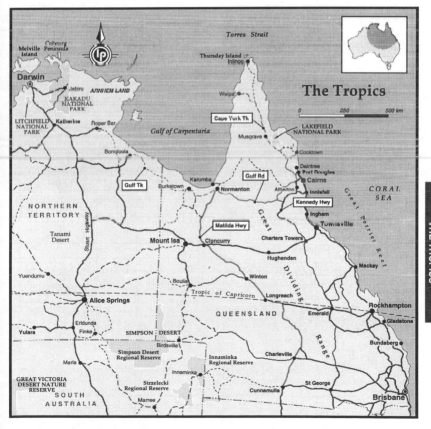

of Arnhem Land and visit the unrivalled Gurig National Park on the Cobourg Peninsula. Access is through Arnhem Land. En route, Kakadu National Park has superb wetlands and Aboriginal art sites, and 4WD tracks to escape the crowds. Litchfield National Park, while only a couple of hours along the bitumen from Darwin, is another great escape. As well as great camping and swimming, the park has some excellent scenery accessible only by well-prepared 4WD vehicles.

Darwin

HIGHLIGHTS

- Sipping champagne and watching the sun set from the cliffs at Nightcliff or Casuarina

- Sampling the offerings of the many and varied food stalls at the Mindil Beach Market (dry season only)

The 'capital' of northern Australia comes as a surprise to many people. Instead of the hard-bitten, rough-and-ready town that you might expect, Darwin (population 82,400) is a lively, modern place with a young population, easy-going lifestyle and cosmopolitan atmosphere. There are between 45 and 60 ethnic groups represented.

Darwin is an obvious base for trips to the Top End's natural attractions. Its remoteness makes it a bit of an oasis too – there are a lot of kilometres to be covered before you get anywhere else, and having reached Darwin, many people rest a bit before leaving.

Information

The Darwin Region Tourism Association Office (☎ (08) 8981 4300; fax 8981 0653) is at Beagle House, on the corner of Mitchell and Knuckey Sts, just around the corner from the end of the mall. It's open from 8.30 am to 6 pm Monday to Friday, from 9 am to 3 pm on Saturday, and 10 am to 2 pm Sunday. It has free maps of the city and several decent booklets.

The main post office (☎ (08) 8980 8200) is at 48 Cavenagh St, on the corner of Cavenagh and Edmunds Sts.

Parks Australia North (PAN; ☎ (08) 8946 4300) is in the Commercial Union building on Smith St between Lindsay and Whitefield Sts.

The Parks & Wildlife Commission (☎ (08) 8999 5511) has its office way out in Palmerston, 20km from the city centre, which is a real nuisance, although they do have a desk at the tourist office in the city centre.

For fossicking permits, the Department of Mines & Energy (☎ (08) 8999 5511) is in the Centrepoint Building, Smith St Mall. For fishing information, the Department of Primary Industry & Fisheries (☎ (08) 8999 5511) has its office in the Harbour View Plaza, Bennett St. The Northern Land Council (☎ (08) 8920 5100; fax 8945 2633) is at 9 Rowling St, Casaurina, Darwin (PO Box 42921, Casuarina, NT 0811).

Other useful addresses include:

Motoring Organisation
   Automobile Association of the Northern Territory, 81 Smith St (☎ (08) 8981 3837)
   Road Service (☎ (08) 8941 0611)
   Wet season road report for Top End (☎ (08) 8922 3394)
Police
   West Lane (☎ (08) 8927 8888)
Medical Facilities
   Ambulance (☎ (08) 8927 9000)
   Royal Darwin Hospital, Rocklands Drive, Casuarina (☎ (08) 8922 8888)
Royal Flying Doctor Service
   Administration Aerial Medical Services (☎ (08) 8922 8110)
   Emergency (☎ (08) 8922 8888, ask for AMS doctor on call).

Bookshops Bookworld on Smith St Mall is a good bookshop. For maps, the NT General Store on Cavenagh St has a good range. Other places to try include the NT Government Publications office or the Department of Lands, Planning & Environment's Maps

NT (☎ (08) 8999 7032) on the corner of Cavenagh and Bennett Sts.

Warning Don't swim in Darwin waters from October to May, when 'stingers' (box jelly-fish) are prevalent. There are crocodiles along the coast and rivers; any crocs found in the harbour are removed, and other beaches near the city are patrolled to mini-mise the risk.

Things to See & Do
There are a number of old buildings in the town centre, including the **Victoria Hotel** on Smith St Mall, the stone **Commercial Bank**, the **old town hall**, **Brown's Mart**, the 1884 **police station** and **old courthouse** at the corner of Smith St and the Esplanade, and **Government House**, built in stages from 1870.

At **Aquascene**, Doctor's Gully, near the corner of Daly St and the Esplanade, fish come in for a feed every day at high tide. Feeding times depend on the tides (☎ (08) 8981 7837 for tide times).

The excellent **Indo-Pacific Marine & Australian Pearling Exhibition** are housed in the former Port Authority garage at the Wharf Precinct. The former displays living coral and its associated life, and the living coral-reef display is especially impressive. The Pearling Exhibition deals with the his-tory of the pearling industry in this area. For Wharf Precinct information ring ☎ toll-free 1800 639 874.

The excellent **Museum & Art Gallery of the Northern Territory** (☎ (08) 8999 8201) is on Conacher St, Fannie Bay, about 4km north of the city centre. It's bright, spacious, well laid out, not too big and full of interest-ing displays. A highlight is the Northern Territory Aboriginal art collection. The **Fannie Bay Gaol Museum** is another inter-esting museum a little further out of town at the corner of East Point Rd and Ross Smith Ave.

Popular beaches include **Mindil** and **Vestey's** on Fannie Bay, and **Mandorah**, across the bay from the city centre.

Places to Stay
Darwin has hostels, guesthouses, motels and holiday flats, as well as a clutch of up market hotels. All of the city's many caravan parks are situated several kilometres out of the city centre.

Camping The closest place to the city is the *Leprechaun Lodge Motel* (☎ (08) 8984 3400), which has a limited number of camping/caravan sites at the rear – enquire at the reception desk. Other camping areas include:

Shady Glen Caravan Park (☎ (08) 8984 3330), 10km east of the city centre, at the corner of Stuart Highway and Farrell Crescent, Winnellie, has campsites at $14 for two ($18 with power) and on-site vans at $40 for two; cramped and crowded.

Lee Point Resort (☎ (08) 8945 0535), Lee Point Rd, 15km north of the city, spacious with good facil-ities, campsites at $14/18, or with ensuite facili-ties for $19; on-site cabins with communal facilities cost around $60 for two.

Overlander Caravan Park (☎ (08) 8984 3025), 13km east of the city centre at 1064 McMillans Rd, Berrimah, has campsites at $12 for two ($14 powered)

Palms Caravan Park (☎ (08) 8932 2891), 17km south-east of town on the Stuart Highway at Berrimah, has campsites at $12 for two ($14.50 powered), on-site vans at $38 and cabins at $68.

Also consider camping at Howard Springs, 26km south-east along the Stuart Highway, where there are two caravan parks.

Hostels There's a host of backpacker-type hostels, with several of the cheapest places on or near Mitchell St, conveniently close to the transit centre. Most places have guest kitchens, and the showers and toilets are almost always communal. Dorm beds are typically $14, while double rooms range from around $35 to $40.

The most popular places include: the purpose-built *Frogshollow Backpackers* (☎ (08) 8941 2600) at 27 Lindsay St; the small and informal *Darwin City Lodge* (☎ toll-free 1800 808 151) at 151 Mitchell St; the recently refurbished *Darwin City Youth Hostel* (☎ (08) 8981 3995) at 69A

THE TROPICS

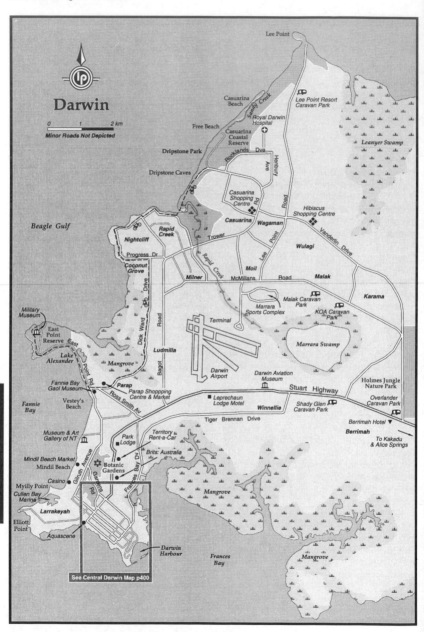

Darwin

0   1   2 km
Minor Roads Not Depicted

Lee Point

Casuarina Beach
Sandy Creek
Lee Point Resort Caravan Park

Free Beach
Royal Darwin Hospital
Casuarina Coastal Reserve

Dripstone Park
Rocklands Dve
Henbury

Dripstone Caves

Leanyer Swamp

Casuarina Shopping Centre
Casuarina
Wagaman
Hibiscus Shopping Centre

Beagle Gulf

Rapid Creek
Nightcliff
Trower
Vanderlin Drive

Progress Dr
Coconut Grove
Rapid Creek
Wulagi

Milner
McMillans
Moil
Road
Malak

Dick Ward Drive
Marrara Sports Complex
Malak Caravan Park
Karama

Military Museum
East Point Reserve
Terminal
KOA Caravan Park

Lake Alexander
East
Ludmilla
Marrara Swamp

Point Rd
Mangrove
Bagot Road

Fannie Bay Gaol Museum
Parap
Darwin Airport
Darwin Aviation Museum

Fannie Bay
Vestey's Beach
Ross Smith Av
Parap Shoppping Centre & Market
Holmes Jungle Nature Park

Stuart Highway
Overlander Caravan Park

Leprechaun Lodge Motel
Winnellie
Shady Glen Caravan Park

Museum & Art Gallery of NT
Park Lodge
Tiger Brennan Drive
Berrimah Hotel

Territory Rent-a-Car
Berrimah

Mindil Beach Market
Mindil Beach
Glinsh Avenue
Brits Australia
To Kakadu & Alice Springs

Casino
Botanic Gardens

Myilly Point
Cullen Bay Marina
Frances Bay Dv
Mangrove

Larrakeyah

Elliott Point
Aquascene
Darwin Harbour

Frances Bay
Mangrove

See Central Darwin Map p400

THE TROPICS

Mitchell St, and *Elke's Inner City Backpackers* (☎ toll-free 1800 808 365) at 112 Mitchell St, just north of Daly St.

Guesthouses Darwin has several small guesthouses which are good for long or short stays. Among those close to the centre is the friendly *Park Lodge* (☎ (08) 8981 5692) at 42 Coronation Drive, Stuart Park. All rooms have fan, air-con and fridge; bathrooms, kitchen, sitting/TV room and laundry are communal. Singles/doubles cost $35/45 daily; weekly rates are cheaper.

Also good is *Robyn's Nest* (☎ (08) 8927 7400) at 19 Harcus Crt, Malak. The two air-con rooms here have good facilities and cost $60 for a double in the Wet, $75 in the Dry.

Motels, Hotels & Holiday Flats The modern *Value Inn* (☎ (08) 8981 4733) on Mitchell St very close to the transit centre has air-con three-bed rooms with attached bath for $64 for up to three people.

The pleasantly tropical *Hotel Darwin* (☎ (08) 8981 9211) on the Esplanade offers good value for money in the heart of the city centre. It has air-con twin rooms from $90 in the Wet.

In the city centre at 35 Cavenagh St, the *Air Raid City Lodge* (☎ (08) 81 9214) has air-con rooms all with shower and toilet, fridge and tea/coffee-making facilities – from $65. Also good and central is the *Mirrambeena Tourist Resort* (☎ toll-free 1800 891 100), which has double rooms at $124, and town houses which sleep up to six people for $151.

There are also places worth considering in the suburbs. The *Parap Village Apartments* (☎ toll-free 1800 620 913) at 39 Parap Rd, Fannie Bay, has fully equipped and furnished two and three-bedroom flats from $140 in the Wet, $155 in the Dry. The *Coolibah Resort* (☎ (08) 8985 4166) at 91 Aralia St, Nightcliff, has single/double/triple one-bedroom apartments from $60/70/80 in the dry season.

Places to Eat
Cafes, Pubs & Takeaways Next to the transit centre on Mitchell St there's a small food centre with a couple of reasonably priced stalls and open-air tables. There's a choice of Asian, vegetarian or pasta, and meals generally cost $5 to $8. At the rear of the arcade is *Coyote's Cantina*, a very popular licensed Mexican restaurant with very reasonable prices.

There's a good collection of fast-food counters in Darwin Plaza towards the Knuckey St end of the Smith St Mall. Further up the mall, the Galleria shopping centre has a few good places. Also on the mall is Anthony Plaza where the *French Bakehouse* is one of the few places you can get coffee and a snack every day. In the Star Village next door, the *Rendezvous Cafe* does great laksa for $7.

Opposite Anthony Plaza is the Victoria Arcade, where the Victoria Hotel has lunch or dinner for around $8 in its *Settlers Bar*. The lunchtime buffet in the bar upstairs is good value at $7, but we're talking quantity rather than quality.

The *Lindsay St Cafe*, at 2 Lindsay St, has a great ambience and an excellent reputation. Expect to pay around $18 for a main course.

Restaurants The *Pancake Palace* on Cavenagh St near Knuckey St is open daily for lunch and in the evening until 1 am. Also on Cavenagh St is *Guiseppe's*, one of the few pasta places in Darwin. Main dishes are in the $10 to $12 range, or there's pizza from $12.

On Smith St, just beyond Daly St, the *Thai Garden Restaurant* serves not only delicious and reasonably priced Thai food but pizzas too! There are a few outdoor tables. There's a takeaway 'Aussie-Chinese' place across the road, and a 24-hour Chinese fast-food joint next door.

At the end of the Stokes Hill Wharf, *The Arcade* is a small, Asian-style food centre, with a number of different shops selling Chinese food, pizza or excellent fish & chips. *Christo's on the Wharf* here is a more

THE TROPICS

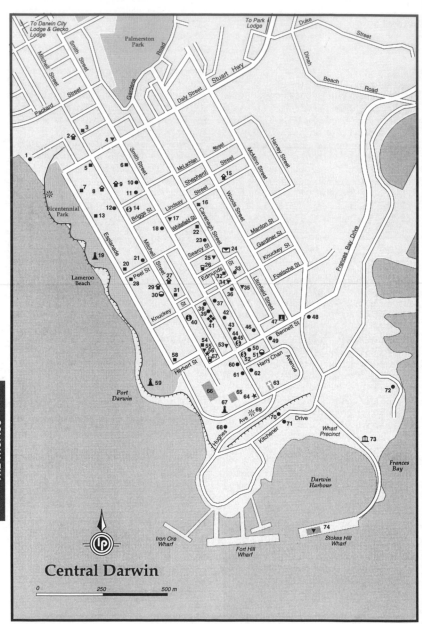

Central Darwin

THE TROPICS

PLACES TO STAY					
2	CWA Banyan View Lodge	53	Victoria Hotel	45	Westpac Bank
3	Elke's Inner City Backpackers	55	Hanuman Restaurant	46	Garuda
5	Top End Hotel	74	The Arcade	47	Chinese Temple
6	Marrakai Serviced Apartments			48	Harbour View Plaza
7	Travelodge	**OTHER**		49	Department of Land, Planning & Environment
8	Globetrotters Hostel	1	Aquascene (Fish Feeding)	50	Qantas
9	Fawlty Towers Hostel	10	Thrifty Rent-a-Car	51	City Bus Depot
13	Beaufort Hotel	11	Nifty Rent-a-Car	52	Commonwealth Bank
15	Frogshollow Backpackers	12	Performing Arts Centre	56	Police Station
16	Mirrambeena Tourist Resort	14	National Bank	57	Petty Sessions Bar
20	Novotel Atrium Hotel	18	AANT & PAN	59	ANZAC Memorial
22	Tiwi Motel	19	Leichhardt Memorial	60	NT Government Publications Centre
27	Holiday Inne	21	McCafferty's Bus Lines	61	Old Town Hall
28	Melaleuca Lodge	23	International Vaccination Clinic	62	Brown's Mart
29	Darwin City Youth Hostel	24	GPO	63	Christ Church Cathedral
31	Value Inn	26	Time (Nightclub)	64	Old Police Station & Courthouse
32	Air Raid City Lodge	30	Transit Centre	65	Supreme Court Building
54	Darwin Plaza Hotel	33	NT General Store	66	Parliament House
58	Hotel Darwin	36	Raintree Gallery	67	Telegraph Cable Memorial
		37	Paspalis Centrepoint	68	Government House
PLACES TO EAT		38	Indigenous Creations	69	Survivors Lookout
4	Thai Garden Restaurant	39	Darwin Plaza	70	WWII Oil Storage Tunnels
17	Lindsay St Cafe	40	Darwin Regional Tourism Association Office	71	Helipad
25	Guiseppe's	41	Galleria Shopping Centre	72	Deckchair Cinema
34	Cafe Capri	42	Ansett Airlines, Anthony Plaza & Rendezvous Café	73	Indo-Pacific Marine & Australian Pearling Exhibition
35	Pancake Palace				
43	Hog's Breath Cafe	44	Bookworld		

up-market place, open for lunch and dinner Tuesday to Friday.

Markets Easily the best all-round eating experience in Darwin is the bustling Asian-style market at Mindil Beach on Thursday nights during the dry season. People begin arriving from 5.30 pm, bringing tables, chairs, rugs, grog and kids to settle under the coconut palms for sunset and decide which of the tantalising food smells has the greatest allure. There are cake stalls, fruit-salad bars, arts & crafts stalls – and sometimes entertainment in the form of a band or street theatre.

Similar food stalls can be found at the Parap market on Saturday morning, the markets at Rapid Creek and Nightcliff on Sunday morning, the Palmerston market on Friday evening (dry season only) and in the Smith St Mall in the evenings (except Thursday), but Mindil Beach is the best for atmosphere and proximity to town. During the Wet, it transfers to Rapid Creek.

Entertainment

Live bands play upstairs at the *Victoria Hotel* from 9 pm Wednesday to Saturday nights. The *Billabong Bar* in the Novotel Atrium Hotel, on the corner of the Esplanade and Peel St, has live bands on Friday and Saturday nights until 1 am.

The *Hotel Darwin* is pleasant in the evening for a quiet drink. There's a patio section by the pool. It's livelier on Friday night when there's a band in the Green

THE TROPICS

Room. The *Rattle and Hum* bar next door on the Esplanade is a very popular backpackers' bar, and often has free live entertainment, disco or barbecue.

The *Brewery Bar* in the Frontier Hotel on the corner of Mitchell and Daly Sts is another good venue for entertainment. The *Beachcomber* bar at the rear is a popular disco and nightclub.

On the small street which runs between Smith and Cavenagh Sts one block from Knuckey St is the *Time* disco. It's about the most popular disco in the city centre, and stays open until very late.

The *Performing Arts Centre* (☎ (08) 8981 1222) on Mitchell St, opposite McLachlan St, hosts a variety of events from fashion award nights to plays, rock operas, pantomimes and concerts.

Finally, there's the *MGM Grand Casino* on Mindil Beach off Gilruth Ave – as long as you're 'properly dressed'. That means no thongs, and long socks for men wearing shorts! However, you don't have to dress up for the free Sunday afternoon jazz concerts out the back (dry season only).

Things to Buy

Aboriginal art is generally cheaper in Alice Springs, but Darwin has a greater variety. The Raintree Gallery on Knuckey St is one of a number of places offering a range of art work for sale; Framed gallery on the Stuart Highway in Stuart Park is another quality outlet.

T-shirts printed with Aboriginal designs are popular but quality and prices vary. Indigenous Creations at 55 Mitchell St has a large range.

Getting Around

The Airport Darwin's busy airport, about 6km from the centre of town, handles international flights as well as domestic ones. The taxi fare into the city centre is about $12.

There is an airport shuttle bus (☎ (08) 8981 5066) for $6, which will pick up or drop off almost anywhere in the centre. If you have a booking at one of the backpacker hostels you can usually travel free from the airport. When leaving Darwin, book a day before departure.

Car Rental Darwin has a couple of cheap local car-rental operators, as well as several of the national companies.

Rent-a-Rocket (☎ (08) 8941 3733), on McLachlan St, offers deals of $35 a day on its mostly 1970s and early 1980s cars, but you are restricted to within 70km of Darwin. This includes 100km free, with a charge of 20c per kilometre beyond that distance. With these deals you can't go beyond Humpty Doo (45km south-east of Darwin along the Arnhem Highway) or Acacia Store (about 70km south of Darwin on the Stuart Highway). The prices drop for longer rentals.

Nifty Rent-a-Car (☎ (08) 8981 2999) offers similar deals, but also has newer, air-con vehicles for around $44 per day.

Territory Rent-a-Car (☎ (08) 8924 2442) at 64 Stuart Highway, Parap, is probably the best value. Discount deals to look for include cheaper rates for four or more days' hire, weekend specials (three days for roughly the price of two) and one-way hires (to Jabiru, Katherine or Alice Springs).

There are also 4WD vehicles available for hire in Darwin. The best place to start looking for a vehical is probably Territory Rent-a-Car, which has several different models – the cheapest, a Suzuki four-seater, costs around $75 a day including insurance, plus 35c a kilometre over 100km.

Brits: Australia (☎ (08) 8981 2081), also on the Stuart Highway in Stuart Park, is best for long-term rentals on 4WDs and campervans, and you can do one-way rentals out of the Northern Territory.

Most rental companies are open every day and have agents in the city centre to save you trekking out to the Stuart Highway. Budget (☎ (08) 8981 9800), Hertz (☎ (08) 8941 0944), Thrifty (☎ (08) 8981 8555) and Territory also have offices at the airport.

Bicycle Darwin has a fairly extensive network of bike tracks. It's a pleasant ride out from the city to the Botanic Gardens, Fannie

Bay, East Point or even, if you're feeling fit, all the way to Nightcliff and Casuarina.

Many of the backpacker hostels have bicycles for hire for a small charge, or occasionally for free.

Litchfield National Park

HIGHLIGHTS

- Taking a walk through the different environments around Florence Falls and Wangi Falls

- Enjoying a refreshing swim in a deep plunge pool

This 650-sq-km national park, 140km south of Darwin, encloses much of the Tabletop Range, a rugged sandstone plateau with eroded cliffs dropping away to blacksoil plains. It is only a couple of hours' drive from Darwin and so is a very popular weekend getaway with the locals.

The main attraction of the park is its superb waterfalls, which tumble down from the plateau, and swimming holes, but the beautiful country, excellent campsites, and the 4WD, bushwalking and photography opportunities are also highlights. It's well worth a few days, although weekends can get crowded.

HISTORY

The Wagait Aboriginal people lived in this area, and the many pools, waterfalls and other prominent geographical features had great significance.

In 1864 the Finniss Expedition explored the Northern Territory of South Australia, as it was then called. Frederick Litchfield was a member of the party, and some of the features in the park still bear the names he gave them.

In the late 1860s copper and tin were discovered, and this led to a flurry of activity with several mines operating in the area. The ruins of two of these are still visible today – at Bamboo Creek (which operated from 1906 to 1955) and Blyth homestead.

The area was then opened up as pastoral leases, and these were in existence right up to the proclamation of the park in 1986.

FLORA & FAUNA

The dominant trees of the open forest are the Darwin woollybutt and the stringybark, while below these, sand palms, banksias, cycads, acacias and grevilleas form the lower level. Around the waterfalls and permanent springs are pockets of surprisingly thick monsoon rainforest.

The more open plains are covered with the high spear grass which is common throughout much of the Top End.

The wildlife of the park is another of its attractions, with the bird life being especially abundant. Two of the most commonly sighted birds are the distinctive red-tailed black cockatoo and the sulphur-crested cockatoo. Smaller parrots such as the beautiful rainbow lorikeet, northern rosella and the red-winged parrot are also often seen.

The jabiru, or black-necked stork, is found in the flooded areas of the park during the Wet, and predatory birds such as black kites, whistling kites and wedge-tailed eagles are often seen soaring in the thermals above the plateau.

The antilopine wallaroo is the largest mammal in the park, but dingoes are also sighted from time to time. Most of the smaller mammals are nocturnal, and so are not often seen. These include the rare northern quoll, the northern brown bandicoot and the northern brushtail possum.

An unusual feature of the park are the so-called magnetic termite mounds found on the blacksoil plains. These mounds are up to 2m high and gain their name from the north-south orientation. It is believed they are aligned this way as a means of controlling temperature – during the hottest part of the day, only the narrow northern edge is exposed to the full sun.

THE TROPICS

INFORMATION

Permits are not required to enter the park, unless you plan to walk and camp in remote areas. There is a ranger station at Batchelor (☎ (08) 8976 0282), about 10km from the eastern edge of the park. If you have an FM radio, information about the park and its attractions is broadcast on 88MHz.

The Parks & Wildlife Commission in Darwin publishes a very good map of the park. If more detail is required, the topographic sheet maps which cover the park are the 1:100,000 *Reynolds River (5071)* and the 1:50,000 *Sheets No 5071 (I-IV)*. These are available from Maps NT (☎ (08) 8999 7032) on the corner of Cavenagh and Bennett Sts in Darwin.

Pets and firearms are prohibited. All dirt roads within the park are closed during the Wet, and usually re-open around the end of May.

THE PARK

There are two routes to Litchfield Park, both about a two-hour drive from Darwin. One, from the north, involves turning south off the Berry Springs-Cox Peninsula road onto the well-maintained Litchfield Park Road, which is dirt but suitable for conventional vehicles except in the wet season. A second approach, also called the Litchfield Park Road, is along a bitumen road from Batchelor into the east of the park. The two access roads join up so it's possible to do a loop from the Stuart Highway.

If you enter the park from Batchelor, it is about 15km to the first major batch of **magnetic termite mounds**, signposted just off to the right of the road.

Another 4km brings you to the **Florence Falls** turn-off on the eastern edge of the plateau. The falls lie in a pocket of monsoon forest 5km off the road along a good track. This is an excellent swimming hole in the dry season, as are the cascades at **Buley Rockhole**, a few kilometres away, where you can also camp.

From Florence Falls a 4WD track takes you north across the Florence Creek to a T-junction, from where you can turn right

(east) and head back to the Litchfield Park Road near the park's eastern boundary.

Back on the main road it's another 4km from the Florence Falls turn-off to the turn-off to the **Lost City**, 10.5km south of the road along a 4WD track. The feature here is the large sandstone block and pillar formations which, with a little imagination, resemble ruined buildings. This track continues another 4km along a *very* rough section as it comes down off the range, to the **Blyth Homestead Ruins**. This homestead was built in 1929 by the Sargent family, and remained in use until the area was declared a national park in 1986. The track then continues another 1.5km, where it joins the Tjaynera Falls track (see below).

Fourteen km beyond the turning to Florence Falls is the turn-off to **Tolmer Falls**, which are a 400m walk off the road. Caves around the gorge here contain major breeding colonies of orange horseshoe-bats and the endangered ghost bat; ancient rock formations take spectacular forms, and the rock pools above the falls are well worth a look. A 1.5km loop walking track here gives you some excellent views of the area. However, the falls and plunge pool are off-limits.

It's another 3km along the main road to **Greenant Creek**, where there's a day-use area and a 1.8km walking trail to **Tjaetaba Falls**, on the north side of the road. Just beyond Greenant Creek is the turn-off to **Tjaynera (Sandy Creek) Falls**, which lie 9km off the road along an often incredibly corrugated 4WD track. From the end of the track it's a 1.7km walk to the falls from the carpark and campsite along a track lined with lofty paperbark trees. The pool here is deep and cool, and is far less crowded than Wangi Falls (see below).

On the way to the falls from the main road, there's a turn-off to the north after 5.4km, and this is the southern end of the Lost City track (see above). After another 2km the track forks, the left (eastern) fork heading to the falls (1.5km), and the right (southern) fork continuing right down through the isolated southern reaches of the park, to a camping ground on the east branch of the

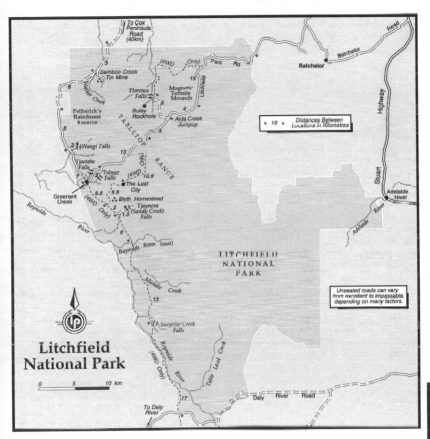

Litchfield
National Park

0   5   10 km

Reynolds River (6km), and then another at **Surprise Creek Falls** (13km). Don't be tempted to swim here as saltwater crocodiles may be lurking. The track crosses the Reynolds River and eventually links up with the Daly River Rd, 17km beyond Surprise Creek. From this intersection you can head east to the Stuart Highway or south-west to Daly River. This track through the south of the park is impassable during the Wet.

The main road continues from the Tjaynera turn-off another 7km to the turn-off to the most popular attraction in Litchfield, **Wangi Falls** (pronounced 'wong-gye'), 2km along a side road. The falls here flow year-round and fill a beautiful plunge pool. There are also extensive picnic and camping areas. This area can really become overrun on weekends, particularly in holiday periods. A marked 3km, 1½-hour walking trail takes you up and over the top of the falls, but it's quite a steep walk. There's an emergency telephone at the carpark – every year a few people get into difficulty while swimming in the pool. It's not possible to swim here in the Wet as the currents are dangerous; markers indicate the when it is safe to swim.

From the Wangi Falls turn-off it's about

5km to **Petherick's Rainforest Reserve**, a small freehold forest reserve which actually lies outside the park. There are waterfalls, some thermal springs and monsoon rainforest, as well as the wreckage of an old Spitfire! An entry fee of $5 is charged, but this is waived if you camp here.

From here the road loops back into the park, and after about 6km there's a turn-off to **Walker Creek**, not far off the road, where there are more rock pools and a campsite. At **Bamboo Creek**, reached along a short 4WD track just north of the Walker Creek side road, remnants of the tin mines which operated here in the 1870s can still be seen.

It's only another 3km to the northern boundary of the park, and from there it's around 40km to the Cox Peninsula road.

ACTIVITIES

During the winter months the rangers conduct a number of activities aimed at increasing your enjoyment and knowledge of the park. On Tuesday at 10 am there's a guided walk to Tolmer Falls, on Wednesday at 8 pm a slide show at the Wangi picnic area, and on Thursday at 10 am the magnetic termite mounds are the feature of a talk.

Excellent wetland cruises on the Reynolds River system are available from the Wangi Kiosk. These run three times daily and take three hours. As they operate on a working cattle station it gives a chance to see another aspect of the Top End. The tours cost $25 and you get picked up (and make bookings) from the Wangi Kiosk

ORGANISED TOURS

There are a few companies offering day trips to Litchfield from Darwin. The cost is typically around $90, and one such company is Coo-ee Tours (☎ toll-free 1800 670 007).

For $99 Travel North (☎ toll-free 1800 089 103) will take you on a tour from Darwin through Litchfield and on to Katherine.

FACILITIES
Camping

The Parks & Wildlife Commission maintains a number of campsites within the park.

Those at *Wangi*, *Florence Falls* (separate 2WD and 4WD areas), *Buley Rockhole* and *Tjaynera Falls* have facilities such as toilets, showers and fireplaces, while the bush camps in the south of the park are very basic. The cost is $4 per person at *Wangi*, $2 at Florence Falls 2WD, and $1 at all the rest. Note that the Wangi campsite usually fills up by mid-afternoon during June, July and August; at other times it's OK.

It's also possible to camp at *Petherick's Rainforest Reserve*, on the western edge of the park, for $5 per person, but the facilities are very basic.

Fuel & Supplies

Fuel is available at Batchelor, or the *Finniss River Store*, which is on the northern access road into the park.

The *Wangi Kiosk* is open year round and does excellent snack meals, such as ripper hamburgers and steak sandwiches.

Batchelor has a *supermarket*, otherwise there's the Finniss River Store.

Kakadu National Park

HIGHLIGHTS

- Visiting one of several superb Aboriginal rock-art sites, such as Ubirr

- Taking a wet-season scenic flight along the Arnhem Escarpment

- Going on a boat cruise on Yellow Water late in the dry season and marvelling at the teeming bird life

Kakadu National Park is one of Australia's natural marvels, and the fact that it contains the entire catchment for a river system (the South Alligator) makes it unique. The longer you stay, the more rewarding it is. It's a very popular destination, and there are some 4WD opportunities, although these are gradually disappearing as tracks are upgraded.

Kakadu stretches more than 200km south from the coast and 100km from east to west, with the main entrance 154km by bitumen road east of Darwin. It encompasses a great variety of superb landscapes, swarms with wildlife and has some of Australia's best Aboriginal rock art.

The name Kakadu comes from Gagadju, one of the local Aboriginal languages, and part of Kakadu is Aboriginal land, leased to the government for use as a national park. There are several Aboriginal settlements in the park, and about half the park rangers are Aborigines. Enclosed by the park, but not part of it, are a few tracts of land designated for other purposes – principally uranium mining leases in the east.

GEOGRAPHY

A straight line on the map separates Kakadu from the Arnhem Land Aboriginal land to its east, which you can't enter without a permit. The Arnhem Land escarpment, a dramatic 100 to 200m-high sandstone cliffline, which provides the natural boundary of the rugged Arnhem Land plateau, winds circuitously some 500km through east and south-east Kakadu.

Creeks cut across the rocky plateau and tumble off the escarpment as thundering waterfalls in the wet season. They then flow across the lowlands to swamp the vast flood plains of Kakadu's four north-flowing rivers, turning the north of the park into a kind of huge vegetated lake. From west to east the rivers are the Wildman, the West Alligator, the South Alligator and the East Alligator. Such is the difference between dry and wet seasons that areas on river flood plains which are perfectly dry underfoot in September will be under 3m of water a few months later. As the waters recede in the Dry, some loops of wet-season watercourses become cut off, but don't dry up. These billabongs are often carpeted with water lilies and are enticing for waterbirds.

The coastline has long stretches of mangrove swamp which are important both for halting erosion and as a breeding ground for marine and bird species. The southern part of the park is drier, lowland hill country with open grassland and eucalypt woodland. Pockets of monsoon rainforest crop up here as well as in most of the park's other landscapes.

In all, Kakadu has over 1000 plant species, and a number of them are still used by the local Aborigines for food, bush medicine and other practical purposes.

SEASONS

The great change between the Dry and the November-March Wet makes a big difference to Kakadu visitors. Not only is the landscape transformed as the wetlands and waterfalls grow, but Kakadu's lesser roads become impassable in the Wet, cutting off some highlights like Jim Jim Falls. The local Aboriginal people recognise six seasons in the annual cycle.

The build-up to the Wet, known as *Gunumeleng*, starts in October. Humidity and the temperatures rise to 35°C or more – and the number of mosquitoes, always high near water, rises to near plague proportions. By November, the thunderstorms have started, billabongs start to be replenished and the waterbirds disperse.

The Wet proper, *Gudjuek*, continues through January, February and March, with violent thunderstorms and an abundance of plant and animal life thriving in the hot, moist conditions. Around 1300mm of rain falls in Kakadu, most of it during this period.

April is *Banggereng*, the season when storms (known as 'knock 'em down' storms) flatten the spear grass, which during the course of the Wet has shot up to 2m or more in height.

Yekke, which lasts from May to mid-June, is the season of mists, and the air starts to dry out. It is quite a good time to visit: there aren't too many other visitors, the wetlands and waterfalls still have a lot of water and most of the tracks are open.

The most comfortable time is the late Dry, July and August – *Wurrgeng* and *Gurrung*. This is when wildlife, especially birds, begins to gather in huge numbers around the

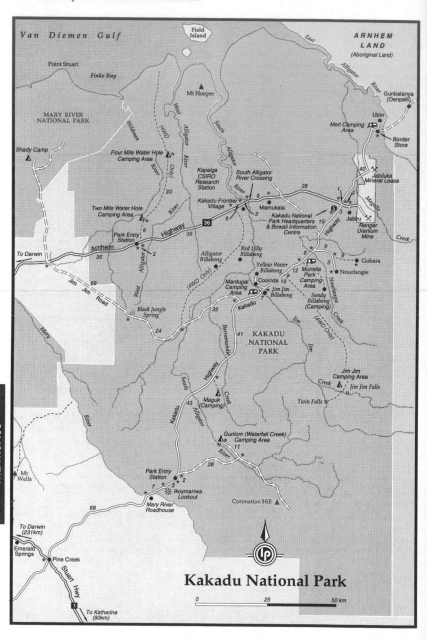

Kakadu National Park

shrinking billabongs and watercourses, but it's also when most tourists come to the park.

FAUNA

Kakadu has about 25 species of frog, 60 types of mammal, 51 freshwater fish species, 75 types of reptile, 280 bird species (one-third of all Australian bird species) and 4500 kinds of insect. There are frequent additions to the list, and a few of the rarer species are unique to the park. You'll only see a tiny fraction of these creatures in a visit to the park since many of them are shy, nocturnal or few in number.

Kakadu's wetlands are on the United Nations list of Wetlands of International Importance, principally because of their crucial significance to so many types of waterbird. Take advantage of talks and walks led by park rangers – mainly in the Dry – to get to know and see more of the wildlife. You can obtain details from the Kakadu Park Information Centre. Cruises are run on the East Alligator River and Yellow Water billabong to see the water life.

Reptiles

The park has both types of Australian crocodile. Twin and Jim Jim falls, for example, both have resident freshwater crocodiles, which are considered harmless, while there are also plenty of the dangerous saltwater variety in the park. You're sure to see a few if you take a South Alligator River or Yellow Water billabong cruise.

Kakadu's other reptiles include several types of lizard, like the frilled lizard, and five freshwater turtle species of which the most common is the northern snake-necked turtle. There are many snakes, including three highly poisonous types, but you're unlikely to see any. Oenpelli pythons, probably unique to the Kakadu escarpment, were only discovered by Europeans in 1973.

Birds

Kakadu's abundant waterbirds reside in beautiful wetland settings and make a memorable sight, particularly late in the dry

Osprey

season. The park is one of the chief refuges in Australia for several bird species, among them the magpie goose, green pygmy goose and Burdekin duck.

Other fine waterbirds include the jabiru, or black-necked stork, with its distinctive red legs and long straight beak, pelicans and darters.

Herons, egrets, ibis and cormorants are common. You're quite likely to see rainbow bee-eaters and kingfishers (of which there are six types in inland Kakadu). Majestic white-breasted sea eagles are often seen near inland waterways too, and wedge-tailed eagles, whistling kites and black kites are common. At night you may hear barking owls calling – they sound just like dogs. Also spectacular is the red-tailed black cockatoo, and there are brolgas and bustards.

Mammals

Nine types of kangaroo and wallaby inhabit the park. You might be lucky enough to see a sugar glider in wooded areas in the daytime. Kakadu is home to 26 species of bat, and a key refuge for four endangered varieties.

Water buffalo, which ran wild after being

introduced to the Top End from Timor by European settlers in the first half of the 19th century, have been virtually eradicated because they were potential carriers of cattle disease and did much damage to the natural environment.

Fish

You can't miss the silver barramundi, which creates a distinctive swirl near the water's surface. It can grow well over a metre long and changes sex from male to female at the age of 5 or 6 years.

ROCK ART

Kakadu has about 5000 Aboriginal rock-painting sites dating from 40,000 or more years ago up to the 1960s. They range from hand prints to paintings of animals, people, mythological beings and European ships, constituting one of the world's most important and fascinating rock-art collections. They provide a record of changing environments and Aboriginal lifestyles over time.

In some places they are concentrated in large galleries, with paintings from different eras sometimes superimposed on one another. Some sites are kept secret – not only to protect them from damage, but also because they are private or sacred to the Aborigines. Some are even believed to be the residences of dangerous beings, who must not be approached by the ignorant. Two of the finest sites, however, have been opened up to visitors, with access roads, walkways and explanatory signs. These are Ubirr and Nourlangie. Park rangers conduct free art-site tours once or twice a day from May to October.

The dominant colours of all the art are yellow, red and white, obtained by grinding natural minerals to powder and mixing them with water.

In the last few decades the rock-painting tradition has all but died out. Aborigines today devote artistic energy instead to painting on eucalyptus bark, often in traditional styles and usually for sale. But they still regard the rock art as important and take care to protect it.

INFORMATION

The excellent Bowali Information Centre (☎ (08) 8938 1121; fax 8938 1123), on the Kakadu Highway a couple of kilometres south of the Arnhem Highway, is open daily from 8 am to 5 pm. Here you'll find informative displays, a video room with several interesting films available, a cafe and resource room. There are details of guided art-site and wildlife walks, and it's also where you pay the $15 entry fee (children under 16 free) if it wasn't collected as you entered the park. This entitles you to stay in the park for 14 days, and there are random checks at various places throughout the park to check tickets.

At Cooinda the Warradjan Aboriginal Cultural Centre gives an excellent insight into the culture of the park's traditional owners. There are intelligent displays, as well as a craft outlet selling locally made items.

THE PARK
Arnhem Highway

From where the Arnhem Highway to Kakadu turns east off the Stuart Highway, it's 121km to the park entrance, and another 105km east across the park to Jabiru, sealed all the way. The Kakadu Highway to Nourlangie, Cooinda and Pine Creek (also sealed) turns south off the Arnhem Highway 2km before Jabiru.

A turn-off to the north, 20km into the park along the Arnhem Highway, leads to campsites at **Two Mile Hole** (8km) and **Four Mile Hole** (38km) on the Wildman River, which is popular for fishing. The track is not suitable for conventional vehicles except in the Dry, and then only as far as Two Mile Hole.

About 35km further east along the Arnhem Highway, a turn-off to the south, again impassable to conventional vehicles in the Wet, leads to campsites at **Alligator** and **Red Lilly** billabongs, and on to the Kakadu Highway.

The **South Alligator River Crossing** is on the highway 64km into the park, about 3km past Kakadu Holiday Village. There's a surfaced boat ramp here and it's a very popular fishing put-in point.

A short side road to the south leads to

Mamukala, 8km east of South Alligator, with views over the South Alligator flood plain, an observation building, a 3km walking trail and bird-watching hides.

Ubirr

This spectacular rock-art site lies 40km north of the Arnhem Highway. The turn-off is 3km before Jabiru and the road to Ubirr is sealed all the way, but there are several creek crossings which make it impassable for a conventional vehicle for most of the wet season – sometimes for 4WD vehicles too. The rock-art site is open daily from 8.30 am to sunset between May and November, 2 pm to sunset the rest of the year.

Shortly before Ubirr you pass the Border Store, near which are a couple of walking trails close to the East Alligator River, which forms the eastern boundary of the park. There is a backpackers' hostel and campsite nearby.

An easily followed path from the Ubirr carpark takes you through the main galleries and up to a lookout with superb views – a 1.5km round trip. There are paintings on numerous rocks along the path, but the highlight is the main gallery with a large array of well-executed and preserved X-ray-style wallabies, possums, goannas, tortoises and fish, plus a couple of *balanda* (white men) with hands on hips.

The Ubirr paintings are in many different styles. They were painted at times ranging from probably 20,000 or more years ago up to the 20th century.

It's worth taking the Guluyambi Cruise (☎ toll-free 1800 089 113) on the East Alligator River close to Ubirr. The 1¾-hour trips are usually accompanied by an Aboriginal guide and the focus is on Aboriginal culture. The tours cost $25 and run daily at 9 and 11 am, and 1 and 3 pm, with pick-up from the Border Store.

Jabiru

The township of Jabiru (population 1450), built originally to accommodate the Ranger Uranium Mine workers but now a major service town, has a supermarket, Westpac bank, chemist, shops, petrol station and a public swimming pool. EFTPOS facilities are available at the supermarket and petrol station.

Jabiru airport is 6km east, and nearby is the **Ranger Uranium Mine**. Minibus tours of the mine ($10) are available twice a day through Kakadu Parklink (☎ (08) 8979 2411).

Nourlangie

The sight of this looming, mysterious, isolated outlier of the Arnhem Land escarpment makes it easy to understand why it has been important to Aborigines for so long. Its long, red, sandstone bulk – striped in places with orange, white and even black – slopes up from surrounding woodland to fall away finally at one end in sheer, stepped cliffs, at the foot of which is Kakadu's best known collection of rock art.

The name Nourlangie is a corruption of *nawulandja*, an Aboriginal word which referred to an area bigger than the rock itself. The Aboriginal name of the rock is Burrunggui. You reach it at the end of a 12km sealed road, which turns east off the Kakadu Highway, 22km south of the Arnhem Highway. Other interesting spots nearby make it worth spending a whole day in this corner of Kakadu. The last few kilometres of the road are closed from around 5 pm daily.

From the main carpark, a round-trip walk of about 2km takes you first to the **Anbangbang shelter**, which was used for 20,000 years as a refuge from heat, rain and the area's frequent wet-season thunderstorms. From the gallery you can walk onto a lookout where you can see the distant Arnhem Land cliffline, including Lightning Dreaming (Namarrgon Djadjam), which is the home of Namarrgon. There's a 12km marked walk all the way round the rock, for which the park office has a leaflet.

Heading back towards the highway, you can take three turn-offs to further places of interest. The first, on the left about 1km from the main carpark, takes you to **Anbangbang Billabong**, with a dense carpet of lilies and a picnic site. The second, also on the left, leads to a short walk up to **Nawulandja**

Lookout, with good views back over Nourlangie Rock.

The third turn-off, a dirt road on the right, takes you to another outstanding – but little visited – rock-art gallery, **Nangaluwurr**. A further 6km along this road, followed by a 3km walk, brings you to **Gubara Pools**, an area of shaded pools set in monsoon forest.

Jim Jim & Twin Falls

These two waterfalls are along a 4WD dry-season track that turns south-east off the Kakadu Highway between the Nourlangie Rock and Cooinda Lodge turn-offs. It is about 60km to Jim Jim Falls, with the last 1km on foot, and about 70km to Twin Falls, where the last few hundred metres are through the water up a snaking, forested gorge – great fun on an inflatable air-bed. Jim Jim – a sheer 215m drop – is awesome during the Wet, but its waters dry up soon after the last storms. However, Twin Falls flows all year round.

Yellow Water & Cooinda

The turn-off to the Cooinda accommodation complex and the superb Yellow Water wetlands is around 52km down the Kakadu Highway from its junction with the Arnhem Highway. It's then 5km to Cooinda, and a couple more to the starting point for the boat trips on Yellow Water. These go three times daily (dry season only) and cost $26.50 ($13.50 for children) for two hours. There are also twice-daily tours (year round) of 1½ hours for $22.50 ($12.50). This trip is one of the highlights of most people's visit to Kakadu. Early morning is the best time to go as the bird life is most active. You're likely to see a saltwater crocodile or two. It's usually advisable to book your cruise the day before at Cooinda – particularly for the early departure.

Yellow Water is also an excellent place for sunsets, particularly in the dry season when the smoke haze from bushfires (common in the Dry) turns bright red in the setting sun. Bring plenty of insect repellent as the mosquitoes are voracious.

Cooinda Turn-Off to Pine Creek

Just south of the Yellow Water and Cooinda turn-off, the Kakadu Highway heads south-west out of the park to Pine Creek on the Stuart Highway, about 152km from Cooinda. On the way there is a turn-off to the very scenic falls and plunge pool at **Waterfall Creek** (also called Gunlom) which featured in the film *Crocodile Dundee*. It's 37km along a dirt road (dry season only).

ACTIVITIES
Walking

Kakadu is excellent but often tough bushwalking country. Many people will be satisfied with the marked trails, which range from 1 to 12km. For the more adventurous there are infinite possibilities, especially in the drier south and east of the park, but take great care and prepare well; tell people where you're going and don't go alone. You need a permit from the park information centre to camp outside the established campsites. The Darwin Bushwalking Club (☎ (08) 8985 1484) welcomes visitors and may be able to help with information too. It has walks most weekends, often in Kakadu. Or you could join a Willis's Walkabouts guided bushwalk (see the following Organised Tours section).

Kakadu by Foot is a helpful guide to the marked walking trails in Kakadu. It is published by PAN but seems to be in short supply; it costs $1.95.

Fishing

Fishing is permitted in most areas, but there are some restricted areas so check at the information centre to be sure. Fishing with anything other than hand lines and rods with lures is not permitted, and the usual Northern Territory bag limits apply.

Crocodiles of course pose a threat to the unwary, so give them a wide berth if you're boating. Boating on the East Alligator River is permitted, but as the river forms the boundary between the park and Arnhem Land, landing on the Aboriginal land on the east bank is not permitted.

There are boat ramps at Yellow Water,

South Alligator River, Mardugal, Jim Jim Billabong and Manbiyarra.

ORGANISED TOURS

There are hosts of tours to Kakadu from Darwin and a few that start inside the park. Two-day tours typically take in Jim Jim Falls, Nourlangie and the Yellow Water cruise, and cost from $220. Companies which seem to be popular include: Hunter Safaris (☎ (08) 8981 2720), $220/320 for two/three days; Kakadu Adventure Safaris (☎ toll-free 1800 672 677), $210/320 for two/three days; and Territory Style Tours (☎ toll-free 1800 801 991), $240 for two days including Jim Jim and Twin falls.

Longer tours usually cover most of the main sights plus a couple of extras. Some combine Kakadu with Katherine Gorge. One of the popular ones is the Blue Banana (☎ (08) 8945 6800), which charges $150 for transport only, and you can get on and off anywhere between Darwin and Katherine as often as you like for three months.

You can take 10-hour 4WD tours to Jim Jim and Twin falls from Jabiru or Cooinda ($120, dry season) with Kakadu Gorge & Waterfall Tours (☎ (08) 8979 2025) or Lord of Kakadu (☎ (08) 8979 2567).

Willis's Walkabouts (☎ (08) 8985 2134) are bushwalks guided by knowledgeable Top End walkers, following your own or preset routes of two days or more. Many of the walks are in Kakadu. Prices vary, but $900 for a two-week trip, including evening meals and return transport from Darwin, is fairly typical.

Magela Cultural & Heritage Tours (☎ toll-free 1800 089 113) is an Aboriginal-owned and run operation, and it offers day tours around Kakadu, concentrating on the less visited sites. The cost is $260 per adult with pick-ups in Jabiru.

Tours into Arnhem Land

A couple of outfits offer trips into Arnhem Land from Kakadu. Kakadu Parklink (☎ (08) 8979 2411) has weekday tours from Jabiru or Cooinda into the Mikinj Valley for $140 ($112 children). The trips are usually accompanied by a local Aboriginal guide.

Scenic Flights

Kakadu Air (☎ (08) 8979 2411) does a number of flights over Kakadu. A half-hour flight from Jabiru costs $60, or it's $100 for an hour.

FACILITIES

There are a number of fuel stations within the park, and there's a wide variety of accommodation. Note that accommodation prices in Kakadu can vary tremendously depending on the season – dry-season prices (given here) are often as much as 50% above wet-season prices.

Fuel & Repairs

Fuel (super, unleaded and diesel) is available at South Alligator River (Kakadu Holiday Village), Jabiru, Cooinda and at the Mary River Roadhouse (☎ (08) 8975 4564), just outside the park's southern boundary on the Kakadu Highway to Pine Creek. The Border Store at Manbiyarra sells diesel and unleaded fuel only (no super).

Mechanical repairs can only be undertaken at Jabiru, although emergency repairs and towing can also be arranged at Cooinda.

Camping

There are sites run by the national parks, and also some (with power) attached to the resorts: *Frontier Kakadu Village*, South Alligator, $10/6 for two with/without power; *Gagadju Lodge Cooinda*, $16/14; and *Frontier Kakadu Lodge*, Jabiru, $10/6 with/without power for two people.

The three main national park campsites that have hot showers, flushing toilets and drinking water, are: *Merl*, near the Border Store; *Muirella Park*, 6km off the Kakadu Highway a few kilometres south of the Nourlangie turn-off; and *Mardugal*, just off the Kakadu Highway, 1.5km south of the Cooinda turn-off. Only the Mardugal site is open during the Wet. The fee for use of these campsites is $7 per person and this is collected at the site.

THE TROPICS

The national parks provide about 15 more basic campsites around the park, and at these there is no fee. To camp away from these you need a permit from the park information centre.

Accommodation
There are a number of accommodation centres around the park.

South Alligator Just a couple of kilometres west of the South Alligator River on the Arnhem Highway is the *Frontier Kakadu Village* (☎ toll-free 1800 818 845), which has twin-bed rooms for $168. The hotel has a restaurant and a basic shop (7 am to 8 pm), and a swimming pool.

Ubirr The basic *Hostel Kakadu* (☎ (08) 8979 2232) has twin-share accommodation at $14 per person. There's a well-equipped kitchen, lounge room and swimming pool. The national park rangers put on a slide show each Thursday evening during the Dry.

The *Border Store* next door has snack food and is open daily until 5 pm.

Jabiru The *Gagadju Crocodile Hotel* (☎ toll-free 1800 808 123) is probably most famous for its design – it's set out in the shape of a crocodile, although this is only apparent from the air. There's nothing very exotic about the hotel itself, although it is comfortable enough. Room prices start at $180/200 for singles/doubles.

The *Frontier Kakadu Lodge* (☎ (08) 8979 2422) has four-bed rooms at $25 per person, or $100 for a whole room. The only cooking facilities are a few barbecues.

Apart from the restaurants at the two resorts, the cafe in the town shopping centre has takeaway burgers and other fast foods. There's also a bakery close by.

Cooinda This is by far the most popular place to stay, mainly because of the proximity of the Yellow Water wetlands and the early morning boat cruises. It gets mighty crowded at times, mainly with camping tours. The *Gagadju Lodge Cooinda* (☎ (08)

8979 0145) has some comfortable units for $110 for up to three people, and much cheaper and more basic air-con 'budget rooms', which are just transportable huts of the type found on many building sites and more commonly known in the Northern Territory as 'demountables', or 'dongas'. For $19 per person they are quite adequate, if a little cramped (two beds per room), although the only cooking facilities are barbecues.

The bistro here serves unexciting and overpriced self-cook barbecue meals at around $15, or there's the more expensive *Mimi Restaurant*.

ALTERNATIVE TRANSPORT
Greyhound Pioneer (☎ toll-free 13 2030) runs daily buses from Darwin to Katherine via Cooinda and Jabiru (and vice versa), with connections from Jabiru to Ubirr.

Cobourg Peninsula

This remote wilderness, 200km north-east of Darwin, includes the **Cobourg Marine Park** and the Aboriginal-owned **Gurig National Park**. It is much more remote than Kakadu and requires a 4WD to access it.

Both parks are on the UN register of Wetlands of International Importance as they are the habitat of a variety of waterfowl and other migratory birds. The coastline here is beautiful and there are some excellent beaches. It's not really possible to explore the inland parts of the park as there are virtually no tracks within the park apart from the main access track.

Gurig is also the home to a wide variety

of introduced animals – Balinese banteng cattle, buffalo, Indian sambar deer and pig – all imported by the British when they attempted to settle the Top End last century.

The park is jointly managed by the Parks & Wildlife Commission and the local Aboriginal inhabitants.

HISTORY

Although European navigators had explored along this coastline, it was the British who tried to make a permanent settlement. After two unsuccessful attempts (at Melville Island and then Raffles Bay on the Cobourg Peninsula), a third attempt was made at Port Essington in 1838. The garrison town was named Victoria Settlement, and at its peak was home to over 300 people. The British intention was that it would become the base for major trade between Australia and Asia, but by 1849, after the settlement had survived a cyclone and malaria outbreaks, the decision was made to abandon it.

INFORMATION

Entry to Gurig is by permit, which has to be obtained well in advance from rangers at Gurig.

You pass through part of Arnhem Land on the way, and the Aboriginal owners here severely restrict the number of vehicles going through – only 15 are allowed in at any one time – so you're advised to apply up to a year ahead for the necessary permit (tce $211 per vehicle for a seven-day stay). Permit forms are available from the tourist office in Darwin, but all applications should be submitted to the rangers at Gurig, either by fax on (08) 8979 0246 or by mail (Black Point Ranger Station, Gurig National Park, Parks & Wildlife Commission, PO Box 496, Palmerston, NT 0831).

At Black Point there is a ranger station and visitor centre (☎ (08) 8979 0244), which has an interesting section dealing with the Aboriginal, European and Maccassan people, and also has a brochure detailing the history of Victoria Settlement and a map of the ruins. No trailers are allowed into the park.

THE PARK

The track to Cobourg starts at Oenpelli and is accessible by 4WD vehicle only – it's closed in the wet season (opening 1 May). The 288km drive to Black Point from the East Alligator River takes about six hours and the track is in reasonable condition – the roughest part coming in the hour or so after the turn-off from Murgenella. The trip must be completed in one day as it's not possible to stop overnight on Aboriginal land.

Victoria Settlement at Port Essington is well worth a visit, but it is accessible by boat only. The ruins still visible include various chimneys and wells, the powder magazine and parts of the hospital. Unfortunately there are no hire boats so it is an option only if you have your own boat.

FACILITIES

There's a *camping ground* with 15 sites about 100m from the shore at Smith Point. It's run by the Parks & Wildlife Commission (☎ (08) 8979 0244) and facilities include a shower, toilet and barbecue. There's no electricity, and generators are banned at night. As many of the shade trees were destroyed by a recent cyclone, it's a good idea to have some portable shade in your gear.

At Black Point there's a small *store* open daily from 3 to 5 pm only. It sells basic provisions, ice, camping gas and fuel (diesel, super, unleaded, outboard mix), and basic mechanical repairs can be undertaken. Be warned that credit cards are not accepted here. Phone the ranger station to check that the store is still open as it has been erratic in the past. If it is closed fuel is usually available through the ranger station, but, again, check in advance.

There's an airstrip at Smith Point which is serviced by charter flights from Darwin.

The fully equipped, four-bed *Cobourg Cottages* (☎ (08) 8979 0214) at Smith Point overlooking Port Essington cost $100 for the whole cottage, but you need to bring your own supplies.

The only other accommodation option is the ultra-luxury, award-winning *Seven Spirit Bay Resort* (☎ (08) 8979 0277), set in secluded

THE TROPICS

wilderness at Vashon Head and accessible only by air or boat. It charges $300 per person, but this includes three gourmet meals. Activities include a day trip to Victoria Settlement, guided bushwalks and fishing. Accommodation is in individual, open-sided, hexagonal 'habitats', each with semi-outdoor private bathroom! Return transfer by air from Darwin costs $250 per person.

Gulf Track

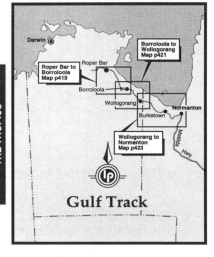

Gulf Track

Steeped in history and lined by unmarked graves, the Gulf Track from Roper Bar in the Northern Territory's Top End to Normanton

in north-west Queensland crosses some of tropical Australia's wildest and most remote country. Until recent times the Track was little more than a set of wheel ruts winding through the endless bush. Those days are gone, but there is still a powerful sense of adventure, thanks to the Gulf's vast untouched forests, the lack of facilities and population, and the saltwater crocodiles that lurk in its numerous rivers. Its attractions include some great fishing opportunities, detours to scenic coastline, abundant wildlife and bush camping beside flowing streams.

For the average traveller, complacency and excessive speed with the road conditions are the Track's major motoring hazards. A 4WD isn't normally required during the dry season unless you plan to take the tracks that lead to the coast from Hell's Gate and Wollogorang. However, conventional vehicles should have good ground clearance and solid suspension – the river crossings are usually no problem by June, when water levels will have dropped to no more than 600mm over the Track.

Traffic on the Gulf Track varies from none in summer to an average of about 30 vehicles per day at the height of the winter tourist season. Travel is not recommended between the beginning of December and the end of March, when extreme heat and humidity make conditions uncomfortable or even dangerous. Apart from that, heavy rain at this time can close the road for lengthy periods. The most pleasant time to visit the Gulf is during the winter months, when you will encounter cool mornings, warm days and balmy evenings.

HISTORY

The Gulf Track more or less follows in the footsteps of the eccentric German explorer Ludwig Leichhardt, who skirted the Gulf of Carpentaria on his trek from Brisbane to newly settled Port Essington (near Darwin) in 1845. Leichhardt was attempting to find an overland trade route to India and many saw the new port becoming the Singapore of

Top: Magnetic termite mounds in Litchfield National Park, Qld
Middle: Lormaieum Lagoon, near the old St Vidgeon homestead, Qld
Bottom: The coastline of Cape York, Qld

Top: Yellow Water in Kakadu National Park, NT
Bottom: Tree roots in the Daintree rainforest, Qld

Australia – 'a safe harbour where the wealth of Asia could be exchanged for grain and horses'. However, Port Essington was abandoned four years later, and the hardships of Leichhardt's route killed any hope that it could be used for trade.

After Leichhardt, the wilderness between Burketown, which was established in 1865, and the Roper lay undisturbed until 1872, when D'Arcy Uhr took 400 head of cattle through to the Top End gold fields. This was no mean feat as, apart from being virtually unknown to white people, the country en route was thickly timbered, poorly pastured and inhabited by thousands of hostile Aborigines. The first drover to follow Uhr starved to death near the Limmen Bight River, after losing his entire mob to Aboriginal attacks, flooded rivers and stampedes.

No further use was made of the route until 1878, when the legendary Nat 'Bluey' Buchanan drove 1200 cattle from Aramac in central Queensland to a station near Darwin. At the Limmen Bight River the drovers returned to camp to find their cook beheaded with his own axe. For hours afterwards the hills echoed with gunfire as the dead man's mates carried out a terrible vengeance.

Three years later Buchanan was back, this time in command of 70 men charged with taking 20,000 head of cattle from St George in south-eastern Queensland to the Daly River near Darwin. To cross the vast sweep of Aboriginal-controlled territory west of Burketown, he separated the cattle into 10 mobs and sent them off a day or two apart. The rigours of the trail claimed many cattle but only one drover, who died of an unknown sickness. It was an epic in Australian droving history and established Leichhardt's hazardous track around the Gulf as the major stock route from Queensland to the Top End.

In 1886 the drovers were joined by a stream of desperadoes and penniless adventurers on their way to the Halls Creek gold rush in Western Australia's Kimberley. The would-be diggers suffered unimaginable privations, and many succumbed to madness, starvation, thirst and Aboriginal spears.

Yet 10 years later, by which time the gold rush and the great cattle drives were over, traffic on the Gulf Track had dwindled to a trickle. It is only in recent times, with the upgrading of the road and the resulting increase in tourism, that you could again describe it as well used. Even so, there are days in the middle of the winter tourist season when you can drive 200km and not see another vehicle.

INFORMATION
Tourist Offices
Croc Spot Tours (☎ (08) 8975 8721) and the Shell Gulf MiniMart (☎ (08) 8975 8790) in Borroloola are the best source of general information on Borroloola and the western end of the Gulf Track. You can also ring the Roper Bar Store (☎ (08) 8975 4636), Wollogorang station (☎ (08) 8975 9944) and Hell's Gate Roadhouse (☎ (07) 4745 8258) for the facts on those particular areas.

The Burketown & Gulf Regional Tourist Information Centre (☎ (07) 4745 5177) is on Musgrave St in Burketown.

For general information on Queensland and the Gulf Savannah area in particular contact:

Gulf Savannah Tourist Association
    PO Box 2312, Cairns, Qld 4870 (☎ (07) 4031 1631; fax 4031 3340)
Far North Queensland Promotion Bureau
    PO Box 865, Cairns, Qld 4870 (☎ (07) 4051 3588; fax 4051 0127)
    Blackall, Qld 4472 (☎ (07) 4657 4255; fax 57 4437)

Road reports can be obtained from the police at Ngukurr, near Roper Bar (☎ (08) 8975 4644), Borroloola (☎ (08) 8975 8770) and Burketown (☎ (07) 4745 5120).

Emergency
There are medical clinics staffed by registered nurses at Ngukurr, Borroloola and Burketown, and a good-sized hospital at Doomadgee. Roper Bar, Hell's Gate and Wollogorang have comprehensive RFDS medical kits and adjoining airstrips.

Absalom's Yabbies

My introduction to Roper Bar was memorable: who should I meet there but the famous Australian bush artist and raconteur Jack Absalom. He and his wife, Mary, were on one of their regular pilgrimages to the Bar. Although it's a long way from their home in Broken Hill, most people who have camped by the Roper River will understand why they do it.

We were on the subject of fishing when Jack started waving his arms about to indicate the size of the local yabbies. I must have looked a bit sceptical because he went straight to his freezer and pulled out the biggest yabby I've ever seen – I didn't know they grew that big! He let me in on a little secret that he promised is much more effective than traps at catching yabbies: simply toss a handful of chook pellets into the water near the bank to attract them, wait a minute, then snaffle them with a throw net.

Denis O'Byrne

Maps

One of the best road guides to use is the 1:750,000 *Gulf Savannah* map which is available from good map shops everywhere. Available widely is the Hema map, *The Top End* which includes the Gulf Track. At the time of this update, Westprint was in the throes of producing a map-guide of the Gulf Track.

The *Northern Territory Fishing Map* with accompanying guide contains plenty of information such as boating and fishing regulations, popular angling species, fishing charters and the location of many fishing spots. You can buy one at newsagencies and tackle shops throughout the Territory, or write to the Department of Primary Industry & Fisheries (☎ (08) 8989 2211), GPO Box 990, Darwin 0801.

Radio Frequencies

For the Track's western half you will need to use the frequencies 6840 and 7975kHz to contact the St John Ambulance base in Darwin (call sign VJY); it operates between 8 am and 5 pm Monday to Friday. These are also after-hours emergency frequencies. You can telephone St John (☎ (08) 8927 911) for service details.

The eastern half of the Track is serviced by the Mount Isa RFDS base (☎ (07) 4743 7887; call sign VJI), which can be contacted on 2020 and 5110kHz in the event of an emergency. RFDS bases in Queensland do not provide a radio telephone (radphone) service.

Telstra provides radphone facilities from its Darwin (call sign VID) and Townsville (call sign VIT) bases. Darwin (Selcalls – Beacon 0599, Operator 0105) has the main frequencies 415, 607, 811 and 1227 while Townsville (Selcalls – Beacon 0999, Operator 0109) has 412, 607, 817, 1229 and 1610.

THE ROUTE
Roper Bar

The place where Leichhardt crossed the magnificent Roper River en route to Port Essington lies 174km by road east of Mataranka on the Stuart Highway. Access from the highway (the turn-off is 6km south of Mataranka) presents no difficulty, as all but the last 40km is sealed.

Over 100m wide at the bar and lined by huge paperbarks, this popular fishing spot lies at the river's tidal limit and has a boat ramp, camping ground, store and airstrip. The road crosses the river here, then continues on for a further 30km to the Aboriginal community at Ngukurr (off limits to visitors). In the early days, steam ships and large sailing vessels tied up at the bar to discharge cargo.

Roper Bar to Borroloola (373km)

Although this section often resembles the twin wheel ruts of earlier times, it mainly presents good going across undulating country carpeted with a mosaic of scrub, tall forest and open parkland. Along the way you pass swamps and spectacular sandstone escarpments, wind through stony hills and ford several rivers. Although the rivers are a magnificent feature of this region, their fording places tend to be disappointing: they're sited at constrictions in the main channels and so feel the full force of wet season flooding. However, the atmosphere and scenery a short distance away on either side are invariably superb. Below the crossings the rivers generally open out into broad stretches of water that take you all the way to the Gulf.

St Vidgeon Ruins Seventy km from Roper Bar, during which there is little to delight the eye, you arrive at the old St Vidgeon homestead – a lonely ruin on a stony rise conjuring up stark images of battlers eking out a scant living from the hostile bush. Bougainvilleas still bloom bravely in the overgrown front yard, providing a splash of vibrant colour in a sea of brown and green. The station is now owned by the Northern Territory government, which is considering creating a

national park in the area. One of the park's gems will be **Lormaleum Lagoon**, a stone's throw from the homestead and only about 1km from the Roper River. Fringed by paperbarks and covered by large water lilies, the lagoon has many birds and a peaceful atmosphere, making it a great spot for a picnic.

Past St Vidgeons, the Track mainly winds about through scrub and forest, with occasional vibrant patches of flowering wattles and grevilleas in late autumn to early winter. Large domed termite mounds and clumps of tall native pine are also of interest.

The Limmen Bight The crossing of the Limmen Bight River, 178km from Roper Bar, is rather a dismal place, thanks to its grey rocks, flood-torn vegetation and a still, dark waterhole that brings lurking crocodiles to mind. The river is much prettier downstream, however, and this area is reached by a 4WD track that turns off on the left about

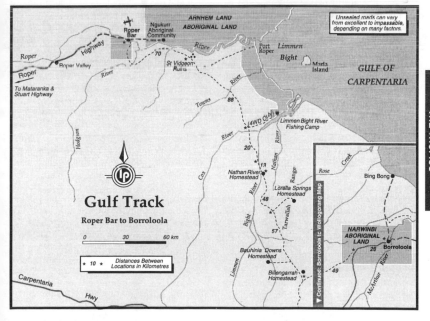

THE TROPICS

20km before the crossing. The track takes you past a permanent **fishing camp**, where payment of a small fee allows you access to shaded campsites and boat-launching points along the river's tidal section. The Gulf of Carpentaria's larger estuaries offer excellent boat fishing, and this one is no exception.

The Limmen Bight marks a change in the country, which to this point is mainly flat to undulating. For about 50km south from here, the road runs up narrow valleys between rugged ridges, with some dramatic scenery along the way.

You pass the turn-off to **Nathan River homestead** 13km from the Limmen Bight crossing. Owned by the Northern Territory government, the station is another proposed national park – contact the Parks & Wildlife Commission's Katherine office (☎ (08) 8973 8888) for an update.

Sixteen km past the homestead a striking grey-and-orange escarpment crowds in on the left. About the same distance further on is one of the Track's most pleasing sights: a large and beautiful parkland dominated by big ghost gums. There are some nice campsites close to the road here, although a nearby swamp means swarms of mosquitoes at night.

Leaving the gums behind, you pass the turn-off to **Lorella Springs homestead**, 239km from Roper Bar, and enter the harsh stony undulations of the Tarwallah Range. **Tarwallah Creek** is 24km further on, and there's a delightful waterhole lined by pandanus palms and overhung by tall river gums and paperbarks. The pool looks ideal for a cooling dip, but up this way, sensible travellers do their swimming in a bucket until they know it's safe to do otherwise.

The next 83km, which takes you to the bitumen Carpentaria Highway, is notable mainly for its suspension-busting washouts and gutters, as the Track winds through harsh, stony hills punctuated by alluvial flats. En route, at the 296km mark from Roper Bar, you pass the turn-off to Daly Waters and **Cape Crawford**, the latter being worth a visit if you're short of fuel or desperate for a cold drink (see the later Detours

section). Once you reach the highway, it's yellow speargrass and low open forest on flat terrain for the remaining 28km to Borroloola.

Borroloola

Until 1885 there were no facilities at all between Burketown (then a busy little port) and the store at Roper Bar. It's true that there were a few widely scattered homesteads along the way, but these were little more than rough forts armed against Aboriginal attack. Then 'Black Jack' Reid brought a ketch loaded with alcohol and supplies up the McArthur River to the Burketown Crossing, where he built a rough store. So Borroloola was born.

A year later, by which time traffic on the Gulf Track had greatly increased, thanks to the Kimberley gold rush, the embryonic township had a population of 150 whites – 'the scum of northern Australia', according to the Government Resident. A decade later, the gold rush and the great cattle drives were over and the white population had shrunk to six. Borroloola probably would have died altogether were it not for its location on one of the Gulf's largest rivers; it survives today as a minor administrative centre and supply point for the region's cattle stations. The town is in the throes of a boom with the development of a giant silver, lead and zinc mine and the creation of a deep-water port on the Gulf.

Sprawled along 2km of wide main street, Borroloola was blown away by Cyclone Kathy in 1984 and much of its old character has been lost in the rebuilding. Its colourful past is preserved mainly in the many interesting displays housed in the **old police station**, which dates from 1886 and is open from noon to 3 pm Monday to Friday. The town is much quieter these days, although bloody re-enactments of what it was like a century ago sometimes take place when the booze is flowing freely, such as on pension days.

Borroloola is connected to the outside world by bitumen roads leading to the Stuart and Barkly highways, and by scheduled

THE TROPICS

daily air services to Darwin and Katherine. The town's population is only about 900, but being an isolated tourism and regional centre, it offers a wide range of government and business services and facilities. These include a medical centre, police station, mechanical repairs, supermarkets, butchery and marine and fishing suppliers.

The Commonwealth, Westpac and ANZ banks have agencies in town, and all three have EFTPOS facilities and take credit cards. The handiest is the Westpac agency at Gulf Mini Mart, which is open seven days a week.

Borroloola attracts around 10,000 visitors annually, most of them coming for the fishing – the **Fishing Classic** held at Easter each year draws a large number of enthusiasts. The McArthur River is tidal as far as the Burketown Crossing near town, and can be accessed by boat from formed ramps at Borroloola and King Ash Bay, about 40km downstream. Anglers with large enough craft

can venture out into the Gulf around the Sir Edward Pellew Group. Don't despair if you don't have a boat: you can catch a wide variety of fish, including barramundi and threadfin salmon, from spots along the river's tidal section, between Batten Point (near King Ash Bay) and the Burketown Crossing. Fishing safaris with a local guide are also available (see Organised Tours).

Borroloola to Wollogorang (258km)
This section of the Track is generally in excellent condition, with long straight stretches that encourage drivers to increase speed until they're bowling along at 100km/h or more. However, it's best to tread lightly on the accelerator pedal, as loose corners and occasional gutters cause numerous accidents each year. The forests are taller between Borroloola and Wollogorang and the river crossings tend to be much more attractive than before. Several offer good campsites near the road.

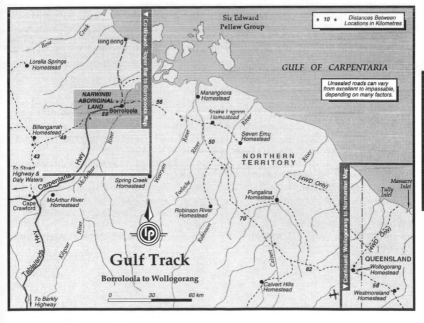

Gulf Track

Borroloola to Wollogorang

Just out of town you leave the blacktop behind and cross the wide bed of the McArthur River. From here the Track spears wide and smooth through a seemingly endless forest of slender stringybarks to the **Wearyan River**, 56km out. Here there is a fine waterhole and a good campsite just upstream from the stony crossing, which in the dry season is about 40cm deep. Of interest are the unusual cycad palms that grow to heights of 6m on either side of the narrow valley.

The Gulf rivers are notable for their wildlife, and the Wearyan River is no exception. If you decide to camp here you're likely to lie awake most of the night listening to mosquitoes whine, dingoes howl, curlews scream, fish splash, flying foxes screech and squabble, and heavy things go thump in the bush. This exercise in insomnia reaches its climax at dawn, when an army of kookaburras cackles loudly in the trees above your head.

The Track narrows past the Wearyan River, crossing the Foelsche River 15km further on. Just past the crossing a track on the left leads to **Seven Emu homestead** (☎ (07) 4742 8258) where, with permission, you can fish and even reach the coast. The main route eastwards continues on through attractive stringybark forest and patches of tropical bush before dropping down into the valley of the **Robinson River**, 105km from Borroloola. You come to the crossing 1km later, where mussel shells, yabby claws and fish scales on the sand give some idea of the river's bounty. Travellers with 4WD vehicles can get access to nice campsites beside shallow flowing water, but the rubbish that's normally strewn about shows that this is also a popular spot for drinking parties.

Robinson River to Wollogorang Seventy km further on you come to the **Calvert River** crossing, where there is a beautiful waterhole bordered by pandanus and low paperbarks. This makes a startling contrast to the stony undulations and low woodland that dominates past the Robinson River. The pink blooms of turkey bush – a nondescript species at other times – are an outstanding feature of these harsher areas in early winter.

Continuing on, you pass a major road junction, 23km from the Calvert River; the little used route on the right heads south-west to the Tablelands Highway. From here the Gulf Track heads east for another 17km or so through low but attractive open forest before entering an area of high, rocky hills. For 20km the Track winds about, a pleasant change from the previous long straights, and crosses spring-fed creeks lined by lush tropical vegetation. Care is needed, as savage washouts and narrow gutters are usually common through the hills.

Sixty km from the Calvert and 4km past the Redbank copper mine turn-off, you arrive on top of the range, to be greeted by the most dramatic scenery between Borroloola and Burketown.

From this lofty summit, a long, steep descent takes you down into a narrow, rugged valley, after which the Track straightens out again for the final 12km to **Wollogorang**. Covering over 7000 sq km, this vast cattle property boasts a fully licensed roadhouse and an 80km frontage of pristine sandy beaches on the Gulf of Carpentaria. The coast can only be reached by 4WD vehicle; a small fee is charged for access (see Detours).

Wollogorang to Burketown (232km)

This section of road was one of the worst in Australia until 1993, when the horrendous bulldust holes on the Queensland side were covered with gravel. Now you can safely sit on 80km/h most of the way – unless, of course, a big Wet has destroyed the government's good work. The country has little going for it in the way of scenery, being mainly flat and covered with scrubby vegetation. In fact, apart from Hell's Gate and the Gregory River, there is little reason to linger on this section.

Hell's Gate You arrive at the Hell's Gate Roadhouse 58km from Wollogorang, located among low outcrops of grey conglomerate that rise like fat dumplings from

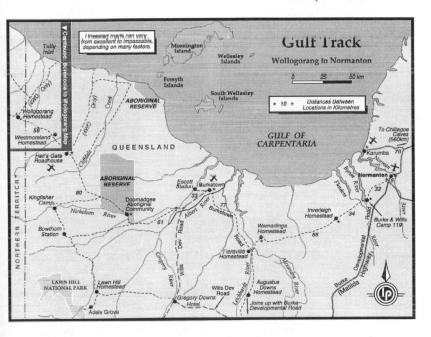

the surrounding bush. In the droving days the police from Turn-Off Lagoon, on the Nicholson River, escorted westbound travellers as far as these rocks, after which they were on their own. Prompted by visions of the spear-wielding warriors who awaited them, they named the place Hell's Gate.

The roadhouse was established by present owners Bill and Lee Olive in 1986, for a very simple reason: the federal government's disease-control programme had reduced the cattle herd on their nearby Cliffdale station from 7000 to 1000 and they needed to find another means of earning a living. The friendly little oasis they've created in the middle of nowhere is a credit to these two battlers.

Bill runs day and half-day tours of the area, and you should ask him about access to the coast, 120km away. The coastal Aborigines lived traditional lifestyles into the 1930s, having managed to survive as a group thanks to good cover and the area's limited value for cattle-grazing. Now their descendants own the coastal strip north of Cliffdale, and the Olives are hoping to negotiate access rights to the beaches and inlets.

Hell's Gate to Doomadgee Other than patches of open forest along occasional creek lines, there is little breaking up the mallee and paperbark scrub all the way to Doomadgee.

The turn-off to **Kingfisher Camp** is on the right, 51km from Hell's Gate. This track heads south to Kingfisher and some fine camping, and then on to Bowthorn station homestead. See under Detours for more information. From the homestead you can continue south to Lawn Hill National Park or head east, joining up with the Gulf Track east of Doomadgee.

The Doomadgee turn-off is passed 29km further on. This Aboriginal community has about 1300 residents, and while you are welcome to shop at the store, camping on the community's land is subject to permission being obtained from the council.

Doomadgee to Burketown Four km past Doomadgee you arrive at the **Nicholson River** crossing, the widest and least attractive of all the Track's fords. The river is about 600m across, and in the dry season its bed of solid rock presents a desolate picture. Scattered small waterholes and low trees do little to gladden the eye – a swim would be nice but signs on the bank warn of saltwater crocodiles. Another 4km further on the turn-off to Bowthorn station homestead is on the right.

In remarkable contrast, the **Gregory River**, 53km further on, presents a lush picture of running water crowded by tropical vegetation. Herons stalk the shallows, and the milky water holds promise of feasts of yabbies. However, motorists must exercise extreme care here – the single-lane concrete crossing has a sharp bend in it and you can't see the other side. If you're towing a caravan, it would be wise to stop before the causeway and send someone across (it's only 200m from bank to bank) to warn any oncoming traffic of your approach.

The deserted **Tirranna Roadhouse** is 1km further on and 8km later there's a major road junction – turn right for the Gregory Downs Hotel (about 90km) and left for Burketown. The dry scrub soon gives way to an open blacksoil plain that keeps you company for the remaining 24km to Burketown.

Approaching Burketown, you pass the turn-off to **Escott Lodge** and cattle station on your left, about 4.5km out of town. The station caters for all travellers, with self-contained rooms available as well as an excellent camping area on the river. The homestead and camping area are 13km from the Gulf Track. Escott Lodge is a top spot to catch a barra, and the property is a working cattle station where every aspect of this hardy life can be experienced by the traveller.

Back on the main track, it is less than 5km to the centre of Burketown.

Burketown

For many, Burketown is 'on the Gulf', but in reality it is over 30km from the coast. The little township shimmers on the biscuit-flat plains that border the waters of the Gulf. Just a stone's throw from the waters of the Albert River, it operated as a port with ships sailing upriver to service the town and its hinterland.

The river was first sighted by Captain John Stokes on the 1841 survey by the HMS *Beagle*. He was enthusiastic about what he thought was a rich region to the south, imagining English villages and church towers dotting the land which he called the 'Plains of Promise'. While Burketown was named after the Burke and Wills expedition of 1860, Burke and his party were really a long way east; other explorers came closer to Burketown and the Albert River.

Founded in 1865, Burketown almost came to a premature end a year later when a fever wiped out most of the residents. Then, in 1887, an extreme tidal surge almost carried the town away. While nothing so dramatic has occurred since, the township is often cut off from the rest of Australia by floods.

Once, by some accounts, the wildest township in Australia, Burketown today is much more peaceful and friendly. Not only is it the administrative centre for a vast region dotted with huge cattle properties, it is also a major supply centre for travellers heading to, from, or along the Gulf. Being such an important centre, it can supply all your normal requirements and, while not pretty to look at, is a good base from which to explore the surrounding area, take in a little fishing or fly out to any of the islands in the Gulf.

As you enter the town, the Burketown & Gulf Regional Tourist Information Centre (☎ (07) 4745 5177), Musgrave St, is on your right, opposite the camping ground. It can help with information and with organising tours and flights. There is a Westpac Bank agency at Nowland Engineering, while the Commonwealth Bank agency is at the post office, in Beames St.

There are a few **historic sites** to see around the place: the old wharves, the boiling-down works (where meat, hooves and hides were processed) and, not far away, the tree emblazoned by the explorer Landsborough. Landsborough had been sent out to try and find the Burke and Wills expedition and had set up a base on the Albert River before pushing south. Like many historic sites, this one is fast decaying under the onslaught of the weather and the white ants. Soon there will be nothing here but a fence around an old tree stump. The cemetery is also interesting. Those with a little more time can head 30km further north, to as close as you can get to the waters of the Gulf.

Lawn Hill National Park and the **Gregory Downs Hotel**, both within a couple of hundred kilometres south, are places worthy of a visit if you are staying in the area for a few days. See Detours later in this section.

Burketown to Normanton (233km)

From Burketown the Track improves as it sweeps across the flat plains of the Gulf to Normanton. The road, which follows the original coach route between Darwin and Port Douglas, was known as the Great Top Road.

Turning right at the pub and heading south, you'll pass the 100-year-old artesian bore on the right, just on the outskirts of town. At Harris Creek, 15km from the centre of town, the dirt begins, and while the bitumen was pleasant, you should be used to the corrugations and the bulldust by now. If you're not, you have another few hundred kilometres to relish the idea. Talking of bulldust, you'll find that on these vast, flat plains, it is finer, deeper and seemingly more enveloping than anywhere else in Australia. The dust hides suspension-wrenching potholes, and if you think it is bad in an air-conditioned 4WD, it is dynamite on a motorcycle!

As you head south on the Burketown Road, most of the creek crossings of any note have been upgraded to a bitumen causeway-type affair. How bad the road is depends on when the graders have been out and how bad the preceding wet season has been – sometimes it can be little better than a track, while at other times it is a wide, graded road interspersed with stretches of corrugations, potholes and bulldust.

Floraville Station The turn-off to Floraville station is at the 73km mark, on the right. A 'Historic Site' sign indicates that this is more than a station track, and it is worth the 1.3km diversion to check the plaque and monument to Frederick Walker, who died here in 1866. He was a wild lad in his time, but a fine explorer who had been sent out to find Burke and Wills. While he didn't find them, he did discover their Camp 119, from which they made their final push to the Gulf.

Walker's monument is found through the gate, heading towards the station. Keep left at the first track junction, about 400m from the road, and turn left again a short time later. By now you should be able to see the monument, down the rise a little, across a narrow creek. Please respect the privacy of the station people and stay away from the nearby homestead.

Leichhardt Falls Just 1km after the turn-off to Floraville, the road drops down the sandy bank of the Leichhardt River and winds its way across the rock bar that makes up the wide bed of the river here. The best place to pull up for a stroll, and probably the best camp on the run between Burketown and Normanton, is at the small, tree-covered island on the left about halfway across and just past the bridge.

From here it is only a short walk downstream to the spectacular Leichhardt Falls. There are pools of water to cool off in (don't swim in the big stretch of water above the road crossing – there are crocs!), the trees offer plenty of shade and the bird life is rich and varied, although the noisy corellas number in the thousands and definitely dominate the scene.

History has it that the falls was a spot where a number of the early explorers camped on their trips through this harsh land. Both McKinlay and Landsborough camped here in 1861 in their separate expeditions to find Burke and Wills, blazing trees in the vicinity of the falls.

THE TROPICS

In a big flood, there is so much water coming down the river that the falls are barely a ripple, as shown by the photos in Burketown's tourist information office. Such floods occur every 10 years or so, and looking down into the gorge below the falls, you see that once-large trees are now just sticks jutting out of the sand. It would be spectacular to fly over the falls when the river was in flood.

The owners of Floraville, who found Walker's grave and erected the monument, are also responsible for the thought-provoking sign near the road crossing in the middle of the riverbed. 'God Is' is all that it says.

Leichhardt Falls to Normanton Once you have climbed the eastern bank of the Leichhardt River, the road winds a short distance and crosses a causeway before reaching a road junction, which can be easy to miss. You are less than 4km from the Floraville station turn-off, less than 2km from the Leichhardt and a total of 77km from Burketown. You need to turn left here for Normanton. Heading south on the better-looking road will take you to the Burke & Wills Roadhouse, 146km away on the Burke Developmental Road (see the Matilda Highway section later in this chapter).

Turn left at the junction, go through the gate, and 500m later you will begin crossing the rough – very rough – bed of the **Alexandra River**.

After the Alexandra, the road continues in a north-easterly direction, crossing the occasional creek (some have a causeway) and ploughing through bulldust and across corrugations. The turn-off to **Wernadinga station** is 16km from the Alexandra River crossing, while the track into Inverleigh station is 85km from the road junction.

You cross the **Flinders River** 28km past the Inverleigh turn-off, and then 3km later the Big Bynoe River. The Little Bynoe River is crossed 2.5km further east. Just up the top of the eastern bank, 500m from the river, is a track heading south (right); it leads less than 2km to Burke and Wills' Camp 119. This is a good spot to have a brew; if you

want to camp, a track leads a short distance back to the edge of the **Little Bynoe**, where you can pitch a tent.

The northernmost camp of the Burke and Wills expedition was **Camp 119**. Leaving their companions, Gray and King, to mind the camels and their equipment, Burke and Wills pushed north across the wet and flooded country to try and reach the waters of the Gulf. It was 11 February 1861. While the water was salty and they observed a rise and fall in the tide, the barrier of mangroves and mud kept them from seeing the actual Gulf.

Returning to their companions at Camp 119, they planned their return to the base camp on Cooper Creek in north-eastern South Australia. No longer an exploratory expedition with mapping and observing a prime consideration, it was now a desperate dash for survival. In the end, only King survived.

Camp 119 is marked by a ring of trees and a centre one all blazed by Burke and Wills. A couple of monuments also mark the spot.

All the rivers previously mentioned are home to salties, so swimming is not advisable. A huge number of cattle use the water for drinking and cooling off, so unless the river is flowing, it's not recommended for drinking either.

Continuing eastwards you reach the bitumen at a road junction 32km east of the turn-off to Camp 119. Turn left here, and 5km later you are in Normanton.

Normanton
On the banks of the Norman River, Normanton is a good base from which to explore the surrounding area. It's a larger town than Burketown and can provide all your requirements, with four pubs and a number of food and fuel outlets. There are also a number of historical places to enjoy.

Don't forget to check some of the **historic buildings** in this once-important port, and if your timing is right, go for a ride on the *Gulflander*, a unique train that runs from the historic railway station to the once-rich gold-mining town of Croydon.

For more information on Normanton, see the Matilda Highway section later in this chapter.

From here you can head south 380-odd km along the all-bitumen Burke Developmental Road to Cloncurry, Mount Isa and beyond, or you can head 300km east to Georgetown and eventually Cairns via the Gulf Developmental Road, which is now (except for about 80km) all bitumen.

Heading north out of town will take you to **Karumba**, on the coast 70km away (see the Matilda Highway section). North of Normanton, on the way to Karumba, you can head off on the dirt and the Burke Developmental Road to Dunbar station and then east to Chillagoe and the coast. This rough, dusty, 560km trip takes you through remote country without any supply points.

DETOURS
Cape Crawford (43km one way)
Nine km past the Bauhinia Downs turn-off and 296km from Roper Bar you arrive at a T-junction; turn right here for the *Heartbreak Hotel* (☎ (08) 8975 9928) at Cape Crawford. The pub has fuel sales (diesel, super and unleaded), takeaway meals, a licensed dining room, air-conditioned motel-style accommodation (starting at $50 a single or $60 for two) and a pleasant caravan park with lawns and shade.

Also available are 4WD tours of two to eight hours' duration that take you to a variety of outstanding attractions, such as strange rock formations, cool ferneries and tumbling waterfalls, none of which are open to the general public. Travellers can also take a scenic flight by helicopter over the spectacular **Lost City**, which rivals the Bungle Bungles and will one day no doubt become a major tourist attraction in the Gulf country. For details of tours and facilities, ring the hotel. Note that despite its name, Cape Crawford is a long way from the coast.

Wollogorang Fishing Excursions
With permission from the Wollogorang Roadhouse (☎ (08) 8975 9944) you can take 4WD tracks to the **Calvert River** (115km one

way) and **Massacre and Tully Inlets** (90km one way) for great fishing and camping in isolated wilderness. A day trip costs $50 a vehicle and is hardly worthwhile, but if you stay more than a couple of days the cost is $20 per day per vehicle.

It takes three hours to get to the river and over two hours to the inlets, each of which includes about 7km of sandy beach driving – there are plenty of marvellous campsites under shady sheoak trees along the beach front. Massacre Inlet was the scene of a slaughter of Aborigines by settlers in the early 1880s – the Aborigines had made the mistake of attacking Westmoreland homestead and killing all the white people living there.

You really need a boat to get good results from the Calvert River, where barramundi is the main attraction. Casting out from the sandy beaches at both inlets yields species such as threadfin salmon, golden snapper, cobia, red bream, queenfish and mangrove jacks. The inlets are also good spots for mud crabs, so take a large metal bucket or drum for cooking your catch.

Hell's Gate
From the Hell's Gate Roadhouse (☎ (07) 4745 8258) you can reach the coast, where there is some very pleasant camping and great fishing. This is Aboriginal land, but you can get permission at the roadhouse – the entry fee is $20 plus $20 per vehicle per day

Kingfisher Camp and Bowthorn Station
Kingfisher Camp is located on the Nicholson River, 40km south of the Gulf Track, and offers visitors fine camping, spectacular river and gorge scenery and delightful bird life. The area has been a fauna reserve since 1983 so traps, nets and firearms are not allowed. People can camp, boat and fish on the river and explore the immediate surrounds on any of the many old 4WD mining tracks in the area.

Kingfisher Camp is part of **Bowthorn station** (☎ (07) 4745 8132), but there are no other facilities here and all visitors must be self sufficient. A small camping fee needs to be paid as well as a deposit – refundable when you return your rubbish to the homestead.

From Bowthorn homestead, 33km south of Kingfisher Camp, you can head east 72km and join up with the Gulf Track east of the Nicholson River, or head south 100km or so to Lawn Hill National Park.

Lawn Hill National Park

This magnificent oasis is an easy 220km from Burketown via the **Gregory Downs Hotel** (☎ (07) 4748 5566), an old Cobb & Co staging post, where fuel and basic (but comfortable) accommodation are available. The Gregory River flows all year past the pub, and there are many excellent campsites along its timbered banks.

Just before Lawn Hill you pass **Adel's Grove** (☎ (07) 4748 5502), where there is a small store and a caravan park. Here you can take a guided tour of a beautiful tropical garden planted by a French botanist in the 1930s. Canoe hire and safe swimming in Lawn Hill Creek are also on offer.

The main attraction at Lawn Hill itself is a rugged gorge where colourful walls tower 60m above deep waterholes fringed by monsoon rainforest. Spectacular range scenery, Aboriginal art and the famous **Riversleigh fossil field** are other major features.

The park's camping ground is extremely busy during the winter months, so you need to book at least six weeks in advance to be sure of securing a site. For details, contact the ranger (☎ (07) 4748 5572).

ORGANISED TOURS
Borroloola

Peter Fittock of Croc Spot Tours (☎ (08) 8975 8721), located at the McArthur River Caravan Park, offers a choice of boat tours, of which his nightly croc-spotting excursions are very popular – for $20 you cruise the river with a spotlight and discover why you should never go swimming there. Peter runs one-day river and reef fishing trips ($75 and $120 per person, respectively), as well as overnight camping safaris (by arrange-

ment) out to the Sir Edward Pellew island group. Minimum numbers apply to all tours. Tackle and bait are provided if required.

Shawflight (☎ (08) 8975 8688; fax 8975 8685) based at Borroloola operates scenic flights, by arrangement, up the McArthur River and over the Sir Edward Pellew Group. The cost is $55 per person, with a minimum of three people for a 45-minute flight.

Wollogorang

Fishing, exploring and pig-shooting safaris operate from the roadhouse, with costs for fishing and exploring tours starting at $120 per person per day. Hunting expeditions are more expensive. These costs do not include meals and accommodation (see Facilities).

Hell's Gate

Bill Olive runs local half-day and full-day 4WD tours for groups of five or more, taking in spectacular escarpment landscapes and lagoons rich in bird life.

Burketown

The Burketown & Gulf Regional Tourist Information Centre (☎ (07) 4745 5177), Musgrave St, Burketown, can supply tourist information and can also organise tours and scenic flights around the area or flights out to Sweers and Mornington islands in the Gulf, through operators such as Escott Barramundi Lodge or Savannah Aviation. For the fishing enthusiasts, the information centre can also arrange boat hire.

FACILITIES
Roper Bar

The *Roper Bar Store* (☎ (08) 8975 4636) caters mainly to tourist traffic and nearby Aboriginal communities. Its services include fuel sales (Avgas is available, subject to a week's notice), a mini supermarket, clothing, fishing tackle, hardware items and a camping ground. Sites in the grassed camping area, which is only about 100m from the river, cost $5 per person.

Borroloola

The *Borroloola Inn* (☎ (08) 8975 8766) has

16 air-conditioned rooms, starting at $45 for a twin room. Its bistro restaurant serves a range of sensibly priced and generous meals, including (of course) local barramundi, while the swimming pool, which is surrounded by large mango trees, is arguably the nicest place in Borroloola.

Just down from the pub, the *Borroloola Holiday Village* (☎ (08) 8975 8742) has air-conditioned units with ensuite, cooking facilities, colour TV and telephone, costing from $97 for a twin room. There are four economy rooms sleeping just one person each ($50), while budget beds in the bunkhouse cost $30. The bunkhouse contains four rooms each sleeping five people, with shared kitchen and laundry. Excellent barbecue facilities with lawn and shade trees are scattered about the complex.

There is little shade at the *McArthur River Caravan Park* (☎ (08) 8975 8734, fax 8975 8706), also in the main street, where powered sites cost $14.50 (add $2.50 if you're using an air-conditioner). Unpowered sites cost $12 for two adults plus $2.50 per extra adult and $1.50 for each child aged under 12. Budget accommodation with shared kitchen facilities costs $30/40 single/double. Fully self-contained cabins sleep up to five and cost between $65 for one person to $85 for a family.

There's good fishing from the river bank at King Ash Bay, where the *Borroloola Boat & Fishing Club* (☎ (08) 8975 9861) has its headquarters. Bush camping is permitted nearby, and if you join the club – a life membership costs $500 and an annual membership $30 – you can make use of its toilet, shower and bar facilities. Otherwise camping will cost you $7 per night, or for a powered site $10 a night. The bar is open from 5 to 8 pm daily.

Wollogorang

Wollogorang Roadhouse (☎ (08) 8975 994), open seven days a week, has a licensed restaurant offering good, wholesome country cooking at reasonable prices. There is also a snack menu (including steak sandwiches, which come highly recommended). The roadhouse has six air-conditioned units, each sleeping three, at $50 a single, $70 a double/twin. Campsites cost $7 per person, kids free. Fuel, including Avgas and jet-A1, is also available, as is takeaway beer.

Hell's Gate

Plates piled high with station-style meals are also a feature at the *Hell's Gate Roadhouse* (☎ (07) 4745 8258), where a licensed restaurant serves breakfast, lunch and dinner – the Sunday-night barbecue should not be missed if you are in the area. There are four two-bed rooms available, costing $25 per person. All fuels, except auto gas, are available, and Avgas can be arranged. The roadhouse is open seven days a week from 7 am to 10 pm (or later). Bookings are recommended for accommodation.

Doomadgee

The well-stocked *Doomadgee Retail Store* sells fuel, meat, groceries, limited hardware items, Aboriginal art and a good range of motoring accessories. It's open from 8.30 am to 5 pm Monday to Friday and from 8.30 to 11.30 am on Saturday.

Burketown

Accommodation is available at the *Albert Hotel/Motel* (☎ (07) 4745 5104; fax 4745 5146). There are four motel units, with all amenities, as well as barbecue and laundry facilities. Singles/doubles cost $65/95. The hotel also has rooms with shared facilities ($35 to $45 a single, $55 to $65 a double).

The *Burketown Caravan Park* (☎ (07) 4745 5010; fax 4745 5145) has powered sites with all amenities, including washing machines and barbecues. Pets are allowed. A tent site costs $9.50 a double, while a powered site is $12.

The *Burketown General Store* can supply most general needs, including fuel.

Escott Lodge (☎ (07) 4748 5577; fax 4748 5551) caters for all forms of travellers. There are self-contained cottages from $30 per person, overnight motel rooms from $45/70 single/double, camping along the river with no facilities for $4.50, and a camping ground with all facilities for $6 per person (power $7.50). There is a licensed dining room, and from here you can organise a safari, a fishing trip, joy flights, boat hire or a trip out to Sweers or Mornington islands.

Normanton & Karumba
There is a good range of facilities in these towns. See the later Matilda Highway section for details.

Bush Camping
For almost its entire length, the Gulf Track passes through station country, and the lease-holders are not likely to be impressed if they find you driving about on their land without permission. However, access to campsites at the various river crossings is generally unre-stricted, except on Aboriginal-owned land surrounding Doomadgee, where a permit is required from the local community council.

The reality of camping in the Gulf country is that you'll be eaten by mosquitoes at night if you don't have adequate protection. Pro-tection from heavy fog and dew is also required, so a canvas tarpaulin or gazebo makes a useful camping accessory.

Cairns

HIGHLIGHTS

- Driving along the coast road between Cairns and Port Douglas at sunrise

- Diving over the Great Barrier Reef

- Swimming in crystal-clear and crocodile-free streams in Daintree National Park

The tourist capital of Far North Queensland and perhaps the best-known city on the Queensland coast, Cairns (population 106,600) has become one of Australia's top travellers' destinations. It is also a staging post for journeys into the wilds of Cape York,

or excursions to the tropical beauty of Cape Tribulation. On the debit side, Cairns' rapid tourist growth has destroyed much of its laid-back tropical atmosphere. It also lacks a beach, but there are some good ones not far north.

Cairns marks the end of the Bruce High-way and the railway line from Brisbane. The town came into existence in 1876 as a beach-head in the mangroves, intended as a port for the Hodgkinson River gold field 100km inland. Initially, it struggled under rivalry from Smithfield and Port Douglas further north, but was saved by the Atherton Table-land 'tin rush' from 1880 and became the starting point of the railway to the tableland.

Information
The Far North Queensland Promotion Bu-reau (☎ (07) 4051 3588) has an information centre on the corner of Grafton and Hartley Sts, open daily from 9.30 am to 5.30 pm.

There are dozens of privately run informa-tion centres, such as the Cairns Tourist Information Centre (☎ (07) 4031 1751), at shop 6 Aplin St, which are basically booking offices for tours. Also good for information are the various backpackers' hostels, as most have a separate tour-booking service. The only problem here is that each booking agent and hostel will be selling different tours, depending on the commission deal they have with the tour companies – shop around.

The GPO on the corner of Grafton and Hartley Sts, has a poste restante service. For general business (stamps etc), there's also an Australia Post shop in the Orchid Plaza on Lake St.

The RACQ office (☎ (07) 4036 6433), 5km out of town at 520 Mulgrave Rd, is a good place to get information on road con-ditions if you're driving up to Cooktown, into Cape York or across to the Gulf of Carpentaria.

The Department of the Environment (☎ (07) 4052 3096), at 10-12 McLeod St, is open weekdays from 8.30 am to 4.30 pm and deals with camping permits for the Frank-land Islands, Lizard Island and Jardine River.

For books, Proudmans in the Pier

complex, and Walkers Bookshop at 96 Lake St, both have a good range. For maps, go to the RACQ, or check Absell's Chart & Map Centre at 55 Lake St.

Things to See

A walk around the town centre turns up a few points of historical interest, although with much recent development the older buildings are now few and far between. The oldest part of town is the **Trinity Wharf** area, but even this has been redeveloped. There are still some imposing neoclassical buildings from the 1920s on Abbott St, and the frontages around the corner of Spence and Lake Sts date from 1909 to 1926. A walk along the **Esplanade**, with views over to rainforested mountains across the estuary and cool evening breezes, is very agreeable.

The **Pier** is an impressive, up-market shopping plaza with expensive boutiques and souvenir shops downstairs, and some interesting eating possibilities upstairs. On Saturday and Sunday mornings there is a food, souvenir and craft market inside. This is known as the Mud Market.

Right in the centre of town, on the corner of Lake and Shields Sts, the **Cairns Museum** is housed in the 1907 School of Arts building, an excellent example of early Cairns architecture. It has Aboriginal artefacts, a display on the construction of the Cairns-Kuranda railway, the contents of a now demolished Grafton St Joss house, exhibits on the old Palmer River and Hodgkinson gold fields, and material on the early timber industry.

A colourful part of town on weekends is the **Rusty's Bazaar** area bounded by Grafton, Spence, Sheridan and Shields Sts. The bustling weekend markets held here are great for people-watching and for browsing among the dozens of stalls full of produce, arts & crafts, clothes and lots of food. The markets are held on Friday night and Saturday and Sunday mornings – Saturdays are the busiest and best.

North-west of town, in Edge Hill, are the **Flecker Botanic Gardens** on Collins Ave. A boardwalk leads through a patch of rainforest to **Saltwater Creek** and the two small **Centenary Lakes**. Collins Ave turns west off Sheridan St (the Cook Highway) 3km from the centre of Cairns, and the gardens are 700m from the turning. Just before the gardens is the entrance to the **Whitfield Range Environmental Park**, with walking tracks which give good views over the city and coast. You can get there with Cairns Trans Buses or the Cairns Explorer.

Also in Edge Hill, the **Royal Flying Doctor Service** visitors' centre, at 1 Junction St, is open weekdays from 8.30 am to 5 pm and weekends from 9 am to 4.30 pm; entry is $5.

Activities

Cairns offers an amazing amount of organised activities for the hordes of adventurous tourists. See the earlier information section for booking details, and shop around before you make a decision.

Diving Cairns is the scuba-diving capital of the Barrier Reef, which is closer to the coast here than it is further south. The competition is cutthroat, and the company offering the cheapest deal one week may be old news the next. A chat with people who have already done a course would be worthwhile.

Prices differ quite a bit, but expect to pay around $350 to $475 for two days in the pool and classroom, one day travelling to the reef and back, and two more days on the reef with an overnight stay on board.

White-Water Rafting Three of the rivers flowing down from the Atherton Tableland make for some excellent white-water rafting. Most popular is a day in the rainforested gorges of the Tully River, 150km south of Cairns. The Tully day trips leave daily from Cairns year-round, and cost about $130. There are cheaper half-day trips on the Barron River (about $70), not far inland from Cairns, or you can make two-day ($220), three-day ($375) or four-day ($730) expeditions on the remote North Johnstone River which rises near Malanda and enters the sea

THE TROPICS

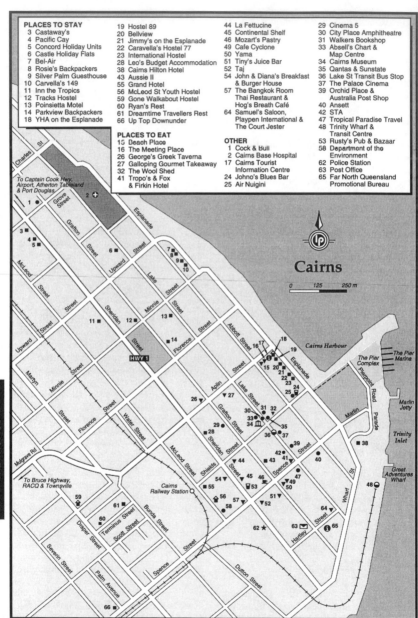

PLACES TO STAY
3   Castaway's
4   Pacific Cay
5   Concord Holiday Units
6   Castle Holiday Flats
7   Bel-Air
8   Rosie's Backpackers
9   Silver Palm Guesthouse
10 Carvella's 149
11 Inn the Tropics
12 Tracks Hostel
13 Poinsietta Motel
14 Parkview Backpackers
18 YHA on the Esplanade

19 Hostel 89
20 Bellview
21 Jimmy's on the Esplanade
22 Caravella's Hostel 77
23 International Hostel
28 Leo's Budget Accommodation
38 Cairns Hilton Hotel
43 Aussie II
55 Grand Hotel
56 McLeod St Youth Hostel
59 Gone Walkabout Hostel
60 Ryan's Rest
61 Dreamtime Travellers Rest
66 Up Top Downunder

PLACES TO EAT
15 Beach Place
16 The Meeting Place
26 George's Greek Taverna
27 Galloping Gourmet Takeaway
32 The Wool Shed
41 Tropo's & Fox
    & Firkin Hotel

44 La Fettucine
45 Continental Shelf
46 Mozart's Pastry
49 Cafe Cyclone
50 Yama
51 Tiny's Juice Bar
52 Taj
54 John & Diana's Breakfast
    & Burger House
57 The Bangkok Room
    Thai Restaurant &
    Hog's Breath Café
64 Samuel's Saloon,
    Playpen International &
    The Court Jester

OTHER
1   Cock & Bull
2   Cairns Base Hospital
17 Cairns Tourist
    Information Centre
24 Johno's Blues Bar
25 Air Nuigini

29 Cinema 5
30 City Place Amphitheatre
31 Walkers Bookshop
33 Absell's Chart &
    Map Centre
34 Cairns Museum
35 Qantas & Sunstate
36 Lake St Transit Bus Stop
37 The Palace Cinema
39 Orchid Place &
    Australia Post Shop
40 Ansett
42 STA
47 Tropical Paradise Travel
48 Trinity Wharf &
    Transit Centre
53 Rusty's Pub & Bazaar
58 Department of the
    Environment
62 Police Station
63 Post Office
65 Far North Queensland
    Promotional Bureau

Cairns

THE TROPICS

at Innisfail. There are also sea-kayaking expeditions on offer.

Other Activities You can go bungy-jumping for $95 or tandem skydiving for $198 to $336. For something a bit more sedate, try a chopper ride over the reef or a wide range of other aerial tours from $80, or go hot-air ballooning over the tablelands for $105 to $170, including a champagne breakfast. Horse rides through the forests around Palm Cove, north of Cairns, cost from $50 to $70. There are also various mountain-bike tours on offer, including a half-day ride to Port Douglas for $69.

Organised Tours

As you'd expect, there are hundreds of tours available from Cairns. Some are specially aimed at backpackers and many of these are pretty good value. Agencies include Tropical Paradise Travel (☎ (07) 4051 9533), at 44 Spence St, and Castaway's (☎ (07) 4041 2480), at 207 Sheridan St, which has a great web site (www.ozemail.com.au/castaway) offering information and booking facilities for tours and accommodation across Australia.

Daintree, Cape Tribulation & Cooktown

Jungle Tours and Tropics Explorer offer good-value and fun-oriented trips north from Cairns.

A day trip to Mossman Gorge and the Daintree River, including a cruise, will cost $84. There are day trips to Cape Tribulation, but you'd be better off taking one of the overnight or longer packages, which cost around $84 for two days, $98 for three days or $122 for five days, and include Mossman Gorge, the Daintree River and accommodation at Crocodylus Village and/or Jungle Lodge and/or PK's Jungle Village. Dan's Mountain Biking (☎ (07) 4033 0128) has day trips from $95.

Barrier Reef There are dozens of options available for day trips to the reef. It's worth asking a few questions before you book, such as how many passengers the boat takes,

what's included in the price (usually at least snorkelling gear and lunch) and how much the extras (such as wetsuit hire and introductory dives) cost, and exactly where the boat is going. Some companies have a dubious definition of outer reef; as a general rule, the further out you go, the better the diving.

Reefmagic (☎ (07) 4031 1588) offers facilities comparable to the larger boats but is less cramped and considerably cheaper at $80 for the trip to the reef, $50 for the first and $25 for the second introductory dive, and $20 for a great snorkelling tour.

Wildlife Spotting Wait-a-While (☎ (07) 4033 1153) runs 4WD tours to rainforest areas around Cairns and Port Douglas for $110. The tours leave Cairns around 2 pm and return around midnight. The highlight is the nighttime search, by spotlight, for rare rainforest mammals such as tree kangaroos, lemuroids, spotted quolls and many others.

Outback There are a number of companies that operate treks and 4WD trips between Cairns, Thursday Island and Darwin, via the Gulf Country, Cape York and Kakadu. Jungle Tours (☎ (07) 4031 1110) has a six-day camping trek from Cairns along the gorges of the beautiful Walsh River in Cape York for $588. Costs include meals.

Billy Tea Bush Safaris (☎ (07) 4032 0077) has six-day ($1399), nine-day ($1499) and 14-day ($1599) fly/drive trips between Cairns and Thursday Island via Cape York. All camping gear, meals and flights are included. Wilderness Challenge (☎ 4055 6504) offers 10-day 4WD safaris from Cairns to Darwin via Normanton, Lawn Hill National Park and Katherine Gorge, for $1595 including all meals and camping gear or $2195 for a 14-day trip which includes Kakadu.

Places to Stay

Cairns has hostels and cheap guesthouses galore, as well as plenty of reasonably priced motels and holiday flats. The accommodation business is extremely competitive and prices go up and down with the seasons.

THE TROPICS

Lower weekly rates are the norm. Prices given here for the more expensive places can rise by 30% or 40% in the peak season, and some of the hostels will charge $1 or $2 less in the quiet times.

Camping There are about a dozen caravan parks in and around Cairns, though none of them are really central. Almost without exception they take campers as well as caravans. The closest one to the centre is the *City Caravan Park* (☎ (07) 4051 1467), about 2km north-west on the corner of Little and James Sts, with tent sites from $6 per person and on-site vans from $30.

Out on the Bruce Highway, about 8km south of the centre, is the excellent *Cairns Coconut Caravan Village* (☎ (07) 4054 6644), with campsites for $17, camp-o-tel units for $24 a double and cabin vans from $49.

Hostels The Cairns hostel scene is constantly changing as new places open up, old ones change hands and others rise and fall in quality and popularity. The type of accommodation is pretty standard – fan-cooled bunk rooms with shared kitchen and bathroom, usually also with sitting areas, laundry facilities and a swimming pool. Unfortunately, you have to beware of theft in some places – use lock-up rooms and safes if they are available.

The Esplanade has the greatest concentration of hostels, and is a lively part of town. The hostels here tend to pack them in, and have very little outside space – any outdoor area is usually cramped with a swimming pool. The hostels away from the city centre offer much more breathing space and are generally quieter, and there are courtesy buses that make regular runs into town.

On the Esplanade, *Caravella's Hostel 77* (☎ (07) 4051 2159), at No 77, is one of the longest established Cairns hostels and has old-fashioned but clean rooms, all with air-con ($15 to $16 per bed in four to six-bunk dorms, singles from $22 to $26, doubles from $30 to $34, or $40 with private bathroom).

Bellview (☎ (07) 4031 4377), at No 85, is a good, quiet hostel with clean and comfortable four-bed dorms from $16 per person, singles from $27 and twin rooms at $36. There are also motel-style units from $49 to $59 a double.

Hostel 89 (☎ (07) 4031 7477 or toll-free 1800 061 712), at No 89, is one of the best kept hostels on the Esplanade. It's a smallish and helpful place, with twin and double rooms and a few three or four-bed dorms, all air-conditioned (from $16 per person, with singles/doubles at $32/34).

At No 93 is *YHA on the Esplanade* (☎ (07) 4031 1919). There are two blocks, one with spacious, airy five-bed dorms with their own bathroom, the other with small twins and doubles. Some rooms have air-con. Dorm beds cost $16 and doubles $36; non-members pay an extra $3.

Rosie's Backpackers (☎ (07) 4051 0235), at No 155, has several buildings with spacious dorms or six-bed flats at $15 per person and doubles at $35. This place is helpful and well run. It has a small pool and a popular Saturday-night barbecue.

Close to the city centre, *Parkview Backpackers* (☎ (07) 4051 3700) is at 174 Grafton St, three blocks back from the Esplanade. This is a very laid-back place where you can relax by the pool and listen to reggae music. It's in a rambling old timber building with a large tropical garden, and four to eight-bed dorms ($14 per person).

At 207 Sheridan St is *Castaway's* (☎ (07) 4051 1238), a quiet and smallish place with dorm beds for $15, singles for $27 and doubles or twins for $32. Some rooms have air-con, all have a fridge, and there's a pool, laundry and courtesy bus. It also has free barbecue nights on Monday, Wednesday and Friday.

Two blocks west of the train station at 274 Draper St, *Gone Walkabout Hostel* (☎ (07) 4051 6160) is one of the best in Cairns. It's small, simple and well run, with a friendly atmosphere. Rooms are mostly twins and doubles ($25), with a few four-bed dorms ($12 per bed), and there's a tiny pool. It's not a place for late partying, however.

THE TROPICS

The YHA *McLeod St Youth Hostel* (☎ (07) 4051 0772), at 20-24 McLeod St, has dorm beds for $16 and singles/doubles for $35; non-members pay $3 extra. The facilities are good and the hostel has parking spaces.

Up Top Downunder (☎ (07) 4051 3636), at 164 Spence St, has clean and spacious three to five bed-dorms for $14, singles for $27 and doubles for $32; $33 with air-con. There is a great pool area, smoking and non-smoking TV rooms and a shuttle bus which runs daily from 7.15 am to 3 am.

Guesthouses A couple of places in this bracket are in the hostel price range, the difference being that their emphasis is on rooms rather than dorms. At 4 Terminus St, *Dreamtime Travellers Rest* (☎ (07) 4031 6753), is a small guesthouse run by a friendly and enthusiastic young Irish/English couple. It's in a brightly renovated timber building and has a good pool (double rooms from $35, or rooms with three or four real beds at $15 per person).

Another good guesthouse with a similar approach is *Ryan's Rest* (☎ (07) 4051 4734), down the road at 18 Terminus St. It's a cosy and quiet family-run place with three good double rooms upstairs at $35, and twins/doubles at $25, and a four-bed dorm at $12 per person downstairs. At 153 the Esplanade, the *Silver Palm Guesthouse* (☎ 4031 6099) is clean with singles/doubles from $29.50/37.50, including the use of a kitchen, laundry, pool and TV room.

Motels & Holiday Flats Holiday flats are well worth considering, especially for a group of three or four people who are staying a few days or more. Expect pools, air-con and laundry facilities in this category. Holiday flats generally supply all bedding, cooking utensils etc.

Castle Holiday Flats (☎ (07) 4031 2229), at 209 Lake St, is one of the city's cheapest places. Self contained flats cost $40 for one bedroom and $60 for two bedrooms. There's a small pool.

There's a string of motels and holiday units along Sheridan St, including the *Pacific Cay* (☎ (07) 4051 0151), at No 193, with one-bedroom holiday units from $55 and two-bedroom units from $70, and the *Concord Holiday Units* (☎ (07) 4031 4522), at No 183, with one-bedroom units; singles/doubles $47/57.

Inn the Tropics (☎ (07) 4031 1088), at 141 Sheridan St, has a good pool, a small guests' kitchen and an open-air courtyard with tables. Clean and modern motel-style rooms with shared bathrooms cost $28/36, or $38/46 with an ensuite.

The *Poinsietta Motel* (☎ (07) 4051 2144), at 169 Lake St, is one of the cheapest central motels, with clean budget rooms for $28/36, with air-con $38/46.

Places to Eat

For a town of its size, Cairns has quite an amazing number and variety of restaurants. Opening hours are long and quite a few places take advantage of the climate by providing open-air dining.

Cafes & Takeaways The Esplanade has a large collection of fast-food joints and restaurants – the stretch between Shields and Aplin Sts is virtually wall-to-wall eateries, where you'll find Italian and Chinese food, burgers, kebabs, pizzas, seafood and ice cream. The *Meeting Place* on Aplin St near the Esplanade is a good food hall with most meals in the $7.50 to $12 range.

The *Galloping Gourmet Takeaway* offers a full breakfast for $5.50, and has a lunch deal for $3.50 – both good value. *Mozart's Pastry*, on the corner of Grafton and Spence Sts, is good for a breakfast croissant and coffee, and also has a range of pastries, cakes and sandwiches. *John & Diana's Breakfast & Burger House*, at 35 Sheridan St, has virtually every combination of cooked breakfast imaginable, for $6.50 or less. Across the road is the *Continental Shelf*, an excellent eat-in deli.

Tiny's Juice Bar, on Grafton St near the Spence St corner, has a great range of fruit and vegetable juices as well as filled rolls and lentil and tofu burgers at good prices. *Cafe Cyclone*, nearby at 49 Spence St, is a friendly

THE TROPICS

little place open for breakfast and lunch, with foccacias, burgers, salads and great coffee at reasonable prices.

Nightclubs & Bars Most of the hostels have giveaway vouchers for cheap meals at various nightclubs, pubs and bars around town, often with free or discounted drinks thrown in. *Samuel's Saloon*, near the corner of Hartley and Lake Sts, and the *Wool Shed*, at 24 Shields St, are two of the most popular places, both serving roasts, pastas and stews for around $4. Both are open from 6 pm till late. They even have buses that collect hungry travellers from the hostels.

The *Beach Place*, a nightclub on the corner of Abbott and Aplin Sts, has very basic food, but it's cheap and a lot of people seem to eat here, again with hostel meal vouchers. The *Fox & Firkin Hotel*, an English-style tavern on the corner of Spence and Lake Sts, also has cheap meals from $4.50.

Restaurants The *Bangkok Room Thai Restaurant*, at 62 Spence St, has a pleasant setting and friendly service, with tasty Thai dishes for around $13. Next door is the popular *Hog's Breath Cafe*, a saloon-style bar and grill. Further along Spence St, the *Taj* serves pretty good Indian food.

La Fettucine at 62 Spence St is a narrow and stylish little BYO place with excellent home-made pastas. *George's Greek Taverna*, on the corner of Grafton and Aplin Sts, is a fairly up-market place with Greek and seafood dishes at around $16. For Japanese food, try *Yama* on the corner of Spence and Grafton Sts.

The Pier complex has a couple of good eating options. The *Pier Tavern* is a popular pub with several bars and outdoor decking overlooking Trinity Bay and the Esplanade. Bistro meals in the Boat Bar are all $9.90 or less, and there are live bands from Wednesday to Sunday. Up on the first level of the shopping plaza is *Donninis*, a smart but casual licensed restaurant with some of the best Italian food (and service) in town:

gourmet pizzas from $9 to $16, pastas around $12 and Italian mains around $17.

Entertainment

Johno's Blues Bar, above McDonald's on the corner of Shields St and the Esplanade, is a big, lively place with blues, rock and R&B bands every night until late. There's a cover charge of $5 on Friday and Saturday nights.

The *Fox & Firkin Hotel*, on the corner of Spence and Lake Sts, and the *Cock & Bull*, on the corner of Grafton and Grove Sts, are both English-style taverns with good atmosphere and affordable meals. Quite a few pubs in Cairns have regular live bands, including the Fox & Firkin, the *Pier Tavern* and *Rusty's Pub* on the corner of Spence and Sheridan Sts.

Cairns' nightclub scene is notoriously wild, especially in the early hours of the morning. A huge complex on the corner of Lake and Hartley Sts houses three places: *Samuel's Saloon*, a backpacker bar and eatery; the *Playpen International*, a huge nightclub that often has big-name bands, stays open until sunrise and charges from $2 to $5 entry; and the more up-market *Court Jester* bar. The *Beach Place* nightclub, on the corner of Abbott and Aplin Sts, is another popular place for a drink and a bop, with a huge video screen, low lighting, loud music and cheap drinks deals. *Tropo's*, next to the Fox & Firkin, has live bands, a disco and a $5 cover charge.

Free lunch-time concerts are held at the *City Place Amphitheatre*, in the mall on the corner of Lake and Shields Sts.

There are two cinemas in town; the *Palace*, on Lake St near the corner of Shields St, and *Cinema 5*, at 108-114 Grafton St.

Things to Buy

Many artists live in the Cairns region, so there's a wide range of local handicrafts available – pottery, clothing, stained glass, jewellery, leather work and so on. Aboriginal art is also for sale in a few places, as are crafts from Papua New Guinea and places further afield in the Pacific. Apart from the many souvenir shops dotted around the town centre, the weekend markets at Rusty's Bazaar and the Pier are all worth a visit.

Getting Around

The Airport The airport in Cairns has two sections, both off the Captain Cook Highway north of town. The main domestic and international airlines use the new section, officially called Cairns international airport. This is reached by an approach road that turns off the highway about 3.5km from central Cairns. The other part of the airport, which some people still call Cairns airport, is reached from a second turning off the highway, 1.5km north of the main one.

The Australia Coach shuttle bus (☎ (07) 4035 9555) from the main terminal costs $4 and will drop you almost anywhere in central Cairns; ring when you're leaving. A taxi (☎ (07) 4051 5333) is about $11.

Local Flights Flights inland and up the Cape York Peninsula from Cairns are shared among a number of small feeder airlines. Sunstate (☎ (07) 4035 9310) flies to Lizard Island ($191.50) and Thursday Island ($202.50). Ansett (☎ (07) 4031 5757) flies to Weipa ($215) and Mount Isa ($532). Flight West (☎ (07) 4035 9511 or through Ansett) operates a service through the Gulf, Cape York Peninsula and to Bamaga ($275).

For a bit of airborne nostalgia, DC3 Australia has daily DC3 flights to Cooktown from $190 return, though these are tours rather than scheduled flights. For something completely different, Cape York Air Services (☎ (07) 4035 9399), the local mail contractor, does mail runs to remote outback stations on weekdays. Space permitting, you can go along on these runs for $195 to $390, depending on the length of the trip.

Car Rental Avis, Budget, Hertz and Thrifty have desks at the international airport terminal. In town, the major firms are along Sheridan St, but local firms have mushroomed all over Cairns and some of them offer good deals, particularly for weekly rental. However, don't be taken in by cut-rates advertising: once you add in all the hidden costs, prices are fairly similar everywhere. Shop around and find the deal that suits. Generally, small cars start from around $50, and regular cars from $65 up. 4WDs start at around $110 – see the Cape York section for details.

The majority of Cairns' rental firms specifically prohibit you from taking most of their cars up the Cape Tribulation road, on the road to Cooktown, or on the Chillagoe Caves road. A sign in the car will sometimes announce this prohibition and the contract will threaten dire unhappiness if you do so. Of course, lots of people ignore these prohibitions, but if you get stuck in the mud halfway to Cape Tribulation, it could be a little embarrassing. Be warned that these roads are fairly rough and sometimes impassable in conventional vehicles.

Bicycle & Motorcycle Rental Most of the hostels and car-hire firms, plus quite a few other places, have bicycles for hire so you'll have no trouble tracking one down. Expect to pay around $15 a day. Jolly Frog (☎ 4031 2379) at 230 Sheridan St has scooters from $29 and larger motorcycles from $65 a day.

Kennedy Highway

HIGHLIGHTS

- Exploring the caves and lava tubes of the Undara Crater National Park
- Fossicking for gems
- Taking a ride on the *Gulflander* train

This 720km route cuts across the rugged verdant tropical ranges just outside Cairns to the drier hills and plains that border the western side of the Great Dividing Range. Beyond Croydon, the vast flat billiard table-like plains of The Gulf begin and extend all the way to Normanton and the sea.

HISTORY

Aborigines inhabited this country for thousands of years before Europeans came along. Dutch navigators sailed the Gulf coast in 1606, while Captain James Cook sailed the east coast in 1770.

Ludwig Leichhardt and Edmund Kennedy passed through this area in the 1840s and in the early 1870s James Venture Mulligan discovered gold. Later, further west, a series of mineral discoveries saw the founding of Georgetown and Forsayth to service the Etheridge Goldfield; Mount Garnet to service the nearby copper and silver mine; Herberton to service the nearby tin fields; Croydon to supply the nearby goldfields; and Chillagoe to support the surrounding copper, silver and tin mines.

Away from the timber mills, mines and mineral fields, sugar is the mainstay of the coastal farming land, while on the Atherton Tablelands, dairy cattle, tobacco and a host of other crops are grown. Further west, cattle are the livelihood of the vast sprawling properties that sometimes cover hundreds of thousands of hectares.

INFORMATION
Tourist Offices

Travellers will find tourist information centres in most of the towns along the route. In addition, information is available from the following tourism bodies:

Far North Queensland Promotion Bureau
  PO Box 865, Cairns, Qld 4870 (☎ (07) 4051 3588; fax 4051 0127)
Gulf Savannah Tourist Association
  PO Box 2312, Cairns, Qld 4870 (☎ (07) 4031 1631; fax 4031 3340)
Outback Queensland Tourism Authority Inc
  PO Box 356, Mount Isa, Qld 4825 (☎ (07) 4743 7966; fax 4743 8746)

For information on any of the national parks, contact the Department of Environment & Heritage in Brisbane (☎ (07) 3227 7111) or Townsville (☎ (07) 4743 2055).

For details and permits on fossicking contact the Mining Registrar in Georgetown, (☎ (07) 4062 1204).

Books & Maps

The Queensland Tourist & Travel Corporation has produced the excellent book *The Reef to the Rock*, while the state mapping authority has produced a map called *North Queensland*. Both are readily available from good book and map shops.

THE ROUTE
Cairns to Ravenshoe (147km)

The easiest route between Cairns and Ravenshoe, and one of the shortest, is to head north on the Bruce Highway and, 13km north of the city centre, veer left towards Kuranda on the Kennedy Highway.

Kuranda, 27km from Cairns, is known as 'the village in the rainforest' and is a popular day trip for those staying in Cairns.

You then come to the outskirts of **Mareeba** about 35km further on and 64km from Cairns. The main business area is to your right and can supply all a traveller requires, but left will continue your trip on the Kennedy Highway south.

At **Atherton**, 30km south of Mareeba, the Gillies Highway comes in from the east but our route continues south along the Kennedy. At the junction of the Kennedy and Palmerston highways, 49km south of Atherton, turn right onto the Palmerston Highway and 4km later you are in the heart of Ravenshoe.

For details on the other routes to Ravenshoe see Detours, later in this chapter.

Ravenshoe

Ravenshoe promotes itself as the gateway to the Gulf. The town can supply all the basic requirements for a traveller, including a range of accommodation. There's plenty to see and do in and around the town and the area is also popular with those looking for **gemstones**.

Just to the south-west of the town is the **Millstream Falls National Park**, protecting the Millstream Falls, the widest in Australia. South of the town is **Tully Gorge National Park** and **Tully Falls**.

THE TROPICS

West to Georgetown (265km)

Heading west on the Kennedy Highway for 29km brings you to **Innot Hot Springs**, where limited accommodation and camping is available. There are mineral springs and mud baths, while nearby, topaz can be found in the gem fields.

Another 15km along the highway you arrive in the old copper town of **Mt Garnet**, now famous for its local gemstones such as sapphires and topaz, found in the nearby **gemfields**. The town offers accommodation and camping, along with limited supplies.

The highway swings south from Mt Garnet and 55km from the town you enter the **Forty Mile Scrub National Park**. This park covers over 4600 hectares and protects subtropical rainforest and vine thickets, and many species of birds can be seen.

Just a few kilometres south and 66km from Mt Garnet you come to a major road junction. Here you need to turn right. Continuing south on the Kennedy takes you, via a more scenic route, The Lynd Junction where you can head west to Einasleigh and Forsayth, joining our route at Georgetown. See Detours at the end of this section for more details.

The road west continues to be good bitumen, even though you have now left the Kennedy Highway and are on the Gulf Developmental Road.

Undara Crater National Park The turn-off to the Undara Crater National Park and the Undara Lava Lodge (☎ (07) 4097 1411; fax 4097 1450) is on the left, 17km from the Kennedy Highway junction. You must take time out to visit this park and the fabulous caves and lava tubes, which lie about 15km from the main road.

The lodge offers accommodation and camping, as well as meals and snacks. A guiding service to visit the lava tubes is available and tours are held each day.

West to Mount Surprise The road continues westward through country that is much drier than before, and 56km from the Kennedy Highway junction you come to the small railway township of **Mount Surprise**.

This small hamlet has limited accommodation and supplies, and offers the traveller access to a number of gem fields, including the **O'Briens Creek Topaz Field**.

The town is also well known for its September **rodeo** and for the **Savannahlander** (☎ (07) 4052 6249 or 13 22 32), a historic train ride between Mount Surprise and Forsayth via Einasleigh. After leaving Mount Surprise the road strikes west through lightly undulating wooded savanna grassland, crossing the Einasleigh River 36km from the town.

Just 5km further on is the turn-off to **Tallaroo Hot Water Springs** (☎ (07) 4062 1221). It's a top spot to pass the heat of the day, and a small kiosk provides light lunches and refreshments.

You cross over the often near-dry bed of the Etheridge River and enter Georgetown, 52km later, or 149km from the Kennedy Highway junction and 265km from Ravenshoe.

Georgetown

Georgetown, with a population of around 300, is the service centre for a large area of surrounding cattle country and the few mines that still dot the region.

There are a number of places to stay in town, including a couple of caravan parks, a hotel and a lodge. All the basic requirements and supplies for travellers can be found here.

There is some excellent **fossicking** in the area for such precious stones as sapphires, topaz, aquamarine and quartz.

Across the Gulf Plains to Normanton (302km)

The bitumen continues as one heads west to the next major town, Croydon. The **Gilbert River** is crossed 74km from Georgetown, and 76km later you arrive in the historic and small town of Croydon.

Croydon This town was established when gold was discovered nearby in 1885 and its longevity seemed assured when the railway

THE TROPICS

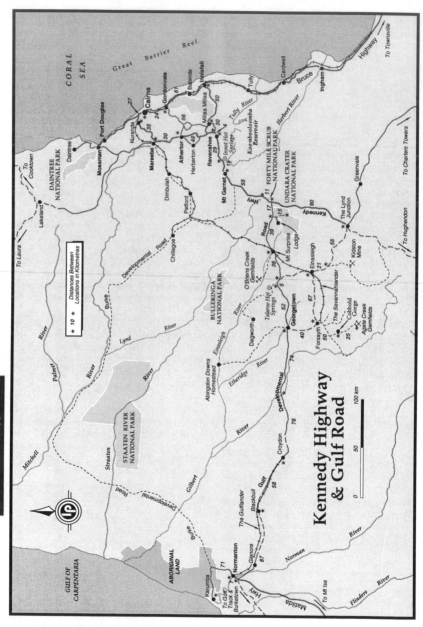

THE TROPICS

Kennedy Highway & Gulf Road

from Normanton was rerouted to Croydon in 1891. By 1925 the gold had petered out and the town was near deserted. The unique and isolated railway, the *Gulflander*, is now a tourist attraction running between Normanton and Croydon once a week.

The town has a pub, a caravan park, and a general store/roadhouse, where you can buy fuel and limited supplies.

West to Normanton Heading on, the road continues to be blacktop, but between here and Normanton expect a few patches of well-maintained dirt, although this is decreasing each year.

The road follows the railway line for most of the way, and 58km later crosses the railway line at **Blackbull**, a deserted railway siding.

Another 61km westward, the road crosses the **Norman River** and a further 26km brings you to a major road junction where you need to veer right. You are in the heart of **Normanton** 7km later, 152km from Croydon and 302km from Georgetown.

There is a wide range of accommodation, general stores and fuel supplies in Normanton, which is the major town on the Gulf. For more information on Normanton see the Matilda Highway section later.

DETOURS
Cairns to Ravenshoe via the Palmerston Highway (165km)
Head out of Cairns, down the Bruce Highway towards **Innisfail**. About 85km from Cairns, at a well signposted junction, turn west onto the **Palmeston Highway**.

For the next 20km or so the road passes through sugarcane fields and then begins to climb the range. For much of the way the route passes through **Bartle Frere National Park**.

Approaching **Millaa Millaa**, farmland again becomes the dominant surroundings and the small township is entered 50km from the Bruce Highway junction.

From Millaa Millaa it is another 30km across undulating rich green country to Ravenshoe.

Cairns to Ravenshoe via Gillies Highway (135km)
Head south on the Bruce Highway for 24km and, close to the town of Gordonvale, turn right onto the Gillies Highway and follow the Mulgrave River valley up into the mountains.

About 10km later the road crosses the Little Mulgrave River and then climbs steeply to the top of the range, passing **Lake Barrine National Park**, and just a few kilometres up the road **Lake Eacham National Park**.

Less than 20km later, and 56km from the Bruce Highway junction, you enter Atherton and come to the main road south – the Kennedy Highway. Here you need to turn left. See the start of this section for details on the route to Ravenshoe.

This is the shortest route to take, and because of the Little Mulgrave River, the lakes and the dams, it is our favourite.

The Etheridge Loop (273km)
Head down the Kennedy Highway from the road junction with the Gulf Developmental Road for another 90km before coming to the small hamlet of The Lynd Junction, where you will find the **Oasis Roadhouse** (☎ (07) 4062 5291). The roadhouse has camping facilities, fuel and limited supplies.

Turn right here onto a good dirt road and head west to Einasleigh. About 55km later you'll pass the turn-off to one of the largest open-cut gold mines in Australia, the Kidson Mine, but there is no public access allowed.

Just over 20km further north, and 76km from the Lynd Junction, you'll enter the small township of **Einasleigh**. The *Central Hotel* (☎ (07) 4062 5222) offers limited accommodation, basic food supplies and fuel.

Head west out of town towards Forsayth and just 67km from the Central Hotel you arrive in **Forsayth** with its *Goldfields Tavern* (☎ (07) 4062 5374) being the only place for a beer, meal, limited accommodation, camping, food supplies and fuel. The town is an excellent base to fossick in the surrounding area.

Agate Creek, 75km south of the town, is a very popular gemfield, but there are no facilities. Cobbold Gorge Tours (☎ (07) 4062 5470) runs boat tours of the gorge of the same name on their property, 50km south of Forsayth.

The 40km to Georgetown from Forsayth continues along a fairly good dirt road and at Georgetown you can turn left to continue the trek west to Normanton.

ORGANISED TOURS
Contact the various tourism bodies and regional tourist information centres for details of local tour operators.

FACILITIES
Atherton
There are a number of motels and inns in Atherton offering a range of accommodation, such as the *Wrights Motor Inn* (☎ (07) 4095 4141), with rooms from $42/45 a single/double.

The *Atherton Woodlands Tourist Park* (☎ (07) 4091 1407) has powered/unpowered sites for $15/12 a double.

Most of the major banks are represented in Atherton, such as the ANZ, Commonwealth, National and Westpac.

The local RACQ depot is the All Wheel Drive Centre, Vernon St (☎ (07) 4091 1555, after hours 4091 4016).

Ravenshoe
There are a number of establishments offering a range of accommodation, such as the *Club* (☎ (07) 4097 6109) and *Kool Moon* (☎ (07) 4097 6407) with rooms costing $30/40 and $38/48 for singles/doubles. It also has a restaurant and fuel sales.

The *Tall Timbers Caravan Park* (☎ (07) 4097 6325) has powered/unpowered sites at $12.50/10 a double.

The banks represented in Ravenshoe include the Commonwealth and National.

The Ravenshoe Foodstore can supply your grocery needs, as can Ladbrook's Foodtown.

Innot Hot Springs
The *Hot Springs Hotel/Motel* (☎ (07) 4097 0203), beside the hot springs, has units for $25/40 a single/double and counter meals are available.

Mt Garnet
The *Norwestgate Travellers Rest Resort & Van Park* (☎ (07) 4097 9249) is also a roadhouse open seven days a week. The resort has a number of units costing $30/40 a single/double, and caravan/campsites at $10/8 a double, powered and unpowered.

The local RACQ depot is Garnet Auto Repairs, Kennedy Highway (☎ (07) 4097 9156 all hours).

Undara Crater National Park
Although this is a national park, the *Undara Lava Lodge* (☎ (07) 4097 1411) has all facilities, with accommodation at $98 a double for bed & breakfast, or you can stay in a tent in the Swags Tent Village for $14 a double. There's another camping area that has most facilities, but no power. Sites cost $16 a double. Bookings are essential for both the lodge and campsites and pets are not allowed.

Mount Surprise
The *Mount Surprise Hotel* (☎ (07) 4062 3118) has rooms available at $20/40 a single/double. The *Shell Service Station and Caravan Park* (tel/fax (07) 4062 3153) can cater for all a traveller's needs, with caravan and campsites at $13/10 a double, powered and unpowered.

Georgetown
The *Wenaru Hotel* (☎ (07) 4062 1208) has accommodation for $25/40 a single/double.

There's a couple of caravan parks in Georgetown – the *Goldfields Caravan Park* (☎ (07) 4062 1269) and the *Midway Caravan Park* (☎ (07) 4062 1219).

Services found in Georgetown include a

bakery and butcher, while the local RACQ depot is Peninsula Freighters, St George St (☎ (07) 4062 1134 all hours).

Local tourist information can be obtained from the Etheridge Shire Council, St George St (☎ (07) 4062 1233).

Croydon

Visitors to Croydon can choose to stay at the *Croydon Club Hotel* (☎ (07) 4745 6184) with rooms costing $25/35 a single/double, or in motel units at the rear of the hotel for $30/45 per single/double. The *Golden Pic-dewehousma Caravan Park* (☎ (07) 4745 6238) has sites from $10.

The *Croydon General Store, Museum & Service Station* (☎ (07) 4745 6163) in Sircom St, can supply all your grocery items and all your vehicle needs. The store is also the local RACQ depot (☎ (07) 4745 6163 all hours).

For further tourist information contact the Croydon Shire Council, Samwell St (☎ (07) 4745 6125).

ALTERNATIVE TRANSPORT
Air

Charter flight is the only way to get around this part of Queensland and there are a number of air charters available, mainly based in Cairns. Contact the tourist information centres or the Far North Queensland Promotion Bureau for details.

Bus

Cairns-Karumba Coachlines (☎ (07) 4041 2295) operates a service from Cairns to Georgetown and Forsayth. The bus departs Cairns on Monday, Wednesday and Thursday at 6.45 am and returns from Georgetown on Tuesday, Thursday and Friday at 1.30 pm. The fare is $64 one way.

Car Rental

There are several car-rental companies in Cairns to choose from. See the Cairns section for details, or contact the Far North Queensland Promotion Bureau.

Cairns to Musgrave via Cooktown

For those who don't have time to travel to the very top of Cape York, but still want to sample the delights of Far North Queensland away from the glitz and glamour of Cairns and Port Douglas, then an interesting loop to do is from Cairns to Cooktown and on to Musgrave via Battle Camp and Lakefield National Park, returning to Cairns via Laura and the Peninsula Developmental Road. For travellers who want to travel to the top of Cape York, but want something a little different to the main road, this route gives a more enjoyable alternative.

The route north from Cairns along the coast to Cape Tribulation and then through the ranges to Cooktown is very scenic and popular. The road north of Cape Tribulation was surrounded by controversy when it was built in the early 1980s because of environmental concerns about the effect it would have on the rainforest. Although the Green movement was out in force, the road was pushed through anyway. Indeed some damage was caused, but for many travellers it offers a chance to see and appreciate this wild part of Australia. The locals in Cooktown also appreciate this shorter access road from Cairns, rather than having to take the corrugated and much longer inland route.

North of Cooktown this route once again

THE TROPICS

cuts across the Great Dividing Range before descending onto the vast flood plains that make up much of Lakefield National Park. During the Wet the rivers often coalesce to make a shallow inland sea, which in turn is replaced during the Dry by a sea of waving grass cut by tree-lined billabongs and lagoons.

At its northernmost point the route passes very close to the shores of Princess Charlotte Bay, before swinging westwards to the Pen insula Developmental Road at the small enclave of Musgrave.

Cooktown is just one of the highlights of this trip, and the natural delights of Lakefield National Park and the Aboriginal rock art in the Laura area are a couple of others. You could easily spend a couple of weeks just in this region of Far North Queensland.

HISTORY

Aborigines occupied much of this land long before the arrival of the Europeans. They inhabited the flood plains and the escarpment country as well as the rainforested mountains along the coast. They travelled the rivers by canoe and at times made forays out to the close offshore islands.

Captain James Cook almost came to grief near Cooktown during his voyage of discovery when he mapped the east coast of Australia. On the night of 11 June 1770 the *Endeavour* hit a reef and it was only after some heavy gear, including a few cannons, were dropped over the side that the ship was refloated. Eleven days later they pulled into the mouth of the Endeavour River and careened their ship for repairs. Cook stayed here until 6 August, his longest foray on the Australian mainland. In that time he managed to repair his ship while his botanist, Sir Joseph Banks, explored the river and collected specimens, including the first kangaroo to be described by a European.

Cook decided to escape the intricate maze of the inner reef. He landed on and named Lizard Island. He was later to come back inside the reef, preferring to navigate the inner reef to the constant danger of being pushed onto the outer reef. With his depar-

ture the Aborigines were left in peace for another 100 years.

In 1865 John Jardine, on his way back from Somerset on the tip of Cape York, sailed up the Endeavour River and later explored and named the Annan River, a little further south. For more information on the Jardine family, see the boxed story on Frank Jardine in the Cape York section.

When James Venture Mulligan discovered gold on the Palmer River in 1873, the area was changed forever. By 1874 over 15,000 men were on the Palmer River gold field, most of them coming via the newly founded port of Cooktown. The town quickly grew and by the end of that year there were supposedly 36 shanties where you could buy grog!

The Aboriginal tribes of the area resisted the invasion of European and Chinese miners every step of the way. In fact the first group of miners (which included a warden and police) to travel to the gold field from Cooktown were attacked by a large group of Aborigines at a place they called Battle Camp. In that battle the Aborigines attacked in waves but were met by a vicious onslaught of gunfire. Repelled, the Aborigines resorted to hit-and-run tactics which over the years left dozens of miners dead. How many Aborigines were killed is impossible to say, but those who survived had to face the more deadly threat of new and potent diseases that the invaders brought with them.

INFORMATION

The distances between fuel stops aren't great and the condition of the road is pretty fair at most times of the year. However, if you break down, you can still be in for a long wait. There is no LPG available beyond Cooktown.

Permits are not required for this route and there's no need to register with police. However, in the Lakefield National Park you do require a camping permit.

Tourist Information

Information sources along the way include:

Far North Queensland Promotion Bureau
     PO Box 865, Cairns, Qld 4870 (☎ (07) 4051 3588; fax 4051 0127)
Department of Environment and Heritage
     Far North Regional Centre, 10-12 McLeod St, PO Box 2066, Cairns, Qld 4870 (☎ (07) 4052 3096; fax 4052 3080)
Cape Tribulation Tourist Information Centre
     Centre Rd, Cape Tribulation, Qld (☎ (07) 4098 0070)
Cook Shire Council
     Charlotte St, PO Box 3, Cooktown, Qld 4871 (☎ (07) 4069 5444; fax 4069 5423)
Croc Shop
     8 Charlotte St, Cooktown (☎ (07) 4069 5880)
Ang-Gnarra Aboriginal Corporation
     Post Office, Laura, Qld 4871 (☎ (07) 4060 3214; fax 4060 3231) – information is available on Aboriginal rock-art sites around Laura, and brochures and maps are available of the sites open to the public

Police

The police can be a good source of information for travellers. The Cooktown police station (☎ (07) 4069 5320) is on Charlotte St. The Hope Vale Aboriginal community police station (☎ (07) 4060 9224) is at 4 Flierl St while the Laura police station (☎ (07) 4060 3244) is on the main road into town.

Medical Services

The Cooktown hospital (☎ (07) 4069 5433) is on Hope St, and there is a dentist (☎ (07) 4069 5679) on Helen St.

There is a clinic (☎ (07) 4060 3320) in Laura.

Books & Maps

There are a number of good maps and guidebooks readily available, especially in the Cairns/Cooktown region. The Hema map *Cape York* and the RACQ maps *Cairns/ Townsville* and *Cape York Peninsula* are the best. Ron & Viv Moon's *Cape York – an Adventurer's Guide* (Kakirra Adventure Publications) is the most comprehensive guidebook for the do-it-yourself camper and 4WD enthusiast.

The best book on Cooktown is the *Queen of the North* by Glenville Pike; *Cape York* by

Hector Holthouse (Australian Geographic) also covers this area.

For the area around the Daintree River and Cape Tribulation, the book *Daintree – Where the Rainforest Meets the Reef* (Australian Conservation Foundation and Kevin Weldon & Associates) is a beauty but may be hard to get.

There are no modern books readily available that give a comprehensive look at the Aboriginal art of the area. Percy Trezise wrote *Quinkan Country* and *Last Days of a Wilderness*, as well as a report titled *Rock Art of South East Cape York*, which was produced some years ago by the Australian Institute of Aboriginal Studies. They are difficult to get now.

THE ROUTE
Cairns to Cooktown via the Coast (254km)

From Cairns you head north along the coast through Mossman towards the tropical village of Daintree. This is one of the most pleasant coastal drives in Australia and it is worth taking your time. For those cycling their way north, the pedalling is pretty easy and there are plenty of places to stop, enjoy the view and rest a while.

Turn off the Daintree Road 25km north of Mossman, 101km from Cairns, onto the Cape Tribulation Road. You cross the **Daintree River** by a small ferry 5km later. The ferry operates from 6 am to 6 pm. The road surface from the river crossing is constantly being worked on, and travellers will find sections of bitumen from here.

The road continues through rainforest and is generally good enough for the family car driven with care. Some of the potholes can make it interesting for a heavily loaded cyclist, but they will be worse further north. Initially, much of the surrounding country is private land and there is little to do but drive, or ride, on.

At **Cow Bay**, 10km north of the ferry and 3km off the main road north, the Cow Bay Hotel provides accommodation and meals. **Thornton Beach** is 20km north of the river crossing. You can launch a boat here and have a meal at the Thornton Beach Kiosk.

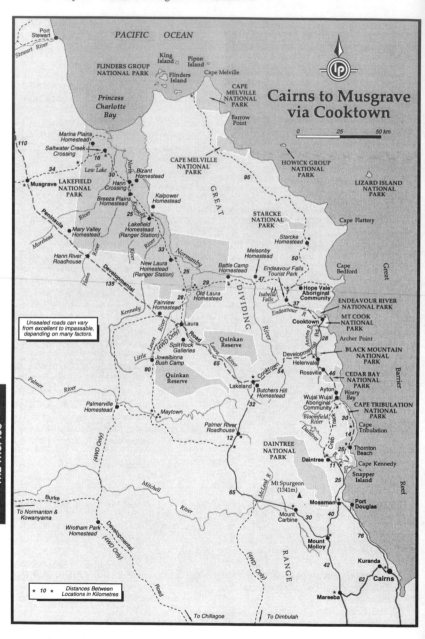

THE TROPICS

Cape Tribulation, 14km further north, is a popular destination, with lush rainforest that tumbles down the hills right to the high-tide mark of a pleasant beach. There is accommodation of all styles and for all budgets. Food and fuel are available from the general store.

North from here the road deteriorates a little, and where it climbs the ranges it becomes a challenge even for a 4WD after any rain. For walkers and those pedalling a mountain bike, the effort is rewarded with magnificent views over the offshore reefs and the surrounding rainforest.

The **Bloomfield River** is crossed 30km north of Cape Tribulation. The crossing has a causeway, but you'll still get your feet or tyres wet.

The **Wujal Wujal Aboriginal community** is on the northern bank of the river. Stick to the main road heading north to Ayton and Cooktown and you won't need a permit. In the tiny hamlet of **Ayton**, accommodation and camping are available at the very pleasant Bloomfield Beach camping ground, or you can stay at the more remote resort of the Bloomfield Wilderness Lodge. Food and fuel are available at the Bloomfield River Inn and the Ayton Store.

The road, which can be dusty, passes through **Cedar Bay National Park**, which stretches inland a short distance. There are no facilities here, and access into the park is either by boat or by walking along numerous small tracks through the bush.

Continue from Cedar Bay National Park to **Rossville**, another small hamlet, and then **Helenvale**, site of the famous **Lion's Den Hotel**, 42km north of Wujal Wujal. There are a couple of lodges around Rossville and Helenvale which offer accommodation and camping.

From Helenvale, it is just 4km to the main Cooktown Road and then another 28km to Cooktown.

Cooktown

The 'Queen of the North', as it is often called, lies on the banks of the Endeavour River, close to where Captain James Cook careened his ship for repairs in 1770. Cooktown is a well-established town with a pervading sense of history. As well as fishing charters to the offshore reefs, it also has one of the best museums in Australia. There is a good range of accommodation options with a number of camping/caravan parks, hotels, motels and lodges to pamper the jaded traveller, as well as all the usual facilities.

History With the discovery of gold on the Palmer River in 1873, Cooktown was founded

---

The Lion's Den Hotel

Built in 1875, the pub has seen little maintenance since then. Its internal decorations have been left by generations of stockmen, tin miners and hippies (from the more recent Cedar Bay days), and the place just oozes character.

On our first trip to Cooktown, back in the 1970s, an army-boot-wearing, moustached, tin-mining lady told me that you haven't been to Cooktown if you haven't been to the Lion's Den. I wasn't game to argue!

Such is the fame of this outback watering hole that Bert Cummings wrote *The Lion's Den – A Pub Yarn* (Angus & Robertson) about it. While the book may not be the complete story of this wild place, it does give you some idea of what has, and does, go on in this hotel that has been on the edge of the frontier for over 100 years.

One thing that does set it apart from the norm is its licensees. The pub was in the same family from 1875 to 1964 and since then all the licensees have been women. Maybe they are the only ones who can hack the pace!

The pub offers accommodation, excellent camping down on the banks of the Annan River, limited supplies and fuel. For more information, see the Facilities section.

Viv Moon

and within a year had grown to a town of 15,000 people. By the turn of the century the population was over 35,000 and there were 65 registered hotels, 20 eating houses and 30-odd general stores. Other ports further south along the coast competed for the prize of being the port to feed the Palmer River gold field. But it was the demise of the gold field due to its lack of rich reef gold that heralded the slow decline of Cooktown.

There was still no road connection to Cooktown in 1930, the town relying on small coastal freighters for its supplies and mail. Cooktown and Laura were connected by a light rail from 1885, but it never reached the Palmer River gold field, despite that being its major destination.

During WWII most of the town population was evacuated and the surrounding area became a forward base for US and Australian servicemen fighting in New Guinea and the Coral Sea.

In 1949 Cooktown suffered a major setback when it was devastated by a cyclone. Much of it was completely flattened and those buildings that remained were badly damaged.

Cooktown, however, refused to die, and in the 1950s the tourists began to arrive. At first it was just a straggle of keen adventurers, but by the 1970s it was a near flood, especially for the months of the dry season.

Today the future of the town is vested in tourism and the vast hinterland that it has served for over 100 years.

Things to See & Do The **waterfront**, which in the past saw so much action, is a pleasant place to wander. At the north end you can check the **old powder magazine** from the days when there was a lot of mining going on, or cast a line from one of the best fishing spots on the coast. Further south you can look over the river to the north bank and the **Endeavour River National Park**, at a scene that has not changed since Cook repaired his stricken ship there.

A number of **monuments** dot the little park that borders the river, not only from Cook's day, but also from more recent times.

In 1889, when Russia was considered a threat, one lone 1803 vintage cannon was installed to defend Cooktown.

The **James Cook Historical Museum** (☎ (07) 4069 5386), on the corner of Helen and Furneaux Sts, should not be missed. It portrays much of the life and times of the early days and has some award-winning displays. The museum is open seven days a week from 10 am to 4 pm.

The **Cooktown Sea Museum** (☎ (07) 4069 5209), on Walker St, has interesting displays of the nautical history of Cooktown and Cape York.

The **lighthouse** on Grassy Hill, named by Cook but no longer grassy, gives a good view of the surrounding area.

The **Cooktown Cemetery** has a unique Chinese shrine and many interesting gravestones, including that of Mrs Watson, the 'Heroine of Lizard Island'.

Many of the **historic buildings** along the main streets are still used commercially. The Westpac Bank building was built in 1878 and is typical of gold-rush buildings – some of the timber work inside is well worth seeing. The Cooktown Hotel, once called the Commercial, was opened in 1875, while the West Coast Hotel had been built a year earlier. The shire offices were erected in 1877 and the post office in 1897. There are many other buildings of historic significance, and just walking around this town is a worthwhile experience.

If you get sick of the historic trail, you can always head for one of the beaches. **Finch Bay**, less than 2km east of the post office, is a popular spot for a dip or a barbecue. **Walker Bay** and **Archer Point**, further south, offer an unspoilt coastline.

The big month to be in Cooktown is June. The **Cooktown Endeavour Festival** is held over the Queen's Birthday weekend, and highlights of the three-day event include a re-enactment of Cook's landing in 1770, along with a colourful gala ball, various sporting events, horse races and rides and a fishing competition. Contact the Cooktown Discovery Festival (☎ (07) 4069 5166), PO Box 630, Cooktown, Qld 4871, for further

Top: Camping on the Little Bynoe River, along the Gulf Track, Qld
Bottom: The Purple Pub, Normanton, Qld

R & V MOON

HUGH FINLAY

Top: The Lost City, NT
Bottom: Young and old participate in traditional dancing, Barunga, NT

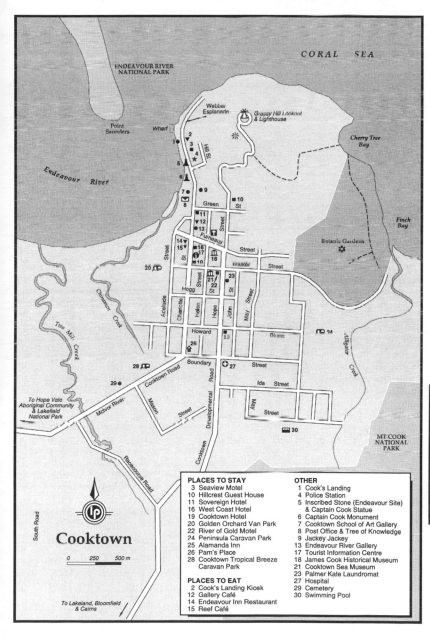

CORAL SEA

ENDEAVOUR RIVER
NATIONAL PARK

Webber
Esplanade

Grassy Hill Lookout
& Lighthouse

Point
Saunders

Wharf

Cherry Tree
Bay

Endeavour River

Finch
Bay

Green
St

Botanic Gardens

Furneaux

Street

Walker   Street

Cinnamon Creek

Hogg

Two Mile Creek

Charlotte

Hope

John

May

Howard

Queen

Boundary

Cooktown Road

To Hope Vale
Aboriginal Community
& Lakefield
National Park

McIvor River

Mason

Street

Ida   Street

May

Street

MT COOK
NATIONAL
PARK

South Road

THE TROPICS

Cooktown

0   250   500 m

To Lakeland, Bloomfield
& Cairns

PLACES TO STAY
3   Seaview Motel
10 Hillcrest Guest House
11 Sovereign Hotel
16 West Coast Hotel
19 Cooktown Hotel
20 Golden Orchard Van Park
22 River of Gold Motel
24 Peninsula Caravan Park
25 Alamanda Inn
26 Pam's Place
28 Cooktown Tropical Breeze
     Caravan Park

PLACES TO EAT
2   Cook's Landing Kiosk
12 Gallery Café
14 Endeavour Inn Restaurant
15 Reef Café

OTHER
1   Cook's Landing
4   Police Station
5   Inscribed Stone (Endeavour Site)
     & Captain Cook Statue
6   Captain Cook Monument
7   Cooktown School of Art Gallery
8   Post Office & Tree of Knowledge
9   Jackey Jackey
13 Endeavour River Gallery
17 Tourist Information Centre
18 James Cook Historical Museum
21 Cooktown Sea Museum
23 Palmer Kate Laundromat
27 Hospital
29 Cemetery
30 Swimming Pool

details. Cooktown has an **art show** in June as well.

The local Turf Club holds two, two-day race meetings a year – in June and August. These are popular events for the locals and the town is crowded with people from the stations as far away as Weipa for the sport and the socialising.

Cooktown to Musgrave (275km)

Once you leave Cooktown you head into the most isolated part of the trip. It is 275km to Musgrave without any fuel stops along the way. For those doing it the hard way – walking or pedalling – the distances between water, especially towards the end of the Dry, can be a fair way and other travellers are few and far between. You must be prepared to carry enough water to get between the permanent water points.

Head out of town along the McIvor River Rd, past the cemetery, racecourse and airport before crossing the **Endeavour River**. The Endeavour Falls Tourist Park is 33km from Cooktown and offers camping and a kiosk for basic supplies (see Facilities later in this section).

There is a junction at the 37km mark. The road to the right leads to the **Hope Vale Aboriginal community**. The Hope Vale Show & Rodeo is staged in July or August each year. The community has artefacts for sale, and you can also buy fuel and supplies. For full details, contact the Administration Clerk (☎ (07) 4060 9185), Hope Vale Aboriginal Community Council, Thiele St, Hope Vale.

Back at the junction that took you to Hope Vale, head west. About 5km further on is a stony river crossing and just downstream is **Isabella Falls**. This is a magic spot; it's worth a stop and even a swim!

Keep left at the next junction 3km up the road. From here the road begins to climb the range and patches of rainforest begin. The turn-off to **Melsonby station** homestead is met some 63km from Cooktown. Peaceful, pleasant camping and tours are available.

The **Normanby River** is crossed less than 2km later. Early in the Dry this river will

have water in it, but by the end of the season it is just a sandy bed. There are pools up and down stream. Keep on the main track heading west across flat country, and 20km from the river crossing you will pass the turn-off to **Battle Camp station**. The mountains to the south are the rugged Battle Camp Range. Less than 3km further on you enter **Lakefield National Park**.

There is a large number of campsites spread along the rivers and billabongs of the park. You will often see tracks leading to these as you travel along the main track. If you want to camp here, you'll need to get a permit. The ranger will let you know the best spot to camp. The ranger station is at **New Laura homestead**, 51km from the park boundary. For more information, see Camping in the boxed story on Lakefield National Park.

The **Laura River** is crossed 25km from the park boundary (114km from Cooktown). This crossing can be a little hairy early in the Dry, but by the end of the season it is generally no problem.

The **Old Laura homestead** on the far bank is worth a good look around. Pioneers lived here and in places like this right through the Cape, and after they had built such a place they thought they were on easy street. Most of us couldn't handle this sort of luxury for too long before we'd be running back to modern civilisation!

Just past the homestead and within 1km of the river crossing, you reach a T-junction. Turning left here will take you south to Laura, 28km away. This is the nearest place for fuel and supplies if you have decided to stay in the park for longer.

Laura This is a good little town in which to enjoy a beer at the pub under the mango trees, or make a base to explore the surrounding area and visit the Aboriginal rock-art galleries. You can also visit the **Jowalbinna Bush Camp**, a wilderness reserve not far from Laura. For further information, see the Organised Tours section.

The Cape York Aboriginal Dance Festival is held near Laura, on the banks of the Laura

Lakefield National Park

Lakefield National Park is the second-largest national park in Queensland and covers over 537,000 hectares. It encompasses a wide variety of country around the flood plains of the Normanby, Kennedy, Bizant, Morehead and Hann rivers.

During the wet season these rivers flood the plains, at times forming a small inland sea. Access during this time is limited or nonexistent. As the dry season begins, the rivers gradually retreat to form a chain of deep waterholes and billabongs. Along these rivers, rainforest patches are in stark contrast to the surrounding grass plains and eucalypt woodland.

Flora & Fauna In the north of the park, around Princess Charlotte Bay, mud flats and mangroves line the coast and the estuaries of the rivers. It might be an area that is full of sandflies, mosquitoes and crocodiles, but this is the nursery for the fish and marine life for which the area is so well known.

As the Dry progresses, the bird life begins to congregate around the permanent waters, and at times thousands of ducks and geese create an unholy noise but a spectacular sight. Groups of brolgas dance on the open plain, and tall stately jabirus stalk their way through the grass. Birds of prey soar on the thermals looking for a meal, while in the deepest, darkest patches of the rainforest, pheasant coucals and Torres Strait pigeons can be found. In all, over 180 species of birds have been identified in the park. At times like these, a small pair of binoculars comes in handy.

Agile wallabies are probably the most commonly seen mammal in the park, but feral pigs are prevalent and a problem for the park staff. Bats make up the largest group of mammals found here. The large flying foxes are an impressive sight as they burst from their roosting spots in their thousands on their evening search for nectar and fruit. You won't forget the sight, the smell, or the damage they can do to the trees in which they roost.

Crocodiles Both freshwater and saltwater (estuarine) crocodiles are found in this park. Lakefield National Park is one of five areas in the state designated as important for the ongoing conservation of the estuarine crocodile in Queensland, and for many people it offers the best chance of seeing one of these animals in the wild.

Fishing Lakefield National Park is one of the few parks in Queensland where you are allowed to fish, and the barramundi is the prize catch. A closed season applies between 1 November and 31 January, and at other times there's a bag limit of two fish per day, with no more than five fish to be taken out of the park. Line fishing is the only method allowed to catch these magnificent fish.

Canoeing & Boating Many of the big waterholes make for excellent canoeing or boating, and you can spend many enjoyable hours paddling a quiet stretch of water, watching birds or the animals as they come down to drink.

It should be noted, however, that the rangers do not recommend canoeing in the park because of the presence of saltwater crocodiles.

Camping Camping is allowed in a number of places, with a permit. A camping fee is payable for each night spent in the park, with a maximum of 21 nights allowed. Permits are available from the rangers at New Laura (☎ (07) 4060 3260) or Lakefield (☎ (07) 4060 3271). Bookings may be made six to 12 weeks in advance by writing to the ranger, Lakefield National Park, PMB 29, Cairns Mail Centre, Qld 4871. Say what you are interested in and the vehicle you have, and the ranger will let you know the best spots to camp. If you have the time, try a couple of different locations. ∎

THE TROPICS

River. It brings together Aborigines from all over Cape York for three days. The festival is usually held every year during the Queensland mid-year or September school holidays, although timing does vary from year to year. Currently, festival times are irregular, but from 1997 it may be held every two years. Contact the Ang-Gnarra Aboriginal Corporation for up-to-date information on festival dates and activities (see the Information section).

The Laura horse races and rodeo are held from Friday to Sunday on the first weekend in July. It is a great weekend where the locals from the surrounding stations show their skills and let down their hair. It has become a tradition on the Cape with people coming from far afield.

Laura to Musgrave To continue to Musgrave and deeper into the Lakefield National Park, turn right at the T-junction where you turned left to go to Laura. The **ranger station** at New Laura homestead is 25km north of the junction.

Heading north, you pass across vast grass plains, bordered by trees that line the rivers. Termite hills tower above the gold of drying grass and occasionally you'll see a shy wallaby skip across the road, or the odd mob of wild pigs. The track can be deep in dust, and walkers and cyclists will find that the sun is unrelenting. After travelling 33km, you will pass the ranger station at **Lakefield homestead**. There is an excellent camping area nearby on the banks of the Normanby River.

The turn-off to **Bizant**, occasionally a ranger station, is 15km past the Lakefield ranger station, with yet another turn-off 10km further on.

Just a few hundred metres past this track junction is the **Hann Crossing** of the North Kennedy River. For travellers passing through the national park, this is a good spot to stop.

Just downstream from the crossing there are a couple of waterfalls that drop into a large pool. The river is tidal to the base of the falls and we wouldn't advise swimming here. If you want to see how many crocodiles can inhabit a small stretch of water, take a spotlight down and check the pool one night. Count the eyes and divide by two!

There is some excellent camping upstream from the crossing. The sites are numbered and at times the place is booked out. It's safe to swim or paddle in the shallows here and the kids will love it.

The crossing itself demands a little care as it has potholes and is rough. Generally it doesn't cause any difficulty.

The **Morehead River** is crossed 13km from the Hann Crossing and is normally an easy crossing. The turn-off to **Low Lake**, a spectacular bird habitat, especially at the end of the Dry, is 15km further on. Continue straight ahead, and in less than 2km you will come to the **Saltwater Creek** crossing. The crossing

is sandy, but it is generally no problem in a 4WD. You can camp around here, but it isn't as good as the Hann Crossing.

The road swings south-west as it begins to head towards Musgrave. Keep to the left at the next few track junctions, as the tracks on the right lead to Marina Plains station. You leave the national park 16km west of Saltwater Creek.

Stick to the main track heading westward and about 8km further on you will come to the access track, on the left, to the **Lotus Bird Lodge**. Overnight accommodation with all meals is available here and the bird-watching is superb.

You will meet with the Peninsula Developmental Road, 34km after leaving the national park, just opposite **Musgrave**. Here you can get fuel, as well as food and accommodation.

Musgrave Direct to Cairns (440km)

This route along the Peninsula Developmental Road is covered in the later Cape York section. While the road is more highly maintained than the tracks you've been on, it is often very corrugated and stony – you'll even wish you were back on a dirt track at times!

ALTERNATIVE ROUTES

From Cairns there's a number of ways to get to historic Cooktown. The main route sweeps inland away from the coast and mountains, while the most scenic is the coast route. The Creb Track requires permission to cross private land at the southern end of the track.

Cairns to Cooktown via the Inland Route (322km)

The route from Cairns to Lakeland is detailed in the Cape York section. Once you reach the small hamlet of **Lakeland**, you can either turn west towards the Cape, or you can continue onwards to Cooktown. From Lakeland, at the junction of the Peninsula Developmental Road and Cooktown Road, it is a corrugated and stony trip for most of the 82km to Cooktown.

Lizard Island

Lizard Island is one of the better known islands of the Great Barrier Reef and it is readily accessible by air or boat from Cairns.

Named by Captain James Cook in 1770 after the big goannas that still roam the island, this speck of rock in a turquoise sea is home to a marine research centre and an upmarket tourist lodge. All but 60 of the island's 1070 hectares is national park and as such is open to anyone who takes the time and effort to travel there. The waters around it are part of the Great Barrier Reef Marine Park.

Most people heading out to Lizard Island are day-trippers on organised tours, or guests staying at the lodge. Don't expect any help from the lodge staff – campers don't rate too highly with them. They might be driving in a similar direction to you but you'll be walking, while the lodge guests get the seats.

Things to See & Do Don't go without taking some snorkelling gear. The waters off Mrs Watson's Beach are alive with coral and fish, as are all the bays and headlands of this island. Spear fishing is not allowed, but the fish are friendly and the snorkelling is safe. Line fishing is allowed except for the area around the Blue Lagoon.

There are any number of walks to enjoy. Don't miss the walk up to Cook's Look, the highest point on the island. This is where James Cook spied his escape from the maze of reefs that surrounded the *Endeavour*.

The remains of Mrs Watson's cottage are at the opposite end of the beach to the camping ground. This remarkable woman lived here in 1881. When her husband was away fishing for bêche-de-mer, she was attacked by Aborigines and her Chinese servant was killed. Fearing more attacks, she collected some provisions and her diary, then with her young child and a wounded servant cast herself adrift in a large boiling-down pot. They drifted north-west at the whim of the currents, finally succumbing on one of the islands near Cape Melville. The last entry in her diary was dated 11 October 1881, a poignant '...nearly dead with thirst'. Her grave, and that of her child, is still well maintained in the Cooktown cemetery.

Accommodation If you have a pocketful of money, you can book and stay in the Lizard Island Lodge (☎ (07) 4060 3999). This upmarket resort is one of the most exclusive and expensive on the reef. Dive trips, fishing, game fishing, sailing and boating are available.

Camping You can camp on the island at the very pleasant designated camping area just behind Mrs Watson's Beach. There are pit toilets, tables and water from a spring. Campers must be self-sufficient, and only charcoal fuel bead fires are permitted – fuel stoves are not allowed on flights to the island and all fallen timber, including driftwood, is protected.

You require a permit ($3 per person per night – maximum stay 10 days) from the Department of Environment & Heritage to camp on the island. You need a permit to board the aircraft as well, so plan ahead. Permits are available from the department's office at 17-19 Sheridan St, Cairns, Qld 4870 (☎ (07) 4052 3096; fax 4052 3080).

Getting There & Away Most people fly to the island, with the only scheduled flight at present being run by Sunstate Airlines (☎ 13 13 13) from Cairns. Probably the best way for campers to get there is with Marine Air (☎ (07) 4069 5915) from Cooktown. The Cooktown Tourism Association (☎ (07) 069 6100) in Charlotte St can arrange permits and organise a flight – you need a minimum of two persons and the cost is around $190 return.

For those short on time, day trips are run by a number of operators including Aussie Airways (☎ (07) 4055 9088, toll-free 1800 620 022) and the Bloomfield Beach Camping Ground (☎ (07) 4060 8207). ■

By the time you reach the **Annan River Crossing** you are looking for a change and the river provides it. You can camp here, but it is close to the road.

Walking downstream a short distance, you come to an impressive narrow gorge and waterfall that really roars when it is in flood. It's worth a look at any time.

The turn-off to **Helenvale** and the famous Lion's Den Hotel is 55km north of Lakeland, and this is a short detour that is well worth the effort. It's just 32km from Helenvale to

Cooktown and the road is bumpy most of the way.

Cairns to Cooktown via the Creb Track (256km)

The Creb Track is maintained by the state electricity authority and you require permission from the landowner (☎ (07) 4098 6107) at the southern end of the route to travel it. While it may be the shortest distance between Cairns and Cooktown, it is also the hardest and the slowest.

From the village of **Daintree**, 110km north of Cairns, you follow the Upper Daintree Road for 17km to near its end. Pass through a gate on your right and you will soon reach the headwaters of the **Daintree River**, which is easily forded in the Dry.

For the next 55km the route is spectacular, taking you over high mountains and across many picturesque creeks. For most of the way, you pass through rich and varied rainforest before coming out on the north side of the **Wujal Wujal Aboriginal community**. From here it is 74km via Helenvale and the Lion's Den Hotel to Cooktown. The track is impassable after rain.

ACTIVITIES

Along the coast, swimming and lazing on the beaches is the way to go. During the summer months, box jellyfish can be a danger. There are enclosures on some of the beaches for protection from these marine 'stingers'. Always seek local advice before plunging in for a cooling dip.

Snorkelling is also pleasant, but the water close to shore can be dirty from recent rain. The offshore reefs and islands are better if you have a boat or can join an organised trip.

Many of the local resorts organise all sorts of activities, and you don't always have to be a guest. See the later Facilities section.

Cape Tribulation

At Cape Tribulation, beach walking and exploring the adjoining rainforest are enjoyable ways to spend a couple of days.

Cooktown

The Cooktown Sport & Gamefishing Club (☎ (07) 4069 5415) runs a number of fishing tournaments between October and December each year. With barramundi and mangrove jack in the rivers and everything up to marlin in the offshore waters, the fishing and the catches can be pretty spectacular.

There is some excellent fishing in and around Cooktown and the nearby Great Barrier Reef. While there are numerous charter boats available in Cooktown, you can also hire yourself a boat from the Hire Shop (☎ (07) 4069 5601), Charlotte St.

Visitors are welcome to join the Cooktown Bushwalkers (☎ (07) 4069 5108, after hours ☎ 4069 5131) on their Sunday walk through Cooktown, taking in the flora, fauna, historical sites and unusual geological features. The group also conducts organised one to three-day walks further afield. For further information write to PO Box 195, Cooktown, Qld 4871.

Lakefield National Park

Lakefield National Park is magnificent for camping, fishing and bird-watching – see the boxed story for further information.

Laura

The small township of Laura is a good base to explore the local area, including Lakefield National Park. There are a number of Aboriginal rock-art galleries in the area that can be visited. At the most popular, Split Rock Gallery, there is a walking trail up onto the escarpment and across the plateau to the Guguyalangi group of galleries. For more details, see the following Cape York section, as well as the boxed story on Quinkan Art.

ORGANISED TOURS

There are a host of tour operators who specialise in Cape Tribulation, Cooktown and Laura. Contact the Far North Queensland Promotion Bureau (☎ (07) 4051 3588) in Cairns for full details.

Cape Tribulation

Companies that specialise in tours to Cape Tribulation include:

Tropical Horizons
    65 Greenbank Rd, Stratford, Cairns, Qld 4870 (☎ (07) 4058 1244; fax 4038 1556)
Billy Tea Bush Safaris
    PO Box 77N, North Cairns, Qld 4870 (☎ (07) 4032 0077; fax 4032 0055)
Australian Wilderness Safaris
    (☎ (07) 4098 1766; fax 4098 1983)
Strikie's Safaris
    Page Rd, Edmonton, Qld 4869 (☎ (07) 4055 4700)
Cape Tribulation Guided Rainforest Walks
    Cape Tribulation Rd, Cape Tribulation (☎ (07) 4098 0070) – also offers a tourist information service
Jungle Tours
    PO Box 179W, Westcourt, Cairns, Qld 4870 (☎ (07) 4031 5315; fax 4031 1880) – specialises in walking treks, bushwalking, sea kayaking and mountain biking

Cooktown

Land Cairns-based operators include the following:

Wilderness Challenge
    PO Box 254, Cairns, Qld 4870 (☎ (07) 4055 6504; fax 4057 7226) – safari tours to Cape Tribulation and Cooktown, extended wilderness adventures to the Cape
New Look Adventures
    PO Box 7505, Cairns, Qld 4870 (☎ (07) 4031 7622; fax 4031 7522)
Wild Track Adventure Safaris
    PO Box 2397, Cairns, Qld 4870 (☎ (07) 4055 2247; fax 4058 1930) – one, two and three-day safaris to Daintree, Cooktown and Laura

You can also join one of the local operators in Cooktown:

Cooktown Tours
    Fisherman's Wharf, Cooktown (☎ (07) 4069 5173) – local bus tours
Pam's Place
    Cnr Charlotte & Boundary Sts, Cooktown (☎ (07) 4069 5166) – tours around Cooktown, as well as 4WD tours to Laura, Cape Tribulation and Laura

Boat There are a number of boat trips out of Cooktown, some specialising in fishing, others in diving, some in both.

MV *Trudena* is a 13.5m charter boat operated by Jim Fairbairn (☎ (07) 4069 5546). There are day cruises to the adjacent reefs for fishing and snorkelling, three-day charter trips to Lizard Island and the nearby reef, or six-day charters to Princess Charlotte Bay and surrounding coast and islands. Write to PO Box 464, Cooktown, Qld 4871.

MV *Reef Safari* (☎ (07) 4069 5605 in Cooktown; (07) 4055 1100; fax 4055 1889 in Cairns), runs seven-day fishing safaris aboard the 16.2m boat. It departs from Cooktown or Lizard Island for Princess Charlotte Bay and the Great Barrier Reef. Write to PO Box 2086, Cairns, Qld 4870.

The *Coral Vista* (☎ (07) 4069 5519) is available for half-day fishing charters from Fisherman's Wharf, Cooktown.

You can also explore and cruise the Endeavour River. For bookings with Cooktown River Cruises, contact Cook's Landing Kiosk (☎ (07) 4069 5101), Webber Esplanade, Cooktown. Endeavour River cruises also depart from Cook's Landing Kiosk. Contact Cooktown Cruises (☎ (07) 4069 5712) for bookings and details.

Air Several companies operate in the Cooktown area:

Endeavour Air
    Charlotte St, Cooktown (☎ (07) 4069 5860) – charter and scenic flights
Aussie Airways
    PO Box 100, Manunda, Qld 4870 (☎ (07) 4055 9088; fax 4055 07075) – operates a one-day Cooktown Heritage tour
Marine Air Sea Planes
    (☎ (07) 4069 5915) – operates trips to offshore islands including Lizard Island

Hope Vale Aboriginal Community

Munbah Cultural Tours (☎ (07) 4060 9173), Post Office, Hope Vale, Qld 4871, is operated by the local Aboriginal community. The programme costs $100 per person per day. Visitors are shown many aspects of traditional life and enjoy a river cruise or bushwalking. Accommodation is provided

THE TROPICS

in bush-timber huts which are on the beach front, and all meals are included in the tour. Pick-up from Cooktown can be arranged. Photography is permitted on the tour.

Laura

The Ang-Gnarra Aboriginal Corporation (see the Information section) has a ranger service based beside the caravan park on the main north-south road. If the ranger is available, a guided tour of the rock-art galleries may be arranged.

Trezise Bush Guide Service (☎ (07) 4060 3236) is based at Jowalbinna, just outside Laura, and specialises in one to four-day trips to some of the magnificent rock-art sites in the area, as well as Daintree, Lakefield National Park and the Deighton River Valley. You can even camp on the property at the bush camp beside the peaceful headwaters of the Little Laura River. A camping fee of $5 per adult applies, while accommodation in a tented camp costs $30. Meals can be provided, with dinner for $20 per person and breakfast and lunch $10 each.

The guide service is $60 per adult per day, $40 a half day, while kids are $10 a day. A 4WD is essential to reach Jowalbinna and maps are available in Laura. Visitors can also fly into Jowalbinna airstrip and stay for a day or overnight.

For more information, phone Jowalbinna or the Cairns office (☎ (07) 4055 1865; fax 4058 1560), or write to PO Box 106, Freshwater, Cairns, Qld 4870.

FACILITIES
North of the Daintree River Ferry

Accommodation & Food From the crossing of the Daintree River to Cape Tribulation there are a number of places tucked away in the surrounding forest and/or close to the beach that make for a pleasant overnight stop.

At Cow Bay, the *Cow Bay Hotel* (☎ (07) 4098 9011) has air-conditioned motel units and a licensed bistro. A single/double unit costs $70/90, including breakfast.

The Rainforest Retreat (☎ (07) 4098 9101) has a range of accommodation and barbecue areas. Self-contained units cost

$50/70 a single/double while a family room is $90. Extra adults cost $10 a person, and kids cost $5. The bunkhouse sleeps 20 with a shared bathroom and costs $15 per person, with linen provided. Although there are no cooking facilities in the dorm or bunkhouse, visitors are welcome to use the dining room kitchen and there is a swimming pool to cool off in.

Less than 3km from the Cow Bay Hotel is the *Crocodylus Village* (☎ (07) 4098 9166) with its backpacker accommodation ranging in price from $15 to $50 for dormitory-style to ensuite cabin-style accommodation. There's a pool, bar, restaurant and a host of activities.

Lync-Haven Rainforest Retreat (☎ (07) 4098 9155) is 16km north of the ferry in 16 hectares of rainforest. There are self-contained cabins which sleep six for $75 a double, $10 for each extra adult and $7.50 per child. If you have your own caravan, a powered site is $16 a double while in the camping area an unpowered site costs $5 per person. There is a licensed restaurant as well as takeaway meals.

The Daintree Wilderness Lodge (☎ (07) 4098 9105) has individual bungalows nestled in the rainforest with all amenities. The cost is $180 for a single/double while extra people in the triple or quad rooms cost an extra $30 a person. The price includes breakfast. A dining room is open for lunch or dinner.

Thornton Beach Kiosk (☎ (07) 4098 9118) is on the beach at Thornton, 20km north of the Daintree River ferry. Good budget-priced meals and refreshments are available from the beach-front bar and cafe.

Fuel Fuel is only available south of Thornton, at the Cow Bay service station on Buchanan Rd, Cape Tribulation.

Cape Tribulation

Accommodation & Food The wide choice of accommodation at Cape Tribulation suits all budgets.

Coconut Beach Rainforest Resort (☎ (07) 4098 0033), with beach frontage, has up-market units, a store, restaurant and bar. Accommodation prices range from $215 to $315 for the luxury villas. Breakfast is included in the price. Activities include 4WD safaris, horse riding, mountain-bike hire, scenic flights, guided rainforest walks, fishing and tours to the reef.

Ferntree Rainforest Resort (☎ (07) 4098 0000; fax 4098 0011) is just five minutes from Cape Tribulation. Accommodation in the resort is available in suites at $275/298 or villas at $195/225 a single/double. The bungalows will set you back $160/185 a time and all rates include breakfast. There are two pools and restaurants, and a number of tours are also available.

PK's Jungle Village (☎ (07) 4098 0040) is on the beach and has a bar and restaurant. The homestead accommodation costs $50 a person while the bungalows with shared amenities are $48 a double, and the dorm beds are $16 a single, which includes linen, shared amenities and a communal kitchen. Camping is $8 per person for an unpowered site. There are reef trips, diving, paddle treks, jungle walks and horse riding available.

Fuel & Supplies The *Masons Store* (☎ (07) 4098 0070) at Cape Tribulation has the normal general store items, food supplies and alcohol. Fuel is only generally available for locals, the closest regular supplies being back at Cow Bay.

Bloomfield River to Helenvale

Accommodation & Food Once north of Cape Tribulation, there is no accommodation until the Bloomfield River.

The Bloomfield Wilderness Lodge (☎ (07) 4035 9166; fax 4035 9180) is set back from the beach on Weary Bay and is surrounded by the Cape Tribulation National Park. This remote resort is only accessible via boat, and the normal tariff includes scenic air transfer, all meals, and accommodation in luxury suites. The lodge offers river cruises, guided rainforest walks, local fishing, reef trips and 4WD safaris. Packages start at $462 per person for two nights up to $1287 for seven nights. If you have a 4WD you can drive and

then catch the boat across the river, and for this you will pay $165 a night per person.

Bloomfield Beach Camping (☎ (07) 4060 8207; fax 4060 8187), 20 Bloomfield Rd, Ayton, is 11.2km north of the Bloomfield River crossing, on the Cooktown side, with 9km of beach front. Grassed areas with plenty of trees make this a very pleasant park. There is a bar and restaurant and all meals, including morning and afternoon tea, are served. All the normal amenities are provided, and camping costs $6/9 a single for an unpowered/powered site. Pets are allowed if kept under control. Accommodation in on-site tents is also available for $15 per person twin share or $18 a single.

Home Rule Rainforest Lodge (☎ (07) 4060 3925; fax 4060 3902) is just south of Helenvale at Rossville. The lodge has a dining room (dinners average $12), games room, licensed restaurant, a small general store and fuel (super, unleaded and diesel). Cabin-style accommodation costs $15 a single, including bed linen, and there is a communal kitchen and laundry facilities. Camping on the river bank, with all amenities, is $6 and children are $3. Activities include horse riding, bushwalking, a nine-hole golf course, river rafting, fishing and access to Cedar Bay National Park.

The *Lion's Den Hotel* (☎ (07) 4060 3911) at Helenvale has cold beer, heaps of character and characters, counter meals and accommodation at $18/25 a single/double. Breakfast, lunch and dinner are available. Camping is allowed behind the hotel beside the Annan River for just $4 per person, with use of the showers at the hotel. It's a top spot to camp. For more information, see the boxed story on the Lion's Den Hotel.

Fuel & Supplies The *Bloomfield River Inn*, Bloomfield Rd, Bloomfield, has motor oils, unleaded, super and diesel fuel, as well as takeaway food, drinks and limited grocery supplies. The *Ayton Store*, West St, Ayton, also has supplies. The *Rossville General Store* has supplies and super, unleaded and diesel fuel. The *Lion's Den Hotel* sells basic food items such as meat, milk and bread, and has super fuel.

Cooktown

Accommodation Cooktown has a wide range of places to stay.

The *Golden Orchid Van Park* (☎ (07) 4069 5641), at the corner of Charlotte and Walker Sts, has sites for $6 per person, power $3 extra. The *Peninsula Van Park* (☎ (07) 4069 5107), Howard St, is set among large shady trees and is a very pleasant place to stop. A range of accommodation with the usual facilities is available, plus barbecue areas. Pets are allowed, under supervision. Self-contained units, including linen, cost $50-60 a double, depending on the size; on-site vans cost $30 a double; the bunkhouse costs $25 a double, including linen; unpowered campsites cost $6 per person, power $3 extra. The weekly fee for camping is six times the day rate.

Tropical Breeze Caravan Park & Holiday Units (☎ (07) 4069 5417), McIvor Rd, has all facilities as well as a fully stocked kiosk. Pets are not allowed. Accommodation in self-contained units ranges from $49 to $64 a double with reduced weekly rates; cabins range from $49 to $59 a double while overnight vans cost $29 a double. Unpowered/powered campsites are $13/15 a double. There are reduced prices for children aged from five to 15.

The *Cooktown Hotel* (☎ (07) 4069 5308), the *Sovereign Hotel* (☎ (07) 4069 5400) and the *West Coast Hotel* (☎ (07) 4069 5350) are all on Charlotte St, the main street of Cooktown. All provide a wide choice of accommodation. Prices for the Cooktown are $15/30 a single/double, while the West Coast has twin rooms for $30. The Sovereign Hotel has a wider choice, from resort rooms with a double and single bed to two-bedroom apartments. Prices range from $95 to $135 a single.

Motels include the *River of Gold Motel* (☎ (07) 4069 5222), on the corner of Hope and Walker Sts, and the *Seaview Motel* (☎ (07) 4069 5377) in Charlotte St. Prices vary from $57 a twin or double room. At the *Cooktown Motor Inn Motel* (☎ (07) 4069 5357), Charlotte St, you can have a choice of backpacker dormitory style accommodation for $14 a single to ensuite motel units that range between $39 and $49, depending on if they are air conditioned and the view from the window.

Pam's Place (☎ (07) 4069 5166), at the corner of Charlotte and Boundary Sts, PO Box 689, offers a range of backpacker accommodation, with the best of shared facilities and linen included in the prices. A single room costs $20, while the dormitory is $10 a night. The lodge also runs organised trips.

The *Alamanda Inn* (☎ (07) 4069 5203), Hope St, offers nice clean self-contained units for $32/40. Rooms are also available in the old style Queenslander house for $32 a double and $25 a single respectively. The Inn has a pool, barbecue facilities, a guest kitchen and laundry.

The *Hillcrest Guest House* (☎ (07) 4069 5305), in the same street, offers accommodation which includes breakfast for $35/45 a single/double. Motel accommodation with all facilities costs $70 a double with breakfast.

The *Endeavour Falls Tourist Park* (tel/fax (07) 4069 5431), PO Box 242, Cooktown, Qld 4871, is 33km north-west of Cooktown, on the McIvor Rd, towards Battle Camp and Lakefield. This picturesque park sits on the banks of the north branch of the Endeavour River and has all amenities, including fuel, a kiosk, takeaway food and barbecues. Pets are permitted on application. Unpowered/powered campsites are $10/12 for a double, plus $3 per extra person. Self-contained holiday units cost $50 a double and $8 per extra person. Swimming and bushwalking are pleasant activities around here.

Fuel & Supplies In Cooktown you will find a butcher, bakery, chemist, dentist and a couple of supermarkets. *Foodstore*, on Helen St, is open seven days a week and has EFTPOS facilities and accepts major credit cards. There are also fruit shops, milk bars and takeaway shops, all centred around Charlotte St.

Fuel is available from a few outlets including Cape York Tyres, Charlotte St, and the Ampol Service Station, Hope St. The Ampol Service Station also has LPG, but remember, it is not available beyond Cooktown.

Post Office & Money The post office offers full postal services and EFTPOS facilities are available at the Commonwealth Bank agency. There is also a Westpac Bank in Charlotte St with full banking facilities.

Airstrip There is a public aerodrome at Cooktown (☎ (07) 4069 5360), which is used regularly by commercial airlines. Aviation fuel can be arranged.

Hope Vale

The Hope Vale Aboriginal community has a number of shops including a hardware, butcher and a general store selling a variety of goods, including Aboriginal artefacts. Fuel (super, unleaded and diesel) is available at the service station.

Laura

Accommodation & Food Apart from camping near the Laura River, you really can only stay at the pub. The *Quinkan Hotel* (☎ (07) 4060 3255) is in the main street and has accommodation in twin rooms for $45 a single, including dinner and breakfast. You can camp; an unpowered site is $5 a single, plus an extra $3 for power, with use of shower facilities. Meals are available and a cool beer can be enjoyed under the mango trees.

Fuel & Supplies All the supplies a traveller needs, including frozen and tinned food and all fuels, are available at the *Laura Store* beside the pub. There is a post office at the store as well. Just north of the Laura River crossing is the *Laura Cafe* where you can get a meal, supplies or fuel.

Airstrip There is a small airstrip just outside town. Aviation fuel can be organised through the Laura Store, but you'll need to give notice beforehand.

Musgrave

There is only one main building in Musgrave – the *Telegraph Station* built in 1887 (☎ (07) 4060 3229). It has very limited supplies, as well as souvenirs, fuel (super, unleaded and diesel), takeaway food, sit-down meals, cold beer and drinks.

Accommodation is available for $20/40 a single/double and breakfast can be arranged. You can also camp at Musgrave for $5 per person.

Airstrip There is an airstrip beside the old telegraph station. If you give the people at Musgrave notice of at least one week, they can arrange a supply of aviation fuel.

ALTERNATIVE TRANSPORT
Air

Flight West Airlines (☎ (07) 4035 9511; fax 4035 9858) has regular scheduled flights from Cairns to Cooktown. Contact the Cairns office for bookings and flight details at PO Box 107, Cairns Mail Centre, Cairns, Qld 4870. The booking agent in Cooktown is at the Seaview Motel & Travel Centre (☎ (07) 4069 5377), Charlotte St.

Cape York Air Services (☎ (07) 4035 9399; fax 4035 9108) calls into Laura on its peninsula mail runs and, subject to space availability, takes passengers. For bookings and flight details, contact the office in Cairns at PMB 13, Cairns Mail Centre, Qld 4871.

Bus

Coral Coaches (☎ (07) 4098 2600; fax 4098 1064), 37 Front St, PO Box 367, Mossman, Qld 4873, runs a bus service six days a week (not on Monday) between Cairns and Cooktown, via Daintree and Cape Tribulation as well as via the inland route. The return fare for the inland route is $92, and the coast route is $99. For details and bookings, you can also contact the agent in Cooktown, the Endeavour Farm Trading Post (☎ (07) 4069 5723), the Cairns office (☎ (07) 4031 7577) or the

Port Douglas office in Grant St (☎ (07) 4099 5351).

Boat

Endeavour Shipping (☎ (07) 4035 1147; fax 4035 1707) has a fortnightly service to Horn Island in the Torres Strait, carrying a couple of passengers as well as general cargo, 4WD vehicles and motorcycles. The vessel calls into Cooktown only by arrangement.

Vehicle Rental

There are a large number of rental companies based in Cairns which have 4WD vehicles available for hire to drive to Cooktown; trying to get a vehicle any further up Cape York is definitely a problem. See the Cairns and Cape York sections for details. In Cooktown there are a couple of places where you can get a vehicle, but again you'll only be able to drive it in the surrounding area, and in some instances even as far as Laura.

Cooktown Motor Inn (☎ (07) 4069 5357), and Endeavour Air (☎ (07) 4069 5860), Charlotte St, Cooktown, have 4WDs for hire.

Cape York

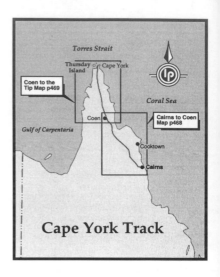

Cape York Track

Cape York is one of the last great frontiers of Australia. It is a vast patchwork of tropical savanna cut by numerous rivers and streams, while along its eastern flank is the northern section of the Great Dividing Range. In amongst these ragged peaks and deep valleys are some of the best and most significant rainforests in Australia. Streams tumble down the rocky mountains to the sea, where just offshore the coral ramparts of the Great Barrier Reef stretch over thousands of square kilometres. The reef is protected in a marine park, and much of the land mass of the Cape is protected in a number of spectacular, rarely visited national parks.

Giving access to that vast natural wonderland is the route to the Cape. Initially the corrugated road you follow is known more officially as the Peninsula Developmental Road, but once that heads away to the mining town of Weipa, you can follow the old and adventurous Telegraph Line Track, or the more sedate 'bypass roads' to the 'Tip'.

From Cairns to the top of Cape York is 952km via the shortest and most challenging route, which is the one we'll describe in detail here. Most travellers will want to visit Cooktown, Weipa and a few other places off the main route, and those diversions will add considerably to the total distance covered.

There are a number of alternative routes. Down south you can choose between the inland route, or the coastal route via Daintree and Cape Tribulation. From Lakeland you can travel straight up the heart of the Cape or go via Cooktown and Battle Camp to Laura or Musgrave. See the earlier Cairns to Musgrave via Cooktown section for more details.

From the Archer River you can head north via Weipa and Stones Crossing, or via the Telegraph Track. Further north again you have the choice of continuing on the Telegraph Track or taking the bypass roads, so called because they pass nearly all of the river crossings – and thereby some of the best spots of the trip north. See the later section on Alternative Routes for more details.

Vast areas of Cape York are also designated Aboriginal land, while the rest is mainly taken up with large pastoral holdings.

Covering an area totalling around 207,000 sq km, or about the same size as the state of Victoria, Cape York has a population of around 15,000 people.

The largest towns in the region are Cooktown, on the south-east coast, and Weipa, a large mining community on the central-west coast. A handful of smaller towns make up the remainder of the communities throughout the Cape.

HISTORY

Before the arrival of Europeans there were a large number of different Aboriginal tribal groups spread throughout the Cape, while a unique group of people inhabited the islands dotted across the reef-strewn Torres Strait. These Torres Strait Islanders came from Melanesia and Polynesia about 2000 years ago and are culturally distinct from the Aborigines. While they had a close affinity with the people further north, they influenced Aboriginal tribal groups near the top of Cape York and vice versa. The further south on the mainland, the less the influence from the north.

For the most part, the tribes of the Cape were aggressive, fighting between themselves and attacking the early European explorers. In fact, there are few accounts of early explorers that do not relate attacks by Aborigines or Islanders.

The rich Aboriginal and Torres Strait heritage is alive and well today and travellers will see much of it on their way through the Cape. Of special importance is one of the world's most significant collections of prehistoric art in the escarpment country surrounding Laura. For further information, see the boxed story on Quinkan Art later in this section.

European history in Australia can trace its beginnings back to the early Dutch navigators who from 1606 explored much of the coastline. These included Janszoon and Tasman, reputedly the first Europeans to report seeing the great south land. (It is unclear whether the Spanish navigator Torres, after whom the strait is named, actually sighted land.) Their exploits are remembered in the names of bluffs and bays dotted down the Gulf side of the Cape.

James Cook mapped the east coast of Australia in 1770, and claimed the continent for England at Possession Island, just off the northerly tip that he named York Cape. Over the next 100 years, other great English navigators, including Bligh, Flinders and King, mapped sections of the coast and bestowed their names upon it.

Ludwig Leichhardt was the first explorer to journey over a section of the Cape during his 1845 expedition from Brisbane to Port Essington on the Cobourg Peninsula in the Northern Territory. South of the Mitchell River they were attacked and John Gilbert, the great collector of animals and birds for the naturalist John Gould, was killed by Aborigines.

Edmund Kennedy and his party had a horrific time in 1848 heading up the east coast along the Great Dividing Range. Continually splitting his party, Kennedy was fatally speared by Aborigines while among the swamps and waterways of the Escape River, south-east of the Tip. Only Jacky Jacky, his Aboriginal guide, reached their destination just a few kilometres north at Albany Passage.

Frank Jardine and his brother led a group taking cattle from Rockhampton to the new government outpost at Somerset in 1863.

This was the start of the Jardine legend on Cape York, with Frank Jardine dominating the top of the Cape until his death in 1917.

Other explorers followed, opening up the region. The discovery of gold on the Palmer River in 1873 was the great catalyst for the development of Cooktown, Laura and, later, Cairns.

In 1887 the Overland Telegraph Line from near Somerset to Palmerville and Cooktown was finally completed, linking the northern-most outpost with Brisbane. This is the route most travellers to Cape York follow today.

During WWII, Cape York was a major staging post for the battles going on in New Guinea and the Coral Sea. Some 10,000 troops were stationed on the Cape from Cooktown in the south to Mutee Heads and Horn Island in the north. Many relics of those days can still be seen, including wrecks of some of the 160-odd aircraft that were reported lost over the region.

Frank Jardine & Somerset

John Jardine, Frank's father, was the government magistrate for the settlement of Somerset when it was established in 1863. Looking at the commercial aspects of the venture, he commissioned Frank and his younger brother Alick, both then aged in their early 20s, to overland a mob of cattle from Rockhampton to the new settlement.

That epic journey was the beginning of the Jardine legend on Cape York. It took them ten months to reach the Top, arriving at Somerset on 13 March 1865. Along the way they overcame lack of water, hostile Aborigines, flooded rivers and the maze of swamps and waterways around the headwaters of the Escape and Jardine rivers.

Later, Frank Jardine took over from his father as government magistrate. Before his arrival at Somerset and during the early part of his stay, attacks by Aborigines and Islanders on Europeans and shipwrecked crews were common. Within a few years of Jardine taking up his post, the attacks stopped. His uncompromising treatment of the Aborigines earned him the name of 'Debil Debil Jardine'.

Jardine established a couple of outstations at Bertiehaugh, Galloway and Lockerbie, where he ran cattle. From his base at Somerset he ran a fleet of pearling luggers throughout Torres Strait. Some say the family treasure came from a Spanish galleon he found wrecked on a remote reef south of New Guinea.

He married a Samoan princess called Sana, whom, the story goes, he kidnapped when she was being taken to New Guinea by missionaries.

When Jardine resigned as government magistrate and the official government residence was moved to Thursday Island, he and Sana took over Somerset as their home. The grove of coconuts they planted, some of which are still standing today, is the most visible reminder of their time at this outpost. The family lived relatively well in this wild place, entertaining ship's captains and any visiting dignitaries, and the Jardine hospitality was legendary.

In 1886, during the building of the Overland Telegraph Line, Jardine was in charge of transporting supplies to the crew building the northernmost section of the line. During that time he explored and named the Ducie River, establishing Bertiehaugh Station on its banks some years later.

In 1890 the *Quetta* sank off the Cape, Queensland's worst shipping disaster. Jardine was responsible for saving many lives. From then on, ships passing through Albany Passage in front of Somerset would dip their flag in salute.

Frank died in 1919 and Sana in 1923. Both are buried on the foreshore at Somerset.

The Jardine story continued in this region until WWII when the family was evacuated from Somerset. Earlier, 'Chum' Jardine, the oldest son of Frank and Sana, had taken the family diaries to his new venture on the Aru Islands further west (now part of Indonesia). In 1942 he was captured by the Japanese and beheaded for 'coast-watching'. The famous diaries and the family treasure, buried before the invasion, were lost.

During the 1920s, the Australian Museum had offered the family over £10,000 for the diaries – an incredible sum for those days. Although the journals are lost, a number of books were written from those historic pages. The most famous writer to have access to them was Ion Idriess, who wrote *The Great Trek, Drums of Mer* and *Head-hunters of the Coral Sea*.

What remained of the house at Somerset was burnt down in 1960, but there is still enough on the hill and down on the beach to remind people of this rich and exciting heritage. It is a great place to spend a few hours. ∎

During the 1950s bauxite was discovered along the coast near Weipa, and by the 1980s it had grown into the world's biggest bauxite mine.

During the late 1980s there was much talk about a space base being built on the Cape, but it seems the plan won't come to fruition. In the early 1990s promises of more national parks were just that, while more and more land was being claimed by Aboriginal groups. It was on the islands of the Straits that the Mabo decision sprang from, while the Wik claim on land around Weipa in late 1996 seemed to challenge every state's right as far as pastoral land and mining tenure was concerned. It seems that Cape York, once a battle ground and then forgotten, has become a 20th Century legal minefield.

INFORMATION

The wet season greatly restricts vehicle movement on Cape York. For that reason the best time to go is as early in the Dry as possible, generally from the beginning of June. The country is greener, there is more water around, there are less travellers and generally the roads are better than later in the season. The peak period is between August and September, with the last travellers being out of the Cape by the beginning of November.

If you plan to visit early or late in the season, it pays to check on the weather and road conditions with locals – contact the police in Coen, Weipa or Cooktown, or the Archer River Roadhouse. Alternatively, you can contact the Queensland Department of Transport (☎ 008 077 247) or the RACQ Road Reports (24 hours ☎ (07) 51 6711, or (07) 11 655).

Occasionally people get caught out by the early rains of the Wet when they're at the very top of Cape York. They'll be looking at either an extended stay or an expensive barge trip with their vehicle back to Cairns.

Of course, you need all the usual gear for travelling in a remote area, and you must carry water. Although you will cross a number of rivers south of the Archer River,

water can be scarce along this section, especially late in the Dry.

It is possible to take a well-constructed off-road trailer all the way to the top, but be prepared to get bogged occasionally. Lesser built trailers will fall apart somewhere along the track. Caravans can make it to Cooktown, driven with care. They can even make it further north to Weipa, but the going is hard and we would not recommend it.

You are also entering saltwater crocodile country so, while there are plenty of safe places to swim, be aware that any deep, dark, long stretch of water can hold a big, hungry saltie.

The most common accidents on the Cape are collisions in the heath country south of the Jardine River. The track is narrow, people travel too fast and sometimes they meet head-on. Nobody has been killed yet – more by sheer luck than anything else. Drive slowly and keep your wits about you.

Tourist Offices

The only official tourist information centre along the route is in Cooktown (☎ (07) 4069 6100) although travellers will find information readily available from the many helpful locals in the roadhouses and towns along the way, such as Coen, Weipa and Bamaga.

The Seisia Camping Ground, at the very top of Australia, is a mine of information. For further details, see the Facilities section.

In Cairns there are a couple of places that can help you with information on travelling Cape York. See Information in the earlier Cairns to Musgrave via Cooktown section.

Police

The police can provide information to travellers on road conditions etc. Contact the following police stations: Coen (☎ (07) 4060 1150); Rocky Point in Weipa (☎ (07) 4069 9119); Lockhart River Aboriginal community (☎ (07) 4060 7120); and Bamaga (☎ (07) 4069 3156).

Medical Services

There are three hospitals on Cape York: Coen (☎ (07) 4060 1141), Rocky Point in Weipa

(☎ (07) 4069 9155), and Bamaga (☎ (07) 4069 3166). There is also a dentist (☎ (07) 4069 9411) at Rocky Point.

Permits

Permits are not required for travelling to Cape York via the main route described.

Once you are north of the Dulhunty River, however, you will need a permit to camp on Aboriginal land, which in effect is nearly all the land north of the river. The Injinoo people are the traditional custodians of much of this land, along with other Aboriginal communities at Umagico and New Mapoon. Please respect the signs and by-laws of the community councils.

Designated camping grounds are provided in a number of areas, including Seisia, Umagico, Pajinka and Punsand Bay. Camping elsewhere in the area requires a permit from the Injinoo Community Council (☎ (07) 4069 3252) or Pajinka Wilderness Lodge. You can write to the Injinoo Community Council, PO Box 7757, Cairns, Qld 4870.

Alternatively, you can wait until you get to the Injinoo owned and operated ferry across the Jardine River. The $80 (return) fee includes the cost of camping at a number of pleasant, isolated sites, and the permit fees.

A plan of management is being developed for the area with a range of access fees, so things may change in the near future.

Travelling across Aboriginal land elsewhere on the Cape may require a permit. Some are easy to obtain while others are difficult – it all depends on the community concerned. It is best to write to the relevant community council stating the reason for you visit, dates etc. Allow plenty of time for an answer.

Books & Maps

A wide range of books and maps on Cape York is available in Cairns, Cooktown and Weipa, and from good bookshops around Australia.

Hema and the RACQ both produce good maps of the region (see Books & Maps in the Cairns to Musgrave via Cooktown section).

For guide books on Cape York, see Books & Maps in the Cairns to Musgrave via Cooktown section. *The Last Frontier: Cape York Wilderness*, written and published by Glenville Pike, really covers the history of the region well. For those interested in the Palmer River gold fields, the book *River of Gold* by Hector Holthouse (Angus & Robertson) is by far the best. If you want to know a little about the flowers of the region, a colourful, small book, *A Wilderness in Bloom*, written and published by B & B Hinton, is a good one to start with.

Radio Frequencies

Unless you are doing something way out of the ordinary, a HF radio, while nice to have, is not really necessary for the Cape.

The RFDS bases in Queensland no longer operate a phone service although they will still respond to medical or emergency calls. The RFDS base in Cairns (call sign VJN) has a primary channel of 5145 and secondary channels of 2260, 4926, 6785 and 7465. The Mount Isa base (call sign VJI) has a primary channel frequency of 5110, with secondary frequencies of 4935, 6965, and 7392.

For those with a Telstra account, Townsville is the base to work through (call sign VIT). The radphone channels available at Townsville include 412, 607, 817, 1231 and 1610. Most of these channels are open from 6 am to 10 pm each day and include voice call, Selcall or Tonecall. Other frequencies are request only. Selcall for the beacon is 0999, while the operator is 0109.

Towing

Should you need a tow to the nearest town, the following towing services will be extremely useful:

Mount Molloy Service Centre & RACQ Service Depot, Brown St, Mount Molloy (24 hours) (☎ (07) 4094 1260)
Lakeland Cash Store & RACQ Service Depot (24 hours) (☎ (07) 4060 2133)
Cooktown Towing & Transport, McIvor Rd, Cooktown (☎ (07) 4069 5545)

THE TROPICS

JBSI Transport, Lot 8 Iraci Ave, Evans Landing, Weipa (24 hours) (☎ (07) 4069 7795; fax 4069 8112) – towing and salvage service anywhere on Cape York, and can arrange to have your vehicle shipped back to Cairns

WRAFTEC Industries, 1 Iraci Ave, Weipa (☎ (07) 4069 7877)

Camping Equipment Rental
Pickers Geo Camping & Canvas (☎ (07) 4051 1944), 108 Mulgrave Rd, Parramatta Park, Cairns, Qld 4870, has a range of camping equipment and accessories for hire.

THE ROUTE
Cairns to Lakeland (244km)
The route from Cairns heads out over the **Atherton Tableland** west of Cairns, and most people travel via Kuranda and Mareeba. This is a scenic drive up and over the Great Dividing Range.

The small township of **Mount Molloy** is 104km north-west of Cairns, or 40km south-west of the sugar port of Mossman. The bitumen continues along the Peninsula Developmental Road and at **Mount Carbine**, 30km north-west of Mount Molloy, you can get fuel and limited supplies from the roadhouse.

The **McLeod River**, about 13km west of the town, is one of the best spots to camp along this section of road and it is popular with travellers.

Further north the road climbs through the DeSailly Range and there are good views from **Bob's Lookout** that are worthy of a quick photo stop. The vegetation is pretty typical of what you will see for much of the trip. Forget deep, dark, impenetrable rainforest. Sure, you will see that, especially if you head off the main track, but jungle of this sort tends to be confined to narrow strips of riverine forest and to a few spots north of the mighty Jardine River. For the most part, the open forests are dominated by stringybarks, ironbarks, bloodwoods and other species of eucalypt.

From Bob's Lookout the road continues to wind through range country, skirting the headwaters of St George Creek before coming to a turn-off west (left) to the **Palmer River gold fields** and **Maytown**, 65km north-west of Mount Carbine and 199km from Cairns.

For travellers with a little time, an excursion to the heart of the gold fields at Maytown is an interesting adjunct to a trip up the Cape. Contact the Queensland Department of Environment and Heritage ranger at Chillagoe (☎ (07) 4094 7163; fax 4094 7213) for a camping permit, information, maps and current track details. There are no facilities at Maytown.

The **Palmer River Roadhouse** is 13km further on overlooking the Palmer River and has fuel, accommodation, beer and limited supplies. There is a museum with a display of Palmer River gold field relics which is well worth a look

Another 32km sees you at **Lakeland** (244km from Cairns), the small rural hamlet at the junction of the roads north-east to Cooktown and north-west to Weipa and the top of the Cape. Lakeland has fuel, food, accommodation, some supplies and repairs.

The surrounding area is heavily farmed with many crops, including sorghum and peanuts. The entrance to **Butchers Hill station** is just across the road from the Lakelands Hotel. This 400,000-hectare property, established in 1874, is not only a successful cattle station and peanut farm, but it also provides accommodation and ranch-style holidays.

Lakeland to the Wenlock River (489km)
A formed dirt road heads north to Laura and the top of the Cape from Lakeland. About 48km north, and 12km south of Laura, is the turn-off to the **Split Rock Gallery**.

These Aboriginal rock-art galleries are well worth a look as they are the most accessible of the 1500 galleries found in this area. Together they represent one of the biggest and most important collections of prehistoric art in the world. See the earlier Cairns to Musgrave via Cooktown section and the boxed story for more on these galleries.

Just a few kilometres further on, north of the Laura River crossing, **Laura** is a well spread-out town with the 'centre' being

Quinkan Art

Quinkan art is one of the great art styles of northern Australia. Vastly different to the X-ray art of Arnhem Land in the Northern Territory, or the Wandjina art of the Kimberley in Western Australia, Quinkan art gets its name from the human-shaped, spirit figures with unusually shaped heads, called Quinkans.

Much study on the sites has been done since 1960 by Percy Trezise, an amateur archaeologist. Over 1200 galleries have been discovered. All of these are around the settlement of Laura, in the escarpment country that surrounds the lowlands along the great rivers of Lakefield National Park.

This great body of art is testimony to the Aborigines who once lived here. When the Palmer River gold rush began in 1873, the Aborigines fought to defend their land against the new invaders. Those who survived the bullets succumbed to disease, and the few remaining Aborigines became fringe dwellers on the outskirts of towns and missions.

The rock-art galleries contain many fine paintings of kangaroos, wallabies, emus, brolgas, jabirus, crocodiles, snakes and flying foxes – in fact, all the wildlife still seen along the rivers and plains.

Spiritual figures and ancestral beings also point to a lifestyle that was rich in culture and religious beliefs. Among the paintings there are 'good' and 'bad' spiritual figures, the 'good' being heroes of old and the figures depicting fertility and ritual increase, while the 'bad' were depicted by spirit figures such as Quinkans.

Other paintings depict tools such as boomerangs and axes, while in some galleries stencils of hands and implements can also be seen. Rock engravings are also found in small numbers, and in a couple of galleries there is evidence of the European invasion with images of horses.

Only the Split Rock and Guguyalangi galleries are open to the public. South of Laura and close to the main road, they are readily accessible, with a walking track joining the two.

There are a number of overhangs in the Split Rock group of galleries, and while Split Rock itself is the most visually stunning, within 100m there are smaller galleries containing flying foxes, tall Quinkans and hand stencils.

The Guguyalangi group consists of over a dozen overhangs that are adorned with a vast array of figures, animals and implements, and are possibly the best of the lot.

A walking trail leads from the carpark at Split Rock, past the galleries in this group and then up onto the plateau to a lookout at Turtle Rock. The view from here is stunning. From this point the trail wanders through the open forest of the plateau for 1km to the Guguyalangi group of galleries. The views here are, once again, spectacular. If you are going to do this walk, save it for the late afternoon or early morning as it can get quite warm wandering across the plateau at midday. Take some water and food and enjoy the art and solitude of this place.

The Giant Horse galleries, across the road from the Split Rock and Guguyalangi sites, are a little harder to see and consist of five shelters depicting many animals, including a number of horses. These galleries can only be visited with a guide from the local community, and pre-arrangement with the ranger is essential.

Percy Trezise and his sons, Steve and Matt, have established a wilderness reserve at Jowalbinna. The Jowalbinna Bush Camp and Deighton River Bush Camps are open to travellers and Steve runs the Trezise Bush Guide Service, specialising in guided walking trips to the many magnificent galleries in the nearby area.

For more information on the Quinkan art around Laura, contact the Ang-Gnarra Aboriginal Corporation on ☎ (07) 4060 3214 or fax 4060 3231. Maps, brochures and information for self-guided walks around the art sites are obtainable from the ranger station, which is beside the caravan park.

It may also be possible to organise a tour of the art sites with a ranger, providing one is available. There is a ranger station, which is usually staffed, at the Split Rock Gallery carpark. Although there is no fee to visit the art sites, visitors are requested to make a donation of $5 per adult.

If you want to join Steve Trezise at Jowalbinna, ring ☎ (07) 4060 3236. Alternatively, contact the Trezise Bush Guide Service (see the Organised Tours section). ■

around the pub. See the Cairns to Musgrave via Cooktown section for more details on Laura and Lakefield National Park.

The road continues to be well-formed dirt as it heads north from Laura, but it can be rough. Most of the creek crossings are dry, but some, such as the Little Laura River, 12km north of Laura, and the Kennedy River, 32km north, often have water and make a good camp.

On the banks of the Hann River, 75km north of Laura, is the **Hann River Road-**

house. Food, fuel, minor repairs and a camping ground are available here.

From here to Musgrave it is 62km of corrugated dirt road that in sections winds through some hilly country. A few bad creek crossings and nasty dips will keep your speed down. About the only spot worth camping at is the **Morehead River**, 29km north of the Hann River.

Musgrave is one of the original fortress telegraph stations that were built along the Overland Telegraph Line and it is the only one you will see easily on the run north. You can get a meal here, as well as fuel and accommodation.

From near Musgrave, tracks run east to the Lakefield National Park (see the Cairns to Musgrave via Cooktown section for more details on this route) or west to Edward River and the Pormpuraaw Aboriginal community.

The road for the next 108km to Coen is little different to what you have experienced before. There may be a few more bulldust patches which can play hell with a motorcycle rider or a low-slung conventional car, but if you've got this far you'll probably make it to Weipa.

About 80km north of Musgrave you meet a road junction. The better, newer road leads left to Coen, while the older, rougher road swings right, crossing the **Stewart River** twice before reaching Coen. With little traffic, the first crossing of the Stewart River makes a fine campsite.

The old road also gives access to the road to **Port Stewart** on the east coast of the Cape where you'll find reasonable camping and some good fishing, especially if you have a small boat.

Coen is the 'capital' of the Cape, and unless you take the turn-off into Weipa, it is the biggest town you'll see north of Cooktown. People have some funny times in this place, all of course in and around the pub, the social heart of any country town.

There is a choice of where to buy food and fuel and even a couple of places offering accommodation, not including the police station with its lock-up, or even the hospital.

About 3km north of Coen, the main road north parallels the **Coen River** and there is some good camping to be found. Toilet facilities are provided.

For the first 23km north of Coen the road is very well maintained, but once you have passed the Coen airfield the road quickly returns to its former standard. About 2km past the airfield you reach the main access track to the Rokeby section of **Mungkan Kaanju National Park**. This park consists of two large separate areas and straddles much of the Archer River and its tributaries. The Rokeby section takes in much of the country from the western edge of the Great Dividing Range almost to the boundary of the Archer Bend section of the same park.

The Rokeby section has excellent camping on a number of lagoons and along the banks of the Archer River. Access to the more remote Archer Bend section of this park is only by rarely given permit. No facilities are provided. The ranger station is about 70km west from the Peninsula Development Road at Rokeby homestead, or see the district ranger based in Coen.

Further north, the main road continues as before, until about 50km north of Coen where it becomes more like a roller coaster.

The excellent **Archer River Roadhouse** is 65km north of Coen and provides food, drinks, fuel, accommodation and camping. Just down the hill from the roadhouse is the magnificent **Archer River**. During the Dry this river is normally just a pleasant stream bordered by a wide, tree-lined, sandy bed. It is an ideal spot to camp, although at times space is at a premium. As with many of the permanent streams on the Cape, the banks are lined with varieties of paperbarks, or melaleucas. Growing to more than 40m, they offer shade for passing travellers and, when in flower, food for hordes of birds and fruit bats that love the, sweet-smelling nectar.

The Archer River crossing used to be a real terror, but now, with its concrete causeway, is quite easy. However, any heavy rain in the catchment will quickly send the water over the bridge, cutting access to Weipa and places further north.

The road north of the Archer and all the

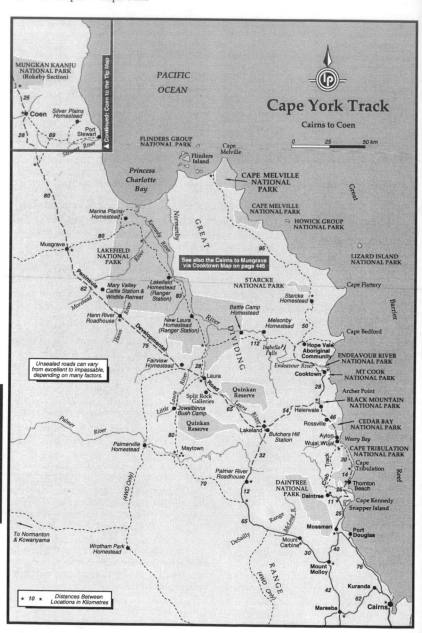

THE TROPICS

MUNGKAN KAANJU
NATIONAL PARK
(Rokeby Section)

*

25

* Coen   Silver Plains
               Homestead
                    Port
                    Stewart
28   69

Stewart River

◄ Continued: Coen to the Tip Map

PACIFIC
OCEAN

Cape York Track

Cairns to Coen

0   25   50 km

FLINDERS GROUP
NATIONAL PARK   Cape
                       Melville
         Flinders
         Island
Princess   CAPE MELVILLE
Charlotte   NATIONAL PARK
Bay
                                 CAPE MELVILLE
                                 NATIONAL PARK
Marina Plains
Homestead   HOWICK GROUP
                                            NATIONAL PARK
80
Musgrave   LIZARD ISLAND
          LAKEFIELD   95   NATIONAL PARK
80   NATIONAL
          PARK
62   Mary Valley   Lakefield   STARCKE   Cape Flattery
      Cattle Station &   Homestead   NATIONAL
      Wildlife Retreat   (Ranger   PARK
      Hann River   Station)   83   Starcke
      Roadhouse   New Laura   Homestead
                         Homestead   Battle Camp
75   (Ranger Station) Homestead   Melsonby   Cape Bedford
                                                        Homestead 50
          Fairview   112 Isabella
          Homestead   28   Falls   Hope Vale
                            Laura   Aboriginal   ENDEAVOUR RIVER
                            Road   Community   NATIONAL PARK
          Split Rock   Quinkan   Endeavour River   MT COOK
          Galleries   Reserve   Cooktown NATIONAL PARK
          Jowalbinna   65   28
          Bush Camp   Archer Point
          Quinkan   80   54 Helenvale BLACK MOUNTAIN
          Reserve   Lakeland   46 NATIONAL PARK
Palmer River   Butchers Hill Rossville CEDAR BAY
          Palmerville   Station   NATIONAL PARK
          Homestead   Maytown   32   Ayton Weary Bay
                                                    Wujal Wujal CAPE TRIBULATION
                                                              30   NATIONAL PARK
                       70   Palmer River   DAINTREE   Cape
To Normanton   Roadhouse   12   NATIONAL   Tribulation 14
& Kowanyama   PARK Daintree Thornton
                       65   11   Beach
                             Wrotham Park   Range   25 Cape Kennedy
                             Homestead   Snapper Island
                                               Mount   Mossman
                             DeSailly   Carbine   30   Port
                                                          30   40   Douglas
                                                    Mount   76
          Unsealed roads can vary   Molloy
          from excellent to impassable,   42   Kuranda
          depending on many factors.   62 Cairns
                                               Mareeba
* 10 * Distances Between
        Locations in Kilometres

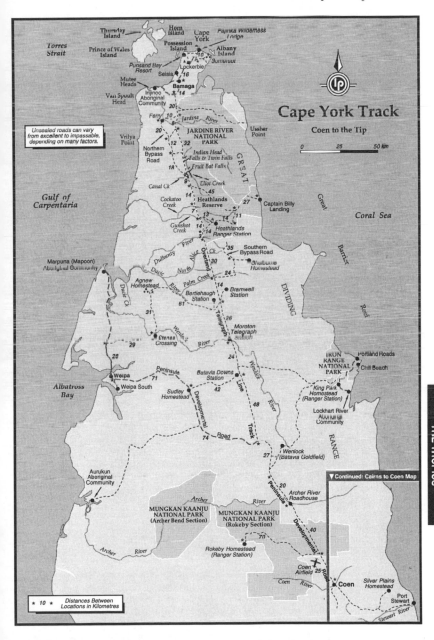

Cape York Track

Coen to the Tip

Unsealed roads can vary from excellent to impassable, depending on many factors.

★ 10 ★ Distances Between Locations in Kilometres

▼ Continued: Cairns to Coen Map

THE TROPICS

way to Weipa is very good, having been re-aligned in recent years away from the flood prone lowlands. The road to Portland Roads, Chili Beach and Iron Range National Park turns east off the main road, 20km north of the Archer, and crosses the Wenlock River, close to the old gold field of Batavia. Many old relics can still be seen here if you take the time to explore the area.

Iron Range National Park is probably the greatest tropical rainforest park in Australia. Forget what you've heard about the Daintree; this place is better and wilder, with more unique animals and plants. There is a rich variety of vegetation, from heathland to dense rainforest.

The rare and vivid eclectus parrot, large palm cockatoo, shy fawn-breasted bowerbird, small red-bellied pitta and giant cassowary are just some of the birds of the forest.

Its mammals include the striped possum, the spotted and southern common cuscus (both a form of possum), and the spiny-haired bandicoot – all are confined to the rainforest habitats of Cape York and New Guinea. Another is the northern quoll, or native cat, which sometimes wanders into camps looking for food. If you're lucky enough to see one you won't forget the encounter – they are beautiful!

Some 10% of Australia's butterflies also reside in this park, including 25 species found no further south, with the park being their stronghold.

There are only a couple of camping areas. Near the East Claudie River and Gordon Creek is the Rainforest Camping Ground, while the other is at Chili Beach on the east coast. Other small campsites are dotted on or near streams along the road. The ranger is based at King Park homestead (☎ (07) 4060 7170) and a permit is needed to camp in the park. You can get a permit from the ranger at King Park or the Queensland Department of Environment & Heritage headquarters in Cairns.

Portland Roads is 135km east of the Peninsula Developmental Road. It is a small fishing port with no facilities for the travel-

ler, except a telephone. The fishing offshore is excellent.

Chili Beach is just a few kilometres south of Portland Roads and is where most travellers camp. Pit toilets are provided. While it is a pleasant spot, it would be even better if the wind would stop blowing – which it does occasionally late in the season. A small boat will give you access to the islands just offshore and to some good fishing.

Lockhart River Aboriginal community is 40km south of Portland Roads and has fuel and limited supplies, although repairs are not available. There is also a police station and a hospital. A permit is not required to enter the community.

Continuing north from the turn-off to Portland Roads, the main Peninsula Developmental Road swings westward to Weipa, 47km north of the Archer River crossing. See the Alternative Routes section for details of the route to Weipa. From this point the route north becomes more of a track, but is still reasonably well maintained.

Batavia Downs station is on the left of the road and marks the second major turn-off to Weipa, 48km north of the first, southernmost one.

The poorly marked **Frenchmans Road** is 2km north of the homestead and leads east from here to meet with the main track to Portland Roads, 56km from that small hamlet. Frenchmans Road crosses the Wenlock River, which has good camping, and the Pascoe River, which doesn't. The latter can also be a little hairy as the river is deep and flows quickly. Take care!

Back on the main route north, the final 22km to the Wenlock River is along a road that is sandy and rough in places.

Wenlock River

The Wenlock River is the first major water challenge you meet on your way north to the Cape. It looks surprisingly easy, but it is astonishing how many people come to grief here. A base of rocks has been put down in the riverbed at the crossing point, and provided it hasn't been washed away in the last wet season, you shouldn't have too much

Walking to the Top

All the early explorers walked to the Top, as did most of the pioneers who followed, searching for gold and rich grazing land. In more recent times, those who 'humped the bluey' are few and far between.

In August 1930, John Carlyon began his walk down the eastern seaboard, a couple of years after Hector Macquarie had made history by being the first to drive a car – a small Austin – to the Top.

In the early 1950s Alex Sklenica and a couple of mates walked from Cairns to Cooktown and on to the Top where they joined the mail boat to travel around Torres Strait.

Sklenica was later to write about the trip:

Cooktown, once a prosperous town with thousands of people and 60 pubs as we were told, was nearly a ghost town now.

A diesel, pulling two cars, maintained a once weekly rail service to Laura. Stockmen and prospectors using the train added to this romantic outback setting. Camping a few days on the Laura River, we shot a few wallabies to prepare jerky and pemmican for the long walk still ahead of us.

Further on the track we met Norman Fisher who offered to take us on his 4WD truck for £5 to Coen. We shared the top of the load with four prospectors who hoped to find a 'pocket' of gold nuggets in creeks around the Wenlock area.

Our travel was reduced sometimes to two miles per hour. We helped to fill holes, cut fallen trees and made a log causeway to enable the 4WD truck to cross the 70 yard wide sandy bed of the Stewart River...

...Supplies diminishing. Walking, we chewed tips of Yakka tree blades, and sticks of dried wallaby meat.

The track along the telegraph line path worsened, the uncut vegetation reaching nearly the wires. Our mainly meat diet lacked sustenance. We craved for carbohydrates, fruit and the kind of vegetables we were used to.

On 15 September, our remaining supplies consisted of half a pound of flour, three-quarters pound of tea, half a pound sugar, 1 spoon of cocoa and 4 spoons of salt.

Arriving at the Jardine River, we saw a small dinghy pulled up on the opposite shore. Nick, the best swimmer among us, brought the dinghy to our side while with Lad we stood guard with rifles. Gear loaded in the small dinghy, we swam across, holding onto the gunnels with one hand.

Later, Mr Cupitt from the Cape York telegraph station told us that he shot recently 14 crocodiles on the spot where we swam the river.

In May 1987 Ian Brown and a couple of friends walked from Coen along much of the Great Dividing Range and the east coast to arrive at the Top. Their trek took 56 days.

In September of that same year Barry Higgins and Steve Tremont began a trek in western Victoria that was to take them 15 months to get to the Top.

In June 1988 Peter Treseder walked and ran from the northernmost tip of Australia to Wilsons Promontory in Victoria. His time? An incredible 41 days – alone and unsupported. While those before him had taken to the coast and untracked wilderness of the range country, Peter had to average 134km a day, and to do that he stayed on the Telegraph Track between the Top and Musgrave. From there he went through Lakefield National Park to Cooktown and south through the Daintree and 50 other odd national parks, before finishing at Australia's southernmost tip.

These recent trips have been sponsored in one way or another by Australian Geographic.

You don't have to join the short list of people who have walked to the Top, but it can be done. In fact, less people have walked to the Cape than have climbed Mt Everest! ■

trouble. If you do bog down, don't despair, you're not the first. The north bank of the Wenlock River is a popular spot to camp and at times it does get crowded. Toilets are provided, as is a telephone. The old telegraph station, 100m up on the north bank, provides homestead accommodation and camping as well as drinks, very limited stores, souvenirs and the like.

Wenlock River to the Jardine River (155km)

The 155km from the Wenlock River to the Jardine River is the best part of the trip, with some great creek crossings and excellent campsites. Take your time and enjoy all the delights the Cape has to offer.

The challenge of following the rough track along the historic Overland Telegraph

Line means that the trip will take at least a very long day, even if all goes well. There are many small diversions from the original route, especially where there is a creek or river to cross. Most of the major creek crossings have water in them; however, it's not the water that is the problem but the banks on each side. Take care. Washaways elsewhere demand you keep your speed down.

Among the scattered timber and blanket of grass you can see zamia, or cycad palms. In places they form quite dense stands, and as they come in male and female forms they must be having quite a party!

The first 40km north of the Wenlock, until the first of the bypass roads leaves the old track, are pretty good.

The turn-offs to **Bramwell station** and **Bertiehaugh station** are 26km north of the Wenlock River. Bramwell station is on the east side of the road and offers very pleasant and reasonably priced accommodation and camping. The route westwards through Bertiehaugh leads to Stones Crossing and then onwards to Weipa.

The first of the major bypass roads, the **Southern Bypass Road**, turns off the Telegraph Track 40km north of the Wenlock. This route to the Top keeps to the high country, staying well away from the many creek crossings the Old Telegraph Line Track makes. See the section on Alternative Routes for more details.

Palm Creek, 43km north of the Wenlock, is followed by Ducie Creek, South Alice Creek and North Alice Creek, before you reach the **Dulhunty River**, 70km north of the Wenlock. This is a popular spot to camp and there are also some lovely places to swim. From this point on you are on land claimed by the Injinoo Aboriginal community and a permit is required to camp.

After crossing another major stream, a road leaves the Telegraph Track 3km north of the Dulhunty and heads for **Heathlands station**, the base for the ranger for Jardine River National Park. This road also bypasses the **Gunshot Creek** crossing. This crossing, just 15km north of the Dulhunty River, used to be one of the hardest and most daunting

on the route north but recent dozer work has made it relatively easy. There's a pleasant spot to camp on the northern side of Gunshot.

Two km north of the Gunshot crossing another track heads east to Heathlands station. The vegetation changes again; no longer is it dominated by straggly eucalypts such as ironbarks and bloodwoods, but instead the country is covered in tall heathland. Take a close look and you'll be surprised at the flowers you can find. The open plains are dominated by grevilleas, hibbertias and small melaleucas, to name just a few, while the creek banks and wetter areas are clothed in banksias and baeckeas.

One of the plants that observant nature lovers will find is the pitcher plant. These are found along the banks of the narrow creeks, Gunshot Creek being a prime spot for them. These special plants trap insects in the liquid at the bottom of the 'pitcher', where their nutrients are absorbed by the plant. It's a unique adaptation to living in an area that is poor in plant food.

After the Gunshot Creek crossing the track is sandy until you come to the **Cockatoo Creek** crossing, 94km north of the Wenlock River. Once again the actual riverbed is no drama, although it is rocky and rough; it's the banks that are the problem. In this case it is the north bank which often has a long haul of soft sand. The Injinoo people have a permanent camp set up on the northern bank of Cockatoo Creek.

For the next 24km the road improves slightly. A couple more creek crossings follow and 14km past Cockatoo Creek the Southern Bypass Road joins up with the Telegraph Track. Just 9km further on, the second major bypass, the **Northern Bypass Road**, heads west away from the Telegraph Track to the ferry that crosses the Jardine River. Stick to the Telegraph Track at this point and keep heading north, even though the track north does deteriorate a little. There are other tracks that lead back to the Northern Bypass Road and the ferry, if you don't want to drive across the Jardine River.

Within 200m a track heads off to the east, taking travellers to **Fruit Bat Falls**. Camping is not allowed here but it is a good spot to stop, have lunch and enjoy the waters of Eliot Creek.

The turn-off to **Indian Head Falls** and **Twin Falls** is 6.5km north of the previous track junction to Fruit Bat Falls. The track leads less than 2km to an excellent camping area. On one side is Canal Creek and the delightful Twin Falls, while on the other is the wider Eliot Creek and Indian Head Falls which drop into a small, sheer-sided ravine.

Pit toilets and showers are set up within the camping area and the ranger from Heathlands keeps the place in good condition, with your help. This is the most popular camping spot on the trip north, and although it gets crowded, it is still very enjoyable. A camping permit is required and a small camping fee payable.

You can spend an enjoyable few days camped here, doing not much else but swimming and lazing in the creeks between lunch and dinner. If you have a mask and snorkel, the water is clear enough for a paddle and there are fish and turtles to watch, or just walk around and enjoy some bird watching.

Back on the Telegraph Track, over the next 10km there are Canal, Sam, Mistake, Cannibal and Cypress creeks to cross. All offer their own sweet challenge. Just south of **Mistake Creek** a track heads west to join up with the Northern Bypass Road, which leads to the ferry across the Jardine River. If you're having fun crossing the creeks, keep heading north at this point, but if you have had enough, it may pay to take the track out to the Northern Bypass Road and the ferry.

From Cypress Creek it is nearly 8km to **Logan Creek**. From here the road is badly chopped up and often flooded in places. You are now passing through the heart of an area the early pioneers called the 'Wet Desert' because of the abundance of water but lack of feed for their stock.

Bridge Creek, or Nolan's Brook, 5.5km further on, once had a bridge, and when you get to it you'll know why. It is an interesting crossing, and though it is short it does demand a lot of care. Less than 2km north of here the last track to the ferry heads west,

while just 4km past this junction the main track veers away from the original telegraph line route to the right and winds for 2km through tall open forest to the Jardine River.

Jardine River

The Jardine River has some magical camping spots along its southern bank, west of the ford. There are no facilities here, and because you are in a national park, a camping permit is required from the ranger at Heathlands station.

The river is wide and sandy. If you want to swim, stick to the shallows where the sandbars are wide. Crocs don't like such open territory but may be lurking in the deep, dark, lily-covered holes that line sections of the river.

Fishing upstream of the crossing is not allowed as you are in a national park. Downstream from this point there is no problem and at times the fishing can be good, although closer to the mouth it is better again.

Jardine River Vehicle Ford The vehicle ford leads out across the wide, sandy bed of the fast-flowing Jardine River. Midway across the river is a steep-sided tongue of sand that constantly changes its position, up and down the river. This tongue of soft sand often causes vehicles to bog in the middle of the stream. The water slowly gets deeper and is at its deepest, generally over a metre deep, within a few metres of the trees on the northern bank. The shallow exit point runs between a corridor of trees. There are some old timbers in this dark water between the trees which can easily stub a toe or hang up a vehicle, so be careful.

Never underestimate this crossing, even if it looks shallow. The 170m between entrance and exit is a long way – certainly most winch cables can't reach you if you stop mid-stream!

Remember, the Jardine River is inhabited by saltwater crocodiles, and although you might not be able to see them they are definitely there. In December 1993 a man was killed by a crocodile while he was swimming to the ferry at the ferry crossing, not far downstream from the vehicle ford.

In recent times the Queensland Department of Environment & Heritage and the Injinoo Aboriginal community have asked that all travellers use the ferry crossing and do not drive across the river at the vehicle ford. For more information on the ferry, see the Northern Bypass section later.

North of the Jardine (69km)

From here to the Top it is less than 70km and for most of the way the track is in good condition.

Once out of the trees bordering the Jardine River, the track swings to the west and finally joins up with the Telegraph Track. A number of minor tracks in this area lead back down to the river and some reasonable campsites.

Turning right, or northwards, and following the old Telegraph Track north brings you to a major crossroad, less than 2km from the exit point on the Jardine. Ignore the Telegraph Track that leads away directly north – this is unused and leads into the heart of the swamp. The main road heading off to the west leads to the main ferry crossing of the river. Turning right, or eastwards, is the main road which will take you to Bamaga.

At the next T-junction, 22km north of the Jardine River, turn right. Left will lead to the coast at the old wartime port of **Mutee Heads**, just north of the Jardine River.

Just 7km further on there is a small carpark beside a fenced area that encloses an **aeroplane wreck**. Dating back to WWII, these remains are of a DC-3, and while this is the easiest aeroplane wreck to see in the area there are a few more scattered around the main airport, which is just a stone's throw away.

A couple of hundred metres past the carpark there is a second T-junction. Right leads to the main airport, while left leads to Bamaga.

Less than 5km from the second T-junction, a signposted road heads off to the right leading to Cape York, Somerset and places close to the Tip. This is the road you will require, but most travellers need fuel and

other supplies, and so continue straight ahead to Bamaga.

Bamaga is the largest community on the northern Cape and is a sprawling town with all the facilities most travellers need. There is a hospital, police station, general store and service station. There is no camping ground at Bamaga, these being located at Seisia (Red Island Point), Umagico and Pajinka Wilderness Lodge at the Tip.

The Islander settlement of **Seisia**, 5km north-west of Bamaga, is an idyllic spot for the weary traveller to relax after the long journey to the Top. There is an excellent foreshore camping ground, a kiosk and service station, and the nearby jetty is a great place for the family to fish.

The **Injinoo Aboriginal community** is 8km south-west of Bamaga, at the mouth of Cowal Creek. Camping is not allowed at Injinoo. However, the settlement of **Umagico** has developed a shady camping area by the beach just north of Injinoo.

The only other official camping areas north of the Jardine River are at the Punsand Bay Private Reserve and the Pajinka Lodge. Camping elsewhere north of the Jardine River is only possible with the permit you received when paying for the ferry ride across the Jardine, or from the Injinoo Community Council. For more details, see the Facilities section.

Just before entering Bamaga, turn north towards the Tip along a well-formed dirt road. The ruins of Jardine's outstation, **Lockerbie**, are 16km north, close to the right-hand side of the road. While the galvanised iron and timber building is a more recent residence, built by the Holland family in 1946, nearby you will find mango trees and pathways established by Frank Jardine. There is usually a small store at the Lockerbie site and visitors are welcome to stop for refreshments, souvenirs and information.

Just north of Lockerbie a track heads west to **Punsand Bay**, about 11 bumpy, sandy kilometres away. A few kilometres later the main track north begins to pass through an area of rainforest called the **Lockerbie**

Scrub. This small patch of rainforest, only 25km long and between 1 and 5km wide, is the northernmost rainforest in Australia.

A Y-junction in the middle of the jungle, 7km from Lockerbie, gives you a choice of veering right for Somerset or left for the top of Australia. Less than 3km from this point on the way to the Top, a track on the left will lead you 7km to the **Punsand Bay Private Reserve** with on-site tents, cabins and camping facilities.

Seven km further on will bring you to the **Pajinka Wilderness Lodge** and the camping area. Here is a small kiosk to service the camping area.

A walking track leads through the forest bordering the camping ground at Pajinka to the beach near the boat ramp. A scattering of mangroves line part of the beach as they do on most of the beaches on the Cape, and sometimes it is almost imperceptible where forest ends and mangroves begin. From the beach you can head overland on the marked trail, or, when the tide is low, you can head around the coast to the northern tip. Both routes are relatively easy walks of an hour or so, depending on how long you dabble your feet in the brine.

The islands of Torres Strait are just a stone's throw away and dot the turquoise blue sea all the way to New Guinea, just over the horizon. Swimming is not recommended here as the tidal stream never seems to stop running one way or the other. The fishing though, can be pretty good. Have your photo taken near the sign proudly proclaiming that you have made it all the way to Australia's northernmost point.

ALTERNATIVE ROUTES
Weipa via the Southern Access Route
Once north of the Archer River, you can head to Weipa instead of heading directly to the Top. Weipa gives you the chance to see something of the Cape's west coast and glimpse what life is like in a remote mining town.

The most direct route to Weipa is the continuation of the Peninsula Developmental Road, which leaves the Overland Telegraph Line route 47km north of the Archer. The Peninsula Developmental Road continues to be a well-maintained dirt road for the 145km to Weipa.

Just over halfway, at the 74km mark, a track which leaves the Telegraph Track at Batavia Downs, south of the Wenlock River, joins up with the Peninsula Developmental Road at Sudley, 71km east of Weipa. This track is often chopped up, but it provides

The Lockerbie Scrub
The Lockerbie Scrub is an important stretch of rainforest, despite being poorly named. It is regularly used as a stopover by migratory birds, and is home to some unique animals and insects. Surprisingly, it has been studied for some time, beginning with naturalists visiting the Jardine family at Somerset and their 'summer residence' at Lockerbie.

Vines and other climbing plants are common in this forest, while hickory ash, paperbark satin ash and cypress pines, which you can see here, were the trees that first established a small logging industry. Probably the most spectacular tree is the fig tree with its large, buttress-type roots. Palms and ferns of all sorts can be commonly found right through the forest, including some huge bird's-nest ferns.

Walking here is really enjoyable, and the thick canopy overhead keeps the area nice and cool. The road passes close to a stream at times and this can easily be followed. Keep an eye out for birds, and with luck you may even see the huge mounds, as tall as 6m or more, of the orange-footed scrub fowl.

You'll no doubt see signs of much rooting around in the leaves and mulch that cover the forest floor. Sadly much of this is due to the wild pigs that infest the area. They are causing untold damage here, and to make matters worse, the introduced cane toad has arrived.

Nature walks and night walks in the forest can be organised by the Pajinka Lodge or Punsand Bay Private Reserve. ■

another option to leave or join the route to the Top.

As you get closer to Weipa, the mining activities increase and the road improves. Heed all the warning signs, especially where the road crosses the mine haulage ways.

Weipa via the Northern Access Route

The route via Stones Crossing, over the Wenlock River, to Agnew and eastwards to the Telegraph Track, south of Bertiehaugh, covers a total distance of 169km.

This track crosses private land and, depending on the owner, access across Bertiehaugh is sometimes open, sometimes closed! This is a good run and well worth the effort, so ask other travellers at each end of the route for the latest advice.

Stones Crossing is 57km north-east of Weipa. First, take the Old Mapoon Road and at the 28km mark veer right at the major Y-junction. The road swings east for 20km before turning north for the last 9km to the crossing of the Wenlock River. This is a magic spot to camp, but remember that the river is tidal as far as the crossing itself and is inhabited by saltwater crocodiles.

From the river, the track deteriorates and heads north for 31km before turning east. **Agnew** was once a wartime airstrip that is now dominated by tall termite mounds. You drive down the edge of the old airstrip before turning eastwards. From here you continue on a rough, sandy track for 50km before coming to a track junction. Keep to the right and after 11km you will meet the Telegraph Track, 26km north of the Wenlock River.

Bypass Roads

The bypass roads avoid most of the creeks and rivers between the Wenlock and Jardine rivers. This route is also called the DCS Road or the 'main' Cairns Road.

Both sections of this road are corrugated and people travel too fast on them. Each year a number of head-on accidents occur, most of those on the Southern Bypass Road. Be careful!

The Southern Bypass This road leaves the Telegraph Track 40km north of the Wenlock River crossing and heads east and then north. The turn-off east to Shelburne station is 24km north of the junction, while another 35km will find you at the junction to Heathlands Ranger Station, 14km to the west.

When you reach a large patch of rainforest, 11km north of the Heathlands turn-off, the bypass road swings north-west, while a track to Captain Billy Landing, on the east coast, continues straight ahead. Keep on the bypass road for the next 45km to rejoin the Telegraph Track 14km north of Cockatoo Creek.

The Northern Bypass This road leaves the Telegraph Track 9km north of where the Southern Bypass Road rejoins the Telegraph Track, north of Cockatoo Creek.

This route heads west away from the Telegraph Track and for 50km winds through tropical savanna woodland to the ferry across the Jardine River. At the 18km and 30km marks, tracks head east to the Telegraph Track.

The Jardine River ferry (☎ (07) 4069 1369) normally operates seven days a week from 8 am to 5 pm, or contact the Injinoo Community Council (☎ (07) 4069 3252) for ferry details. A fee is charged to use the ferry, which includes your permit and access and camping fees.

ACTIVITIES
Seisia

The Red Island Point jetty at Seisia is one of the top fishing spots in Australia, and Gebadi's Tackle Shop nearby can supply any gear or bait you need.

Gary Wright's Wilderness Safaris (☎ (07) 4069 3400; fax 4069 3155) has sportfishing and outdoor trips as well as a small boat for hire and is based at the camping ground at Seisia. Recognised as an expert on the region, Gary can get you offshore or down into the hot spots of the Jardine River and other top end streams, chasing barra, queenfish and other fantastic game fish.

Each year the Cape York Fishing Classic

is run out of Seisia, normally during August or September. People come from all over to fish the surrounding waters and a great time is had by all.

Weipa

Around Weipa itself, and the areas north, there are some excellent fishing spots. Full/half-day river fishing safaris, costing $140/70 with all gear supplied, can be booked from the Pax Haven Campground (see the Facilities section), but you can hire a boat yourself from either the camping ground or the Weipa Snack Shack & Boat Hire Service (☎ (07) 4069 7495) at the Evans Landing wharf. The latter has 4m aluminium boats, and it's best to ring and pre-book a boat during the tourist season. Cost is $70/50 per day/half day. The Shack also sells bait and fishing accessories and can give you information on the best spots to fish.

Bamaga

The Bamaga Festival, with its rodeo and rich Aboriginal and Torres Strait Islander culture, is normally run in September each year.

ORGANISED TOURS

For most people travelling to the Cape, Cairns is the stepping-off point. It is a major city with everything you need to organise a trip north. Rental vehicles, camping equipment rental and guiding services are available, as well as a host of tour operators to organise part, or all, of your trip to the Cape.

A number of tour operators work from Seisia offering a wide range of tours, including bird-watching, nature tours, fishing and hunting safaris. Contact the Seisia Camping Ground (☎ (07) 4069 3243) for details.

Guide Services

One of the most popular ways to see the Cape is in the company of a tag-along operator. Some companies supply a cook and all the food, while others only act as guides, supplying information, permits, HF radio facilities and recovery expertise. While they do not supply a vehicle, if you need to hire one they can organise it for you. Otherwise rental companies can supply vehicles. See the earlier Cairns section or the later 4WD Rentals section.

Most tag-along companies operate out of Cairns and include the following:

Cape York Connections
    PO Box 371, Port Douglas, Qld 4871 (tel/fax (07) 4098 4938, mobile (015) 63 3332)
Guides to Adventure
    PO Box 908, Atherton, Qld 4883 (☎ (07) 4091 1978; fax 4091 2545)
Oz Tours
    PO Box 6464, Cairns, Qld 4870 (☎ (07) 4055 9535; fax 4055 9918)

Motorcycle guide services include the following:

Cape York Motorcycle Adventures
    PO Box 103, Clifton Beach, Cairns, Qld 4879 (☎ (07) 4059 0220)
2 Wheel Adventures
    146 Sheridan St, Cairns, Qld 4870 (☎ (07) 4031 5707)

There are quite a number of operators running tours to Cape York in 4WD vehicles and coaches. For a comprehensive list of established and well-known tour operators, contact the Far North Queensland Coach & Off Road Association. See Information in the Cairns to Musgrave via Cooktown section.

Boat

With magnificent offshore reefs and islands, the coast of Cape York is a popular destination for fishing enthusiasts and divers. Many charters and safaris operate from Cairns. Contact the Far North Queensland Tourist Bureau for details (see Information in the Cairns to Musgrave via Cooktown section).

The *El-Torito* operates out of Cairns to Thursday Island and cruises the Torres Strait. For cruise details and bookings, contact Jardine Shipping in Cairns (☎ (07) 4035 1900; fax 4035 1685), or the Jardine Hotel (☎ (07) 4069 1555; fax 4069 1470) on Thursday Island.

Capricorn Mist, operated by Carpentaria

THE TROPICS

Seafaris (☎ (07) 4096 5632; fax 4096 5151), PO Box 787, Malanda, Qld 4885, operates from its base at Seisia. The cost is $2145, with a minimum of four people, for an eight-day trip fishing the Gulf coast of Cape York.

Gary Wright's Wilderness Safaris (☎ (07) 4069 3400; fax 4069 3155) is based at Seisia.

For information on fishing safaris on the *Reef Safari*, see Organised Tours in the Cairns to Musgrave via Cooktown section.

FACILITIES
Fuel
Diesel, unleaded and super are generally readily available along the route to the Cape, but there is no LPG after Cairns, except at Cooktown. Prices for fuel will vary between fuel stops and can be quite expensive in places. Weipa and Bamaga always seem to be the cheapest.

Money
Probably the best option is to have a pass-book account with the Commonwealth Bank, which enables you to withdraw cash at any post office. Banking facilities are very limited on Cape York, and full banking facilities are only available at three banks in Weipa, Cooktown and Thursday Island.

Cheques are not normally accepted, but major credit cards, such as Bankcard, MasterCard and Visa, are accepted widely for most services. EFTPOS terminals are becoming more widespread and are available in Weipa and Cooktown. Australian travellers cheques are also exchanged in some places along the way. However, in many places cash is still the only form of currency accepted.

Telephones
STD phones are located at most roadhouses and certainly in the towns.

Mount Carbine
The *Mt Carbine Roadhouse* should once again be open and dispensing fuel (diesel, unleaded and super), as well as limited repair facilities. What other facilities will be available aren't known.

The *Mt Carbine Village and Caravan Park* (☎ (07) 4094 3160) has campsites for $10, powered sites for $12 and self contained cabins for $42 a double. Free caravan storage is available here. The *Mt Carbine Hotel-Motel* (☎ (07) 4094 3108) has single rooms for $25 a night while doubles costs $40.

Palmer River
The *Palmer River Roadhouse* (☎ (07) 4060 2152) has fuel and accepts only travellers cheques or cash. It is also licensed, and refreshments, snacks and evening meals are available. With miners from the local area, it can be a colourful night's stay.

There is a caravan and camping park behind the roadhouse (no dogs allowed). Cost is $3 per person for a campsite and $7 for a caravan site.

Lakeland
The small township of Lakeland caters for surrounding properties and travellers, and most facilities are available. The *Lakeland Cash Store* (☎ (07) 4060 2133) is a general store and service station. It has a good range of food supplies, takeaway food etc, and the service station supplies fuel, mechanical repairs, welding and tyres and is the RACQ Service Depot. It is open seven days a week and accepts major credit cards.

The store also runs a caravan and camping park with on-site vans, powered and unpowered sites, hot showers and laundry facilities. Camping costs $5 per person for an unpowered site, or $12 per couple for a powered site (children half price). It is also possible to store your caravan here. Dogs are allowed, under control.

The *Lakeland Hotel-Motel* (☎ (070) 4060 2142) has refreshments, snacks, counter lunches and teas. Accommodation is available for $38/55 a single/double. Breakfast can also be arranged. Most major credit cards are accepted.

The *Lakelands Roadhouse* (☎ (07) 4060 2188; fax 4060 2165), on the Peninsula Developmental Road, has all fuels, tyres, batteries, camping gas etc. It can make emergency mechanical repairs and the restaurant serves a range of meals and snacks. Shower facilities are also available. Open from 7 am to 9 pm, it has EFTPOS facilities and accepts major credit cards.

Laura

See Facilities in the Cairns to Musgrave via Cooktown section.

Hann River

The *Hann River Roadhouse* (☎ (07) 4060 3242) has fuel and does minor repairs, and has limited food supplies, snacks and a licensed restaurant. It even has its own airstrip. The combination of a camping ground with all amenities, including powered sites, and the nearby permanent water and fishing make it a pleasant spot to camp. Campsites cost $5 a single, with power costing an extra $2. You can contact the roadhouse by writing to PMB 88, Cairns Mail Centre, Qld 4870.

Musgrave

The historic *Musgrave Telegraph Station* (tel/fax (07) 4060 3229) sells fuel, refreshments, meals, takeaway food and cold beer. Accommodation is available for $20/30 a single/double and breakfast can be arranged. It is also possible to camp at Musgrave for $5 per person.

An airstrip runs beside the station, and aviation fuel can be organised if you notify the station at least one week before you intend flying in.

Coen

Coen is a major town on the Cape and caters for most travellers' needs. The *Clark's General Store & Garage* supplies groceries, fuel, gas refills for camping bottles, mechanical repairs and welding. The store is open seven days a week but the workshop is not usually open on Sunday.

Ambrust & Co General Store (☎ (07) 4060 1134; fax 4060 1128) has food supplies, and doubles as the post office with a Commonwealth Bank agency. There is also a fax facility. Fuel and camping gas is avail-

able. It is the agent for aviation fuel, although you will need to contact them beforehand to arrange supply and fuelling. The store runs a camping ground with most amenities for $5 per person for an unpowered site (power is $1 extra); there are special rates for children and families. Dogs are allowed, under control.

Counter or dining-room meals and accommodation are available at the *Exchange Hotel* (☎ (07) 4060 1133), with a choice of hotel rooms or motel units from $25/35 a single/double in the hotel or $35/45 in the motel.

You can also stay at the very pleasant *Homestead Guest House* (☎ (07) 4060 1157) for around $30/50. It also serves meals and morning and afternoon teas.

Archer River

The *Archer River Roadhouse* (tel/fax (07) 4060 3266) near the river is a great place to stop and enjoy a cold beer and friendly company, along with the famous Archer Burger. General food supplies, takeaway food, snacks, books and maps can be purchased, along with fuel. Very limited repairs can also be carried out. It is open from 7 am to 10 pm.

Campers can pitch tents in the camping ground and use all the amenities for $5 ($2 for children). Accommodation is also available in units for $30 per single, $40 a twin/double, $60 for a family. Dogs are allowed, under control.

There is an airstrip near the roadhouse and aviation fuel can be supplied, but only if you give them plenty of warning to get fuel flown in. You can contact the roadhouse by writing to PMB 77, Cairns Mail Centre, Qld 4870.

Weipa

Weipa is the largest town on the Cape, and because it is a mining town, all facilities are available. These include a Commonwealth Bank agency located in the post office which handles most banking and credit-card requirements, a chemist, a large supermarket in the suburb of Nanum, and numerous mechanical service centres.

THE TROPICS

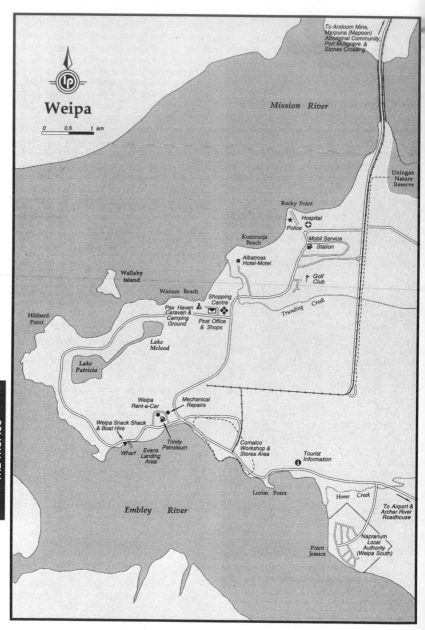

Weipa

Top: Lizard Island, Qld – punishment after all those kilometres trekking across desert Australia!
Bottom Left: Fish feeding at Aquascene, Darwin, NT
Bottom Right: Canoeing is a great way to explore Lawn Hill Creek and gorge, Qld

RICHARD NEBESKY

PETER ROBINSON

JEFF WILLIAMS

Goldfields
Top Left: British Arms Hotel, Kalgoorlie, WA
Top Right: Closed shop, Silverton, NSW
Bottom: Remains of the Old Halls Creek post office, WA

The *Pax Haven Caravan & Camping Ground* (☎ (07) 4069 7871; fax 4069 8211) offers all amenities, including hot showers and green lawns. Dogs are allowed on leashes. Costs are around $7 per person for an unpowered site, plus $2 for power. Tours of Comalco's mining operations are conducted daily during the tourist season while river fishing trips, boat hire, boat trailer hire and scenic flights can all be organised through the camping ground.

The *Albatross Hotel-Motel* (☎ (07) 4069 7314; fax 4069 7130), Trunding Point, has motel rooms and bungalows. Prices range from $90 for a single motel room, or bungalows from $50 a single to $130 for a family. Meals are served in the restaurant, or the family bistro.

Lockhart River Aboriginal Community

Visitors to the Aboriginal community at Lockhart River are welcome to stop for fuel and supplies, but are asked to respect the community's privacy. Use of cameras and videos is not permitted. You can contact the Lockhart River Community Council (☎ (07) 4060 7144; fax 4060 7139).

The *General Store* (☎ (07) 4060 7192) can supply most food items, including meat, fruit and vegetables, as well as fuel (which is expensive). It also has a post office with a Commonwealth Bank agency.

There are no camping facilities, but accommodation is available at the *guest-house* (☎ (07) 4060 7144) and it is best to book ahead. The house is self-contained, but you need to supply your own linen. It costs $40 per person per day.

Jardine River

The *Jardine River Roadhouse*, on the south bank of the river at the ferry crossing, has had a chequered history since it opened a few years ago. When it is operating it supplies fuel and has a camping area around the back. Contact the Injinoo Community Council (☎ (07) 4069 3252) for further details.

Bamaga

A wide range of facilities are available in Bamaga, the largest community on the northern Cape. The *Bamaga Service Centre* (☎ (07) 4069 3275; fax 4069 3335) has fuel available and can provide mechanical repairs, along with ice and camping-gas refills. It is open from Monday to Friday, and Saturday and Sunday mornings, and accepts major credit cards.

A reasonably well-stocked *supermarket* is open seven days a week during the tourist season, with limited trading hours on the weekend. There is also a National Australia Bank agency within the store (passbook only accepted).

The post office (☎ (07) 4069 3126) is also the Commonwealth Bank agency (again passbook only).

Beer and wine can be purchased from the *Bamaga Canteen*, fresh bread from the bakery, and ice from the ice works. There is also a snack bar and newsagency.

Seisia

The *Seisia Camping Ground* (☎ (07) 4069 3243; fax 4069 3307) is definitely the place to go and see about what is happening in and around the top end of Cape York. It is the booking agent for most tours, the ferry service and anything else that is available. You can get up-to-date fishing information and maps, along with general tourist information.

The camping ground overlooks the islands of Torres Strait and features palm-thatched picnic shelters, hot showers, washing machines and calm-water boating. Camping fees are $7 per person, power $3 extra. Self contained air-conditioned cabins are also available for $38, twin share, or $55 a single. Dogs are allowed. During the tourist season the Seisia Island Dancers give regular performances.

Seaview Lodge is part of the camping ground complex and has well set up air conditioned rooms for $48 twin share, or $65 sole occupancy. The lodge has a fully equipped communal kitchen, barbecue area and laundry. Bookings are essential.

The *Seisia Kiosk* is open seven days a week. Hot food and meals are served in the

THE TROPICS

restaurant, and snacks and takeaway food are available.

A laundromat and taxi service (☎ (07) 4069 3400) also operate out of Seisia and are located close to the camping ground.

Fuel & Repairs Seisia Marine Engineering (☎ (07) 4069 3321; fax 4069 3278) provides general fabrication and engineering, gas refills for camping bottles, aluminium welding, boat repairs, trailer and suspension repairs, and radiator clean-outs and repair. Major credit cards are accepted.

Top End Motors, on Tradesmans Way, is the place to go for all mechanical and welding repairs to your vehicle, along with batteries, tyres, oils and a range of spare parts.

The Seisia Palms Service Station (☎ (07) 4069 3172) is Australia's northernmost service station and can supply super, unleaded and diesel fuel, outboard oils and marine products.

Injinoo Aboriginal Community

The small township of Injinoo is 8km south-west of Bamaga. It has a general store, Commonwealth Bank agency, fuel and mechanical repair facilities. For information, phone the Injinoo Community Council (☎ (07) 4069 3252).

New Mapoon

Facilities are limited at this small settlement, with only general food items and ice available. However, a new camping ground is proposed in the area with beach frontage. For further information, contact the New Mapoon Community Council (☎ (07) 4069 3277).

Umagico

Limited facilities, including a general food store and canteen, are available at this small community. A pleasant beachside *camping ground* has been established at Umagico. With showers and toilets the camping fee is $7 a person.

For more details, contact the Umagico Community Council (☎ (07) 4069 3251).

Punsand Bay

On a north-facing beach just a few kilometres from the tip of Cape York is the *Punsand Bay Private Reserve* (☎ (07) 4069 1722 or 4055 9535; fax 4069 1403). Facilities include hot showers, laundry, kiosk with basic food supplies, ice, a licensed bar and a dining room serving meals for breakfast, lunch and dinner. An EFTPOS service is also available.

Activities include night walks, day tours to Cape York and the surrounding area and cruises to the offshore islands including Thursday Island. There is also a resident fishing guide with blue water and river fishing trips from $60 a half day, all gear supplied.

Those with a tent can camp; an unpowered site costs $8 per person. There are a limited number of powered sites available. Accommodation is also available in on-site tents with beds for $95 and cabins $135 per person including all meals. On-site tents are also available with no meals supplied. Communal cooking is available in the barbecue area.

There is a regular return ferry service, six days a week, from the resort to Thursday Island.

For further information or bookings, write to Punsand Bay Private Reserve, Wilderness Base Camp, Punsand Bay, Via Bamaga, Cape York, Qld 4876.

Pajinka Wilderness Lodge

The Pajinka Wilderness Lodge (☎ (07) 4069 2100; fax 4069 2110) is run by the Injinoo Aboriginal community and is only 400m from the northernmost tip of Australia. There is a resident naturalist and fishing guide, and 4WD tours with Aboriginal guides can be organised. The lodge is accessible all year round by air.

Cabin-style accommodation is available, and prices range from $230 each for triple share to $270 single occupancy. The tariff includes all meals. A fully licensed bar and pool are available for lodge guests.

Camping costs $8 per person in the *camping ground*, with unpowered sites only available. Normal amenities are provided for campers, and a licensed kiosk supplies limited stores, takeaway food and ice.

For bookings or further information, contact the Cairns office (☎ 1800 802 968, or (07) 4031 3988) at 125 Abbot St, Cairns, Qld 4870.

Station Properties

There are a number of properties that cater for the traveller, offering camping and accommodation, and organising tours.

These include: Bramwell station (☎ (07) 4060 3237), north of Wenlock River; Butchers Hill station (☎ (07) 4060 2155), near Lakelands; Melsonby station (☎ (07) 4060 2259), west of Cooktown; Mary Valley Cattle Station & Wildlife Retreat (☎ (07) 4060 3254), near Musgrave, with its own airstrip; and Silver Plains homestead (☎ (07) 4060 3228), east of Coen on the coast.

Airstrips

There are four public aerodromes, at Cooktown, Coen, Iron Range and Laura, while throughout Cape York there are small, privately owned and maintained airstrips on station properties. Aviation fuel can be organised from most of the airstrips, but give prior notice of your requirements.

Coen aerodrome (☎ (07) 4060 1136) is 24km north of Coen on the Peninsula Developmental Road. Lockhart River airfield (☎ (07) 4060 7121) is 5km from the Lockhart River Aboriginal community.

Weipa has a major airport with aviation fuel available. Jacky Jacky airfield is 9km south-east of Bamaga and is the main airport for the Top.

ALTERNATIVE TRANSPORT
Air

A wide range of charter aircraft operate all over Cape York with most based in Cairns. Each company usually has its own scheduled scenic flights and safari tours. Contact the Far North Queensland Tourist Bureau for full details (see Information in the Cairns to Musgrave via Cooktown section).

Cape York Air Services operates the Peninsula mail run, the world's longest, dropping into remote cattle stations and towns (see Alternative Transport in the Cairns to Musgrave via Cooktown section).

Flight West Airlines (☎ (07) 40 35 9511) has flights from Cairns to Cooktown, Kowanyama, Edward River, Coen, Lockhart River, Bamaga, Horn Island and Thursday Island. For details on prices and current flight schedules, write to PO Box 107, Cairns Mail Centre, Cairns, Qld 4870.

Sunstate Airlines and Qantas (☎ 13 1313) have flights from Cairns to Lizard Island, Bamaga and Thursday Island. Ring for current flight details and reservations.

Ansett Australia (☎ 13 1300) has a daily flight from Cairns to Weipa.

Skytrans (☎ (07) 4035 9444; fax 4035 9699) has flights twice weekly from Weipa to Bamaga and Thursday Island, while from Cairns it flies to Lockart River, Coen, Aurukun and Yorke Island. For more information, see Alternative Transport in the Cairns to Musgrave via Cooktown section.

Falcon Airlines has flights from Horn Island to all the islands around the top of Cape York. Contact them on Thursday Island (☎ (07) 4069 2777; fax 4069 2255) for flight details, costs and flight times, or call the main office in Cairns (☎ (07) 4035 9359).

Bus

No bus company actually runs a service all the way to the top of Cape York, but a number of companies run services from Cairns to Cooktown or Weipa.

Coral Coaches (☎ (07) 4098 2600; fax 4098 1064), 37 Front St, Mossman, Qld 4873, operates a daily bus service from Cairns to Cooktown. See Alternative Transport in the Cairns to Musgrave via Cooktown section for full details.

Cape York Coaches (☎ (07) 4093 0176), 21 Vievers Drive, Kuranda, Qld 4891, operates a weekly service from Cairns to Weipa on Friday, and Weipa to Cairns on Saturday.

Boat

A number of shipping companies service the coast of Cape York carrying a variety of cargo and stores. While many can transport vehicles, only a couple take passengers.

Jardine Shipping (☎ (07) 4035 1900) operates a weekly service from Cairns to Thursday Island and Bamaga, taking vehicles, general cargo and passengers.

Endeavour Shipping (☎ (07) 4035 1147) operates a regular service from Cairns to Bamaga carrying freight and vehicles.

Sea Swift (☎ (07) 4035 1234) has a weekly service from Cairns to Lockhart River, Bamaga and Thursday Island carrying freight, vehicles and passengers.

Thursday Island Ferry Service Peddell's Ferry & Tourist Service (☎ (07) 4069 1551; fax 4069 1365), based on Thursday Island, operates a regular ferry service between Seisia and Thursday Island. During the peak tourist season, from June to October, the ferry runs from Monday to Saturday, leaving the jetty at Seisia at 8 am and stopping at Punsand Bay and the Pajinka Wilderness Lodge to pick up passengers. An adult return fare (same day) costs $65, one way costs $45, and kids cost $45 return. Bookings are essential and can be made through Peddell's direct or at the Seisia Camping Ground, Punsand Bay or Pajinka Lodge. Peddell's also operates a bus tour of Thursday Island in conjunction with the ferry service.

4WD Rental
There are a number of companies that hire 4WDs to travellers over 25 years of age, but the majority will only let you take them as far as Cooktown and Laura. Only a few companies, based in and around Cairns, will allow you to take the vehicle all the way to the Top. These include:

Brits Rentals
    411 Sheridan St, Cairns (☎ (07) 4032 2611) – 4WDs and 4WD campervans available
Cairns Leisure Wheels
    196A Sheridan St, Cairns (☎ (07) 4051 8988) – 4WDs available for hire from Cairns to Weipa, and the Top, to drivers over 26 years of age
Cairns OffRoad Accessories 4WD Hire
    55 Anderson St, Manunda, Cairns (☎ (07) 4051 0088; fax 31 1804)

Crocodile Car Rentals
    50 Macrossan St, Port Douglas (☎ (07) 4099 5555)
Hertz 4WD Rentals
    37 Sheridan St, Cairns (☎ (07) 4031 2260)

There are other companies that hire cars in Cooktown (see the Cairns to Musgrave via Cooktown section for details), Weipa and Seisia. However, you can only use the vehicles in the local area.

Seisia Hire Cars (☎ (07) 4069 3368) operates from Seisia and has 4WDs available for daily or weekly hire. Visitors can use the vehicles to explore the surrounding area, including the Tip, Bamaga and areas north of the Jardine River. Ring and book ahead to ensure a vehicle is available.

Weipa Rent-A-Car (☎ (07) 4069 7311; fax 4069 7435), is at the airport and has 4WD vehicles available for touring around Weipa.

Motorcycle Rental
It is very difficult to hire a motorcycle to take up to the top of Cape York. However, those travelling to Cooktown or Chillagoe can hire motorcycles (250cc to 600cc) from 2 Wheel Adventures (☎ (07) 4031 5707).

Tour operators like 2 Wheel Adventures and Cape York Motor Cycle Adventures can rent a motorcycle to you for use on their guided tours to Cape York. For more information, see the Organised Tours section.

Thursday Island & Torres Strait

HIGHLIGHTS

- Experiencing one of Australia's most cosmopolitan atmospheres on tiny Thursday Island

- Enjoying a beer or cold drink at the beachside Federal Hotel

- Visiting the Japanese cemetery with its memorial to those who died searching for the elusive pearl

THE TROPICS

No visit to the top of the Cape would be complete without a visit to Thursday Island, or 'TI' as it is more often called by locals and visitors alike.

There are a number of islands scattered across the reef-strewn waters of Torres Strait, and they exhibit a surprising variety in form and function. There are three main types: the rocky, mountain-top extension of the Great Dividing Range makes up the western group that includes TI and Prince of Wales Island; the central group of islands that dot the waters east to the Great Barrier Reef are little more than coral cays; while the third type of islands are volcanic in origin and are in the far east of the strait, at the very northern end of the Great Barrier Reef. These Murray Islands are some of the most spectacular and picturesque in the area.

While TI is the 'capital' of Torres Strait, there are 17 inhabited islands, the northernmost being Saibai and Boigu islands, a couple of kilometres from the Papua New Guinea coast.

HISTORY

There were often bloody tribal conflicts across the islands before the Europeans arrived, but inevitably the Islanders came off second-best against the weaponry of the whites.

When pearl shell was discovered in the waters of the strait during the 1860s, it led to an invasion of boats and crews in search of this new form of wealth. It was a wild and savage industry with 'blackbirding', a form of kidnapping for sale into slavery, and killing being common. Being on the very edge of the frontier, the strait and all those who worked in it and plundered its resources were out of reach of the law.

Around the same time, the missionaries arrived and they were obviously successful, as the Islanders are still one of the most church-going populations in Australia.

During the first half of this century the pearling industry was the lifeblood of the area. It was a dangerous job as there was little knowledge of the physiological aspects of deep diving, and death from the bends, or decompression sickness, was common. Poor equipment and the odd storm or cyclone were also perils that the divers and crews faced. In fact, it was a cyclone in March 1899 that caused the biggest loss of life and devastated the industry. That cyclone struck Bathurst Bay where 45 boats from the TI pearling fleet were anchored, and in the following hours only one boat survived and over 300 men were killed.

While a number of nationalities made up the working population, the Japanese were considered by many to be the best divers. The price they paid for their expertise is evident in the TI cemetery where over 500 are buried.

In WWII Torres Strait and the islands were part of Australia's front line in the battle against the Japanese. Horn Island, in essence TI's airport, was bombed a number of times in 1942, but TI never had a bomb dropped on it. Some say that was due to the legend that a Japanese princess was buried on the island, but it was more than likely the fact that there was a large population of Japanese living on TI.

After the war, plastics took over where pearl shell left off. A number of cultured pearl bases still operate around the waters of TI, but the 100 or more boats that once worked the beds have long since disappeared.

In 1975 Papua New Guinea became independent. Though there was some dispute over international boundaries, all the islands up to 2km off the Papua New Guinea coast remained Australian.

Today much of the wealth of the area still comes from the sea in the form of prawns from the Gulf, for which TI is a major port, and crayfish from the reefs of the strait. Tourism is also playing its part in this region of Australia that is so vastly different to the mainland.

THURSDAY ISLAND

The island is little more than 3 sq km in area, with the town of TI on its southern shore. The population is less than 2500.

There are a few stores, including a general

store, chemist, takeaways and a branch of the National Bank (with full banking facilities). There are also four hotels, three with accommodation as well as a cold beer. There is intense but friendly rivalry between the hotels, with each supporting a local Rugby League football club. TI also has a police station (☎ (07) 4069 1520) and a hospital (☎ (07) 4069 1109).

Things to See
The **Quetta Memorial Church** was built in 1893 in memory of the *Quetta*, wrecked three years earlier with over 130 lives lost. The **cemetery**, with its Japanese graves and the more recent Japanese Pearl Memorial for those who lost their lives diving for shell, is a poignant place. **Green Hill Fort**, on the west side of town, was built in the 1890s when the Russians were thought to be coming.

While there are places of interest around TI, it is the atmosphere of the island and the people that set it apart from the rest of Australia.

Special Events
The Torres Strait Cultural Festival is held annually in May and numerous activities are organised such as art exhibitions, traditional singing, ceremonial dancing and cooking, along with a colourful procession. Visitors can also wander through the many stalls set up during the festival, many of which have local art & craft displayed. For further information contact ☎ (07) 4069 1698; fax 4069 1658, or write to PO Box 42, Thursday Island, Qld 4875.

The Coming of the Light Festival is held in July with traditional singing and chorus hymns.

Places to Stay
The *Federal Hotel* (☎ (07) 4069 1569) is on the beach front at Victoria Parade. The *Torres Hotel* (☎ (07) 4069 1141) is back one street from the water on the corner of Douglas and Normanby Sts, while the more up-market *Jardine Hotel* (☎ (07) 4069 1555) is on the corner of Normanby St and Victoria Parade. Prices range from $40 to $130 for a single.

There are also a couple of centrally located hostels on TI: the *Jumula Dubbins Hostel* (☎ (07) 4069 2212) and the *Mura Mudh Hostel* (☎ (07) 4069 1708). Prices range from $25 a bed to $50 a single with full board.

Places to Eat
Each of the hotels offer counter meals. In the evening, most have a better class of meal in their respective restaurants.

In the main area of Douglas St are a number of milk bars and takeaway places. Don't expect these to be open outside business hours – this is TI!

Getting There & Away
You can either fly to TI or catch the ferry that runs between Seisia and TI. Even if you fly you will still be up for a ferry ride as the plane lands on Horn Island, separated from TI by the 1.5km-wide Ellis Channel.

Flight West and Sunstate Airlines have regular flights to TI. For flight details and reservations, contact Flight West Airlines in Cairns (☎ (07) 4035 9511) or their TI office (☎ (07) 4069 1325); and Sunstate (☎ 13 13 13).

The most popular way to get to TI is via Peddell's Ferry Service which leaves the mainland from the jetty at Red Island Point, adjacent to the camping area at Seisia. For details, see under Boat in the earlier Cape York section.

Getting Around
To see the island, you can grab a local taxi (☎ (07) 4069 1666) or join any of the tours that generally meet the ferry from the mainland, such as Peddell's Wongai Isle Bus Tours and Willie Nelson's TI Tours. You can book the Peddell's tour through the TI office (☎ (07) 4069 1551) or with their agents at Seisia, Punsand Bay or Pajinka camping grounds (see under Facilities in the earlier Cape York section). For bookings and details for Willie Nelson's tour contact ☎ (07) 4069 1588.

Alternatively, you can hire a car from TI

Travel (☎ (07) 4069 1264) or R & F Self-Service Store (☎ (07) 4069 1173).

OTHER ISLANDS

The other inhabited islands of the strait are isolated communities wresting a living from the surrounding reef-strewn sea. The Islanders who inhabit them are fiercely proud of their heritage, with a separate identity to the Australian Aborigines.

Outside of TI the largest group of people are found on Boigu, close to the Papua New Guinea coast, where the population numbers less than 400. Most of the inhabited islands have populations between 100 and 200 people.

Information & Facilities

Getting around and staying on the other islands of Torres Strait is really for the adventurous traveller. To visit any of the islands you need a permit, and as these are issued by the local council they may not be easy to get. Contact the Islanders Community Council (☎ (07) 4069 1446) at their office in Summers St, Thursday Island.

Accommodation on these islands is very limited. The community on Yorke Island, 110km north east of TI, runs a small, self-contained *guesthouse*. Cost is $35 a single ($45 with meals). Intending visitors should first write to the community council stating details of their visit. For further details, contact the Yorke Island Community Council on (☎ (07) 4069 4128).

Accommodation is also available on Horn Island at the *Gateway Torres Strait Resort* (☎ (07) 4069 1902) and the *Wongai Tavern* (☎ (07) 4069 1683).

Getting There & Away

Once you have a permit you have a choice of who to fly with.

Air Cairns has a number of charter planes based around the straits while Falcon Airlines operates regular flights servicing many of the islands. Skytrans has direct flights to Yorke Island from Cairns on each Saturday between March and November.

For further information and reservations,

contact Air Cairns (☎ (07) 4035 9003), or Falcon Airlines at its Horn Island office (☎ (07) 4069 2777) or in Cairns (☎ (07) 4035 9359) or the Skytrans agent on TI (☎ (07) 4069 1473) or its Cairns office (☎ (07) 4035 9444).

The regular ferry or boat services to the outer islands do not take passengers.

Matilda Highway

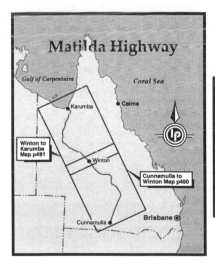

HIGHLIGHTS

- Experiencing railroading history on the tiny *Gulflander* train between Normanton and Croydon

- Discovering how the outback was developed at the Stockman's Hall of Fame in Longreach

Outback Queensland is a place where dinosaurs once roamed, the inspiration for Waltzing Matilda, the birthplace of Qantas and the home of the Stockman's Hall of Fame. It has many attractions for travellers with a sense of history and an appreciation of nature.

The all-bitumen, 1674km Matilda Highway is the name given to a route made up of sections of the Mitchell Highway, the Landsborough Highway and the Burke Developmental Road. It begins at Cunnamulla, and it takes you north from the vast open plains of south-western Queensland to Karumba, a prawn fishing centre on the Gulf of Carpentaria.

HISTORY
Aborigines inhabited this country for thousands of years, and saw the comings and goings of animals that are now preserved in the stones of Riversleigh, a monumental deposit of fossils near Lawn Hill National Park, north-west of Mount Isa, and easily accessible from this route.

Dutch navigators were the first Europeans to sight this land, when Willem Janszoon sailed the Gulf coast in 1606. Others followed but found little to interest them, and it wasn't until the great British navigator Matthew Flinders sailed along the Gulf coast, careening his ship on Sweers Island in November 1802, that the British crown showed any interest in this region.

Ludwig Leichhardt crossed the Gulf plains on his way to Port Essington in the Northern Territory in 1844. Over the next 20 years, some of Australia's greatest explorers, including Thomas Mitchell (later knighted for his exploration achievements), Burke and Wills, William Landsborough, Augustus Gregory and John McKinlay, crisscrossed the vast plains and the low rugged ranges of outback Queensland. In the process they opened up this land to the sheep and cattle graziers who quickly followed.

INFORMATION
Tourist Offices
Travellers will find tourist information centres in most towns along the route. In addition, information is available from the following tourism bodies, which also publish some very good, readily available booklets:

Outback Queensland Tourism Authority Inc, PO Box 356, Mount Isa, Qld 4825 (☎ (07) 4743 7966; fax 4743 8746)
Outback Queensland Tourism Authority Inc, PO Box 295, Blackall, Qld 4472 (☎ (07) 4657 4255; fax 4657 4437)
Gulf Savannah Tourist Association, PO Box 2312, Cairns, Qld 4870 (☎ (07) 4031 1631; fax 4031 3340)

For information on any of the national parks, contact the Department of Environment & Heritage in Brisbane (☎ (07) 3227 7111) or the regional headquarters in Townsville (☎ (07) 4743 2055).

Books & Maps
The Queensland state mapping authority's map *The Matilda Highway* can be purchased from Sunmap centres or agencies and good book/map shops.

THE ROUTE
Cunnamulla
The southernmost town in western Queensland, Cunnamulla (population 1700) is on the Warrego River 120km north of the Queensland/New South Wales border. It lies 805km west of Brisbane via St George and 1034km north-west of Sydney via Bourke (254km away).

The town was gazetted in 1868, and in 1879 Cobb & Co established a coaching station here. In the 1880s, an influx of farmers opened the country up to the two million sheep that graze the open plains today. The train arrived in 1898, and since then Cunnamulla has been a major service centre for the district; in good years it is Queensland's biggest wool-loading railyard.

For information on Cunnamulla, contact the tourist information centre (☎ (07) 4655 2121; fax 4655 1647) at the shire hall.

The town has two hotel/motels, four hotels, one motel and one caravan park, as well as a number of service stations, supermarkets and the like.

There is the **Historical Society Display**,

THE TROPICS

telling the story of the pioneers of the district, and the **Robbers Tree**, a reminder of a bungled robbery in the 1880s. Another tree at the civic centre takes some importance from the fact that it is a yapunyah tree, floral emblem of the Paroo Shire – it was planted by royalty!

In late August/early September the town celebrates the Cunnamulla-Eulo Festival of the Opal, a week-long festival with arts & crafts, lizard racing, woodchopping, sandhill digging and ironman competitions, a parade and ball. Another major event is the annual Show, held in May.

Cunnamulla to Augathella (281km)

From Cunnamulla you can head east along the Balonne Highway to Brisbane, or go west to Thargomindah and on past the Jackson Oil Fields to Innamincka, in north-eastern South Australia – see the Strzelecki Track section in the Central Deserts chapter.

Eulo, 64km west of Cunnamulla, is on the Paroo River close to the Yowah opal fields. In late August/early September it hosts the **World Lizard Racing Championships**. The **Destructo Cockroach Monument** was erected in memory of a racing cockroach who died when a punter stood on it; this granite plinth must be the only cockroach memorial in the world.

Our route from Cunnamulla lies north along the Mitchell Highway, paralleling the Warrego River off to the west. The railway follows a similar route. A couple of railway sidings, the odd station homestead and tiny **Wyandra**, with the obligatory hotel and general store, make up the habitation profile of the 197km trip to Charleville. For the most part, the mainly flat country is clothed in mulga.

Charleville One of the largest towns in outback Queensland, Charleville is 760km west of Brisbane and situated on the Warrego River. Edmund Kennedy passed this way in 1847, and the town was gazetted in 1868, six years after the first settlers had arrived. By the turn of the century it was an important service centre for the outlying sheep stations.

Cobb & Co began building coaches at Charleville in 1893, and these coaches, especially designed for Australian conditions, were built here until 1920. The last official service by coach ran from Yuleba to Surat just four years later.

Aviation history was being made at the same time. In 1921 Qantas (Queensland & Northern Territory Aerial Services) was founded in Winton, and in November of the following year the carrier's first fare-paying passengers flew between Charleville and Cloncurry, further north on our trip to the Gulf.

The tourist information centre (☎ (07) 4654 3057) in the Billabong Park on Cunnamulla Road, and the Western Travel Service (☎ (07) 4654 1026) in Alfred St have details of points of interest and things to do in and around Charleville.

The town has a couple of hotel/motels, four motels and two caravan parks, as well as service stations, general stores, supermarkets, chemists and butchers – in fact, everything a traveller (or a remote outback community) needs.

Apart from its links with the stagecoach days and the birth of Qantas, Charleville offers history buffs the **Historic House Museum**, the **Steiger Vortex Gun** (invented in an attempt to break the great drought of 1902) and the **Landsborough Tree** (marked by the explorer William Landsborough in 1862, a few kilometres south of town on the edge of the river).

The **RFDS base** (☎ (07) 4654 1341) and the **School of the Air** (now called the School of Distance Education) are both open to visitors. On the east side of town, the National Parks & Wildlife Service's **research centre** (☎ (07) 4654 1255) has a breeding programme for the endangered bilby, sometimes called the rabbit-eared bandicoot.

Situated in a specially built observatory at the Charleville airport, **Outback Queensland Skywatch** (☎ (07) 4654 1260) offers visitors guided tours of the night skies through powerful telescopes.

A number of events are held at Charleville during the year. In May the annual Show

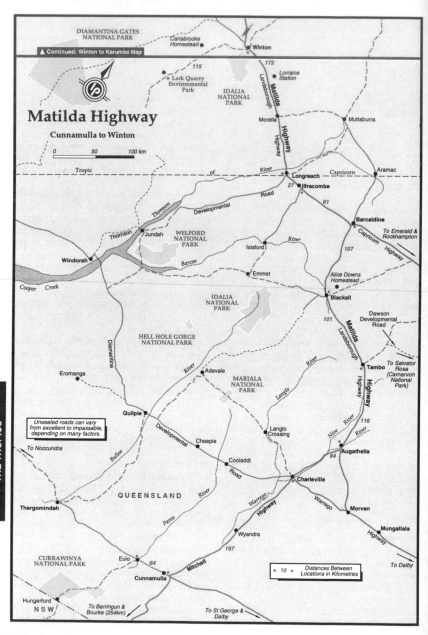

Matilda Highway

Cunnamulla to Winton

0   50   100 km

DIAMANTINA GATES
NATIONAL PARK

Carisbrooke
Homestead

Winton

▲ Continued: Winton to Karumba Map

115   172   Lorraine
                     Station

Lark Quarry
Environmental
Park

IDALIA
NATIONAL
PARK

Morella   Muttaburra

Tropic   of   River   Longreach   Capricorn   Aramac

27 Ilfracombe

Developmental   Road   81

Thomson   Barcaldine   To Emerald &
                                 Rockhampton

Thomson   Jundah   WELFORD
                     NATIONAL
                     PARK

River   Capricorn   Highway

Isisford   107

Windorah   Barcoo   Emmet   Alice Downs
                                 Homestead

Cooper   Creek   Blackall

IDALIA
NATIONAL
PARK   101   Dawson
                 Developmental
                 Road

HELL HOLE GORGE
NATIONAL PARK   Landsborough

Diamantina   Eromanga   River   Adavale   MARIALA
                                         NATIONAL
                                         PARK   River   Tambo   To Salvator
                                                                     Rosa
                                                                     (Carnarvon
                                                                     National Park)

Langlo   116

Quilpie   Highway

Unsealed roads can vary
from excellent to impassable,
depending on many factors.   Developmental   Cheepie   Langlo
                                                         Crossing   Nive   River

Bulloo   Road   Cooladdi   84   Augathella

To Noccundra   River   Charleville

QUEENSLAND   Warrego   Highway   Warrego   Morven

Thargomindah   Paroo   River   Mungallala

Highway   To Dalby

Wyandra   197

CURRAWINYA
NATIONAL PARK   Eulo   64   Mitchell   ★ 10 ★   Distances Between
                                                       Locations in Kilometres

Cunnamulla

Hungerford   To Barringun &
N S W   Bourke (254km)   To St George &
                           Dalby

THE TROPICS

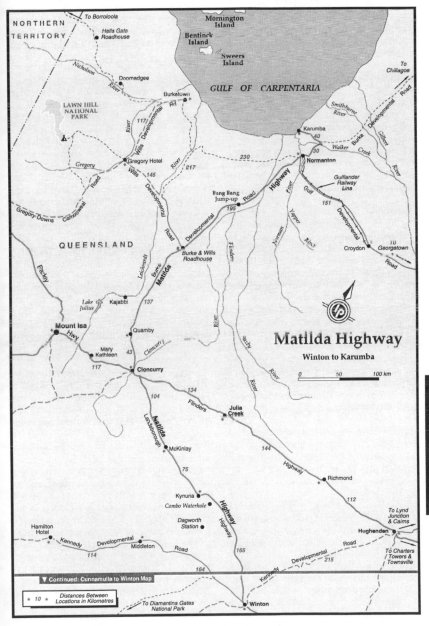

NORTHERN TERRITORY

To Borroloola

Hells Gate Roadhouse

Mornington Island

Bentinck Island

Sweers Island

GULF OF CARPENTARIA

Nicholson River

Doomadgee

LAWN HILL NATIONAL PARK

Burketown

Burketown Rd

Smithburne River

Karumba
40
30

Normanton

Walker Creek

Burke

Gilbert River

To Chillagoe

Developmental Road

Wills Developmental

117

Gregory Hotel
145
£17

Gregory

Wills

River

230

Bang Bang Jump-up

Road

Highway

Norman River

Gulf

Yappar

Gulflander Railway Line

151

Developmental

Croydon

To Georgetown
10

QUEENSLAND

Gregory-Downs

Cahooweal

Gregory Road

Developmental Road

195

Burke & Wills Roadhouse

Flinders River

Leichhardt River

Eyre Matilda

River

Leichhardt

River

Flinders River

Yamman River

Saxby River

Cloncurry River

Parley

Lake Julius

Kajabbi
137

Mount Isa
Hwy

Quamby

Matilda Highway

Winton to Karumba

0   50   100 km

Mary Kathleen
117

43

Cloncurry

104

134

Flinders

Julia Creek

Matilda

Landsborough

McKinlay

75

144

Highway

Richmond

Kynuna

Combo Waterhole

Dagworth Station

Highway

112

To Lynd Junction & Cairns

Hughenden

Hamilton Hotel

Kennedy

Developmental

Middleton

Road

114

165

Developmental Road
215

To Charters Towers & Townsville

164

Kennedy

▼ Continued: Cunnamulla to Winton Map

To Diamantina Gates National Park

Winton

* 10 *   Distances Between Locations in Kilometres

THE TROPICS

takes place, and in September there is a rodeo, and the Booga Woongaroo Festival, with historic displays and a fishing competition as part of the festivities.

North of Charleville From Charleville you can head east to Brisbane via Roma, or west to Quilpie, Windorah and Bedourie via the Diamantina Developmental Road.

Our route, however, continues northwards along the Mitchell Highway, paralleling the Warrego River. The river offers opportunities to dangle a line for Murray cod, yellowbelly, golden perch (one of the tastiest freshwater fish in Australia) or catfish.

Augathella

The town of Augathella is 84km north of Charleville. It lies at the junction of the Mitchell Highway and the road south-east to Morven and the route to Brisbane. Southeast Queensland travellers heading north to Mount Isa, the Gulf or the Northern Territory often join the Matilda at this junction.

Surveyed in 1880, Augathella began as a bullock team camp beside the Warrego River. Today it's a service centre for the surrounding sheep properties.

This small country town has one hotel, one motel and a caravan park, with fuel and supplies from the shops in town. Tourist information can be obtained from Russell's Roadhouse (☎ (07) 4654 5255).

Augathella to Barcaldine (324km)

At Augathella you change highways, continuing north-west on the Landsborough Highway; 116km north of Augathella is the small township of **Tambo**, on the banks of the Barcoo River.

Tambo is surrounded by perhaps the best grazing land in western Queensland, and this small hamlet also has some of the earliest historic buildings in the region. In the main street are timber houses that date back to the town's earliest days in the 1860s, while the 'new' post office has been operating since 1904. The **old post office**, built in 1876 and at that time the main repeating station for south-west Queensland, is now a museum.

The town has a couple of hotels and motels and a caravan park. It can supply all you require, including LPG. The information centre is at the shire council chambers (☎ (07) 4654 6133).

Tambo promotes itself as 'the friendly town of the west', and each year races are held at the local track, a tradition dating back to the formation of the Great Western Downs Jockey Club, in 1865.

From Tambo you continue northwards, but if you're looking for a good excursion, there is access to the **Salvator Rosa** section of Carnarvon National Park. The Salvator Rosa park is 120km east of Tambo via the Dawson Developmental Road and the Cungelella station, generally a 4WD route.

Discovered and named by the explorer Thomas Mitchell in 1846, the same year he discovered the downs on which Tambo is situated, Salvator Rosa's 26,000 hectares protect a maze of sandstone escarpments and gorges. It's a spectacularly rugged area with few facilities, and you need a permit from the national parks to camp. Try the park office (☎ (07) 4684 4086) or the regional office in Longreach (☎ (07) 4658 1761) for more information.

Continuing northwards along the Landsborough Highway, it's a pleasant run of 101km to the town of Blackall. The **Barcoo River** is crossed 59km north of Tambo; there's an excellent spot to camp off the eastern side of the road.

The Barcoo is one of the great rivers of western Queensland, and must be the only river in the world that in its lower reaches becomes a creek! The Barcoo initially flows north-west past Blackall, then swings south-west through Isisford and into the Channel Country of south-western Queensland, where it becomes Cooper Creek, probably the most famous of Australia's inland rivers.

While Mitchell had waxed lyrical about this river in 1846, thinking it was a route to the Gulf, it was left to his second-in-command Edmund Kennedy (later of Cape York fame) to discover the real course of the river and to call it the Barcoo in 1847.

Both Banjo Paterson and Henry Lawson

mention the Barcoo in their writings. The name has also entered the Australian idiom, appearing in the *Macquarie Dictionary* in such terms as 'Barcoo rot' (basically scurvy), the 'Barcoo salute' (the waving about of hands to keep flies away from the face) and the 'Barcoo spews' (vomiting caused by the heat).

Gazetted in 1868, **Blackall** is named after the second governor of Queensland, Samuel Blackall. The town is a pleasant spot to stop on trips north or south along the Matilda. It can provide a wide range of accommodation in its two motels, four hotels and one caravan park, while fuel and supplies are available from a good range of outlets.

The town prides itself on the fact that, in 1892 at nearby Alice Downs station, the legendary shearer Jack Howe set his world record of shearing 321 sheep in less than eight hours, with a set of hand shears! The record still stands today – even shearers using machine-powered shears didn't reach that number until 1950. Acclaimed as the greatest 'gun' (the best in the shed) shearer in the world, Jackie's name lives on in the working man's blue singlet which he made popular. After his shearing days were over, he ran one of the hotels in Blackall, and is buried there.

Blackall was the site of the first artesian well to be drilled in Queensland, although the well didn't strike water at first and when it did the product was undrinkable. After you use the bore water for washing or whatever, you'll probably agree with most travellers and say it stinks a little. Locals reckon it's got a bit of 'body'.

North-east of Blackall is the **Blackall Woolscour**, the only steam-driven scour (wool-cleaner) left in Queensland. It stopped operating in 1978, but guided tours of the operation are run by the local tourist office.

Annual events in Blackall include the Claypan Bogie Country Music Festival (in late Feb/early March) and the Show (in May). In October every even-numbered year, the Barcoo Rush Festival takes place featuring the Jackie Howe run and shearing competition.

For more information on Blackall, contact the Blackall Community Tourist Office (tel/fax (07) 4657 4637).

From Blackall you can travel into the Channel Country of south-west Queensland by heading out to Isisford or Windorah (115km and 337km west of Blackall, respectively). Our route, though, lies north along the Landsborough Highway.

North of Blackall Travelling these roads at night is not recommended. Kangaroos often reach plague proportions out in western Queensland, and the edge of the bitumen is a place where water gathers from any rain and where green feed is more readily available. At night in a 100km section of this road, you can see in excess of 1000 animals.

An hour's travelling on the bitumen across flat, lightly treed plains brings you to Barcaldine, 107km north of Blackall.

Barcaldine

Barcaldine lies at the junction of the Landsborough and Capricorn highways, 575km west of Rockhampton via Emerald and is surrounded by sheep and cattle stations. It's known as the 'Garden City of the West', with good supplies of artesian water nourishing orchards of citrus fruits – Barcaldine was the first town in Australia to realise its underground bounty, in 1887.

Established in 1886 when the railway arrived, Barcaldine gained a place in Australian history in 1891 when it became the headquarters of the historic shearers' strike during which over 1000 men camped in and around the town. That confrontation saw troops called in, and the formation of the Australian Workers' Party, the forerunner of today's Australian Labor Party. The **Tree of Knowledge**, near the train station, was the meeting place of the organisers, and still stands as a monument to workers and their rights. The **Australian Workers' Heritage Centre** (☎ (07) 4651 1422), opened by the prime minister in 1991, also commemorates the struggle – this complex includes a number of exhibition halls.

Barcaldine's other attractions include the

THE TROPICS

folk museum, historic **Beta Farm** (dating from the 1880s) and a number of National Trust buildings. The annual Show is held in May, while the town's Artesian Festival with its mardi gras, golf tournaments and more is usually held in June.

A good range of accommodation is available in Barcaldine's six hotels, four motels and two caravan parks. There's also the normal range of stores and outlets for fuel, food and other supplies and facilities. Tourist information is available from the information centre (☎ (07) 4651 1724) in Oak St.

Barcaldine to Winton (280km)
From Barcaldine you can head east to Rockhampton and the coast, or you can head north through the small but interesting towns of Aramac and Muttaburra to Hughenden, 357km north of Barcaldine. The unsealed road from Muttaburra to Hughenden passes through flat country and can be a bit rough in places, but is usually quite manageable in a conventional vehicle with sufficient ground clearance. For more information contact the local shire office (☎ (07) 4651 3311).

From Hughenden, you can head east along the sealed Flinders Highway to Charters Towers and Townsville, or continue up the Kennedy Developmental Road to the bitumen at the Lynd Junction and on to Cairns – an interesting route that takes you past the stunning Porcupine Gorge. This road is rocky and rougher than the previous section, but is usually OK in a conventional vehicle driven with care.

Our route from Barcaldine, however, lies west along the Landsborough Highway, across the wide open plains towards Longreach.

Ilfracombe, a hamlet 81km from Barcaldine, contains several historic buildings and a good folk museum. The hotel offers accommodation and camping, while the general store provides fuel and takeaway food. Contact the shire council office (☎ (07) 4658 2233) for tourist information.

Longreach Longreach, 27km further west,

is on a 'long reach' of the Thomson River. Apart from Mount Isa further north, it's western Queensland's largest town, with a population of around 3500.

The surrounding region was explored by Augustus Gregory in 1858 and 1859, and though the area was settled in the 1870s, the town was not officially gazetted until 1887.

It was in 1870 that Harry Redford stole 1000 head of cattle from Mount Cornish, an outstation of Bowen Downs, north of Longreach, and drove them down the Thomson River and its continuation, Cooper Creek, to the present site of Innamincka. From there he followed the Strzelecki Creek south, finally selling his ill-gotten gains to a station owner north of Adelaide. His exploit opened up a new stock route south, and when he was finally brought to justice, in Roma in 1873, he was found not guilty by the admiring public!

The railway arrived in 1892, and during the early years of the 20th century, the wool boom made Longreach into the town you see today.

In February 1921 the first **Qantas** flight left here for Winton, and the following year Longreach became the operational base for the fledgling airline founded in Charleville. The first seven aircraft built in Australia were constructed here, between 1922 and 1930.

Located in the heart of Queensland's outback and at the crossroads of some of the great cattle stock routes, it is no wonder that Longreach is the site of the **Australian Stockman's Hall of Fame**. Opened in 1988, the brainchild of artist Hugh Sawrey, it is one of the finest museums in the country, honouring the explorers, stockmen, shearers, pastoralists and everyday folk who helped open up outback Australia. It's a place that should not be missed.

The recently opened **Qantas Founders' Outback Museum** is situated in the Qantas hangar at Longreach airport and houses, among other exhibits, a full-size replica of an Arvo 504K, the first type of passenger aircraft used by Qantas. Also worth a visit is the **Longreach Powerhouse Museum** in Swan St. The powerhouse supplied electricity to the area from 1921 to 1985 and generators and associated equipment from each phase of its development are still in place.

A number of events are held in Longreach during the year. The **Outback Muster & Drovers Reunion** is normally run in April while the Thomson River Campdraft and the annual Show take place in May. During July there are shearing championships, as well as the Waltzing Matilda Endurance Ride, run between Winton and Longreach. Every even-numbered year the Starlight Stampede Festival is held in September.

There are also a number of other points of interest in and around the town and, of course, the river provides an opportunity for canoeing and fishing. A number of tours are available to historic or scenic attractions in the surrounding area, and there are enjoyable cruises on the river as well. Most of these are for two or three hours; try the 'Sunset Cruise'.

As is to be expected in such a large and important town, there is everything a traveller needs. Accommodation-wise there is a wide choice, with five hotels, five motels, two caravan parks and a backpackers' hostel. For local information contact the Longreach Outback Travel Centre (☎ (07) 4658 1776; fax (07) 4658 1794) in Eagle Street.

Longreach to Winton From Longreach you can head south along the Thomson Developmental Road to Windorah and places further south along Cooper Creek. Northwards you can head to Muttaburra and to Hughenden, 380km west of Townsville.

For those travelling the Matilda, head north-west out of Longreach along the Landsborough Highway; just out of town you cross the Thomson River.

The little township of Winton is entered nearly 48km further on, 172km north of Longreach.

HUGH FINLAY

Stockman's Hall of Fame

Winton

At the crossroads of the Landsborough Highway and the east-west Kennedy Developmental Road, Winton was settled in 1875 and now services the surrounding sheep and cattle stations.

This outback town has its fair share of claims to fame, with Banjo Paterson and Qantas figuring prominently. Back in 1895 the original North Gregory Hotel in Winton was the venue for the first public performance of Paterson's *Waltzing Matilda*, which he had written after a visit to Combo Waterhole on Dagworth station (where a local shearer had committed suicide), 140km north-west of Winton. Since then the song has become the country's unofficial anthem, recognised around the world as pure Australian. An annual bush-verse competition, The Bronze Swagman Award, attracts interest from all over Australia, keeping alive the Banjo Paterson tradition and celebrating its influence on Australian literature. The Waltzing Matilda Festival held in April of each year features a race meeting, a rodeo and bush poetry.

Australia's major airline, Qantas, began in Winton – the first board meeting occurred in the Winton Club in 1921.

With those two events in mind, it's no surprise that the local museum is called **Qantilda Pioneer Place**, and it's worth more than a cursory look. As with any country town that has been around for over 100 years, Winton has its share of country architecture, with the open-air **Royal Theatre** testimony to the fine weather and just one of the interesting buildings in town.

South-west of the town is **Lark Quarry Environmental Park**, where fossilised footprints testify to a stampede of small dinosaurs 100 million years ago. It's a well-signposted trip of 115km each way on dirt roads to the site, which has no facilities other than a toilet and a rainwater tank.

The Diamantina Lakes National Park (☎ (07) 4657 3024) is located 290km south-west of Winton and is accessed via the Kennedy Developmental Road. It is a great bird habitat.

With a population of 1200, Winton has three motels, four hotels, two caravan parks, a good selection of stores for supplies, and a choice of fuel outlets. The Gift & Gem Centre (☎ (07) 4657 1296) in Elderslie St is the local tourist information centre.

Winton to Cloncurry (344km)

Heading north-west out of town on the Landsborough Highway, the country is rolling grassland dotted with the occasional mesa or patch of breakaway country. The wide thoroughfare is a recognised stock route, and it's not unusual to see cattle and drovers wandering the 'long paddock'. In those cases where there are sheep or cattle spread all over the road, you should slow down to a crawl, stopping if necessary, and let the people and dogs handling the stock work their way around you. Enjoy the passing parade – it is a way of life that brings back images of Australia's pioneering past.

The turn-off to Paterson's Combo Waterhole is signposted, 145km north of Winton. After another 20km you come to tiny **Kynuna**, where you can get fuel and limited supplies. Kynuna is dominated by the 100-year-old **Blue Heeler Hotel**. It's a top spot for a cool beer, and also offers meals and accommodation.

McKinlay, 75km north of Kynuna, can also supply fuel and limited stores. Named after the explorer who passed through this region in the 1860s after searching for Burke and Wills, it's a little bigger than Kynuna, but that is not saying much! It has a top pub that you need to turn off the main highway to visit; once it would rarely see any passing traffic, but since it became **Walkabout Creek Hotel** in the quintessentially Australian film *Crocodile Dundee*, life has never been the same. It's an inviting place, dispensing cold beer, good meals and friendly banter. The pub also offers accommodation, and there is a small caravan/camping ground just out the back.

The country begins to change north of McKinlay, the flat plain giving way first to low rolling hills and then to ever more rugged country. By the time the road crosses the railway to Cloncurry and Mount Isa and then, soon after, joins with the Flinders Highway just 14km east of Cloncurry, you are surrounded by low, craggy hills, scoured with veins of bare rock and cut by narrow, convoluted creeks that tear out the earth after any heavy rain.

The country remains the same for the run into Cloncurry, 344km north of Winton.

Cloncurry

Cloncurry traces its European heritage back to the days of the ill-fated Burke and Wills expedition, which passed this way in 1861 and named the Cloncurry River, on whose banks the town was built. There are a number of monuments to these explorers in and around the town.

Founded a few years later, Cloncurry had one of the world's biggest copper mines, ensuring its early prosperity. The **Great Australia Mine**, just a little to the south of town, operated until the early 1920s. Visitors can wander over the old workings and around the ruins.

As you come into town, it's hard to miss the **Mary Kathleen Memorial Park & Museum** on the left. It preserves relics of the uranium-mining town of Mary Kathleen, now just a spot on the map about 60km west towards Mount Isa. The park is a beauty, and the museum has many reminders of the region's interesting history.

Apart from the museum, Cloncurry's major attraction is **John Flynn Place**. This museum tells the history of the RFDS, which was founded in this town by the Reverend John Flynn, a minister of the Presbyterian Church working for the Australian Inland Mission (which he also helped set up). In 1928 the first flight of the RFDS was from Cloncurry to Julia Creek, 134km to the east. Just a couple of years earlier, Alfred Traeger, an Adelaide radio engineer, had developed a 'pedal wireless', with Flynn's support, and with such technology the 'mantle of safety' Flynn wanted for the pioneers in the outback was about to be put into place.

There an **RFDS Historical Museum** in the town, and an original Qantas hangar. The

Afghan and Chinese cemeteries here are a little different from the more commonly seen Christian ones, and are testimony to the area's rich cultural heritage. The town is also noteworthy for having recorded the highest shade temperature in Australia: 53.1°C (more than 130°F) in 1889. As in much of the north, the best time to visit is in the cooler winter (dry) season.

With a population of around 2000, and catering for a vast pastoral and mining region, Cloncurry can meet a traveller's every need. The town has a couple of hotel/motels, a motel and a caravan park, and good choices of fuel outlets and places to buy supplies or takeaway food. Cloncurry also has a tourist information centre (☎ (07) 4742 1361).

Tours are available in the local area and as far afield as **Kajabbi** (100km north-west of Cloncurry) and **Lake Julius** (40km west of Kajabbi). For the do-it-yourselfer, there is fishing in the river and trips to the old mining areas dotted through the ranges. The town is a good base from which to explore the surrounding area or even take a day trip to Mount Isa.

Cloncurry to Karumba (445km)

While the Matilda Highway continues northwards, Cloncurry is a major stepping-off point for those heading west to Mount Isa and the Northern Territory. Eastwards, the Flinders Highway stretches all the way to the coast at Townsville, 770km away.

Once across the Cloncurry River the Matilda Highway breaks away from the Flinders Highway and takes to the narrower Burke Developmental Road. It's not long before you leave the gentle pastoral country well and truly behind.

Quamby, just 8km north of the tiny hamlet of Urquhart, is a total of 43km north of Cloncurry. Once a Cobb & Co coach stop and a centre for the gold mining that helped develop the region, Quamby now has nothing but the historic Quamby Hotel. You'll enjoy a beer here and fuel is also available.

Continuing north across the rolling hills

dotted with low, spindly gums, you reach the turn-off to **Kajabbi** 29km north of Quamby. Once the focus of the area, Kajabbi has been all but forgotten. The town was once the railhead for this part of the Gulf's cattle industry and the nearby copper mines, but all that has long since disappeared. The Kalkadoon Hotel (☎ (07) 4742 5979) is the focal point for locals and visitors alike. From here there is much to explore, including the Mt Cuthbert Mine site, and the site of the last stand of the Kalkadoon people, who resisted the white invasion in bloody battles during the 1880s.

Just before the Burke & Wills Roadhouse along the Burke Developmental Road, 180km north of Cloncurry, the Wills Developmental Road from Julia Creek comes in from the right.

Nearly everyone stops at the **Burke & Wills Roadhouse** (☎ (07) 4472 5909) where there's a little shade, ice creams to buy from the well-stocked store and, if you really need it, fuel. Accommodation, camping and supplies are also available.

From the roadhouse you can strike northwest along the Wills Developmental Road to the fabulous Gregory River, where there is some excellent bush camping, and the famous **Gregory Downs Hotel** (☎ (07) 4748 5566). From there a reasonable dirt road leads north to friendly Burketown or westwards to the impressive **Lawn Hill National Park** (☎ (07) 4748 5572) – see the Gulf Track section earlier in this chapter.

For those travelling the Matilda, the route continues in a more northerly direction towards the Gulf. The country remains reasonably flat, but once you get to **Bang Bang Jump-Up** and descend about 40m to the Gulf plains proper, you really know what 'flat' means. This near-sheer escarpment vividly marks where the high country ends, 80km north of the roadhouse.

From this point the road stretches across vast, billiard-table-flat plains covered in deep grass, which in the Dry is the colour of gold. Dotted here and there are clumps of trees, and wherever there is permanent water or shade there are cattle. In this country the cattle stand out – during the day. At night, as everywhere in outback Queensland, they can make driving on the roads very hazardous.

Normanton On the Norman River 375km from Cloncurry, Normanton marks the end of the 195km stage from the roadhouse. The most important town in the Gulf region, Normanton was established in 1868 and really boomed during the 1890s gold rush to the Croydon gold fields, 150km inland. So rich were these fields that the railway which was supposed to be built from Normanton south was eventually pushed through to Croydon. Today, the *Gulflander*, as it is called, is an isolated offshoot of the main Queensland railway network and caters more for tourists than for locals. Every Wednesday it leaves Normanton at 8.30 am on the trip to Croydon. It leaves Croydon the following morning, getting back to Normanton early or mid afternoon. It's a beauty – don't miss it.

Since those heady days, the town has existed as a major supply point for the surrounding cattle stations, and as the shire centre. It has a couple of hotel/motels and a caravan park, and has several fuel outlets and places to stock up on supplies. Several of its historic buildings are still in use, including the Carpentaria Shire Council offices and Burn Philps store, down towards the river end of the town. The shire council (☎ (07) 4745 1166; fax 4745 1340) can help with information.

Travellers may also be interested in the Normanton Rodeo & Gymkhana held in June, the area's biggest social and sporting event of the year. In August the races and a ball take place.

As a base for fishing, Normanton is hard to beat, with the Norman River producing some magic-size barramundi. From here it's just a hop, step and jump across the plains to the Gulf port of Karumba.

Normanton to Karumba Heading out of town, the Burke Developmental Road soon crosses the Norman River and, less than 29km up the road, a major tributary of the river, Walker Creek. At the 30km mark is a major intersection. Veer left here, sticking to the bitumen, and the road quickly swings almost due west.

Traversing these great plains, it is not hard to imagine that during the torrential rains of the wet season, this area becomes one huge lake. At times, with king tides backing up the waters of the rivers, the floods isolate towns like Normanton for weeks at a time.

The bird life is rich and varied – this region is the best in Australia to see the stately brolga and the very similar sarus crane – a recent natural invader from South-East Asia. Another large bird which you'll see is the magpie-coloured jabiru, certainly one of the most majestic birds of the tropics.

Karumba

Karumba, 70km from Normanton, is right beside the Gulf of Carpentaria and the Norman River. Originally established as a telegraph station in the 1870s, it became a stopover for the flying boats of the Empire Mail Service in the 1930s. The discovery of prawns in the Gulf in the 1960s brought Karumba alive, and today that industry keeps the town humming. You certainly can't miss seeing the boats as they sit beside the jetty, draped with nets, just a stone's throw from the pub and the centre of town.

There's a hotel/motel here and a couple of caravan parks; the former can really be jumping when the boats come in for a short break or for resupply. There are also a number of holiday cabins available. The town can supply basic travelling requirements like fuel and food, as well as nearly everything for the fishing person.

Festivals held during the year include the Karumba Kapers (in July), the Barra Ball (in November) and the Fisherman's Ball (in December).

The town lives and breathes fish and fishing, prawns and prawning. If you aren't interested in these things, you won't stay long. Sure, you can actually get to the sea at Karumba – one of the few places around the Gulf that you can – but once you've checked the town, been to the beach at Karumba Point

and enjoyed a prawn or two at the pub, there is not much else to hold your attention. Of course, you could always fly to Mornington or Sweers islands out in the Gulf, but once again, these are favoured fishing haunts and you need to love fishing to fully appreciate these wild, remote places.

If you don't have your own boat, you can hire one from Karumba Boat Hire (☎ (07) 4745 9132) at Karumba Point. There are also a number of boating and fishing tours run from Karumba, and Air Karumba (☎ (07) 4745 9354) has flights to Mornington and Sweers islands, as well as further afield around the Gulf. Contact the Carpentaria Shire Council in Normanton (☎ (07) 4745 1166) for full details.

Karumba marks the end of the Matilda, and if you have been travelling it from its humble origin in Cunnamulla, 1674km south, you have experienced one of the best bitumen trips in Australia. Like anything fine, it is to be savoured slowly – take your time and enjoy!

ORGANISED TOURS

Contact the various tourism bodies and regional tourist information centres for details of local tour operators.

FACILITIES
Cunnamulla

There is a range of accommodation to choose from at such establishments as the *Billabong Hotel/Motel* (☎ (07) 4655 1225) and the *Corella Motor Inn* (☎ (07) 4655 1593) where rooms cost $40/50 a single/double. There is also the *Jack Tonkin Caravan Park* (☎ (07) 4655 1421), where dogs are allowed (under control) and sites cost $12/10 powered/unpowered, while accommodation in the park cabin section costs $28 a double.

The local RACQ depot is Bill's Auto (☎ (07) 4655 1407).

Eulo

Travellers can stay at the *Eulo Queen Hotel* (☎ (07) 4655 4867), or at the *Eulo Caravan Park* (☎ (07) 4655 4890) with powered and unpowered sites at $10/7, and pets are

THE TROPICS

allowed. The *Carpet Springs Tourist Retreat* (☎ (07) 4655 4604) near Eulo has dormitory style accommodation for five people, costing $90 a single per day all meals inclusive.

Charleville

Accommodation is available at the *Charleville Motel* (☎ (07) 4654 1566) with room only for $45/55 a single/double; *Charleville Waltzing Matilda Motor Inn* (☎ (07) 4654 1720) with rooms for $35/40 a single/double; and *Warrego Motel* (☎ (07) 4654 1299) at $55/65 a single/double. The *Bailey Bar Caravan Park* (tel/fax (07) 4654 1744) has a park cabin section from $40/41 a single/double and on-site vans from $25 a double, while powered and unpowered sites are $12/10 a double. There is also the *Cobb & Co Caravan Park* (☎ (07) 4654 1053) with on-site vans from $26 a double and powered/unpowered sites $12/10 a double. Pets are allowed at both parks.

The local RACQ depot is Bert's Body Shop (☎ (07) 4654 1733, after hours 4654 1214).

Augathella

Travellers can stay at the *Augathella Motel/Caravan Park* (☎ (07) 4654 5177) with a choice of units from $45/55 a single/double, or powered/unpowered sites at $12/10 a double. Dogs are allowed (on a leash).

Tambo

A choice of accommodation is available at the *Club Hotel/Motel* (☎ (07) 4654 6109) where a unit costs $30/45 a single/double or budget hotel room is $12 for a single; the *Royal Carrangarra Hotel* (☎ (07) 4654 6127) has rooms only for $10/20 a single/double; and the *Tambo Mill Motel* (☎ (07) 4654 6466) has rooms only from $48/58 single/double. The *Tambo Caravan Park* (☎ (07) 4654 6463) caters for campers and also has overnight vans.

The RACQ depot is Ricks Tyre Centre (☎ (07) 4654 6276) in Arthur St.

Blackall

A number of hotels and motels offer accommodation, such as the *Barcoo Hotel* (☎ (07) 4657 4197), the *Blackall Motel* (☎ (07) 4657 4611) and the *Coolibah Motel* (☎ (07) 4657 4380), with prices for a room ranging from $39 a single to $55 a double. Cabins (from $30 double) are available at the *Blackall Caravan Park* (☎ (07) 4657 4816), as are on-site vans from $22 a double and caravan and campsites $12/10 a double power/unpowered. Pets are allowed only on application. *Avington Station Homestead* (☎ (07) 4657 5952), 75km north-west of Blackall, offers double rooms and shearing shed accommodation from $50/90 a single/double for bed & breakfast.

Banks represented in Blackall are the Commonwealth, National Australia and Westpac. The local RACQ depot is Wood's Mechanical Repairs (☎ (07) 4657 4100, after hours 4657 4400).

Barcaldine

There is a wide range of accommodation to choose from, including the *Barcaldine Motel* (☎ (07) 4651 1244), *Commercial Hotel* (☎ (07) 4651 1242), *Globe Hotel* (☎ (07) 4651 1141), and *Lee Garden* (☎ (07) 4651 1488), with prices for a room only ranging from $30 for a single to $68 a double. There are also two caravan parks: the *Showgrounds* (☎ (07) 4651 1211) and the *Homestead* (☎ (07) 4651 1308). Cabins are also available at the Homestead from $28/32 a single/double, or on-site vans at $28 a double, while sites are $13/11 for a double with or without power. Pets are allowed (on application only). *North Delta station* (☎ (07) 4651 1634), east of the town, has a cottage with everything supplied from $120 a double, as well as bunkhouse accommodation.

The banks represented are the Commonwealth and Westpac. The RACQ depot is Barcaldine Engineering Works (☎ (07) 4651 1337, after hours 4651 1544).

Ilfracombe

You can choose to stay in the *Wellshot Hotel* (tel/fax (07) 4658 2106), or in an on-site van at the *Teamster's Rest Caravan Park* (☎ (07) 4658 2295) for $?? a double. The park also has campsites at $10/8 a double with or without power.

Longreach

The town has a large choice of accommodation, including the *Longreach Motor Inn* (☎ (07) 4658 2322), *Longreach Motel* (☎ (07) 4658 1996), *Starlight Motel* (☎ (07) 4658 1288), *Albert Park Motel* (☎ (07) 4658 2411), *Jumbuck Motel* (☎ (07) 4658 1799), *Commercial Hotel/Motel* (☎ (07) 4658 1677) and *Aussie Betta Cabins* with prices from $50 to $70 a single/double for rooms only. The *Hallview Lodge* (☎ (07) 4658 3777) offers family, twin-room and share accommodation, a laundry and a barbecue area, and meals. The cost is $45/58 a single/double for bed & breakfast.

The *Gunnadoo Caravan Park* (☎ (07) 4658 1781) and the *Longreach Caravan Park* (☎ (07) 4658 1770) have all camping and caravan facilities, and pets are allowed. Cabins or on-site vans are also available from $45 and $28 a double respectively, while powered/unpowered sites begin at $13/10 a double.

All the major banks have branches in Longreach – ANZ, Commonwealth, National Australia and Westpac. The RACQ depot is Mobil Midtown Service Station (☎ (07) 4658 1747, after hours 4658 1080).

Winton

Travellers can stay in the *Outback Motel* (☎ (07) 4657 1422), *Matilda Motel* (☎ (07) 4657 1433), *Australian Hotel* (☎ (07) 4657 1214), *North Gregory Hotel* (☎ (07) 4657 1375) or *Banjo's Motel/Cabins* (☎ (07) 4657 1213), with rooms ranging from $40 a single to $50 a double.

The *Matilda Country Caravan Park* (☎ (07) 4657 1607) has both on-site vans and a cabin section, with prices at $25 and $50 a double respectively, while the *Pelican Fuel Stop Caravan Park* (☎ (07) 4657 1478) has units from $20 a double. Both have powered and unpowered sites from $9/12 double, and pets are allowed on application.

The National Australia and Westpac banks have branches in Winton. The local RACQ depot is Winton Fuel & Tyre Service (☎ (07) 4657 1305).

Kynuna

The *Blue Heeler Hotel* (☎ (07) 4646 8650) has motel and hotel rooms available at $50/55 and $30/35 single/double respectively. The *Jolly Swag Van Park* has an on-site van and campsites for $10/8 a double with/without power. Pets are allowed. The Kynuna Roadhouse runs the *Never Never Caravan Park* (☎ (07) 4646 8683) which has cabins for $30 double and campsites for $8 double ($10 with power). Pets are allowed. Meals are available in the roadhouse from 6 am to 9 pm daily.

McKinlay

The *Walkabout Creek Hotel Caravan Park* (☎ (07) 4746 8424) provides accommodation with room rates at $38/46 a single/double, or you can stay in the camping area at the back of the hotel where sites with/without power cost $12/10. Pets are allowed.

Cloncurry

The *Cloncurry Motel* (☎ (07) 4742 1268), *Oasis Hotel/Motel* (☎ (07) 4742 1366), *Leichhardt Hotel/Motel* (☎ (07) 4742 1389), *Post Office Hotel* (☎ (07) 4742 1411), and the *Wagon Wheel Motel* (☎ (07) 4742 1866) offer a range of accommodation, with rooms from $35 a single to $55 a double.

Gilbert Park Cabins (☎ (07) 4742 2300) has cabins with all amenities from $48 a double. Cabins and on-site vans cost $35 and $30 a double respectively at the *Cloncurry Caravan Park Oasis* (☎ (07) 4742 1313). Caravan/campsites, powered and unpowered, cost $14/10 double at Cloncurry, where no pets are allowed, or you can pitch a tent at the *Great North West Caravan Park* (☎ (07) 4742 2300) where sites are $14/10 and pets are allowed on application.

The National Australia and Westpac banks have branches in Cloncurry. The RACQ depot is Nevs Auto Repair (☎ (07) 4742 1243).

Normanton

Accommodation is available at the *Albion Hotel* (☎ (07) 4745 1218), *Central Hotel* (☎ (07) 4745 1215), *Gulflander Motel* (☎ (07) 4745 1290) and *National Hotel* (☎ (07) 4745 1324), commonly called the Purple Pub. Room only rates range from $45 single to $60 double.

The council's *Normanton Caravan Park* (☎ (07) 4745 1121) has all facilities, including a heated pool, with powered/unpowered sites at $13/10 a double. Pets are allowed on leashes.

The Normanton Travel Service (☎ (07) 4745 1200) can help with information and can organise tours and flights. The Westpac Bank has full banking facilities, while the Commonwealth Bank agency is at the post office. The RACQ depot is Gulf Service Station (☎ (07) 4745 1221).

Karumba

Accommodation is available at the *Karumba Lodge Hotel* (☎ (07) 4745 9121), where a unit costs $55/65 for singles/doubles. Cabins, at $28/40 a single/double, are available at the *Gulf Country Caravan Park* (☎ (07) 4745 9148). Pets are allowed on application. Campers and caravanners can select a site for $12/10 with/without power.

The *Karumba Point Tourist Park* (☎ (07) 4745 9306) also has on-site vans from $30 double, or campsites at $13/11 a double. Campsites cost $12/9 at the *Sunset Caravan Park* (☎ (07) 4745 9277) at Karumba Point. There are a number of holiday cabins for rent at Karumba and Karumba Point – contact the shire office in Normanton (☎ (07) 4745 1166) for a full listing.

B & B Supermarket (☎ (07) 4745 9242) has just about everything you may need, including newsagency, cafe, fishing tackle, taxi service and EFTPOS facilities.

The Westpac Bank in Karumba is open only on Tuesday and Thursday, and there's a Commonwealth Bank agenct at the post office.

ALTERNATIVE TRANSPORT
Air

Flight West Airlines (reservations within Queensland ☎ 13 23 92, Australia wide 1800 77 78 79) has flights servicing Charleville, Blackall, Barcaldine, Longreach, Winton, Normanton and Karumba.

Ansett Australia (☎ 13 13 00) operates daily flights between Brisbane and Mount Isa.

There's a number of charter operators – contact the tourist information centres for details. Air Mount Isa (☎ (07) 4743 2844) does mail runs and supply flights to isolated mines, and takes tourists for a negotiable fee.

Bus

Greyhound Pioneer (☎ 13 20 30 or Townsville (07) 4771 2134) services all towns between Townsville and Mount Isa on the Flinders and Barkly highways. McCafferty's Express Coaches (☎ (07) 4772 5100) service all towns on the Warrego, Landsborough and Capricorn highways between Brisbane and Mount Isa, as well as Rockhampton and Longreach.

Campbell's Coaches (☎ (07) 4743 2006), based at Mount Isa, travels once a week from Mount Isa to Cloncurry, Quamby, Burke & Wills Roadhouse, Normanton and Karumba.

Train

Queensland Rail Traveltrain (☎ 13 22 32, in Townsville ☎ (07) 4772 8211) operates rail services from Brisbane to Charleville on the *Westlander* with bus connections to Cunnamulla and Quilpie, from Brisbane to Longreach on the *Spirit of the Outback* with a bus connection to Winton, from Townsville to Mount Isa on the *Inlander*, and from Normanton to Croydon on the wonderful *Gulflander*. For further information you can contact the Queensland Rail Travel Centre (☎ (07) 3235 1323).

Car Rental

Offices of Avis (☎ 1800 225 533) and Hertz (☎ 13 30 39) can be found in the larger towns, such as Charleville, Longreach and Mount Isa.

Gold Fields & Ghost Towns

Gold – when driving through the outback, you begin to imagine what lured thousands to seek it in the gullies, along river banks and underground. The dust that now covers this exciting part of history bites into your nostrils. The history, the remnants of the rush that never ended, the ghost towns (some rejuvenated and others not), are all still there to explore.

As you drive off the beaten track, chances are it is to a Hill End, Just in Time, Old Halls Creek or Palmer River. More than likely the road you are following is there as a direct result of the search for gold. And if you are off-track and *lost*, think of Harry Lasseter in search of his elusive reef.

Our 4WDs are a far cry from the wheelbarrows that Russian Jack pushed, our burden is much lighter than the heavy swags the miners carried and metal detectors are a

Gold Fields &
Ghost Towns

503

great deal more sophisticated than the pick, shovel and cast-iron gold pan. Today, in remote places, only the gravestones and ruins of the gold rushes protrude through encroaching sand and weeds.

History of the Rushes

The first recorded find of gold in Australia was in 1823 in New South Wales, but it was not until early 1851, when Edward Hargraves vigorously promoted his meagre finds at Ophir, near Bathurst, that the first real rush started. By May that year, there were over a thousand diggers in the creeks around Ophir. A licensing system was introduced whereby each person paid 30 shillings, both to limit the diggers and to encourage the unsuccessful to return to their jobs.

When the gold at Ophir ran out, diggers had already found more on the Turon (Sofala) – soon there were six or seven thousand miners there. The area around Bathurst teemed with hopefuls toiling in rugged creekbeds.

The drift of the population northwards to the gold fields of New South Wales prompted the Victorian government, on 9 June 1851, to offer a £200 reward for the discovery of a payable gold field within 200 miles of Melbourne. Early in the following month, the finds of James Esmond at Clunes were made public. In August, diggers were flocking to Ballarat, later to be one of the greatest sources of gold. In September, the rush was to the shallow fields around Mt Alexander (later Castlemaine). There were 20,000 diggers spread out around there and as far north as Bendigo by December.

Prospectors had been working at Bendigo during October and November. A lack of water prevented development but by May the following year, there was a rush to the rich discoveries in Eaglehawk Gully. A small rush to the largely inaccessible creeks around Omeo, in Gippsland, followed. The year 1853 saw minor rushes to other regions, including the Buckland River on the rugged Ovens field and in 1854, Maldon, Avoca, Maryborough and Ararat were opened up.

The diggers came from all parts of the world and a range of professions. They included people from England, continental Europeans (especially Germans), veterans of the Californian gold fields (the '49ers') and impoverished Chinese from Kwangtung province.

Melbourne was the new San Francisco, teeming with diggers infected with a golden wanderlust. Between Princes Bridge and the bay beaches, Canvas-Town, a sea of tents, was established to accommodate the migrants before they began the hazardous journey to the gold fields.

The introduction of a licence fee on the Victorian fields was met with resentment. The issue flared up after a visit to the Ballarat gold fields by the new governor, Charles Hotham, who resolved to strictly enforce the collection of fees with biweekly licence hunts. After a number of niggling incidents which inflamed the predominantly Irish miners of the Eureka lode near Ballarat, two mass meetings were held on Bakery Hill on 11 and 29 November; licences were burned at the second meeting.

The following day, the authorities, in a show of force, went on a licence hunt. The diggers resolved to make a stand and erected the Eureka Stockade as a symbol of their own protection. Peter Lalor led the diggers' oath of allegiance to the flag of the Southern Cross. There were about 120 diggers in the stockade when it was attacked by soldiers and police on 3 December 1854. In the ensuing melee, about 30 miners and five soldiers were killed; Peter Lalor was shot in the shoulder and Captain Wise of the 40th Regiment was mortally wounded. None of the protesters was convicted and the diggers' stand hastened reform on the gold fields. The following year 'miner's right' was introduced.

In 1858, diggers were being transported north, to the Tropic of Capricorn, to Rockhampton (also called Fitzroy, or Canoona). In the autumn of 1860, Victorians crossed the border and climbed high into the Snowy Mountains to the alpine rush at Kiandra. Winter snows forced the diggers to look elsewhere, which they did with success – Forbes and Young became rich fields.

Queensland's turn for such frenzy came in 1867, when the white quartz reefs of Gympie were uncovered. Four years later, it was the rich fields of Charters Towers, then the steamy tropical forests of the Palmer River and the fields on Cape York, which lured only the desperate.

Discoveries in the Northern Territory followed and a workable gold field at Pine Creek was announced in August 1872. Isolation, the high costs of mining, and the marauding Aborigines were problems. Coolies, or indentured, labourers were brought in to work the fields, and when the work stopped, they went over the alluvial deposits for a second time. At about this time, interest in gold mining began to decline for a while.

A resurgence came in 1886 and the Croydon field was opened about 500km north-west of Charters Towers. Gold was discovered at Halls Creek in the remote Kimberley in 1885 and in 1886, diggers on the Queensland fields made the anticlockwise trek to the new riches. The terrain in the Kimberley was inhospitable and the track from the wharves at Wyndham and Derby was the most ferocious that miners in Aus-

tralia had yet negotiated. Still, they pushed across it and, unbelievably, miners walked to it from the Queensland fields.

The Pilbara was the next to reveal its riches. The year 1888 saw diggers pouring over Pilbara Creek and fanning out through the dry gorges to Marble Bar, Nullagine and the Ashburton River. Despite the intense heat, the lure of gold held them fast and some diggers were rewarded with finds of huge nuggets.

Gold was found inland from Geraldton, near Nannine, in 1890. The Murchison field now bloomed and Cue, Day Dawn, Payne's Find, Lake Austin and Mount Magnet joined the huge list of gold towns in the outback.

More discoveries followed, especially around Southern Cross in Western Australia's Yilgarn district, first opened in 1888. Major strikes were made in 1892 at Coolgardie and nearby Kalgoorlie, the only large town left today in the Western Australian gold fields.

Coolgardie's period of prosperity lasted only until 1905; many other gold towns went from nothing to populations of 10,000 then back to nothing in just 10 years. Western Australia profited from the gold boom for the rest of the 19th century (and it still profits today). It was gold that put the state on the

Lasseter's Lost Reef
The gold prospector Lewis Hubert (Harold Bell) Lasseter (1880?-1931) is immortalised as one of Australia's great hopefuls. We still know of him today because of Ion Idriess' *Lasseter's Last Ride* (1931); otherwise he would probably have faded into the red dust of the Petermann Range. But Lasseter claimed to have found, sometime between 1897 and 1911, the richest gold reef in Australia, some 23km in length. The diminutive Lasseter had supposedly been looking for rubies when he stumbled upon gold as thick as 'plums in a pudding'. It was in the remote, arid Petermann Range in central Australia on the Northern Territory/South Australia border.

In 1930 the Central Australian Gold Exploration Company was formed, with Lasseter as a guide. The expedition was well equipped with an aeroplane, trucks and wireless. But things started to go wrong: the aircraft crashed near Ayers Rock, and Fred Blakeley, the expedition leader, abandoned it at Ayers Rock. Lasseter, after an argument with another hopeful prospector, Paul Johns, headed out alone to look for the reef.

Lasseter died of starvation in January 1931 near Shaws Creek and his body was found by Bob Buck in March; his diaries were retrieved and in them he claimed to have pegged the reef. Idriess used these diaries to write the above-mentioned book.

Subsequent attempts to find Lasseter's lost reef have been unsuccessful. His name is perpetuated in the Lasseter Highway, which runs from the Stuart Highway to Uluru (Ayers Rock). ∎

map and finally gave it the population to make it viable in its own right, rather than just an offshoot of the east-coast colonies.

Depressions and unemployment often attracted fossickers back to the gullies and rivers, especially during the Great Depression in the 1930s. In other places, like the Golden Mile in Kalgoorlie-Boulder, mining never actually stopped.

WESTERN AUSTRALIA
Old Halls Creek

This town is a fascinating reminder of the Kimberley gold rush. All that is left is heaps of broken bottles where the pub used to be, the crumbling walls of the old post office, cemetery and a failed tourist venture – the modern building that sits forlornly at the top of the hill. This ghost town is about 14km east of modern-day Halls Creek, actually on the banks of the creek. In the new town is a statue of Russian Jack.

Gwalia

This twin town of Leonora, 237km north of Kalgoorlie, is another ghost town worth visiting. Gold was discovered here in 1896 and mined until 1963 in the Sons of Gwalia mine (it recently reopened with the benefits of the new open-pit technology). It was the largest mine outside Kalgoorlie-Boulder's Golden Mile. The 25m headframe still stands; its construction in 1898 was supervised by the first mine manager, Herbert Hoover, who became president of the USA in 1929. The town was once so prosperous that it ran the state's first electric trams.

Many of the mine buildings are still intact and there is an interesting museum. Gwalia is a good example of a modern ghost town.

Gwalia's centenary was celebrated in 1996 and a project was initiated where old buildings were bought and restored and furnished to what was thought to be their original state. The old store was also part of the project and visitors are now allowed to look inside.

There are many more ghost towns in the area – Ora Banda, Niagara, Menzies, Kanowna and Broad Arrow. Get a copy of the

Gold Rush Country pamphlet from the Kalgoorlie tourist centre.

Kalgoorlie-Boulder

Kalgoorlie-Boulder is hardly a ghost town, but its rich and turbulent history, swayed by gold prices and discoveries, has seen its fortunes both soar and slump. It was the site of a major gold rush after prospector Paddy Hannan found gold there in 1893. As in so many places, the surface gold soon dried up, but at Kalgoorlie the miners went deeper and more and more gold was found. The storybook chunky nuggets of solid gold weren't found – Kalgoorlie's gold had to be extracted from the rocks by a costly and complex processes of grinding, roasting and chemical action – but there was plenty of the metal.

With the substantial increase in gold prices since the mid-1970s, mining of lower-grade deposits has become economical and Kalgoorlie is again the largest producer of gold in Australia. Large mining conglomerates have been at the forefront of new open-cut mining operations in the Golden Mile – gone are the old headframes and corrugated iron homes. Mining, pastoral development and a busy tourist trade ensure Kalgoorlie's continuing importance as an outback centre.

One of Kalgoorlie's biggest attractions is the **Hannan's North Tourist Mine**. You can take the lift cage down into the bowels of the earth and make a tour around the drives and crosscuts of the mine. The **Super Pit** is the world's biggest open-cut mine. The lookout, just off the Goldfields Highway, near Boulder, is open from 6 am to 6 pm daily.

The impressive Ivanhoe mine headframe, at the northern end of Hannan St, marks the entrance to the excellent **Museum of the Goldfields**. A block back, north-west of Hannan St, is Hay St, one of Kalgoorlie's most famous 'attractions'. Although it's quietly ignored in most tourist brochures, Kalgoorlie has a strip of **brothels** with true-blue, and pink, Aussie galvanised-iron doorways. Kalgoorlie also has a legal **two-up school** in a corrugated-iron amphitheatre 6km north of town.

The Pittman-Walsh Murders

On Hopkins St, Boulder, is the Cornwall Hotel, which was involved in the notorious Pittman and Walsh murders.

During April 1926, Detective Sergeant Pittman of the Gold Stealing Detection staff and Inspector John Walsh went missing. They were found shot, dismembered, partially burnt and dumped in a mineshaft.

The police were determined to get the killers and did, eventually, when Teddy Clarke, licensee of the Cornwall and a gold stealer, turned King's evidence. His barman Phillip Treffene and one William Coulter, a punter and backer of bookies, were found guilty of the murders and hanged at Fremantle gaol. ∎

There's a helpful tourist office (☎ (08) 9021 1966, 9021 1413), on the corner of Hannan and Cassidy Sts, where you can get a good free map of the city. It is open from 8.30 am to 5 pm Monday to Friday, from 9 am to 5 pm on weekends.

Coolgardie

Coolgardie is a ghost of its former self – you only have to glance at the town hall, warden's court and post office to appreciate its former size.

A reef of gold was discovered here in 1892, by the prospector Arthur Bayley and his mate Bill Ford, and called 'Bayley's Reward' By the turn of the century, the population of Coolgardie had boomed to 15,000, there were two stock exchanges, six newspapers, over 20 hotels and three breweries. The gold then petered out and the town withered away just as quickly. However, there's still plenty of interest for the visitor.

The **Goldfields Exhibition**, in the same building as the tourist office, is open daily and has a fascinating display of gold-fields memorabilia. You can even find out about US president Herbert Hoover's days on the Western Australian gold fields. It's an interesting museum, worth the $2.50 entry.

One km west of Coolgardie is the **town cemetery**, which includes many old graves such as those of explorer Ernest Giles (1835-

97) and several Afghan camel drivers. It's said that 'one half of the population buried the other half' because of unsanitary conditions and violence in the gold fields.

NORTHERN TERRITORY

Pine Creek

This town, 245km south of Darwin, has been a ghost town, but in recent years has had a new lease of life because of a large open-cut mine which opened nearby. It is in the centre of a number of Top End ghost towns, including Yam Creek, 40km to the north. Pine Creek, surrounded by mullock heaps, has many reminders of the gold rushes, including corrugated iron buildings. Ah Toy's store is reminiscent of the time when Chinese outnumbered Europeans on these gold fields. The old train station has been restored as an information centre, while a museum can be found on Railway Parade.

Arltunga

Probably the most isolated gold fields were centred around Arltunga, on the Hale River north-east of Alice Springs, in the MacDonnell Ranges. Gold was struck at Paddy's Waterhole in 1887, but mining petered out by 1908. All supplies for this field had to be hauled 650km from Oodnadatta over a dangerous track.

QUEENSLAND

This state is replete with abandoned gold-mining towns. Once all the gold was taken, there was often no reason for a town's existence.

Croydon

This town, 500km north-west of Charters Towers, was proclaimed a gold field in January 1886, but gold had been discovered there three years earlier. In its day, it was one of the richest fields in Australia and the centre of Queensland's north-west. It even boasted two newspapers, the *Golden Age* and *Mining News*. All that is left now is a pub (the Club Hotel), general store, courthouse, mining warden's office and a tin railway shed. Not much is left of the fabulous Golden

Russian Jack

The gold fields and the rushes produced many heroes: successful speculators, the 'lucky' who found nuggets or struck it rich, Peter Lalor and the diggers of Eureka Stockade, the knucklemen, the Mountain Maid and the extremely odd and unusual.

Russian Jack was the Kimberley's hero, renowned for his feats of strength and endurance. He is believed to have carried a sick friend over 300km in his rough-and-ready wheelbarrow. He had originally pushed his barrow, with its 2m Derbyshafts and extra-wide wheel for the sandy tracks, all the way from Derby loaded with food, tools, blankets and water.

His loyalty to his mates and the job became legendary. One day he fell to the bottom of an open pit at Mount Morgan in Western Australia, about 23m down. After lying there injured for three days, his only comment when they pulled him out was, 'I've missed a shift'. ∎

Gate mine, except for a few rusting remains. See the Matilda Highway section in the Tropics chapter for details about the *Gulflander* train between Croydon and Normanton.

Palmer River

The Palmer River gold fields hide many once-thriving towns. At the start of the rush, the diggers got to these towns from **Cooktown**, itself a great example of gold-fields architecture, via a rugged packhorse road. Later, **Laura**, the railhead of the line from Cooktown, handled 20,000 passengers a year. Today it has only a few houses, including a pleasant pub, a general store and a small museum. Many people come to the area today to see the Quinkan Aboriginal paintings west of Lakeland, believed to be 15,000 years old. There are ruins at **Maytown** and **Palmerville**, south of Laura, about 70km west of the Palmer River crossing on the Cairns-Cooktown inland road.

NEW SOUTH WALES

New South Wales has a number of ghost towns, but the only ones in the outback are Milparinka and Tibooburra. **Milparinka**, 315km north of Broken Hill, was alive in 1880 after the first nugget was found near Mt Poole, a few miles west. Once it was the main town in the centre of the field but is now a beleaguered place, the very epitome of a ghost town.

About 40km north is **Tibooburra**, which became part of the 1880s rush in this region. The lack of water militated against success and the fields had a short life. Tibooburra is today a centre for tourists visiting Corner Country – Cameron's Corner (where New South Wales, South Australia and Queensland meet) and Sturt National Park.

SOUTH AUSTRALIA

The South Australian gold rushes are probably the least known, as copper is the main metal sought there. **Waukaringa** is about all that is left of the 1880s gold rush. The rush began in 1886, when miners flocked to the Teetulpa gold fields. The town is eerie, isolated out on the wide, open plain. To get to the mine ruins, turn north at the town of Yunta on the Barrier Highway, between Broken Hill and Peterborough.

Checklists

Before You Go

- [ ] Pre-plan – where, time of year, time needed, distance, fuel range.
- [ ] Research – things to see and do, history, fuel availability, resupply, road conditions.
- [ ] Make an itinerary – and use it as a guide only. Keep it flexible to allow for breakdowns, advice or ideas you receive while underway and places you fall in love with.
- [ ] Apply for permits – to national parks and Aboriginal land. Some parks operate on a ballot system in the busy seasons so it's wise to enquire about bookings well in advance. Restrictions are also placed in parks such as Gurig in the Northern Territory, where bookings must be made at least 12 months in advance because only 15 vehicles are allowed in at any one time.
- [ ] Book accommodation – if you want to stay at a popular spot, for instance Monkey Mia in Western Australia over the school holidays, you may want to book. Remember that if you book too many places, your flexible itinerary will go out the window.
- [ ] Let someone know your itinerary – if you change it greatly, let them know so they don't hit the panic button. Keep in touch with someone at home at prearranged intervals.

Always Carry

- [ ] basic recovery gear (see below)
- [ ] first aid kit plus manual (see the Health section in the Facts for the Visitor chapter)
- [ ] fire extinguisher
- [ ] HF radio if you're heading to remote country
- [ ] vehicle tools and spare parts (see below)
- [ ] plenty of water (at least 5L of drinking water per person per day)
- [ ] good maps
- [ ] matches
- [ ] compass
- [ ] torch (flashlight) & spare batteries
- [ ] knife
- [ ] space blanket

Camping & Personal Gear

- [ ] tent, swag and/or stretcher (camp bed)
- [ ] sleeping gear
- [ ] mosquito net (fine mesh)
- [ ] broad-brimmed hat (maybe with fly net)
- [ ] good-quality sunglasses
- [ ] wet-weather gear

- [ ] portable light (gas, spirit or electric – one that operates off the car battery)
- [ ] portable fridge or ice chest ('Esky')
- [ ] folding chairs
- [ ] folding table
- [ ] heavy-duty plastic rubbish bags
- [ ] toilet paper
- [ ] toiletries bag
- [ ] clothes (including sweater)
- [ ] camera, film and spare batteries
- [ ] sunscreen lotion (rated 15+)
- [ ] insect repellent
- [ ] paper and pencils
- [ ] string
- [ ] plastic sheet
- [ ] tarpaulin
- [ ] poles, ropes & pegs
- [ ] 10L bucket (square packs best)
- [ ] clothesline, pegs and detergent
- [ ] long-handled shovel
- [ ] axe or bow saw (latter is far safer)

Campfire Cooking Equipment (Essential)

- [ ] medium to large cast-iron camp oven – pack carefully so it doesn't bounce around and crack
- [ ] two or three steel saucepans or billies of varying size, with lids. Choose saucepans that will fit inside one another for better packing
- [ ] at least one large steel billy with lid
- [ ] large, steel frying pan
- [ ] steel barbecue plate with legs
- [ ] heat-resistant gloves with lower-arm protection (eg welding gloves)
- [ ] long-handled shovel

Campfire Cooking Equipment (Not so Essential)

- [ ] cake rack or similar to place in the bottom of your camp oven
- [ ] jaffle iron
- [ ] toasting forks
- [ ] metal fire grate with legs (preferably adjustable)
- [ ] long-handled barbecue utensils
- [ ] natural-fibre brush – to brush coals off camp oven lid
- [ ] fire starters

General Cooking Items

- [ ] gas stove
- [ ] eating utensils
- [ ] plates, bowls, cups (plastic is best)
- [ ] sharp knives
- [ ] mixing bowls
- [ ] flat plastic grater
- [ ] sieve
- [ ] chopping board
- [ ] can opener, bottle opener, corkscrew
- [ ] peeler
- [ ] small measuring cup
- [ ] small plastic funnel
- [ ] large mixing spoons
- [ ] aluminium foil
- [ ] plastic food-wrap
- [ ] snap-lock plastic bags
- [ ] heavy-duty plastic rubbish bags
- [ ] tea towels
- [ ] dishwashing detergent (concentrated)
- [ ] pot scourer
- [ ] sponges (for dishwashing)
- [ ] square 10L bucket (for dishwashing)

Car Tools

- [ ] repair manual
- [ ] set of ring and open-end spanners (to suit your vehicle)
- [ ] adjustable spanner
- [ ] plug spanner
- [ ] wheel brace, jack and jacking plate (30cm square x 2.5cm thick board)
- [ ] 1m length of steel pipe (to fit over handle of wheel brace for extra leverage when removing stubborn wheel nuts)
- [ ] screwdrivers (selection of standard and Phillips head)
- [ ] Allen keys (if applicable)
- [ ] hammer, chisel
- [ ] hacksaw and spare blades
- [ ] file, including a points file
- [ ] thread file
- [ ] pliers and wire cutters
- [ ] tie wire, nylon 'zip-ties'
- [ ] heavy-gauge low-tensile wire (handy for tying broken bits together)
- [ ] Araldite epoxy resin
- [ ] feeler gauges
- [ ] tyre levers
- [ ] bead breaker (if required)
- [ ] good-quality tyre pump and pressure gauge
- [ ] tube/tyre repair kit
- [ ] battery jumper leads
- [ ] WD40, or similar
- [ ] funnel and hose

- [ ] rags
- [ ] octopus straps and spare rope

Car Spares

- [ ] radiator hoses
- [ ] heater hoses
- [ ] fan belts
- [ ] fuses
- [ ] globes
- [ ] electric wire
- [ ] electrical insulation tape
- [ ] thread sealing tape
- [ ] spark plugs (petrol engine)
- [ ] plug leads (petrol engine)
- [ ] points (petrol engine)
- [ ] coil (petrol engine)
- [ ] condenser (petrol engine)
- [ ] tyre tube, valves and caps
- [ ] bolts, nuts, self-tapping screws, washers etc
- [ ] grease
- [ ] gasket cement
- [ ] second spare wheel (for remote areas)

It's always wise to carry some extra fuel and engine oil. On longer trips, you could include a more comprehensive range of tools and spares, such as a socket set plus any of the commonly needed special tools for your vehicle, exhaust sealant, wheel bearings, air filters and gear oil. It's easy to carry too much, though, so be critical. If there are similar vehicles in your group, save weight by sharing.

Car Recovery Gear

- [ ] snatch strap
- [ ] two 'D' shackles
- [ ] long-handled shovel
- [ ] axe
- [ ] jack and jacking plate (to provide a stable base for jacking in mud or sand)

The above are the basics. Depending on the nature of the trip and the problems likely to be encountered, you could add:

- [ ] Tirfor (or similar) hand winch, or power winch
- [ ] tree protector strap
- [ ] winch extension straps
- [ ] snatch-block
- [ ] extra 'D' shackles
- [ ] high-lift jack and base plate
- [ ] air-bag jack (particularly good in sandy areas)
- [ ] chainsaw (with fuel, spare chain, chain file etc)

Glossary

amber fluid – beer
ankle-biter – small child, *tacker*, *rug rat*
arvo – afternoon
avagoyermug – traditional rallying call, especially at cricket matches
award wage – minimum pay rate

back o' Bourke – back of beyond, middle of nowhere
backblocks – *bush* or other remote area far from the city
bail up – hold up, rob, *earbash*
bail out – leave
Balmain bug – see *Moreton Bay bug*
banana bender – resident of Queensland
banker – a river almost overflowing its banks (as in 'the Cooper is running a banker')
barbie – barbecue (BBQ)
barra – barramundi (prized fish of the north)
barrack – cheer on a team at sporting event, support (as in 'who do you barrack for?')
bastard – general term of address which can mean many things. While mostly used as a good-natured form of greeting ('*G'day*, you old bastard!'), it can also denote the highest level of praise or respect ('He's the bravest bastard I know!') or it can be the most dire of insults ('You lousy, lying bastard!')
bathers – swimming costume (Victoria, Western Australia)
battler – hard trier, struggler (the outback is full of 'great Aussie battlers')
beaut, beauty, bewdie – great, fantastic
big bikkies – a lot of money, expensive
big mobs – a large amount, heaps
bikies – motorcyclists
billabong – waterhole in dried-up riverbed, more correctly an ox-bow bend cut off in the dry season by receding waters
billy – tin container used to boil tea in the bush
bitumen – asphalt, surfaced road
black stump – where the *back o' Bourke* begins
blaze – (a blaze in a tree) a mark in a tree trunk made by cutting away bark, indicating a path or reference point; also 'to blaze'
bloke – man
blowies – blowflies, bluebottles
bludger – lazy person, one who won't work and lives off other people's money (originally, a prostitute's pimp)
blue (ie **have a blue**) – to have an argument or fight
bluey – *swag*; also nickname for a red-haired person
bonzer – great, *ripper*
boomer – very big; a particularly large male kangaroo
boomerang – a curved flat wooden instrument used by Aborigines for hunting
booze bus – police van used for random breath testing for alcohol
boozer – pub
bottle – 750ml bottle of beer
bottle shop – liquor shop
bottlo – *bottle shop*
bowser – fuel pump at a service station (named after the US inventor SF Bowser)
brumby – wild horse
bruss – brother, *mate* (used by central Australian Aborigines)
Buckley's, Buckley's chance – no chance at all ('Across the Tanami? They've got Buckley's in that *shitbox*'). The origin of this term is unclear. Maybe it derives from the Melbourne department store of Buckley's & Nunn; or from the escaped convict William Buckley, whose chances of survival were considered negligible but who ended up living with Aborigines for 20 years; or from the Sydney escapologist Buckley, who had himself chained-up in a coffin and thrown into Sydney Harbour, with dire results
bug – see *Moreton Bay bug*
Bulamakanka – place even beyond the *back o' Bourke*, way beyond the black stump (see *never-never*)
bull bar – outsize front bumper on car or truck used as the ultimate barrier against animals on the road

bull dust – fine, powdery and sometimes deep dust on outback roads, often hiding deep holes and ruts that you normally wouldn't drive into; also bullshit

bunfight – a quarrel over a frivolous issue or one that gets blown out of proportion

bungarra – any large (1.5m-plus) goanna, but specifically an Aboriginal name for Gould's goanna, prized as food

bunyip – mythical bush spirit said to inhabit Australia's swamps

burl – have a try (as in 'give it a burl')

bush – country, anywhere away from the city; *scrub*

bush (ie **go bush**) – go back to the land

bushbash – to force your way through pathless bush

bushranger – Australia's equivalent of the outlaws of the American Wild West (some goodies, some baddies) – the helmeted Ned Kelly was the most famous

bush tucker – food available naturally

BYO – Bring Your Own (booze to a restaurant, meat to a barbecue etc)

caaarn! – come on, traditional rallying call, especially at football games (as in 'Caaarn the Crows!')

cackle-berries – eggs; also 'hen-fruit', 'chook-nuts' and 'bum-nuts'

camp draft – Australian rodeo, testing horse rider's skills in separating cattle or sheep from a herd or flock

camp oven – large, cast-iron pot with lid, used for cooking in an open fire

cask – wine box (a great Australian invention)

Chiko roll – vile Australian junk food

chocka – completely full (from 'chock-a-block')

chook – chicken

chuck a U-ey – do a U-turn

chunder – vomit, technicolour yawn, pavement pizza, curbside quiche, liquid laugh, drive the porcelain bus, call Bluey

clobber – clothes

cobber – *mate*

cocky – small-scale farmer; cockatoo

come good – turn out all right

compo – compensation such as workers' compensation

cooee – shouting distance, close (to be within cooee of ...)

cop, copper – police officer (not uniquely *strine* but very common nevertheless); see *walloper*

counter meal, countery – pub meal

cow cocky – small-scale cattle farmer

cozzie – swimming costume (New South Wales)

crook – ill, badly made, substandard

crow eater – resident of South Australia

culvert – channel or pipe under road for rainwater drainage

cut lunch – sandwiches

cut snake – see *mad as a ...*

dag, daggy – dirty lump of wool at back end of a sheep; also an affectionate or mildly abusive term for a socially inept person

daks – trousers

damper – bush loaf made from flour and water and cooked in a *camp oven*

Darwin stubby – 2L bottle of beer sold to tourists in Darwin

dead horse – tomato sauce

deli – delicatessen; milk bar in South Australia

digger – Australian or New Zealand soldier or veteran (originally, a miner); also a generic form of address assuming respect, mainly used for soldiers/veterans but sometimes also between friends

dijeridu – cylindrical wooden musical instrument played by Aboriginal men

dill – idiot

dingo – indigenous wild dog

dink – carry a second person on a bicycle or horse

dinkum, fair dinkum – honest, genuine ('fair dinkum?' – really?)

dinky-di – the real thing

distillate – diesel fuel

divvy van – police divisional van

dob in – to tell on someone

Dog Fence – the world's longest fence, erected to keep *dingoes* out of south-eastern Australia

donga – small transportable hut; also the

bush, from the name for a shallow, eroded gully, found in areas where it doesn't rain often, so people don't go there

donk – car or boat engine

don't come the raw prawn – don't try and fool me

down south – the rest of Australia, viewed from the Northern Territory or anywhere north of Brisbane

drongo – foolish or worthless person

droving – moving livestock a considerable distance

Dry, the – the dry season in the north

duco – car paint

duffing – stealing cattle (literally: altering the brand on the 'duff', or rump)

dunny – outdoor lavatory

dunny budgies – *blowies*

earbash – talk non-stop

eastern states – the rest of Australia viewed from west of Queensland.

Esky – trademark name for a portable ice box used for keeping beer etc cold

fair go! – give us a break!

fair crack of the whip! – *fair go!*

feeding the ants – being in a very deceased condition out in the *donga*

FJ – most revered classic Holden car

flagon – 2L bottle (of wine, port etc)

flake – shark meat, often used in fish & chips down south

floater – meat pie floating in thick pea soup

flog – steal; sell; whip

fluke – undeserved good luck ('they had three flat tyres, no spare, no puncture kit, no water, but they fluked a lift into town on the monthly mail truck. Otherwise they'd still be there *feeding the ants*')

fossick – hunt for gems or semi-precious stones

from arsehole to breakfast – all over the place

furphy – a misleading statement, rumour or fictitious story, named after Joseph Furphy, who wrote a famous Australian novel, *Such is Life*, then reviewed the book for a literary journal of the time and criticised it; the public bought it by the ton. Or maybe this is a furphy and the term instead derives from the water or sewerage carrier made by his brother's company in Shepparton, Victoria; in WWI these carriers were places where the troops met, swapped yarns and information and no doubt construed a few furphies

galah – noisy parrot, thus noisy idiot

game – brave (as in 'game as Ned Kelly')

gander – look (as in 'have a gander')

garbo – person who collects your garbage

gibber – Aboriginal word for stone or boulder; gibber plain – stony desert

gidgee – a type of small acacia

give it away give up

g'day – good day, traditional Australian greeting

good on ya – well done

grade – (to grade a road) to level a road, usually by means of a bulldozer fitted with a 'blade' that scrapes off the top layer and pushes it to the side

grazier – large-scale sheep or cattle farmer

Green, the – term used in the Kimberley for the wet season

grog – general term for alcoholic drinks

grouse – very good, unreal

homestead – the residence of a *station* owner or manager

hoon – idiot, hooligan, *yahoo*; also 'to hoon' or 'hooning around', often in a vehicle – to show off in a noisy fashion with little regard for others

how are ya? – standard greeting – expected answer: 'Good, thanks, how are you?'

how ya goin'? – *how are ya?*

HQ – second-most revered Holden car

Hughie – the god of rain and surf ('Send her down, Hughie!', 'Send 'em up, Hughie!'); also God when things go wrong ('It's up to Hughie now')

humpy – Aboriginal bark hut ('it was so cold, it would freeze the walls off a bark humpy')

icy-pole – frozen *lolly water* or ice cream on a stick

jackaroo – young male trainee manager on a *station*

jaffle – sealed toasted sandwich

jerky – dried meat

jillaroo – young female trainee on a *station*

jocks – men's underpants

joey – young kangaroo or wallaby

journo – journalist

jumped-up – arrogant, full of self-importance (a 'jumped-up petty Hitler')

jump-up – escarpment

kiwi – (also 'kay-one-double-you-one') New Zealander

knackered – exhausted, very tired

knock – criticise, deride

knocker – one who *knocks*

Koori – Aborigine (mostly south of the Murray River)

lair – layabout, ruffian

lairising – acting like a *lair*

lamington – square of sponge cake covered in chocolate icing and coconut

larrikin – a bit like a *lair*; rascal

lay-by – put a deposit on an article so the shop will hold it for you

lemonade – Australian Seven-Up

lock-up – *watch house*

lollies – sweets, candy

lolly water – soft drink made from syrup and water

lurk – a scheme

mad as a cut snake – insane, crazy; also insane with anger

mallee – low, shrubby, multi-stemmed eucalypt. Also 'the mallee' – the *bush*

manchester – household linen

March fly – horsefly, gadfly

mate – general term of familiarity, whether you know the person or not (but don't use it too often with total strangers)

Matilda – *swag*

middy – 285ml beer glass (New South Wales, Western Australia)

milk bar – general store

milko – milkman

mob – a herd of cattle or flock of sheep while *droving*; any bunch of people (group, club, company)

Moreton Bay bug – (also known as *bug* or *Balmain bug*) an estuarine horseshoe crab closely related to the shovel-nosed lobster (good *tucker* with an unfortunate name)

mozzies – mosquitoes

mud map – map drawn on the ground with a stick, thus any rough map drawn by hand

mulga – arid-zone acacia; the *bush*, away from civilisation (as in 'he's gone up the mulga')

Murri – Aborigine (mostly in Queensland)

muster – round up livestock

mystery-bags – sausages

never-never – a place even more remote than *back o' Bourke*

no-hoper – hopeless case

northern summer – summer in the northern hemisphere

north island – mainland Australia, viewed from Tasmania

no worries – *she'll be right*, that's OK

nulla-nulla – wooden club used by Aborigines

ocker – an uncultivated or boorish Australian

ocky strap – octopus strap: elastic strap with hooks for tying down gear and generally keeping things in place

off-sider – assistant or partner

on the piss – drinking alcohol ('they're on the piss tonight')

O-S – overseas (as in 'he's gone O-S')

outstation – an outlying *station* separate from the main one on a large property

OYO – own your own (flat or apartment)

Oz – Australia

pad – animal track ('cattle pad')

paddock – a fenced area of land, usually intended for livestock (paddocks can be huge in Australia)

pal – *mate*

pastoralist – large-scale *grazier*

pavlova – traditional Australian meringue and cream dessert, named after the Russian ballerina Anna Pavlova

perve – to gaze with lust

pineapple, rough end of – *stick, sharp end of*

piss – beer

pissed – drunk

pissed off – annoyed

piss turn – boozy party

plonk – cheap wine

pocamelo – camel polo

pokies – poker machines

pom – English person

pommy's towel – a notoriously dry object ('the Simpson Desert is as dry as a pommy's towel')

possie – advantageous position (pronounced 'pozzy')

postie – mailman or woman

pot – 285ml beer glass (Victoria, Queensland)

push – group or gang of people, such as shearers

quid – literally: a pound, $2. Still a common term in the *bush* for a non-specified amount of money, as in 'can you lend me a quid?' (enough money to last me until I'm no longer *skint*)

rapt – delighted, enraptured

ratbag – friendly term of abuse (friendly trouble-maker)

rat's coffin – meat pie of dubious quality

ratshit (R-S) – lousy

razoo – a coin of very little value, a subdivision of a rupee ('he spent every last razoo'). Counterfeit razoos made of brass circulated in the gold fields during *two-up* sessions, hence 'it's not worth a brass razoo'

reckon! – you bet!, absolutely!

rego – registration (as in 'car rego')

ridgy-didge – original, genuine, *dinky-di*

ripper – good, great (also 'little ripper')

road train – *semi-trailer*-trailer-trailer

roo bar – *bull bar*

root – have sexual intercourse

ropable – very bad-tempered or angry

rubbish (ie **to rubbish**) – deride, tease

rug rat – small child, *ankle-biter*, *tacker*

salvo – member of the Salvation Army

sandgroper – resident of Western Australia

sanger – sandwich

scallops – fried potato cakes (Queensland), the edible muscle of certain molluscs (north Queensland), shellfish (elsewhere)

schooner – a 425ml beer glass in New South Wales, or a 285ml glass in South Australia (where a 425ml glass is called a 'pint')

scrub – stunted trees and bushes in a dry area; a remote, uninhabited area

sealed road – tarred road

sea wasp – box jellyfish

sedan – a closed car seating four to six people

see you in the soup – see you around

seismic line – *shotline*

semi-trailer – articulated truck

septic tanks – (also 'septics') rhyming slang for Yanks

session – lengthy period of heavy drinking

shanty – pub, usually unlicensed (proliferated in gold-rush areas)

sheila – woman, sometimes derogatory

shellacking – comprehensive defeat

she'll be right – *no worries*, it'll be OK

shitbox – neglected, worn-out, useless vehicle

shonky – unreliable

shoot through – leave in a hurry

shotline – straight trail through the bush, often kilometres long and leading nowhere, built by a mining company for seismic research

shout – buy round of drinks (as in 'it's your shout')

sickie – day off work through illness or lack of motivation

singlet – sleeveless shirt

skint – the state of being *quidless*

slab – package containing four six-packs of *tinnies* or *stubbies*, usually encased in plastic on a cardboard base; also called a 'carton' when packaged in a box (Victoria, Western Australia)

sleep-out – a covered verandah or shed, usually fairly open

sling off – criticise

smoko – tea break

snag – sausage

sport – *mate*

spunky – good looking, attractive (as in 'what a spunk')

squatter – pioneer grazier who occupied land as a tenant of the government

squattocracy – Australian 'old money' folk, who made it by being first on the scene and grabbing the land

squiz – a look (as in 'take a squiz')

station – large sheep or cattle farm

stick, sharp end of – the worst deal

stickybeak – nosy person

stinger – box jellyfish

stoush – fist fight, brawl (also verbal)

stretcher – camp bed

strides – *daks*

strine – Australian slang (from how an *ocker* would pronounce the word 'Australian')

Stubbies – trademark name for rugged short shorts

stubby – 375ml bottle of beer

sunbake – sunbathe (well, the sun's hot in Australia)

super – superannuation (contributory pension)

surfaced road – tarred road

surfies – surfing fanatics

swag – canvas-covered bed roll used in the outback; also a large amount

swaggie, swagman – itinerant worker carrying his possessions in a *swag* (see *waltzing Matilda*)

ta – thanks

table drain – rainwater run-off area, often quite deep and wide, along the side of a dirt road

tacker – small child, *ankle-biter*, *rug rat*

takeaway – fast food, or a shop that sells it

tall poppies – achievers (*knockers* like to cut them down)

Taswegian – resident of Tasmania

tea – evening meal

terrorist – tourist

thingo – thing, whatchamacallit, hooza meebob, dooverlacky, thingamajig

thirst you could paint a picture of – the desire to drink a large quantity of foaming, ice-cold, nut-brown ale

thongs – flip-flops

tinny – 375ml can of beer; also a small aluminium fishing dinghy

Tip, the – the top of Cape York

togs – swimming costume (Queensland, Victoria)

too right! – absolutely!

Top, the – the tip of Cape York

Top End – northern part of the Northern Territory, sometimes also Cape York

Troopie – Toyota Landcruiser Troopcarrier (seats up to 11 people)

trucky – truck driver

true blue – *dinkum*

tucker – food

two-pot screamer – person unable to hold their drink

two-up – traditional heads/tails gambling game

uni – university

up north – New South Wales and Queensland when viewed from Victoria

ute – utility, pickup truck

vegies – vegetables

waddy – wooden club used by Aborigines

wag – to play truant ('to wag school')

wagon – station wagon, estate car

walkabout – lengthy walk away from it all

wallaby track, on the – to wander from place to place seeking work (archaic)

walloper – police officer (from 'wallop', to hit something with a stick)

waltzing Matilda – to wander with one's *swag* seeking work or a place to settle down (archaic)

washaway – washout: heavy erosion caused by running water across road or track

watch house – temporary prison at a police station

weatherboard house – wooden house clad with long, narrow planks

Wet, the – rainy season in the north

wharfie – dock worker

whinge – complain, moan

willy-willy – whirlwind, dust storm

woof wood – petrol used to start a fire (also 'bushman's lighter fluid')

woolly rocks – sheep

wowser – spoilsport, puritan

wobbly – disturbing, unpredictable behaviour (as in 'throw a wobbly')

wobbly boot – (as in 'to put on the wobbly boot') to have consumed too much alcohol

woomera – stick used by Aborigines for throwing spears

yabby, yabble – small freshwater crayfish

yabby, to – to catch yabbies, a relaxed activity often involving *mates* and a *slab* or two ('they're going yabbying this *arvo*')

yahoo – noisy and unruly person, *hoon*

yakka – work (from an Aboriginal language)

youse – plural of you (pronounced 'yooz')

yobbo – uncouth, aggressive person

yonks – ages, a long time

yowie – Australia's yeti or bigfoot

Index

Maps

Text

LONELY PLANET PHRASEBOOKS

Nepali phrasebook

Ethiopian Amharic phrasebook

Latin American Spanish phrasebook

Ukrainian phrasebook

Greek phrasebook

Vietnamese phrasebook

Building bridges,
Breaking barriers,
Beyond babble-on

Listen for the gems

Speak your own words

Ask your own questions

Master of your own image

- handy pocket-sized books
- easy to understand Pronunciation chapter
- clear and comprehensive Grammar chapter
- romanisation alongside script to allow ease of pronunciation
- script throughout so users can point to phrases
- extensive vocabulary sections, words and phrases for every situations
- full of cultural information and tips for the traveller

'...vital for a real DIY spirit and attitude in language learning' – Backpacker

'the phrasebooks have good cultural backgrounders and offer solid advice for challenging situations in remote locations' – San Francisco Examiner

'...they are unbeatable for their coverage of the world's more obscure languages' – The Geographical Magazine

---

Arabic (Egyptian)
Arabic (Moroccan)
Australia
  Australian English, Aboriginal and Torres Strait languages
Baltic States
  Estonian, Latvian, Lithuanian
Bengali
Burmese
Brazilian
Cantonese
Central Europe
  Czech, French, German, Hungarian, Italian and Slovak
Eastern Europe
  Bulgarian, Czech, Hungarian, Polish, Romanian and Slovak
Egyptian Arabic
Ethiopian (Amharic)
Fijian
French
German
Greek

Hindi/Urdu
Indonesian
Italian
Japanese
Korean
Lao
Latin American Spanish
Malay
Mandarin
Mediterranean Europe
  Albanian, Croatian, Greek, Italian, Macedonian, Maltese, Serbian, Slovene
Mongolian
Moroccan Arabic
Nepali
Papua New Guinea
Pilipino (Tagalog)
Quechua
Russian
Scandinavian Europe
  Danish, Finnish, Icelandic, Norwegian and Swedish

South-East Asia
  Burmese, Indonesian, Khmer, Lao, Malay, Tagalog (Pilipino), Thai and Vietnamese
Spanish
Sri Lanka
Swahili
Thai
Thai Hill Tribes
Tibetan
Turkish
Ukrainian
USA
  US English, Vernacular Talk, Native American languages and Hawaiian
Vietnamese
Western Europe
  Basque, Catalan, Dutch, French, German, Irish, Italian, Portuguese, Scottish Gaelic, Spanish (Castilian) and Welsh

---

LONELY PLANET JOURNEYS

JOURNEYS is a unique collection of travel writing – published by the company that understands travel better than anyone else. It is a series for anyone who has ever experienced – or dreamed of – the magical moment when they encountered a strange culture or saw a place for the first time. They are tales to read while you're planning a trip, while you're on the road or while you're in an armchair, in front of a fire.

JOURNEYS books catch the spirit of a place, illuminate a culture, recount a crazy adventure, or introduce a fascinating way of life. They always entertain, and always enrich the experience of travel.

ISLANDS IN THE CLOUDS
Travels in the Highlands of New Guinea
Isabella Tree

Isabella Tree's remarkable journey takes us to the heart of the remote and beautiful Highlands of Papua New Guinea and Irian Jaya – one of the most extraordinary and dangerous regions on earth. Funny and tragic by turns, *Islands in the Clouds* is her moving story of the Highland people and the changes transforming their world.

Isabella Tree, who lives in England, has worked as a freelance journalist on a variety of newspapers and magazines, including a stint as senior travel correspondent for the *Evening Standard*. A fellow of the Royal Geographical Society, she has also written a biography of the Victorian ornithologist John Gould.

'One of the most accomplished travel writers to appear on the horizon for many years . . . the dialogue is brilliant' – Eric Newby

---

SEAN & DAVID'S LONG DRIVE
Sean Condon

Sean Condon is young, urban and a connoisseur of hair wax. He can't drive, and he doesn't really travel well. So when Sean and his friend David set out to explore Australia in a 1966 Ford Falcon, the result is a decidedly offbeat look at life on the road. Over 14,000 death-defying kilometres, our heroes check out the re-runs on tv, get fabulously drunk, listen to Neil Young cassettes and wonder why they ever left home.

Sean Condon lives in Melbourne. He played drums in several mediocre bands until he found his way into advertising and an above-average band called Boilersuit. *Sean & David's Long Drive* is his first book.

'Funny, pithy, kitsch and surreal . . . This book will do for Australia what Chernobyl did for Kiev, but hey you'll laugh as the stereotypes go boom'
– Time Out

LONELY PLANET TRAVEL ATLASES

Lonely Planet has long been famous for the number and quality of its guidebook maps. Now we've gone one step further and in conjunction with Steinhart Katzir Publishers produced a handy companion series: Lonely Planet travel atlases – maps of a country produced in book form.

Unlike other maps, which look good but lead travellers astray, our travel atlases have been researched on the road by Lonely Planet's experienced team of writers. All details are carefully checked to ensure the atlas corresponds with the equivalent Lonely Planet guidebook.

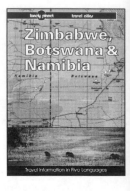

The handy atlas format means no holes, wrinkles, torn sections or constant folding and unfolding. These atlases can survive long periods on the road, unlike cumbersome fold-out maps. The comprehensive index ensures easy reference.

- full-colour throughout
- maps researched and checked by Lonely Planet authors
- place names correspond with Lonely Planet guidebooks
  – no confusing spelling differences
- legend and travelling information in English, French, German,
  Japanese and Spanish
- size: 230 x 160 mm

Available now:
Chile & Easter Island • Egypt • India & Bangladesh • Israel & the Palestinian Territories •Jordan, Syria & Lebanon • Kenya • Laos • Portugal • South Africa, Lesotho & Swaziland • Thailand • Turkey • Vietnam • Zimbabwe, Botswana & Namibia

---

LONELY PLANET TV SERIES & VIDEOS

Lonely Planet travel guides have been brought to life on television screens around the world. Like our guides, the programmes are based on the joy of independent travel, and look honestly at some of the most exciting, picturesque and frustrating places in the world. Each show is presented by one of three travellers from Australia, England or the USA and combines an innovative mixture of video, Super-8 film, atmospheric soundscapes and original music.

Videos of each episode – containing additional footage not shown on television – are available from good book and video shops, but the availability of individual videos varies with regional screening schedules.

Video destinations include: Alaska • American Rockies • Australia – The South-East • Baja California & the Copper Canyon • Brazil • Central Asia • Chile & Easter Island • Corsica, Sicily & Sardinia – The Mediterranean Islands • East Africa (Tanzania & Zanzibar) • Ecuador & the Galapagos Islands • Greenland & Iceland • Indonesia • Israel & the Sinai Desert • Jamaica • Japan • La Ruta Maya • Morocco • New York • North India • Pacific Islands (Fiji, Solomon Islands & Vanuatu) • South India • South West China • Turkey • Vietnam • West Africa • Zimbabwe, Botswana & Namibia

The Lonely Planet TV series is produced by:
Pilot Productions
The Old Studio
18 Middle Row
London W10 5AT UK

For video availability and ordering information contact your nearest Lonely Planet office.

Music from the TV series is available on CD & cassette.

PLANET TALK

Lonely Planet's FREE quarterly newsletter

We love hearing from you and think you'd like to hear from us.

When...is the right time to see reindeer in Finland?
Where...can you hear the best palm-wine music in Ghana?
How...do you get from Asunción to Areguá by steam train?
What...is the best way to see India?

For the answer to these and many other questions read PLANET TALK.

Every issue is packed with up-to-date travel news and advice including:

- a letter from Lonely Planet co-founders Tony and Maureen Wheeler
- go behind the scenes on the road with a Lonely Planet author
- feature article on an important and topical travel issue
- a selection of recent letters from travellers
- details on forthcoming Lonely Planet promotions
- complete list of Lonely Planet products

To join our mailing list contact any Lonely Planet office.

Also available: Lonely Planet T-shirts. 100% heavyweight cotton

---

LONELY PLANET ONLINE

Get the latest travel information before you leave or while you're on the road

Whether you've just begun planning your next trip, or you're chasing down specific info on currency regulations or visa requirements, check out Lonely Planet Online for up-to-the-minute travel information.

As well as travel profiles of your favourite destinations (including maps and photos), you'll find current reports from our researchers and other travellers, updates on health and visas, travel advisories, and discussion of the ecological and political issues you need to be aware of as you travel.

There's also an online travellers' forum where you can share your experience of life on the road, meet travel companions and ask other travellers for their recommendations and advice. We also have plenty of links to other online sites useful to independent travellers.

And of course we have a complete and up-to-date list of all Lonely Planet travel products including guides, phrasebooks, atlases, Journeys and videos and a simple online ordering facility if you can't find the book you want elsewhere.

www.lonelyplanet.com
or
AOL keyword: lp

LONELY PLANET PRODUCTS

Lonely Planet is known worldwide for publishing practical, reliable and no-nonsense travel information in our guides and on our web site. The Lonely Planet list covers just about every accessible part of the world. Currently there are eight series: *travel guides*, *shoestring guides*, *walking guides*, *city guides*, *phrasebooks*, *audio packs*, *travel atlases* and *Journeys* – a unique collection of travel writing.

EUROPE

Amsterdam • Austria • Baltic States phrasebook • Britain • Central Europe on a shoestring • Central Europe phrasebook • Czech & Slovak Republics • Denmark • Dublin • Eastern Europe on a shoestring • Eastern Europe phrasebook • Estonia, Latvia & Lithuania • Finland • France • French phrasebook • German phrasebook • Greece • Greek phrasebook • Hungary • Iceland, Greenland & the Faroe Islands • Ireland • Italian phrasebook • Italy • Mediterranean Europe on a shoestring • Mediterranean Europe phrasebook • Paris • Poland • Portugal • Portugal travel atlas • Prague • Russia, Ukraine & Belarus • Russian phrasebook • Scandinavian & Baltic Europe on a shoestring • Scandinavian Europe phrasebook • Slovenia • Spain • Spanish phrasebook • St Petersburg • Switzerland • Trekking in Greece • Trekking in Spain • Ukrainian phrasebook • Vienna • Walking in Britain • Walking in Switzerland • Western Europe on a shoestring • Western Europe phrasebook

Travel Literature: The Olive Grove: Travels in Greece

NORTH AMERICA

Alaska • Backpacking in Alaska • Baja California • California & Nevada • Canada • Florida • Hawaii • Honolulu • Los Angeles • Mexico • Miami • New England • New Orleans • New York City • New York, New Jersey & Pennsylvania • Pacific Northwest USA • Rocky Mountain States • San Francisco • Southwest USA • USA phrasebook • Washington, DC & the Capital Region

CENTRAL AMERICA & THE CARIBBEAN

Bermuda • Central America on a shoestring • Costa Rica • Cuba • Eastern Caribbean • Guatemala, Belize & Yucatán: La Ruta Maya • Jamaica

SOUTH AMERICA

Argentina, Uruguay & Paraguay • Bolivia • Brazil • Brazilian phrasebook • Buenos Aires • Chile & Easter Island • Chile & Easter Island travel atlas • Colombia • Ecuador & the Galápagos Islands • Latin American Spanish phrasebook • Peru • Quechua phrasebook • Rio de Janeiro • South America on a shoestring • Trekking in the Patagonian Andes • Venezuela

Travel Literature: Full Circle: A South American Journey

ANTARCTICA

Antarctica

ISLANDS OF THE INDIAN OCEAN

Madagascar & Comoros • Maldives• Mauritius, Réunion & Seychelles

AFRICA

Africa - the South • Africa on a shoestring • Arabic (Moroccan) phrasebook • Cape Town • Central Africa • East Africa • Egypt • Egypt travel atlas• Ethiopian (Amharic) phrasebook • Kenya • Kenya travel atlas • Malawi, Mozambique & Zambia • Morocco • North Africa • South Africa, Lesotho & Swaziland • South Africa, Lesotho & Swaziland travel atlas • Swahili phrasebook • Trekking in East Africa • West Africa • Zimbabwe, Botswana & Namibia • Zimbabwe, Botswana & Namibia travel atlas

Travel Literature: The Rainbird: A Central African Journey • Songs to an African Sunset: A Zimbabwean Story

MAIL ORDER

Lonely Planet products are distributed worldwide. They are also available by mail order from Lonely Planet, so if you have difficulty finding a title please write to us. North American and South American residents should write to Embarcadero West, 155 Filbert St, Suite 251, Oakland CA 94607, USA; European and African residents should write to 10 Barley Mow Passage, Chiswick, London W4 4PH; and residents of other countries to PO Box 617, Hawthorn, Victoria 3122, Australia.

NORTH-EAST ASIA

Beijing • Cantonese phrasebook • China • Hong Kong • Hong Kong, Macau & Guangzhou • Japan • Japanese phrasebook • Japanese audio pack • Korea • Korean phrasebook • Mandarin phrasebook • Mongolia • Mongolian phrasebook • North-East Asia on a shoestring • Seoul • Taiwan • Tibet • Tibet phrasebook • Tokyo

Travel Literature: Lost Japan

MIDDLE EAST & CENTRAL ASIA

Arab Gulf States • Arabic (Egyptian) phrasebook • Central Asia • Iran • Israel & the Palestinian Territories • Israel & the Palestinian Territories travel atlas • Istanbul • Jerusalem • Jordan & Syria • Jordan, Syria & Lebanon travel atlas • Lebanon • Middle East • Turkey • Turkish phrasebook • Turkey travel atlas • Yemen

Travel Literature: The Gates of Damascus • Kingdom of the Film Stars: Journey into Jordan

ALSO AVAILABLE:

Travel with Children • Traveller's Tales

INDIAN SUBCONTINENT

Bangladesh • Bengali phrasebook • Delhi • Hindi/Urdu phrasebook • India • India & Bangladesh travel atlas • Indian Himalaya • Karakoram Highway • Nepal • Nepali phrasebook • Pakistan • Rajasthan • Sri Lanka • Sri Lanka phrasebook • Trekking in the Indian Himalaya • Trekking in the Karakoram & Hindukush • Trekking in the Nepal Himalaya

Travel Literature: In Rajasthan • Shopping for Buddhas

SOUTH-EAST ASIA

Bali & Lombok • Bangkok • Burmese phrasebook • Cambodia • Ho Chi Minh City • Indonesia • Indonesian phrasebook • Indonesian audio pack • Jakarta • Java • Laos • Lao phrasebook • Laos travel atlas • Malay phrasebook • Malaysia, Singapore & Brunei • Myanmar (Burma) • Philippines • Pilipino phrasebook • Singapore • South-East Asia on a shoestring • South-East Asia phrasebook • Thailand • Thailand's Islands & Beaches • Thailand travel atlas • Thai phrasebook • Thai audio pack • Thai Hill Tribes phrasebook • Vietnam • Vietnamese phrasebook • Vietnam travel atlas

AUSTRALIA & THE PACIFIC

Australia • Australian phrasebook • Bushwalking in Australia • Bushwalking in Papua New Guinea • Fiji • Fijian phrasebook • Islands of Australia's Great Barrier Reef • Melbourne • Micronesia • New Caledonia • New South Wales & the ACT • New Zealand • Northern Territory • Outback Australia • Papua New Guinea • Papua New Guinea phrasebook • Queensland • Rarotonga & the Cook Islands • Samoa • Solomon Islands • South Australia • Sydney • Tahiti & French Polynesia • Tasmania • Tonga • Tramping in New Zealand • Vanuatu • Victoria • Western Australia

Travel Literature: Islands in the Clouds • Sean & David's Long Drive

THE LONELY PLANET STORY

Lonely Planet published its first book in 1973 in response to the numerous 'How did you do it?' questions Maureen and Tony Wheeler were asked after driving, bussing, hitching, sailing and railing their way from England to Australia.

Written at a kitchen table and hand collated, trimmed and stapled, *Across Asia on the Cheap* became an instant local bestseller, inspiring thoughts of another book.

Eighteen months in South-East Asia resulted in their second guide, *South-East Asia on a shoestring*, which they put together in a backstreet Chinese hotel in Singapore in 1975. The 'yellow bible', as it quickly became known to backpackers around the world, soon became *the* guide to the region. It has sold well over half a million copies and is now in its 9th edition, still retaining its familiar yellow cover.

Today there are over 240 titles, including travel guides, walking guides, language kits & phrasebooks, travel atlases and travel literature. The company is the largest independent travel publisher in the world. Although Lonely Planet initially specialised in guides to Asia, today there are few corners of the globe that have not been covered.

The emphasis continues to be on travel for independent travellers. Tony and Maureen still travel for several months of each year and play an active part in the writing, updating and quality control of Lonely Planet's guides.

They have been joined by over 70 authors and 170 staff at our offices in Melbourne (Australia), Oakland (USA), London (UK) and Paris (France). Travellers themselves also make a valuable contribution to the guides through the feedback we receive in thousands of letters each year and on our web site.

The people at Lonely Planet strongly believe that travellers can make a positive contribution to the countries they visit, both through their appreciation of the countries' culture, wildlife and natural features, and through the money they spend. In addition, the company makes a direct contribution to the countries and regions it covers. Since 1986 a percentage of the income from each book has been donated to ventures such as famine relief in Africa; aid projects in India; agricultural projects in Central America; Greenpeace's efforts to halt French nuclear testing in the Pacific; and Amnesty International.

'I hope we send people out with the right attitude about travel. You realise when you travel that there are so many different perspectives about the world, so we hope these books will make people more interested in what they see. Guidebooks can't really guide people. All you can do is point them in the right direction.'

– **Tony Wheeler**

LONELY PLANET PUBLICATIONS

Australia
PO Box 617, Hawthorn 3122, Victoria
tel: (03) 9819 1877 fax: (03) 9819 6459
e-mail: talk2us@lonelyplanet.com.au

USA
Embarcadero West, 155 Filbert St, Suite 251,
Oakland, CA 94607
tel: (510) 893 8555 TOLL FREE: 800 275-8555
fax: (510) 893 8563
e-mail: info@lonelyplanet.com

UK
10 Barley Mow Passage, Chiswick,
London W4 4PH
tel: (0181) 742 3161 fax: (0181) 742 2772
e-mail: lonelyplanetuk@compuserve.com

France:
71 bis rue du Cardinal Lemoine, 75005 Paris
tel: 1 44 32 06 20 fax: 1 46 34 72 55
e-mail: 100560.415@compuserve.com

World Wide Web: http://www.lonelyplanet.com
or *AOL keyword: lp*